Women and Religion in the Ancie

Studies in Ancient Near Eastern Records

General Editor:
Gonzalo Rubio

Editors:
Nicole Brisch, Eva Cancik-Kirschbaum, Petra Goedegebuure, Amélie Kuhrt(†), Peter Machinist, Piotr Michalowski, Cécile Michel, Beate Pongratz-Leisten, D. T. Potts, and Kim Ryholt

Volume 30

Women and Religion in the Ancient Near East and Asia

Edited by
Nicole Brisch and Fumi Karahashi

DE GRUYTER

ISBN 978-1-5015-2360-1
e-ISBN (PDF) 978-1-5015-1482-1
e-ISBN (EPUB) 978-1-5015-1453-1
ISSN 2161-4415

Library of Congress Control Number: 2022950059

Bibliographic information published by the Deutsche Nationalbibliothek
The Deutsche Nationalbibliothek lists this publication in the Deutsche Nationalbibliografie; detailed bibliographic data are available on the internet at http://dnb.dnb.de.

This volume is text- and page-identical with the hardback published in 2023.
Typesetting: Integra Software Services Pvt. Ltd.

www.degruyter.com

To the memory of our mothers

Foreword and Acknowledgements

This book and all its contributions originated in the discovery in 2015 that Chuo University in Tokyo and the University of Copenhagen are partner universities. As we discovered this connection, an idea began to take shape that we wanted to use a small subject like Assyriology to create a platform for knowledge exchange between Japan and Denmark, two countries that are commonly counted among the periphery of academia in general and Assyriology in particular, even though both countries have long traditions in the study of the ancient Near East.

It so happened that we were both researching the roles of women in ancient Mesopotamia, and so we decided to hold two workshops on the topic of women and their interaction with the sphere of the religious in ancient Mesopotamia, a topic that, to our mind, had not received enough attention (see below).

The first workshop took place in 2015 and was funded by the Asian Dynamics Initiative (ADI), a cross-faculty initiative at the University of Copenhagen that seeks to facilitate exchange in research and teaching and has the goal to "grasp the dynamics of Asia" for which it is necessary to "both understand and learn from Asia."[1] The second workshop took place in 2017 and was funded by Faculty of Letters and Institute of Cultural Science at Chuo University and the Japan Society for the Promotion of Science (JSPS).[2] While intellectual traditions and societal dynamics are very different in Japan and Denmark, the study of the ancient Near East, including ancient Egypt, in both countries can offer a platform for an exchange of knowledge of a third cultural area that is geographically, culturally, and chronologically remote from both of these countries.

The two workshops as well as this volume would not have been possible without the help of the abovementioned sponsors and the speakers and contributors. We would like to sincerely thank them. We are also very grateful to the Department of Cross-Cultural and Regional Studies of the University of Copenhagen and the Department of Western History at Chuo University for their logistical support. This publication would not have been possible without the generous support from the Wissenschaftskolleg zu Berlin / Institute for Advanced Study, which hosted Fumi Karahashi in February 2020 as a guest of Nicole Brisch. This made it possible for us to get started with our editorial duties. We would also like to express our sincere gratitude to Gonzalo Rubio and the staff at DeGruyter for having accepted our book for publication. And finally, we are very grateful to Simone

---

1 See the web portal of the Asian Dynamics Initiative https://asiandynamics.ku.dk/english/about-asian-dynamics-initiative/ (accessed on May 14, 2021).

2 JSPS Grants-in-Aid of Scientific Research C, No. 16K03095.

https://doi.org/10.1515/9781501514821-202

Willemoes Skjold Sørensen for having helped with the book in the final stages of preparing the manuscripts for publication. This book would not have been possible without the brilliant support we received from everyone mentioned here and we are extremely grateful.

Please note: unless stated otherwise, abbreviations follow the *Assyrian Dictionary of the University of Chicago* (CAD) or the list of abbreviations on the Cuneiform Digital Library Initative (CDLI) (https://cdli.mpiwg-berlin.mpg.de/abbreviations).

Contents

Foreword and Acknowledgements — VII

Nicole Brisch and Fumi Karahashi
Introduction — 1

Yuko Matsumoto
Women's History and Gender History in Japan — 11

Part I: **Businesswomen, Empresses, and Royal Women**

Agnès Garcia-Ventura and Fumi Karahashi
Socio-Economic Aspects and Agency of Female Maš-da-ri-a Contributors in Presargonic Lagash — 25

Katsuji Sano
The Role of Women in Assyrian Foreign Policy — 45

Yoko Watai
Women Involved in Daily Management in Achaemenid Babylonia: The Cases of Rēʾindu and Andiya — 63

Huang Haijing
Wu Zetian's Buddhist Policy: A New Perspective — 81

Part II: **Priestesses**

Seraina Nett
The Office and Responsibilities of the En Priestess of Nanna: Evidence from Votive Inscriptions and Documentary Texts — 95

Nicole Brisch
High Priestesses in Old Babylonian Nippur: The NIN and NIN-dingir Priestesses of Ninurta — 121

Ada Taggar-Cohen
Hittite Royal Ideology and the Uniqueness of the Priestess Titled NIN.DINGIR — 141

Ulla Koch
The Roles of Women in the Practice of Ancient Mesopotamian Divination — 163

Part III: **Goddesses**

Sophus Helle
Enheduana's Invocations: Form and Force — 189

Piotr Michalowski
On Language, Gender, Sex, and Style in the Sumerian Language — 209

Troels P. Arbøll
Venomous Scorpions and Venerable Women: The Relationship Between Scorpions, the Goddess Išḫara, and Queens in the Neo-Assyrian Period — 263

Carolina López-Ruiz
The Networks of Ashtart-Aphrodite and the Archaic Mediterranean *Koiné* — 289

Nozomu Kawai
The Lioness Goddess Statuary from the Rock-Cut Chambers at Northwest Saqqara and Their Cult in Middle Kingdom Egypt — 303

Index — 339

Nicole Brisch and Fumi Karahashi

Introduction

> Es obliegt mir nicht, zu werten. Ich sammle, ich ordne,
> ich teile ein, ein bescheidener Diener im Hause des Wissens;
> ich deute und versuche, die Gestalt der Dinge darzustellen
> und ihren Lauf zu verzeichnen. Doch das Wort hat sein eignes
> Leben: es läßt sich nicht greifen, halten, zügeln, es ist doppeldeutig,
> es verbirgt und enthüllt, beides; und hinter jeder Zeile lauert Gefahr.
> *Stefan Heym, Der König David Bericht*

In times of the MeToo movement and the backlashes the movement has provoked, adding historical dimensions to the roles of women in the most ancient history takes on renewed importance. The gender theorist and philosopher Judith Butler recently published an opinion piece in The Guardian, in which she specifically addressed the backlash to gender studies in a global perspective (Butler 2021). Butler's opinion piece mentions, among others, Denmark, whose parliament recently passed a resolution against excessive activism by scholars employed at public universities, a move seen by many as an attack by politicians on freedom of research in Denmark.[1]

It should be stated in the beginning that gender studies has had an immensely positive effect on research in historical subjects such as Assyriology and Egyptology. Theoretical perspectives from gender studies further our understanding of women's roles in antiquity, whose importance for ancient societies has often been downplayed in favor of traditional histories of "big men."

The importance of historical gender studies in general and the study of women in antiquity becomes also clear when considering how studies of women continue to shape images and behaviors of women in today's world, as discussed by Mary Beard in two lectures that she held at the invitation of the London Review of Books (Beard 2018). The study of women and gender in the past can be used to justify or challenge the status quo of today's world. We will only mention one example here: women acting in religious functions in the ancient Near East were often interpreted as "temple prostitutes," a designation that can be traced back to Herodotus's description of Babylonian women who prostituted themselves in front of the temple. Modern studies of prostitution and sex work have

1 We decided to include a brief discussion of some political dimensions in our introduction, because universities are asked more and more to show the relevance and value of research for modern societies. Additionally, we believe it is important for scholars in the humanities to situate their research in current debates.

https://doi.org/10.1515/9781501514821-001

sometimes used the ancient Near East to destigmatize modern sex work by showing that it was not defamed in the past.[2] However, a closer examination of the women that have been interpreted as temple prostitutes shows that such an interpretation is far from clear.[3] The past becomes an arena that shapes the present and the future. This illustrates the need for more detailed, historical studies of women and gender with sound methodologies and theoretical frameworks. Though the contributions in this volume focus on women in antiquity, the study of gender is equally important, for example, regarding complex goddesses as Ištar and the priestly offices associated with her. However, it would go beyond the framework of this book to discuss this complex issue in detail.

As detailed in the foreword, this book is a result of a Danish-Japanese collaboration. In the 2022 Global Gender Gap Index, Denmark is ranked number 32 (score 0.764; score change −0.004 compared to 2021).[4] Perhaps it is for this reason that it is not surprising that gender studies has recently come under attack by Danish politicians, such as Morten Messerschmidt from the Danish People's party or Henrik Dahl from the party Liberal Alliance, two politicians that proclaim their worry that Danish universities will be driven by left-wing activists who disguise their activism as scholarship.[5] Dahl has been most vocal in this context and described disciplines such as gender studies as "nonsense" subjects, "pseudoscience," and disciplines that are filled with "bullshit" (Friis 2021). The terminology used here is not new and in fact already dates back at least to the 1990s, when the "Sokal affair" led to debates within academia on the nature of what is scientific and what is not. It should be noted that such debates are not just confined to the humanities and social sciences but have also taken place (and still are taking place) within the natural sciences, for example, relating to questions about the replicability of experiments ("replication crisis"), or the falsification of scientific data.[6] Yet, Dahl and others only selected

2 See, for example, Sanders et al. 2009: 1. While the wish to destigmatize modern sex work is understandable, it is problematic to use the interpretation of ambiguous data from the past to do so.

3 The question of temple prostitution is difficult and cannot be discussed in detail here; for two recent studies in which alternative interpretations were offered see Karahashi 2017 and Brisch 2021, with further literature.

4 See https://www3.weforum.org/docs/WEF_GGGR_2022.pdf. Denmark also ranks well below other Nordic countries, to which it is commonly compared.

5 See also Heeger and Billingsøe 2021. It is unclear what qualifies these politicians to judge the scientific quality of scholarship in the humanities.

6 The latter is well known in Denmark from the case of Milena Penkowa, a neuroscientist, who was found to have engaged in scientific misconduct.

disciplines in their diatribes that they seem to find politically objectionable, such as gender or migration studies.

Such political attacks on selected research subjects or individual researchers represent a severe setback from achievements of postwar European democracies, in which academic freedom from political meddling became one of the cornerstones of democratic societies based in the rule of law.[7] While it remains unclear what qualifies a politician to make such assessments, buzzwords such as "pseudoscience" are sure to attract the attention of the media in a destructive manner.

Yuko Matsumoto's contribution in this volume, written before these recent attacks in Denmark, offers an important counterpoint to some of the claims that have been made about gender studies. Far from being a topic that is the domain of the "West," whatever those using the term mean by it, it is a research discipline that not only transcends academia and is directly relevant to gender equality in the societies that we live in; it also transcends cultural and geopolitical boundaries, as Matsumoto shows by underlining the importance of gender studies for Japan.

In her contribution to this volume, Matsumoto gives an overview of history and current situation of women's studies and gender studies in Japan including feminist influence and political backlash against everything gender.[8]

It is a well-known fact that Japan is far behind in gender equality and ranked 116 as of 2022 (score 0.650; score change 0.006 compared to 2021). As Matsumoto points out, the idea of "men's public role vs. women's private role" is still deeply rooted in the people's mind in Japan, even though the idea is not from time immemorial. Its lingering influence can be seen from polls that show that 40% of men and 30% of women in Japan accept this idea as of 2019.[9] This is reflected not only in the low proportions of women administrative/managerial workers, political representatives, and researchers but also in the despicable sexist comments, "women

---

7 In Germany, for example, the freedom of academia and the arts is enshrined in the constitution (Grundgesetz), §5.3. See the recent debates surrounding questions of academic and artistic freedom by the initiative GG 5.3.

8 See also Ueno (2011), which is the collection of her essays about her feminist activities and political backlash against her since the 1970s.

9 The answers can be broken down as follows: men: agree 8.6 %, somewhat agree 30.8% (total 39.4%); women: agree 6.5%, somewhat agree 24.6% (total 31.1%) to the statement "Regarding the idea that "husbands should work outside and wives should take care of their home (2019)." See the White Paper on Gender Equality 2020–Summary– (July 2020 Gender Equality Bureau, Cabinet Office, Government of Japan) https://www.gender.go.jp/english_contents/about_danjo/whitepaper/pdf/ewp2020.pdf, accessed on August 21, 2021.

talk too much," by Yoshiro Mori, the former Japanese prime minister, who was forced to resign as the president of the Tokyo 2020 Olympic organizing committee (Rich 2021).

Matsumoto also emphasizes the inclusion of historical studies of women in the field of gender studies. Therefore, we would like to emphasize in the beginning of this introduction that researching gender and gaining a better understanding of the role of women in the most ancient high civilizations in world history is not only solid research using well established methods of philology, history, social sciences, and archaeology, and other fields; the research contributions collected in this volume also add important dimensions to how we write history and therefore on how we can shape our future.

A recent volume in this series (Lion and Michel 2016) assembled an impressive array of scholars writing on the topic of women and work in the ancient Near East, a topic that has been neglected in the past. As Lion's and Michel's (2016: 1–7) introduction included a brief history of research on the topic, there is no need to repeat their overview here. Since then, a number of important publications have appeared, such those from the Gender and Methodology workshops (Svärd and Garcia Ventura 2018; Budin et al. 2018), as well as Michel's book on women in the Old Assyrian texts from Kanesh (Michel 2020) and a collection of articles on the subject of powerful women in antiquity (Droß-Krüpe and Fink 2021).

The volume presented here and the contributions in it are meant to add further dimensions to this ongoing research on women by highlighting the role of women in the sphere of ancient religions. The exceedingly complex topic of ancient religions cannot be discussed adequately within the framework of this short contribution, and we will only be able to highlight some aspects. It is often assumed that the most ancient religions did not distinguish between the sacred and the profane, between piety and ethics, between the supernatural and the natural world: according to these views, everything in the ancient world was sacred and imbued with divinity or divine spirits. More often than not, such notions of religions are rooted in Eurocentric visions of "true religion" (as explained, e.g. by Assmann 2008; Assmann 2018), which created the distinction between "true" and "false" religion and whose beliefs were shaped through the written word ("holy scriptures"). In many cases, history has identified charismatic men, be they historical or not, that were the founding figures of these religions (e.g. Moses, Jesus, Lao Tsu, Buddha, Mohammed), while female aspects of religious beliefs and practices or female agents within religions are often backgrounded.[10]

10 See, however, the research focus on women and gender in Biblical studies https://www.oxfordbibliographies.com/view/document/obo-9780195393361/obo-9780195393361-0246.xml.

It is the goal of the contributions gathered in this book to highlight the historical roles of women as agents within ancient religions, to emphasize female participation and agency in religions (see, e.g. Garcia Ventura and Karahashi, this volume), and hence to begin moving away from the standard history of ancient religions that focus on male perspectives of religion and anachronistically transplant modern notions of writing to arrive at evolutionary assessments of ancient religions.

Businesswomen and Empresses

Economy and politics in ancient Mesopotamia, as in ancient Egypt, are often discussed separate from ancient religion. Yet, as the contributions to the first part of this volume illustrate, much is to be gained in embedding the study of economic or socio-political roles of women in a history of religion. This applies especially to the study of women in the early phases of Mesopotamian history, that is the third and early second millennia BCE, when the priesthood and other offices related to the temple economy offered women a pathway to political and economic influence (Pollock 1991). A good example in this context is a particular kind of gift that supported religious festivals in Early Dynastic Lagash (Garcia Ventura and Karahashi, this volume). Why should businesswomen only be a phenomenon of the 21th century CE? Although festival provisions were donated by a majority of men, elite women also were active contributors to these festivals, thus proving that women had the means to make such contributions. By focusing on women's agency in the Early Dynastic period, Garcia-Ventura and Karahashi are able to offer a more refined and less monolithic picture of ancient religious economies: elite women were agents and active participants in the ancient religious economy and society.

Similarly, women in the first millennium BCE also participated actively in the economic sphere, as Yoko Watai shows in her contribution on the economic management of wealthy urban families in Achaemenid Borsippa. The wealth of these families originated in lucrative temple offices (e.g. the brewer's prebend), and although women were generally not allowed to hold such offices, they were agents in managing the family business. Watai takes a close look at the two women belonging to such families, Rē'indu and Andiya. The former was attested as wife of the head of family, and the latter may have been as well. It seems most likely that both were capable of writing letters. Watai's in-depth studies of their family archives show that these women were engaged not only in daily housework but also in economic management of the household, playing an active role in public and private transactions.

Women in the political sphere can also not be completely dissociated from the religious sphere in ancient Mesopotamia. The expansion and foreign policy of the Assyrian empire was seen as a fulfillment of the divine command of the god Assur to expand Assyria's territory; most often this command was fulfilled through military conquests. Yet, Katsuji Sano (this volume) explores the role of daughters of Assyrian kings as well as foreign rulers and nobles during the Neo-Assyrian period and their significance for establishing political relations. He points out that Assyrian rulers employed a variety of strategies involving these women to establish and consolidate their empire, to which previous studies have not paid sufficient attention, because wars and deportations were the focal points. Princesses were exchanged between Assyria and other powerful states, Assyrian princesses were given to foreign puppet rulers, and women together with dowries were sent from foreign rulers or nobles to Assyria. Sano concludes that keeping these women and strategies in mind, it will be necessary to reconsider Assyrian policies of domination.

Another example of the intricacies of the relationship between politics and religion comes from ancient China. Huang Haijing explores this relationship in her study of Wu Zetian, the only empress in the history of China. She points out that previous studies have focused mostly on ideological aspects of the empress's rule. Haijing instead offers a new approach, which takes into consideration the empress' economic policy. From her detailed analyses emerges a more complete picture, in which the empress effectively organized her project of translating Buddhist sutras and utilized the project's core members as well as the wealth of Buddhist temples in order to consolidate her political power.

Priestesses

The contributions of the second part explore aspects surrounding women as officials in ancient religious worship. In the early phases of ancient Mesopotamian history, especially in the third and early second millennia, women are frequently attested as holders of temple offices. These were often women of high standing; in several cases they were members of the royal family. Sometime in the course of the second millennium, the role of priestesses changed, with the result that in the first millennium, women were no longer allowed to actively participate in religious rituals in the temple. In some cases, the old titles of priestesses were reinterpreted as "temple prostitutes." Yet, what were the roles of these priestesses?

Seraina Nett offers a detailed study of the high priestess of the moon god Nanna at Ur during the Ur III period. Nett's study shows clearly that the high priestess is only rarely mentioned in the administrative record of the Ur III period when adjusted for the frequent attestations in year names that mention the appointment of the high priestess. Nett's discussion of this absence of high priestesses in the documentary record raises important points that are relevant for our understanding of priestesses: Nett suggests as a possible explanation that this lack of attestations may be due to the administrative structures of the Ur III state as well as the gaps in the textual record from Ur, which seems to cluster around the end of the Ur III state.

Nicole Brisch traces the titles of two high priestesses of the god Ninurta in Nippur, the religious center of early Mesopotamia, to gain a better understanding of how to evaluate the data on these high priestesses. Brisch, like Nett (and others), also notes the rarity of attestations of high priestesses in the administrative record from Nippur. Brisch offers a critical evaluation of the available textual sources to show that the role of women in the priesthood may have undergone historical changes and that lexical lists should be used with care when attempting to establish the correct readings of some of these priestly titles.

Interestingly, high priestesses in Hittite records in the second half of the second millennium show that these priestesses were still of high standing in Asia minor, which is, perhaps, in contrast to the role of high priestesses in Mesopotamia. Ada Taggar-Cohen explores unique aspects of the Hittite NIN.DINGIR priestess in relation to the Hittite royal ideology/family structure. The royal family was the prime apparatus of authority, which they propped up through performing various cultic activities. In prescribed cultic texts the NIN.DINGIR, being the only priestess with this title at a given time, appeared together with king, queen, and crown-prince and played an important role. Taggar-Cohen concludes that the NIN.DINGIR was the most important female member of the royal house, either the daughter of the ruling king and the sister of the crown-prince or the daughter of the previous king and the sister of the ruling king.

An important branch of ancient religions was divination, a means of communicating with the gods and foretelling the future. Ulla Koch explores the roles of women in divination throughout Mesopotamian history, a topic that has not received much attention thus far. This is perhaps due to only very few attestations of women as professionals in divination, a traditionally male dominated sphere, yet, as Koch's contribution to this volume shows, though women are attested rarely as experts in divination, there do not seem to be any differences in their ability to communicate with the divine to that of male experts.

Goddesses

The third part with the title "Goddesses" explores various aspects in literature, language, rituals and worship surrounding goddesses in ancient Mesopotamia, Egypt, and the Mediterranean. Sophus Helle discusses new aspects of a well-known hymn to the goddess Inanna, composed by (or attributed to) the high priestess Enheduanna, the first named author in world history. The hymn analyzed by Helle was written in praise of the goddess Inanna and vividly describes a dire situation that the priestess found herself in. Helle convincingly shows that invocations of the goddess functioned as a literary device (or "event" in Helle's words) that were designed to create divine proximity, perhaps both for the author and for their audience.

Michalowski's contribution explores the Sumerian dialect of Emesal, which has variously been dubbed a sociolect or genderlect. Michalowski, referencing recent typological studies of genderlects in linguistics, questions the existence of a genderlect in Sumerian, though Emesal seems to be predominantly the language used by goddesses in some mythological texts as well as the language of mourning and lamentation. Though Michalowski's study of Emesal is predominantly a linguistic investigation, it was decided to place his contribution in the section on goddesses, because, as just mentioned, it is the language that is frequently used by goddesses in mythological and other religious texts. An investigation of the literary situations in which Emesal words are used leads Michalowski to suggest that Emesal may better be described as an emotive language, used in certain situations that evoke strong emotions, such as love-making or mourning.

Troels Arbøll offers a study of scorpions and their religious and symbolic aspects. In ancient Mesopotamia, the scorpion was associated with the goddess Išḫara, originally an aspect of the goddess Ištar. Scorpions also had a strong association with fertility. Arbøll argues convincingly that the association with fertility may be based on behaviors observed in scorpions, whose females carry their offspring on their backs and defend them using their venom, thus creating a strong association of protectiveness and defense mechanisms against the dangers that mothers and their offspring faced in antiquity.

The goddess Ištar (the Semitic equivalent of the Sumerian goddess Inanna) in her Phoenician incarnation as Aštart and the transmission of the worship of these goddesses throughout the Mediterranean, is the topic of Carolina López-Ruiz's article. López-Ruiz's "brief *tour de force*" traces the Phoenician goddess Aštart from the Levant and Cyprus through the Aegean and to the central and western Mediterranean and shows that the goddess Aštart and her incarnations as Aphrodite, Tanit, Venus, and other local goddesses were often at the heart of the hybrid cultures of these communities, mediating the cultural transactions as well as overseeing the major religious and commercial centers, in the eighth-seventh centuries BCE. López-Ruiz shows that "the networks of Aštart" are female counterparts of the pan-Mediterranean networks of the Tyrian god Melqart, to whom Herakles was assimilated.

The lioness goddess, probably to be identified as the Egyptian goddess Bastet, is the main topic of Nozomu Kawai's article, which deals with terracotta and clay statues excavated at Northwest Saqqara by the Japanese archaeological mission. There are five statues of a lioness goddess among them. Kawai concludes that two of these statues, which had a figure of a child-king at each side, were originally the dyads of Bastet and king Khufu, to which Pepy I added his own figures. Kawai reconstructs the life history of these statues from the Fourth Dynasty to the end of the Middle Kingdom and relates them to the cult of the lioness goddess in the Memphite Necropolis, and through this he explores the nature of the cult of the lioness goddess in the region.

The contributions gathered in this volume should be seen as a starting point for further research and the selection presented here does not aim at offering a complete overview of this topic. Much work remains to be done on the topic of women in religion and many more in-depth studies are needed, as several of the individual contributions in this volume indicate.

Bibliography

Assmann, Jan. 2008. *Of God and Gods. Egypt, Israel, and the Rise of Monotheism*. Madison, Wisconsin: The University of Wisconsin Press.

Assmann, Jan. 2018. *The Invention of Religion. Faith and covenant in the Book of Exodus*. Translated by Robert Savage. Princeton, New Jersey: Princeton University Press.

Beard, Mary. 2018. *Women & Power. A Manifesto. Updated*. London: Profile Books London Review of Books.

Brisch, Nicole. 2021. Šamhat. Deconstructing Temple Prostitution One Women at a Time. Pp. 77–90. In *Powerful Women in the Ancient World. Perception and (Self)Presentation. Proceedings of the 8th Melammu Workshop, Kassel, 30 January – 1 February, 2019*, edited by Kerstin Droß-Krüpe and Sebastian Fink. Melammu Workshops and Monographs, 4. Münster: Zaphon Verlag.

Budin, Stephanie L., Megan Cifarelli, Agnès Garcia-Ventura, and Adelina M. Albà (eds.) 2018. *Gender and Methodology in the Ancient Near East. Approaches from Assyriology and Beyond*. Barcino Monografica Orientalia, 10. Barcelona: Edicions de la Universidat de Barcelona.

Butler, Judith. 2021. Why is the idea of 'gender' provoking backlash the world over? *The Guardian*, October 23, 2021. https://www.theguardian.com/us-news/commentisfree/2021/oct/23/judith-butler-gender-ideology-backlash.

Droß-Krüpe, Kerstin, and Sebastian Fink (eds.). 2021. *Powerful Women in the Ancient* World. *Perception and (Self)Presentation. Proceedings of the 8th Melammu Workshop, Kassel, 30 January – 1 February, 2019*. Melammu Workshops and Monographs, 4. Münster: Zaphon Verlag.

Friis, Rasmus. 2021. Værdikrigeren Henrik Dahl blæser til angreb på «Nonsensfag» og «Krænkelsessyge». *Uniavisen*, October 8, 2021. https://uniavisen.dk/vaerdikrigeren-henrik-dahl-blaeser-til-angreb-paa-nonsensfag-og-kraenkelsessyge/.

Heeger, Troels, and Esben Vest Billingsøe. 2021. Morten Messerschmidt i krig med kønsforskere: «Det er føleri, det er politik, det er sniksnak». *Berlingske*, March 6, 2021. Opinion, p. 8–9.

Karahashi, Fumi. 2017. Royal Nurses and Midwives in Presargonic Lagaš Texts. Pp. 159–71. In *The First Ninety Years: A Sumerian Celebration in Honor of Miguel Civil*, edited by Lluís Feliu, Fumi Karahashi and Gonzalo Rubio. SANER, 12. Berlin: De Gruyter.

Lion, Brigitte, and Cécile Michel (eds.). 2016. *The Role of Women in Work and Society in the Ancient Near East*. SANER, 13. Berlin: DeGruyter.

Michel, Cécile. 2020. *Women in Assur and Kanesh. Texts from the Archives of Assyrian Merchants*. Writings from the Ancient World, 42. Atlanta, Georgia: SBL Press.

Pollock, Susan. 1991. Women in a Men's World: Images of Sumerian Women. Pp. 366–87 in *Engendering Archaeology: Women and Prehistory*, ed. Joan M. Gero and Margaret W. Conkey. Oxford: Basil Blackwell.

Rich, Motoko. 2021. Tokyo Olympics Chief Resigns over Sexist Comments. *The New York Times*, February 11, 2021. https://www.nytimes.com/2021/02/11/world/asia/yoshiro-mori-tokyo-olympics-resigns.html.

Sanders, Teela, Maggie O'Neill, and Jane Pitcher. 2009. *Prostitution, Sex Work, Policy and Politics*. London.

Svärd, Sanaa, and Agnès Garcia-Ventura (eds.). 2018. *Studying Gender in the Ancient Near East*. University Park, Pennsylvania: Eisenbrauns.

Ueno, Chizuko. 2011. 不惑のフェミニズム [Forty years of feminism]. Tokyo: Iwanami Shoten.

Yuko Matsumoto

Women's History and Gender History in Japan

1 Women's History and Gender History in Japan

1.1 Women's History in Japan

Japan has a long tradition of research on Japanese women's history. Already in the prewar period, both male and female scholars of Japanese history were interested in the history of customs, family structures, and features of everyday life such as clothes and food, which was thought to be the history of the female sphere. After World War II, Marxist historians began to pay some attention to women's history for the purpose of women's liberation. Afterwards, there arose various arguments over women's "subordinate position." At the same time, a long succession of works was produced by local, mostly amateur, historians. These historians, mainly women who were leaders in community activities and volunteer work, recorded everyday lives in various localities and noted the engagement of farmers' wives or female workers in the activity of their communities.

Based on this long tradition, since the 1970s, historians who are interested in women's history in Japan have produced various works. This upsurge in the study of women's history was partly influenced by Western feminism and Japanese feminist activities. Established historians in the field of Japanese history, however, did not readily integrate the above-mentioned works into the mainstream description of Japanese history. Scholars who regarded the power relations between men and women as naturally derived advanced the criticism that works of so-called feminist historians overestimated the historical roles of female activists and feminist movements (Wakita and Osa 2002).

In the late 1970s, under the influence of new trends in social history, sociology, and women's studies in the U.S. and European countries, Japanese scholars who study Western history began to reexamine women's history from a new point of view. They aimed at reexamining women's positions in the context of the larger society, not necessarily to pursue feminist goals, but primarily to illuminate women's history as part of the mainstream of historical description. Scholars who specialize in Japanese history began to write women's history from the same point of view in the 1980s. In 1982, the Research Society for Women's History published five volumes on Japanese women's history (Research Society for Women's History 1982). This project motivated further work on the history of women in Japan for

https://doi.org/10.1515/9781501514821-002

two reasons. First, many contributors to this project who had not necessarily been interested in women's history began to pay attention to it. The other reason is that this project shed light on the productive work of independent scholars who did not hold positions at universities. Since then, gradually, works on women's history have become acknowledged in Japanese academia, but women's history is still regarded as a supplementary history that fills in gaps in the mainstream description of Japanese history (Wakita and Osa 2002: 160–62; Nagano 2006: 77–84).

1.2 Gender History in Japan

Gender history is not synonymous with women's history. "Gender" signifies a socially constructed difference of the sexes. In other words, gender is a view of sexual difference that is not necessarily grounded in the facts of biology but rather rooted in social structure. The most well-known example of socially constructed gender difference is the idea of the separate spheres of the two sexes. The idea of separate spheres in modern era is that men should earn a living for their families and participate in activities such as politics in the public sphere while women should be in the private sphere engaged in activities like taking care of domestic chores and bringing up children. Since the 1970s, feminists in Japan, like feminists all over the world, have raised their voices against this unequal gender system. Nowadays, the idea of the separate sphere is no more openly advocated as the major social norm in Western societies. Even today, however, the idea of separate spheres still remains in Japanese society and prevents the achievement of job equality among the sexes and social advancement of women.

On the basis of the above-mentioned meaning of gender, various methods of analyzing gender history have been developed. A historian's task is to reveal how the gender system based on the power relationships between the sexes has been constructed. Around the 1980s, directly influenced by the upsurge of interest in theories and history of gender in the Western world, Japanese scholars who studied Western history and historical sociology introduced gender history approaches into Japanese academia. For instance, one of the Japanese pioneers in the study of gender history of the United States translated Joan Scott's *Gender and the Politics of History* (1988) into Japanese in 1992. Since then, scholars who try to use gender analysis to study Japanese history have also cited Scott's definition of gender in their works.

Some historians who led the study of Japanese women's history tended to distance themselves from gender history approaches at first, mainly because they thought that the gender analysis might marginalize the historical agency of women. They have made efforts to disclose historical cases concerning past discrimination against women or women's contribution to society. They worried that these historical case studies might be lightly treated in the gender analysis, since the objective of gender history is to study the history of social systems or social norms. Also, they were concerned that the social construction theory which gender historians often utilized tended to de-emphasize the evidence-based approach of historical studies. Nevertheless, the idea of gender as a tool for historical analysis is gradually penetrating into Japanese academia, especially among scholars of women's history (Kurushima, Nagano, and Osa 2015).

While scholars of Japanese women's history have taken the initiative in promoting studies of gender history in Japan, the subjects that had been discussed in Japanese women's history have been sometimes treated from a different perspective in the studies of gender history. For instance, Japan's unique *ie* ("family") system has been discussed in studies of both women's history and gender history in Japan as a major theme. This system was based on primogeniture, characterized by priority given to the eldest male child and by strong authority of the male head of the household. In this patriarchal system, social customs dictated that the wife of the eldest son had to serve not only her husband but also her parents-in-law, her husband's siblings, and his close relatives. This *ie* system functioned in the premodern era and was legislated in the Civil Code that went into effect in 1898. Although this system was legally abolished after World War II, it still has some impact on individual families. The power relations between the two sexes in this patriarchal system continue to regulate gender relations as customs or social norms in modern Japanese society, exerting significant influence even today. Therefore, in studies of Japanese women's history, the *ie* system has been discussed as one of the major causes for the subordination of Japanese women from the premodern feudal era until the present time.[1] After WWII, for instance, there was a controversy among historians over whether the common people practiced the *ie* system willingly, or whether alternatively the system of the upper class was imposed upon the common people at some point in Japanese history (Wakita and Osa 2002: 160–61). In studies from a gender perspective, however, the fact that the *ie* system was legislated in the Civil Code that went into effect in 1898, nine years after the promulgation of the Meiji Constitution, attracted a great deal of attention. Scholars argue from a gender perspective that the *ie* system constituted a basis for constructing the state system of the Meiji era. These scholars do not necessarily

1 To understand the *ie* system in comparison with the Western concept of the family, for instance, the impact of both that concept and the *ie* system on Japanese immigrants in the United States before WWII is informative (Matsumoto 2016).

deny the significance of the historical fact that the *ie* system functioned in various forms in the premodern era, but they try to reexamine the *ie* system as a modern concept by using a gender approach (Ochiai 1997: 85–89).

Scholars who study gender history in Japan have tried to reexamine themes of mainstream historical description such as politics, construction of the modern state, and imperialism. Studies of the history of masculinity also have developed, because men as well as women are gendered historical subjects and masculinity takes on a meaning only in relation to femininity (e.g., Ujiie et al. 2003; Muta 1996). Furthermore, in recent studies of modern Japanese history based on gender analysis, it has become clear that women have not always been victims to be liberated. Scholars of Japanese gender history describe how Japanese women played an aggressive role during Japanese colonial rule and argue that women share responsibility for actions in World War II (Wakita and Osa 2002: 168–69).

As for education, several universities in Japan have established gender study centers in which historians also participate. Almost every university has courses or lectures related to gender, although most of the courses are taught from a sociological rather than a historical viewpoint. In 2004, the Gender History Association of Japan was organized and now has around 400 members from various disciplines, including Japanese, Asian, and Western history, literature of various areas in the world, cultural anthropology, sociology, and comparative art history.

However, it cannot be said that the concept of gender is recognized in the mainstream Japanese academic world as an analytical tool. History textbooks for high schools, which must be approved by the government of Japan, have not incorporated works on gender history and women's history (Nagano and Himeoka 2011). Furthermore, the term "gender" has been criticized by some conservative politicians, media, and social groups in Japan. They believe mistakenly that the term "gender" implies a refusal to recognize sexual differences in public places such as restrooms or changing rooms and permission for unrestrained sexual activity. Above all, they fear that ideas based on gender analysis might destroy the traditional family system. In Japan, which ranks 116th in the world in terms of gender disparity according to the World Economic Forum's *Global Gender Gap Report 2022*, it is difficult to obtain acknowledgement of the concept of gender from either academia or society. Nonetheless, historians in Japan who recognize the significance of the concept of gender as an analytical tool are striving to apply the gender approach to the rewriting of mainstream Japanese historical interpretation.

2 Women's and Gender History of Ancient Japan

Theories and textbooks on gender theory and gender history, such as the books by Joan Scott or Sonia O. Rose, mostly start their analysis from the modern era. They refer to the premodern era or to ancient history only when searching for the origin of gender relations in the modern era. In the field of Japanese history also, the gender approach was utilized most actively by scholars of modern history when the concept of gender was first introduced. How then can we apply the gender approach to premodern or ancient history? In 2019, four volumes of *Gender History: Critical Readings* were published (Smith 2019). These volumes are anthologies consisting of 60 excerpts from works on women's history and gender history extending from prehistory to contemporary society and coming from all over the world. Despite the editor's consciousness about the necessity of a gender approach, however, most of the works on the ancient and premodern periods in these anthologies are women's history. This enormous project demonstrates that the utilization of a gender approach to the premodern era may be difficult not only in Japan, but also all over the world. Because of the insufficiency of historical materials, above all, it is hard to write either gender history or women's history for ancient periods.

Despite these difficulties, works on women's history and gender history in ancient or classical Japan[2] have been produced steadily, and the controversy over the views on women's roles in ancient society has been heated at times. Scholars utilize a wide variety of primary sources such as official family registries, anecdotes, literature, wood strips that were used for routine records, ink writing on earthenware, epigraphs and archeological sources, and official books on history, in order to search for traces of the lives of ancient women.[3] Since I am not a specialist in ancient history, I am not qualified to offer a review of works on the subject. Nevertheless, there are interesting issues in the study of ancient women's and gender history which have received attention from today's society and scholars of modern history as well as from scholars of ancient Japanese history. I would like to mention some of these issues as examples of the way in which ancient Japanese women's history and gender history have been discussed.

---

2 Around the beginning of the first century, a description of people who lived in the Japanese archipelago appeared in an official Chinese history text. Broadly speaking, therefore, the extent of the ancient or classical period of Japanese history that can be studied through written records is from around the beginning of the first century to around the 10th or 11th century.

3 For a detailed introduction to recent works on gender history in ancient Japan written in English, see Yoshie 2019.

2.1 Religious and Political Roles of Women in Ancient Japanese Society

The religious role of women, and their relation to magic, has been one of the major issues in Japanese ancient history. According to an official Chinese record written at the end of the third century, a queen called Himiko ruled Yamatai-koku (the Yamatai kingdom) in Japan with her brother. Although we are not sure where Yamatai-koku was located and how it related to the sovereignty of Yamato, which was a coalition government of local kingdoms, Yamatai-koku is regarded as a significant kingdom in ancient political history. In the mainstream interpretation, Himiko had shamanistic powers and did not show herself in public, while her brother wielded the actual political power. According to Akiko Yoshie, a scholar who reexamined this mainstream interpretation of the history of Himiko from a gender perspective, there are two gender-biased premises in this mainstream interpretation (Yoshie 2005). One is the biologically determined hypothesis that shamanistic power originated in an attribute of biological femaleness. For instance, a scholar who studies Shinto shrine maidens in antiquity explains that they had shamanistic power because shamanism was related to women's wombs (Iinuma 1997). According to Japanese records written in the eighth century, however, kings in the fifth century were also thought to have magical powers (as well as political and military power) and they did not show themselves to foreign envoys (Yoshie 2005). Thus, sacred or magical power in ancient times was not necessarily attributed to a biological difference between the sexes.

The other premise is the assumption that political power belonged to men. Mainstream historians emphasize that Himiko's supposed magical powers did not provide her with "real" power (Yoshie 2010: 33–46). According to recent studies, however, Himiko was a regular queen who wielded political power. Archeological findings indicate that from the third to the fifth century there were small kingdoms in Japan, half of which were ruled by queens who had political power and directed military affairs (Yoshie 2005).

Political power and the political role of women in the later periods have also been the focus of controversy. As mentioned above, until the fifth century, both queens and kings ruled small kingdoms and both had political power. In other words, gender difference was not a major factor in electing rulers. Around the sixth and seventh centuries, a unified kingdom based on hereditary transfer was established. This kingdom was sometimes ruled by empresses. Some scholars who study dynastic succession in this period argue that empresses ruled the kingdom only on an interim basis when there was a succession problem with the male line, and assert that only the rule of emperors was legitimate. Others, especially those focusing on the political roles of women, claim that the kingdom was not organized along patrilineal lines, but rather bilateral ones that esteemed both the mother's and father's lines. In this view, the succession of sovereignty was not limited to male lines, and female successors and kings' mothers could also hold political power (Yoshie 2017; Fukuto 2004).

2.2 Economic Roles of Women and the Patriarchal System

The economic roles of ordinary women in ancient Japanese society have not been studied as thoroughly as the religious and political roles of the empresses, due mainly to the scarcity of historical sources. Nevertheless, some scholars discuss women's economic roles in relation to the development of the patriarchal system. It is a matter of course that most ordinary women worked and participated in some economic activities throughout the whole course of premodern history. One of the major questions concerning the history of women's economic activities in ancient times, however, is the extent to which women could maintain active or independent roles in economic activities. To answer this question, scholars with an interest in women's economic activities in antiquity emphasize the significance of studying the history of the patriarchal system, since the household was the main economic institution in the premodern era, and women's independence was supposed to be difficult under the rule of the male head in the patriarchal household.

A focal point of discussion is when the patriarchal system was fully established. According to the mainstream description of ancient Japanese history, society from early times consisted of patrilineal families, and the male head of the family managed the patriarchal household. Scholars who focus on the history of women and the family system in ancient society, however, have tried to reexamine this thesis. For instance, before World War II, Itsue Takamure, one of the pioneering researchers in the field of Japanese women's history, studied a large volume of sources about the family system in the Heian period (eighth to eleventh centuries) and argued that ancient Japanese society was based on a matrilineal family structure and that a matrilocal system of marriage prevailed in which the husband visited the wife at home. She asserted that this marriage system and the family structure indicated that women in ancient society were independent economically and socially (Takamure 1938; 1953). Now, it is well known that Takamure, as an amateur scholar, did not utilize historical materials correctly and that her works were partly fictional (Kurihara 1997). Nevertheless, her work is regarded as epochal because for the first time, Takamure suggested the possibility of challenging the mainstream historians who regarded the patrilineal family system as natural.

Scholars of ancient women's and gender history have inherited Takamure's iconoclastic spirit. Although they criticize her thesis about the matrilineal family system, they point out that ancient society had diverse types of family. They maintain that the patrilineal family and the patriarchal household, which were regarded as natural in the mainstream description of Japanese ancient history, did not become the social norm at least until the eighth century, when the *ritsuryō* bureaucratic system was imported from China (Nishino 1997). In the sixth and seventh centuries, when the unified kingdom was established, according to recent studies, both men and women who originated from local clans became bureaucrats in the imperial court. Historical sources indicate the existence of female leaders of local clans and villages (Ijuin 2016; Sekiguchi 2018: 59–66). In this period, women and men both participated in the work of village communities. Although there was a division of labor based on gender, no hierarchy of merit can be found among the kinds of labor. Furthermore, according to folkloric sources such as anecdotes, some women operated commercial ventures or managed property independently from their husbands (Sekiguchi 2018: 63–66). In a word, the patriarchal form of family was not the social norm and women in antiquity were able to play active economic roles before the *ritsuryō* system was introduced.

The reason why scholars regard the introduction of *ritsuryō* system as an epochal event is that Japanese written documents about the system as well as Chinese history books indicate that its basis was the patriarchal household. However, some Japanese scholars emphasize the gap between the written records or codes of the *ritsuryō* system and real lives as seen in the folkloric sources and other written local records. In the eighth century, when the *ritsuryō* system was introduced, according to some historical sources, husbands and wives jointly ran their property. Although the *Nihon Shoki*, the official Japanese history book written in the eighth century, introduced the Chinese concept of gendered division of labor, namely that "men farm and women weave," women chieftains played a major role in agricultural management and the supervision of labor in rural society at that time. There are some historical records suggesting that women had active economic roles in local communities even in the ninth century (Sekiguchi 2018; Yoshie 2007; Yoshie 2019).

These findings about women's active economic activities in the beginning of the *ritsuryō* period deepen the discussion not only about the time when the patriarchal system was established but also about the historical meaning of the patriarchy itself. Some scholars argue that the patriarchal system was fully established much later, because women were able to play active economic roles even in the 9th century. In this interpretation, the subordination of women to the male head of the family is the key factor for understanding the patriarchal system. Criticizing this argument, however, other scholars assert that what is significant is that women could not be the head of the family after around the end of the eighth century, even though they could play a major role in agricultural management. In this interpretation, the power structure rather than concrete activities is the most significant factor for understanding the history of the patriarchal system (Fukuto 2004). Thus, the discussion will no doubt continue.

3 Conclusion: Ancient and Modern History

In history textbooks, ancient history and modern history seem to be totally different, even though we know about historical continuity. The studies on ancient Japanese women's history and gender history, however, demonstrate how the interpretation of ancient history has been influenced by the contemporary ideas and politics about gender relations. For instance, Yoshie (2005) compared the history books in which Himiko was described until the end of the Edo period (1603–1868) with the mainstream description of Himiko after the Meiji Restoration in 1868. She discovered that the interpretation that Himiko had religious power while her brother had the actual political power cannot be found until the end of the Edo period. Mainstream historians began to argue that Himiko had shamanistic power only after the idea of shamanism was introduced by western anthropologists in the Meiji period. In other words, a new mainstream interpretation concerning Himiko and her rule appeared in the Meiji period when the modern imperial regime was established. Since the imperial state before WWII was based on the *ie* system and the patrilineal succession of the emperor (*tennō*), political power, it was thought, must have belonged to men. According to Yoshie, the mainstream description of Himiko and her rule may have been influenced culturally and politically by the contemporary politics and society (Yoshie 2005). I am not qualified to evaluate Yoshie's thesis about the political construction of the mainstream interpretation of Himiko or to examine the history books that she utilized. But her work proposes a significant question about the description of ancient history influenced by the politics of the contemporary society.

The argument about the political role of empresses in ancient history has also drawn the attention of modern society. The above-mentioned argument about whether empresses ruled the kingdom only as interim successors with no real power, or whether they wielded real political power, is directly relevant for the problem of the imperial succession in today's society. The imperial system of the modern state was established in the Meiji period on the basis of the idea that the state of Japan was founded and developed by successive emperors (*tennō*) in a patrilineal system. It was necessary for political leaders to receive confirmation from historians that this *tennō* system was historically legitimate, and consequently the mainstream interpretation of ancient history before WWII supported the *tennō* system. Accordingly, since the Meiji period only males have been allowed to become the *tennō*. In recent times, as succession based on the male line encounters difficulties, politicians, bureaucrats, and intellectuals who discuss the problem of the succession of the *tennō* try to find answers in ancient history. While people who deny the possibility of a female *tennō* emphasize the mainstream interpretation of the Meiji period as the only Japanese tradition, others (including some mainstream historians), who support the interpretation that the empress in antiquity was a legitimate ruler, recognize the possibility of a female *tennō*. In other words, interpretations of the ancient Japanese history have become politicized.

In a sense, early Japanese studies of women's history were also influenced by the contemporary politics on gender relations. Takamure's attitude toward women's history is a well-known example. It is said that Takamure began her research because she appreciated the ideas of Raicho Hiratsuka, who led the Japanese feminist movement before World War II and in 1911 published the famous sentence, "In the beginning, woman was the sun" in the first issue of a feminist magazine that she launched. As mentioned above, Takamure tried to search for historical proof that women were independent "in the beginning" of Japanese history. In addition to her thesis about the matrilineal family structure, she asserted that the sacred role of women was evidence that women had political power in the ancient period. Takamure accepted the mainstream idea that the sacred roles of women in antiquity originated in their intrinsic femaleness but reached a contrary conclusion (Takamure 1954; Tabata, Ueno, and Fukuto 1997).

In comparison with studies of European and American women's history and gender history, the high level of interest among Japanese scholars in the development of the patriarchal system is notable. This also partly reflects the interest of Japanese feminists who try to challenge the prevailing social norms on gender relations affected by the *ie* system in today's society.

It goes without saying that scholars in the fields of women's and gender history studying ancient Japanese society base their arguments on historical evidence. The mainstream description of Japanese ancient history especially after WWII has not been homogeneous, and there is a splendid body of work. Nonetheless, as both the mainstream description concerning gender relations in ancient history that has been accepted since the Meiji period and Takamure's works demonstrate, ancient history can convey strong political messages to the contemporary society.

A direct connection between ancient history and modern history in the case of the history of the *tennō* might be exceptional in comparison with the history of other areas. As has been noted, however, various traditions were invented in every country for the purpose of building modern nation states (Hobsbawm and Ranger 1983), and ancient civilizations provided significant source materials for the newly invented traditions. By paying attention to the women's history and gender history of ancient times, therefore, we may be able to learn whether interpretations of ancient history were used to invent the "traditions" on which gender relations in modern societies are based.

Bibliography

Fukuto, Sanae. 2004. 女性史とジェンダー [Women's history and gender]. ジェンダー史学 [Gender history] (journal of the Gender History Association of Japan) 1: 23–31.

Hobsbawm, Eric and Terence Ranger (eds.). 1983. *The Invention of Tradition*. Cambridge: Cambridge University Press.

Iinuma, Kenji. 1997. 女性史から見た「道鏡事件」 [The "Dokyo Incident" from the viewpoint of women's history]. Pp. 24–41 in ジェンダーと女性 [Gender and women], ed. Yasuko Tabata et al. Tokyo: Waseda University Press.

Ijuin, Yoko. 2016. 日本古代女官の研究 [A study of female bureaucrats in Japanese antiquity]. Tokyo: Yoshikawa Kobunkan.

Kurihara, Hiroshi. 1997. 高群逸枝の女性史像 [Women's history as studied by Itsue Takamure]. Pp. 234–47 inジェンダーと女性 [Gender and women], ed. Yasuko Tabata et al. Tokyo: Waseda University Press.

Kurushima, Noriko, Hiroko Nagano, and Shizue Osa (eds.). 2015. ジェンダーから見た日本史 [Japanese history from the viewpoint of gender]. Tokyo: Otsuki Shoten.

Matsumoto, Yuko. 2016. Americanization and Beika: Gender and Racialization of the Issei Community in California Before World War II. Pp. 161–82 in *Trans-Pacific Japanese American Studies*, ed. Yasuko Takezawa and Gary Y. Okihiro. Honolulu: University of Hawai'i Press.

Muta, Kazue. 1996. 戦略としての家族 [The family as a strategy]. Tokyo: Shinyosha.

Nagano, Hiroko. 2006. ジェンダー史を学ぶ [Learning gender history]. Tokyo: Yoshikawa Kobunkan.

Nagano, Hiroko and Toshiko Himeoka (eds.). 2011. 歴史教育とジェンダー [History education and gender]. Tokyo: Seikyusha.

Nishino, Yukiko. 1997. 古代女性史の現状と課題 [The current situation and current issues in ancient women's history]. Pp. 7–23 in ジェンダーと女性 [Gender and women], ed. Yasuko Tabata et al. Tokyo: Waseda University Press.

Ochiai, Emiko. 1997. 女性史における近代家族と家 [The modern family and the *ie* system]. Pp. 73–98 inジェンダーと女性 [Gender and women], ed. Yasuko Tabata et al. Tokyo: Waseda University Press.

Research Society for Women's History. 1982. 日本女性史 [Japanese women's history]. 5 volumes. Tokyo: Tokyo University Press.

Rose, Sonia O. 2010. *What is Gender History?*. New York: Polity Press.

Scott, Joan. 1988. *Gender and the Politics of History*. New York: Columbia University Press.

Sekiguchi, Hiroko. 2018. 日本古代女性史の研究 [Women's history in Japanese antiquity]. Tokyo: Hanawa Shobo.

Smith, Bonnie G. (ed.). 2019. *Gender History: Critical Readings*. New York: Bloomsbury Academic.

Tabata, Yasuko, Chizuko Ueno, and Sanae Fukuto (eds.). 1997. ジェンダーと女性[Gender and women]. Tokyo: Waseda University Press.

Takamure, Itsue. 1938. 母系制の研究 – 大日本女性史 [A study of matriliny: Japanese women's history]. Tokyo: Koseisha.

Takamure, Itsue. 1953. 招婿婚の研究 [A study of matrilocal marriage]. Tokyo: Rironsha.

Takamure, Itsue. 1954. 女性の歴史 [Women's history]. Tokyo: Kodansha.

Ujiie, Mikito et al. (eds.) 2003. 日本近代国家の成立とジェンダー [Gender and the formation of the modern Japanese state]. Tokyo: Kashiwa Shobo.

Wakita, Haruko and Shizue Osa. 2002. ジェンダー史と女性史 [Gender history and women's history]. Pp. 160–72 in 現代歴史学の成果と課題、1980–2000年, I 歴史学における方法的転回 [Historical studies in Japan from 1980 to 2000: Trends and perspectives I, methodological turns in historical thinking], ed. The Historical Science Society of Japan. Tokyo: Aoki Shoten.

Yoshie, Akiko. 2005. つくられた卑弥呼 [The constructed image of Himiko]. Tokyo: Chikuma Shobo.

Yoshie, Akiko. 2007. 日本古代女性史論 [A study of ancient Japanese women's history]. Tokyo: Yoshikawa Kobunkan.

Yoshie, Akiko. 2010.「聖なる女」の思想的系譜 [The theoretical lineage of "the sacred woman"].
Pp. 28–48 in 思想と文化: ジェンダー史叢書3 [Thoughts and cultures: Gender history series 3], ed. Kazuko Takemura and Akiko Yoshie. Tokyo: Akashi Shoten.

Yoshie, Akiko. 2017. 日本古代女帝論 [A study of the empress in ancient Japanese history]. Tokyo: Hanawa Shobo.

Yoshie, Akiko. 2019. Gender in Early Classical Japan: Marriage, Leadership and Political Status in Village and Palace. Pp. 60–92 in *Gender History: Critical Readings*, vol. 2, ed. Bonnie G. Smith. New York: Bloomsbury Academic.

Part I: Businesswomen, Empresses, and Royal Women

Agnès Garcia-Ventura and Fumi Karahashi

Socio-Economic Aspects and Agency of Female Maš-da-ri-a Contributors in Presargonic Lagash

Presargonic texts from the so-called **E_2-MI_2** archive from Girsu, part of the city-state of Lagash, record some women who made a special kind of contribution, called a **maš-da-ri-a** (see §2.1 below). No matter how these women are listed, either along with their husband or separately, they are always listed with their own **maš-da-ri-a**. Although women's participation in **maš-da-ri-a** contributions has been recognized by Yvonne Rosengarten (1960: 16), Julia Asher-Greve (2013: 365), and most recently by Walther Sallaberger (2018: 185), their role as contributors has not been sufficiently explored. In this paper[1] we aim to highlight the active role these women had in the socio-economic sphere. To do so we present, first, a synopsis of the use of agency in ancient Near Eastern studies. Second, we concentrate on the primary sources, presenting first an overview of the **maš-da-ri-a** contributions followed by a focus on six female **maš-da-ri-a** contributors selected as specific case studies. Third, we discuss some aspects of the **maš-da-ri-a** contributors using agency as an analytical tool with the aim of shedding some additional light on the interpretation of the sources.

1 Preliminary versions of some topics developed in this paper were presented by Fumi Karahashi at the workshop on "Women's Religious and Economic Roles in Antiquity" held at Chuo University in Japan on Nov. 10–11, 2017 (funded by Japan Society for the Promotion of Science: Grants-in-Aid of Scientific Research C, No. 16K03095 and Chuo University) and by Karahashi and Agnès Garcia-Ventura in two separate papers at the *Third Workshop on Gender, Methodology and the Ancient Near East* (GeMANE 3) held in Ghent in April 2019. We thank the organizers and attendees at both meetings for giving us the chance to launch our joint work on these topics and for their constructive feedback. We also thank Frederick W. Knobloch for language check, helpful discussion and comments, while preparing this article. Last but not least, we would like to express our gratitude to Nicole Brisch and the anonimous reviewer for their insights, which helped us to improve our paper.

Abbreviations used in the present study follow the Cuneiform Digital Library Initiative (http://cdli.ox.ac.uk/wiki/abbreviations_for_assyriology).

https://doi.org/10.1515/9781501514821-003

1 Agency in Ancient Near Eastern Studies

The use of "agency" as an analytical tool has been growing in ancient Near Eastern studies since the beginning of the 21st century.[2] On the one hand there are the studies revolving around visual culture, such as the ones by Julia Asher-Greve (2013) or by Claudia Suter (2017, 2018). Despite the differences and nuances between these and other comparable studies, a common ground underlies all of them: the debate about whether the visibility and presence of women in images might be interpreted as proof of a potentially high degree of agency, while their absence might be interpreted as proof of a potentially low one. This is particularly emphasized when dealing with the way elite men and women are portrayed exercising political and religious power.

On the other hand there are the studies based on textual sources. They analyze agency as linked to two main contexts or sets of activities: first, writing; and second, economic activities.[3] With regard to writing, it is worth noting the contributions of Brigitte Lion and Eleanor Robson on women scribes (see, for instance, Lion and Robson 2005) as well as the work of Saana Svärd on the roles of women as authors (see, for instance, Svärd 2013; Halton and Svärd 2018, especially pp. 27–30). The economic and trade studies by Allison K. Thomason (2013), Cécile Michel (2016, 2020),[4] and Katrien De Graef (2018), all concentrate on textual sources from the beginning of the second millennium BCE, highlighting the active role of ancient Near Eastern women in textile production and trade, or as *nadītu* priestesses. Also worth noting is the analysis of Matteo Vigo (2016) on the explicit and implicit agency of women in Hittite sources.[5]

All the previously mentioned studies applying agency to the scrutiny of visual and textual ancient Near Eastern sources focus on women or female agency. This is not by chance, as the incorporation of this analytical tool is clearly linked

2 For an overview of the use of agency in this milieu as well as for definitions, state of the art, and some examples of case studies dealing mainly with object agency, see Downes 2019.

3 Here we do not offer a comprehensive state of the art, but a selection of authors, publications and approaches to agency in ancient Near Eastern studies that we consider to be illustrative for better framing of our case study. In most cases we selected only those authors explicitly using the word *agency* when dealing with the topic here under discussion. However, we also include Lion and Robson (2005) and Michel (2016) because they were pioneers in the approach summarized, although they did not explicitly use *agency* in their papers.

4 Michel has published extensively on the role of women in Old Assyrian trade. See Michel 2020 for a compendium of sources and for references to her previous works.

5 Vigo takes as a theoretical framework a proposal by Svärd to define women as explicit or implicit agents (see Vigo 2016: 332–33 for more details of the proposal as well as for further references).

to an interest in women's history and/or gender studies (leaving aside the fact that almost all the scholars mentioned so far are women). When incorporating agency, thus, the main aim is to detect a potentially active role of women often neglected in previous studies (see Bahrani 2001: 32–33). Doing so implies, at least to a certain extent, questioning the public/private, institutional/non-institutional, and active/passive divides as well as their link to men and women. In other words, the aim is deconstructing preconceptions about the allegedly active and public role of men, that is the existence of men's agency (or male agency), as opposed to the supposedly private and passive roles of women, that is the lack of women's agency (or female agency).[6]

We see then that the use of agency in the framework of women's studies and of gender studies is frequent and considered appropriate for the abovementioned reasons. However, there are also critical voices about the use of agency, precisely from gender studies. The pioneer of gender archaeology Joan Gero (1944–2016) summarized some of these criticisms in her paper eloquently titled "Troubled Travels in Agency and Feminism" (Gero 2000). The kernel of these criticisms is that because agency has been usually associated with active males, when used for females it gives even more value to the traditional stances that gender archaeology questions. Along these lines she wonders why we are so interested in agency, traditionally linked to men, rather than in empathy, traditionally linked to women (Gero 2000: 35). Although we consider such criticisms[7] here and think that it is important to take them into account, we counter that using agency as a category of analysis might help to overcome these assumptions "from the modern Assyriologists' point of view," in Thomason's words (2013: 106). For this purpose we take as starting point the definition of agency provided by Sharon R. Steadman and Jennifer C. Ross in the introduction to the volume titled *Agency and Identity in the Ancient Near East: New Paths Forward*: "the human capacity for motivated, reflexive action having some consequence (if not always an expected or intended outcome). Agency pertains to individuals and groups" (Steadman and Ross 2010: 1).[8]

---

6 As can be seen, here we only concentrate on human agency, but it is worth mentioning that particularly in the applications of agency to archaeological research, material and non-human agency has been also a field of scrutiny and work. See, for instance, Knappett and Malafouris 2008.

7 These are not the only criticisms of agency as it has been applied, in particular, to archaeological research. For an overview and discussion of these possible flaws, see Dobres and Robb 2000.

8 For a critical overview of several definitions of agency and their applicability to the study of the past, as well as a summary of main features of the first definitions of agency suggested by the sociologists Pierre Bourdieu and Anthony Giddens in the 1970s, among others, see Dobres

2 The Sources: Maš-da-ri-a Contributions in Presargonic Lagash

2.1 Maš-da-ri-a Contributions: An Overview

Walther Sallaberger has recently discussed the goddess Baba's festival extensively with a focus on the **maš-da-ri-a** in his article "Festival Provisions in Early Bronze Age Mesopotamia."[9] Confirming Rosengarten's conclusion,[10] Sallaberger (2018: 173 with n. 6 with further previous references), translates the term **maš-da-ri-a** as "festival provisions," and states that "the *mašdaria* was collected as a kind of tax on production, delivered to the political center, and there used to equip festivals."[11] Many texts recording **maš-da-ri-a** deliveries[12] are preserved from the reigns of the last two rulers of the Lagash I dynasty, Lugalanda and Urukagina,[13] and their respective queens, Baranamtara and Sasa.[14] There are short memos recording only one or a couple of deliveries, as well as longer compiled documents recording multiple deliveries. These documents basically tell us what was brought or delivered (Sumerian verb DU) by whom and to/for whom as well as often the month, occasion, and/or place in which the delivery was made. A representative format that opens the document is: delivered item(s) / **maš-da-ri-a** / PN (contributor) / occupation title or family affiliation.[15] A typical **maš-da-ri-a** consisted of a kid, lamb, or sheep, sometimes accompanied by comestibles such as bread,

---

and Robb 2000 (particularly pp. 4–6); Dornan 2002. For the classic works of the abovementioned sociologists, see Bourdieu 1977; Giddens 1979.

9 *KASKAL* 15 (2018), which was published in 2020.

10 About Rosengarten's research and career, see Garcia-Ventura 2019.

11 For **maš-da-ri-a**, see also Nett in this volume.

12 The number of **maš-da-ri-a** texts is given as 68 (Beld 2002: 9 with n. 9) and as over 80 (Prentice 2010b: 187).

13 On these rulers and the dates of their reigns, see Sallaberger and Schrakamp 2015: 70–74, 82 table 18, 135–136 table 39.

14 However, Nik 1: 158 at least is an exception to this. This document is dated to year 1, presumably of Enentarzi (no ruler's name was written), in which a person called **NI-a-a** appears in the context of a **maš-da-ri-a** contribution: "one ram was the **maš-da-ri-a** of **NI-a-a. Mu-ni-na-ga-me** gave it to **Ki-ti** from the **E$_2$-MI$_2$**." Selz (1995: 212) has identified **NI-a-a** with Dimtur, queen of Enentarzi. Note also attestations such as **ab$_2$ NI-a-a-kam** "(they are) the cows of **NI-a-a**" in DP 233 obv. i 4 (dated to Enentarzi 4); **šuku NI-a-a-kam** "(it is) the sustenance fields of **NI-a-a**" in MLVS 6 rev. iii 1 (dated to year 5; no ruler's name was written but certainly year 5 of Enentarzi). In another text dated to the same year, animals of the **ensi$_2$**'s possession and those of **Ni-a-a** were listed (Nik 1: 188).

15 For more formulaic details, see Rosengarten 1960: 15–16.

beer, vegetables, dairy products,[16] and fish (Prentice 2010b: 189). The recipient of the **maš-da-ri-a** goods was generally the queen[17] in the **E_2-MI_2** or in the palace,[18] but also the dead ancestors[19] as well as the ruler[20] or royal children[21] are named as recipients. The delivered goods were utilized for festivals and celebrations, stored for future use, given to royal children, and so forth (Rosengarten 1960; Sallaberger 2018). The majority of the contributors were male: some 120 different men are attested in the **E_2-MI_2** archive.[22] Of these, one group consists of chief administrators (**sanga**) of various temples in the city-state of Lagash and officials in important positions (Prentice 2010: 191; Sallaberger 2018: 178 table 3), and the other consists of cowherds and fishermen as well as overseers of several types (Sallaberger 2018: 176–77 table 2 [3–4], 188 table 6). On the other hand, only about twenty distinct female contributors are attested. From a quantitative point of view, the proportion of male and female contributors reveals a clear imbalance favoring males: 85% of male contributors versus only about 15% of female contributors.

---

16 On the term **kig_2-gur-ra**, see Karahashi 2011: 6 ad 403 ("a kind of milk product, cheese?") and 10 n. 12; see also Sallaberger 2018: 176.

17 In one text a total of 68 wool sheep brought as **maš-da-ri-a** was defined as "sheep, property (**udu u_2-rum**) of Baranamtara" (VS 14: 73 rev. i 1–3).

18 Other locations are also mentioned; for instance, Nina (DP 131 rev. iii 4), the temple of **^{d}Nin-mar^{ki}** (DP 213 obv. i 4), and the **abzu** of the river bank (DP 214 obv. ii 5; DP 217 obv. ii 1), where ceremonies were held.

19 In most cases these were Dudu the **sanga** and Enentarzi, the former being probably Enentarzi's father (Beld 2002: 166–67). Note that in Genava 26: 1, which recorded a **maš-da-ri-a** brought to Dudu (obv. iii 3–4; rev. iii 3–4 **Du-du / mu-na-DU**), a woman named Munussaga is mentioned as another recipient (obv. iii 14–15 **Munus-sa_6-ga / mu-na-DU**). DP 40, dealing with the ruler's offerings which were brought for Dudu the **sanga** (**nig_2-giš-tag-ga / $ensi_2$-ka-kam / Du-du / sanga / mu-na-DU** in rev. iii 2–6), also records that the offerings were brought for a woman named Ninmezida (**Nin-me-zi-da-ra / mu-na-DU** in obv. v 1–2); here the conjugation prefix is not **e-** as in Balke 2017: 341 but is clearly **mu-**. Munussaga and Ninmezida are to be identified with the dead members of Dudu and Enentarzi's family who were listed as recipients of offerings of garments and jewelry in DP 73 and DP 76.

20 E.g., Lugalanda (DP 59 rev. vii 6); when only the phrase "in the palace" is written with no name of recipient (e.g., DP 210 rev. i 1), it could be either the queen or the ruler.

21 E.g., **$Geme_2$-^{d}Nanshe**, daughter of Lugalanda (Nik 1: 176), who was not only given a share from the **maš-da-ri-a** of the ruler (rev. i 5–8) but also recieved **maš-da-ri-a** goods by herself (obv. iii 3–6, rev. ii 4–iii 1); and **Šubur-^{d}Ba-ba_6**, son of Urukagina (VS 14: 62).

22 Note that the ruler (**$ensi_2$**) is also attested as contributing sheep for feasting, once at the river bank and once at the **ki-a-nag**-chapel (DP 80 obv. i 2; ii 1) although his and others' contributions were not described as **maš-da-ri-a**.

2.2 Female Maš-da-ri-a Contributors

When a woman, especially one who was married, acted in a patriarchal society, we must wonder the extent to which she exercised agency over her activities, if at all; the general assumption is that she acted as a proxy for a man, namely, her husband. Prentice (2010: 184), speaking of women's role in the "holy milk and holy malt" (**ga-ku$_3$ munu$_4$-ku$_3$**) texts,[23] states as follows:

> In other contexts women are referred to by their personal name even when they are further identified as the wife of someone, but in the milk and malt documents none of the women who receive milk and malt are recorded by their personal name, instead, they are identified as the wife ('dam') of the holder of a specific (and important) office or profession. Therefore, it is probable that the women receive on behalf of their husbands, or more precisely their husband's office, rather than in their own right.

Is it justifiable to infer the role of women based only on the way they were identified even in a case such as this? It may not necessarily be so. It should be remembered that it was the custom (until very recently in many societies and even now in some) to identify married women by their husband's name and/or occupation, and this custom concealed women's (actual) socio-economic activities. Indeed, this is also what might have happened when dealing with the **maš-da-ri-a** contributions, since the twenty or so female contributors are always linked to the name and/or profession of their husbands.

In contrast to Prentice and others (Prentice 2010: 184 n. 76), Beld (2002: 133), from the perspective of social integration, has already drawn attention to the importance of the participation of elite women in religio-social ceremonies and to the function of queen who organized them. Along similar lines, Sallaberger (2018: 195) writes on the festival of Baba as follows: "[b]y contributing a share of the food and drink consumed during the feasting, everyone became an active member and assumed a host-like role, thus it became his or her celebration as well." Pursuing this line of interpretation, we further suggest that the elite women of Lagash had the socio-economic means to enable them to play a public role.

To address this, materials concerning female **maš-da-ri-a** contributors are ideal because a discussion of them inevitably leads us to issues of the agency of women.[24] We have selected six women among some twenty female **maš-da-ri-a** contributors about whom more information is available. They are discussed in §2.2.1–§2.2.6 below. In the first five cases, we will describe who these women

23 On these texts, see also Selz 1995: 73–78.

24 For a possible iconographic representation of such a female contributor, coming from Girsu, see Prentice 2010b: 289 with n. 781.

were and evaluate whether they had the economic means to contribute their own gifts.[25] Although the amounts of the **maš-da-ri-a** brought by these women were small, as was often also the case for other male contributors (Prentice 2010b: 190; Sallaberger 2018: 180), they must have had the means to make their own contributions. As for the last case of these six women, we will analyze the arrangement, wording, and expressions used in the text to see how the wife's deliveries were recorded in relation to her husband.

2.2.1 Bara$_2$-a-ra$_2$-nu$_2$, Wife of Lugal-mu-da-kuš$_2$

Baraaranu (**Bara$_2$-a-ra$_2$-nu$_2$**), the wife of Lugalmudakush (**Lugal-mu-da-kuš$_2$**), brought a **maš-da-ri-a** of flour and two kinds of beer (DP 59 rev. ii 15–19).[26] That she was a prominent figure, perhaps belonging to the ruling family, can be deduced from her position in the so-called **ereš-dingir** ration lists.[27] In three out of four such documents she is listed[28] second only to the **ereš-dingir**-priestess of the goddess Baba and heads the group of nine **lukur** women.[29] However, Baraaranu was not a sister of the ruler because in the fourth document (DP 127) she appears (obv. iii 5–6) outside of a group consisting of **Geme$_2$-ub$_5$-ku$_3$-ga**, queen's mother, and the seven (**lukur**-)women designated here as ruler's sisters (**nin ensi$_2$-ka-me**) (obv. ii 11). Baraaranu is also attested in a document as holding 9 **iku**[30] of leased fields (**gan$_2$ apin-la$_2$**),[31] which might mean that she was engaged in a sort of agribusiness, enabling her to use part of the profit to procure **maš-da-ri-a** goods. In fact, almost 60 years ago, Yomokuro Nakahara, a pioneer of cuneiform studies

25 Note that Asher-Greve (2013: 365) has already pointed out, "some women, mostly wives of important, high status men, had the means to provide 'mašdaria,' presumably an obligatory 'gift' used for sacrifices."

26 She is counted as a "named woman" in Sallaberger 2018: 185 table 5.

27 On these lists, see Beld 2002: 184–87.

28 RTC 61 obv. i 12; DP 134 obv. i 13; Nik 1: 53 obv. i 12.

29 For these high-ranking **lukur**-women, see Steinkeller 1981a: 85. A certain **Gan-^{d}Ba-ba$_6$**, who is also thought to have been a high-ranking **lukur**, appeared as a witness in a document of house purchase by Enentarzi (DP 31 obv. iii 12–13); cf. other (perhaps lower-ranking) **lukur** attested in the **E$_2$-MI$_2$** archive such as **Nin-šu-sikil** (Balke 2017: 349) and **Ama-numun-zi** (Balke 2017: 86). For more on **lukur**, see Sharlach 2008, 2017; Huber Vulliet 2010; Goodnick Westenholz 2013, among others.

30 1 **iku** is an ancient Mesopotamian unit of area equivalent to ca. 0.36 ha; see "ED IIIb metrology: texts from Lagaš" (http://cdli.ox.ac.uk/wiki/doku.php?id=ed_iii_metrological_systems).

31 Her field was described as **tab-ba** (RTC 75 obv. iv 6–rev. i 1). For this terminology, see Foster (1980); Maekawa 1982: 102.

in Japan, discussing the land system of Presargonic Lagash, pointed out that a woman named **Sa$_6$-sa$_6$** herself paid part of her field rent (DP 555 obv. iii 2–4)[32] and suggested that men and women[33] gained profits from leased fields by having their servants or slaves work on them or by subleasing them (Nakahara 1961: 85–88). Further, Baraaranu was allotted onion fields (**ki-šum$_2$-ma**) measuring 1 **iku.**[34] This is an important piece of information because, firstly, only royal family and a small number of the elite were allotted onion plots,[35] onions being a restricted crop; secondly, onions were occasionally brought as **maš-da-ri-a** goods; and thirdly, part of the onion crop was handled by the chief merchant **Ur-e-muš** for purchase/exchange (**nig$_2$-sam$_2$-ma**) purposes (Prentice 2010a, 2010b: 127–29). While certain onion plots were intended to produce onions for **maš-da-ri-a** as Prentice (2010a: 259–60) suggests, it is also possible that the individuals who were allotted onion plots benefitted from them.[36] Thus we may suggest at least two scenarios although these are not attested: Baraaranu might have brought onions harvested from her own plots as **maš-da-ri-a**; and/or she might have used part of the profit from the onion plots to procure other **maš-da-ri-a** goods of her own. We will see later a woman named **Nin-bur** who brought onions as her **maš-da-ri-a** (§2.2.4).

2.2.2 Ku$_3$-ge-pa$_3$, Wife of Du-du, Scribe

The (unnamed) wife of the scribe Dudu (**Du-du**) appeared as a **maš-da-ri-a** contributor with one [sheep, lamb, or kid] in a text dated in Lugalanda 6 (RTC 44 obv. iii 8–iv 1).[37] In a text of a couple of years later, dated to Urukagina **lugal**-

32 On the rent of the **gan$_2$ apin-la$_2$**, see Maekawa 1977, which includes a discussion of the aforementioned RTC 75; differently, Steinkeller 1981b. For women who are attested as holders of land in the **E$_2$-MI$_2$** archive, see Karahashi 2016b.

33 Nakahara particularly mentioned **Ku$_3$-ge-pa$_3$**, who held a large acreage of leased fields (see §2.2.2 below).

34 DP 406 obv. i 1–2; also note DP 385 rev. i 3, which refers to “onion (**šum$_2$**) of Baraaranu.” On “the Onion Archive” from Sargonic Nippur, see Gelb 1965; Westenholz 1987: 87–98.

35 E.g., DP 394 (queen’s mother and the chief administrator **En-ig-gal**); VS 27: 8 (royal children).

36 Prentice (2010a: 265–67) states that onions served as an exchange commodity in Presargonic Lagash and that the **E$_2$-MI$_2$** and the palace monopolized the market. However, the possibility that those who were allotted onion plots also claimed their share or a profit cannot be dismissed.

37 RTC 44 mentions three more female **maš-da-ri-a** contributors: the wife of a **sa$_{12}$-du$_5$**-official with one sheep and one kid (obv. iv 4–5), **Nin-bur** with one sheep (see §2.2.4), and **Nin-u$_3$-ma** with one sheep (see §2.2.6).

year 1, the wife of the scribe Dudu was identified by the name Kugepa (**Ku$_3$-ge-pa$_3$**) and was allotted 18½ **iku** of leased fields.[38] This Kugepa is most likely the **Ku$_3$-ge-pa$_3$** who is mentioned as **lukur**[39] and ruler's sister[40] in the **ereš-dingir** ration lists.

2.2.3 Bara$_2$-ir-nun, Wife of Al-la, Rope-Maker

Alla's (**Al-la**) wife Barairnun (**Bara$_2$-ir-nun**) brought a **maš-da-ri-a** of one sheep and beer (VS 14: 159 obv. vi 8–11). It is known from another text that her husband Alla was a rope-maker (**tug$_2$-du$_8$**) and that she gave birth to a child in Lugalanda year 4.[41] This year also witnessed queen Baranamtara's giving birth to a daughter.[42] No other women except for these two are remembered with such details in the **E$_2$-MI$_2$** archive. The special attention paid to Barairnun and her childbirth implies her high status. Consequently, it is most likely that this Barairnun was the **Bara$_2$-ir-nun** who is listed as a **lukur**[43] and as one of sisters of the ruler.[44] She is not attested in any land allotment texts, but it is highly probable that she was allotted some land like the abovementioned Kugepa and other female members of the ruling family.[45]

2.2.4 Nin-bur, Wife of Lugal-ša$_3$-su$_3$, Field Surveyor

The **maš-da-ri-a** records concerning Ninbur (**Nin-bur**), the wife of the field-surveyor (**lu$_2$-eš$_2$-gid$_2$**) Lugalshasu (**Lugal-ša$_3$-su$_3$**), have survived in a greater

38 18½ **iku / gan$_2$ apin-la$_2$ / Ku$_3$-ge-pa$_3$ / dam Du-du dub-sar** (HSS 3: 40 rev. ii 13–16).

39 Nik 1: 53 obv. iii 2; RTC 61 obv. iii 7; DP 134 obv. iii 2.

40 DP 127 obv. ii 6.

41 DP 219 obv. i 2–5; for Alla and his wife Barairnun, see Karahashi 2016a: 55–56.

42 Nik 1: 209 obv. ii 1–2; DP 218 rev. iii 7–iv 2.

43 Nik 1: 53 obv. iii 4; RTC 61 obv. iii 9; DP 134 obv. iii 4. If Barairnun continued serving as **lukur** after giving birth in Lugalanda 4 (which cannot be proven because two of these texts are dated to Lugalanda 1 and the last is missing the year), we would have an additional piece of evidence for Steinkeller's (1981a: 85) understanding that the Lagashite **lukur** could be married and have children.

44 DP 127 obv. ii 8.

45 Another possible example is **Gišgal-ir-nun**, a **lukur** (Nik 1: 53 obv. iii 6; RTC 61 obv. iii 11; DP 134 obv. iii 6) and sister of the ruler (DP 127 obv. ii 10), who might be the same person as a **Gišgal-ir-nun** whose 8½ **iku** of barley fields was taken over (**e-dab$_5$**) by another person (Nik 1: 30 rev. iii 5, rev. iv 2–3; Selz 1989: 188–89).

number than those of any other woman,[46] a total of seven.[47] Her **maš-da-ri-a** usually consisted of one sheep,[48] but in a document recording **maš-da-ri-a** of onions she delivered 72 **$sila_3$** (DP 89 obv. ii 4–rev. i 2), the other contributors being two **sanga**-administrators.[49] Although we do not possess any documentation that would suggest her financial situation, it is not unlikely that she had been allotted leased fields and onion plots, as was Baraaranu (see §2.2.1).

2.2.5 Hal-hal, Wife of En-ig-gal, Chief Administrator

Halhal (**Hal-hal**), the wife of the chief administrator Eniggal (**En-ig-gal**), is attested as a **maš-da-ri-a** contributor in several texts, bringing one kid (DP 86 obv. ii 4–rev. i 2) or one lamb (Nik 1: 172 obv. i 1–ii 2; VS 14: 179 obv. v 3–5).[50] In contrast to those cases in which Halhal was listed without her husband, in VS 14: 159 she and her husband appear with their respective **maš-da-ri-a** goods: his **maš-da-ri-a** consisted of one sheep and 10 **sa_2-dug_4**[51] of beer (obv. i 3–6), and hers was one sheep and 5 **sa_2-dug_4** of beer (obv. v 5–9). No preserved text testifies that Halhal held any kind of land. It is worth noting, however, that the (unnamed) wife of another chief administrator was allotted 12 **iku** of (leased fields from) palace land.[52] Since Halhal was the wife of the most active and

46 Taking **Nin-bur** to be a short form of **Nin-bur-šu-ma** (Foxvog 2011: 63–64); cf. Balke 2017: 319, which lists only one attestation (MLVS 916) under the name **Nin-bur**.

47 Nik 1: 168 obv. i 1–4 is heavily broken but included in this number, following the reconstruction in CDLI.

48 DP 90 obv. i 1–4; VS 14: 179 obv. i 5–7; RTC 44 rev. i 5–7. In DP 86 obv. i 1–3 and MLVS 916 obv. ii 5–6, her delivered item is missing or unclear but most likely to be one small animal in both cases. Note that the additional two **maš-da-ri-a** contributors mentioned in DP 86 are also women: (name broken), wife of the chief scribe **Amar-šuba** (obv. i 4–ii 3) and **Hal-hal,** wife of the chief administrator **En-ig-gal** (see §2.2.5).

49 Prentice (2010a: 261) analyzes the professions of those who brought onions as **maš-da-ri-a**: they were **sanga**-administrator of temples, **agrig**-official, scribe, field measurer of Ningirsu, head ploughman (**sag-apin**), farmer (**engar**), doctor (**a-zu**), and **nu-$banda_3$**. She discusses DP 89 with no mention to Ninbur among the onion **maš-da-ri-a** contributors (p. 261 n. 45).

50 VS 14: 179 mentions 26 contributors of **maš-da-ri-a** in total, among whom are eleven (possibly twelve) women, including Halhal; the other women are Ninbur (§2.2.4), three women we will discuss later (§2.2.6), wife of the **sanga**-administrator of the palace **$Ša_3$-TAR**, wife of the **sanga**-administrator of **^{d}Nin-dar**, wife of the scribe **A-gub_2-ni-du**, **Ama-nagar**, wife of the trader (**ga-$eš_8$**), wife of the farmer (**engar**) **Lu_2-^{d}Ba-ba_6**, and wife of the **sanga**-administrator of **^{d}Ga_2-tum_3-du_{10}**.

51 A liquid measurement: 1 **sa_2-dug_4** = 18 liters or 24 liters in Powell 1987–90: 507.

52 12 **iku e_2-gal-kam / dam Šubur /** [**nu**]-**$banda_3$** (VS 14: 156 obv. iii 8–iv 1).

powerful chief administrator of the **E_2-MI_2**, it would not be surprising if she had been allotted land as well, making her able to afford her own goods for **maš-da-ri-a**. We will come back to the co-appearance of the couple later (§2.2.6).

2.2.6 Gan-šubur, Wife of Sig_4-ki-be_2-gi_4, Sanga-Administrator of the Goddess Nanshe

The last of the six women is the wife of the **sanga**-administrator of the goddess Nanshe. We take up with her because the way in which her deliveries were recorded seems to reveal the record keeper's view that her and her husband's deliveries were independent.

According to DP 206 (dated to Lugalanda 5), the wife of the **sanga**-administrator of the goddess Nanshe brought a **maš-da-ri-a** two times, and her husband four times. Her first **maš-da-ri-a** delivery corresponded to his second, and her second delivery to his fourth:

> One lamb the wife of the **sanga**-official of the goddess Nanshe / one kid for the *second* time / the **sanga**-official of the goddess Nanshe;[53]

> One sheep for the *second* time / the wife of the **sanga**-official of the goddess Nanshe / one kid for the *fourth* time / the **sanga**-official of the goddess Nanshe.[54]

By this way of specification each one's delivery was clearly distinguished, and the wife appears to have been as much an active contributor as her husband.

The wife of the **sanga**-administrator of the goddess Nanshe can be easily identified as Ganshubur (**Gan-šubur**) based on a text dated to Lugalanda 4,[55] while the identification of her husband is somewhat confusing. On the one hand, the **sanga**-administrator of Nanshe is identified as **Sig_4-ki-be_2-gi_4** in a text dated to Lugalanda 4,[56] as **Sig_4-be_2-gi_4** in a text dated to Lugalanda 3,[57] and as **Sig_4-ki** in two texts dated to year 3 of a ruler who is most likely to be Lugalanda.[58] These texts seem to mention one and the same person, **Sig_4-ki-be_2-gi_4**, for which **Sig_4-ki** was a short form (Foxvog 2011: 64). On the other hand, another text dated to

---

53 1 **$sila_4$ dam sanga ^{d}Nanše** / 1 **maš 2-kam-ma-ka** / **sanga ^{d}Nanše** (DP 206 obv. ii 3–5).

54 1 **udu** 2-**kam-ma-kam** / **dam sanga ^{d}Nanše** / 1 **maš** 4-**kam-ma** / **sanga ^{d}Nanše** (DP 206 obv. iii 6–iv 2).

55 **Gan-šubur** / **dam sanga ^{d}Nanše** (Nik 1: 214 rev. i 2–3).

56 DP 205 obv. i 3–4.

57 DP 59 obv. ii 2; see Balke 2017: 380.

58 DP 41 obv. ii5–6; RTC 59 obv. ii 6–rev. i 1; the ruler's name under whom these tablets were written was not noted.

Lugalanda 3, VS 14: 179, refers to two **sanga**-administrators: a certain **Sig$_4$-ki**, who was the **sanga**-administrator of **Pa$_4$-pa$_4$** of Lagash (obv. i 9–ii 1)[59] and an unnamed **sanga**-administrator of the goddess Nanshe (obv. ii 4). On this occasion the latter brought a **maš-da-ri-a** of one sheep and two lambs,[60] and his wife (unnamed), who was listed separately, brought one sheep, one kid, and one lamb.[61] The date of the document points to the interpretation that this unnamed **sanga**-administrator of the goddess Nanshe was **Sig$_4$-ki(-be$_2$-gi$_4$)**,[62] and if so, his wife was Ganshubur. Further, **Sig$_4$-ki** the **sanga** (with no specifics as to **sanga** of which temple) and his wife appear in a document, one following the other: he is bringing his **maš-da-ri-a** of [one] sheep, and she is bringing her **maš-da-ri-a** of one sheep and one lamb.[63] This couple is most likely **Sig$_4$-ki-be$_2$-gi$_4$** the **sanga**-administrator of the goddess Nanshe and his wife Ganshubur.

Other elite couples who appeared together or separately in a single document are:

- **Sag-^{d}Nin-gir$_2$-su-da**, the **sanga**-administrator of the **E$_2$-babbar$_2$** Temple, and his wife. They were listed together, one after the other, with their respective **maš-da-ri-a** contributions,[64] while they were listed separately in another text;[65]
- The **sanga**-administrator **Gu$_2$-bi**[66] and his wife **Nin-u$_3$-ma**, who were listed together, one following the other with their respective **maš-da-ri-a** contributions of one sheep each;[67]
- The chief administrator Eniggal and his wife Halhal (see §2.2.5);
- The herald **La-la** and his wife **Nin-u$_3$-ma**. They were listed separately, the former bringing one kid[68] and the latter one sheep.[69]

59 All attestations of **Pa$_4$-pa$_4$** are dated from the reign of Lugalanda and this designation was used to refer to Baranamtara (Rosengarten 1960: 15; Selz 1995: 272).

60 1 **udu** 2 **sila$_4$** / **sanga ^{d}Nanše** (VS 14: 179 obv. ii 3–4).

61 1 **udu** 1 **maš** 1 **sila$_4$** / **dam sanga ^{d}Nanše** (VS 14: 179 obv. iii 1–2).

62 Hence it can be concluded that the **sanga**-administrator of **Pa$_4$-pa$_4$** of Lagash had a name similar to that of the sanga-administrator of the goddess Nanshe if they were not the same individual.

63 [1] **udu** / [**maš**]**-da-ri-a** / **Sig$_4$-ki** / **sanga** / 1 **udu** 1 **sila$_4$** / **dam Sig$_4$-ki** / **sanga** (DP 216 obv. i 1–7; date missing).

64 [goods] / **sanga E$_2$-babbar** / 1 **udu** / **dam Sag-^{d}Nin-gir$_2$-su-da** / **sanga** / **E$_2$-babbar$_2$** (DP 216 obv. ii 9–iii 3).

65 1 **udu sanga E$_2$-babbar$_2$** (VS 14: 179 obv. ii 5); 1 **udu dam sanga E$_2$-babbar$_2$** (obv. v 2).

66 He is specified as "**Gu$_2$-bi, sanga** of **^{d}Nin-mar^{ki}**" elsewhere (e.g., BIN 8: 351 obv. i 2–3).

67 1 **udu Gu$_2$-bi** / **sanga** / 1 **udu Nin-u$_3$-ma** / **dam Gu$_2$-bi** (VS 14: 179 obv. iv 8–v 1).

68 1 **maš La-la** / **nimgir** (RTC 44 obv. iv 2–3).

69 1 **udu Nin-u$_3$-ma** / **dam La-la** / **nimgir** (RTC 44 rev. ii 4–6).

When the husband-and-wife pairs are listed in one and the same tablet recording **maš-da-ri-a** deliveries, some appear together while others separately. At this point, we can think of at least two rather obvious scenarios to explain the difference in how they appear in tablets: (1) the husband and the wife came together with their respective **maš-da-ri-a** and were listed together; or (2) the husband and the wife came on different occasions with their respective **maš-da-ri-a**, and thus were listed separately in a *Sammeltafel*. In both scenarios, however, there is no difference as to the question of each bringing his/her own goods. This assumption is strongly backed up by the independent counting of the deliveries of the couple.

3 Assessing Women's Agency in Presargonic Lagash Through maš-da-ri-a Contributions

After this overview of the sources, let's consider again the definition of agency cited before: "the human capacity for motivated, reflexive action having some consequence (if not always an expected or intended outcome). Agency pertains to individuals and groups" (Steadman and Ross 2010: 1). Starting from this definition allows us to highlight three issues relevant to the present case. First, what is crucial in this definition is "capacity" rather than "action." Second, and clearly linked to the first, when analyzing our case study, the question is not if women "had" agency but what degree of agency they were capable of exercising or enacting. In this direction we align with the idea that agency, as power, is exercised, rather than possessed.[70] Taking these two premises into account, we can state that the abovementioned women (especially the first five) were capable of exercising a certain degree of agency, since all seem to have had, in one way or another, the financial means to procure **maš-da-ri-a** goods.

Third and last, we defend that this definition, particularly its last part ("agency pertains to individuals and groups"), helps to counteract what we may call the "fantasy of individuality," that is the illusion of individual free will as an impulse for agency. Echoing the proposals coined by the archaeologist Almudena Hernando, we prefer a relational approach to agency, rather than an

70 For an overview of different sociological approaches to power, such as the ones by Max Weber and by Michael Mann, with remarks about their applicability to ancient Near Eastern studies, see Svärd 2015: 23–39. See also Bahrani 2001, particularly pp. 20–23, for some remarks based on proposals by Michel Foucault.

individual one.[71] In a similar way, the archaeologist Joanna Brück (2001: 655) states that agency is "located not simply within bounded human bodies but within the wider set of social relationships that make up the person." Seen from this perspective, the information about the six women of Presargonic Lagash selected here provides some insights into their lives as individuals but also into the network that they were part of. All of them were women of the elite, and this hierarchical position gave them a certain degree of agency, regardless of their gender.

It should be noted that to make **maš-da-ri-a** contributions possible it was necessary to carry out other activities. To better assess the degree of agency, then, it is also useful to identify and list the activities carried out by elite women besides properly managing the **maš-da-ri-a** contributions. Some of these activities and actions might seem, at first sight, not necessarily related to the contributions, but when we view these activities as part of a larger network, these other activities are fundamental for obtaining the bigger picture. Moreover, doing so renders visible the role of these women as agents in scenarios where they have often been invisible in scholarship. This strategy has proven relevant in two articles devoted to the scrutiny of the economic agency of women at the beginning of the second millennium BCE, both quoted above (§1), authored by Thomason (2013) and by De Graef (2018). Thomason (2013: 97) lists up to 28 activities women developed as enterpreneurs and producers: from writing and receiving letters to marrying Anatolian husbands or buying wool. De Graef analyzes sales, loans, and leases to make evident the role of women as active parties in all these transactions.

With regard to the case study discussed here, some of the activities carried on by elite women as witnessed in the Presargonic Lagash texts are:[72]

1) Maintaining diplomatic relations
2) Owning domestic animals
3) Holding leased fields
4) Holding sustenance fields
5) Buying goods and property, including slaves
6) Actively participating in decision making related to profit management

71 See Hernando 2018, applying the relational/individual divide to identity. Cf. also Knapp 2010, especially pp. 194–95 for the difficulties of applying certain ideas about identity linked to agency when studying the past.

72 Needless to say, not all elite women engaged in the same activities, and some of the listed activities are attested only for the queen. However, we collect here a wide arrange of activities to highlight its potentiality and also to reinforce our approach to the degrees of agency, directly depending on the number and kind of activities developed.

7) Holding titles, such as **ereš-dingir** and **lukur**
8) Organizing religious ceremonies and processions
9) Receiving offerings
10) Managing offerings and contributions such as the **maš-da-ri-a**
11) Gestating and giving birth to children, thus ensuring the continuity of the elite through heirs[73]

This provisional list of actions and activities, which includes also the **maš-da-ri-a** deliveries, gives testimony to the quite high degree of agency of elite women in the economic, political, social, and religious milieux. If compared with the situation of their male counterparts, we suggest that there is a quantitative rather than a qualitative difference regarding their agency. If we consider the frequency of the deliveries performed by the contributors in the whole corpus, as pointed out above (§2.1) only about 15% were female. If we consider this datum, it might seem that the degree of agency of female **maš-da-ri-a** contributors was lower than that of male ones. However, on the other hand, if we focus on the content of the gifts and on the economic means of the contributors, we realize that there was not so much difference between male and female contributors. As these are qualitative factors, we may conclude that from the qualitative point of view the degree of agency of female **maš-da-ri-a** contributors was not radically different from that of male ones. At this point it is interesting to note that the same was suggested by Svärd in her paper about women's agency as authors (Svärd 2013: 269–70). Svärd also points out that if there was a gender difference in terms of the degree of agency, it might not be due to qualitative factors. In sum, we acknowledge a divergence between qualitative and quantitative interpretations of the data. However, this divergence does not call into question the capacity of female contributors of **maš-da-ri-a** for motivated action. This is important because women's agency, as pointed out above, tends to be questioned and needs to be proven, something that does not happen with male agency.

At this point, one may wonder why we tend to pose research questions about the agency of elite women while we do not ask the same with regard to elite men. Why is agency as an analytical tool almost exclusively applied to research on women in ancient Near Eastern studies? We propose here two possible entangled

---

73 These activities have been often naturalized and thus not considered as relevant from an economic or political point of view. However, in the framework of women's studies and gender studies several voices claim that there is a need to consider such activities, including the (re)productive ones, like others linked mainly or exclusively to women, as productive work. As an example in ancient Near Eastern studies, see, for instance, Michel (2016: 199), who presents as "unrecognized and unpaid work" the "manifold activities of women as housewives."

answers. First, we still look for women's agency in order to counteract the tendency to associate women with passive private roles and men with active public roles. This is clear when, to explain the presence of women as contributors, the hypothesis of these women acting as proxies of their husbands is put on the table. Consequently, it seems we need more evidence to prove the presence of women in roles depicted as active and/or as public than is needed to prove the presence of men in the same circumstances. In previous joint research we also verified this situation when dealing with the overseers of textile production in Presargonic Lagash: men were the expected overseers, while women were not (for the selection of texts and development of this argument, see Karahashi and Garcia-Ventura 2016).

Second, and clearly linked to the first answer, is that still nowadays the agency of elite men needs only to be "found" (it is assumed to be there), while the agency of elite women needs to be proved (because its existence is not assumed). As summarized by Bahrani (2001: 46), "archaeologists have either argued for an unrecorded female agency or have assumed that women have none." Also along these lines, it is illuminating to see how for decades the study of ancient Near Eastern Early Dynastic sculpture has been approached with certain assumptions about male and female donors, conditioning not only the interpretation of the materials but even their reconstruction and preservation.[74] As has been pointed out by Jean Evans (2012: 190) in her study on the topic, "the sculpture fragments belonging to female figures were more likely to remain fragments, whereas many statues of male figures were reconstructed. This attitude obscured a full assessment of Early Dynastic dedicatory practices in the Diyala region with respect to gender."

Nevertheless, it is interesting to note that this situation has been denounced in various fields, and thus it is not a peculiarity of ancient Near Eastern studies. A good example of this is the now-classic work by the U.S. writer Joanna Russ (1937–2011) ironically titled *How to Suppress Women's Writing* (2018, originally published in 1983). Russ puts on the table several frequent statements posed in secondary literature when analyzing women's writing or women as authors. All these statements start from a premise: men are the expected authors, while women are not. For this reason, when women are authors, scholars tend to look for an explanation for a situation perceived as an anomaly. Some of Russ' statements might also help to reflect on the case study of the **maš-da-ri-a** contributors, for instance these two: "she wrote it, but she wrote only one of it" or "she

---

74 For an exhaustive analysis and overview with special emphasis on gender aspects, see Evans 2012: 179–202.

wrote it, but there are very few other."[75] If we change "wrote" to "brought" and consider "she" to refer to an elite woman of Presargonic Lagash, we have some of the arguments often advanced to downplay the potential degree of agency of these women.

4 To Conclude

Summing up the available evidence as a whole, it seems certain that female contributors of **maš-da-ri-a** in Presargonic Lagash, who were themselves members of the ruling family and/or wives of high-ranking oficials, had the socio-economic means to procure their own **maš-da-ri-a** goods. That they were active contributors just like their husbands can be corroborated through the arrangement, wording, and expressions used in the documents to record such deliveries. On these grounds, we conclude that, first, from the qualitative point of view there are no significant differences with regard to the degree of agency of female and male **maš-da-ri-a** contributions; and second, that agency is a useful analytical tool to highlight the effective and active role of women in several milieux.

All in all, we argue that we always need a thorough scrutiny of the texts combined with theoretically informed research, as we have aimed to do here, to shed new light on women in Presargonic Lagash in particular and on ancient Near Eastern sources in general.

Bibliography

Asher-Greve, Julia M. 2013. Women and Agency: A Survey from Late Uruk to the End of Ur III. Pp. 359–77 in *The Sumerian World*, ed. Harriet Crawford. London: Routledge.
Bahrani, Zainab. 2001. *Women of Babylon. Gender and Representation in Mesopotamia.* London: Routledge.
Balke, Thomas E. 2017. *Das altsumerische Onomastikon: Namengebung und Prosopografie nach den Quellen aus Lagas.* dubsar 1. Münster: Zaphon.
Beld, Scott G. 2002. The Queen of Lagash: Ritual Economy in a Sumerian State. Ph. D. dissertation. The University of Michigan.
Bourdieu, Pierre. 1977. *Outline of a Theory of Practice.* Cambridge: Cambridge University Press.

75 See particularly the beginning of chapter 8 where Russ (2018 [1983]: 92) summarizes most of the statements she takes as starting points for her analyses in previous chapters.

Brück, Joanna. 2001. Monuments, Power, and Personhood in the British Neolithic. *Journal of the Royal Anthropological Institute* 7: 649–67.
De Graef, Katrien. 2018. Puppets on a String? On Female Agency in Old Babylonian Economy. Pp. 133–56 in *Studying Gender in the Ancient Near East*, ed. Saana Svärd and Agnès Garcia-Ventura. University Park, PA: Eisenbrauns and Penn State University Press.
Dobres, Marcia-Anne, and John Robb. 2000. Agency in Archaeology: Paradigm or Platitude? Pp. 3–17 in *Agency in Archaeology*, ed. Marcia-Anne Dobres and John Robb. London: Routledge.
Dornan, Jennifer L. 2002. Agency and Archaeology: Past, Present, and Future Directions. *Journal of Archaeological Method and Theory* 9/4: 303–29.
Downes, Sophy. 2019. Agency. Pp. 333–57 in *A Companion to Ancient Near Eastern Art*, ed. Ann C. Gunter. Hoboken, NJ: Wiley Blackwell.
Evans, Jean M. 2012. *The Lives of Sumerian Sculpture: An Archaeology of the Early Dynastic Temple*. Cambridge: Cambridge University Press.
Foster, Benjamin R. 1980. "Land of Both Types" at Sargonic Umma. *ASJ* 2: 225–26.
Foxvog, Daniel A. 2011. Aspects of Name-Giving in Presagonic Lagash. Pp. 59–97 in *Strings and Threads: A Celebration of the Works of Anne Draffkorn Kilmer*, ed. Wolfgang Heimpel and Gabriella Frantz-Szabó. Winona Lake, IN: Eisenbrauns.
Garcia-Ventura, Agnès. 2019. Vida y obra de la asirióloga francesa Yvonne Rosengarten, "un bon chercheur entièrement voué à son travail." *Aula Orientalis* 37: 25–39.
Gelb, Ignace J. 1965. The Philadelphia Onion Archive. Pp. 57–62 in *Studies in Honor of Benno Landsberger on His Seventy-Fifth* Birthday, *April 21, 1965*, ed. Hans G. Güterbock and Thorkild Jacobsen. AS 16. Chicago: University of Chicago Press.
Gero, Joan M. 2000. Troubled Travels in Agency and Feminism. Pp. 30–39 in *Agency in Archaeology*, ed. Marcia-Anne Dobres and John Robb. London: Routledge.
Giddens, Anthony. 1979. *Central Problems in Social Theory: Action, Structure and Contradiction in Social Analysis*. London: Macmillan.
Goodnick Westenholz, Joan. 2013. In the Service of the Gods: The Ministering Clergy. Pp. 246–74 in *The Sumerian World*, ed. Harriet Crawford. London: Routledge.
Halton, Charles, and Saana Svärd. 2018. *Women's Writing of Ancient Mesopotamia: An Anthology of the Earliest Female Authors*. Cambridge: Cambridge University Press.
Hernando, Almudena. 2018. *La fantasía de la individualidad. Sobre la construcción sociohistórica del sujeto moderno*. 2nd ed. Madrid: Traficantes de Sueños.
Huber Vulliet, Fabienne. 2010. Un festival nippurite à l'époque paléobabylonienne. Pp. 125–50 in *Your Praise is Sweet: A Memorial Volume for Jeremy Black from Students, Colleagues and Friends*, ed. Heather D. Baker, Eleanor Robson, and Gábor Zólyomi. London: British Institute for the Study of Iraq.
Karahashi, Fumi. 2011. "An Early Dynastic Tablet in Ancient Orient Museum, Tokyo," *Bulletin of Ancient Orient Museum* 32: 1–16.
Karahashi, Fumi. 2016a. Some Professions with Both Male and Female Members in the Presargonic E_2-MI_2 Corpus. *Orient* 51: 47–67.
Karahashi, Fumi. 2016b. Women and Land in the Presargonic Lagaš Corpus. Pp. 57–70 in *The Role of Women in Work and Society in the Ancient Near East*, ed. Brigitte Lion and Cécile Michel. Boston and Berlin: De Gruyter.
Karahashi, Fumi, and Agnès Garcia-Ventura. 2016. Overseers of Textile Workers in Presargonic Lagash. *KASKAL: Rivista di storia, ambienti e culture del Vicino Oriente Antico* 13: 1–19.

Knapp, A. Bernard. 2010. Beyond Agency: Identity and Individuals in Archaeology. Pp. 193–200 in *Agency and Identity in the Ancient Near East: New Paths Forward*, ed. Sharon R. Steadman and Jennifer C. Ross. London: Equinox Publishing.

Knappett, Carl, and Lambros Malafouris. 2008. Material and Nonhuman Agency: An Introduction. Pp. ix–xix in *Material Agency: Towards a Non-Anthropological Approach*, ed. Carl Knappett and Lambros Malafouris. New York: Springer.

Lion, Brigitte, and Eleanor Robson. 2005. Quelques textes scolaires paléo-babyloniens rédigés par des femmes. *JCS* 57: 37–54.

Maekawa, Kazuya. 1973–74. The Development of the é-mí in Lagash during Early Dynastic III. *Mesopotamia* 8–9:77–144.

Maekawa, Kazuya. 1977. The Rent of the Tenant Field (gán-APIN.LAL) in Lagash. *Zinbun* 14: 154.

Maekawa, Kazuya. 1982. The Agricultural Texts of Ur III Lagash of the British Museum (II). *ASJ* 4: 85–127.

Michel, Cécile. 2016. Women Work, Men are Professionals in the Old Assyrian Archives. Pp. 193–208 in *The Role of Women in Work and Society in the Ancient Near East*, ed. Brigitte Lion and Cécile Michel, SANER 13. Boston: De Gruyter.

Michel, Cécile. 2020. *Women of Aššur and Kaneš: Texts from the Archives of Assyrian Merchants*. Writings from the Ancient World. Baltimore, MD: SBL Press.

Nakahara, Yomokuro. 1961. シュメール土地制度における託営地について[On allotted land in Sumer land system]. *Seiyoshigaku* 50: 83–94.

Powell, Marvin A. 1987–90. Maße und Gewichte. Pp. 457–516 in *Reallexikon der Assyriologie und Vorderasiatischen Archäologie*, vol. 7. Berlin: de Gruyter.

Prentice, Rosemary. 2010a. A Prohibition on Onion Growing in Pre-Sargonic Lagaš? Pp. 255–67 in *Your Paise Is Sweet: A Memorial Volume for Jeremy Black from Students, Colleagues and Friends*, ed. Heather D. Baker, Eleanor Robson, and Gábor Zólyomi. London: British Institute for the Study of Iraq.

Prentice, Rosemary. 2010b. *The Exchange of Goods and Services in Pre-Sargonic Lagash*. AOAT 368. Münster: Ugarit-Verlag.

Rosengarten, Yvonne. 1960. *Le régime des offrandes dans la société sumérienne d'après les textes présargoniques de Lagaš*. Paris: E. de Boccard.

Russ, Joanna. 2018 [1983]. *How to Suppress Women's Writing*. Austin, TX: University of Texas Press.

Sallaberger, Walther. 2018. Festival Provisions in Early Bronze Age Mesopotamia. *KASKAL: Rivista di storia, ambienti e culture del Vicino Oriente Antico* 15: 171–200.

Sallaberger, Walther, and Ingo Schrakamp. 2015. Philological Data for a Historical Chronology of Mesopotamia in the 3rd Millennium. Pp. 3–136 in *History and Philology*, ed. Walther Sallaberger and Ingo Schrakamp. ARCANE 3. Turnhout: Brepols.

Selz, Gebhard J. 1989. *Altsumerische Verwaltungstexte aus Lagaš*. Teil 1: *Die altsumerischen Wirtschaftsurkunden der Ermitage zu Leningrad*. FAOS 15/1.

Selz, Gebhard J. 1995. *Untersuchungen zur Götterwelt des altsumerischen Stadtstaates*. Occasional Publications of the Samuel Noah Kramer Fund, 13. Philadelphia: University of Pennsylvania Museum.

Sharlach, Tonia M. 2008. Priestesses, Concubines, and the Daughters of Men: Disentangling the Meaning of the Word lukur in Ur III times. Pp. 177–83 in *On the Third Dynasty of Ur: Studies in Honor of Marcel Sigrist*, ed. Piotr Michalowski. Boston: American Schools of Oriental Research.

Sharlach, Tonia M. 2017. *An Ox of One's Own: Royal Wives and Religion at the Court of the Third Dynasty of Ur*. SANER 18. Berlin: de Gruyter.

Steadman, Sharon R., and Jennifer C. Ross. 2010. *Agency and Identity in the Ancient Near East: New Paths Forward*. London: Equinox Publishing.

Steinkeller, Piotr. 1981a. More on the Ur III Royal Wives. *ASJ* 3: 77–92.

Steinkeller, Piotr. 1981b. The Renting of Fields in Early Mesopotamia and the Development of the Concept of "Interest" in Sumerian. *JESHO* 24: 113–45.

Suter, Claudia E. 2017. On Images, Visibility, and Agency of Early Mesopotamian Royal Women. Pp. 337–62 in *The First Ninety Years: A Sumerian Celebration in Honor of Miguel Civil*, ed. Lluís Feliu, Fumi Karahashi, and Gonzalo Rubio. SANER 12. Boston: de Gruyter.

Suter, Claudia E. 2018 Feasting and Elite Women in Early Mesopotamia: A Contribution from the Visual Record. *KASKAL. Rivista di storia, ambienti e culture del Vicino Oriente Antico* 15: 139–54.

Svärd, Saana. 2013. Female Agency and Authorship in Mesopotamian Texts. *KASKAL. Rivista di storia, ambienti e culture del Vicino Oriente Antico* 10: 269–80.

Svärd, Saana. 2015. *Women and Power in Neo-Assyrian Palaces*. State Archives of Assyria Studies 23. Winona Lake, IN: Eisenbrauns.

Thomason, Allison K. 2013. Her Share of the Profits: Women, Agency, and Textile Production at Kültepe/Kanesh in the Early Second Millennium BC. Pp. 93–112 in *Textile Production and Consumption in the Ancient Near East: Archaeology, Epigraphy and Iconography*, ed. Marie-Louise Nosch, Henriette Koefoed, and Eva A. Strand. Oxford: Oxbow Books.

Vigo, Matteo. 2016. Sources for the Study of the Role of Women in the Hittite Administration. Pp. 328–53 in *The Role of Women in Work and Society in the Ancient Near East*, ed. Brigitte Lion and Cécile Michel. SANER 13. Boston: de Gruyter.

Westenholz, Aage. 1987. *Old Sumerian and Old Akkadian Texts in Philadelphia, Part Two: The "Akkadian" Texts, the Enlilemaba Texts, and the Onion Archive*. CNI Publications 3. Copenhagen: Museum Tusculanum Press.

Katsuji Sano

The Role of Women in Assyrian Foreign Policy

1 Introduction

In the Neo-Assyrian period (934–609 BC), Assyria not only regained the territories lost during the invasions of the Aramaeans in the end of the Middle-Assyrian period, but also continued to expand beyond traditional borders, and dominated the entire Near East ranging from Egypt to Elam during the reign of Assurbanipal (668–631/627? BC).[1] The Assyrian royal inscriptions, which record the achievements of the Assyrian kings, contain the detailed accounts of the kings' conquest activities in their military campaigns, and these accounts confirm that they carried out deportations of many enemies in the process of Assyrian expansion. Oded (1979: 20), who systematically investigated the Assyrian deportations on the basis of a variety of historical sources, mainly Assyrian royal inscriptions, counted Assyria as having carried out 157 mass deportations over three centuries, in which an estimated total of 4.5 million people were deported. Many Assyriologists explain that the Neo-Assyrian Empire was built through the continuous implementation of mass deportations of enemies, citing the study of Oded. In this context, it is rare to find a mention of domination policies other than mass deportations, or of diplomacy. Therefore, in this article, I focus on "foreign policy (domination and diplomacy) using women" that we speculate was carried out in the process of Assyrian expansion, and I attempt to reveal the political role that these women played. By this I would like to emphasize the fact that the Neo-Assyrian Empire was built based on much more complex human movements than has been so far envisaged, and to propose that the conventional simple Assyrian image needs to be reviewed. The women considered in this article are, strictly speaking, the daughters of the Assyrian kings and the female relatives of foreign rulers and nobles (*rabûti*) who were presented to the Assyrian kings.

1 This article is a revised version of the manuscript read at the International Workshop "Women's Religious and Economic Roles in Antiquity" (Nov. 10–11, 2017, Chuo University). The aforementioned manuscript was prepared based on my German article published in 2015, namely "Die den Assyrerkönigen übersandten ausländischen Frauen mit Mitgift in neuassyrischer Zeit," *Kaskal* 12: 383–89. I would like to thank Dr. Nicole Brisch, Prof. Andreas Fuchs, Prof. Fumi Karahashi, and an anonymous reviewer for reading the manuscript and providing valuable comments.

https://doi.org/10.1515/9781501514821-004

2 The Role of the Daughters of the Assyrian Kings

The daughters of Assyrian kings were used for two political purposes. That is, maintaining a peace treaty concluded with rival lands (Babylonia, Elam) or one strong land (Scythia) located far away, and strengthening relations between Assyria and her vassal states. Historically, Assyria engaged in repeated military conflicts with rival lands and competed for political influence, but sometimes Assyria also concluded peace treaties, when the political situation required it. In the reigns of Adad-nērārī II (911–891 BC) and Esarhaddon (680–669 BC), it is confirmed that the daughters of the Assyrian kings were used in cases of this kind. At some point between 893 and 891 BC, Adad-nērārī II fought with the Babylonian king Nabû-šuma-ukīn I, conquered the cities of Babylonia and carried away goods and people as booty. Afterward, in 891 BC, the two kings finally concluded a peace treaty and defined a new boundary between Assyria and Babylonia. At that time, they exchanged their daughters as marriage partners.[2] The friendly relations established by this diplomatic marriage lasted for about 80 years until the reign of Šamšī-Adad V (823–811 BC).[3] As well as Babylonia, Elam was also a powerful rival land for Assyria, and in the reigns of Sargon II (721–705 BC) and Sennacherib (704–681 BC), Assyria had repeated military conflicts with Elam. However, Esarhaddon chose to conclude a peace treaty with Elam in 674 BC. From the letter that Esarhaddon sent to Urtaku, the king of Elam, it is confirmed that the kings had mutually exchanged their sons and daughters as political collateral for maintaining the treaty.[4] This is quite different to the arrangement with Babylonia, and it clearly shows how important the improvement of relations with Elam was for

---

2 Grayson 1975: 166–67 Chronicle 21 iii 10–21; Glassner 2004: 180–81 iii 10–21.

3 Briefly, there were no military campaigns to Babylonia in the reigns of Tukultī-Ninurta II (890–884 BC) and Assurnasirpal II (883–859 BC), and Shalmaneser III (858–824 BC) responded to the request of Babylonian King Marduk-zākir-šumi who was rebelled against by his brother Marduk-bēl-usāte, and Shalmaneser III advanced to Babylonia in 851 BC to help him. Regarding the relevant expedition of Shalmaneser III, see Grayson 1996: 30 A.0.102.5 iv 1–5; 37 A.0.102.6 ii 41–44; 46 A.0.102.8, 23′–24′; 52–53 A.0.102.10 iii 31–34; Grayson 1975: 167 Chronicle 21 iii 28–34; Glassner 2004: 182–83 iii 28–34.

4 Luukko and Buylaere 2002: 4 no. 1, 1–13. Also, in the letter of crown prince to Šulmu-bēli-lušme (Reynolds 2003: 7–9 no. 7, 3–10) it is mentioned that the king of Elam and the king of Assyria have become treaty partners, having repeatedly negotiated, and a festival was held to celebrate it. The liver omen text (Starr 1990: 84 no. 74) shows that Esarhaddon asked Šamaš before the start of negotiations, whether Urtaku's proposal for concluding a peace treaty was sincere. Regarding a peace treaty between Assyria and Elam, see also Parpola and Watanabe 1988: XVI–XVIII.

Assyria. Because of exchanging more than one royal family member as political collateral, that is, sons and daughters of both kings, a stronger effect on compliance with the treaty could be expected than that achieved by diplomatic marriage involving only the daughters. It is assumed that Esarhaddon adopted this special policy for the purpose of removing the conflict with Elam before undertaking the expedition against Egypt in 671 BC. It is especially important to note that this diplomacy is not accurately reported in the inscription of Esarhaddon, and it is described that the king of Elam, afraid of Assyria, voluntarily dispatched his messenger to Assyria for friendship and peace, and he swore an oath by the great gods.[5] From this description it is understood that the Assyrian royal inscriptions were created to represent the "strength of the Assyrian king" maximally, and that therefore concessions to other lands should not be recorded, even if it was temporarily necessary diplomatically in the process of the expansion of the empire. Although I mentioned earlier that the Assyrian and Babylonian kings exchanged their daughters for the maintenance of the peace treaty, evidence suggests the existence of another case to show the implementation of a similar policy in the reign of Esarhaddon. The case comes from the liver omen text that Esarhaddon, or strictly speaking, his augur, asked questions of the Sun-god Šamaš.[6] From this text, we know that Esarhaddon received a message from the Scythian king Bartatua that he wanted to take one of Esarhaddon's daughters as his wife, and that Esarhaddon asked Šamaš whether he should accept Bartatua's request, whether Bartatua would comply with the treaty, and whether this treaty would benefit Esarhaddon. Because the answer from Šamaš is not recorded, we do not know how Esarhaddon answered. Starr (1990: LXII), the editor of this text, assumes that Esarhaddon accepted the request of Bartatua and that the alliance established between Assyria and Scythia continued until the reign of Madyes, the son of Bartatua, because Assyria was released from Median pressure at least temporarily when Madyes attacked the Median troops. Also, the German archaeologist Boehmer (2001: 60) thinks that the incident described in Herodotus (I. 103) that Madyes came to the aid of Assyria during the last battle over Nineveh probably reflects a historical fact, and that Esarhaddon gave his daughter in response to the request of Bartatua and also received a daughter of Bartatua in return. The reason why Boehmer believes that Esarhaddon received Bartatua's daughter

5 Leichty 2011: 22 no. 1 v 26–33. Strictly speaking, in the relevant passage of this inscription, the king of Elam is mentioned together with a Gutian king in the third person plural. That is, two kings concluded peace treaties with Esarhaddon.

6 Starr 1990: 24–26 no. 20. Although no. 21 is considered to be a text concerning the same matter, it is not possible to confirm the name of Bartatua, because the text is damaged. See Starr 1990: LXII.

derives from two archeological finds. According to Boehmer (2001: 58), the fact that a dragon-shaped handle of a gold jug, found in Bronze Coffin 2 in Tomb III under the Northwest Palace at Nimrud, resembles closely the appearance of a dragon seen in the golden sheath of Akinakes, an iron dagger excavated from Kelermes, indicates the possibility that both artefacts were created in the same place.[7] Also the morphological features of a woman's skull found in Bronze Coffin 3 (containing bones of five adults) at the same site suggests that she came from eastern Anatolia, the Caucasus, or the Asian steppe between the Caspian Sea and the Amu-Darya.[8] The hypothesis of Boehmer is sufficiently convincing and can be supported.

So far, we have seen the role of the daughters of the Assyrian kings used for the construction of friendships with rival lands (Babylonia, Elam) and one strong land (Scythia) located far away. Next, we will look at the second political purpose, that is, the role of the kings' daughters used to strengthen relations between Assyria and her vassal states. In the time of Tiglath-pileser III (744–727 BC), Assyria began to annex the lands located outside the traditional borders, and increased the area under direct control as Assyrian provinces. As a result, Assyria gradually approached the powerful rival lands geographically, and Sargon II tried to place one extremely loyal vassal state as a buffering state between Assyria and those rival lands. Sargon II utilized his own daughter as one of means to realize this purpose.[9] That is, Sargon II permitted Ḫullī, the king of Bīt-Purutaš who was deported to Assyria by Shalmaneser V (726–722 BC) to return to Bīt-Purutaš in order to maintain Bīt-Purutaš located in south-central Anatolia as an obedient buffer state against the land Mušku (Phrygia), and educated Ambaris (or Amris), the son of Ḫullī, at the Assyrian court.[10] After the death of Ḫullī, Sargon II appointed Ambaris

7 Regarding the gold jug from Coffin 2, see also Damerji 1998: 9, Abb. 48–52; Collon 2008: 115–17, pl. VII; Hussein 2016: 34, pls. 134–37.

8 Schultz and Kunter 1998: 114; Boehmer 2001: 60. One may wonder why a gold jug, thought to belong to the burial goods of a woman buried in Coffin 3, was found in Coffin 2. However, this is not so surprising, because the individuals found from three Coffins in Tomb III were in all likelihood originally buried another place. See Schultz and Kunter 1998: 103; Boehmer 2001: 57.

9 When Sargon II suppressed the rebellion of the Land Mannea, he also exceptionally allowed the revolting king of that land to remain on the throne, in order to make his land an obedient buffer state against Urartu, Assyrian rival land. Also, a little later, the people who had been deported to Assyria as punishment for the revolt were allowed to return. See Fuchs 1998: 24, 54 II.d Ass.1–11.

10 Gadd 1954: 182–83 Nimrud Prisms D & E v 16; Fuchs 1994: 123–24, 323 Ann. 194–197; Fuchs 1998: 42, 71 VI.c 6–11.

as the king of Bīt-Purutaš and gave him his own daughter and the land Ḫilakku.[11] Sennacherib also educated the Egyptian princes caught in the field near the city of Eltekeh in 701 BC at the Assyrian court and he planned to appoint them as Egyptian kings when Assyria conquered Egypt in the future.[12] In the record of house purchase in Nineveh, Šusanqu, who is identified as one of the Egyptian princes, appears as one of the witnesses, with the description "Witness Šusanqu, the son-in-law of the king" (IGI ᵐ*šu-sa-an-qu ḫa-at-na* MAN).[13] From this description

---

11 Gadd 1954: 182–83 Nimrud Prisms D & E v 17; Fuchs 1994: 124, 323 Ann. 197–198; 199, 344 Prunk 29–30. Although the hypothesis identifying the daughter of Sargon II given to Ambaris as Aḫāt-abīša is widely accepted (see Aro and Nissinen 1998: 59), Fuchs (2012: 155) is skeptical of this idea, because there is no evidence directly indicating it.

12 See Radner 2012: 475–76. Regarding the battle near Eltekeh and the capture of the Egyptian princes on the field, see Grayson and Novotny 2012: 64–65 no. 4, 44–45; 96 no. 15 iii 18′–25′; 115 no. 16 iii 50–58; 132 no. 17 iii 14–21; 150 no. 18 ii 1‴–3‴; 176 no. 22 ii 82–iii 6; 193 no. 23 ii 77–iii 5; Grayson and Novotny 2014: 184 no. 140 rev. 8–9; 189 no. 142, 14′–17′; 239 no. 165 iii 32–39.

13 Kwasman and Parpola 1991: 125 no. 142 rev. 12. The term *ḫatanu* means "relative by marriage" and can be translated as "son-in-law," "brother-in-law," or "bridegroom." See CAD H: 148a and AHw: 335b. Note that *ḫatānu* in the CAD entry is an error and should be corrected as "*ḫatanu*." In this regard, see Goetze 1947: 246–47, and von Soden 1995: 16. Kwasman and Parpola (1991: 125) opt to translate this term (in the "Glossary" of their book as *hatannu* listed) as "brother-in-law." On the other hand, Radner (2012: 472–73) translates the passage as "Šusanqu, the king's in-law" and states as follows: "Although it is the most likely scenario, Shoshenq was not necessarily married to a daughter of Sennacherib as the term *hatannu* designates more generally a man linked by marriage to a certain family. Therefore, he could have been married to one of Sennacherib's sisters or even a more distant female relative of the king." In my opinion, there is no other possibility than that Šusanqu was given a daughter of the king. So far as I know, no case of the Assyrian king's sister being used to contract an international political marriage has been confirmed from any historical sources. Furthermore, if we take into account that Sennacherib intended to make Egypt not an ally of equal status with Assyria but a vassal state after its future conquest, we understand that it is unlikely that one of Sennacherib's sisters could have been given in marriage to Šusanqu. In forming an alliance with an independent land equal to Assyria, one might think the king's sister a suitable choice for the construction of a brother-in-law relationship, but Sennacherib's aim was to construct an unequal relationship (a parent-child relationship in law) with Šusanqu, one of the Egyptian princes, whom Sennacherib schemed to appoint as one of the Egyptian kings in the future. Therefore, the translation of *ḫatanu* in the concerned passage must be "son-in-law." Also, Radner points to "a more distant female relative of the king" as one of the possible candidates, but I reject this idea because it is known that Ambaris of Bīt-Purutaš was given a daughter by Sargon II, the predecessor of Sennacherib. If Šusanqu, who had the possibility of becoming one of Assyria's vassal kings in the future, were given a distant female relative of the king, he would not necessarily feel that he was the person most favored by the king among the many Assyrian vassals, even if it was an honor. In other words, from the perspective of maintaining loyalty, constructing a relationship through a distant female relative of the king cannot be expected to be as effective as the construction of a relationship through a daughter of the king.

it is understood that Sennacherib gave Šusanqu his daughter.[14] Šusanqu was later appointed as one of Egyptian kings together with other Egyptian princes when Esarhaddon, the successor of Sennacherib conquered Egypt in 671 BC.[15] The Egyptian princes, like the successors of Assyrian vassal states, were educated at the Assyrian court so as to become faithful vassals in the future; more precisely speaking, so as to have an identity as elite members of the Assyrian Empire rather than the identity of local kings.[16] The Assyrian kings gave their daughters to realize this aim more effectively, only to the persons of strategically important lands. Only two cases have been attested, and this attempt was not always necessarily successful after the return of the princes to their homelands as Assyrian vassal kings, but it can be said that it is one of the important dominance policies that should not be overlooked when trying to understand the establishment of the Assyrian imperial rule.

3 The Role of Foreign Women Presented to the Assyrian Kings

From the Neo-Assyrian royal inscriptions several cases are confirmed that Assyrian kings received women with dowries (*nudunnû*, *terḫatu*)[17] from foreign rulers

In any case, Radner considered the most plausible candidate to be a daughter of the king. Therefore, I would like to note here when I cited her article and introduced her idea in my 2016 article (Sano 2016: 253), I wrote that Šusanqu was given the king's daughter without mentioning other candidates whom she mentioned as possibilities.

14 It is only Šusanqu that we can confirm from the historical sources was given the princess by Sennacherib. Sennacherib must have tried to make the Egyptian princes compete in loyalty to him so as not to unite against him, for which purpose, giving the princess only to particularly loyal person(s) would have functioned well.

15 Novotny and Jeffers 2018: 233–34 no. 11 i 90–113. Šusanqu is called Susinqu in the Royal Inscription (i 110).

16 Sano 2016: 253–54. The list of Errata for this article is uploaded in my page of Academia.edu.

17 Although in the royal inscriptions of the Assyrian kings before Assurbanipal, only the term *nudunnû* (Ass. *nudnû*) CAD N/2: 310a–12a is used to mean "dowry," in the royal inscriptions of Assurbanipal the term *terḫatu* CAD T: 353b–54a "dowry, bridal gift" instead is sometimes used. See the first translation of Case 13 and the first translation of Case 14 in the Appendix. Although I translated *terḫatu* as "bridal gift" in the aforementioned Cases, in the following discussion I refer to women with *nudunnû* or *terḫatu* as "women with dowries" without distinguishing "women with dowries" and "women with bridal gifts," because I assume that *terḫatu* is used in the royal inscriptions as a synonym for *nudunnû*. Regarding *nudunnû* and *terḫatu* used in parallel, see footnote 39 below.

or nobles.[18] Although various studies have explored the role of women at the Assyrian court,[19] few researchers have investigated the phenomenon of foreign rulers and nobles presenting their own female relatives with dowries to Assyrian kings, in connection with the Assyrian policy of domination. This remains a blind spot in the field of women's studies.[20]

Female relatives of foreign rulers or nobles were presented to the Assyrian kings in the following five different situations: (1) during a military campaign without a battle, (2) after a battle that could not be resolved, (3) during a battle to suppress rebellion against Assyria, (4) and (5) in normal times. The case numbers of the individual events (Cases 1–16) in the categories below (1)–(5) correspond to the case numbers in the Appendix, in which the date of the event, the historical source, and the translation of the text are presented for every Assyrian king.

(1) A land that rebelled against Assyria or an enemy land that never belonged to Assyria, in fear of an Assyrian military expedition, presents one or more women with dowries to the Assyrian king, namely (a) the daughter of the ruler (Shalmaneser III: Cases 4, 5, and 6; Shalmaneser IV: Case 9), (b) the sisters of the ruler (Tukultī-Ninurta II: Case 1), (c) the sister or daughter of the ruler, as well as the daughters of nobles (Assurnasirpal II: Case 2; Shalmaneser III: Case 7), or (d) the niece of the ruler (Assurnasirpal II: Case 3), to demonstrate loyalty to Assyria.

(2) In the case that Assyria was unable to conquer a hostile land by military means, the hostile ruler or the new ruler presents his daughter(s) (Sennacherib: Case 10; Assurbanipal: Case 16) to the Assyrian king after the return of the Assyrian troops, having decided to obey Assyria.

(3) In case an Assyrian vassal state rebelled against Assyria and Assyria could not rapidly conquer the vassal state's capital despite laying siege to it because of its strong defenses or due to the necessity to march to another main target, the hostile ruler presents (a) his daughter(s) with dowry(ies) (Shalmaneser III: Case 8; Esarhaddon: Case 11) or (b) his daughter and the daughters

---

18 Only one case is confirmed in which the nobles of the subjugated land presented women with dowries to the Assyrian king. See Case 2 in the Appendix.

19 As to the relevant studies, see Parpola 1988; Dalley 1998; Novotny 2001; Melville 2004; Melville 2005; Parpola 2012; Svärd 2012; Kertai 2013; Svärd 2015a; Svärd 2015b; Stol 2016.

20 Svärd (2015a: 128–30) collected data on women who appeared in the royal inscriptions, and arranged them in a table by each king's reign. Svärd's table provides us with accurate information on the women presented to the Assyrian kings, but beyond simple data collection, no special consideration has been given to these women. I should also point out that I missed two cases in my German article published in 2015, and therefore have added these cases (Cases 8 and 9 in the Appendix) newly in this article.

of his brothers with dowries (Assurbanipal: Case 13) to the Assyrian king to show his will to obey Assyria.

(4) A foreign ruler who is afraid of Assyria and would like to avoid a future Assyrian military campaign against him, decides to obey Assyria and presents his daughter with dowry as a token of his loyalty to the Assyrian king (Assurbanipal: Cases 14 and 15).

(5) The Assyrian vassal brings his daughter with dowry to the Assyrian king to show his further loyalty (Assurbanipal: Case 12).

First, it is necessary to mention the daughters of Hezekiah of the land Judah (Sennacherib: Case 10) and the daughter of Uallî of the land Mannea (Assurbanipal: Case 16) in category (2) because it is not mentioned in the royal inscriptions that they had dowries. As for the daughters of Hezekiah, it is assumed that the scribe of the Rassam Cylinder made in 700 BC had simply forgotten to mention the term "dowries" and that the scribes of the later inscriptions retained the notation on the Rassam Cylinder. Also, concerning the daughter of Uallî of the land Mannea, we can attribute likewise that the reason for the absence of the term "dowry" is due to the oversight of the scribes, because Prisms B, C, F, and A, which report about the daughter of Uallî, explicitly mention the daughters of other foreign rulers using the description "(his) daughter, his offspring, with a bountiful dowry" (Cases 12–15).[21] Since the texts of the Assyrian royal inscriptions are not necessarily perfect, it is not appropriate to think that the daughters of Hezekiah and the daughter of Uallî were excluded from the possibility of political marriage.

Although some scholars regard the role of foreign women with dowries as that of hostages (sg. *līṭu*, pl. *līṭū*/ SB *līṭī*),[22] one should not misunderstand their roles. Because unlike the persons who were taken as hostages by Assyrian kings, in my opinion, the women with dowries did not have the value of a political guarantee. With the marriage, they became a part of the family into which

21 Although an explanation may not be needed, "(his) daughter" and "his offspring" are in apposition.

22 See Radner 2004: 161; Lanfranchi 2010: 45; Cogan 2014: 72. It remains unclear to whom *līṭu* "hostage" refers because the royal inscriptions do not specify. While Zawadzki (1995: 456) assumes that hostages were usually members of king's sons, in particular successors to the throne, and other royal families except for the kings and the daughters of the kings, I consider *līṭu* to mean only the potential successor of king or ruler. For this, see Sano 2015c: 169. Therefore, regarding the Case 3 in which the Assurnasirpal II took hostages (*līṭī*) from Lubarna, King of Patinu, I assume that hostages were the sons of Lubarna who have the right to succeed to the throne.

they had married, therefore, killing them for the punishment against their fathers would have been useless. In fact, women with dowries are never referred to as hostages in Assyrian royal inscriptions.

As a result of an Assyrian king receiving a female relative or relatives of a foreign ruler, a relationship was established between the rulers of both lands. The construction of this relationship was one of Assyria's domination policies aimed at preventing the rebellion of lands that became vassal states. However, the domination policy depended on the establishment of a relationship through sister(s) or daughter(s) of a foreign ruler, and nieces were thought to have little value in helping Assyria maintain indirect control over its vassal states. This can be understood from the case of Lubarna, king of Patinu, who did not have a daughter of his own and instead gave his niece to Assurnasirpal II under threat of an Assyrian military expedition, but nonetheless had hostages taken (perhaps his sons) by Assurnasirpal II (Case 3). Although it remains unclear from the historical sources who these women with dowries were married to, it can be assumed that they were married to the Assyrian king himself or to one of his male relatives, perhaps the king's brothers, sons or nephews.[23] It is likely that a marriage with a member of the Assyrian elite, who was not a member of the royal family, could have posed a threat to the Assyrian king. However, it is possible that daughters of foreign nobles could have married into the Assyrian elite. This is inferred from the fact that the daughters of nobles were merely an addition to the female relatives of the foreign rulers (Assurnasirpal II: Case 2; Shalmaneser III: Case 7), and that it is not confirmed in any case that they were presented alone to Assyrian kings.

The role played by female relatives of foreign rulers seems to differ greatly between the reigns of the kings before Assurbanipal and the reign of Assurbanipal. Because, regarding the women with dowries presented to Assurbanipal, it is described in his royal inscriptions as follows: he (the foreign king) brought to Nineveh[24] (his) daughter, his offspring, (and the daughters of his brothers)[25]

23 The family backgrounds of most Neo-Assyrian queens are unclear. The only exception is Mullissu-mukannišat-Nīnua, the queen of Assurnasirpal II who is called in her funerary inscription (Al-Rawi 2008: 124) "daughter of Aššur-nīrka-da"inni, chief cupbearer of Assurnasirpal, king of Assyria." Regarding this, see Kertai 2013: 110–11.

24 Other variations include "brought before me" and "sent me."

25 Among the foreign rulers it is only Ba'alu, king of Tyre who presented both his own daughter and also nieces to Assurbanipal (Case 13). Probably at that time Ba'alu had only one daughter of a marriageable age because he had presented his daughters to Esarhaddon, the predecessor of Assurbanipal, when he submitted to him (Case 11). Originally, in Case 13, he should have submitted more than one daughter to Assurbanipal, but since it was impossible, he must have presented also his nieces. However, Ba'alu was fully aware that even if he added (each) with a bountiful dowry (*nudunnû, terḫatu*)[26] to serve as (a) female servant(s) (*ana epēš abrakkūti*) (Assurbanipal Cases 12, 13, 14, 15, and *16*). The term *abrakkūtu* means "service and status of a female steward at the Assyrian court,"[27] i.e., in all likelihood they stayed as female servants at the Assyrian court. However, why did the daughters of the foreign rulers have to work at the court despite arriving in Assyria with bountiful dowries and why was such a thing not mentioned in royal inscriptions before Assurbanipal? The Assyrian historical sources offer no answer to this question, and therefore we must depend on speculation. In my opinion, Assyrian kings before Assurbanipal presumably tried to strengthen the relations between Assyria and its vassal states by forming a relationship immediately after the reception of the women with dowries. However, Assurbanipal, through the use of the daughters as female servants, made all his vassals (subjugated foreign rulers) recognize that they should be the vassals that serve Assurbanipal and had to remain loyal. If they remained loyal, their daughters might have married Assurbanipal as secondary wives, or they might have married a relative of Assurbanipal,[28] and through

---

his nieces to his daughter, it would not be equivalent to presenting his own daughters, because, as I already mentioned, Assyria did not regard the establishment of a relationship through the niece of a foreign ruler as a valid domination policy (Case 3). Therefore, it is convincing that Ba'alu tried to submit his son to Assurbanipal. In other words, Ba'alu's nieces were politically less valuable to both kings and originally they should not have been presented to Assurbanipal.

26 Regarding *nudunnû* and *terḫatu*, see also footnote 17 above.

27 CAD A/I: 61b–62a. AHw I: 3b, s.v. *abarakkatu* translates the term as "Hausverwalterin, Schaffnerin" and *abarakkūtu* as "Schaffnerinnendienst" (AHw I: 4a, s.v. *ab(a)rakkūtu*). The German term "Schaffnerin" is an outdated designation for a domestic, i.e. someone who organizes and keeps a household. Here I translate *ana epēš abrakkūti* into German as "um einen Dienst auszuüben" or "um als Dienerin(nen) tätig zu sein." Svärd (2015a: 128) reads MUNUS.AGRIG-*ú-ti* of the passage *ana epēš* MUNUS.AGRIG-*ú-ti* as MÍ.IGI.DUB-*ú-ti* and translates this passage as "to make into a *masennutu*," and regarding these women she says briefly that "the *masennutu* was to be married in Assyria." Novotny and Jeffers translate the aforementioned passage as "to serve as (a) housekeeper(s)."

28 In my German article published in 2015, I pointed to only Assurbanipal's male relatives as possible marriage partners of the daughters of foreign rulers presented to Assurbanipal, because the Assyrian kings had officially only one wife, and it was already confirmed that Assurbanipal had been married to Libbāli-šarrat when he was a crown prince. However, as Kertai (2013: 121) argues "Sargon and Sennacherib must have had (at least) another consort in addition to the queen," so the possibility cannot be completely excluded that Assurbanipal also had secondary wives, although their existence has not been confirmed from any available historical sources. Therefore, I decided to add Assurbanipal himself to the set of possible of marriage partners of these women in this article. Regarding Libbāli-šarrat, see Ambos 2001: 660–61.

this their fathers would have been able to acquire an advantage, namely a higher status among many vassal states. Such a use of the daughters of foreign rulers at the Assyrian court reflects the strong kingship of Assurbanipal, who brought Assyria to the zenith of its long history.

4 Conclusion

The prevalent discourse stating that the Assyrian Empire was built by the continued mass deportations of foreign enemies has been accepted by many Assyriologists for decades. The study of the role of women in foreign policy presented here adds a new facet to our understanding of the Assyrian empire. It is important that we consider the roles that these women played in the political construction of Assyria. Through my study I have been able to show that Assyria did not establish imperial rule by means of mass deportations alone, but that the Assyrian kings also used other means of establishing and consolidating their empire.

Appendix: Cases in which the Assyrian Kings received foreign women

1. Tukultī-Ninurta II, 885 BC, Grayson 1991: 176 A.0.100.5, 97–102
Moving on from the city Rummunina I approached the city Sūru of Bīt-Ḫalpê which is upon the River Ḫabur. 20 minas of gold, 20 minas of silver, (. . .), **his two sisters with their bountiful dowries** – (this was) the tri[bute from Ḫamat]āiu, the Laqean.
2. Assurnasirpal II, 879 BC, Grayson 1991: 211 A.0.101.1 ii 118–125[29]
The nobles of Amme-ba'lī, a man of Bīt-Zamāni, rebelled against him and killed him. I marched to avenge Amme-ba'lī. They took fright before the brilliance of my weapons and the terror of my dominion (and) I received harnessed chariots, equipment for troops (and) horses, (. . .), **his sister with her bountiful dowry, (and) the daughters of his nobles with their bountiful dowries.**

29 Regarding this case, see also Grayson 1991: 251–52 A.0.101.1.17 iv 109–120; 261 A.0.101.19, 85–90.

3. Assurnasirpal II, 875–869 BC, Grayson 1991: 217–18 A.0.101.1 iii 72–77
Moving on from the River Aprê I approached the city Kunulua, the royal city of Lubarna, the Patinean. He took fright in the face of my raging weapons (and) fierce battle and submitted to me to save his life. I received as his tribute 20 talents of silver, 1 talent of gold, (. . .), 10 female singers, **his brother's daughter with her bountiful dowry**, a large female monkey, (and) ducks. As for him, I showed him mercy. I took with me the chariots, cavalry, (and) infantry of the Patinean (and also) took **hostages** from him.
4. Shalmaneser III, 858 BC, Grayson 1996: 16 A.0.102.2 i 40–41
Moving on from the city Paqaraḫubunu, I approached to the cities of Mutallu, the Gurgumite. I received tribute – silver, gold, oxen, sheep, wine, (and) **his daughter with her bountiful dowry** – from Mutallu, the Gurgumite.
5. Shalmaneser III, 857 BC, Grayson 1996: 18 A.0.102.2 ii 21–24
I received from Qalparunda, the Patinean, 3 talents of gold, 100 talents of silver, (. . .), **his daughter with her bountiful dowry**, (. . .). I imposed upon him as annual tribute 1 talent of silver, 2 talents of red purple wool, (and) 100 cedar beams, (and) I regularly received (it) in my city Aššur.[30]
6. Shalmaneser III, 857 BC, Grayson 1996: 18 A.0.102.2 ii 24–27
I received from Ḫaiānu, the man of Bīt-Gabbari, which is at the foot of the Amanus range, [N] talents of silver, 90 talents of bronze, (. . .), (and) **his daughter with her dowry.**[31] I imposed upon him as tribute 10 minas of silver, 100 cedar beams, (and) 1 homer of cedar resin, (and) I received (it) annually in my city Aššur.
7. Shalmaneser III, 857 BC, Grayson 1996: 18–19 A.0.102.2 ii 27–29
I received from Sangara, the Carchemishite, 2 talents of gold, 70 talents of silver, (. . .), **his daughter with (her) dowry, 100 of his nobles' daughters**, 500 oxen, (and) 5,000 sheep. I imposed upon him as tribute 1 mina of gold, 1 talent of silver, (and) 2 talents of red purple wool, (and) I received (it) annually.
8. Shalmaneser III, 839, 836, or 835 BC, Grayson 1996: 119 A.0.102.40 iii 5–8
I marched to the lands Que (and) Tabal, I conquered those lands (and) turned (them) into ruin hills. I confined Katî, the perverse enemy, to the city Paḫru, his royal city. My lordly brilliance overwhelmed him. I brought **his daughter with her dowry** to the city Calah (and) he submitted to me.

30 Grayson thinks of *am-da-ḫar* in line 24 as the present tense and translates it as "I regularly receive (it) in my city, Aššur." But in my opinion *am-da-ḫar* (*amdaḫḫar*) is the preterite tense of Gtn-stem. Therefore, it should be translated as "I received it regularly in my city Aššur." This also applies to the last lines of Case 6 and Case 7.

31 The translation of Grayson, that is, "his daughter with her rich dowry" is not appropriate, because the adjective *ma'di* "rich, bountiful" is not written in the text. See Grayson 1996: 18 A.0.102.2 ii 26.

9. Shalmaneser IV, 773–772 BC, Grayron 1996: 240 A.0.105.1, 4–10
When Šamšī-ilu, the field marshal, marched to the land Damascus, the tribute of Ḫadiānu, the Damascene – silver, gold, copper, his royal bed, his royal couch, **his daughter with her bountiful dowry,** the property of his palace without number – I received from him (Ḫadiānu).
10. Sennacherib, 701 BC, Grayson and Novotny 2012: 65–66 no. 4, 52–58[32]
As for him (Hezekiah), I confined him inside the city Jerusalem, his royal city, like a bird in a cage. (. . .) As for him, Hezekiah, fear of my lordly brilliance overwhelmed him and, after my (departure), he had the auxiliary forces (and) his elite troops whom he had brought inside to strengthen the city Jerusalem, his royal city, and who had provided support, (along with) 30 talents of gold, (. . .), together with **his daughters**, his palace women, male singers, (and) female singers brought into Nineveh, my capital city, and he sent his mounted messenger to me to pay tribute and to do obeisance.[33]
11. Esarhaddon, 671 BC, Leichty 2011: 76 no. 30 rev. 1′–7′
[. . . Ba'alu, the king of Ty]re, who dwells [in the midst of the sea, . . .] who threw off [my] yo [ke, . . .] the god Aššur, the king of the gods, and the splendor of my lordship [. . .] kneeling and beseeched [my] lord[ship . . .] heavy [tribu]te, **his daughters with [their] dowr[ies, . . .]** all of his [annu]al [giving] which he had stopped, [. . .] (and) he kissed my feet.
12.[34] Assurbanipal, ca. 662 BC,[35] Novotny and Jeffers 2018: 236 no. 11 [Prism A] ii 63–67[36]
(As for) Yakīn-Lû, the king of the land Arwad, who dwells in the midst of the sea, who had not bowed down to the kings, my fathers, he bowed down to my yoke. **He brought to Nineveh his daughter with a bountiful dowry, to serve as a female servant,** and kissed my feet.

32 See also Grayson and Novotny 2012: 97 no. 15 iv 18–14′; 115–16 no. 16 iv 8–37; 133 no. 17 iii 52–81; 151 no. 18 iii 27–31; 162–63 no. 19 i 3′–14′; 176–77 no. 22 iii 18–49; 194 no. 23 iii 24–42; Grayson and Novotny 2014: 80–81 no. 46, 28–32.

33 Although Grayson and Novotny translate *a-na na-dan man-da-at-ti ù e-peš* ARAD-*ú-ti iš-pu-ra rak-bu-šú* in the last line of text describing this event (line 58 in no. 4) as "he sent a mounted messenger of his to me to deliver (this) payment and to do obeisance," I interpret this as meaning that "a mounted messenger" of Hezekiah was not sent to carry people and expensive gifts mentioned in the preceding lines but he was sent to Assyria to convey the message that they would obey Assyria and pay annual tribute from then onwards.

34 Regarding this case, see also the third translation of Case 14.

35 It was 667 BC when the land Arwad became a vassal state of Assyria. For this, see Sano 2015b: 168–69.

36 See also Novotny and Jeffers 2018: 276 no. 13 [Prism J] iii 9′–13′.

13. Assurbanipal, ca. 662 BC, Novotny and Jeffers 2018: 61–62 no. 3 [Prism B] ii 38–62[37]

On my third campaign, I marched against Ba'alu, the king of the land Tyre who dwells in the midst of the sea. Because he did not obey my royal command (and) did not listen to the pronouncement from my lips, I set up outposts against him. To prevent his people from leaving, I reinforced (its) garrison. By sea and dry land, I took his routes (and) cut off (all) access to him. (. . .) **[He brou]ght before me his daughter, his offspring, and the daughter(s) of his brothers to serve as female servants.** He b[ro]ught his son, who had [nev]er crossed the se[a], to do obeisance to me. **I received from him [his] dau[ghter a]nd the daughters of his brothers (each) with a bountiful bridal gift.** I had mercy on him and I gave (his) son, his offspring, back to him. (. . .) I received from him his substantial tribute. I returned safely to Nineveh, my capital city.

Novotny and Jeffers 2018: 268 no. 12 [Prism H] ii 14′–24′

(As for) Baʾalu, the king of the land Tyre who did not obey my royal command (and) did not listen to the pronouncement from my lips, I set up outposts against him. (. . .) I made them bow down to my yoke. **He brought before me his daughter and the daughters of his brothers to serve as female servants,** together with his substantial tribute.

14. Assurbanipal, ca. 662 BC, Novotny and Jeffers 2018: 236 no. 11 [Prism A] ii 68–74

(As for) Mugallu, the king of the land Tabal who had spoken with disrespect to the kings, my fathers, **he brought to Nineveh (his) daughter, his offspring, with a bountiful bridal gift, to serve as a female servant,** and he kissed my feet. I imposed upon Mugallu large horses as tribute yearly.

Novotny and Jeffers 2018: 309 no. 23 [IIT] 139–141

[(As for) Mugallu, the king of of the land Taba]l, who spoke to the kings, [my] fathers, with disrespect, fear of (the god) Aššur (and) the goddess Mullissu, my lords, [overwhelmed him, and . . .], who had not bowed down to the yo[k]e, sent **(his) [daug]hter,** his offspring, together with large horses, as his su[bstant]ial tribute, and kissed my feet.

Novotny and Jeffers 2018: 62 no. 3 [Prism B] ii 63–74[38]

Rulers of the midst of the sea and kings who dwell in the high mountains saw the might of these deeds of mine and became frightened of my lordly majesty. (As for) Yakīn-Lû, the king of the land Arwad, Mugallu, the king of the land Tabal, (and) Sanda-šarme of the land Ḫilakku, who had not bowed down to the kings, my fathers, they bowed down to my yoke. **They brought to Nineveh (their) daughters, their offspring, (each) with a [bou]ntiful dowry and a bountiful bridal gift, to serve as female servants, and they kissed my feet.**[39] I imposed upon Mugallu large horses as tribute yearly.

37 Regarding this case, see also Novotny and Jeffers 2018: 120 no. 6 [Prism C] iii 58′–88′; 193–94 no. 9 [Prism F] i 55–68; 236 no. 11 [Prism A] ii 49–62.

38 Regarding this case, see also Novotny and Jeffers 2018: 120–21 no. 6 [Prism C] iii 89′–105′; 194 no. 9 [Prism F] i 69–76.

39 Based on the sentence highlighted in bold one might think that the daughters of the foreign rulers were presented to Assurbanipal with both dowries (*nudunnû*) and bridal gifts (*terḫatu*).

15.[40] Assurbanipal, ca. 662 BC, Novotny and Jeffers 2018: 236–37 no. 11 [Prism A] ii 75–80
(As for) Sanda-šarme of the land Ḫilakku, who had not bowed down to the kings, my fathers, (and) had not pulled their yoke, **he brought to Nineveh (his) daughter, his offspring, with a bountiful dowry, to serve as a female servant**, and he kissed my feet.
16. Assurbanipal, ca. 660 BC, Novotny and Jeffers 2018: 65 no. 3 [Prism B] iii 80–92[41]
Afterwards, Uallî, his son, sat on his throne. He saw the might of the deities Aššur, Bēl, (. . .), and bowed down to my yoke. For the preservation of his life, he opened up his hands to me (and) made an appeal to my lordly majesty. He sent Erisinni, his successor, to Nineveh and he kissed my feet. I had mercy on him. I dispatched my messenger of goodwill to him. **He sent me (his) daughter, his offspring, to serve as a female servant**. (As for) his former tribute, which they had discontinued in the time of the kings, my fathers, they carried (it) before me. I added thirty horses to his former tribute and imposed (it) upon him.

Bibliography

Al-Rawi, Fadhil N. H. 2008. Inscriptions from the Tombs of the Queens of Assyria. Pp. 119–38 in *New Light on Nimrud: Proceedings of the Nimrud Conference 11th–13th March 2002*, ed. John Curtis et al. London: British Institute for the Study of Iraq in association with the British Museum.

Ambos, Claus. 2001. Libbāli-šarrat. Pp. 660–61 in *The Prosopography of the Neo-Assyrian Empire, Volume 2, Part II: L–N*, ed. Heather D. Baker. Helsinki: The Neo-Assyrian Text Corpus Project.

Aro-Valjus, Sanna and Martti Nissinen. 1998. Aḫāt-abīša. P. 59 in *The Prosopography of the Neo-Assyrian Empire, Volume1, Part I: A*, ed. Karen Radner. Helsinki: Neo-Assyrian Text Corpus Project.

Boehmer, Rainer Michael. 2001. Eine goldene Kanne aus Nimrud. Pp. 57–65 in *Lux Orientis: Archäologie zwischen Asien und Europa. Festschrift für Harald Hauptmann zum 65. Geburtstag*, ed. Rainer Michael Boehmer and Joseph Maran. Rahden: Verlag Marie Leidorf.

But I want to point out that the daughter of each foreign ruler was presented to Assurbanipal with *nudunnû* or *terḫatu*. This is clear from other Cases mentioned for each land. That is to say, the daughter of Yakīn-Lû with *nudunnû* (Case 12), the daughter of Mugallu with *terḫatu* (the first translation of Case 14), the daughter of Sanda-šarme with *nudunnû* (Case15). Therefore, in my opinion, we should interpret this sentence as meaning that Assurbanipal received two daughters with *nudunnû* and one daughter with *terḫatu* from foreign rulers.

40 For this case, see also the third translation of Case 14.

41 Regarding this case, see also Novotny and Jeffers 2018: 123 no. 6 [Prism C] iv 73″–v 5; 195–96 no. 9 [Prism F] ii 41–52; 239 no. 11 [Prism A] iii 11–26.

Borger, Riekele. 1996. *Beiträge zum Inschriftenwerk Assurbanipals*, Wiesbaden: Harrassowitz Verlag.

Cogan, Mordechai. 2014. The Author of Ashurbanipal Prism A (Rassam): An Inquiry into his Plan and Purpose, with a note on his Persona. *Orient* 49: 69–83.

Collon, Dominique. 2008. Nimrud Treasures: Panel Discussion. Pp. 105–18 in *New Light on Nimrud: Proceedings of the Nimrud Conference 11th–13th March 2002*, ed. John Curtis et al. London: British Institute for the Study of Iraq in association with the British Museum.

Dalley, Stephanie. 1998. Yabâ, Atalyā and the Foreign Policy of Late Assyrian Kings. *SAAB* 12/2: 83–98.

Damerji, Muayad Said Basim. 1998. Gräber assyrischer Königinnen aus Nimrud. *Jahrb. RGZM* 45: 1–84.

Fuchs, Andreas. 1994. *Die Inschriften Sargons II. aus Khorsabad*. Göttingen: Cuvillier Verlag.

Fuchs, Andreas. 1996. Die Inschrift vom Ištar-Tempel. Pp. 258–96 in Rykle Borger, *Beiträge zum Inschriftenwerk Assurbanipals*. Wiesbaden: Harrassowitz Verlag.

Fuchs, Andreas. 1998. *Die Annalen des Jahres 711 v. Chr. nach Prismenfragmenten aus Ninive und Assur*. SAAS 8. Helsinki: Neo-Assyrian Text Corpus Project.

Fuchs, Andreas. 2012. Urartu in der Zeit. Pp. 135–61 in *Biainili-Urartu: The Proceedings of the Symposium Held in Munich 12–14* October *2007*, ed. Stephan Kroll et al. Acta Iranica 51. Leuven: Peeters.

Gadd, Cyril John. 1954. Inscribed Prisms of Sargon II from Nimrud. *Iraq* 16: 173–201.

Glassner, Jean-Jacques. 2004. *Mesopotamian Chronicles*. Atlanta, GA: Society of Biblical Literature.

Goetze, Albrecht. 1947. Short or Long *a*? (Notes on Some Akkadian Words). *OrNS* 16: 239–50.

Grayson, Albert Kirk. 1975. *Assyrian and Babylonian Chronicles*. TCS 5. New York: J.J. Augustin.

Grayson, Albert Kirk. 1991. *Assyrian Rulers of the Early First Millennium BC I (1114–859 BC)*. RIMA 2. Toronto: University of Toronto Press.

Grayson, Albert Kirk. 1996. *Assyrian Rulers of the Early First Millennium BC II (858–745 BC)*. RIMA 3. Toronto: University of Toronto Press.

Grayson, Albert Kirk, and Jamie Novotny. 2012. *The Royal Inscriptions of Sennacherib, King of Assyria (704–681 BC), Part 1*. RINAP 3/1. Winona Lake, IN: Eisenbrauns.

Grayson, Albert Kirk, and Jamie Novotny. 2014. *The Royal Inscriptions of Sennacherib, King of Assyria (704–681 BC), Part 2*. RINAP 3/2. Winona Lake, IN: Eisenbrauns.

Hussein, Muzahim Mahmoud, with translation and initial editing by Mark Altaweel, and editing and additional notes by McGuire Gibson. 2016. *Nimrud: The Queens' Tombs*. Chicago: Baghdad: Iraqi State Board of Antiquities and Heritage, and Chicago: The Oriental Institute.

Kertai, David. 2013. The Queens of the Neo-Assyrian Empire. *AoF* 40/1: 108–24.

Kwasman, Theodore, and Simo Parpola. 1991. *Legal Transactions of the Royal Court of Nineveh, Part I: Tiglath-Pileser III through Esarhaddon*. SAA 6. Helsinki: Helsinki University Press.

Lanfranchi, Giovanni Battista. 2010. Greek Historians and the Memory of the Assyrian Court. Pp. 39–65 in *Der Achämenidenhof / The Achaemenid Court: Akten des 2. Internationalen Kolloquiums zum Thema „Griechische und lateinische Überlieferung und Altvorderasien", Landgut Castelen bei Basel, 23. –25. Mai 2007*, ed. Bruno Jacobs and Robert Rollinger. CLeO 2. Wiesbaden: Harrassowitz.

Leichty, Erle. 2011. *The Royal Inscriptions of Esarhaddon, King of Assyria (680–669 BC)*. RINAP 4. Winona Lake, IN: Eisenbrauns.

Luukko, Mikko, and Greta Van Buylaere. 2002. *The Political Correspondence of Esarhaddon*. SAA 16. Helsinki: Helsinki University Press.
Melville, Sarah. 2004. Neo-Assyrian Royal Women and Male Identity: Status as a Social Tool. *JAOS* 124/1: 37–57.
Melville, Sarah. 2005. Royal Women and the Exercise of Power in the Ancient Near East. Pp. 219–28 in *A Companion to the Ancient Near East*, ed. Daniel Snell. Oxford: Blackwell.
Novotny, Jamie. 2001. Daughters and Sisters of Neo-Hittite and Aramaean Rulers in the Assyrian Harem. *BCSMS* 36: 175–84.
Novotny, Jamie, and Joshua Jeffers. 2018. *The Royal Inscriptions of Ashurbanipal (668–631 BC), Aššur-etel-ilāni (630–627 BC), and Sîn-šarra-iškun (626–612 BC), Kings of Assyria, Part 1*. RINAP 5/1. University Park, PA: Eisenbrauns.
Oded, Bustenay. 1979. *Mass Deportations and Deportees in the Neo-Assyrian Empire*. Wiesbaden: Reichert Verlag.
Parpola, Simo. 1988: The Neo-Assyrian Word for "Queen". *SAAB* 2/2: 73–76.
Parpola, Simo. 2012. The Neo-Assyrian Royal Harem. Pp. 613–26 in *Leggo! Studies Presented to Frederick Mario Fales on the Occasion of His 65th Birthday*, ed. Giovanni B. Lanfranchi et al. LAOS 2. Wiesbaden: Harrassowitz.
Parpola, Simo and Kazuko Watanabe. 1988. *Neo-Assyrian Treaties and Loyalty Oaths*. SAA 2. Helsinki: Helsinki University Press.
Radner, Karen. 2004. Assyrische Handelspolitik: die Symbiose mit unabhängigen Handelszentren und ihre Kontrolle durch Assyrien. Pp. 152–69 in *Commerce and Monetary Systems in the Ancient* World: *Means of Transmission and Cultural Interaction: Proceedings of the Fifth Annual Symposium of the Assyrian and Babylonian Intellectual Heritage Project Held in Innsbruck*, Austria, *October 3rd–8th, 2002*, ed. Robert Rollinger and Christoph Ulf. Oriens et Occidens 6. Stuttgart: Steiner.
Radner, Karen. 2012. After Eltekeh: Royal Hostages from Egypt at the Assyrian Court. Pp. 471–79 in *Stories of Long Ago. Festschrift für Michael D. Roaf*, ed. Heather D. Baker et al. AOAT 397. Münster: Ugarit-Verlag.
Reynolds, Frances. 2003. *The Babylonian Correspondence of Esarhaddon and Letters to Assurbanipal and Sin-šarru-iškun from Northern and Central Babylonia*. SAA 18. Helsinki: Helsinki University Press.
Sano, Katsuji. 2015a. Die den Assyrerkönigen übersandten ausländischen Frauen mit Mitgift in neuassyrischer Zeit. *Kaskal* 12: 383–89.
Sano, Katsuji. 2015b. Die Tochter des Jakinlû. *NABU* 2015/4, no. 101: 168–69.
Sano, Katsuji. 2015c. Wer ist in den assyrischen Königsinschriften mit *līṭu* gemeint? *NABU* 2015/4, no. 102: 169.
Sano, Katsuji. 2016. Die Eroberungen von Ägypten durch Asarhaddon und Aššurbanipal. *UF* 47: 251–63.
Schultz, Michael, and Manfred Kunter. 1998. Erste Ergebnisse der anthropologischen und paläopathologischen Untersuchungen an den menschlichen Skeletfunden aus den neuassyrischen Königinnengräbern von Nimrud. *Jahrbuch RGZM* 45: 85–128.
Starr, Ivan. 1990. *Queries to the Sungod: Divination and Politics in Sargonid Assyria*. SAA 4. Helsinki: Helsinki University Press.
Stol, Marten. 2016. *Women in the Ancient Near East*. Berlin: De Gruyter.
Svärd, Saana. 2012. Women, Power, and Heterarchy in the Neo-Assyrian Palaces. Pp. 507–18 in *Organization, Representation, and Symbols of Power in the Ancient Near East:*

Proceedings of the 54th Rencontre Assyriologique Internationale at Würzburg 20–25 July 2008, ed. Gernot Wilhelm. Winona Lake, IN: Eisenbrauns.

Svärd, Saana. 2015a. *Women and Power in Neo-Assyrian Palaces*. SAAS 23. Helsinki: The Neo-Assyrian Text Corpus Project.

Svärd, Saana. 2015b. Changes in Neo-Assyrian Queenship. *SAAB* 21: 157–71.

von Soden, Wolfram. 1995. *Grundriss der Akkadischen Grammatik. 3., ergänzte Auflage unter Mitarbeit von Werner R. Mayer*. AnOr. 33. Rome: Editrice Pontificio Instituto Biblico.

Zawadzki, Stefan. 1995. Hostages in Assyrian Royal Inscriptions. Pp. 449–58 in *Immigration and Emigration within the Ancient Near East*, ed. Karel van Lerberghe and Antoon Schoors. OLA 65. Leuven: Uitgeverij Peeters en Departement Oriëntalistiek.

Yoko Watai

Women Involved in Daily Management in Achaemenid Babylonia: The Cases of Rē'indu and Andiya

1 Introduction

Babylonia from the seventh to the fourth century BCE, in the Neo-Babylonian and Achaemenid periods, has provided us with an abundance of cuneiform tablets: according to the estimate of M. Jursa (2005: 1 and 2010: 6), more than 16,000 legal or administrative documents have been published, with tens of thousands of unpublished texts housed in museum collections around the world.[1] Most of these documents deal with everyday practical matters, and can be classified as economic texts, familial documents (marriage contracts, documents of division of succession and of transfer of properties, testaments, etc.), administrative records, and letters, mostly drafted in the "long sixth century" (Jursa 2010: 4–5) that lasted about 140 years between the fall of the Neo-Assyrian Empire (620 BCE) and the "end of archives" in the second year of Xerxes (484 BCE).[2] Although far fewer women appear in these texts than men, we estimate that at least several thousand women are mentioned. Most of them were inhabitants of Babylonian cities like Babylon, Borsippa, Uruk, and Sippar, and they represent various social strata: women of free status from urban families, slaves, and oblates at temples. The corpus constitutes, therefore, a good basis for discussing the role, status, situation, and activities of women in the social, economic, and familial frameworks.

We find that quite a few women, mainly those of free status, participated in economic activities such as the management of fields, lending and borrowing of silver or commodities, buying of slaves and real estate, transfer of properties, and house rentals. Unfortunately, most of these practical texts do not provide

1 This work is supported by JSPS KAKENHI Grant Number JP 19K13361.

Abbreviations used in the present study follow the Cuneiform Digital Library Initiative (CDLI; abbreviations are listed at http://cdli.ox.ac.uk/wiki/abbreviations_for_assyriology).

2 For more detail on the "end of archives" and its connection with the Persian king's suppression of revolts in the second year of Xerxes, see Waerzeggers 2003/2004; Oelsner 2007; and Baker 2008.

https://doi.org/10.1515/9781501514821-005

us with the detailed context of their activities. However, "archive studies"[3] allow us to reconstitute the family history of some urban families and the background of some women's activities. We know that some women (especially wives and widows) enjoyed economic autonomy and managed their properties on their own initiative, while others participated in economic activities for the family's benefit, and still others are mentioned, but without any description of their activities (Watai 2016).

In general, the majority of women, who are "invisible" in terms of textual evidence, presumably were engaged in daily house-based work, such as taking care of the family, managing the domestic area, preparing meals, and weaving clothes – activities that are not usually mentioned in documents. We do have, however, some possible attestations of the domestic activities of women, which suggest that at least some women carried out an important role in the domestic area. In this paper, we focus on the activities of two women, Rē'indu and Andiya, who lived in Borsippa in the Achaemenid period (from the sixth to the fifth century BCE). This study makes use of memoranda and letters, which by their nature preserve only restricted information in obscure contexts. Hence, we cannot clarify the situation of the two women completely, and our conclusions are necessarily limited. However, this study will throw light on the role and the activities of women, especially wives of the family heads, in the economic sphere of the urban families.

2 The Case of Rē'indu

2.1 The Archive and Activities of the Family

Rē'indu[4] is mentioned in ten texts, of which seven are memoranda: VS 6: 191; 303; 315; VS 4: 193; 202; VS 3: 204; OECT 12: A 182, and three are letters: *AfO* 19, no. 36 (= Hackl, Jursa, and Schmidl 2014, no. 126); OECT 12: C 6 (= Hackl, Jursa, and Schmidl 2014, no. 130); HSM 1899.2.262 (= Hackl, Jursa, and Schmidl 2014, no. 131).[5]

3 See, for example, Joannès 1989 on the Ea-ilûta-bāni family (Borsippa), Wunsch 2000 and Abraham 2004 on the Egibi family (Babylon), and Baker 2004 on the Nappāḫu family (Babylon).

4 This name is derived from the verb *râmu* "love," and means "beloved one." It was a popular name for free women of this period.

5 *AfO* 51, no. 27 mentions a woman called Rē'indu, but we cannot be sure she is our Rē'indu.

They belong to what is known as the "Ilušu-abušu A" archive, according to the nomenclature of M. Jursa (2005: 88–89).[6]

The archive consists of twenty-six texts from Borsippa that cover the period from year 7 of Darius I (515 BCE) to year 2 of Xerxes (484 BCE), with the exception of one earlier text that is dated in the 40th year of Nebuchadnezzar (564 BCE) (Hackl in Jursa 2010: 633 and 637). The main figure in the archive is Rēmūt-Bēl, head of the Ilušu-abušu family. However, not all of the texts mention him, and some other persons appear frequently. One of these is Rē'indu.

Rēmūt-Bēl, as well as another family member, owned a brewer's prebend[7] at Ezida, the main temple of Borsippa. His archive itself does not relate to the activities of the prebend, but another group of texts, that of Balāṭu, a slave of Rēmūt-Bēl, shows that Balāṭu was in charge of the brewing of beer for offerings on behalf of his master.[8]

A major part of the archive of Rēmūt-Bēl deals with accounts of silver expenses (*tēlītu*) for the purchase of various foodstuffs and everyday objects.[9] There is a very wide range in the amounts of silver mentioned in the documents. Some large payments of silver were undoubtedly related to temple administration, such as "payments connected with tax and service obligations owed to the crown by the temple community of Ezida," as noted by J. Hackl (Hackl in Jursa 2010: 639). In fact, Rēmūt-Bēl travelled at least once to Susa,

6 Concerning this archive, see also Jursa 2010: 633–41 (the section contributed by J. Hackl); Waerzeggers 2010a: 437–41; Jursa 2013; Hackl, Jursa, and Schmidl 2014: 240–48.

7 The "prebend" is of course generally a term related to the Christian church, but we use it for the Babylonian system of *isqu* "share" for convenience. A Babylonian prebend gives its titleholder the privilege of entering the temple and performing various kinds of duties for the divinities, for which the titleholder is rewarded. Thus, the "prebendaries," (also called "priests," "clergy") were in charge of preparations for rituals. For example, in order to prepare and serve meals for the divinities, prebendary bakers, brewers, butchers, and oil pressers performed their respective tasks. We also find prebendary singers, launderers, gatekeepers, metalworkers, reed workers, carpenters, barbers, etc. They were all citizens, and most lived outside of the temples. The prebend was usually inherited from generation to generation as family property, but it was sometimes sold and purchased. Recent studies on the prebend include: van Driel 2002: 31–151; 2005; Corò 2005; Démare-Lafont 2010; Jursa 2010: 155–68; Waerzeggers 2010a; Frame and Waerzeggers 2011; Monerie 2014, 2018.

8 Balāṭu acted as "an entrepreneur in the prebendary sphere" (Jursa 2005: 88), and "developed certain lines of business in margins of the sacrificial economy and even participated in more central areas of the priestly trade" (Waerzeggers 2010a: 437–38). However, Balāṭu's file is found separately from the archive of Rēmūt-Bēl.

9 For a list of commodities and goods for which silver is disbursed, see Hackl in Jursa 2010: 638–39 table 98.

one of the capitals of Achaemenid Persia,[10] as a member of Borsippa's delegation to the Achaemenid court. This is attested by, for example, a letter which Nabû-aḫḫē-iddin, a governor of Borsippa, who had been "a former travel companion who recently returned home," (Jursa 2013: 5) sent to Rēmūt-Bēl when the latter was in Susa (OECT 12: AB 252 = Hackl, Jursa, and Schmidl 2014, no.128). High-quality foodstuffs and drink must have been purchased for the Achaemenid court and brought there by the Borsippean delegation, including Rēmūt-Bēl (Hackl in Jursa 2010: 639; Jursa 2013: 7). Thus, Rēmūt-Bēl participated in the administrative sphere of the temple.

However, some of the purchases may have been for the private use of the family. Texts include mention of payments of small sums of silver, less than one shekel.[11] In addition, some of the texts use forms with first and second person pronouns. These facts indicate that these texts are from a private archive rather than administrative documents of the temple (Jursa 2005: 89; Hackl in Jursa 2010: 638).

That silver served not only for high-range expenditures (for "mass consumption" at the palace or temple), but was also used for paying small daily expenses in the private sphere (Jursa 2010: 629–41 and 772–83; Jursa 2016), indicates the existence of a true monetary system of silver in Babylonia in the sixth century, as indicated by Jursa, although it is true that these documents reflect the life of a high-ranking family, rather than that of ordinary people.

2.2 Who Was Rē'indu?

Rē'indu's relation to the Ilušu-abušu family requires some comment. In some letters that she wrote, Rē'indu calls Rēmūt-Bēl "my brother" (OECT 12: C 6 = Hackl, Jursa, and Schmidl 2014, no. 130; HSM 1899.2.262 = Hackl, Jursa, and Schmidl 2014, no. 131). However, we do not need to take this literally, since women frequently addressed males as "my brother" in letters, and in fact one text, VS 6: 315, identifies Rē'indu (who was likely the same person as our Rē'indu) as the "daughter of Bazuzu." This makes it doubtful that Rē'indu was the sister of Rēmūt-Bēl, because his father was Iddin-Nabû (or Iddinaya, abbreviated form of Iddin-Nabû).[12] Rē'indu was certainly married because one text (VS 4: 193) tells us

10 "Possibly, Rēmūt-Bēl was in charge of the organization of one or several of these trips, which took place in the spring of Xer 01-02 (VS 4: 194; VS 6: 194)" (Waerzeggers 2010a: 437). On the travel of Babylonians to Susa, see Waerzeggers 2010b.

11 1 shekel ≈ 8.3 g; 1 mina = 60 shekels ≈ 500 g.

12 However, we cannot exclude the possibility that Iddin-Nabû had another name, Bazuzu. The phenomenon of double names has been recorded for several persons belonging to notable families.

that she was the mother of two sons (probably grown-up) in the first year of Xerxes, although the name of her husband is never mentioned. We can suppose that since her husband was known to the members of the Ilušu-abušu family, it was not necessary to identify him in these documents. Although we do not have clear evidence of it, Rē'indu was very likely the wife of Rēmūt-Bēl, as Jursa (2013: 4) has indicated, given her important role in the economic sphere of the family, as we will see below.[13]

2.3 Activities of Rē'indu

In most of the documents in which she appears, Rē'indu is the receiver of silver (VS 6: 303; 315; 191; VS 4: 202; OECT 12: A 182), or barley (VS 3: 204).

(1) VS 6: 303

VS 6: 303[14] (cf. San Nicolò and Ungnad 1935, no. 854)
(1) 7 shekels of silver for Rē'indu, (2) of which 1 shekel (3) was paid to the weaver on day 20 of the fourth month; (4) ½ shekel of silver for Iddinaya, (5) offspring of Iqīša-[Bēl], to be paid to the messenger (6) of the governor, on day 28 of the fourth month; (7) five shekels of silver, for the second time, (8) for Iddinaya, offspring of Iqīša-Bēl, (9) [to be paid] to the messenger (10) of the governor; [. . . . . .] (11) [2 or 3] cuts of meat for Rēmūt-[. . .] (12) on day 10 of the third month; (13) two cuts of meat for the same person on day 12; (14) three cuts of meat for the same person on day 14; (15) two cuts of meat for the same person on day 14 of the fourth month; (16) three cuts of meat for the same person on day 18; (19) 3? cuts of meat for the same person on day 24; (18) two (or three) cuts of meat for the same person on day 28; (19) three cuts of meat for the same person (20) on day [x] of the fifth month; (21) in total twenty-one cuts of meat.

VS 6: 303 tells of 7 shekels of silver for Rē'indu, one of which was given to a weaver (lines 1–3). This implies that Rē'indu bought cloth made by the weaver.

13 It is curious that we find no indication of her husband, but probably there was no need to specify the matrimonial relationship in memoranda belonging to the private archive of the family.
14 (1) 7 GÍN KÙ.BABBAR *ana* ^{MÍ}*re-['indu]* / (2) *a-di* 1 GÍN *šá a-na* / (3) ^{LÚ}UŠ.BAR SÌ-*nu* ITI ŠU U$_4$ 20.KAM / (4) ½ GÍN KÙ.BABBAR *a-na* ^{I}SÌ-*na-a* / (5) A ^{I}BA-*šá*-[^{d}EN] *šá a-na* ^{LÚ}KIN.GI$_4$.A / (6) *šá* ^{LÚ}NAM SÌ-*nu* ITI ŠU U$_4$ 28.KAM / (7) 5 GÍN KÙ.BABBAR *šá-nu-ú* KÁ / (8) *a-na* ^{I}SÌ-*na-a* A ^{I}BA-*šá-a*-^{d}EN / (9) *a-na* ^{LÚ}KIN.GI$_4$.A / (10) *šá* ^{LÚ}NAM [. . . . . .] / (11) [(2 or 3?) U]ZU ^{I}*re-mu[t . . .]* / (12) ITI SIG$_4$ U$_4$ 10.K[AM] / (13) 2 UZU ^{I}ditto U$_4$ 12.KAM / (14) 3 UZU ^{I}ditto U$_4$ 14.KAM / (15) 2 UZU ^{I}ditto ITI ŠU U$_4$ 14.KAM / (16) 3 UZU ^{I}ditto U$_4$ 18 / (17) 3? UZU ^{I}ditto U$_4$ 24 / (18) 2 (or 3)? UZU ^{I}ditto 28 / (19) 3 UZU ^{I}ditto / (20) ITI NE U$_4$ 1+[x] / (21) PAP 21 UZU (Where not otherwise noted, transliteration of the Akkadian is my own).

Since generally women may have woven cloth for their family, it must have been a luxury to buy cloth.

The text next mentions some payments for "the messenger of the governor" (lines 4–10). The cuts of meat listed in lines 12–21 seem to concern the sale of sacrificial meat which was redistributed as prebendary income. After sacrificial sheep were slaughtered for daily offerings (*ginû*), they were carved into small pieces in specified ways by prebendary butchers, and then the meat was distributed to prebend holders, according to their rank.[15] Certain prebend holders received quite a large amount of meat, at least in Ezida, and they would have sold this in the market or to a merchant (Waerzeggers 2010a: 268–71). This text seems to concern the sale of sacrificial meat; it may show that the Ilušu-abušu family sold sacrificial meat which it received as prebendary remuneration. In this case, a person called Rēmūt-[. . .] mentioned in the eleventh line may have been a merchant.

(2) VS 6: 315

VS 6: 315[16] (cf. San Nicolò and Ungnad 1935, no. 862)
(1) ⅔ mina and 1 shekel (= 41 shekels) of silver was available for Bēl-iddin, (2) of which 6 shekels was spent by Bēl-ibni. (3) The remaining ½ mina and 5 shekels (= 35 shekels) of silver, from the hands of Bēl-iddin, (4) was at your disposal including 1½ shekels of silver, "deficit" (which may mean "unspecified expenditure"). (5) 6 ½ shekels of silver (was at the disposal of?) Rē'indu, daughter of Bazuzu. (6) ¼ (shekel) was for fish and ¼ for *parīdu* (-berries?). (7) The remaining ½ mina and 3 shekels (= 33 shekels) of silver (was) at the disposal of Bēl-[šar?- . . .] (8) on day 26 of the fourth month, including the expense [. . .]. (9) 7 shekels of silver for 2 *kandu*-jars of wine – (10) of which one was for Nergal-nāṣir, boatman (?), (11)and another was sold, a total of 2 *kandu*-jars of wine – (9) was paid. (12) 5 shekels of silver (is given) (13) for Urbanu, (12) for reed and timber (or beams) (13) of the *bīt šutummu* of the king. (14) 12 shekels of silver was paid for 2 *kandu*-jars of wine. (15) Of the second pair of wine jars, one was for Bēl-aṣûa, (16) and the other was for Bēl-zēra-

15 Concerning the distribution of meat, see, for example; van Driel 1993; Joannès 2000; Corò 2004; Waerzeggers 2010a: 258–60.

16 (1) ⅔ MA.NA 1 GÍN KÙ.BABBAR *šá ina pa-ni* ^{Id}EN-MU / (2) *ina lìb-bi* 6 GÍN KÙ.BABBAR KI ^{Id}EN-DÙ *e-pu-uš* / (3) *re-ḫi* ½ MA.NA 5 GÍN KÙ.BABBAR *ina* ŠU^{II} ^{Id}EN-MU / (4) IGI-*ka ina lìb-bi* 1 ½ GÍN KÙ.BABBAR *ba-ab-tu* / (5) 6 ½ GÍN KÙ.BABBAR ^{MÍ}*re-'i-in-du* DUMU.MÌ *šá* ^{I}*ba-zu-zu* / (6) 4-*tú a-na* KU$_6$.ḪI.A 4-*tú pa-ri-du* / (7) *re-ḫi* ½ MA.NA 3 GÍN KÙ.BABBAR *ina* IGI ^{Id}EN-[LUGAL$^?$- . . .] / (8) ITI ŠU U$_4$ 26.KAM *ina lìb-bi te-lit* [. . .] / (9) 7 GÍN KÙ.BABBAR *a-na* 2 ^{DUG}*kan-du* GEŠTIN *n*[*a-din*] / (10) *ina lìb-bi* 1 *a-na* ^{Id}U.GUR-PAP ^{LÚ}MÁ.[LAḪ$_4$$^?$] / (11) *ù* 1 *a-na* KÙ.BABBAR *na-din* PAP 2 ^{DUG}*kan-d*[*u* GEŠTIN] / (12) 5 GÍN KÙ.BABBAR *a-na* GI *u* GIŠ.ÙR / (13) *a-na* ^{I}*ur-ba-nu-ú šá* É *šu-tùm*^{um}*-mu šá* LUGAL / (14) 12 GÍN *a-na* 2 ^{DUG}*kan-du* GEŠTIN *na-din* / (15) 2-*ú* KÁ *ina lìb-bi* 1 ^{Id}EN-*a-ṣu-u-ú-a* / (16) *ù* 1 ^{Id}EN-NUMUN-MU PAP 2 ^{DUG}*kan-du te-lit-tú* / (17) PAP ⅓ MA.NA 4 GÍN KÙ.BABBAR *te-lit-tu*$_4$ / (18) TA IGI ^{Id}EN-DÙ EN 1 GÍN KÙ.BABBAR / (19) TA *re-*⌜x-x⌝ ^{Id}EN-DÙ / (20) *pu-ut* ḪA.LA-*šú šá* ^{DUG}*kan-du*

iddin; total expense: 2 *kandu*-jars. (17) Total: ⅓ mina and 4 shekels (= 24 shekels) of silver spent (18) by Bēl-ibni, with 1 shekel of silver, (19) from the rest (?) of Bēl-ibni, (20) his share of *kandu*-jars (?).

VS 6: 315 tells of 41 shekels of silver, of which 6 shekels were spent by Bēl-ibni (line 2). Of the remaining 35 shekels of silver, 1½ shekels was used for an unspecified expenditure (line 4). Apparently, 6½ shekels of silver was at the disposal of Rē'indu (line 5), but she actually spent only ½ shekel. She paid this ½ shekel of silver for fish and a type of berry, probably for household consumption (line 6). Rē'indu seems to have been in charge of the daily provision of food for the family, as well as clothing.

Additionally in this text, silver is used to pay for four jars of wine, which were purchased for distribution or sale, but the payment was not made by Rē'indu. The text also mentions the purchase of reeds and timber for the *bīt šutummu* of the king. The *bīt šutummu* was a private storehouse for the use of prebend holders in the Ezida temple.[17] The family may have been in charge of the construction of the *bīt šutummu* on behalf of the king. We also find the name of another key person in this text, Bēl-iddin (lines 1 and 3), probably a younger brother of Rēmūt-Bēl.[18]

(3) VS 6: 191

VS 6: 191[19] (13/v/ [Xer?] 1) (cf. San Nicolò and Ungnad 1935, no. 797)
(1) Three minas (= 180 shekels) of silver (2) brought (1) for ḪAR.ḪAR ("chain"? uncertain) (2) to Rē'indu, (3) of which 17 shekels of silver (4) was brought (3) to the gate of the [. . .]-canal (4) with me. The remaining (5) 2⅔ minas [and 3 shekels] (= 163 shekels) of silver and 2½

17 Joannès 1982: 306; 1984: 146–47; Watai 2012: 212–14.

18 He calls Rēmūt-Bēl "my master" in letters, but M. Jursa indicates that he is possibly a younger brother or son of Rēmūt-Bēl. In their letters addressed to Rēmūt-Bēl, Bēl-iddin writes: "I am fine. Rē'indu, my brothers and sister are fine" (*AfO* 19, no. 36 = Hackl, Jursa, and Schmidl 2014, no. 126), while Rē'indu writes: "I am fine. Bēl-iddin, his brothers and sisters are fine" (OECT 12: C 6 = Hackl, Jursa, and Schmidl 2014, no. 130; HSM 1899.2.262 = Hackl, Jursa, and Schmidl 2014, no. 131). This means that the family is composed of Rēmūt-Bēl, Rē'indu, Bēl-iddin and his brothers and sister(s). If Bēl-iddin is Rēmūt-Bēl's son, Rē'indu is apparently not his biological mother, since he never calls her "my mother." If we consider Rē'indu to be the wife of Rēmūt-Bēl, it seems most natural to identify Bēl-iddin as Rēmūt-Bēl's brother. See also Jursa 2013: 4.

19 (1) 3 MA.NA KÙ.BABBAR *šá a-na* ḪAR.ḪAR [x] / (2) *a-na* ^{MÍ}*re-'i-in-<du> šu-bu*[*l*] / (3) *ina lìb.bi* 17 GÍN KÙ.BABBAR KÁ I_7.⸢x x⸣ / (4) ⸢*it*⸣*-ti-iá na-ši re-ḫi* / (5) 2⅔ MA.NA [3 GÍN KÙ.BABBAR] *ù* 2 MA.NA / (6) 6 GÍN KÙ.BABBAR *šá* TA IGI ^{Id}⸢EN⸣-[x x]-*a* / (7) *ina lìb-bi* 1½ MA.NA 8 [GÍN$^{?}$ . . .] / (8) [. . .] 9 GÍN ⸢KÙ$^{?}$.BABBAR$^{?}$ x x⸣ [. . .] / (9) [. . .] ⸢x x x x x⸣ [. . .] / (10) ⸢*re*⸣*-ḫi* 58 GÍN KÙ.BABBAR [. . .] / (11) PAP 3 ⅔$^{!}$ MA.NA 1 GÍN KÙ.BABBAR *ina* IGI / (12) ^{MÍ}*re-'i-in-du* ITI ŠU U_4 2.KAM / (13) *ina lìb-bi* 15 GÍN KÙ.BABBAR *a-na* GU_4 / (14) *a-na ki-na-a-a-tú na-din* / (15) 1 MA.NA KÙ.BABBAR *ina* igi ^{Id}AG-*it-tan-na* / (16) A ^{I}*la-a-ba-ši* ⅔ MA.NA KÙ.BABBAR / (17)

minas (6) 6 shekels (= 156 shekels) of silver (were brought) from Bēl-[. . .]*a*; (7) of which 1½ minas and 8 shekels (= 98 shekels) of silver . . . . . . (8) 9 shekels [of silver . . . (9) . . .]. (10) The remaining 58 shekels of silver [. . .]. (11) A total of 3⅔ minas and 1 shekel (= 221 shekels) of silver was at the disposal of (12) Rē'indu on day 2 of the fourth month, (13) of which 15 shekels of silver (14) was spent (13) for an ox (14) as (or: and for) a *kīnayātu*-gift; (15) 1 mina of silver was available for Nabû-ittanna, (16) offspring of Lābāši; ⅔ mina (= 40 shekels) of silver (17) (was carried by?) Rēmūt-Bēl (to) Babylon (?). (18) A total of 1 mina and 55 shekels (= 115 shekels) of silver was spent. (19) The remaining 1⅔ mina and 6 shekels (= 106 shekels) of silver, (20) (including?) 9 shekels (of silver) purified (?), is available for Rē'indu. (21) On day 13 of the fifth month of the first year (22) the account was made.

VS 6: 191 is an interesting account drafted by someone who brought some silver to Rē'indu. First, 180 shekels of silver was given to Rē'indu, of which 17 shekels was taken away by the writer. The remainder was 163 shekels (lines 1–5a). Next, 156 shekels of silver was brought from someone, of which 98 shekels was spent. The remainder was 58 shekels (156 shekels minus 98 shekels) (lines 5b–10). A total of 221 shekels (163 shekels + 58 shekels) was at the disposal of Rē'indu (lines 11–12), of which 15 shekels was spent for an ox, 1 mina of silver was available for someone, and 40 shekels was perhaps carried by Rēmūt-Bēl to Babylon. Thus, a total of 1 mina 55 shekels (= 115 shekels) of silver was spent (lines 13–18). The remaining 106 shekels (221 shekels minus 115 shekels) was available to Rē'indu (lines 19–20). The text illustrates that Rē'indu was entrusted with management of money for the family.

(4) VS 4: 193

VS 4: 193[20] (30/viii/Xer 1) (cf. San Nicolò and Ungnad 1935, no. 574)
(2) Nabû-kuṣuranni (4) received (1) 15 shekels of silver, as silver for sacrificed sheep for the regular offering, (2) at the order of Rēmūt-Bēl, (3) and on behalf of Rē'indu, mother of Marduk-balāssu-iqbi and Nabû-nādin-šumi, (4) from the hands of Nabû-erība. (5) Month 8, day 30, year 1 of Xerxes, (6) king of Persia and Media, (7) [king of Ba]bylon and lands.

In VS 4: 193, a person called Nabû-kuṣuranni receives 15 shekels of silver, "silver for sheep for sacrifices (UDU.SISKUR.MEŠ)" from Nabû-erība "under the order of" (*ina qībi ša*) Rēmūt-Bēl, and "on behalf of" (*ina našparti ša*) Rē'indu. The silver seems to be the price of the sheep. We have seen that Rēmūt-Bēl's family participated in transactions involving meat in VS 6: 303. The sheep mentioned

^{I}*re-mut-*^{d}en *a-na* E^{KI} ⌜x⌝ / (18) PAP 1 MA.NA 55 GÍN KÙ.BABBAR *te-[lit]* / (19) *re-ḫi* 1 ⅔ MA.NA 6 GÍN KÙ.BABBAR / (20) 9 GÍN *me-su ina* IGI ^{MÍ}*re-'i-[in-du]* / (21) ITI ⌜AB⌝ U$_4$ 13.KAM MU 1.KAM / (22) NÍG.KA$_9$ *ep-ši*

20 (1) 15 GÍN KÙ.BABBAR *i-na* KÙ.BABBAR *šá* UDU.SISKÚR.MEŠ / (2) ^{Id}AG-*ku-ṣur-an-ni in qí-bi šá* ^{I}*re-mut-*^{d}EN / (3) *ina na-áš-par-tu*$_4$ *šá* ^{MÍ}*re-'i-in-du* AMA *šá* ^{Id}AMAR.UTU-DIN-*su-iq-bi u* ^{Id}AG-*na-din-*šeš / (4) *ina* ŠU^{II} ^{Id}AG-*eri-ba ma-ḫi-ir* / (5) ITI APIN U$_4$ 30.KAM MU 1.KAM ^{I}*ak-ši-ia-ar-šú* / (6) LUGAL *par-ša-a u ma-da-a-a* / (7) [LUGAL KÁ].DINGIR.RA *u* KUR.KUR

in this text seem also to have been received as prebendary income[21] and then sold by Rēmūt-Bēl. He very likely was travelling to Susa at this time, and so in his absence Rē'indu took charge of the transaction on behalf of her husband. In this context, Nabû-erība must have been the purchaser of the sheep.

(5) VS 4: 202; VS 3: 204; OECT 12: A 182

In VS 4: 202 (cf. San Nicolò and Ungnad 1935, no. 793),[22] Rē'indu receives 10 shekels of silver from a person called Nabû-tāriṣ, and in VS 3: 204 (cf. San Nicolò and Ungnad 1935, no. 790), she receives 5 kur of barley from another person, Ana-muḫḫi-Nabû-taklāk.[23] We do not know the dates or context of the transactions in these texts. In OECT 12: A 182,[24] dated in the second year of Xerxes, Rē'indu received 9¼ shekels of silver from Nabû-erība, whom we encountered in VS 4: 193. There is another payment addressed to Rēmūt-Bēl and Bēl-iddin, two other central figures of the archive, although we do not know what the silver was used to buy.

(6) Letters

Next, we will examine some letters that Rē'indu wrote to Rēmūt-Bēl during his stay in Susa. In OECT 12: C 6 (= Hackl, Jursa, and Schmidl 2014, no. 130), Rē'-indu reports that the citizens of Borsippa were discontented because the income from prebends was not distributed correctly.

OECT 12: C 6 (Hackl, Jursa, and Schmidl 2014, no. 130)[25]

Letter from Rē'indu to Rēmūt-Bēl, my brother. May the goddesses Nanaya and Sutīti ordain my brother's health and well-being! Thanks to the protection of the gods, I am fine. Bēl-iddin, his brothers and sisters are fine. The whole family is well.

You should know: all prebendary income of the Borsippeans has been withheld and (people say): "Let's see whether I can get even one-third of [. . .]." However, no one has held the *takkassû* (-bread) and they say: "If you had met the accountant (?), all of us would have held one third of a cut of [. . .]-meat. . . . (broken)."

---

21 According to the remark of Waerzeggers (2010a: 265–66), animals offered during festivals (*guqqû*) were not carved and were distributed whole in Borsippa.

22 (1) 10 GÍN KÙ.BABBAR ^{MÍ}*re-'i-in-du* / (2) *ina* ŠU^{II} ^{Id}AG-LAL-*iṣ* ITI GAN U$_4$ 20[.KAM] / (3) 1 GÍN 4-*tú* KÙ.BABBAR *šá* ITI APIN / (4) *ina* IGI ^{Id}AG-LAL-*iṣ*

23 (1) 5 GUR ŠE.BAR *ina* ŠU^{II} / (2) ^{I}*a-na-muḫ-ḫi-*^{d}AG-*tak-lak* / (3) ITI NE U$_4$ 15.KAM / (4) ^{MÍ}*re-'i-in-du* / [*ma-ḫir* ?]

24 (1) 9 GÍN 4-*tù* KÙ.BABBAR *šá gin-nu* (?) / (2) ^{MÍ}*re-'i-in-du maḫ-rat* / (3) *ina* ŠU^{II} ^{Id}AG-SU / (4) *e-lat te-lit šá* ^{I}*re-mut-*^{d}EN / (5) *ù* ^{Id}EN-SÌ-*na* / (6) ITI GU$_4$ U$_4$ 22.KAM / (7) MU 2.KAM ^{I}*ak-ši-ia-ar-šú* / (8) LUGAL KUR *par-su u* KUR *ma-da-a-a* / (8) LUGAL KÁ.DINGIR.RA *u* KUR.KUR

25 Transliteration and translation of OECT 12: C 6 are available in Jursa 2013: 7 and Hackl, Jursa, and Schmidl 2014: 246–47.

The problem concerning the prebendary income is also visible in another letter (HSM 1899.2.262 = Hackl, Jursa, and Schmidl 2014, no. 131), although it is described on an individual level. In this letter, Rē'indu complains that she cannot receive sheep, probably as prebendary income.

HSM 1899.2.262 (Hackl, Jursa, and Schmidl 2014, no. 131)[26]
Letter from Rē'indu to Rēmūt-Bēl, my brother. May the goddesses Nanaya and Sutīti ordain the health and well-being of my brother. Thanks to the protection of the god, I am fine. Bēl-iddin, his brothers and sisters are fine. The whole family is well. On the fourteenth and seventeenth day of every month, I ask [Mār-bīti] for your well-being, my brother. [. . .] I have neither sheep before the goddess Sutīti, nor before the pedestal of Marduk.

M. Jursa points out that these letters[27] demonstrate a tense relationship between the Achaemenid king and the citizens of Borsippa because of the interruption of the payment of prebendary incomes just before Babylonian revolts broke out in 484 BCE.[28]

Under these circumstances Rē'indu sent letters to Rēmūt-Bēl in his absence and reported the situation of the family and other prebendaries of the city.[29] Although we cannot affirm that Rē'indu wrote these letters by herself, it seems probable that some women knew how to write cuneiform on the basis of studies of women in the Old Assyrian Period. Certain women probably wrote letters by themselves.[30]

---

26 The transliteration and translation are available in Jursa 2013: 3 and Hackl, Jursa, and Schmidl 2014: 247–48.

27 See also the letter OECT 12: C 4 = Hackl, Jursa, and Schmidl 2014, no. 129 (Jursa 2013: 8; Hackl, Jursa and Schmidl 2014: 245).

28 According to Jursa (2013: 10), " . . . at least at one point during the very last years leading up to the rebellions against Xerxes, perhaps just a few months before the outbreak of the uprisings, the payment of prebendary income in Ezida had been interrupted, or at least severely curtailed, on the order of a royal official."

29 We find a certain number of women who sent or received letters, although their number is much less than that of men. Among the 242 private letters collected in Hackl, Jursa and Schmidl 2014, thirteen were sent by women and sixteen were received by women, including two letters where both the sender and recipient were women. For women's letters, see Hackl, Jursa, and Schmidl 2014: 53–58.

30 According to the studies of women in Old Assyrian Period, certain women of the merchant families likely wrote letters by themselves (Michel 2009, and see also Michel 2013. Concerning letters sent by women, see Michel 2001: 419–511).

2.4 Conclusion on Rēʾindu

The documents related to Rēmūt-Bēl illustrate many interesting points: the existence of a true monetary system based on silver, the critical situation of Borsippa on the eve of revolts against the Persians, and the roles of women in the family. Rēʾindu, surely the wife of the head of the family, was entrusted with the management of silver. This was spent for the purchase of foodstuffs, drinks, and daily goods.[31] Since these memoranda include both expenditures for the temple administration and for the consumption of the family at the same time, it is occasionally difficult to distinguish the type of the purchases; but Rēʾindu seems to participate in purchases for the family. Additionally, she is involved in activities related to the family's prebend. She also wrote, maybe by herself, to her husband while he was in Susa to inform him of the situation of the family and of the citizens of Borsippa.

The role that she played in the family seems surprising, since these types of activities are not frequently demonstrated in the records. Perhaps it was usual for women, especially wives of the head of families, to manage their households, participate in the management of the family budget, and to represent their husbands in their absence in activities concerning the family business.[32]

3 The Case of Andiya

The second woman we will discuss is Andiya.[33] We find six documents mentioning her: five receipts (*AfO* 51, nos. 65, 74, 92, 93; *AfO* 51: 148) and a letter

31 One text (BM 64153 in Jursa 2000) indicates that a woman walking along the street with her female servant fell victim to violence. This text suggests that women went out, for example to the market for shopping by herself. See also Joannès 2016.

32 See also a letter which Itti-Marduk-balāṭu of the Egibi family sent to Iddin-Marduk, his father-in-law (CT 22: 110 = Hackl, Jursa, and Schmidl 2014, no. 23). In this letter, Itti-Marduk-balāṭu wrote that 85 shekels of silver were at the disposal of Nūptaya, his wife, in the house (lines 12–14). We also find that in the Old Assyrian period "Épouses de marchands souvent absents, les Assyriennes sont amenées à prendre seules les décisions concernant leur famille, leur maison ou leur situation financières" (Michel 2009: 253).

33 This name means "servant of the goddess" (whose name is not explicitly mentioned), normally an abbreviated form of Amat-DN or Andi-DN. Her name is written with logograms GÉME-*ia*, except in one text (*AfO* 51, no. 74) that uses the syllabic spelling *an-di-ia* (/*iá*). Amtiya and Andiya are also possible as the transcription of GÉME-*ia*. We use Andiya in this paper, following *AfO* 51, no. 74

(Hackl, Jursa, and Schmidl 2014, no. 155). The five receipts were published by R. Zadok (2005) and belong to a group of texts concerning Nabû-ēṭir.[34]

3.1 The Archive of Nabû-ēṭir

The archive of Nabû-ēṭir is chronologically distributed from year 25 to year 28 of Darius I (497-493 BCE), but the majority of the texts are dated from years 26 and 27 of Darius (496-494 BCE) and very likely originated in Borsippa. The archive includes 197 documents (letters, orders, receipts, and records) referring to the delivery of foodstuffs, principally bread and cuts of meat, but also spices, oil, wine, beer, and other materials like silver and wool. The central figures in the archive, Nabû-ēṭir and his agent Bēl-ēṭir, take part in various transactions, receiving foodstuffs and other items from one person and giving them to another person.

According to Zadok (2005: 187), these deliveries may be linked to the performance of the prebendary duties of preparing divine meals in the Ezida temple, because some texts allude to the supplying of foodstuffs for divine meals and offerings. He suggests that half of these texts belong to the archive of Šaddinnu, the prebendary baker.[35] Waerzeggers (2010a: 197–98 n. 762), however, points out that the subject of the archive is not the prebendary baker, because "the scope of these texts . . . surpasses the affairs of the baker," and "a varied clientele benefited from these allowances, including women and messengers, people who were by definition not counted among the prebendary personnel."

F. Joannès (2013) proposes that these texts concern the exchange or the practical commercial distribution of foodstuffs in a private context. Foodstuffs offered as divine meals were redistributed to prebendaries, and a part of these foodstuffs may have been circulated as commodities on the market, as we have seen in the case of Rē'indu. Nabû-ēṭir may have been a merchant or an intermediary in the sales and purchases of foodstuffs.

We find 14 women among the 128 persons appearing in the archive. They took part in the transactions either as receivers or as deliverers. Some of them

34 BM 96363 is presented in his paper (Zadok 2005: 148), but it does not belong to the archive of Nabû-ēṭir, but rather to the Šaddinnu archive.

35 Bēl-ēṭir, one of central figures of the archive of Nabû-ēṭir, and Andiya, who appears frequently in the archive, and Šaddinnu are mentioned in a text (BM 96363) (Zadok 2005: 148).

appear in several texts, both as receivers and as deliverers.[36] However, Andiya seems to have had an exceptional position among these women.

3.2 Activities of Andiya

In three texts, Andiya appears as a receiver. In *AfO* 51, no. 65, a person called Ubār receives six cuts of meat "at the order of Andiya" from Bēl-ēṭer, agent of Nabû-ēṭir; in *AfO* 51: 148 (BM 96363), her agent receives three cuts of meat from Bēl-ēṭer; and in *AfO* 51, no. 92, her agent Nāṣiru receives 16 cuts of meat, which are given to another person.

***AfO* 51, no. 65 (BM 96486)**
Ubāru received from Bēl-ēṭer at the order of Andiya six (unspecified) cuts of meat. Month 9, day 22, year 26[+½(?)]. Four (unspecified) cuts of meat and two (loaves of) *ṣibtu*-bread[37] Dani[ya(?)] on behalf (?) of the daughter(?) of Ezida (received). (The reading and interpretation are obscure.) Three shekels of white silver are/were at the disposal of Nabû-silim. Two shekels of silver are/were at disposal of Gūzānu. Nabû-uṣuršu on behalf of Nabû-silim received one kur of dates.

***AfO* 51: 148 (BM 96363)**
Three (unspecified) cuts of meat (were delivered) by Bēl-ēṭer (to) Ana-Nabû-taklāk (?) on behalf of Andiya.
One (for) Atete (?), month 12, day 6.
Two shank meat cuts (delivered) by Itti-Nabû-gūzu(?) were taken by ᶠ[. . .]*tā*.
2 *sūt* of wine – Nabû-iddina, son of Bēl-iqīša, month 12, day 3, year 26.
Bēl-ēṭer received 0.75 shekels of silver from Andiya; month 12, day 12, account settled.
Six (unspecified) cuts of meat – Šaddinnu the baker.

***AfO* 51, no. 92 (BM 29271)**
Nāṣiru, on behalf of Andiya, received 16 cuts of (unspecified) meat from Nanaya-tāqiš, which were given to Rēmūt, son of Taklāk-ana-Bēl. Month 8, day 2, year 27.

In two texts, she appears as a deliverer. In *AfO* 51, no. 74, she distributes a total of about 720 liters of dates to some people via Bēl-ēṭir, and in *AfO* 51, no. 93, bread and cuts of meat were given to a messenger on her orders.

36 For example, in a text (*AfO* 51, no. 13 = BM 29309), Nabû-ēṭir orders to Bēl-ēṭir to give two loaves of bread in exchange for wool to a woman called Mullissu-silim. In this text, Mullissu-silim gives wool, and receives bread. In another text (*AfO* 51, no. 12 = BM 29504), Nabû-ēṭir orders Bēl-ēṭir to give dates to Mullissu-silim, in exchange for bread, which was given to another woman. In this text, Mullissu-silim gives bread, and receives dates.
37 The term *ṣibtu* means a type of bread, which is a principal category of bread offering (Waerzeggers 2010a: 116). See also CAD Ṣ: 162–63.

***AfO* 51, no. 74 (BM 29188)**
Dates from Andiya, which are at the disposal of Bēl-ēṭir on behalf of Andiya, that Ardi-Nergal and his son received from Bēl-ēṭer. First installment: 1 *kur* 5 *sūt*; second installment: two kur. Months 4 and 5, year 26. [1+?]1 *kur* of barley in Babylon.

***AfO* 51, no. 93 (BM 96543)**
One (loaf of) *ṣibtu*-bread (and) one (unspecified) cut of meat at the order of Andiya, [to$^{!?}$][38] daughter(s?) of ^{f}Hiptaya. Month 1, year 27.

Two shank meat cuts (and) one (loaf) of *ṣibtu*-bread which were given to a messenger (*mār šipri*) at the order of Andiya.

In all these cases, either as a receiver or as a deliverer, Andiya gives orders to male agents. She also sent a letter (Hackl, Jursa, and Schmidl 2014, no.155) to Bēl-ēṭir. In the letter, she asked Bēl-ēṭir to cut meat and preserve it in salt if he could do so, or to give the meat to another agent if he could not do it.

Hackl, Jursa, and Schmidl 2014, no. 155 (BM 29255)
Letter from Andiya to Bēl-ēṭer. Now, if you can, cut up[39] the meat at your disposal and put it in salt. If you cannot, give it to Nāṣir from the ninth day so that he can cut it up. As you see, I have written you through Itti-Nabû-gūzu.

Apparently, Andiya took charge of the conservation and storage of meat, probably to be distributed.

3.3 Who Was Andiya?

Although the familial background of Andiya was not clearly mentioned in texts, the circumstantial evidence strongly suggest that she was the wife of Nabû-ēṭir, the key person in the archive.[40] There are three reasons for believing so. First, Nabû-ēṭir is not mentioned in the same texts as Andiya, implying perhaps that she acts in his stead. Second, Bēl-ēṭir, the agent of Nabû-ēṭir, also acts as the agent of Andiya. Third, she was clearly in a position to take the initiative in the management of meat within the business of Nabû-ēṭir.[41]

---

38 According to R. Zadok, the transliteration of line 2 is: *šá* ^{MÍ}GÉME-*iá* DUMU.MUNUS* (text MEŠ) *šá* ^{f}*hi-ip-ta-a*. He read this phrase as "of Andiya, daughter of ^{MÍ}Hiptaya," but I suspect that *ana* "to" is missing between ^{MÍ}GÉME-*iá* (Andiya) and DUMU.MUNUS.MEŠ ("daughters"), so that we can interpret this as "at the order of Andiya, to daughters of Hiptaya."

39 Understanding *šupallika* as an ŠD imperative of *palāku*. Cf. GAG § 95b ("zerlege!") and CAD P: 50b ("divide (?)").

40 Perhaps one text mentions her mother, but this is not certain (see n. 37 above).

41 Another possibility is that she is the owner of the prebend. Women can possess prebends, but cannot perform the tasks. Maybe, therefore, Andiya managed it through agents.

3.4 Conclusion on Andiya

If indeed she was the wife of Nabû-ēṭir, Andiya is another example of a woman who participated in the business of her husband, namely in the circulation of offerings redistributed for prebend holders on the private level. We can also suppose that the family's funds were at her disposal, since she appears separately from her husband in texts, and gives orders to agents in her own name.

4 Conclusion

The activities of Rē'indu and Andiya provide glimpses of the position and activities of women in the economic sphere of the urban family in a patriarchal society, where women were not very visible. Rē'indu was in charge of the family budget for buying foodstuffs and other things for daily life, and in charge of the family business concerning meat from offerings redistributed to prebend holders on behalf of her husband. Andiya played an important role in the commercial distribution of meat which came from the temple, likely with a certain amount of authority in the economic activities of the family.

Both women were recognized by their husbands and by their agents or business partners as being capable of taking responsibility in the economic sphere of the family, taking initiatives in transactions, and writing letters. They functioned as part of the circulation of commodities related to the temple.

It was possible for women, especially the spouses of the head of the family, to play an important part in the management of familial property. We can assume that the role and activities of Rē'indu and Andiya were not exceptional cases, but rather usual among notable urban families in Borsippa, although that is not normally visible in the documents.

Bibliography

Abraham, Kathleen. 2004. *Business and Politics under the Persian Empire. The Financial Dealings of Marduk-nāṣir-apli of the House of Egibi (521-487 B.C.E)*. Bethesda: CDL Press.

Baker, Heather, D. 2004. *The Archive of the Nappāḫu Family*. AfO Beiheft 30. Wien: Institut für Orientalistik der Universität Wien.

Baker, Heather. 2008. Babylon in 484 BC: the excavated archival tablets as a source for urban history. *ZA* 98: 100–16.

Corò, Paola. 2004. Meat, Prebends and Rank: A Short Note on the Distribution of Sacrificed Meat in Seleucid Uruk. Pp. 257–67 in *Food and Identity in the Ancient World*, ed. Cristiano Grottanelli and Lucio Milano. History of the Ancient Near East, Studies 9. Padova: Sargon Editrice e Libreria.

Corò, Paola. 2005. *Prebende templari in età seleucide*, History of the Ancient Near East, Monographs 8. Padova: Sargon Editric e Libreria.

Démare-Lafont, Sophie. 2010. Les prébendes dans la Mésopotamie du Ier Millénaire avant J.-C. Pp. 3–17 in *L'organisation matérielle des cultes dans l'Antiquité*, ed. Barbala Anagnostou-Canas. Paris: Editions Cybèle.

Frame, Grant and Caroline Waerzeggers. 2011. The Prebend of Temple Scribe in First Millennium Babylonia. *ZA* 101: 127–51.

Hackl, Johannes, Michael Jursa, and Martina Schmidl. 2014. *Spätbabylonische Privatbriefe*. AOAT 414/1. Münster: Ugarit Verlag.

Joannès, Francis. 1982. *Textes Économiques de la Babylonie Récente*. Étude Assyriologiques, Cahier n° 5. Paris: Éditions Recherche sur les civilisations.

Joannès, Francis. 1984. Les archives d'une famille de notables babyloniens du VIIe au Ve siècle avant Jésus-Christ. *Journal des Savantes* 3–4: 135–50.

Joannès, Francis. 1989. *Archives de Borsippa, la famille Ea-ilûta-bâni*. Hautes Études Orientales 25. Genève: Librairie Droz.

Joannès, Francis. 2000. Découpage de la viande en Mésopotamie. Pp. 333–43 in *Les animaux et les hommes dans le monde syro-mésopotamien aux époques historiques*, ed. Dominique Parayre. Topoi Supplément 2. Paris: De Boccard.

Joannès, Francis. 2013. La Place des femmes dans l'économie domestique néo-babylonienne, contribution for the first workshop of the French-Japanese research project "Le Rôle Économique des Femmes en Mesopotamie Ancienne (=REFEMA)" (November 2012, Nanterre). https://refema.hypotheses.org/202

Joannès, Francis. 2016. By the Street of Babylon. Pp. 127–38 in *Parcours d'Orient: Recueil de textes offert à Christine Kepinski*, ed. Bérengère Perello and Aline Tenu. Oxford: Archeopress.

Jursa, Michael. 2000. *ṭerdu*. Von Entführung in Babylon und Majestätsbeleidigung in Larsa. Pp. 497–514 in *Studi in Vicino Oriente antico dedicati alla memoria di Luigi Cagni*, ed. Simonetta Graziani. Napoli: Istituto Universitario Orientale.

Jursa, Michael. 2005. *Neo-Babylonian Legal and Administrative Documents, Typology, Contents and Archives*. Münster: Ugarit-Verlag.

Jursa, Michael. 2010. *Aspects of the Economic History of Babylonia in the First Millennium BC*. AOAT 377. Münster: Ugarit-Verlag.

Jursa, Michael. 2013. Epistolographic Evidence for Trips to Susa by Borsippean Priests and for the Crisis in Borsippa at the Beginning of Xerxes' Reign. *Arta* 2013.003, 1–12.

Jursa, Michael. 2016. Silver and Other Forms of Elite Wealth in Seventh Century BC Babylonia. Pp. 61–71 in *Silver, Money and Credit, A tribute to Robartus J. van der Spek on the Occasion of His 65th Birthday*, ed. Kristin Kleber and Reinhard Pirngruber. PIHANS 128. Leiden: Nederlands Instituut voor het Nabije Oosten.

Jursa, Michael. with contributions by Waerzeggers, Caroline. 2009. On Aspects of Taxation in Achaemenid Babylonia: New Evidence from Borsippa. Pp. 237–69 in *Organisation des pouvoirs et contacts culturels dans les pays de l'empire achéménide*, ed. Pierre Briant and Michel Chaveau. Persika 14. Paris: De Boccard.

Michel, Cécile. 2001. *Correspondance des marchands de Kaniš au début du IIe millénaire avant J.-C.* LAPO 19. Paris: Les éditions du Cerf.
Michel, Cécile. 2009. Les femmes et l'écrit dans les archives paléo-assyriennes. Pp. 253–72 in *Femmes, cultures et sociétés dans les civilisations méditerranéennes et proche-orientales de l'Antiquité*, ed. Françoise Briquel-Chatonnet, Saba Farès, Brigitte Lion and Cécile Michel. Topoi Supplément 10. Paris: De Boccard.
Michel, Cécile. 2015. Women in the Family of Ali-ahum son of Iddin-Suen (1993 Kültepe archive), Pp. 85–93 in *Proceedings of the 1st Kültepe International Meeting, Kültepe, 19–23 September, 2003. Studies Dedicated to Kutlu Emre*, ed. Fikri Kulakoğlu and Cécile Michel. Kültepe International Meetings 1. *Subartu* 35. Turnhout: Brepols.
Monerie, Julian. 2014. Women and Prebends in Seleucid Uruk. Pp. 526–42 in *The Role of Women in Work and Society in the Ancient Near East*, ed. Brigitte Lion and Cécile Michel. SANER 13. Berlin: De Gruyter.
Monerie, Julian. 2018. *L'économie de la Babylonie à l'époque héllenistique (IVème – IIème siècle avant J. C.)*. SANER 14. Berlin: De Gruyter.
Oelsner, Joachim. 2007. Das zweite Regierungsjahr des Xerxes (484/3 v.Chr.) in Babylonien. Pp. 289–303 in *Festschrift für Hermann Hunger zum 65. Geburtstag gewidmet von seinen Freunden, Kollegen und Schülern*, ed. Markus Köhlbach, Stephan Procházka, Gebhard J. Selz, and Rüdiger Lohlker. WZKM 97. Wien: Selbstverlag des Instituts für Orientalistik.
San Nicolò, Mariano, and Arthur Ungnad. 1935. *Neubabylonische Rechts- und Verwaltungsurkunden*. Leipzig: J. C. Hinrichs'sche Buchhandlung.
Ungnad, Arthur. 1959/60. Neubabylonische Privaturkunden aus der Sammlung Amherst. *AfO* 19: 74–82.
Van Driel, Govert. 1993. Bones and the Mesopotamian State? Animal Husbandry in an Urban Context. *BiOr* 50: 545–63.
van Driel, Govert. 2002. *Elusive Silver*. PIHANS 95. Leiden: Nederlands Instituut voor het Nabije Oosten.
Waerzeggers, Caroline. 2003. The Babylonian revolts against Xerxes and the 'End of archives.' *AfO* 50: 150–73.
Waerzeggers, Caroline. 2010a. *The Ezida Temple of Borsippa, Priesthood, Cult, Archives*, Achaemenid History 15. Leiden: Peeters Publishers.
Waerzeggers, Caroline. 2010b. Babylonians in Susa. The Travels of Babylonian Businessmen to Susa Reconsidered. Pp. 777–813 in *Der Achämenidenhof. The Achaemenid Court*. ed. Bruno Jacobs and Robert Rollinger. Classica et Orientalia 2. Wiesbaden: Harrassowitz.
Watai, Yoko. 2012. Les maisons néo-babyloniennes d'après la documentation textuelle. Thèse de doctorat (Université Paris 1).
Watai, Yoko. 2016. Economic Activities of Women in 1st Millennium Babylonia. Pp. 494–511 in *The Role of Women in Work and Society in the Ancient Near East*, ed. Brigitte Lion and Cécile Michel. SANER 13. Berlin: De Gruyter.
Wunsch, Cornelia. 2000. *Das Egibi Archiv I. Die Felder und Gärten*, 2 tomes. CM 20. Groningen.
Zadok, Ran. 2005. The Text Group of Nabû-ēṭir. *AfO* 51: 147–97.

Huang Haijing

Wu Zetian's Buddhist Policy: A New Perspective

1 Preliminary

Wu Zetian 武則天 (ca. 624–705) is the only empress in the history of China.[1] She was the queen of Li Zhi 李治 (628–83), who became the third emperor of the Tang唐 dynasty as Gaozong 高宗 (reign 649–83). Since her husband was suffering from an unknown illness called *fengji* 風疾, Wu Zetian was entrusted to manage political affairs after the Xianqing 顯慶 period (656–60). In the first year of Zaichu 載初 (690) she changed the title of the dynasty from Tang to Zhou 周 (690–705) and moved the capital from Chang'an 長安 to Luoyang 洛陽. It is assumed that in the following year she reversed the traditional religious policy held from the beginning of the Tang dynasty, in which Taoism 道教 had been given precedence over Buddhism, and elevated the status of Buddhism above that of Taoism.[2]

The majority of previous studies on the Wu Zhou revolution 武周革命 have argued that Wu Zetian utilized Buddhism to legitimize her seizure of political power.[3] After briefly reviewing the previous studies, I will provide a new perspective on the relationship between Wu Zetian and Buddhism.[4]

2 Previous Studies on Wu Zetian's Buddhist Policy and Some Issues

2.1 Previous Studies

Yabuki (1927: 685–761) argued that because Wu Zetian did not find any teaching or thought in traditional Confucianism or Taoism that would help to legitimize her claims to the power, she relied on works of foreign origin such as the

1 Translated from Japanese by Fumi Karahashi with the help of Frederick W. Knobloch.
2 *Jiu tangshu* 旧唐書, vol. 6; *Zetian huanghou benji* 則天皇后本紀.
3 For example, Yokota 1956; Guisso 1978; Forte 1976 and 1988; Kaneko 1986; Ōmuro 1994; Kamata 1994; Kegasawa 1995; Sun 2014; Wang and Liang 2014.
4 This paper is largely based on my doctoral dissertation (Huang 2016).

https://doi.org/10.1515/9781501514821-006

Buddhist *Dayun jing* 大雲経 and *Baoyu jing* 宝雨経. Although the *Dayun jing* talks about the appearing of a female sovereign, it does not specifiy who the woman would be. Forte (1984: 173–206) demonstrated that it was the *Dayun jingshu* 大雲経疏, commentaries to *Dayun jing*, not the *Dayun jing* that would make the identification of that woman possible, and that the commentaries were made immediately before her seizure of power. Jin and Liu (2009: 31–46), based on their research on the good omens and prophecies mentioned in *Dayun jingshu*, suggested that Wu Zetian utilized prognostications with the intention to legitimize her power.

Some scholars, like Chen (1935: 137–47), Rao (1974: 397–418), and Nishimura (1976: 25–40), ask whether Wu Zetian made use of Buddhism simply to serve her political aims, or whether she herself had a strong faith in Buddhism. Chen explored the relationship between Wu Zetian and Buddhism by asking how much influence the Buddhist beliefs of the clan of her mother, Lady Yang 楊氏, exerted upon her, and how she proved her claim to special political status from the Buddhist perspective.

Ōuchi (1998: 449–70), focusing on the way in which Wu Zetian's government organized the state project of translating Buddhist sutras, studied *Da Zhou kanding zhongjing mulu* 大周刊定衆経目録, which was completed by Mingquan 明佺 of the Foshouji Temple 仏授記寺 in Luoyang and his colleagues in the first year of Tiance wansui 天册萬歳, and concluded that temples located in Luoyang, especially the Dafuxian Temple 大福先寺,[5] were central to the translation project carried out during Wu Zetian's reign.

As for the relationship between Wu Zetian and the Buddhist monks and sects, Im (1990: 1–16) focused on the editors of *Dayun jingshu*, and Tsukamoto (1944: 1–50) on the nationwide construction of Dayun temples 大雲寺, which was closely related to Wu Zetian's Buddhist policies.

Wen (1989: 119–27) discussed the carving of Buddhist images on niches at the Longmen Grottoes in relation to Wu Zetian's religious policy and suggested that she utilized belief in Maitreya 弥勒 to legitimize her seizing of power.

Kou (1999: 19–26) discussed the reason why Wu Zetian conceived of the religious policy of "Buddhism over Taoism" 仏先道後 and where to find reflections of it.

5 For this temple, see Huang 2007; Ando 1952.

2.2 Issues Not Addressed in Previous Studies

As seen from the overview in §2.1, most of the previous studies on Wu Zetian's Buddhist policy have argued that she utilized Buddhist thought and teachings to legitimize her claims to political power and secure her control. These studies, in general, analyze the writings of the Buddhist writings such as *Dayun jing*, *Dayun jingshu*, and *Baoyu jing*, and regard them as the theoretical basis of her claims. Along these lines, Sun (2013: 78–88; 2014), through his analysis of honorary titles, argued that Wu Zetian utilized the idea of the *chakravartin* 転輪王 'ideal universal ruler' as political propaganda.

Most of the previous studies that have focused on Wu Zetian's utilization of Buddhism have discussed how Buddhist thought or her faith influenced her politics. Certainly, Buddhist thought and teachings may have helped her to achieve her goals. The question arises, however, as to whether people could have been persuaded to accept her authority on the basis of Buddhist ideology only.

3 A New Perspective

Although previous scholarship viewed the Buddhist groups as central to the state project of translating Buddhist sutras, a project which Wu Zetian held to be very important, the influence of these groups on the situation and politics of that time has hardly been explored. Given that the translation of Buddhist sutras was a national enterprise of great importance, it appears to be meaningful and necessary to examine the manner in which Buddhist groups participated in Wu Zetian's translation project. Consequently, I would like to argue that she not only utilized Buddhist thought and teachings, but also was keen to take control of the economic power and social influence of the Buddhist temples, which could be utilized for pragmatic ends.

When investigating Wu Zetian's Buddhist policy from the viewpoint of the relationships between the Buddhist groups and her translation project, the first question to be addressed is who the individual participants were. One of the historical sources available to me for this purpose is what is called in Japanese the *Yakujo retsui* 訳場列位, colophons in the translated sutras that enumerate the names of the monks and government officials who were directly involved in the project.[6] These texts provide me with important information by revealing the extent to which Buddhist groups were connected to Wu Zetian's administration.

6 For the *Yakujo retsui*, see Ikeda 1990: 14.

3.1 The State Organization for Translating Buddhist Sutras

The above-mentioned *Yakujo retsui* clearly show that translater-monks called *fanjing* 翻経 *shamen* 沙門 (*śramaṇa*) or *fanjing* 翻経 *dade* 大徳 (*bhadanta*) who were chosen by the authorities, as well as government officials, participated the translation project in a systematic way. The following is a brief overview of persons of special importance whom Wu Zetian particularly valued.

When the monk Yijing 義浄[7] returned to Luoyang from India in the first year of Zhengsheng 証聖 (695), Wu Zetian went out in person from the Shangdong Gate 上東門 to meet him. He brought back many Buddhist sutras with him, joined Wu Zetian's translation project, and devoted himself to it. In the year of his return he succeeded in deciphering the twelve signs inscribed on the *Jade Plate* 玉冊which was in the possession of Wu Zetian. In so doing, he proved and proclaimed Wu Zetian's legitimate right to power. In other words, he actively co-operated with her policies. In his early years in Luoyang, he joined the *yichang* 訳場 ("place of translation") directed by Śikṣānanda 実叉難陀 (see below). Beginning in the year Jiushi久視 (700) Yijing himself became the main translator and significantly advanced the translation project.

Dharmaruci 達摩流支 was renamed Bodhiruci 菩提流志 by Wu Zetian.[8] He was a *sanzang* 三蔵 born in southern India and had knowledge of magic, *yingyang* 陰陽, and divination. In the second year of Changshou 長寿 (693), he came to Luoyang and translated into Chinese the ten volumes of *Baoyu jing* and the two volumes of *Wenshu shili suoshuo busiyi fojingjie jing* 文殊師利所説不思議仏境界経 in the Foshouji Temple and the Dafuxian Temple. It is well known that *Baoyu jing* and *Dayun jing* contain descriptions of the reign of the empress.

Śikṣānanda, who was originally from Khotan 于闐, was a *sanzang-fashi* 三蔵法師 (*tripiṭaka* master).[9] Wu Zetian sent a delegation to Khotan to obtain the original text of *Dafangguangfo huayan jing* 大方広仏華厳経 in order to make a new and complete Chinese translation of it. Śikṣānanda arrived at Luoyang in 695 and at the request of Wu Zetian started translating *Dafangguangfo huayan jing* at the Dabiankong Temple 大遍空寺 with the above-mentioned Yijing and Bodhiruci. Wu Zetian regarded these texts as very important, to the extent that she herself

7 See *Kaiyuan shijiao lu* 開元釈教録vol. 9; *Taisho shinshu daizokyo* 大正新修大蔵経 vol. 55: 568–69; Huang 2017; Sun 2014.

8 For Bodhiruci, see *Song gaoseng zhuan* 宋高僧伝vol. 3; *Tang luojing changshousi putiliuzhi zhuan* 唐洛京長寿寺菩提流志伝, in *Taisho shinshu daizokyo*, vol. 50: 720.

9 For Śikṣānanda, see *Song gaoseng zhuan*, vol. 2; *Tang luojing da biankongsi shichanantuo zhuan* 唐洛京大遍空寺実叉難陀伝 in *Taisho shinshu daizokyo*, vol. 50: 718–19.

wrote the introduction. Yijing and Bodhiruci also produced a *xuanfanben* 宣梵本 (a phonetic transcription of the Sanskrit original) of *Dafangguangfo huayan jing*.

In the second year of Shengli 聖暦 (699), the monks Fuli 復礼, Fazang 法蔵, and others completed translating *Dafangguangfo huayan jing* at the Foshouji Temple. In the following year, *Dasheng rulengqie jing* 大乗入楞伽経 was translated at the Sanyang Palace 三陽宮, and *Wenshu shouji* 文殊授記 and some other Buddhist sutras were translated at the Qingchan Temple 清禅寺 in Xijing 西京 (i.e., Chang'an) and the Foshouji Temple in Dongdu 東都 (i.e., Luoyang). The monks Bolun 波崙, Xuangui 玄軌, and others worked as *bishou* 筆受 "scribes," the abaove-mentioned Fuli and others as *zhuiwen* 綴文 "composition binders," and the monks Fabao 法宝, Hongjing 弘景, and others as *zhengyi* 証義 "lexicon checkers." Jia Yingfu 賈膺福, who held the title of *taizi zhongshe* 太子中舍, served as supervisor.

Fazang (643–712) of Huayan 華厳,[10] who was originally from Kangju 康居 and who was given various responsibilities by Wu Zetian, also played an important role in the translation project. It is well known that Wu Zetian became a devout believer because of him. About the same time that the Xitaiyuan Temple 西太原寺 was built in 670, Fazang was chosen to take the tonsure in the palace and entered the Xitaiyuan Temple. Later Wu Zetian ordered the Jingcheng shidade 京城十大徳 "ten authorized monks" to give him the *manfenjie* 満分戒 "perfect religious precepts" and the title of *xianshou*賢首. Further, upon receiving an imperial decree, he joined the group led by the Khotan *sanzang* Śikṣānanda to translate *Dafangguangfo huayan jing* at the Dabiankong Temple in Luoyang. It was said that when Fazang was giving a lecture on *Dafangguangfo huayan jing* after receiving another imperial decree, the lecture hall and the entire temple shook. This incident was interpreted as a good omen and reported to the palace by Hongjing. These accounts clearly show that the organization for translating Buddhist sutras abetted Wu Zetian's policy. She appointed Fazang to the rank of *xianshou pusajieshi* 賢首菩薩戒師 "master of Bodhisattva vow," and later he became the director of the Xitaiyuan Temple.

Other monks such as Chuyi 処一, Degan 徳感, Zhijing 知静, Huiyan 恵儼, Faming 法明, Huileng 慧稜, and Xinggan 行感 were also involved in offering *Dayun jing* and translating *Baoyu jing* and were given the title of *kaiguogong*

---

10 For Fazang, see *Song gaoseng zhuan*, vol. 5 ; *Zhou luojing foshoujisi fazang zhuan* 周洛京仏授記寺法蔵伝 in *Taisho shinshu daizokyo*, vol. 50: 732; *Datang da jianfusi gu dade kangzang fashi zhibei* 大唐大薦福寺故大徳康蔵法師之碑 completed by *mishu shaojian* Yan Chaoyin 秘書少監閻朝隠撰 in *Taisho shinshu daizokyo*, vol. 50: 280; *Fozu tongji* 仏祖統紀, vol. 39 in *Taisho shinshu daizokyo*, vol. 49: 370.

開国公 (duke or founder of a principality).[11] Among them Degan and Huiyan also participated in later Buddhist sutra translations in the capacity of *fanjing dade* 翻経大徳 "*bhadanta* of Buddhist sutra translation." With the help of Śikṣānanda and Yijing, they worked together with Fuli 復礼, Fabao 法宝, Hongjing, Bolun 波崙, and Fazang to advance Wu Zetian's policy.

Apart from the monks who did the translation work, the above-mentioned bureaucrat named Jia Yingfu[12] has also drawn my attention because he makes numerous appearances in the *Yakujo retsui*. Nevertheless, he has never attracted much attention when considering the relationship between Buddhism and Wu Zetian's policy. In addition to his involvement in Wu Zetian's translation project, Jia Yingfu was in charge of composing and writing the inscription of the Dayun Temple located in Henei 河内 (Huaizhou 懷州), which was one of the Dayun temples that Wu Zetian built all over the country as a means to consolidate her power. I argue that together with the monks who did the translation work and thus spread the claim of legitimacy of the Wu Zhou revolution, Jia Yingfu helped the Wu Zhou government maintain power. It should be noted that he had a close connection with a Buddhist sect called Sanjiejiao 三階教.

I would like to suggest that the organization established for the purpose of translating Buddhist sutras during the reign of Wu Zetian was not just an academic institution but was committed to supporting her with propaganda and acting in accordance with her political agenda (Huang 2012, 2017).

3.2 The Wu Zhou Government and the "Inexhaustible Deposit" of the Huadu Temple

As mentioned above, in accordance with Wu Zetian's policy of preferential treatment for Buddhism, numerous statues and temples were erected, and monks were ordained in great numbers. Consequently, this period saw Buddhism increasingly flourish, and temples gradually accumulated wealth.

Sanjiejiao 三階教, which was the most powerful Buddhist sect at that time, is especially noteworthy for its extensive economic activities. As a result, the Wujinzang 無尽蔵 "Inexhaustible Deposit" of the Sanjiejiao Huadu Temple 化度寺 in Chang'an, where the sect's headquarters was located, had enormous financial strength.[13] Volume three of *Liangjing xinji* 両京新記, edited by Weishu 韋述,

11 See the *Yakujo retsui* of *Foshuo baoyu jing* 仏説宝雨経, vol. 9; Ikeda 1990: 240–41; Forte 1984.

12 On this person, see Li 1998: 231–37; Huang 2012.

13 For the Inexhaustible Deposit, see Tsukamoto 1975: 191–207.

contains a description of the Wujinzang of the Sanjiejiao Huadu Temple in the Yining Quarter 義寧坊 as follows:

> 義寧坊. 南門之東, 化度寺. (中略) 寺内有無盡藏院, 即信行所立. 京城施捨, 後漸崇盛. 貞觀之後, 錢帛金玉積聚, 不可勝計. 常使名僧監藏, 供天下伽藍修理. 藏内所供, 燕 涼 蜀 趙, 咸來取給, 每日所出, 亦不勝數. 或有擧便亦不作文約, 但往, 至期還送而已. 貞觀中, 有裴玄智, 戒行修謹, 入寺灑掃十數年間. 寺内徒衆以其行無玷玦, 使守此藏. 後密盜黃金, 前後所漸, 略不知數. 寺衆莫之知也. 遂便不還. 衆驚, 觀其寢房, 内題詩云「將羊遣狼放, 置骨狗前頭. 自非阿羅漢, 誰能免作偷.」竟不知所之. 武太后移此藏於東都福先寺, 天下物産, 遂不復集. 乃還移舊所. 開元元年, 勑令毀除, 所有錢帛, 供京城諸寺修緝毀壞. 其事遂廢. (Xin 2006: 57)

> The Yining Quarter. The Huadu Temple is situated in the eastern lot of the south gate . . . Xinxing 信行 established the Inexhaustible Deposit in the temple. Donations by the people of the capital increased in course of time, so that by the end of the Zhenguan 貞観 period, it was impossible to count the money, silk, gold, and jade that had accumulated. Management of the Inexhaustible Deposit was always assigned to a distinguished monk who was responsible for managing the expense of repairing temple buildings all over the country. People from Yan 燕 (Heibei Province 河北省), Liang 涼 (Gansu Province 甘粛省), Shu 蜀 (Sichuan Province 四川省), and Zhao 趙 (Shanxi Province 山西省) all came to receive money and goods from it. The amount of money and goods that were provided every day was again too much to count. Money and goods were lent out with no written contract and only had to be returned by a deadline. A certain Pei Xuanzhi 裴玄智 was there in the Zhenguan period. He was a modest person who trained himself following the commandments and was engaged in cleaning of the temple for more than ten years. Since there were no problems with his behavior, people of the temple appointed him as the manager of the Inexhaustible Deposit. But later he secretly stole gold. His stealing increased more and more to the point where it was impossible to know how much he had stolen, but none of the temple personnel noticed. One day, he went out from the temple and did not come back, which surprised people. They went to check his bedroom and found a poem on the wall: "You let a sheep loose in front of a wolf, and leave a bone in front of a dog: except for an arhat, who in the world would not steal?" Pei Xuanzhi's whereabouts were never discovered. Wu Zetian moved the Inexhaustible Deposit to the Dafuxian Temple 大福先寺 in Luoyang, but products from all over the land were never again brought together in one place. Later the Wujinzang was moved back to its original place, and in the first year of Kaiyuan 開元 (713) it was demolished by imperial ordinance. The money and goods that had been collected in it were given to temples in the capital, Chang'an, so that they could be used for repairs. The Inexhaustible Deposit was abolished in this way.

According to this text, the Inexhaustible Deposit of the Huadu Temple, which was established by Xinxing, a Sanjiejiao monk, became prosperous during the Tang period. The Huadu Temple in the capital, which was the main temple of Sanjiejiao, collected an enormous amount of money and goods in the Inexhaustible Deposit through people's donations, and money was lent out in a huge quantity to many entities. Such activities by the Inexhaustible Deposit of Sanjiejiao, which some scholars view as nothing more than economic activities

(Nishimoto 1998), were widely known at that time throughout the country. The sect had a strong influence on society and received deeply felt support from the people.

As is clear from the above-mentioned episode of Pei Xuanzhi, the money and goods accumulated in the Inexhaustible Deposit of the Huadu Temple were so attractive that even monks who were trying to observe the precepts of Buddhism could not resist the urge to steal from it. This was also true of those in power.

According to *Datang jingyusi gu dade Fazang chanshi taming bingxu* 大唐浄域寺故大德法藏禅師塔銘並序 in Jinshi *cuibian* 金石萃編, vol. 71, which was inscribed on the tower of a monk of Sanjiejiao, Fazang *chanshi* 法藏禅師, this monk himself inspected and supervised the Inexhaustible Deposit on two occasions by the order of Wu Zetian: the first time in the first year of Ruyi 如意 (692) in the Dafuxian Temple, to which Wu Zetian had relocated the Inexhaustible Deposit, and the second time during the Chang'an period (701–04) in the Huadu Temple after the Wujinzang was moved back to its original place.

It is noteworthy that Wu Zetian moved the Inexhaustible Deposit from the Huadu Temple in Chang'an to the Dafuxian Temple in Luoyang. Her motivation for doing so may be sought in the close connection she had with the latter. This temple was the former Dongtaiyuan Temple 東太原寺 (Eastern Taiyuan Temple), which used to be the residence of Wu Zetian's mother, Lady Yang. It is assumed that the creation of the Dongtaiyuan Temple followed the precedented case of the Xitaiyuan Temple (Western Taiyuan Temple), which had been converted to a temple in 670 from the former residence of Yang Gongren 楊恭仁, a relative of Wu Zetian's mother, which was located in the Xiuxiang Quarter 休祥坊 in Chang'an. Wu Zetian established the Dongtaiyuan Temple when she transferred the political center to Luoyang. Her intention was probably to relocate the activity of the Taiyuan Temple 太原寺, which had played an important role in copying Buddhist sutras during the Gaozong Period, from Chang'an to Luoyang. The Dongtaiyuan Temple then became the center of her translation project and occupied a key position in her Buddhist policy (Huang 2007). It was to this temple, renamed the Dafuxian Temple, that the Inexhaustible Deposit was brought from the Huadu Temple of Sanjiejiao. As already mentioned, however, Wu Zetian moved the Inexhaustible Deposit back to the Huadu Temple after gross misuse of funds and failure in management.

Previous studies have already pointed out that Wu Zetian relied upon Buddhism to legitimize her seizure of political power. I would like to suggest that she utilized for her purposes the financial strength of the Inexhaustible Deposit of the Huadu Temple of Sanjiejiao and the sect's influence in society. Further, I believe that she was very keen to take control of Buddhist temples, which had considerable economic strength and exerted influence over society that could be put to practical use. This is clearly seen in the way in which she employed monks and officials in her project of translating Buddhist sutras.

4 Conclusions

A detailed analysis of some monks and government officials involved in the translation project who are mentioned in the *Yakujo retsui* and of the relevant accounts of the 'Inexhaustible Deposit' in vol. 3 of Liangjing xinji suggests that Wu Zetian effectively used Buddhism for her political purposes by placing under her tight control the economic resources of the Inexhaustible Deposit of the Huadu Temple of Sanjiejiao and the sect's strong influence over individuals and society. This paper has shed light on the practical aspects of Wu Zetian's Buddhism policy, which have not previously been discussed. They, together with the ideological aspects discussed by previous studies, help us to gain a more complete picture of her policy.

Bibliography

Andō, Kōsei. 1952. 洛陽大福先寺考 [On the Dafuxian Temple in Luoyang]. *Kodai* (Journal of the Archaeological Society of Waseda University) 7/8: 1–6.

Chen, Yinque. 1935. 武曌与仏教 [Wu Zhao and Buddhism]. *Zhongyang yanjiuyuan lishi yuyan yanjiusuo jikan* (*Bulletin of the Institute of History and Philology, Academia Sinica*) 5/2: 137–47.

Forte, Antonino. 1976. *Political Propaganda and Ideology in China at the End of the Seventh Century*. Napoli: Istituto Universitario Orientale.

Forte, Antonino. 1984. 大雲経疏をめぐって [On *Dayun jingshu*]. Pp. 173–206 in 敦煌と中国仏教 [Dunhuang and Buddhism in China], ed. Tairyo Makita and Fumimasa Fukui. Tokyo: Daito Shuppansha.

Forte, Antonino. 1988. *Mingtang and Buddhist Utopias in the History of the Astronomical Clock*. Rome: Istituto Italiano per il Medio ed Estremo Oriente.

Huang, Haijing. 2007. 武則天の仏教政策: 太原寺の役割を中心に [On the Buddhist policy of Wu Zetian: With a focus on the role of the Taiyuan Temple]. *Graduate School of Chuo University Ronkyu* 40: 79–98.

Huang, Haijing. 2012. 武周政権における仏教の役割: 訳場列位に登場する賈膺福を中心とした一考察 [The role of Buddhism in the Wu Zhou administration: Some notes on the Jia Yingfu who is mentioned in the *Yakujo retsui*]. *Chūgoku: Shakai to Bunka* (Journal of the Association for Studies of Chinese Society and Culture) 27: 288–307.

Huang, Haijing. 2016. 武則天仏教政策の新研究 [A new study of the Buddhist policy of Wu Zetian], Ph.D. Dissertation, Chuo University, Japan.

Huang, Haijing. 2017. 武周政権の訳経組織: 義浄を中心とした一考察 [The Wu Zhou administration's organization for translating Buddhist sutras, with a focus on Yijing]. Pp. 133–60 in 川越泰博教授古稀記念アジア史論叢 [Studies on Asian history in honor of the seventieth birthday of Professor Kawagoe Yasuhiro], ed. Department of Asian History of Chuo University. Tokyo: Hakuto Shigakkai of Chuo University.

Ikeda, On. 1990. 中国古代写本識語集録 [Collected colophons from ancient Chinese manuscripts]. Tokyo: Institute for Advanced Studies on Asia of University of Tokyo.

Im, Dae Heu. 1990. 武周革命に協力した仏教宗派—大雲経疏からの検討 [Buddhist sects cooperating with the Wu Zhou revolution: A study on *Dayun jingshu*]. *Bulletin of the Faculty of Humanities, Ibaraki University: Studies in Humanities* 23: 1–16.

Jin, Yingkun and Liu Yonghai. 2009. 敦煌本大雲経疏新論: 以武則天称帝為中心 [A new study on *Dayun jingshu* in the Dunhuang version, with a focus on Wu Zetian, who became empress]. *Wenshi* 4: 31–46.

Kamata, Shigeo. 1994. 中国仏教史第五巻　隋唐の仏教 [Buddhism in the Sui and Tang dynasties. History of Buddhism in China, vol. 5]. Tokyo: University of Tokyo Press.

Kaneko, Shūichi. 1986. 則天武后の明堂について [The Bright Hall of empress Wu Zetian]. Pp. 359–89 in 律令制: 中国朝鮮の法と国家 [The *Ritsuryō* system: The law and state in China and Korea], ed. The Historical Society of the Tang Period. Tokyo: Kyuko shoin.

Kegasawa, Yasunori. 1995. 則天武后 [Empress Wu Zetian]. Tokyo: Hakuteisha.

Kou, Yanghou. 1999. 「武則天与唐中宗的三教共存与仏先道後政策: 唐代三教並行政策形成的第二階段」[Three religions and the policy of "Buddhism over Taoism" during the reigns of Wu Zetian and emperor Zhongzong: The second phase of the policy of coexisting of the three religions during the Tang dynasty]. *Shanxi shifan daxue xuebao (Journal of Shanxi Normal University: Philosophy and Social Science Edition)* 3: 19–26.

Li, Fang. 1998. 関于風峪石経中的監護官員:兼談唐前期写経使及判官 [On the supervisors of "Fengyu Shijing": Sutra-copying officers and sutra-copying judges in the first half of the Tang dynasty]. Pp. 231–37 in 武則天研究論文集 [Collected research papers on Wu Zetian], ed. Zhao Wenrun and Li Yuming. Shanxi: Shanxi guji chubanshe.

Nishimoto, Teruma. 1998. 三階教の研究 [*A Study of the San-Chieh-Chiao*]. Tokyo: Shunjusha.

Nishimura, Genyū. 1976. 武周革命における仏教政策とその政治的背景 [The Buddhist policy during the period of the Wu Zhou revolution and its political background]. *Bulletin of Buddhist Cultural Institute of Ryukoku University* 15: 25–40.

Ōmuro, Mikio. 1994. 檻獄都市: 中世中国の世界芝居と革命 [Prison cities: the drama of the world and revolution in medieval China]. Tokyo: Sanseido.

Ōuchi, Fumio. 1998. 大周刊定衆経目録の成立と訳経組織: 訳経従事者の所属寺院を中心として [The creation process of *A Catalogue of Da Zhou Kanding Zhongjing Sutras* and the state organization for translating Buddhist sutras: On the temples to which the monks participating in the translation project belonged]. Pp.449–70 in七寺古逸経典研究叢書第6巻 中国·日本経典章疏目録 [A catalogue of Buddhist sutras and commentaries in China and Japan], ed. Tairyō Makita and Toshinori Ochiai. Studies on the Ancient Texts Found in the Nanatsudera Temple, vol. 6. Tokyo: Daito Shuppansha.

Rao, Zongyi. 1974. 從石刻論武后之宗教信仰 [On questions of Empress Wu's religious beliefs as reflected on some stone inscriptions]. *Zhongyang yanjiuyuan lishi yuyan yanjiusuo jikan* (*Bulletin of the Institute of History and Philology, Academia Sinica*) 45/3: 397–418.

Guisso, Richard. W. L. 1978. *Wu Tse-t'ien and the Politics of Legitimation in T'ang China*. Bellingham,Wash.: Western Washington University.

Seo, Tatsuhiko. 2005. 唐長安史研究と韋述両京新記 [Study of the history of Chang'an in the Tang period and the *Liang Jing Xin Ji* written by Weishu]. Pp. 1–35 in 東アジアの都城と渤海 [The capital cities in East Asia and Bohai], ed. Tamura Koichi. Tokyo: Toyo Bunko.

Sun, Yinggang. 2013. 転輪王与皇帝:仏教対中古君主概念的影響 [Chakravartin and emperor: Buddhist influence over the mediaeval concept of the prince]. *Shehui kexue zhanxian* 11: 78–88.

Sun, Yinggang. 2014. 神文時代: 讖緯, 術数与中古政治研究 [The Shenwen period: studies on prophecy, divination, and politics in medieval China]. Shanghai: Shanghai guji chubanshe.

Tsukamoto, Zenryū. 1974. 国分寺と隋唐の仏教政策並びに官寺 [Kokubunji temples and Sui-Tang policy on Buddhism and state temples]. Pp. 1–50 in日中仏教交渉史研究 [Studies on the history of Buddhist interaction between Japan and China]. 塚本善隆著作集第六 [Collected Papers of Tsukamoto Zenryū, vol. 6]. Tokyo: Daito Shuppansha.

Tsukamoto, Zenryū. 1975. 信行の三階教団と無尽蔵について [On the Sanjiejiao sect of Xinxing and Inexhaustible Deposit]. Pp. 191–207 in 中国中世仏教史論考 [Studies on Buddhist history in mediaeval China]. 塚本善隆著作集第三 [Collected papers of Tsukamoto Zenryū, vol. 3]. Tokyo: Daito Shuppansha.

Wang, Shuanghuai and Liang Yongtao (eds.). 2014. 武則天与広元 [Wu Zetian and Guangyuan]. Beijing: Wenwu chubanshe.

Wen, Yucheng. 1989. 試論武則天与竜門石窟 [A study on Wu Zetian and the Longmen Grottoes]. *Dunhuangxue jikan* 1: 119–27.

Xin, Deyong. 2006. 両京新記輯校· 大業雑記輯校 [Edited and collated *Liangjing xinji* and *Daye zaji*]. Xi'an: Sanqin chubanshe.

Yabuki, Keiki. 1927. 三階教之研究 [A study on the Sanjiejiao]. Tokyo: Iwanami Shoten.

Yokota, Shigeru. 1956. 武周政権成立の前提 [Background of empress Wu's power]. *Tōyō-shi Kenkyū* (*The Journal of Oriental Researches*) 14/4: 273–94.

Part II: **Priestesses**

Seraina Nett

The Office and Responsibilities of the En Priestess of Nanna: Evidence from Votive Inscriptions and Documentary Texts

One of the few areas where the evidence from documentary texts is complemented by the presence of other sources (in particular, royal inscriptions and year names) to help our understanding of women and religion, are sources about women who have obtained priestly offices.[1] Of particular importance in this context is the office of the **en** priestess of the moon god Nanna, as the high priestess of the city god of the capital city arguably the highest religious office that could be held by women, at least under the rule of the Third Dynasty of Ur (Ur III, 2112–2004 BCE).

I will in what follows discuss the evidence at hand for the women holding this important office, beginning by summarizing the information that is available based on royal inscriptions, votive texts and year names. These texts tend to be very formulaic in nature and rarely provide more information about the role of the **en** priestess than their name, filiation and titles.

To complement this, I will then examine the – comparatively scarce – evidence from the large corpus of Ur III documentary texts that mention the title of the **en** priestess of Nanna and attempt to reconstruct what can be gleaned from the sources at hand concerning the specific functions and responsibilities that were attached to the office of the **en** priestess of Nanna.

1 Women in Priestly Offices in Early Mesopotamia

It is clear from the available evidence that women were represented at all levels of the Mesopotamian religious hierarchy, from workers in the temple workforce to the highest priestly offices as **en** priestesses of the great gods.[2]

1 I would like to thank the editors of the present volume for their patience and their helpful and constructive comments and feedback. Work on this article was greatly facilitated by the use of the Database of Neo-Sumerian Texts (BDTNS), an incredibly useful resource hosted by the Consejo Superior de Investigaciones Científicas, Spain. This article is based on work undertaken in the course of the project *Counting Sheep: Temple Economy and the State in Third Millennium Mesopotamia*, funded by the Danish Council for Independent Research (DFF-FKK) for 2015–17.

2 See the detailed discussion of the different offices and their responsibilities in Huber Vulliet 2019; Sallaberger and Huber Vulliet 2005: 625–635; Westenholz 2006; Stol 2016: 555–77. See

https://doi.org/10.1515/9781501514821-007

Of the priestly titles that women can hold, the most frequently attested title in the Ur III corpus is the title of the **en**, often translated "high priest(ess)," Akk. *enum* and *entum*, respectively, which occurs more than 6000 times in the Database of Neo-Sumerian Texts (BDTNS). This total number includes both the female and the male **en** priests and is vastly inflated due to the occurrence of the title in many Ur III year names – only a fraction of this total number of texts mentions the title outside the year names. The second most frequently held title in the Ur III corpus is the title of **ereš-dingir** priestess, with 370 attestations. The list contains **ereš-dingir** priestesses of various deities, but the vast majority of these texts stems from Girsu and nearly a third of these attestations refer to the **ereš-dingir** priestess of the goddess Baba.

The third priestly title that is well-attested in the Ur III corpus is the title of the **egi-zi** priestess, which occurs in 49 instances. Another priestly office, that of the **lukur**, has been discussed by Sharlach (2008) where she lists the known **lukur** priestesses, considered the gods' secondary wives. The use of the term **lukur** during the Ur III period is complicated by Šulgi's use of the term to designate his secondary wives.

2 The en Priestesses of Nanna in the late Third Millennium BCE

The office of the **en** priestess of the moon god Nanna/Sîn is well-documented in year names and votive inscriptions from the Akkade-period to the Early Old Babylonian period.[3]

I will in what follows discuss the two genres that yield information concerning the office and function of the **en** of Nanna separately, beginning with a discussion of the evidence available to us from year names and votive inscriptions, to establish an overview of the names of the **en** priestesses known to us and the

also the discussion of the terminology surrounding the titles of high priestesses of Ninurta in Nippur in Brisch, this volume. A possible origin for the title of the **en** priestess has been put forth in Steinkeller 1999.

3 For an early outline of the **en** priestesses of Nanna in the Akkade and Ur III periods, see Sollberger 1954–56: 23–29. For an overview of priestesses from the Akkade royal family in particular, see Weiershäuser 2008: 249–59.

For an updated discussion of the Ur III **en** priestesses, see also Huber Vulliet 2019: 170–82; Weiershäuser 2008: 242–44. The known **en** priestesses from the Isin-Larsa Period are discussed in Renger 1967: 114–34. Also note the suggestion by Winter (1987: 195–200) that **en** priestesses are already depicted in Mesopotamian art since the Early Dynastic period.

chronology of their time in office (for the individual priestesses and the respective sources, see Table 1). This will provide the backdrop for further analysis based on the evidence from the documentary texts.

Table 1: The **en** priestesses of Nanna in Ur known from year names and royal and votive inscriptions.

Name	Filiation	Titles	Accession	Texts
En-he$_2$-du$_7$-an -na	dumu šar-ru-GI	zirru$_x$, dam ^{d}Nanna	unknown	RIME 2.1.1.16 RIME 2.1.1.2003 RIME 2.1.1.2004 RIME 2.1.1.2005
En-men-an-na	DUMU.MUNUS-*su* (viz. Naram-Sîn)	zirru$_x$, dam ^{d}Nanna, en ^{d}EN.ZU *in* URI$_5$^{ki}	Naram-Sîn	RIME 2.1.4.33 RIME 2.1.4.34
En-an-ne$_2$-pa$_2$- da	dumu ur-^{d}ba-ba$_6$	en ^{d}Nanna, zirru$_x$, dam ^{d}Nanna	unknown	RIME 3/1.1.6.12 RIME 3/1.1.6.13
En-nir-gal$_2$-an- na	dumu ki-ag$_2$-ni (viz. Ur-Namma)	en-^{d}nanna	unknown	RIME 3/2.1.1.54
En-nir-zi- an-na	not specified	en ^{d}Nanna	Š15 (sel.) / Š17 (inst.)	RIME 3/2.1.2.87 UET 3: 1320 UET 3: 911 UET 9: 415
En-ubur-zi-an- na	not specified		unknown	AUCT 1: 327
En-mah-gal-an -na	not specified	en ^{d}Nanna	AS4	
En-an-na- tum$_2$-ma	dumu ^{d}iš-me- ^{d}da-gan	zirru$_x$, en ^{d}Nanna; en ki-ag$_2$- ^{d}Nanna, en ^{d}Nanna; en ki-ag$_2$- ^{d}Nanna	Išme-Dagan 1 (?)	RIME 4.1.4.3 RIME 4.1.4.4.
En-ša$_3$-ki- ag$_2$-^{d}Nanna			Sûmû-El 23	
En-an-e-du$_7$	dumu ku-du-ur- ma-bu-uk	en ^{d}Nanna	Warad-Sîn 7	RIME 4.2.13.15 RIME 4.2.13.32 RIME 4.2.14.20 UET 5: 544

2.1 The en Priestesses of Nanna Before the Reign of the Third Dynasty of Ur

The earliest attested and certainly most well-known royal daughter holding the office of **en** priestess was Enheduanna (**En-he$_2$-du$_7$-an-na**), the daughter of Sargon of Akkade. Only very limited contemporary evidence for her role as **en** priestess of Nanna exists, limited to the famous Disc of Enheduanna, which provides her filiation as the daughter of Sargon and listing her titles as **zirru** (see the discussion of the use of this title further below) and wife of Nanna, but not using the title **en**,[4] as well as three inscribed seals belonging to her entourage.[5] Additionally, the literary works traditionally ascribed to her are known from later copies.[6]

Another Sargonic princess, a daughter of Naram-Sin with the sacerdotal name Enmenanna (**En-men-an-na**), is mentioned in two inscriptions and on a cylinder seal.[7] Her installation is also commemorated in a year name of Naram-Sin.[8]

The next **en** priestess of Nanna mentioned in the sources is a daughter of Ur-Baba of Lagaš, Enannepada (**En-an-ne$_2$-pa$_3$-da**), known from two inscriptions on several vessels found in Ur.[9] Nothing else is known about this priestess, and her name does not occur in any documentary texts. Due to the lack of sources and also due to our still limited understanding of the chronology of the period in question, it is difficult to assess when she was installed as **en** priestess and if she was the direct successor of Naram-Sîn's daughter Enmenanna. As far as we know, Enannepada was the only princess from the Lagaš II dynasty to hold the office of **en** of Nanna in Ur. This is particularly interesting considering the importance of the office during the Akkade and Ur III periods and suggests

4 The inscription reads **en-he$_2$-du$_7$-an-na, zirru ^{d}Nanna, dam ^{d}Nanna, dumu šar-ru-GI, lugal KIŠ** (RIME 2.1.1.16: 1–7). Next to the disc excavated in Ur, the inscription is also known from an Old Babylonian copy.

5 The seals RIME 2.1.1.2003–2005. None of these three seals uses Enheduanna's title, but two of them provide her filiation as daughter of Sargon.

6 For Enheduanna in general, see Westenholz 1989, for her literary production and the associated question of authorship, see Helle 2020. For the depiction of Enheduanna in Mesopotamian art, see Collon 1999: 20–21; Winter 1987: 190–95.

7 RIME 2.1.4.33 (royal inscription on a tablet fragment from Ur), RIME 2.1.4.34 (her name inscribed on a door socket, also from Ur), RIME 2.1.4.2019 (cylinder seal of her servant).

8 **mu en-^{d}nanna na-ra-am-^{d}EN.ZU maš-e ib$_2$-dab$_5$-ba** "Year in which Naram-Sin chose the **en** priestess of Nanna by omens" (OIP 97, p. 82 n. 10).

9 RIME 3/1.1.6.12 (on two fragments of limestone bowls) and RIME 3/1.1.6.13 (on three vessel fragments and an alabaster vase).

that the kings of Lagash in this time period may have considered themselves the successors of the kings of the Akkade dynasty.

2.2 The en Priestesses of Nanna in Ur during the Reign of the Third Dynasty of Ur

The **en** priestesses of Nanna under the Third Dynasty of Ur are significantly better represented in the contemporaneous evidence. The first royal daughter we see ascend to the office is a daughter of Ur-Namma with the name Ennirgalanna (**En-nir-gal$_2$-an-na**). No year name commemorating her accession is preserved, which makes it difficult to assess when during Ur-Namma's reign her installation took place, but in light of the Old Akkadian and later Ur III evidence, it seems likely that such a year name once existed. A votive inscription by Ennirgalanna with a dedication to the goddess Ningal, preserved in two copies on a fragmentary stone cone and on the fragments of a limestone vessel, are the only documents mentioning this priestess by name.[10]

The next **en** priestess of Nanna we find in the sources is Ennirzianna (**En-nir-zi-an-na**). The year name Š15 commemorates her selection for the office and the year Š17[11] her installation as **en**-priestess. She was in all likelihood a daughter of Šulgi, although this is not explicitly stated, and no votive inscriptions in her name are known. Next to the impression of the seal of her scribe found on a tablet from Ur,[12] her name also occurs in two documentary texts found at Ur, once in a receipt for flour products "for the field of Ennirzianna"[13] and once in fragmentary context in an inventory list.[14] In this context, it is worth discussing a short votive inscription by a daughter of Šulgi, ME-Enlil. The inscription, RIME 3/2.1.2.89, was found in two duplicates: one, inscribed on a bowl which also bears a previous inscription by Naram-Sîn, was found within the Gipar, the residence of the **en** priestess, as has already been pointed out by Weadock (1975: 107). The other duplicate, on a calcite vessel, was excavated within the confines of the Enunmah, also within the temple precinct of Nanna. Considering the two find spots and their close association with the living and working quarters of the **en** priestess, it is tempting to

---

10 RIME 3/2.1.1.54, from Ur.

11 Š15: **mu en-nir-zi-an-na en-^{d}nanna maš$_2$-e i$_3$-pa$_3$** "Year Ennirzianna, the **en** priestess of Nanna, was chosen by omens." Š17: **mu en-nir-zi-an-na en-^{d}nanna ba-hun-ga$_2$** "Year Ennirzianna, the **en** priestess of Nanna, was installed."

12 UET 3: 1320 (dated Š37). The seal inscription is also edited as RIME 3/2.1.2.87.

13 **0.0.2 zi$_3$ sig$_{15}$ 0.0.4 dabin a-ša$_3$ En-nir-zi-/an-na-še$_3$** (UET 3: 911 rev. 3–5, not dated).

14 **[En-n]ir-zi-an-na** (UET 9: 415 obv. ii' 3′, date not preserved).

consider the name of this princess the birth name of one of the **en** priestesses – either Ennirzianna,[15] her successor Enuburzianna (**En-ubur-zi-an-na**), or another unattested daughter of Šulgi.

Ennirzianna likely died between Š37 (the date of the sealed tablet UET 3: 1320[16]) and the year Š43, which commemorates the selection of the next **en** of Nanna, Enuburzianna.[17] Enuburzianna's installation did not form the subject of a separate year name,[18] although Sollberger (1954–56: 23) suggested that this priestess was identical to Enmahgalanna (**En-mah-gal-an-na**) whose installation as **en** priestess is recorded in the year name AS4. However, following this, one would have to accept a lengthy period of nine years between the selection and the installation of the **en** priestess, as well as a change of the sacerdotal name of the **en** priestess within this timeframe, neither of which is otherwise attested. Thus, I will in what follows consider Enuburzianna and Enmahgalanna separate individuals who were chosen for the office in quick succession.

Enuburzianna is only known from the year name referring to her selection as **en** priestess, no votive inscriptions mention her name and she does not occur by name in the documentary texts, except possibly in fragmentary context in a receipt for cattle and sheep (AUCT 1: 327) dating to the year AS3 and discussed further below.

The installation of her successor, Enmahgalanna, is commemorated in the year name for the fourth year of Amar-Suen.[19] Beyond the year name, her name only

---

15 Note, however, Huber Vulliet's (2019: 172) observation that ME-Enlil is attested in Umma during the tenure of Ennirzianna as **en** priestess. However, this does not necessarily preclude an identification of ME-Enlil with Ennirzianna's successor, Enuburzianna.

16 Naturally, the seal could have remained in use after Ennirzianna's death, but considering the installation of another **en** priestess in Š43, the date tallies well with the chronology of the Ur III period.

17 Š43: **mu en-ubur-zi-an-na en-^{d}nanna maš-e maš$_2$-e i$_3$-pa$_3$** "Year Enuburzianna, **en** priestess of Nanna, was chosen by omens."

18 Huber Vulliet (2019: 175–76) has suggested that the phrase **en ki en-na du-še$_3$** "when the **en** priestess went to the place of the **en**" in UET 3: 1221 obv. 3 (Š44) could refer to the installation of Enuburzianna as **en** priestess and her moving into the Gipar.

19 AS4: **mu en-mah-gal-an-na en-^{d}nanna ba-hun-ga$_2$** "Year Enmahgalanna, **en** priestess of Nanna, was installed." A year formula mentioning the selection (instead of the installation) of Enmahgalanna as **en** priestess is only attested in two texts (CTPSM 1: 61; SNAT 159. NRVN 1: 211 also presents a corrupted form of this year name) and is most likely a mistake and not a variant year name for an earlier year. A further group of texts (Santag 6: 133; AAICAB 1/2, Ashm. 1935-522; SAT 2: 785; Nisaba 24: 15; AUCT 2: 266) list the identical year name ("year in which Enmahgalanna was chosen by omens") but with Enmahgalanna's title given as **en** priestess of Inanna instead. These are likely also mistakes rather than evidence for the existence of a priestess of Inanna with the same name.

occurs in an inscription on a stone bowl excavated within the Gipar (RIME 3/ 2.1.3.19), only including her name and her title as **en** priestess of Nanna.

No further **en** priestesses of Nanna in Ur occur in the year names of the subsequent rulers of the Ur III dynasty[20] or can be identified in royal and votive inscriptions.

2.3 The en Priestesses of Nanna in the Early Old Babylonian Period

The next **en** priestess of Nanna in Ur appears in a year name[21] for the accession year of Išme-Dagan of Isin.[22] The year names do not provide the name of this **en** priestess, but it seems likely that this is the priestess with the sacerdotal name Enannatumma (**En-an-na-tum$_2$-ma**) who is also known from a range of votive inscriptions and documentary texts. Two inscriptions on bricks and clay cones, attested in multiple copies from Ur, list her titles as the **en** priestess of Nanna as well as her filiation as the daughter of Išme-Dagan and attest to her extensive building activities.[23] She is also the author of a votive inscription to Ningal on a statue

20 A list of Ur III year names (UET 1: 292) lists the selection of a second Ennirzianna as **en** priestess of Inanna for the tenth year of Ibbi-Sîn. However, this year name is unattested outside this particular list and it seems likely that the entry is corrupted. For the time being, I see no reason to amend the entry to the title of **en** of Nanna, also considering that we then would end up with two **en** priestesses of Nanna with the identical sacerdotal name within a short period of time. For a more detailed discussion including references, see Weiershäuser 2008: 243; Huber Vulliet 2019: 180.

21 Contrary to Renger 1967: 118–19, there is no evidence for a daughter of Išbi-Erra selected as **en** priestess of Nanna, rather, the year name in question (Išbi-Erra 22) should, following Sallaberger 1995: 20–21, be read **mu en-bara$_2$-zi$^?$ dumu-munus lugal egi$_2$-zi-an-na maš$_2$-e i$_3$-pa$_3$** "Year Enbarazi? the daughter of the king was chosen as **Egizianna**-priestess."

22 Both the accession year of Išme-Dagan (**mu ^{d}iš-me-^{d}da-gan lugal-e en-^{d}nanna uri$_5$^{ki}-ma ba-hun-ga$_2$** "Year king Išme-Dagan installed the **en** priestess of Nanna in Ur") and the two following years (**mu us$_2$-sa ^{d}iš-me-^{d}da-gan lugal-e en-^{d}nanna uri$_5$^{ki}-ma ba-hun-ga$_2$** "Year after the year king Išme-Dagan installed the **en** priestess of Nanna in Ur" and **mu us$_2$-sa ^{d}iš-me-^{d}da-gan lugal-e en-^{d}nanna uri$_5$^{ki}-ma ba-hun-ga$_2$ mu us$_2$-sa-a-bi** "Second year after the year king Išme-Dagan installed the **en** priestess of Nanna in Ur") refer to the installation of the **en** priestess.

23 RIME 4.1.4.3, found on one stamped and nine inscribed bricks from Ur (to the eight listed in RIME p. 29, add now also an additional copy in the collection of the National Museum of Denmark [NMC 8869]) and two clay cones. RIME 4.1.4.4 is Enannatumma's standard inscription found on 21 stamped bricks from Ur (where known) which deviates slightly from the text of RIME 4.1.4.3, most importantly in her titles as **en** priestess (RIME 4.1.4.3 gives the title **zirru**, which in RIME 4.1.4.4 is replaced by **en ki-ag$_2$-^{d}Nanna**).

found within the Ningal temple in the Gipar (RIME 4.1.4.13). We know that Enannatumma remained in office after the death of her father and the conquest of Ur by the Larsa dynasty from two inscriptions dedicated by her to Dagan and Utu, respectively,[24] for the life of king Gungunum of Larsa, here styled "king of Ur." Interestingly, Enannatumma is the only known **en** priestess who seems to have had issue: a sealing on two tablets gives the name and filiation of her son **A-ab-ba.**[25] It is unclear if this concerns a biological child or possibly a case of adoption, but the find spot of one of the sealed tablets in the Enunmah in the temple precinct of Nanna strongly suggests that the mother Enannatumma is indeed identical with the priestess of the same name.

Enannatumma seems to have remained in office for a relatively long time. Only in year Sûmû-El 23[26] do we see the next installation of an **en** priestess: Enšakiag-Nanna (**En-ša$_3$-ki-ag$_2$-^{d}Nanna**), a daughter of Sûmû-El.[27] The following six years (Sûmû-El 24–29) are also named after this event. It is unclear how long Enannatumma had remained in office – there are no further texts referring to her by name after the clay cones dating to the reign of Gungunum mentioned above. However, as Renger (1967: 119–20) has pointed out, texts referring to the **ki-a-nag**, the place for the funerary offerings, for Enannatumma appear for the first time in the year Sûmû-El 10. Whether the office of the **en** priestess remained vacant between the death of Enannatumma and the installation of Enšakiag-Nanna or if there was another **en** priestess who only held the office for a relatively brief period of time and was not mentioned in Sûmû-El's year names, cannot be determined. However, even if we assume a date during the year Sûmû-El 9 for the death of Enannatumma, she was the **en** priestess with the longest time in office, spanning more than 60 years and coinciding with the rule of Išme-Dagan, Lipit-Ištar, Gungunum, Abi-sare, and the first ten years of the reign of Sûmû-El.

No further information is known about Sûmû-El's daughter Enšakiag-Nanna apart from the year name in question and she seems to have remained in office until the installation of her successor Enanedu (**En-an-e-du$_7$**), a daughter of Kudur-Mabuk and sister of Warad-Sîn and Rīm-Sîn, commemorated in the year

---

24 RIME 4.2.5.1 on several clay cones from Ur, detailing the construction of the **e$_2$-eš$_3$-me-dagal-la**, his splendid storehouse (**e$_2$-šutum$_2$-ku$_3$-ga-ni**) for Dagan and RIME 4.2.5.2 on several clay cones from Ur, relating the construction of the **e$_2$-hili**, his splendid storehouse (**e$_2$-šutum$_2$-ku$_3$-ga-ni**) for Utu.

25 RIME 4 1.4.14: (1) **a-ab-ba** (2) **dumu en-an-na-tum$_2$-ma** (3) **en ^{d}Nanna.**

26 **mu en-^{d}nanna en-ša$_3$-ki-ag$_2$-^{d}nanna ba-hun-ga$_2$** "Year the **en** priestess of Nanna, Enšakiag-Nanna, was installed."

27 RIME 4.2.13.15: Frag. 8, 1–2.

name Warad-Sîn 7.[28] However, as Renger (1967: 120) has pointed out, she occurs together with her predecessor in the text UET 5: 544, a list of offerings of metal objects by the king (not mentioned by name but likely referring to Warad-Sîn) and various members of the royal family, including the future king Rīm-Sîn and both **en** priestesses, Enšakiag-Nanna and Enanedu, albeit without mention of their titles. The order of the persons involved here is interesting: Enšakiag-Nanna is listed directly after the king, while Enanedu is listed last, but already bearing her sacerdotal name. It cannot be ascertained at this moment whether this indicates an overlap or a "co-regency" between the two **en**-priestesses, but it is worth considering Charpin's argument (2017: 76) that this list does not necessarily record donations that occurred at the same point in time, as Etellum, the vizier of king Gungunum, who is listed in line 10 would have been close to a hundred years old if the text, as commonly thought, dates to the early years of Warad-Sîn's reign.[29]

Enanedu is also the author of a large stone tablet, excavated in Ur and now in Philadelphia, dating to the reign of Warad-Sîn.[30] The fragmentary text relates the restoration of a building – likely the Gipar – by Enanedu and also makes reference to several of her predecessors, providing the correct filiation, including Enannatumma, the daughter of Išme-Dagan, and Enšakiag-Nanna, the daughter of Sûmû-El, as well as another **en** priestess whose name and filiation are mostly lost.

Another lengthy inscription on a clay cone, probably dating to the reign of Rīm-Sîn, is also authored by Enanedu and gives a detailed account of her rebuilding work in the cemetery for the **en** priestesses, which she says to have surrounded by a wall and purified.[31]

An inscription by Enanedu is also mentioned by Nabonidus in the text relating the selection and installation of his daughter as **en** priestess of Nanna in Ur.[32] Nabonidus claims in this text to have found an inscription by Enanedu – likely the inscription on the clay cone RIME 4.2.14.20.[33]

---

28 **mu en-an-e-du$_7$ en-^{d}nanna uri$_2$^{ki} ba-hun-ga$_2$** "Year Enanedu, **en** priestess of Nanna in Ur, was installed."

29 Thus, for example, Gadd 1951: 30–32; van de Mieroop 1989: 401.

30 RIME 4.2.13.15. The text is heavily fragmented. For a proposed reconstruction of the text, see RIME 4 pp. 224–25 with a discussion of a reconstruction of the tablet and references to previous literature.

31 RIME 4.2.14.20, inscription on the cone head.

32 RINBE 2 Nabonidus 34: i 44–ii 4.

33 For the similarities between the Enanedu clay cone inscription and the Nabonidus cylinder, see Schaudig 2003: 482–85.

Enanedu is also the only **en** priestess for whom a seal is known. The inscription, reconstructed from sealings on a fragment of a tablet envelope dated to the year Rīm-Sîn 11 found in Ur (UET 1: 303 / UET 5: 272), reads "En-an-e-du$_7$, **en** priestess of Nanna in Ur, daughter of Kudur-Mabuk, brother (sic) of Warad-Sîn, king of Larsa."[34]

The name of Enanedu occurs in two additional documentary texts: in CUSAS 36: 101 she appears as the sender of a letter to a certain Lipit-Ištar concerning sheep and in UET 5: 343, she is listed as the issuer of a silver loan, together with another individual, to a group of people.

Enanedu is the last **en** priestess known by name until Nabonidus' resurrection of the office in the first millennium BCE.

2.4 Summary: The en Priestess of Nanna in Year Names and Votive Inscriptions

Based on year names and royal inscriptions, we can thus reconstruct a sequence of **en** priestesses from the reign of Sargon to the reign of Warad-Sîn, but it is difficult to establish with any degree of certainty whether this list is complete.

Only in the Sargonic and early Old Babylonian Periods do the **en** priestesses list their filiation and in all the cases where their filiation is known, they are daughters or sisters of the ruler at the time of entering into office. In turn, none of the **en** priestesses from the Ur III period with the exception of Ennirgalanna mention their filiation, but it seems reasonable to assume that they were close relatives (daughters, possibly sisters) of the kings of Ur. As Michalowski (2013: 289) has pointed out, familial relationships are scarcely mentioned in the Ur III corpus, even for kings. While the **en** priestesses undoubtedly were members of the royal family, it is difficult to identify them among the numerous known Ur III princesses, as their names were changed upon accession (with the possible example of Šulgi's daughter ME-Enlil discussed above).

In addition to the absence of the filiation, the Ur III texts differ from their earlier and later counterparts in one more crucial aspect: the use of the titles.

34 UET 1: 303 / UET 5: 272, for the content of the letter (transfer of an orchard), see Charpin 1986: 60–61. For the seal inscription, see RIME 4.2.13.32: **[en-a-ne-du$_7$] [en]-^{d}[Nanna] Uri$_5$^{ki}-[ma] dumu ku-du-ur-ma-bu-[uk] šeš IR$_3$-^{d}EN.[ZU] lugal Larsa^{ki}-[ma].**

While both Sargonic **en** priestesses use the titles **zirru**$_x$,[35] **dam** ^{d}**Nanna** "wife of Nanna," and **en** ^{d}**Nanna** "**en** priestess of Nanna," the first two titles seem to fall out of use in the Ur III period: all Ur III inscriptions simply use the title **en** ^{d}**Nanna**, and the title **zirru** is not attested in the Ur III corpus at all. Interestingly, it then reappears in the Early Old Babylonian corpus where it is used by Enannatumma, but not by her successors.

Most of the texts discussed so far mentioning the different priestesses by name are votives in their name or secondary references to the priestesses in question in royal and votive inscriptions of other individuals. As such, they yield relatively limited information regarding the function the **en** priestesses fulfilled in the cult and in the daily administration of the temple. From the little evidence that is available, we can at least conclude that the **en** priestess could be involved in building and renovation activities within the temenos (as evidenced, for example, by Enannatumma's brick inscriptions and the lengthy description by Enanedu of her renovation of the Gipar in RIME 4.2.14.20). It is interesting to note in this context that inscriptions of this nature – the **en** priestess being involved in building activities in her own right – are absent from the earlier corpora dating to the Sargonic and Ur III periods. It is tempting to speculate that this increase in building inscriptions is evidence for a change in the role of the **en** priestess to one involving more agency in the transition from the Ur III to the Early Old Babylonian period, but conclusive evidence is so far lacking.

2.5 Excursus: The en Priestesses of Nanna in Karzida

The matter of the **en** priestesses of Nanna is further complicated by the fact that, beginning early in the reign of Amar-Suen, two **en** priestesses of Nanna are attested: the **en** priestess of Nanna in Ur and the **en** priestess of Nanna of Karzida, in Gaeš, the location of the Akitu-house just outside of Ur (Sallaberger 1993: 170–72).

Two **en** priestesses of Nanna of Karzida are known by name from Ur III year names and votive inscriptions[36]: Enagazianna (**En-aga-zi-an-na**) is known from a building inscription by king Amar-Suen on several foundation tablets (RIME 3/2.1.3.17), although her accession is not commemorated in a year name. It is

35 A difficult title, the interpretation of which is not quite clear. For a discussion, see most recently Steinkeller 1999: 121 n. 61; Marchesi 2004: 170 n. 109. On the relationship between the titles **zirru**, **en** and **dam** ^{d}**Nanna**, and the etymology, history and usage patterns of these titles, see also Huber Vulliet 2019: 163–70.

36 For the two well-known **en**s of Karzida, see now also Huber Vulliet 2019: 222–27.

interesting to note in this context that Amar-Suen claims in the inscription that "since distant days, no Gipar had been built in Karzida, and no **en** had lived there."[37]

In light of text PDT 2: 767 which lists provisions for the installation of a new **en** priestess (discussed further below), Sallaberger (1992: 132–33) has plausibly suggested that this text refers to the installation of Enagazianna, also commemorated in the royal inscription.

Amar-Suen's ninth year is named after the installation of another **en** priestess by the name of En-Nanna-Amar-Suen-kiagra (**En-^{d}Nanna-^{d}Amar-^{d}Suen-ki-ag$_{2}$-ra**)[38] whose name is mentioned in the seal inscription of her cup-bearer on UET 3: 155 and to whose accession rites several of the documentary texts may be referring.

No further **en** priestesses of Nanna in Karzida are known from the Ur III evidence, but Renger (1967: 119–20) has suggested that the **en** priestess Enmegalanna, who is not known from other sources and for whom funerary offerings are recorded in the Early Old Babylonian period,[39] may have been in office in Karzida and not in Ur.

3 The en Priestesses of Nanna in the Ur III Documentary Texts

As demonstrated in the cursory overview of the **en** priestesses of Nanna given above, a reasonable amount of information concerning the priestesses can be gathered from year names and royal inscriptions. It is evident that the selection and installation of a new **en** priestess of Nanna was a momentous occasion, important enough to be commemorated in the year name of at times several years. It is, however, striking how little is known concerning the ritual and economic functions of the **en** priestesses themselves from the documentary texts.

Using the abundant documentary texts dating to the reign of the third dynasty of Ur to trace women in general and priestesses in particular presents certain problems. First and foremost, the Sumerian language does not use grammatical gender and many personal names (unless they contain gendered

37 **u$_{4}$ ul-li$_{2}$-a-ta kar-zi-da gi$_{6}$-par$_{4}$ nu-du$_{3}$ en nu-un-til$_{3}$-a** (RIME 3/2.1.3.17: 13–16).

38 Year name 9c. **mu en-^{d}nanna-^{d}amar-^{d}suen-ki-ag$_{2}$-ra en-^{d}nanna ga-eš^{ki} / kar-zi-da^{ki}-ka a-ra$_{2}$ 3(diš)-kam ba-hun** "Year En-Nanna-Amar-Suen-kiagra, the en of Nanna in Karzida was installed for the third time."

39 The texts in question are UET 1: 238; UET 5: 737; 750; 753; 754; 758; 788; 759; Nisaba 5-2: 88.

elements such as GEME$_2$, "female worker") do not indicate whether the bearer was male or female. Furthermore, filiations and titles are rarely given, making it difficult to differentiate between several individuals bearing the same name.

While a search in the Database of Neo-Sumerian Texts (BDTNS) for the title **en ^{d}Nanna** yields 3158 results, the vast majority of texts in which the phrase occurs refers to one of the year names commemorating the choosing or installation of the **en** priestess mentioned above. Only a few dozen texts provide information beyond the year names and only a limited number of them gives further information concerning the **en** priestesses' duties and associated rituals. A further handful of texts, mostly from Ur, mention some of the **en** priestesses by name instead of by title (see the list of texts in Table 2).[40]

Table 2: Documentary texts listing the en priestess of Nanna by name or by title.

Publication	Provenance	Date	Content
AAICAB 1/2: Ashm. 1954-208	Puzriš-Dagan	SS07-10-07	Mašdaria-delivery
AOS 32: L20	Puzriš-Dagan	IS02-1-00	Mašdaria and siškur-offering of the king, when the en of Nanna of Urum was chosen
ASJ 8: pp. 346–47	Girsu	–	Transfer of fields
AUCT 1: 327	Puzriš-Dagan	AS03-1-05	One sheep for Enuburzianna
AUCT 3: 326	Puzriš-Dagan	AS07-08-00	Mašdaria-delivery
BIN 3: 352	Puzriš-Dagan	AS08-11-00	Cattle to choose the en by means of extispicy
BPOA 6: 111	Puzriš-Dagan	IS02-10-11	Mašdaria-delivery
BPOA 10, p. 479 Phillips 13	Puzriš-Dagan	SH26?-12-00	Precious objects disbursed on occasion of a feast
CUSAS 3: 1478	Irisaĝrig	SS06-02-17	Personal name (En-Nanna-ra-kal-la the barber)

40 **En-nir-zi-an-na**: UET 3: 911; 1320, UET 9: 415; **En-ubur-zi-an-na**: AUCT 1: 327; **En-mah-gal-an-na**: UET 3: 45; 52; 1717; UET 9: 1156; **En-^{d}Nanna-^{d}Amar-^{d}Suen-ki-ag$_2$-ra**: MVN 15: 365; UET 3: 155.

Table 2 (continued)

Publication	Provenance	Date	Content
CUSAS 40-2: 7	Irisaĝrig	SS0-03-13	Personal name (En-Nanna-ra-kal-la the barber)
Fs. Neumann, p. 203 I.A.7 NUL 05	Puzriš-Dagan	IS02-10-11	Mašdaria-delivery
ITT 3: 6557	Girsu	–	Ditila, Sammelurkunde
JCS 52, p. 11 no.45	Puzriš-Dagan	SS07-01-06	Mašdaria-delivery
Kyoto 46	Puzriš-Dagan	SS09-01-07	Mašdaria-delivery
Mesopotamia 5-6: p. 300	Girsu	SH36-00-06	Transfer of field
MVN 7: 286	Girsu	–	Temple personnel (šabra en ^{d}Nanna)
MVN 9: 184	unknown	–	Receipt for textiles
MVN 13: 376	Girsu	–	List of expenses (grain and beer)
MVN 15: 365	Puzriš-Dagan	AS08-12-14	Offerings in connection with installation of the en of Nanna in Karzida
Nisaba 15/2: 310	Irisaĝrig	SS05-02-07?	Personal name (En-Nanna-ra-kal-la the barber)
Nisaba 15/2: 361	Irisaĝrig	SS06-02-00	Personal name (En-Nanna-ra-kal-la the barber)
OIP 121: 463	Puzriš-Dagan	AS06-10-00	30 sheep as regular deliveries for the en of Nanna in Karzida
Ontario 1: 82	Puzriš-Dagan	AS09-01-05	Mašdaria-delivery when the en of Nanna went to Eridu
PDT 2: 767	Puzriš-Dagan	AS02-12-00	Accession ritual expenses for the en of Nanna in Karzida
PDT 2: 1213	Puzriš-Dagan	IS02-10-11	Mašdaria-delivery
Princeton 1: 122	Puzriš-Dagan	SH48-08-29	receipt of lambs in Tummal
RSO 83, p. 346 no. 20	Puzriš-Dagan	SS01-10-00	Mašdaria-delivery
SACT 1: 165	Puzriš-Dagan	AS08-11-29	Cattle for the ki-Utu rites of the en of Nanna in Karzida

Table 2 (continued)

Publication	Provenance	Date	Content
SACT 1: 189	Puzriš-Dagan	–	Title: šabra en ^{d}Nanna Uri$_{5}^{k}$
Trouvaille 4	Puzriš-Dagan	AS09-01-16	Delivery of cattle, possibly relating to the installation of the en of Nanna in Karzida
UET 3: 45	Ur	IS14-09-00	Legal document: court case involving Enmahgalanna, brought before the king
UET 3: 52	Ur	–	Enmahgalanna mentioned in broken context
UET 3: 155	Ur	IS06-06-00	Title: seal of the cup-bearer (sagi) of the en of Nanna in Karzida
UET 3: 911	Ur	XX-01-00	Receipt of flour for the field of Ennirzianna
UET 3: 959	Ur	XXX	Lamb for the šuku of the en of Nanna
UET 3: 1306	Ur	IS07-06-16	Personal name: En-^{d}Nanna-ar-i$_{3}$-DU
UET 3: 1320	Ur	SH37-12-00	Title: seal of the scribe of Ennirzianna
UET 3: 1717	Ur	IS06-09-00	Expenditure of a textile for Enmahgalanna
UET 9: 40	Ur	IS17-12-00	House of the en of Nanna (⸢e$_{2}$⸣ en ^{d}Nanna-ka) mentioned in broken context
UET 9: 103	Ur	–	Pisandubba: grain rations of the house of the en of Nanna
UET 9: 415	Ur	–	Ennirzianna mentioned in broken context
UET 9: 934	Ur	–	Personal name: En-^{d}Nanna-ar-i$_{3}$-DU
UET 9: 1136	Ur	–	Text listing ovines, fragmentary context
UET 9: 1156	Ur	IS14-00-00	= UET 3: 45
WMAH 164	Puzriš-Dagan	AS09-10-07	Mašdaria-delivery

Of the 40 documentary texts referring to the title of the **en** priestess of Nanna outside the year names, three are too fragmentary to draw further conclusions and six list the title of the **en** priestess of Nanna as part of a personal name, the name of **En-^{d}Nanna-ra-kal-la**, a barber (**šu-i**) who was active in Irisagrig during the reign of Šu-Sîn.

A further four texts do not refer to the **en** priestess directly, but rather refer to people in her employ: Two seal impressions from Ur belong to servants of **en** priestesses. The sealing on UET 3: 155 reads "The **en** priestess of Nanna Amar-Suenra-kiaganna, **en** priestess of Nanna in Karzida, **A-a-dingir-mu**, the cup-bearer, is her servant." **A-a-dingir-mu** is otherwise known from a dozen administrative documents from Puzriš-Dagan, Ur and Girsu.

Another seal inscription mentioning an **en** priestess is found on UET 3: 1320, with an inscription of the scribe **Giri$_{3}$-ni-i$_{3}$-sa$_{6}$**, servant of Ennirzianna.[41]

Two more texts mention the **šabra**, or household administrator, of the **en** priestess of Nanna. MVN 7: 286 (undated, from Girsu) lists the receipt (**mu-ku$_{x}$**) of linen and oil by the **šabra** of the **en** priestess of Nanna. SACT 1: 189, a livestock inventory from Puzriš-Dagan, records several types of small cattle for Ur-Bilgames, the **šabra** of the **en** priestess of Nanna. The date formula of this text is broken, but Maeda (1992: 159 n. 26) has dated the text to the last half of the reign of Šu-Sîn based on the individuals who appear within the document.

3.1 Mašdaria-Deliveries

Of the remaining 25 texts, a significant group concerns the royal mašdaria-deliveries to the **en** priestess of Nanna.[42] To the five texts collected in Sallaberger (1993: 92 Table 53), we can now also add AAICAB 1/2: Ashm. 1954-208 (dating to ŠS7), AUCT 3: 326 (AS7), BPOA 6: 111 (IS2), Fs. Neumann, p. 203: NUL 5 (AS7), *JCS* 52, p. 11 no. 45 (AS7), and *RSO* 83, p. 346 no. 20 (ŠS1) leaving us with a total of eleven texts, ranging in date from AS7 to IS2.[43]

41 See also RIME 3/2.1.2.87 for the seal inscription.

42 For the **maš-da-ri-a** deliveries and their relation to the different festivals, see Sallaberger 1993: 160–70.

43 To this, we can probably add UET 3: 1563, a mašdaria-delivery of textiles "for the **en** priestess" (**ki en-na-še$_{3}$**) possibly ritual garments for the Akitu-festival, discussed by Huber-Vulliet (2019: 173–74), which uses slightly different terminology, most importantly not specifying the **en** in question (although with the text stemming from Ur, it is likely to be the **en** of Nanna) and not qualifying the mašdaria-delivery as a "royal mašdaria-delivery" (**maš-da-ri-a lugal**).

This group of texts is relatively homogeneous in structure, giving a variation of the phrase **maš-da-ri-a lugal ki en-^{d}Nanna-šè**, "royal mašdaria-delivery for the **en** priestess of Nanna." All of the texts belong to the cattle archive of Puzriš-Dagan and most refer to transactions taking place in Gaeš or, in the case of AAICAB 1/2: Ashm. 1954-208 and WMAH: 164, in Ur.[44]

Following Sallaberger's (1993: 169–70) interpretation of the mašdaria-deliveries not as offerings, but rather as a cattle resource to be used during the festivals and to a particular degree to be disbursed to members of the royal family, it seems possible that the **en** priestesses did not necessarily receive these deliveries as part of their religious function, but rather as members of the royal family.

Only AOS 32: L20[45] explicitly states which festival the delivery was intended for – the **še-KIN-ku$_5$** festival at the beginning of month i – but the dates of three of the remaining texts, dated to month i, strongly suggest an association with the same festival and for the remaining six texts, dated to month x, we can assume a connection to the **ezem-mah** festival of month x.

As Farber and Farber (2018: 204) have pointed out, three texts (BPOA 6: 111; Fs. Neumann, p. 203: NUL 5; PDT 2: 121) in this small group of documents are dated to the same day: the 11th day of **ezem-mah** (month x) in the year Ibbi-Sîn 2. BPOA 6: 111 is a large account recording cattle expenditures for various deities (including, several times, for Nanna) and institutions (including the Dublamah and the Nanna temple in general). After the entry concerning the mašdaria-delivery of 2 fattened oxen and 6 fattened sheep, Aradmu is noted as the **maškim** official. Immediately after the mašdaria entry follows the total of 4 oxen and 26 sheep as a "royal gift" (**niĝ$_2$-ba lugal**), of which the delivery is part. The account is conducted with Du$_{11}$-ga the **ša$_3$-tam** official as the **kišib** official, but with ^{d}Suen-ILLAT the **šar$_2$-ra-ab-du** official as conveyor (**giri$_3$**), and the tablet is sealed by the same ^{d}Suen-ILLAT.

Fs. Neumann, p. 203: NUL 5 is a receipt for small cattle as mašdaria-delivery and for other purposes and exhibits striking parallels with BPOA 6: 111. Aradmu is again listed as the **maškim** official for the delivery, which in this case consisted

44 Two of the texts, AOS 32: L20 and AUCT 3: 326 do not specify the location of the transaction, but AUCT 3: 326 specifically indicates the **en** priestess of Nanna of Karzida as the recipient. The fact that most of the text note Gaeš as the location of the transaction is striking, especially in light of Sallaberger's assertion that the **ezem-mah** festival was mostly celebrated in Ur itself although Gaeš was also included on occasion (1993: 170–71). The situation is further complicated by the existence (at least from the reign of Amar-Suen onwards) of two **en** priestesses, one in Ur and one in Gaeš, and the texts mostly do not specify which **en** priestess is the recipient.

45 Note, however, that according to Weiershäuser 2008: 244, this text refers to the **en** of Nanna in Urum, a different priestess.

of ten undetermined small cattle (the text is broken) and four goats. The subsequent lines specify that this is a royal gift as well. The transaction is recorded as having been withdrawn (**ba-zi**) by Urkununna (**Ur-ku$_3$-nun-na**), with Ahuwaqar (*A-ḫu-wa-qar*), the **šar$_2$-ra-ab-du**, and Duga (**Du$_{11}$-ga**), the **ša$_3$-tam**, as conveyors (**giri$_3$**). The tablet is sealed by Ahuwaqar.

PDT 2 121 only contains one transaction, a receipt of small cattle (one grass-fed sheep and two grass-fed billy-goats) as a mašdaria-delivery. Aradmu again acts as **maškim**, and the amount is again withdrawn by Urkununna. Ahuwaqar the **šar$_2$-ra-ab-du** is again the conveyor, but this time together with Nur-Sîn (*Nu-ur$_2$-Suen*), the **ša$_3$-tam** official, who also sealed the tablet.

The texts seem to record three separate transactions, as we can see from the different animals that are listed – albeit recorded by some of the same officials – and illustrate the complexities of the administration at Puzriš-Dagan. With regard to the mašdaria-deliveries in particular, it is interesting that these are here recorded as royal gifts and not as a mandatory contribution to the festival.

Another text from the *Schatzarchiv* of Puzriš-Dagan, BPOA 10, p. 479 Phillips 13, dating to the reign of Šulgi,[46] lists precious objects (jewelry, metal vessels, textiles, furniture, and foodstuff) for the king, queen, members of the royal family and high-ranking priests and officials.[47] The **en** priestess of Nanna is listed, together with several other **en** priestesses, as a recipient of precious garments. The objects are listed in connection with a feast hosted by a high-ranking individual, which the royal family and high officials attended. Based on the presence of the cultic personnel and the date of the text, Paoletti (2012: 324) suggests that this event could have taken place in connection with the harvest-Akitu-festival.

3.2 Documentary Texts Referring to the Selection, Accession and Funerary Rites for the en Priestess of Nanna

As Sallaberger (1995: 19) points out, three Puzriš-Dagan texts (BIN 3: 352; SACT 1: 165; MVN 15: 365), all dating to the year AS8, likely refer to the omens and rites that were involved in selecting a new **en** priestess of Nanna in Karzida, although only MVN 15: 365 explicitly states this.

---

46 Weiershäuser (2008: 171 n. 732) dates the text to Š47, after information from Volk who was able to read the date after cleaning the tablet. BDTNS tentatively dates it to Š26. Paoletti dates the text to Š27, see Paoletti 2012: 321 for a discussion of the date.

47 For a detailed discussion of this unique document, see Paoletti 2012: 316–24.

Equally, the delivery of cattle to the **en** of Nanna at Gaeš, recorded in Trouvaille 04, which dates to the first month of AS9, could belong to the installation of the new **en** priestess after whom the year is named.[48]

A large tablet from Puzriš-Dagan (PDT 2: 767) listing sacrificial animals mentions the phrase **nig$_2$-dab$_5$ en ^{d}Nanna Kar-zi-da hun-ga$_2$** "requisitioned items when the **en** priestess of Nanna in Karzida was installed."[49] The tablet dates to the second year of Amar-Suen and thus presumably refers to the selection of Enagazianna as **en** priestess of Nanna in Karzida. The text lists a total of 40 heads of cattle for various tasks and rituals associated with the accession of the new **en** priestess, including **en-e uru šu$^!$ ni$_{10}$$^!$-ni$_{10}$$^!$-da** "when the **en** goes around the city" (obv. i 3), **ka$_2$ gi$_6$-par$_4$$^!$** "at the gate of the Gipar" (obv. ii 2 & rev. i 1) and **e$_2$ ama en-e-ne ^{d}Nin-sun$_2$** "at the temple of the mother of the **en** priestesses, Ninsun" (obv. ii 15).[50] The text also lists **siškur$_2$ ki-^{d}Utu en-na** (obv. i 10), sacrifices to be conducted in connection with the ritual purification of the **en.**[51]

Finally, Sallaberger (1995) argues convincingly that the text UET 3: 335 (dating to the year AS8), although it does not mention the name or title of an **en** priestess, lists the grave goods (various gold objects) that were given to a deceased priestess during her funeral rites. Based on the date of the text shortly before the selection and installation of the new **en** priestess as well as the location of the transaction in Gaeš, Sallaberger suggests that the precious objects are indeed the funerary offerings for the deceased **en** priestess of Nanna in Karzida, the otherwise scarcely attested Enagazianna (Sallaberger 1995: 19). Furthermore, another text, OIP 121: 463, lists 30 sheep as **sa$_2$-du$_{11}$**, regular delivery, for the **en** of Nanna in Gaeš. The text dates to month 10 of the year Amar-Suen 8 and may thus also be referring to the funerary cult, as **sa$_2$-du$_{11}$** offerings are usually limited to deities and deceased royalty.[52]

---

48 Sallaberger 1995: 19. Note also that Ontario 1: 82, one of the royal mašdaria-deliveries discussed above, dates to the first month of year AS9 and also seems to refer to the **en** of Nanna at Gaeš, as the transaction took place in Gaeš (rev. 1). This delivery was made "when the **en** of Nanna went to Eridu(?)" (**en ^{d}Nanna NUN!?-na / du-ni**, l. 6), which suggests that one of the very first tasks of the newly instated **en** involved travel to Eridu.

49 PDT 2: 767 obv. ii 17, rev. i 3, ii 8. My interpretation here is based on the transliterations given in Yildiz and Gomi 1988: 21–2, Huber Vulliet 2014: 36–44, and in the BDTNS database, as no photos or hand copies are available. See also the comments by Sallaberger (1992: 132–33). For an in-depth discussion of this text in the context of the installation of the high clergy during the reign of Ur III, see Huber Vulliet 2014.

50 For a detailed reconstruction of the rituals associated with the accession of the **en** based on PDT 2: 767 and other sources, see Westenholz 2006: 35–36.

51 On the **ki-utu** rituals, see Sallaberger 1993: 215–26.

52 For a different interpretation, see Huber Vulliet 2019: 223 who suggests that this unique document was issued by the cattle administration in Puzris-Dagan and not by the local administration

Only one additional Ur III-period text explicitly refers to funerary offerings for the deceased **en** priestess: TIM 6: 8 mentions the **ki-a-nag en-na**, the location for the funerary libation of the **en**. The text, however, does not specify the **en** priest or priestess of which deity is mentioned here.[53]

3.3 Other References to the en Priestess of Nanna in Documentary Texts

A few scattered texts from Ur also refer to the **en** priestess of Nanna by her title. They do not form a coherent group, but rather contain scattered references to transactions having taken place.

As Huber Vulliet (2019: 183) points out, an amount of 660 litres of grain listed in UET 9: 958, an account of grain for a range of purposes, including for the **sa$_2$-du$_{11}$** of Nanna, was likely destined for the consumption of the **en** priestess for a year and separate from specific deliveries for festival and special occasions.

Two texts refer to the house of the **en** of Nanna: UET 4: 40 (IS17) mentions the house of the **en** of Nanna in a transaction (because of the broken state of the text, it is unclear what goods are involved) and UET 9: 103 is a pisandubba-label mentioning barley in the house of the **en** of Nanna in Karzida.

Another text, MVN 9: 184, of unclear provenance but with the transaction recorded having taken place in Ur, lists a delivery of different textiles and mentions the title of the **en** of Nanna in broken context. UET 3: 959, lists one lamb as the **šuku** (food allocation) for the **en** of Nanna and UET 3: 76 lists oil for the maintenance of the boat of the **en** priestess.[54]

While most of the documentary texts mentioning the **en** priestess of Nanna stem from Puzriš-Dagan and Ur, we also find her title in a smaller number of documents from Girsu. ITT 3: 6557 is a *Sammelurkunde* of court protocols (**di-til-la**). The specific case that mentions the title of the **en** of Nanna is unfortunately completely broken.

Two texts from Girsu concern fields belonging to the **en** of Nanna. *Mesopotamia* 5–6: p. 300 (Š36), a long list of fields in the possession of Girsu, mentions the transfer (**i$_3$-dab$_5$**) of a field located between the Nun-canal and the Nanna-Gugal-

in Ur due to the vacancy of the office and that it simply records the regular deliveries for the **en** priestess.

53 Note here also the evidence for the funerary offerings for the deceased **en** priestesses in the evidence from the Early Old Babylonian period, see Charpin 1986: 208.

54 For the latter text, see also the discussion in Huber Vulliet 2019: 184.

canal to the **en** of Nanna. *ASJ* 8: pp. 346–47 is a near complete duplicate of this text, including the same officials, but with some differences in the numbers.[55]

MVN 13: 376, also from Girsu, is a large fragmentary tablet with a balanced account listing beer and cereal expenses, mentioning an amount of groats for the **en** of Nanna in Karzida.

The few texts mentioning the priestesses by name instead of title do not provide us with much further evidence either. Ennirzianna occurs in a receipt (**ba-zi**) for different types of flour (UET 3: 911) and in fragmentary context in a tablet listing bronze vessels (UET 9: 415). Enuburzianna is the recipient of a sheep, likely for sacrifice during the **še-KIN-ku$_5$**-festival in the text AUCT 1: 327, dated to the year AS3, her last year in office.[56] Enmahgalanna occurs by name in several documents. UET 3: 1717 (IS6) is a receipt (**ba-zi**) for a ceremonial garment, UET 3: 45 a legal document mentioning Enmahgalanna's name. Unfortunately, the text is heavily damaged, but it seems to concern a court case involving Enmahgalanna which had been brought before the king. Enmahgalanna is furthermore mentioned twice in UET 3: 52. The text is heavily broken and the context in which Enmahgalanna is mentioned is unclear.[57]

3.4 Summary: The en Priestesses of Nanna in the Ur III Documentary Texts

Unfortunately, no clear picture emerges looking at the evidence for the cultic and secular functions in the documentary texts.

As we can expect, it seems that the **en** priestesses of Nanna predominantly appear in the Puzriš-Dagan texts in connection to matters of national importance and in connection with the involvement of the king. These texts refer to the royal deliveries as part of important festivals and to the rites that were involved in the choosing and installation of the priestesses. In turn, the group of texts from Ur at least in part concerns the local administration and the daily workings of the

55 For these two texts, see also the discussion in Huber Vulliet 2019: 182 who suggests that the fields in question were originally the property of the **en** priestess Enannepada, the daughter of Ur-Baba of Lagash.

56 Huber Vulliet (2019: 177–78) suggests that this text and TAD 47 (covering the same time frame) may be connected to the selection or installation of Enuburzianna's successor that may have taken place during the **še-KIN-ku$_5$**-festival.

57 It is unclear whether UET 3: 52 is, in fact, the recto of UET 3: 45, for a summary of the arguments, see Huber Vulliet 2019: 179–80.

temple: we see receipts for smaller deliveries of various goods, such as textiles, and the **šabra** of the **en** priestess acting on her behalf.

4 Conclusion

What is striking in the evidence discussed in this contribution is the relative scarcity of references to the titles (or sacerdotal names) of the **en** priestess, particularly in the documentary evidence. The prominence of the office in the year names of the Ur III dynasty stands in stark contrast to the very limited textual evidence referring to the cultic and economic activities tied to the office.

One may of course argue that there undoubtedly existed a range of officials carrying out administrative duties on behalf of the priestess herself. Three **šabra** "household administrators" are attested in the Nanna precinct during the Ur III period: one for the **en** priestess of Nanna, one for Nanna himself, and one for Nanna's consort, Ningal. Two **šabra** of the **en** priestess are known by name, but they are only attested in a couple of documents. The **šabra** Ur-Bilgames is mentioned in SACT 1: 189 (the livestock inventory from Puzriš-Dagan mentioned above) and the **šabra** Ur-Ningublaga appears in PDT 2: 767 (the text connected to the accession rituals discussed above) and in another document, BIN 3 198, an account of cattle from Puzriš-Dagan.[58]

The **šabra** of Nanna, on the other hand, is significantly better attested, and Huber Vulliet (2019: 160–63) has been able to reconstruct a sequence of four consecutive officials in this role spanning the time period from Š43–IS2. While the **šabra** of Nanna does occur in Ur, the majority of the documents concern livestock deliveries for offerings to Nanna from the cattle administration in Puzriš-Dagan. One might speculate that the relative scarcity of documentary sources for the **en** priestess and her **šabra** – and the connection of the documentation to accession rites and specific festivals – may be due to the specific rites and tasks performed in the context of the Gipar not involving sacrifice of livestock, and thus not being recorded in the Puzriš-Dagan archives. The **šabra** of Nanna was thus in charge of the regular cult in the main temple, whereas the **šabra** of the

58 For the **šabra** of the **en** priestess of Nanna, see also Huber Vulliet 2019: 181–82. Another official that we can specifically connect to the en of Nanna is her cup-bearer (although equally scarcely attested), see Huber Vulliet 2019: 182.

en priestess was concerned with matters directly relating to the household of the **en** priestess itself, and not its cultic functions.[59]

But considering the fact that the **en** priestesses presumably were members of the royal family, and we have ample evidence for royal women participating in economic activities in their own right (Sharlach 2017: 306–307), their apparent lack of agency warrants an explanation. Was it then, presumably, the religious nature of her office that precluded the **en** priestess from taking a more active role? This does not seem likely, seeing as we have ample evidence for priests – male and female – engaging beyond the realm of the cult: the title of the **en** of Inanna is well-attested in Ur III documentary texts also outside the year names[60] and we find numerous references to the various **ereš-dingir** priestesses.

Weiershäuser (2008: 242) suggests two possible explanations for the absence of the **en** priestess of Nanna from the documentary texts: either the texts refer to her under a different name than the sacerdotal name we know from the year names and royal inscriptions or her estate was not provided for by the cattle administration in Puzriš-Dagan. The former explanation seems rather unlikely, considering that there are a number of texts – albeit only very few – that do refer to the **en** priestess by her sacerdotal name, alongside a larger number of texts that mention her title. The latter suggestion has more merit, especially if we take into account – as pointed out above – that other priestly offices as well as other members of the royal family do indeed appear in the Puzriš-Dagan documentation. We would then have to look for additional documents elsewhere, very likely in Ur itself.

The relative scarcity of texts from Ur in general may be partially to blame for the lack of more texts dealing with the daily workings of the Gipar[61] and the cultic and economic role of the **en** priestesses. Of the more than 100,000 texts currently listed in the database of Neo-Sumerian texts, a mere 5% stem from Ur. In addition, the texts from Ur are – for the most part – concentrated towards

---

59 To what extent this indicates whether or not the **en** priestess was cloistered within the Gipar is difficult to ascertain based on the available evidence. The **en** priestess certainly travelled outside the Gipar, at least during the major festivals, and also, at least in the case noted in Ontario 1: 82, to Eridu.

60 Weiershäuser (2008: 241) has pointed out that the **en** of Inanna appears in over 100 **mu-ku$_x$** deliveries in the Puzriš-Dagan corpus. Currently, a cursory search reveals a total of 375 texts referring to the **en** of Inanna outside the year names in the BDTNS corpus.

61 It is important to note, however, that the Gipar does occur in a sizeable number of texts from the administrative corpus from Puzriš-Dagan and also in a handful of texts from Ur itself. Even though these texts mostly refer to events occurring in the **ka$_2$ gi$_6$-par$_4$-ra**, the gate of the Gipar, it cannot be excluded that the household of the **en** priestess could have been summarily referred to as the Gipar, not mentioning the title of the **en** priestess of Nanna explicitly.

the very end of the Ur III dynasty, with peaks during the early reign of Ibbi-Sîn (Years IS1– IS8) and in the year Ibbi-Sîn 15. Considering the precarious state in which the Ur III kingdom seems to have been already in the early years of Ibbi-Sîn, it is also worth considering to what extent these texts really are representative of the wealth and importance of the office of the **en** priestess in the Ur III kingdom as a whole.

While documentary texts can further help us investigate the cultic function and economic role of what was one of the most important female religious figures in Ur III Mesopotamia to a certain degree, even more information concerning her role and her level of agency in economic activities still remains lacking.

Abbreviations

AS	year name of king Amar-Suen
IS	year name of king Ibbi-Sîn
RIME 2	Frayne 1993.
RIME 3/1	Edzard 1997.
RIME 3/2	Frayne 1997.
RIME 4	Frayne 1990.
RINBE 2	Weiershäuser and Novotny 2020.
Š	year name of king Šulgi
ŠS	year name of king Šu-Sîn

Bibliography

Charpin, Dominique. 1986. *Le clergé d'Ur au siècle d'Hammurabi (XIXe-XVIIIe siècles av. J.-C.).* Geneva & Paris: Droz.

Charpin, Dominique. 2017. En marge d'Archibab, 25: une offrande à Ur d'Etellum, ministre du roi de Larsa Gungunum. *NABU* 2017: 75–77.

Collon, Dominique. 1991. Depictions of Priests and Priestesses in the Ancient Near East. Pp. 17–46 in *Priests and Officials in the Ancient Near* East. *Papers of the Second Colloquium on the Ancient Near East – The City and its Life held at the Middle Eastern Culture Center in Japan (Mitaka, Tokyo), March 22–24,1996*, ed. Kazuko Watanabe. Heidelberg: Winter.

Edzard, Dietz Otto. 1997. *Gudea and His Dynasty*. RIME 3.1. Toronto: University of Toronto Press.

Farber, Gertrud and Walter Farber. 2018. The Cuneiform Tablets at Northwestern University Library. Pp. 195–226 in *Grenzüberschreitungen: Studien zur Kulturgeschichte des Alten Orients. Festschrift für Hans Neumann zum 65. Geburtstag am 9. Mai 2018*, ed. Kristin Kleber et al. Dubsar 5. Münster: Zaphon.

Frayne, Douglas. 1990. *Old Babylonian Period (2003–1595 BC)*. RIME 4. Toronto: University of Toronto Press.
Frayne, Douglas. 1993. *Sargonic and Gutian Periods*. RIME 2. Toronto: University of Toronto Press.
Frayne, Douglas. 1997. *Ur III Period (2112–2004 BC)*. RIME 3/2. Toronto: University of Toronto Press.
Gadd, Cyril J. 1951. En-an-e-du. *Iraq* 13: 27–39.
Helle, Sophus. 2020. The Birth of the Author. *Orbis Litterarum 75:* 55–72.
Huber Vulliet, Fabienne. 2014. De la ville au temple: L'intronisation du haut-clergé babylonien à la fin du troisième millénaire av. J.-C. Pp. 25–46 in *Life, Death, and Coming of Age in Antiquity: Individual Rites of Passage in the Ancient Near* East *and Adjacent* Regions / *Vivre, grandir et mourir dans l'antiquité: rites de passage individuels au Proche-Orient ancient et ses environs*, ed. Alice Mouton and Julie Patrier. PIHANS 124. Leiden: Nederlands Instituut voor het Nabije Oosten.
Huber Vulliet, Fabienne. 2019. *Le personnel cultuel à l'époque néo-sumérienne (ca. 2160–2300 av. J.-C.)*. BPOA 14. Madrid: Consejo Superior de Investigaciones Científicas.
Maeda, Tohru. 1992. The Defense Zone during the Rule of the Ur III Dynasty. *ASJ* 14: 135–72.
Marchesi, Gianni. 2004. Who Was Buried in the Royal Tombs of Ur? The Epigraphic and Textual Data. *OrNS* 73: 153–97.
Michalowski, Piotr. 2013. Of Bears and Men. Thoughts on the End of Šulgi's Reign and on the Ensuing Succession. Pp. 285–320 in *Literature as Politics, Politics as Literature. Essays on the Ancient Near East in Honor of Peter Machinist*, ed. David S. Vanderhooft and Abraham Winitzer. Winona Lake, Indiana: Eisenbrauns.
van de Mieroop, Marc. 1989. Gifts and Tithes to the Temples in Ur. Pp. 397–401 in *Dumu-e$_2$-dub-ba-a: Studies in Honor of Åke W. Sjöberg*, ed. Hermann Behrens et al. Occasional Publications of the Samuel Noah Kramer Fund 9. Philadelphia, Pennsylvania: The University Museum.
Paoletti, Paola. 2012. *Der König und sein Kreis. Das staatliche Schatzarchiv der III. Dynastie von Ur*. BPOA 10. Madrid: Consejo Superior de Investigaciones Científicas.
Renger, Johannes. 1967. Untersuchungen zum Priestertum in der altbabylonischen Zeit. 1. Teil. *ZA* 58: 110–88.
Sallaberger, Walther. 1992. Review of F. Yildiz. & T.Gomi: Die Puzriš-Dagan-Texte der Istanbuler Archäologischen Museen. Teil II: Nr. 726–1376 (= FAOS 16). *ZA* 82: 131–37.
Sallaberger, Walther. 1993. *Der kultische Kalender der Ur III-Zeit*. UAVA 7. Berlin and New York: de Gruyter.
Sallaberger, Walther. 1995. Eine reiche Bestattung im neusumerischen Ur. *JCS* 47: 15–21.
Sallaberger, Walter, and Fabienne Huber Vulliet. 2005. Priester A.1. Mesopotamien. *RlA* 10: 617–40.
Schaudig, Hanspeter. 2003. Nabonid, der "Archäologe auf dem Königsthron". Zum Geschichtsbild des ausgehenden neubabylonischen Reiches. Pp. 447–97 in *Festschrift für Burkhart Kienast zu seinem 70. Geburtstage dargebracht von Freunden, Schülern und Kollegen*, ed. Gebhard J. Selz. AOAT 274. Münster: Ugarit-Verlag.
Sharlach, Tonia M. 2008. Priestesses, Concubines, and the Daughters of Men: Disentangling the Meaning of the Word lukur in Ur III Times. Pp. 177–83 in *On the Third Dynasty of Ur. Studies in Honor of Marcel Sigrist*, ed. Piotr Michalowski. JCSSS 1. Boston, Massachusetts: American Schools of Oriental Research.

Sharlach, Tonia M. 2017. *An Ox of One's Own. Royal Wives and Religion at the Court of the Third Dynasty of Ur*. SANER 18. Berlin and Boston: de Gruyter.

Sollberger, Edmond. 1954–56. Sur la chronologie des rois d'Ur et quelques problèmes connexes. *AfO* 17: 10–48.

Steinkeller, Piotr. 1999. On Rulers, Priests, and Sacred Marriage. Tracing the Evolution of Early Sumerian Kingship. Pp. 103–37 in *Priests and Officials in the Ancient Near* East. *Papers of the Second Colloquium on the Ancient Near East – The City and its Life held at the Middle Eastern Culture Center in Japan (Mitaka, Tokyo), March 22–24,1996*, ed. Kazuko Watanabe. Heidelberg: Winter.

Stol, Marten. 2016. *Women in the Ancient Near East*. Boston & Berlin: De Gruyter.

Weadock, Penelope N. 1975. The Giparu at Ur. *Iraq* 37: 101–28.

Weiershäuser, Frauke. 2008. *Die königlichen Frauen der III. Dynastie von Ur*. GBAO 1. Göttingen: Universitätsverlag.

Weiershäuser, Frauke and Jamie Novotny. 2020. *The Royal Inscriptions of Amēl-Marduk (561–560 BC), Neriglissar 559–556 BC), and Nabonidus (555–539 BC), Kings of Babylon*. RINBE 2. Winona Lake, Indiana: Eisenbrauns.

Westenholz, Joan Goodnick. 1989. Enheduanna, En-Priestess, Hen of Nanna, Spouse of Nanna. Pp. 539–56 in *Dumu-e$_2$-dub-ba-a: Studies in Honor of Åke W. Sjöberg*, ed. Hermann Behrens et al. Occasional Publications of the Samuel Noah Kramer Fund 9. Philadelphia, Pennsylvania: The University Museum.

Westenholz, Joan Goodnick. 2006. Women of Religion in Mesopotamia: The High Priestess in the Temple. *C.S.M.S. Journal* 1: 31–44.

Winter, Irene J. 1987. Women in Public. The Disk of Enheduanna, the Beginning of the Office of En-Priestess, and the Weight of Visual Evidence. Pp. 189–201 in *La femme dans le Proche-Orient antique. Compte-rendu de la XXXIIIe Rencontre Assyriologique Internationale (Paris, 7–10 juillet 1986)*, ed. Jean-Maria Durand. Paris: Editions Recherche sur les Civilisations.

Nicole Brisch

High Priestesses in Old Babylonian Nippur: The NIN and NIN-dingir Priestesses of Ninurta

The gender theorist Judith Butler has pointed out that the oppression of women is not a historical universal that can or should be read into the historical record but that needs to be studied within a concrete cultural context (Butler 1990: 5–8).[1] Zainab Bahrani made a very similar point in her discussion of feminist scholarship and the applicability of feminist methodologies to the study of women in the historical record (Bahrani 2001: 7–27). These are significant points when it comes to studying and interpreting the role of women as actors with ancient Mesopotamian religions: it is important for scholars to be aware of his or her own notions on gender, and I would add here, also on religions, in order to avoid reading interpretations into the ancient written record that are rather based on modern notions of gender and women's roles as actors within religions. Moreover, it is of utmost importance to include a careful source critique that is particularly sensitive to gender aspects in the written record. All too often, one interpretation is presented as fact without even raising, let alone discussing other possible interpretations. For example, it is often assumed that priestesses were not allowed to marry, because they are identified in documents as the daughters of PN rather than the wife of PN, as is customary. Yet is this a conclusion that has been proven, or should it not be critically examined?

Among the most controversial issues regarding the reconstruction of Mesopotamian religious beliefs and practices is the role that priestesses played as active participants in religious rituals. Priestesses are often either categorized as temple prostitutes or celibate nuns, with little or no nuances in between. The recent years have, however, seen several more nuanced and detailed studies of priestesses (e.g. Barberon 2012; Huber Vulliet 2019; De Graef 2016, 2018), while

1 I am very grateful to Fumi Karahashi for her feedback on this article. Mistakes are of course entirely my own. I am also very grateful to Fumi for the wonderful invitation to Tokyo and for having organized a stimulating workshop at Chuo University. Furthermore, I would like to acknowledge the online research tools (The Electronic Pennsylvania Dictionary and the Electronic Text Corpus of Sumerian Literature), which have greatly helped in researching this paper. All abbreviations follow the list of abbreviations on the Cuneiform Digital Library Initative (CDLI: https://cdli.ox.ac.uk/wiki/abbreviations_for_assyriology).

https://doi.org/10.1515/9781501514821-008

the pioneering works, in particular of Rivkah Harris (1964, 1975), Elizabeth Stone (1982), and Marten Stol (2016)[2] should also be acknowledged.

As more studies and primary data on priestesses in ancient Mesopotamia are emerging, it becomes evident that there were considerable local differences in the practice of religion within the common cultural area of southern Mesopotamia. This is also apparent in the study of priestesses, who had different titles depending on their geographical location as well as the deity that they served. For example, it was long assumed that *nadītum* priestesses were not allowed to marry or had to remain childless, yet, it is clear that the *nadītum* priestesses of Marduk in Babylon did marry, and now there is also an example of a **lukur** priestess of the god Lugalaba in Old Babylonian Nippur, who was married and adopted a son (Goddeeris 2016: 361).

This is not an article about priestesses in general, but an attempt at a detailed study of high priestesses of the god Ninurta in Old Babylonian Nippur, in particular of the high priestesses with the title **NIN** and **NIN-dingir**, as indicated in the title to this contribution. As some of the current scholarship on priestesses tends to mix data from three millennia without acknowledging historical or geographical differences, I will rely in the following primarily on data that are directly relevant to high priestesses Old Babylonian Nippur, in particular the Old Babylonian documentary data from Nippur itself but also other relevant sources.[3] I believe it is important to attempt to *untangle* the available data to gain a better understanding of historical and localized traditions regarding priestesses in ancient Mesopotamia.

Studying priestesses in Old Babylonian Nippur is an undertaking that is not as straightforward as it might sound, in part this is also due to the high number of deities that were worshipped in Nippur. As the religious center of early Mesopotamia, Nippur was also the home to two of the most important deities in ancient Mesopotamia, Enlil, the highest head of the pantheon, and Ninurta, his son, who was the patron deity of Nippur (Sallaberger 1997). The first complications already arise when trying to establish the various priestly titles, both in Sumerian and in Akkadian, of Ninurta's high priestesses (see already Stol 2000; Huber Vulliet 2010, 2019). A certain amount of confusion about the titles of Ninurta's priestesses already may have existed in antiquity. According to our

---

2 Stol's 2016 book is a comprehensive study of women in the Ancient Near East, including several chapters on priestesses. However, Stol focused on bringing diverse sources of information together for a comprehensive synthesis. This contribution, by contrast, seeks to *untangle* the sources on high priestesses of Ninurta at Nippur.

3 The Old Babylonian data from Nippur can be found mainly in Robertson 1981; Sigrist 1984; Goddeeris 2016.

current state of knowledge, there was no **en**-priestess in service of the god Ninurta, though there was an **en**-priestess for Enlil (Huber Vulliet 2019: 52–60). Perhaps it was for this reason that Ninurta's temple was not assigned an **en**-priestess, though this is speculative. However, there is an unidentified year name, possibly of an Isin king, which mentions an **en**-priest or **en**-priestess of Ninurta, yet not much more is known about this singular attestation.[4]

That there are no **en** priestesses attested for Ninurta is, perhaps, unusual, because the office of the **en** is generally considered to have been the highest in the priestly hierarchy, and there are indications that the **en** was usually of the opposite sex than the deity they served (Renger 1967: 116). Yet, it is also possible that there were historically different titles and traditions in Nippur (see below). It has been suggested that the office of the high priest of Enlil was, at least at times, held by a man (Renger 1967: 116; J. Goodnick Westenholz 1992: 306),[5] yet this has been called into question more recently (Huber Vulliet 2019: 54 and n. 146).

Priestesses with the Titles NIN ^{d}nin-urta and NIN-dingir ^{d}nin-urta

There have been suggestions that the titles **NIN ^{d}nin-urta** and **NIN-dingir ^{d}nin-urta** were in fact variations of the same title (Such Gutierrez 2003: 147 and n. 602). Stol (2000: 457–60) has affirmed that Ninurta did indeed have a priestess with the title **NIN**, while Huber Vulliet (2019: 108) suggested that the title **NIN** was replaced with **NIN-dingir** in the first half of the second millennium BCE, though the evidence for this assessment is not clear. However, given that there was no **en** priestess of Ninurta and given that there both titles are attested frequently enough to exclude an abbreviation in writing, at least in the Old Babylonian period, the possibility must be taken seriously that these were in

4 The year name reads: **mu** *na-aḫ-ma-tum* **en ^{d}nin-urta ba-hug̃-g̃á** "the year that Nahmatum, the **en**-priestess of Ninurta, was appointed." The year name is attested on the tablet NBC 9198, see Beckman 1995: 108; Richter 2004: 60 n. 271. It is not clear whether this singular attestation may have been a faulty writing of the title **NIN**.

5 J. Goodnick Westenholz's (1992: 310) claim that there was a **NIN-dingir** (*ugbabtum*?) of Enlil at Nippur is incorrect, see already Sigrist 1977: 179; Sigrist 1984: 162. The text in question is PBS 13: 61 (=CBS 14217 + CBS 8550) = Sigrist 1977; PBS 13: 61 does not mention a **NIN-dingir** of Enlil, only 6 **NIN-dingir**, who appear in connection with the Nuska temple (col. viii line 20, not col. vi line 1, as incorrectly stated in Renger 1967: 146 n. 252 and Sigrist 1984: 162). The original transliteration of PBS 13: 61 assigned the columns incorrectly, see Sigrist 1977.

fact two different titles and that these two titles continued throughout the Old Babylonian period, though, as Stol has already pointed out, they were sometimes confused already in antiquity.[6]

The title **NIN** appears to be exclusive to the Nippur clergy, and within Nippur it is only connected to Enlil and Ninurta. The title **NIN** $^{\mathbf{d}}$**nin-urta** is attested at least two times in the third millennium, both texts are from Nippur (Huber Vulliet 2019: 108). An Old Akkadian account mentions one goat and one male sheep for the high priestess (ECTJ 176 obv. i 1, = Aa. Westenholz 1975), while she receives one sheep in an Ur III account (TMH NF 1-2: 275 obv. 3, no date).

In the early second millennium, the high priestess appears frequently in year names of the Isin dynasty (Išbi-Erra 7;[7] Šu-ilišu 3;[8] and Išme-Dagan N and O[9]). In addition to the year names, the **NIN**-priestess of Ninurta is mentioned in a text of unknown provenience (YOS 14: 312), which is a receipt of semolina (**dabin**) for the regular offerings (**sa**$_{\mathbf{2}}$**-dug**$_{\mathbf{4}}$) of the **NIN** priestess of Ninurta.[10] In this attestation she is mentioned both in the text itself and in the year name on the document (Išme-Dagan N), it is therefore very unlikely that this is a typo for the title **NIN-dingir**, and we have to assume that this office still existed in the Old Babylonian period.[11] A further possible Old Babylonian attestation of the title **NIN** of Ninurta may have been a misreading.[12]

The title **NIN** is also used in connection with the high priestess of Enlil in the Old Akkadian record (Huber Vulliet 2019: 53 and n. 136), but, as mentioned above, appears to be a variant spelling of the Akkadian title *ēntum* and it seems not to have been used later (Huber Vulliet 2019: 54).

---

6 Stol 2000: 457 n. 5: "Die damaligen Schreiber hatten also selbst Schwierigkeiten mit dem ungewöhlichen Titel NIN."

7 In the year name Išbi-Erra 7, there are variants that write **NIN-dingir** $^{\mathbf{d}}$**nin-urta**, see Sigrist 1988: 13.

8 Sigrist 1988: 22; De Boer 2021: 11.

9 See De Boer 2021: 14 and n. 32, who suggested that the priestly title in the year name might be emended to ereš-<dingir>.

10 For a detailed list of attestations and misreadings of the title **NIN** $^{\mathbf{d}}$**nin-urta** in Old Babylonian year names see Stol 2000: 457–59 n. 5.

11 Contra Richter 2004: 60 and n. 270. Also see De Boer 2021: 14 n. 32.

12 Stol (2000: 458 n. 9) noted an Old Babylonian account from Nippur (N. 2426 = Çiğ 1992: 94; Huber Vulliet 2010) about the disbursal of animals and cuts of meat to various temple officials and others that mentions the house or household of the **NIN** priestesses of Enlil and Ninurta. See Çiğ 1992: Ni. 2426 iv 1-2: 3(diš) uzu gu$_4$ e$_2$ NIN ^{d}en-lil$_2$-la$_2$, 3(diš) uzu gu$_4$ e$_2$ NIN ^{d}nin-urta. The text is dated to the year Rīm-Sîn 21. However, as Huber Vulliet (2010: 147 n. 137) pointed out, Stol (1998–2001: 541) emended the **é NIN** to **é-sikil**. Regardless, it is important to properly collate this tablet before drawing any firm conclusions.

The title **NIN-dingir ^{d}nin-urta** is also very rarely attested. The possibly earliest attestation of the title can be found in an Ur III document from Puzriš-Dagan dating to the year Šulgi 43, which recorded the delivery of a lamb from the **NIN-dingir** of Ninurta (Koslova n.d.).[13] There are two confirmed attestations in the Old Babylonian period: an Old Babylonian tablet (dating to the year Išbi-Erra 19) mentions a **NIN-dingir** of Ninurta in the context of leather bags that the Ensi of Nippur received,[14] and another Old Babylonian text of unknown provenience, kept at the Louvre Museum, mentions a field that borders the field (?) of the **NIN-dingir** of Ninurta.[15] This tablet is dated to the year Enlilbani E. Furthermore, the tablets that belong to the so-called *sattukku* archive also mention a **NIN-dingir** of Ninurta (Sigrist 1984: 162).[16]

Another tablet from Nippur that mentions the priestess was published by Çiğ (1992) and edited by Huber Vulliet (2010). The tablet Ni 2446, dated to the year Rim-Sin 21, was part of the administration of animal offerings at Nippur. It mentions a **NIN-dingir ^{d}nin-urta** among the recipient of redistributed meat offerings (Ni 2446 obv. i 10), together with other high priestesses.[17] Moreover, the lexical list of professional titles OB Nippur Lu (Q000047) distinguishes the titles **NIN ^{d}nin-urta** and **NIN-dingir ^{d}nin-urta** very clearly (lines 224–225, also see below).[18] Though these attestations are but few, again they should allow us to conclude that Ninurta had both, a **NIN** and a **NIN-dingir** priestess at Nippur.[19] Whether the title **NIN-dingir ^{d}nin-urta** is secondary or substituted the title **NIN** cannot be established at this point due to the paucity in attestations. If the attestation in the Ur III tablet mentioned above is correct, then it may have been an office that may have been newly introduced during that time.

---

13 Koslova n.d. obv. 5. The line is unfortunately partially broken; it is also possible that the title has to be restored as **NIN ^{d}nin-urta.**

14 BIN 9: 216, see Van De Mieroop 1987: 111.

15 Charpin and Durand 1981: 18 = AO 5419.

16 I hope to publish the *sattukku* archive fully in the very near future.

17 It would have been helpful, if Huber Vulliet's edition had represented the tabular format, in which the tablet was written. Whether the tablet also mentions a **lukur** of Ninurta (Ni 2436 obv i 9), as suggested by Huber Vulliet (2019: 148 and n. 142), is subject to collation of this tablet. Such far-reaching emendations should be made only after careful collation.

18 See the DCCLT on Oracc (http://oracc.museum.upenn.edu/dcclt/index.html), s.v. OB Lu.

19 The text traditions of priestesses in the lexical corpus and in divinatory texts, in particular of the first millennium, need to be sorted out carefully and separately, which would go beyond the scope of this contribution. See however a few remarks further below.

The Reading of NIN

The difficulties in studying ancient Mesopotamian priestesses already start with the correct readings of their titles. This is true for some of the most ancient titles of high priestesses (and priests) in the very earliest written record from ancient Mesopotamia, and a confusion about certain titles already seems to have existed in antiquity, when some of them may no longer have been understood. Additionally, there are also local differences in the priestly titles in the earliest periods: high priests and priestesses held different titles depending on which deity they served and where they were located. Steinkeller (1999: 120 n. 53), Marchesi (2004: 186–89) and others have proposed the reading **ereš/eriš** for the sign **NIN** in certain contexts. According to Marchesi (2004: 186), the sign **NIN** should be read **ereš** when it designates the word "queen" (Akkadian *šarratum*) or "lady" (Akkadian *bēltum*).[20] Similarly, Stol (2000, with further references) also indicated, albeit with caution, that the priestly titles **NIN** and **NIN-dingir** could be read **ereš** and **ereš-dingir** respectively. Moreover, as Civil (2011: 258 n. 58) has pointed out, the entry for the title **NIN-dingir** in the Emesal vocabulary (II 76–77) has generally been ignored and would point to an equally valid reading of **nin-dingir**.

It is clear from several attestations from sign lists that the sign combination **NIN(SAL.TUG$_2$)** had two readings, **nin** and **ereš** (see, for example, Proto-Ea, lines 419–420, Civil 1979: 48; = Q000055 [OB Nippur Ea]), yet it is far from clear when the sign should be read **nin** and when it should be read **ereš.** We see the reading of **NIN** as **ereš** most frequently in the name of the netherworld goddess Ereškigal(a) "Lady of the great earth (=netherworld)" (Wiggerman 1998–2001: 220). The reading of the sign **NIN** as **ereš** is indicated from a syllabic spelling of her name in the (late) myth Nergal and Ereškigal from Tell el-Amarna (EA 357, see Izreel 1997: 51–61). Ereškigal appears for the first time in the Old Akkadian period, in a royal inscription of Lu-Utu, a local governor of Umma (= *RIME* 2.11.6.2 = Frayne 1993: 265–66). Katz (2003: 386) noted her absence in the Early Dynastic god lists, speculating that the queen of the underworld may have been known under a different name then. In the Old Babylonian period, there is very little evidence that the goddess was worshipped at all, and she mainly seems to occur in literary texts.

That **nin** and **ereš** were, perhaps, synonymous can be seen from the Emesal form of Ereshkigal's name, which is given as **^{d}ga-ša-an-ki-gal** "Lady of the underworld," though this may be a folk etymological interpretation. However, as

20 Also see Marchesi 2006: 73 n. 382.

gašan is a well-known Emesal form of Emegir **nin** (for example, in the divine name Inanna, whose Emesal equivalent is **^{d}ga-ša-an-an-na** "Lady of the heavens"), the distinction between when to read **nin** or **ereš** cannot be semantic, as seemingly suggested by Marchesi (2004: 186). A possible distinction between reading **nin** or **ereš** connected to whether a deity or a human is designated, is equally difficult to reconcile with the available data. Bauer (2019: 90) pointed to an Early Dynastic spelling of a personal name that would confirm the reading **ereš** (**ereš-šè-an-su**[21] "the Lady knows him/her (?)"). Here the word **ereš** functions as an epithet for a divinity (see Limet 1968: 323).

The word **nin** may originally have indicated both "lord" and "lady" (Bauer 1998: 435), and here it was pronounced **nin** because of alternate spellings with the sign **nig̃$_2$**, for example, in the name Ningirsu (**^{d}nig̃$_2$-g̃ir$_2$-su** "Lord of Girsu") (Bauer 1998: 435). Early Dynastic personal names indicate moreover that the word **nin** appeared in personal names instead of **lugal** "king" (**lugal-dingir-g̃u$_{10}$** and **nin-dingir-g̃u$_{10}$**, the latter as the (presumably) female equivalent, see Bauer 1998: 520). More recently, Attinger (2021: 807 n. 2419) also acknowledged that it can be difficult to know when to read "**nin**" or "**eriš**." Given that it is not possible to distinguish when to read **nin** or **ereš** in general, this insecurity should also be acknowledged in the reading of the priestly title **NIN-dingir**.

The suggestions to read the priestly title as **ereš-dingir** are primarily based on lexical lists and a handful of second millennium syllabic spellings, with only a single syllabic spelling dating to the third millennium, which occurs in the Ebla sign list (see Marchesi 2004: 186 with further references). The Ebla spelling is furthermore without context and only indicates a possible reading for the sign **NIN** by itself but not in the combination with **dingir**. The same is true for other syllabic spellings of the sign **NIN** by itself, for example, in Old Babylonian literary texts. In other words, the syllabic spelling from Ebla and other places is not necessarily an indication that the sign **NIN** should be read **ereš** in the sign-combination **NIN-dingir**.

Another important indication for the reading of **NIN** as **ereš** in the priestly title is found in a syllabic spelling from a lexical text from Emar (see Fleming 1992: 80–82). The lexical exercise, formerly identified as Ura XIX, now identified as Middle Babylonian Ura 11b (Veldhuis 2014: 290–91), shows the syllabic spelling of the sign combination **NIN-dingir-ra** as **i-ri-iš-ti-gi-ra** and translates the term as *i-ti*, which presumably stands for *ēntu* (lines 43 and 47 in Msk 74149, see Arnaud 1987: 135; Veldhuis 2014: 291). The unusual exercise tablet, in which lines that began on the obverse were continued directly onto the

21 For the personal name see VS 25: 69 obv. iv 19 = P020275.

reverse (Veldhuis 2014: 290–91), offers a clear syllabic spelling of the sign **NIN** in the combination **NIN-dingir**. However, a word of caution may be added: given that the difficulties in reading and understanding the titles of priestesses already began in the Old Babylonian period, or perhaps as early as the Old Akkadian period, the question should be raised again, whether the reading **ereš** for the sign **NIN** in the priestly title is original or a late re-interpretation.

It is therefore important to add a historical perspective on the reading and interpretation of priestly titles, some of which already appear in the proto-cuneiform texts.[22] Stol (2016: 426) has already pointed out that some of the older titles of ancient Mesopotamian women and priestesses were often lumped together with words that can be translated as "prostitutes" after the Old Babylonian period. The closer one looks at the titles of women and priestesses, the more complicated the picture becomes, with clear difficulties in establishing correct readings and interpretations of titles already in antiquity. A further complication arises from some priestly titles also appearing as epithets of goddesses, such as the title **nu-gig**, which originally served as a professional title for midwives or wet nurses but was also used as an epithet of goddesses.[23]

As the title **NIN** for high priestesses may have been confined to (or typical for) Nippur, it is difficult to distinguish the roles of priestesses with the title **NIN** from those with the title **NIN-dingir**. The title **NIN** was not confined to Ninurta,[24] the Old Babylonian version of the lexical list Lu from Nippur (Q000047) mentions both titles (see above). The titles appear in a section on priestly titles, including those of female temple officials. Yet, a word of caution about the use of lexical lists for establishing correct readings of priestly titles should be added. As Civil (1969: 25–26) has already pointed out, the list Old Babylonian Lu list is not entirely thematic (see also Veldhuis 2014: 160–62) and contains some terms that do not designate professions but entries that were thematic, graphic, or grapho-thematic associations (Civil 1969: 25). This can also be seen in the section that lists the titles of priestesses, where a few lines (237–240) have Akkadian glosses of female body parts. According to Civil (1969: 26), these glosses indicate that the original

---

22 For example, the title **lukur**, in Akkadian *nadītum*, is mentioned for the first time in an Uruk III grain account (ca. 3100-2900 BCE), see Monaco 2016: 107. The title **zirru** (or **nunuz-zi nanna**) of the high priestess of Ur also appears in Uruk III and Early Dynastic I texts, see Lecompte (2013: 159–60) with further references and other early priestly titles.

23 On the Early Dynastic meaning of the title **nu-gig** see now Karahashi 2017.

24 Also see below. A **NIN** of Enlil is also mentioned in an Ur III account, in which the priestess is assigned a field. See Maekawa 1997: 135 text no. 120 (=P102677) obv. iii 6: **2(bur$_3$) a-ša$_3$ NIN ^{d}en-lil$_2$-le**, an account of land allotments (Maekawa 1997: 113–14). I would like to thank Fumi Karahashi for this reference.

meaning of entries that were originally titles of priestesses was not always preserved. Perhaps this also shows that already by the Old Babylonian period some of the titles were no longer understood and hence received re-interpretations.

A Middle Assyrian version of the Lu list shows, albeit in a different sequence, the following Akkadian equivalents, further adding to the complication and confusion surrounding the reading of the **NIN** and the priestly titles that were written with that sign:[25]

Col. I

1	[nin]	*be-e[l-t]u*
2	[nin]-dingir	MIN
3	[x] bi-zi	MIN
4	[ni]n$^{e\text{-}[r]i\text{-}iš}$	MIN
5	[ni]n	*en-tu*
6	[nin]-dingir	MIN
7	[nin]-dingir	*gu-bab-tu*
8	[nin] ⸢^{d}⸣nin-urta	*en-ti* ^{d}nin-urta
9	[nin-dingir?] ⸢^{d}⸣nin-urta	*gu-bab-ti* MIN
10	[nin-dingir?] ⸢^{d}⸣ba-ba$_6$	*šá-ḫi-it-tu*

This Middle Assyrian version of the Lu list shows that the reading and translation of **NIN** and **NIN-dingir** different Akkadian translations for the same words: although it is partly broken, on the basis of this passage we can assume that **nin**, **nin-dingir**, and **ereš** all were translated as *bēltu* "lady." Moreover, the priestly titles **NIN** and **NIN-dingir** were both translated as *ēntu* "En-priestess," and **NIN-dingir** could also be translated as *ugbabtu*. Nevertheless, whether the translation of the title **NIN ^{d}nin-urta** with *ēntu* and of **NIN-dingir ^{d}nin-urta** with *gubabtu* (=*ugbabtum*) of Ninurta can also be presumed for the Old Babylonian periods or the third millennium is far from clear.[26] It is also far from clear whether the pronunciation gloss /**ereš**/ for **nin** = *bēltum* presented in the text above should be applied to all the previous and following entries and all of the priestly titles or not.

The equation of the priestly title **NIN** with *ēntum* occurred for the first time in the Old Akkadian period in reference to the title of the high priestess of Enlil at Nippur. It appears that in Old Akkadian texts and year names, the titles **en**, **NIN** and *ēntum* were used interchangeably, at least in reference to the high

25 VAT 9558 = *MAOG* 13/2, 38–43, pl. 4. A photograph and transliteration of this tablet can be found on CDLI = P282499. See MSL 12: 128, tablet IV lines 1–10.

26 For the Akkadian equivalent, see further Renger 1967: 134–135; Stol 2000; CAD E, s.v. *ēntu*; CAD U/W, s.v. *ugbabtu*, including the discussion sections. Also see above.

priestess of Enlil at Nippur (Huber Vuillet 2019: 53–55). The Old Akkadian spelling variations of the title of the high priestess of Enlil may have further added to misunderstandings and confusion surrounding the proper reading and translation of these titles.

In other cases, the earliest priestly titles were written with **diri**-sign combinations, whose correct readings are often established on the basis of lexical texts that date to a much later period. A case in the point is the title **zirru**, written with different sign combinations, with recent suggestions that the title should be read **nunuz-zi nanna** instead.[27] In her study of priestly titles in the Ur III period, Huber Vulliet (2019) illustrates the regional and chronological variations of titles and the complications associated with establishing their readings in an exemplary manner.

Stol (2000: 462–63) discussed the problems in how to establish when the Sumerogram **NIN-dingir** should be translated into Akkadian as *ēntum* or *ugbabtum* and concluded that context is the most important factor. If the royal appointment of a **NIN** or **NIN-dingir** priestess is mentioned in a year name, it is likely that the priestess here should be understood as *ēntum*, the higher-ranking priestess. When a greater number of **NIN-dingir** priestesses is mentioned, especially in the context of administrative or legal tablets, it is more likely that these were *ugbabtum* priestesses, who ranked lower in the hierarchy than the *ēntum*. Yet, this suggestion is not without problems, because these high priestesses only appear very rarely in administrative and legal texts. Therefore, the context is not always easily established. Moreover, in year names the two titles were sometimes used interchangeably, as already mentioned above, and so it is not always clear whether the Sumerian equivalents designated the *ēntu* or the *ugbabtu* priestess.

While the reading **ereš-dingir** has become widely accepted in the secondary literature, the reading of the title **NIN** as **ereš** or **eriš** has not. It is this kind of inconsistency that should be addressed in a larger, international effort at establishing values for the reading of Sumerian signs and sign combinations. For the reasons outlined above, in particular the cautionary notes regarding the transmission and understanding of priestly titles, I have decided to read the titles of these priestesses as **NIN** and **NIN-dingir** in this contribution, knowing full well that they *may* have been read **ereš** and **ereš-dingir**.

---

27 For the reading of the various sign combinations as **zirru** see Marchesi 2004: 170 n. 109; Lecompte 2013: 160. Also see the readings **en-zirru**, **en-(nu)nuzzi**, **en-ukurrim**, and **en-šennu** in Civil 1969: 41.

High Priestesses of Ninurta at Nippur

Stol (2000: 463) suggested that at Nippur the title **NIN**, **NIN-dingir**, and **lukur** of Ninurta were sometimes used interchangeably. While a confusion of the titles **NIN** and **NIN-dingir** can sometimes be observed in year names, a confusion of these two titles with the title **lukur** is unlikely. Stol's suggestion was based on the observation that the title **NIN-dingir** only occurs in the *sattukku* archive but never appears in any of the available administrative and legal texts. By contrast, the title **lukur** of Ninurta occurs frequently in administrative and legal texts at Nippur[28] but is never mentioned in the *sattukku* archive. However, upon further examination this presumed pattern turns out to be incorrect. As mentioned above, there are a couple of attestations of the title **NIN-dingir** **^{d}nin-urta** in Old Babylonian administrative documents, as mentioned above. Additionally, the *sattukku* texts that Sigrist (1984: 31–33) called "4-column tablets," which deal with the redistribution of food offerings, actually do mention a **lukur**-priestess of Ninurta (Brisch 2021a: 587). It is unclear how this group of texts should be dated as most of their year dates are broken, though there is one fragment which has a Sin-iqišam year date.[29]

One interpretation may be that the 4-column tablets date to a time when the title **lukur** was being substituted for the title **NIN-dingir**, which would be most likely well after the reign of Enlilbani or sometime in the reign of Rim-Sin I, and that therefore the **NIN-dingir** of Ninurta was not mentioned anymore. This is unlikely as there seems to have been but one **NIN-dingir** of Ninurta at any given time, at least in the *sattukku* archive, as opposed to several **lukur**/*nadītum* priestesses that were attested over longer periods of time.[30] Another possible explanation may be that these priestesses lived and acted in very different spheres and that **NIN-dingir** priestesses simply may not have needed to be mentioned in legal or administrative records due to the nature of their duties.

Were the **NIN** and the **NIN-dingir** priestesses of Ninurta one and the same? Huber Vuillet (2019: 108–109) indicated that the title **NIN-dingir** of Ninurta replaces the title **NIN** of Ninurta in the first half of the second millennium,

---

28 See, for example, Stone, 1982; 1991; Robertson 1992; Goddeeris 2016.

29 4-column tablets do not mention the term **$sá$-dug_4** but their archaeological context suggests that they were related to the Sattukku archive. In addition, they mention redistributions of food offerings, though their purpose is not entirely clear.

30 See Goddeeris 2016: vol. II pp. 449–50, they are attested for the reigns of Warad-Sin, Rim-Sin, and Samsuiluna. Thus, the attestations of the **lukur** priestesses overlap chronologically with the Sattukku archive.

referencing the Old Babylonian temple archive of Ninurta's temple at Nippur, studied by Sigrist (1984). However, there are several problems with this suggestion. First, it is not clear at all whether the archive studied by Sigrist is in fact the archive of the Ninurta temple. The *sattukku* archive's affiliation is still a matter of dispute for several reasons: F.R. Kraus (1985: 533) already pointed out that the name of Ninurta's temple, the Ešumeša, is never mentioned in the archive, which instead mentions the E'igišugalamma. Moreover, Zettler (2003: 11–13) suggested that the archaeological context indicates that the archive may have been kept near or in the Inana temple in Nippur and may be an example of cross-institutional collaboration. The latter suggestion is not unlikely. It is possible that the archive did not belong to a single temple but instead may have been part of a centralized or semi-centralized administration of food offerings (Brisch 2017: 45). If that was indeed the case, then perhaps the highest priestess of Ninurta, the **NIN** priestess, may appear in other archival texts from Nippur. This brings me to the second point, which makes the suggestion that the title **NIN** was replaced by **NIN-dingir** in Old Babylonian Nippur problematic: a substantial number of administrative records from Old Babylonian Nippur are still unpublished, in particular those from the pre-World War II excavations. The archival documents at the Penn Museum, studied by Robertson (1981) remain unpublished, as do the records from the administration of animal offerings that are now kept at Istanbul Archaeological Museums (see Çiğ 1992). As long as these substantial records remain unpublished, it is difficult to draw firm conclusions. The attestations of the titles **NIN ^{d}nin-urta** discussed above would make it hard to argue that it was the same as the title **NIN-dingir ^{d}nin-urta**.

As presented earlier, the title **NIN** of Ninurta is attested from the Old Akkadian to the Old Babylonian period and appears both in year names and independently of years names in administrative documents. The title **NIN-dingir** of Ninurta is attested in the Ur III and Old Babylonian periods and also appears both in year names and independent of year names in the administrative record, even though the office of the **NIN-dingir** priestess itself is older. The confusion of the titles **en**, **NIN** and *ēntum* seems to have begun in the Old Akkadian period, when Tuṭṭanapšum, daughter of Naram-Sin, was appointed high priestess of Enlil at Nippur. She is attested with the titles **en**, **NIN**, and *ēntum*, which all seem to indicate the highest priestly office of Enlil (Huber Vulliet 2019: 53). Perhaps the title **NIN**, originally the title of the highest priestess of Ninurta at Nippur, began being used for other gods, including Enlil, and then became identified with the Akkadian title *ēntum*, yet this has to remain speculative. It is possible that changes in the priestly hierarchy necessitated the introduction of another priestess of Ninurta, who then received the title **NIN-dingir** in the Ur III period.

We know from other cases that Ur III kings created new offices of **NIN-dingir** priestesses for their own worship as divine kings (Brisch 2006), so the possibility that a new priestly office was created during the Ur III period is not entirely unlikely. By the Old Babylonian period, when the titles of priestesses already began being forgotten or not transmitted properly (see above), **NIN** and **NIN-dingir** may have begun being confused at times, which may explain the different identifications with the Akkadian titles *ēntum* and *ugbabtum*. Although the overall number of attestations of these priestly titles is rather small, I believe it still is important, especially if and when more data are uncovered, to firmly distinguish between these two titles and to assume for the time being that these were two distinct priestly offices.

Possible Duties of the NIN and NIN-dingir Priestesses

What were some of the possible functions of the **NIN** or **NIN-dingir** priestess of Ninurta at Nippur? According to Renger (1967: 143), the **NIN-dingir** appears to have been lower in status than the **en**-priestess, though the latter is mostly attested for the highest gods, while the **NIN-dingir** is also attested for lower gods. However, as Sigrist (1984: 162) has already remarked, one can hardly refer to Enki, Ninurta, and Sîn as lower gods. Renger (1967: 144) suggested some kind of involvement in the sacred marriage rite, but, as he himself admitted, there is no direct evidence for this. And, moreover, Steinkeller (1999: 121) has already underlined that it is unlikely that she would have served as a god's spouse, since this priestly office is attested both for male and female deities. He indicated instead that the priestess may originally have served as a deity's servant (ibid.). As mentioned above, in the Ur III period, some **NIN-dingir** priestesses were assigned to attend to the worship of deified kings, and this appears to have included both the rituals surrounding living and deceased deified kings (Brisch 2006).

Several scholars have speculated about the roles that the high priestesses played in religious rites. In some cases, modern scholars have embellished her role with various sexual aspects that have little or no basis in the evidence, and I will only mention two examples here: the first one is Igor Diakonoff, who speculated that **NIN-dingir** priestesses at Ur worked as prostitutes in a bordello, which was located in Pater Noster row 8–10 (Diakonoff 1986). Stol's (2000: 462 n. 36) succinct assessment is cited here: "Die Beweisführung überzeugt indes nicht." Though Diakonoff may not be representative of current scholarship, priestesses are still discussed frequently in the context of temple prostitution, be it to affirm or refute the notion of women as sacred prostitutes.[31]

On the opposite end of the spectrum is the scholarly literature expressing the opinion that high priestesses had to remain celibate or were not allowed to have children, an opinion that is mainly based on the mythological tale of Atramhasis, the Babylonian story of the flood. At the end of the myth, several priestly offices (*ugbabtu, ēntu*, and *igiṣītu* priestesses) were created. The priestesses were designated as taboo (*ikkibu*) as a means to curb childbirth and hence population growth. Yet, from documentary sources we know that some priestesses had children, adopted children, or married. Already in the Old Akkadian record there are attestations that the famous **en**-priestess of Enlil in Nippur, Tuṭṭanabšum, had at least one child, thus making it unlikely that the **en** of Enlil in Nippur was required to remain celibate (J. Goodnick Westenholz 1992: 303; N.L. Kraus 2020: 92). Additionally, several "laws" of the Code of Hammurabi discuss circumstances surrounding the marriages of **lukur**/*nadītum* priestesses and their children.[32] Literary texts and the Code of Hammurabi are not unbiased sources, but data from legal and administrative texts offer increasing substantiation that at least some priestesses got married, had children, and even adopted children, though, admittedly, it is not clear whether **NIN** and **NIN-dingir** priestesses were allowed to do the same.

There are strong indications that high priestesses had to undergo elaborate purification rituals as part of their initiation (J. Goodnick Westenholz 1989: 546), perhaps even involving the shaving ceremony. Huber Vulliet (2014) reconstructed installation rituals of high priests and priestesses on the basis of two administrative documents of the Ur III period. If her reconstruction is correct, the high priests and priestesses also had to undergo ritual cleansing, shaving, and nail clipping before being installed in their offices. From the first millennium, we know that such purification rituals enabled priests and other persons of special relevance (e.g. carpenters that had to repair a divine statue) to enter into the inner sanctum of the temple. Only few people were allowed to enter

31 For a more detailed discussion of temple prostitution see Brisch 2021b with further literature.

32 A paragraph in the Laws of Ur-Namma is unfortunately too broken to offer a sound interpretation. Civil (2011: 247) transliterates and translates: "tukum-bi ereš-dingir [. . .]-ba lú úr-na ba-ná . . . (no satisfactory reconstruction). If someone sleeps with a high-priestess . . ." Civil (2011: 258) suggested that the break may have included either punishment for the man or provisions for the children resulting from the encounter. Civil also pointed to the Laws of Lipit-Eštar (§22, see Roth 1997: 30), which provides the following statement: "If a father, during his lifetime, consents for his daughter (to become) a **NIN-dingir**, a **lukur**, or a **nu-gig** priestess, they shall divide the estate (treating her) like an heir."

into the innermost parts of the sanctuary and those that were allowed to enter had to undergo purification first (Löhnert 2010; Waerzeggers and Jursa 2008). In the first millennium, women were not allowed to serve in these rituals (Waerzeggers 2010; Monery 2016), yet, the purification rituals of priestesses in the third and second millennia strongly indicate that priestesses were able to enter into the proximity of the divine, perhaps to offer foods to the gods for their daily meals.[33] For example, one of the hymnic texts about Enheduanna (J. Goodnick Westenholz 1989: 552–55, text B) mentions her undergoing purification rituals and being involved in the preparation of food offerings. If indeed the **NIN** of Ninurta was the equivalent of the **en**/*ēntum* of other deities, she may also have overseen, among other things, the god's daily meals, perhaps ensuring the correct presentation of the foods. Perhaps the **NIN-dingir** priestess may have assisted the **NIN** originally, or, as a kind of "lady-in-waiting," she may have been in charge of other aspects of presenting the daily meals, yet this all remains speculative. However, if some of the reconstructions outlined above are correct, these priestesses were charged with the performance of some of the most sacred rituals in the temple. This might explain why these women only appear relatively rarely in the documentary record that dealt with the more mundane aspects of the acquisition of food offerings or other ritual paraphernalia. Thus far, we have no knowledge of whether **NIN** and **NIN-dingir** priestesses lived in separate living quarters. Nippur texts mention a place called **ki-lukur-ra**, literally the "place of the **lukur** priestesses," yet there are clear indications that this was not a living quarter in Nippur that was reserved only for sacred women (Brisch 2021a: 590).

Conclusions

The titles **NIN** and **NIN-dingir** of the god Ninurta offer an opportunity to discuss the roles of women serving as priestesses in ancient Mesopotamia. While already the correct reading of these titles poses many challenges and while I do not wish to exclude the possibility that the titles were read **ereš** and **ereš-dingir** respectively, it is also important to acknowledge the general difficulties in the reading of these priestly titles and to acknowledge possible historical changes and reinterpretations. The Akkadian glosses of female body parts to what were originally titles of priestesses in the Old Babylonian Lu list show that

33 I will discuss this further in my forthcoming book on *Feeding the Gods*.

at least some titles were no longer understood by the time lexical lists received glosses, syllabic spellings, and translations into other languages.

Additionally, the available data cannot be used to argue that these women, often women of high standing, were either sacred prostitutes or celibate, childless virgins. Instead, it is necessary to further explore possible alternative explanations for their roles as temple officials. That they received rations as part of the redistribution of food offerings, coupled with their having to undergo ritual purification shows that they were able to approach the divine and thus were active participants in rituals, perhaps even in the ritual of offering foods to the gods. As such, high priestesses would have been part of a select group of individuals that were allowed to enter into the inner sanctuary of the temple, perhaps an equivalent of the *ērib bīti* of the first millennium.

To return to the starting point for this contribution: if one were to read the oppression of women into the historical record, one could argue that high priestesses were temple prostitutes or celibate nuns. Yet, this image needs to be subjected to a rigorous methodological examination, and this examination will uncover that the evidence for high priestesses having been temple prostitutes or celibate nuns is rather thin if not non-existent, and that to the contrary, there is actual evidence that at least some priestesses had children and got married. To separate out modern interpretation of ancient sources, to subject these sources to a rigorous source critique, and to contemplate alternative explanations (instead of the obvious ones) should be the historian's task.

Bibliography

Arnaud, Daniel. 1987. *Recherches au pays d'Aštata*. Emar VI/4. Paris: Editions Recherche sur les civilisations.

Attinger, Pascal. 2021. *Glossaire sumérienne-français principalement des textes littéraires paléobabyloniens*. Wiesbaden: Harrassowitz.

Bahrani, Zainab. 2001. *Women of Babylon. Gender and Representation in Mesopotamia*. London: Routledge.

Barberon, Lucile. 2012. *Les religieuses et le culte de Marduk dans le royaume de Babylone*. Archibab, vol. 1. Paris: SEPOA.

Bauer, Josef. 1998. Der vorsargonische Abschnitt der Mesopotamischen Geschichte. Pp. 429–585 in Robert K. Englund, Manfred Krebernik, Josef Bauer, *Mesopotamien. Späturuk-Zeit und Frühdynastische Zeit*. Mesopotamien, 1. Freiburg, Schweiz: Universitätsverlag.

Bauer, Josef. 2019. Zum altsumerischen Onomastikon. *OrNS* 88: 83–93.

Beckman, Gary. 1995. *Old Babylonian Archival Texts in the Nies Babylonian Collection*. Catalogue of the Babylonian Collections at Yale, 2. Bethesda, Maryland: CDL Press.

Brisch, Nicole. 2006. The Priestess and the King: The Divine Kingship of Šū-Sîn of Ur. *JAOS* 126: 161–76.

Brisch, Nicole. 2017. To Eat Like a God: Religion and Economy in Old Babylonian Nippur. Pp. 43–53 in *At the Dawn of History: Ancient Near Eastern Studies in Honour of J.N. Postgate*, ed. Yağmur Heffron, Adam Stone, and Martin Worthington. Winona Lake, Indiana: Eisenbrauns.

Brisch, Nicole. 2021a. The Marginalization of Priestesses in Ancient Mesopotamia. Pp. 585–94 in *Pearls, Politics and Pistachios: Essays in Anthropology and Memories on the Occasion of Susan Pollock's 65th Birthday*, ed. Aydin Abar, et al. Berlin: ex oriente e.V.

Brisch, Nicole. 2021b. Šamhat: Deconstructing Temple Prostitution One Woman at a Time. Pp. 77–90 in *Powerful Women in the Ancient World: Perception and (Self)Presentation. Proceedings of the 8th Melammu Workshop, Kassel, 30* January *– 1 February 2019*, ed. Kerstin Droß-Krüpe and Sebastian Fink. Melammu Workshops and Monographs, 4. Münster: Zaphon.

Butler, Judith. 1990. *Gender Trouble, Feminism and the Subversion of Identity*. New York: Routledge.

Charpin, Dominique, and Jean-Marie Durand. 1981. Textes paléo-babyloniens divers du Musée du Louvre. *RA* 75: 15–29.

Çiğ, Muazzez İ. 1992. Eski Babil Çağina ait iki Tüketim Listesi. Pp. 91–96 in *Hittite and Other Anatolian and Near Eastern Studies in Honour of Sedat Alp*, ed. Heinrich Otten et al. Ankara: Türk Tarih Kurumu Basımevi.

Civil, Miguel. 1969. *The Series lú = ša and Related Texts*. MSL 12. Rome: Pontificium Institum Biblicum.

Civil, Miguel. 1979. *Ea A = nâqu, Aa A = nâqu, with their Forerunners and Related Texts*. MSL 14. Rome: Pontificium Institutum Biblicum.

Civil, Miguel. 2011. The Law Collection of Ur-Namma. Pp. 221–89 in *Cuneiform Royal Inscriptions and Related Texts in the Schøyen Collection*, ed. Andrew R. George. CUSAS, 17. Bethesda, MD: CDL Press.

De Boer, Rients. 2021. Studies on the Old Babylonian Kings of Isin and Their Dynasties with an Updated List of Isin Year Names. *ZA* 111: 5–27.

De Graef, Katrien. 2016. *Cherchez la femme!* The Economic Role of Women in Old Babylonian Sippar. Pp. 270–95 in *The Role of Women in Work and Society in the Ancient Near East*, ed. Brigitte Lion and Cécile Michel. SANER, 13. Berlin: DeGruyter.

De Graef, Katrien. 2018. *In Taberna Quando Sumus*. On Taverns, *Nadītum* Women, and the *Gagûm* in Old Babylonian Sippar. Pp. 77–115 in *Gender and Methodology in the Ancient Near* East. *Approaches from Assyriology and Beyond*, ed. Stephanie L. Budin et al. Barcino Monographica Orientalia, 10 Barcelona: Edicions de la Universitat de Barcelona.

Diakonoff, Igor M. 1986. Women In Old Babylonia Not under Patriarchal Authority. *JESHO* 29: 225–38.

Fleming, Daniel. 1992. *The Installation of Baal's High Priestess at Emar. A Window on Ancient Syrian Religion*. HSS, 42. Atlanta, Georgia: Scholars Press.

Frayne, Douglas R. 1993. *Sargonic and Gutian Periods (2334-2113 BC)*. RIME, 2. Toronto: The University of Toronto Press.

Goddeeris, Anne. 2016. *The Old Babylonian Legal and Administrative Texts in the Hilprecht Collection Jena*. Texte und Materialien der Frau Professor Hilprecht Collection of Babylonian Antiquities im Eigentum der Friedrich Schiller Universität Jena, 10. Wiesbaden: Harrassowitz.

Goodnick Westenholz, Joan. 1989. Enheduanna, En-Priestess, Hen of Nanna, Spouse of Nanna. Pp. 539–56 in *Dumu-E_2-Dub-Ba. Studies in Honor of Åke W. Sjöberg*, ed. Hermann Behrens et al. OPKF, 11. Philadelphia: The University Museum.

Goodnick Westenholz, Joan. 1992. The Clergy of Nippur: the Priestess of Enlil. Pp. 297–310 in *Nippur at the Centennial. Papers Read at the 35e Rencontre Assyriologique Internationale, Philadelphia, 1988*, edited by Maria DeJ. Ellis. OPKF, 14. Philadelphia: The Museum of the University of Pennsylvania.

Harris, Rivkah. 1964. The *Nadītu* Woman. Pp. 107–35 in *Studies Presented to A. Leo Oppenheim. June 7, 1964*. Chicago: The Oriental Institute of the University of Chicago.

Harris, Rivkah. 1975. *Ancient Sippar. A Demographic Study of an Old Babylonian City, 1895-1595 B.C.* PIHANS, vol. 35. Istanbul: Nederlands Historisch-Archaeologisch Instituut Te Istanbul.

Huber Vulliet, Fabienne. 2010. Un festival Nippurite à l'époque paléobabylonienne. Pp. 125–50 in *Your Praise is Sweet. A Memorial Volume for Jeremy Black from Students, Colleagues and Friends*, ed. Heather Baker et al. London: The British Institute for the Study of Iraq.

Huber Vulliet, Fabienne. 2014. De la ville au temple: l'intronisation du haut-clerge babylonien à la fin dy troisième millenaire av. J.-C. Pp. 25–46 in *Life, Death, and Coming of Age in Antiquity: Individual Rites of Passage in the Ancient Near East and Adjacent Regions*, ed. Alice Mouton and Julie Patrier, 25–42. PIHANS, 124. Leiden: Nederlands Instituut Voor Het Nabije Oosten.

Huber Vulliet, Fabienne. 2019. *Le personnel cultuel à l'époque néo-sumérienne (ca. 2160-2003 av. J.-C.)*. BPOA, 14. Madrid: Consejo Superior de Investigaciones Científicas.

Izreel, Shlomo. 1997. *The Amarna Scholarly Tablets*. CM, 9. Groningen: Styx Publications.

Karahashi, Fumi. 2017. Royal Nurses and Midwives in Presargonic Lagaš Texts. Pp. 159–71 in *The First Ninety Years: A Sumerian Celebration in Honor of Miguel Civil*, edited by Lluís Feliu et al. SANER, 12. Berlin: De Gruyter.

Katz, Dina. 2003. *The Image of the Netherworld in the Sumerian Sources*. Bethesda, Maryland: CDL Press.

Koslova, Natalya. n.d. Heremitage 3, 110. http://cdli.ucla.edu/P212090.

Kraus, Fritz R. 1985. Eine altbabylonische Buchhaltung aus einem Amtsarchiv in Nippur. *BiOr* 42: 522–41.

Kraus, Nicholas L. 2020. Tuṭṭanabšum. Princess, Priestess, Goddess. *JANEH* 7: 85–99.

Lecompte, Camille. 2013. *Archaic Tablets and Fragments from Ur (ATFU). From L. Woolley's excavations at the Royal Cemetery*. Nisaba, 25. Messina: DiCAM.

Limet, Henri. *L'Anthroponomymie sumerienne dans les documents de la 3re dynastie d'Ur*. Paris: Société d'Édition «Les Belles Lettres».

Löhnert, Anne. 2010. Reconsidering the Consecration of Priests in ancient Mesopotamia. Pp. 183–91. In *Your Praise is Sweet. A Memorial Volume for Jeremy Black from Students, Colleagues and Friends*, ed. Heather Baker et al. London: The British Institute for the Study of Iraq.

Maekawa, Kazuya. 1997. The Agricultural Texts of Lagash in the British Museum (XI). *ASJ* 19: 113–45.

Marchesi, Gianni. 2004. Who Was Buried in the Royal Tombs of Ur? The Epigraphic and Textual Data. *OrNS* 73: 153–97.

Marchesi, Gianni. 2006. *Lumma in the Onomasticon and Literature of Ancient Mesopotamia*. HANES 10. Padova: S.A.R.G.O.N.

Monaco, Salvatore F. 2016. *Archaic Cuneiform Tablets from Private Collections*. CUSAS 31. Bethesda, MD: CDL Press.

Monery, Julien. 2016. Women and Prebends in Seleucid Uruk. Pp. 526–42 in *The Role of Women in Work and Society in the Ancient Near East*, ed. Brigitte Lion and Cécile Michel, SANER, 13. Berlin: DeGruyter.

Renger, Johannes. 1967. Untersuchungen zum Priestertum in der altbabylonischen Zeit, Teil 1. *ZA* 58: 110–88.

Richter, Thomas. 2004. *Untersuchungen zu den lokalen Panthea Süd- und Mittelbabyloniens in altbabylonischer Zeit. 2., verbesserte und erweiterte Auflage*. AOAT, 257. Münster: Ugarit-Verlag.

Robertson, John F. 1981. Redistributive Economies in Ancient Mesopotamian Society. A Case Study from Isin-Larsa Period Nippur. PhD dissertation, University of Pennsylvania.

Robertson, John F. 1992. The Temple Economy of Old Babylonian Nippur: the Evidence for Central Management. Pp. 177–88 in *Nippur at the Centennial. Papers Read at the 35^{e} Rencontre Assyriologique Internationale, Philadelphia, 1988*, ed. Maria DeJ. Ellis. OPKF, 14. Philadelphia: The Museum of the University of Pennsylvania.

Roth, Martha T. 1997. *Law Collections from Mesopotamia and Asia Minor*. "2. " edition. WAW, 6. Atlanta, GA: Scholars Press / Society of Biblical Literature.

Sallaberger, Walther. 1997. Nippur als religiöses Zentrum Mesopotamiens im historischen Wandel. Pp. 147–68 in *Die Orientalische Stadt: Kontinuität, Wandel, Bruch*, ed. Gernot Wilhelm. CDOG, 1. Saarbrücken: SDV Saarbrücker Druckerei und Verlag.

Sigrist, Marcel. 1977. Offrandes dans le temple de Nusku à Nippur. *JCS* 29: 169–83.

Sigrist, Marcel. 1984. *Les satukku dans l'Ešumeša durant la periode d'Isin et Larsa*. Bibliotheca Mesopotamica, 11. Malibu, CA: Undena.

Sigrist, Marcel. 1988. *Isin Year Names*. Institute of Archaeology Publications, Assyriological Series, vol. II. Berrien Springs, Michigan: Andrews University Press.

Steinkeller, Piotr. 1999. On Rulers, Priests and Sacred Marriage. Tracing the Evolution of Early Sumerian Kingship. Pp. 103–37 in *Priests and Officials in the Ancient Near* East. *Papers of the Second Colloquium on the Ancient Near East – The City and Its Life, held at the Middle Eastern Culture Center in Japan (Mitaka, Tokyo), March 22–24, 1996*, ed. Kazuko Watanabe. Heidelberg: Universitätsverlag C. Winter.

Stol, Marten. 1998–2001. Nippur. A.II. Altbabylonisch. *RlA* 9: 539–44.

Stol, Marten. 2000. Titel altbabylonischer Klosterfrauen. Pp. 457–66 in *Assyriologica et Semitica. Festschrift für Joachim Oelsner*, ed. Joachim Marzahn and Hans Neumann. AOAT, 252. Münster: Ugarit-Verlag.

Stol, Marten. 2016. *Women in the Ancient Near East*. Translated by Helen and Mervyn Richardson. Berlin: DeGruyter.

Stone, Elizabeth. 1982. The Social Role of the Nadītu in Old Babylonian Nippur. *JESHO* 25: 50–70.

Such-Gutiérrez, Marcos. 2003. *Beiträge zum Pantheon von Nippur im 3. Jahrtausend*. Teil 1. MVS, 9/1. Rome: Università degli Studi di Roma "La Sapienza."

Van De Mieroop, Marc. 1987. *Crafts in the Early Isin* Period. *A* Study *of the Isin Craft Archive From the Reigns of Išbi-Erra and Šū-ilišu*. OLA, 24. Leuven: Department Oriëntalistiek.

Veldhuis, Niek. 2014. *History of the Cuneiform Lexical Tradition*. GMTR, 6. Münster: Ugarit-Verlag.

Waerzeggers, Caroline. 2010. *The Ezida Temple of Borsippa. Priesthood, Cult, Archives*. Achaemenid History, XV. Leiden: Nederlands Instituut voor het Nabeje Oosten.

Waerzeggers, Caroline, with a contribution of Michael Jursa. 2008. On the Initiation of Babylonian Priests. *Zeitschrift für Altorientalische und Biblische Rechtsgeschichte* 14: 1–38.
Westenholz, Aage. 1975. *Early Cuneiform Texts in Jena: Pre-Sargonic and Sargonic Documents from Nippur and Fara in the Hilprecht Sammlung Vorderasiatischer Altertümer, Institut für Altertumswissenschaften der Friedrich Schiller Universität, Jena*. Copenhagen: The Royal Academy / Munksgaard.
Wiggerman, Frans A.M. 1998–2001. Nergal. A. Philologisch. *RlA* 9: 215–23.
Zettler, Richard. 2003. Reconstructing the World of Ancient Mesopotamia: Divided Beginnings and Holistic History. *JESHO* 46: 3–45.

Ada Taggar-Cohen

Hittite Royal Ideology and the Uniqueness of the Priestess Titled NIN.DINGIR

1 Introduction to the Hittite NIN.DINGIR

The Hittite NIN.DINGIR has been my "friend" for a long time, in fact ever since I started studying the Hittite priesthood.[1] I was fascinated by her, especially since she was never named as a person, nor as a historical figure, although her prescribed performances are included in the category of royal cultic texts. According to these texts, she was to perform together with figures titled as the king, queen and crown-prince; together with them she officiated in the main state festivals. While kings, queens, and crown princes were recorded as historical figures of the Hittite kingdom in other genres apart from the cultic corpus, the NIN.DINGIR appears only in prescribed cultic texts originating from the royal archives of Ḫattuša, without any reference to a specific historical period or a historical name.[2]

1.1 The Background of Hittite Royal Ideology

As is well known to those who study Hittite texts, these texts originate from royal archives, reflecting the concerns of the ruling elite and the Hittite royal administration. In many cases, the Hittite rituals found in these texts also fall into the

1 I wish to thank Prof. Theo van den Hout, Chief Editor of the Chicago Hittite Dictionary, for letting me use the Hittite Dictionary files at the Oriental Institute of the University of Chicago during my Sabbatical period as a visiting scholar of the Department of NELC in 2014. The follow-up research was supported by a grant from the Japan Society for the Promotion of Science for the years 2017–2021 (17K02234). I also thank Prof. Fumi Karahashi for inviting me to read a first draft of this article in the international workshop on "Women's Religious and Economic Roles in Antiquity" in November 10–11, 2017 at Chuo University.

In this paper the transliteration of the title of the priestess follows the way Hittitologists use. Any Sumerian cuneiform sign is transliterated in capital letters thus – NIN.DINGIR/EREŠ.DINGIR.

2 The most comprehensive and detailed work on this Hittite title appears in my book, showing her to have been a royal priestess, Taggar-Cohen 2006a: 384–422. See also my study of the title NIN.DINGIR among the Hittites in relation to Mesopotamian titles and the Sumerian title nin-dingir, Taggar-Cohen 2006b. I would like to indicate here that all texts mentioning the NIN. DINGIR come from the capital Ḫattuša main archives: largely from Büyükkale, the scriptorium in the House on the Slope and the magazines of the main temple.

https://doi.org/10.1515/9781501514821-009

category of administrative texts, since they were prepared and copied for administrative use, prescribing the enactment of rituals whenever the circumstances demanded their performance by the royals.

We now know the Hittites who spoke the Hittite language were of Indo-European origin. They arrived in central Anatolia at the turn of the second millennium and became assimilated with the indigenous inhabitants who were of Ḫattian origin, while retaining their language and customs. From the Ḫattians they received the essential elements of their religion which directly reflected their idea of royal ideology as depending on the divine world and the kings' and queens' relations with it (Beckman 1995: 529–43).

The Hittite archives reveal texts written in several languages: Hittite is the main one, but within the Hittite texts the use of the Ḫattian language (one of the most ancient languages of Anatolia known to us today), Ḫurrian, and Luwian can also be found, as well as texts originating from Mesopotamia, or translated from Hittite, written in the Sumerian and Akkadian languages. It seems that the Hittites (probably like many other royal courts in the ANE) collected religious, mythological and historical texts from their surrounding cultures. In some ways, these collections might be misleading because when we come across such material, we incorporate it into our analysis of Hittite culture. As has been shown recently by Theo van den Hout, some of the texts of foreign origin, that is Sumero-Akkadian or Ḫurrian, may have belonged to the scholarly elite of scribes who studied these texts with the aim of broadening their own knowledge (Van den Hout 2009, 2015). In this context what was the place of the ritual genre within the ideological work of the elite, serving their royal family?

An overview of the religious developments in Hittite history shows that early on the Hittites had an obvious cultural acceptance of the indigenous people of central Anatolia – the Ḫattians – from whom their concept of royal ideology stems, but then there was a phase of strong Ḫurrian religious influence on the royal house from around 1400 BCE until the end of the kingdom in 1180 BCE. Meanwhile there was also constant influence of the Luwian religion on the Hittite royal family, as Luwians formed a large part of the population of the kingdom especially during the New Kingdom (Collins 2007: 157–58; Hutter 2003: 216–19).

Hittite royal ideology relied on two important sources of authority for its legitimacy: the gods of kingship, mainly the Storm-god of Ḫatti and the Sun-goddess of the city Arinna, and a group of ancient Ḫattian gods, especially the goddess Ḫalmaššuitt – the deity represented by the throne (Collins 2007: 92–98; Gilan-Mouton 2014). Hittite royalty also worshiped some of their deified ancestors, spanning several hundred years of royal history (Collins 2007: 193–95). The mundane existence of the kings depended on the realms of the divine world.

This can be clearly seen in the constant communication of the kings with their gods through oracles and prayers, and their dedication to worshipping the gods.

The two sources of the divine realm – the gods and the deified royal ancestors – were the center of royal worship, which was prescribed for them and written down by the scribes of the kingdom.[3] The actions of the royal family – king, queen, crown-prince – together with specific cult personnel as well as important figures of the court are prescribed in detail in these recorded texts for each festival and ritual. Among these state festival-texts a person with the title of NIN.DINGIR appears as an officiating member, next to other royal figures.

1.2 The Title NIN.DINGIR

The Sumerograms NIN.DINGIR in Hittite texts are part of large number of Sumerograms that entered the Hittite writing system, due to Hittite scribes mostly using them as logograms to be read with Hittite language equivalents. The Sumerograms could come with or without a Hittite complement, such as NIN.DINGIR with no case complement versus NIN.DINGIR-*aš* (nom.); NIN.DINGIR-*an* (acc.) etc. with the case complement. Unfortunately, so far, we have no parallel text that reveals the Hittite title behind the Sumerograms NIN.DINGIR.

The Hittite writing system was developed based on the system of Old Babylonian cuneiform used in Alalaḫ in the first part of the second millennium (Van den Hout 2009: 71–96; Weeden 2011b: 603). Therefore, the way of reading the signs refers back to the Old Babylonian period. Still, it has been shown in recent research that the Hittites had their own way of using Sumerian and Akkadian words as logograms. As indicated by Weeden, at the same time the Hittites incorporated the cuneiform system from north Syria, they also used logograms from the Akkadian language as Akkadian words, while the Sumerograms were understood as logograms for Hittite words (Weeden 2011a: 333–84).[4]

In recent Mesopotamian research the reading of the title of the NIN.DINGIR priestess in Sumerian was changed to EREŠ.DINGIR, although some scholars still maintain the reading of NIN.DINGIR (Stol 2016: 566). Scholars of Hittite seem to have adopted this new reading. However, I argue that we should keep the reading NIN.DINGIR in the Hittite texts for the following reasons:

---

3 For a description of the rituals and festivals of the Hittites and the different terminology used see Schwemer 2016.

4 For a recent detailed and enlightening study of the literacy in the Hittite kingdom, see Van den Hout 2020. On the adoption of the cuneiform script by the Hittite, see pp. 101–19.

The Sumerogram NIN (MUNUS+TÚG), the first of the combination NIN.DINGIR is used in Hittite to indicate "sister." It is used in Hittite texts next to other Sumerograms for family members such as wives, sons, daughters, and brothers, and is read as the Hittite word "*nega-/neka-*".[5] The combination NIN.DINGIR in Hittite should then be considered in relation to other titles written Sumerographically in Hittite relating to the royal family. Other Sumerograms relating to royalty, that are combined in order to indicate titles for a profession or function, are as follows in the Hittite corpus; the way they are transliterated by scholars indicates what the scholars think they represent in Hittite:

^{d}UTU-*ŠI* = "my sun-god" (the title for the Hittite great king) written with Sumerogram and Akkadogram the king uses this to speak of himself, and his subjects also refer to him with this title[6]
LUGAL GAL = "great king" (a noun and an adjective in hit. *šalli-*"great" *ḫaššu-* "king")
MUNUS.LUGAL = within the category of king, she is the female[7] (MUNUS in hit. *kuwan* "woman")[8]
DUMU.LUGAL= within the category of king, he is a child/son (DUMU-*laš*, hit. unknown[9])
DUMU.MUNUS.LUGAL = within the category of child(ren) of the king, she is female
AMA.DINGIR = within the category of divine/deity, she is a mother (hit. "*šiwanzanna-*")[10]

5 CHD, L-N: 425–28. The importance of family relations within the royal ranks may be hinted at in a letter from Puduḫepa the queen to Tattamaru (KUB 23.85), who has taken in marriage the daughter of the sister of Puduḫepa, thus becoming an in-law of the queen, written in the text in Akkadogram ^{LÚ}*ḪA-TÁ-NU* (in Akkadian the husband of one's daughter – here for the sister of the queen not of the queen herself!). For the edition of this letter see Hoffner 2009: 364–65. More on this below.

6 The Hittite reading is not recorded. The Akkadian reading of this title is *Šamšī*, which is already found in Old Babylonian texts and was used to refer to Zimrilim king of Mari. Beckman (2002: 15–21) suggests the reading of *ištanuš-miš* in Hittite. For attestations, see Weeden 2011a: 642–46.

7 Ašmunikkal, the Hittite queen of the 14th century BCE, calls herself: MUNUS.LUGAL GAL "great queen": see the opening to her decreed instructions in KUB 13.8 obv. 1: *UM-MA* ^{MUNUS}*AŠ-MU*-^{d}NIN.GAL-aš MUNUS.LUGAL GAL "Thus (says) Ašmunikkal, the Great Queen." For more attestations, see Weeden 2011a: 585.

8 The assumed reading of the Hittite noun for a queen is **ḫaššuššara-*, however, this noun has never appeared in the texts up to now. See Kloekhorst 2008: 328, and HW^2 H: 457. For a recent study of *kuwan-*, see Süel and Weeden 2019.

9 The Sumerogram DUMU seems to stand for "child" and "son" while female had to be indicated with MUNUS.DUMU. See Weeden 2011a: 202; and for the treatment of DUMU.LUGAL/DUMU.MUNUS.LUGAL, see pp. 210–11.

10 For a discussion of the historical formation of the Sumerograms, see Taggar-Cohen: 2006a: 30–31.

NIN.DINGIR = within the category of divine/deity, she is a sister (NIN= hit. "*nega-/neka*")[11]
LÚ.SANGA / MUNUS.SANGA = male priest (hit. *šankuni-*) / female priest (hit. unknown)[12]
LÚ ^{d}U / MUNUS ^{d}U = in regard to the Storm-god, he is a man / she is a woman

The relations between the Sumerograms are either of an adjectival or of genitival construction "of." In any case the combinations are of two nouns. If read as a genitival construction, NIN.DINGIR in Hittite should be translated as "the sister of the deity (god/goddess)." This stands in correlation with AMA.DINGIR (=Mother.Deity) which is read in Hittite *šiwanzanna-* and which some scholars translate as "the mother of the deity"; this would indicate the family relationship of the two priestesses to the divine world. But if we look at MUNUS.LUGAL, the result is "female of king" or "royal woman." Thus, it is possible to read AMA.DINGIR in an adjectival form "divine(ly) mother." For NIN.DINGIR, an adjectival construction would then be "divine sister."[13] Of course, we could say that since this relationship is metaphorical, it can be interpreted both ways. But if we look carefully at the examples, it seems that titles related to the royal family and those related to the gods should not be interpreted differently. That is, we have a family construction for royal family members officiating in the cult. As I have already noted in the past (Taggar-Cohen 2006a: 366–68) the Sumerogram combination ama-dingir is not found in Sumerian as a priestly title and neither is it used in Akkadian texts as a priestly title.[14] It could therefore be an innovation of Hittite scribes. I have indicated that this combination starts sometime in Middle Hittite texts as a replacement for the older title for a priestess MUNUS.SANGA. It is therefore part of those family titles relating to the divine world.[15]

---

11 Regarding the title that appears only in relation to the divine world in Hittite, we have the Sumerograms DAM.DINGIR = within the category of divine/deity, she is the wife. This should be translated as the "wife of the god (+name of god/ or city)." In Ebla this title was used for a priestess who was a daughter of the king, see Archi 1998: 43–53.

12 See CHD Š: 182ff. SANGA may also stand for another Hittite word in different period. *šankuni-* appears in the new kingdom texts.

13 For the reading of *šiwanzanna-* as adjectival form deriving from *šiwant-*, see Kloekhorst 2008: 765. It has to be pointed out here that the adjectival reading in Hittite does not correlate with the grammatical form in Sumerian that reads NIN-dingir as "lady/wife of a god," for which see Steinkeller 1999, 121.

14 In Sumerian texts mentioning **ama-dingir**, the combination does not seem to refer to a title for a female cult professional. See examples in the URL: http://bdtns.filol.csic.es/index.php?p=home.

15 Hittite titles may be written with one Sumerogram and can also be written with two or more Sumerograms. There is a question whether it was represented in Hittite with one word or with two, a direct translation from the original Sumerogram. So far Hittitologists were not able to show a systematic pattern. For detailed discussion of this complicated situation, that may have had also been developed over time, being influenced from differing cultural regions (Old

1.3 Royal Titles in Cultic Texts

In Hittite prayers, the king and queen are titled as priests of the gods; the king is titled a SANGA and the queen is an AMA.DINGIR-*LIM*.[16] This indicates that both of them are seen as officiating priests in the service of all the gods of the kingdom, even when in a prayer they may pray to one specific god or goddess. However, in all prescribed rituals in which they are to take part, they are referred to with the titles LUGAL for the king (or with another ancient title *Tabarna*) and MUNUS. LUGAL (or *Tawananna*) for the queen, not with the titles of priests; the officiating priests in these rituals appear with their professional titles such as LÚ.SANGA (of god X) or LÚ.GUDU$_{12}$ and other priestly titles.[17] This, to my understanding, is in order to distinguish clearly between the officiating functionaries. The king and queen are in their priestly capacity but it is not their position in society. Their position is at the head of the royal house. The crown-prince, titled DUMU.LUGAL, appears also with the title *tuḫ(u)kanti-/taḫukanti-* which is the title kept for the crown prince alone.[18] In these rituals' context the NIN.DINGIR is part of the royal family.

2 The Uniqueness of the NIN.DINGIR as a Royal Figure in Hittite Texts

NIN.DINGIR appears in all texts as a single officiating person.[19] All verbs indicating her actions are in the singular, and in the texts, she appears next to the king,

Assyrian, Old Babylonian, Alalah, etc.), see the careful description and treatment by Weeden 2011a: 30–38, 333–36.

16 Their titles always appear written Sumerographically. The female title uses in all forms, the Akkadogram *-LIM* standing for the genitive ending of the word *ilu-* "god" in Akkadian. For more detailed discussion, see Taggar-Cohen 2006a: 369ff.; Weeden 2011a: 146–47.

17 For the discussion on the Hittite-Luwian origin of the titles *tabarna-* "(the) powerful (one)" and *tawananna-* "(the) righteous (one)," see Melchert 2003: 18–20. He concludes: "The titles of both Hittite king and queen are thus Luwian, while that of the crown-prince [LÚ]*ta/uḫ(u)kanti-* and the word for the 'throne' *ḫalmaššuitt-* are Hattic. [. . .] Such a fusion of Hattic and Luwian elements appears more generally in Hittite notions of kingship." For more details on the main priestly titles, see Taggar-Cohen 2006a.

18 The difference in use between the titles of the prince is not clear to us. For a recent survey on the title, see Bilgin 2018: 27–36. The festival for the crown prince titled DUMU.LUGAL in CTH 647 is treated by Taracha 2017.

19 I have dedicated an entire chapter to the NIN.DINGIR in my book 2006a. In the appendix to this chapter, I have listed all the texts I used where the title NIN.DINGIR appeared. Since the publication of the online catalogue of Hittite texts http://www.hethport.uni-wuerzburg.de/HPM/index-en.php)

queen and the crown-prince in the most important state festivals. Like the king and queen, she is not identified as a NIN.DINGIR of a specific deity or a specific town, in contrast to the SANGA and $GUDU_{12}$- priests who are identified as priests to a certain god or goddess many times. The NIN.DINGIR worships all the kingdom's deities, although as will be seen in the following list of ritual festivals, she performs in a special festival dedicated to a deity named Tetešḫapi. She is attested to in the following festival texts, according to CTH numbers[20]:

627 KI.LAM- festival (A festival of the town Ḫattuša in the spring)
625&621 AN.TAḪ.ŠUM-festival (The most important state spring festival)
626 *nuntarriyašḫa* – (The most important state fall festival)
649 Fragments of festival(s) including the title NIN.DINGIR (the main source of descriptions of her)
682 Festival for the protective god(s) ^{d}LAMMA
738 Festival of the goddess Tetešḫapi (seems to be an important goddess for the NIN. DINGIR)

Of all these festivals, the most important and those dated to the Old Hittite and Middle Hittite periods are the Festival for Tetešḫapi and the Festival of the KI. LAM. Also, the fragments mentioning her, manifest an origin in the Old Hittite ductus, but it is not clear to which festival they belong.

The NIN.DINGIR appears in texts dated to the Old Hittite period, but also in texts copied in later Hittite periods; a copy of an important state festival in which she is mentioned through her Tutelary Deity, is according to its colophon, from the time of the new kingdom, since the head scribe named in it belonged to the 13th century.[21] I thus determine that the office indicated with the title NIN.DINGIR prevailed throughout the existence of the Hittite kingdom. Through the detailed studies of Hittite festival texts conducted in recent years it has become clear that these texts underwent editing and changes throughout the years of their use. It is certainly becoming apparent that the state cult festivals evolved from an accumulation of local festivals thus becoming long festivals

it has become clearer to which larger texts, many of the small fragments I used then, now belong. I stressed then and I stress now that firstly, the title stands for a female, and secondly, that she is a single person in that office in the kingdom, for which see below.

20 The texts are basically prescribed rituals for the way in which the festivals are to be conducted, therefore they describe the parts the NIN.DINGIR takes in the festivals. For examples, see 3.2 below.

21 The text KBo 19.128 ii 11 mentions the NIN.DINGIR ^{d}Zitḫariya for which, see McMahon 1991: 23 with note 125. The colophon of KBo 19.128 rev. vi 37′ mentions the head scribe Anuwanza, who is known to have worked during the reign of the Hittite kings Ḫattušili III and his son Tudḫaliya IV. See Van den Hout 1995: 238–42; Torri 2010: 389–96.

with the royal family engaged in conducting celebrations in Ḫattuša as well as throughout the core land of Ḫatti.[22]

2.1 The NIN.DINGIR's Status within the Cult

The royal status of the Hittite NIN.DINGIR meant that she had possessions, although there is no exact mention of this. Two points however may support this supposition: the first one is based on comparing her with the queen, who controlled a large part of the possessions of the kingdom and was able to use them with her own seal.[23] It seems that the NIN.DINGIR was also capable of owning estates. But as indicated we have no seals or administrative or legal documents mentioning a NIN.DINGIR in such capacities.[24] The second is a mention in one of the texts of the fall festival *nuntarriyašḫa-*. The text, after indicating that the king is leaving Ḫattuša for the city of Ḫarranašši to celebrate the festival, mentions the NIN.DINGIR going to celebrate in the house of the charioteers:

> She offers to the gods in succession. For her eating and drinking there are three palaces available – the palace of Ninašša, the house of T[uwanuwa] and the palace of Ḫupišna. Day 12. (KUB 10.48 ii 6–9)[25]

This text does not decree the availability of the houses but rather indicates that those palaces are for the NIN.DINGIR as her own resources. This is clearly a consequence of her parallel status to the king and queen and crown prince in the cultic texts.[26]

---

22 See Torri 2015: 289–300 for the *purulli* festival with Klinger 2009: 99–100. And, also Galmarini 2014: 277–95 on the festivals for Mount Puškurunuwa.

23 This is observed in different texts but especially in the prayer of Muršili II, who apologizes for having to expel the queen mother from her office which included her priestly office as AMA.DINGIR-priestess. He accuses her of using the treasures of the land under her control in wrong ways; CTH 71 translation by Singer 2002: 75–79. In the same way Ḫattušili I accuses his sister and especially daughter for exploiting Ḫattuša economically, thus plotting against him (Beckman 1997: 80–81 §§13–18). See on that below under 4.

24 Generally speaking, the Hittite archives revealed very little economic and legal material.

25 For the edition of the text, see Nakamura 2002: 20–22.

26 Siegelová 2015 presented textual material that points to the economic independence of the queen interpreted by her as a separate house income from the system of the state economy or that of the king. Vigo (2016: 351), based on the study of the "inventory tablets" records of goods transferred to the royal treasury and the great number of bullae found at Nişantepe in Ḫattuša, both including names of females of the royal house involved in the transfer of those goods, concludes: "it is noteworthy that, among the Hittites, women and men seem to operate

2.2 On the NIN.DINGIR's Cultic Activity: Textual Evidence of the Royal Priestly Role

Here follow examples of rituals in which the activity of the NIN.DINGIR is prescribed.[27]

1) The following prescribed ritual is from the state festival recorded on KUB 56.46 (a text belonging to CTH 627 KI.LAM festival with rituals in which the NIN.DINGIR officiates):

KUB 56.46 ii 1′ -7′:

> The cupbearer gives thick bread to the king. The king breaks (it). The cupbearer holds to the king a thick bread and he brings (it) forward. When they hold the cups for the king and the queen, as well as the NIN.DINGIR, the INANNA lyres they repeatedly play, (and) the *arkammi*-instrument they beat, the *ḫapiya*-men dance.[28]

2) In the text KUB 11.32, a festival for the deity Tetešḫapi (CTH 738 I.24.A[29]), we learn of the form in which the NIN.DINGIR participates in the festival:

> (iii 5–28) The SANGA-priest lifts the deity Tetešḫapi. They turn forth the carriage, and the NIN.DINGIR sits down (in it). Then she enters the city of Dawiniya. The Lords of the affair, too, proceed.

The NIN.DINGIR is treated royally by the cult members manifested by her riding in the royal carriage (^{GIŠ}*ḫuluganni*-[30]) and by the way the Lords of the city welcome her into the city. After this the women singers named *zintuḫi*- welcome her with singing in the Ḫattic language. As the festival proceeds, this female chorus continues to accompany her.

KUB 25.51 iv 8–10:

> Then the NIN.DINGIR arrives at the *arzana*-house, the *zintuḫi*-women go back to the temple.

side by side. We would cautiously suggest that, according to the little evidence we have, neither the male nor the female world was exclusive to one gender or another."

27 For more detailed quotes, see Taggar-Cohen 2006a: 390–417.

28 For a recent transliteration, see Tischler 2016: 83.

29 The text is made up as follows: KUB 25.51+KUB 20.17+ KUB 11.32+IBoT 3.68+KBo 37.51.

30 The royal or light carriage in Hittite ^{GIŠ}*ḫuluganni*- is one of the royal insignia the Hittite king boasted receiving from the Throne goddess Ḫalmaššuitt in the mythological account of establishing a house for the king recorded in CTH 414, for which see the following footnote.

And again, in KUB 11.32 v 8′–14′:

> When however, the NIN.DINGIR arrives at the temple of the deity Tetešḫapi, she descends from the carriage and enters the temple, and she bows down to the deity. 'To eat' one calls out. To all the gods she offers to drink in succession.

3) KBo 25.48 ii 1–17 (CTH 738.I.12)

> [The NIN.DINGIR] comes out. She si[ts herself] in the carriage. She goes to the temple of the deity Tetešḫapi. The NIN.DINGIR steps down [of the carriage and enters the temple]. She bows to the deity. They seat the palace attendants. They seat the overseer of the *ḫapiya*-men, the second in command [of the *ḫapiya*-men], the scepter bearer, the leopard-man, the SANGA-priest of the deity Tetešḫapi, the *menea*-man, and the man of the spear. She drinks seated the deity Mezzulla and the Sun-god. The cupbearer gives the NIN.DINGIR [some bread]. The NIN.DINGIR breaks (it). The cupbearer holds the thick bread for the NIN.DINGIR, and he carries (it) forth. The *taḫukanti* takes it from the cupbearer and places it on the wood of the beam. The table man takes two loafs of thick bread from the table and he gives to the NIN.DINGIR. The NIN.DINGIR breaks it. The table-man puts the two loafs of the thick bread on the table.

This kind of ritual takes place for a number of deities, mainly Ḫattian ones; among the most important is Ḫalmaššuit (the throne goddess). On the reverse of KBo 25.48, with no parallel texts, the following text is read in broken form:
(rev. iii 3′–10)

> [. . .] towards the deity Šiu [. . .]. Further the *zintuḫi*-women [. . .] sing in the Ḫattic (language): "*ililuwaai*"[. . .] "*ililuwaiya*". A daughter of a poor-man [. . .]. The NIN.DINGIR dan[ces] towards [her?]. The palace attendants hold the NIN.DINGIR [. . .]. The scepter bearer holds. Then further to the courtyard (of the temple) they go [. . .].

Previously, the appearance of the ^{LÚ}MASDA = the poor-man in this text, made Pecchioli Daddi connect this festival ritual with the myth told by the GUDU$_{12}$-priest named Kella during the spring *purulli*-festival (Pecchioli Daddi 2014). In this mythological account, the priest recites how the fight between two important gods, the Storm-god and the god Illuyanka, the serpent/monster of the sea, ended in the victory of the Storm-god brought about by him marrying the daughter of a poor-man who bore him a son who married the daughter of the serpent, and thus helped his father subdue the serpent. The story was chanted by the priest, and it may very well be that the NIN.DINGIR was part of this myth performance by her dancing assisted by the palace attendants and other personnel, including the *zintuḫi*-women singing and the *ḫaliyari* men and the *ḫapiya* men acting in various other ways. Her actions in this role, performed in the presence of the *taḫukanti* (= crown-prince), as well as mentions in other texts of her being together with the king and queen, shows her manifested connection with the royal family, i.e., the head cultic officiators of the royal family. The myth telling of the war between the two gods, however, is told as a war between two families, in which the daughter and the son of the two gods play a very important role in giving the victory for kingship to the Storm-god.

3 In What Way Does the NIN.DINGIR Support Hittite Royal Ideology?

The Hittite texts that describe her actions in the festival texts manifest origins in Old Hittite texts; such as, for example, the old version of the KI.LAM festival, which may have originated in the northern part of the Hittite land and was incorporated during the New Kingdom period into the KI.LAM festival of the capital Ḫattuša, and the same is also the case for the fall festival the *nuntariyašḫa-*. The NIN.DINGIR is described in these texts as part of the royal family as she rides to the palace in the royal carriage with the king and the queen. The idea of the family – and especially the royal family – plays a central role in Hittite royal ideology as is seen in the ritual for establishing a royal house/temple (CTH 414[31]).

This ritual starts with a ceremony worshiping the Storm-god and the Sun-goddess (the gods of kingship). Then the king speaks to the divine throne as follows (quotes from the text translated by Beckman 2010: 72–75):

> Come let us go! You will step behind the mountains . . . be my equal, be my friend.[32]

This means that the goddess is requested to support the king, and in the next few lines it is explained that the Storm-god and the Sun-goddess allotted the land and the house to the king. It continues declaring that: "From the sea, the Throne (goddess Ḫalmaššuitt) brought the rule and the royal carriage (^{GIŠ}*ḫuluganni-*) to me". The king and the Throne go to the forest and the Throne allows the king to cut down trees to build the house. In the next parts of the ritual the king is protected with charms, and to ensure his future health the following words are recited: "May the gods turn over to evil and crush whoever should seek evil for the king."

31 CTH 414 is one of several building texts (Beckman describes eleven, 2010: 71–89, 451–55), which suggest the background beliefs of the king building a palace or a temple both written in the text in the Sumerogram É for "house." Torri and Görke (2014) have studied five of these building ritual texts.

32 I have treated this text in detail, and specifically this phrase, as part of Hittite royal ideology in a forthcoming article (Taggar-Cohen, Forthcoming).

The text concludes with instructions regarding "when the king builds a palace in a town," and a description of the royal family entering that palace.[33] Their central place of gathering within the house is the hearth (regarded as a deity), and the family is seated around it as follows:

> The gods are seated, and the owners of the building – the King and the Queen and the secondary wives – take their seats. And they sway like gazelles(?). Then the daughters of the household take their seats. The *tuḫḫan* are in place and the *šaḫuwan* is set below. Groats are placed (on them?). The Hearth says, 'This is good for me.' Then the paternal brothers take their seats and they frolic like eagles. The Hearth says, 'This is good for me.'

Then at the end of this scene all participants kneel down at the hearth, saying:

> 'May the male and female children be numerous to the first and second generation.'
> The Hearth says, 'This is good for me.'

At the end of the ritual they offer sheep and breads to the Hearth.

Hittite royal ideology regards two things as important: firstly, the designation of the king by the Storm-god and the Sun-goddess of the town Arinna, and by the supporting partner to rulership, the Throne deity (Ḫalmaššuitt) and secondly, that rulership is a consequence of the royal family, at the head of which stand the king and queen, and next their children. In all categories, both divine and human, the male and female elements are evident.

The Hittites indeed emphasized the idea of a royal family, as we can see in two important texts. The first text is the proclamation of king Telipinu, where in the description of the previous generations he explains the strength of the kingdom due to the strong unity and loyalty of the royal family.[34]

> §1(1–4) [Fo]rmerly, Labarna was Great King, and his [son]s, [brother]s, as well as his in-laws, his (further) family members and his troops were united.[35] §2(1:5–6) The land was small but wherever he went on campaign, he held the enemy country subdued by (his) might. §3(1:7–9) He destroyed the lands, one after another, stripped(?) the lands of their power and made them the borders of the sea. When he came back from campaign, however, each (of) his sons went somewhere to a country: §4(1:10–12) The cities of Ḫupišna, Tuwanuwa, Nenašša, Landa, Zallara, Paršuḫanta (and) Lušna, the(se) countries they each governed and the great cities made progress.[36]

---

33 Some scholars suggested that this tablet is composed of two different mythical rituals. For that, see Torri and Görke 2014: 289.

34 Translation by Van den Hout 1997: 194–98.

35 Hittite: [*ka*]-*ru-ú* ^{m}*La-ba-ar-na* LUGAL GAL *e-eš-ta n*[*a*]-*pa* [DUMU]^{MEŠ}-*ŠU* [ŠEŠ]^{MEŠ}-*ŠU* LÚ^{MEŠ} *ga-e-na-aš-še-eš-ša* LÚ^{MEŠ}*ḫa-aš-ša-an-na-aš Ú* ERIN^{MEŠ}-*ŠU ta-ru-up-pa-an-te-eš e-še-ir*.

36 Interestingly the first three towns in the list are the towns where the palaces supporting the NIN.DINGIR are mentioned in KUB 10.48 ii 6–9 (see 2.1 above).

Trouble started when members, by marriage, of the family assassinated king Muršili I.

> §10 (31–33) Ḫantili the cupbearer married Ḫarpašili the sister of Muršili.
> And Zitanda had a wife the daughter of Ḫantili. Together they committed the crime.

The second text – and the older one – is known as the "Testament of Ḫattušili I," in which he explains his reasons for his decision to install Muršili (a grandchild) as his heir over his adopted son of his sister. From his *Annals'* text we learn that his father took over the throne, in special circumstances, and that he was the "son of the brother of Tawananna." He passed over his sister's son, deposed him and chose his grandson Muršili.[37] It seems, from this text, that the sister of the king had certain rights and power within the royal family that allowed her to control some of the administration especially in the capital Ḫattuša.[38] The fact that in the festivals in which the NIN.DINGIR takes part, the three important figures are the king, queen and *tuḫukanti* illustrates, to my understanding, the structure of the family:

> LUGAL (king) – MUNUS.LUGAL (Queen) // DUMU.LUGAL (*tuḫukanti*) – NIN.DINGIR
> Father – Mother // son = crown prince – sister = daughter of the king

The NIN.DINGIR could be the sister or the daughter of the king. It could be that it was originally a title for the king's sister, but it may have been transferred to a daughter. In any case we are dealing with titles that cover a family metaphor.

3.1 The Singleness of the Office of the NIN.DINGIR in the Hittite Kingdom

In my previous study on the Hittite NIN.DINGIR I presented the Hittite texts according to which I tried to define the status and position in Hittite society of the

37 For the translated text see Goedegebuure 2006: 222–28. For the direct speech specifically of Ḫattušili I regarding the status of his heir as adopted son of his sister, see §2: "I, the king apprehended him and had him brought to my couch: 'Why? Should no one ever again raise his sister's son?'" (p. 224). In an article on royal rhetoric Hoffner (2013:140–41) also emphasizes the family relations in the text, translating from §§8–9: "Your clan shall be [united] like that of a *wetna*-animal [. . .] His (i.e., Muršili I's) subjects are born [of one mo]ther."

38 Goedegebuure 2006: 226 §§13–18. Ḫattušili I accused her of causing harm to the people of Ḫattuša.

female Hittite functionary written Sumerographically NIN.DINGIR, a well-known title from Mesopotamian texts of the third through the first millennia (Taggar-Cohen 2006a). My conclusion was that "only one female at a time served as a Hittite NIN.DINGIR in Ḫattuša, and we do not hear of other NIN.DINGIRs in other towns. She is of royal decent, possibly the daughter of the king. Her cultic activity resembles that of other royal family members such as the king, queen and crown prince, with whom she performs rituals to the divine" (Taggar-Cohen 2006b: 324).

Mark Weeden, in his recent book published on the Hittite logograms in use in Hittite texts, indicated a fragment of an Old Hittite text on which he based his claim that the NIN.DINGIR title appears as a noun in the plural form (Weeden 2011a: 148). In this section I would like to examine his suggestion and argue against his conclusion, keeping the designation of the Hittite NIN.DINGIR as a single female member of the royal family, acting in the state cult as a priestess to the gods.[39]

The KI.LAM festival was regarded as one of the most important and elaborate festivals celebrated by the Hittite king and the royal family in the capital Ḫattuša. During this festival the Hittite king would host representatives from different towns in Ḫattuša, in contrast to the other large festivals during which he and the royal family had to travel between the religious cities of central-northern Anatolia to visit the gods' temples and celebrate the festival. The first comprehensive edition of the KI.LAM festival published by Itamar Singer (1983–4) reveals a festival celebrated for several days with the participation of the Hittite great king, the queen and the NIN.DINGIR, next to a large number of cult personnel and the guests from the different cities. The text, preserved on several different tablets, some of Old Hittite ductus and some from the late Hittite kingdom, prescribes in detail the rituals to be carried out during the festival. Detlev Groddek (2004) edited the fragment KBo 38.12 as part of an old version of the KI.LAM festival (CTH 627).

39 This is in contrast to the Mesopotamian NIN.DINGIR of Old Babylonian time, who were numerous, and who already in the third millennium were installed as priestesses to specific gods in different cities in Sumer. It is important to note that the Hittite NIN.DINGIR is never identified as a NIN.DINGIR of a specific deity. The reading of Johan de Roos 2007: 115 for KUB 15.23 12′–13′: *A-NA* NIN.DINGIR ^{d}<URU> Ku-uš-ša-ra-x is mistaken as the sign is not NIN but DAM. According to the texts of vows, the queen is giving presents to gods not to priests. I therefore find no reason why she would dedicate the precious present to a NIN.DINGIR rather than to the deity who is the wife of the god of the town Kuššar, the hometown of the first king of the dynasty, Ḫattušili I.

The fragment KBo 38.12 records the last lines of the ritual, where the colophon indicates that it belongs to the KI.LAM-festival. Together with a small fragment KBo 20.27 these lines were read by Groddek as follows:[40]

rev. iv
12' [nu N]IN.DINGIR-aš ^{GIS}BA[NŠUR]-ša$^{?}$-x-x da-a-i tu-uš-ta
13' [p]é-e-ta-an-[zi] te-eš-ta pa-a-an-zi LÚ.MEŠ ḫa-a-pí-eš
14' pa-a-an-zi [$^{M]EŠ}$ NIN.DINGIR-an EGIR-*ŠU* SÌR^{RU}

Colophon :
15' [ ] ma-a-an LUGAL-uš
16' [KI.LA]M-ni III-*ŠU* e-ša

This tablet determined in its colophon: "[ ] when the king sits three times at the [gate]house", thus showing that it is part of the KI.LAM-festival. Groddek compared the entire tablet to the other OH text of the ritual treated by Singer, ABoT 1.5(+), and was able to show that they are the same text, thus determining that this is the description of the second day of the festival activities.

The tablet, then, describes the second day's activities of the king and queen together with all participating cult personnel. It includes the NIN.DINGIR next to the king and queen.

The NIN.DINGIR appears in this text several times (iii 7′, 13′, 46′, iv 12′, 14′). In all occurrences except for iv 14′ the noun NIN.DINGIR indicates the singular form of the nominative case: NIN.DINGIR-*aš* NIN.DINGIR-*ša/a*; we know that it is singular because of the verb used in the two cases to indicate her activities (e-ša "sits"). In the other copy, ABoT 1.5 (+), she is also mentioned as drinking to the gods like the king and queen. Only in iv 14′ is she indicated with the complement NIN.DINGIR-an (accusative case); preceding the title, according to Groddek, is a broken sign of the plural indicator -MEŠ and at the end of the sentence a verb in the plural form SÌR-*RU* "they sing." Groddek translates:

> Die *ḫapiia*-Leute gehen. [ ] . . . die Gottesherrin, man singt hinter ihr

He thus understands the plural form of the verb as denoting someone else singing behind the NIN.DINGIR. In his interpretation of the ideogram NIN.DINGIR, Mark Weeden (2011a: 148) reads the end of the line as follows:

---

40 The tablet is composed of four columns.

> The plural form, $^{\text{[MUNUS.]MEŠ}}$ EREŠ.DINGIR.DINGIR (nom. pl. KBo 38.12 rev.$^{?}$ iv$^{!}$ 14, OS or MS), also indicates a discrete Sumerian concept: "the lady-gods, divine ladies", not the "lady of the gods". Contrast the plural of ^{MUNUS}AMA.DINGIR-*LIM* which only once substitutes the determinative MEŠ for the Akkadographic phonetic complement *LIM*, in the form $^{\text{MUNUS.MEŠ}}$AMA.DINGIR^{MEŠ} in a MS text.

Weeden therefore considers the noun NIN.DINGIR with the complement sign -*an* as representing the Sumerogram DINGIR (god); thus, he suggests reading DINGIR.DINGIR (the Sumerogram twice over, used for plurality), and he takes the verb in the plural form at the end of the line SÌR-*RU* to indicate the activity of these NIN.DINGIRs.

3.2 There Are Several Points Begging Discussion

1) Does the Sumerogram NIN.DINGIR appear in other places in this ritual text?
2) Is it necessary to read the complement to the noun NIN.DINGIR as a Sumerogram?
3) What are her activities in this ritual?
4) Is the sign before the noun NIN.DINGIR to be read indeed as the plural MEŠ?

The ideogram compound NIN.DINGIR appears in this text of the KI.LAM festival four more times besides column iv line 14′:[41] iii 7′, 13′, 46′; iv 12′; in all these cases the NIN.DINGIR is a singular noun indicated by the verb in the singular. The noun is in the nominative case, NIN.DINGIR-aš. Checking the other copies of the KI.LAM festival published by Singer 1984: 209, the NIN.DINGIR also appears as a singular noun in the following cases: NIN.DINGIR with no case indication, which is clearly the nominative case; NIN.DINGIR-š(a) nominative singular, once as NIN.DINGIR-aš, but unclear whether nominative or genitive; once as NIN.DINGIR-*ri* indicating dative-locative singular, and twice as NIN.DINGIR-ya not indicating case (-ya standing for the conjunction "and"). So, except for the case of iv 14′ that Weeden reads as plural, the NIN.DINGIR does not appear in a plural form in the KI.LAM-festival.

Looking at the general attestations (apart from the KI.LAM-festival) of the noun NIN.DINGIR the cases indicated are:

---

41 See Groddek's edition, ibid, p. 67.

Nom. sg. NIN.DINGIR / NIN.DINGIR-*aš* / NIN.DINGIR-*ša*/ NIN.DINGIR-*aš-ša*
Acc. sg. NIN.DINGIR-*an* – (only once) KBo 25.48 iii 8′ (MS)[42]
Gen. sg. NIN.DINGIR-*aš* (only a small number of attestations)
Dat.-loc. sg. NIN.DINGIR / NIN.DINGIR-*i* / NIN.DINGIR-*ri*[43]
The noun shows a stem ending with -a or -ra if we take the Dat. loc. -ri.

It is important to indicate that in most attestations the noun, NIN.DINGIR has no indication of a case marker. We can find the forms: NIN.DINGIR-*ma*, NIN.DINGIR-*ya*, NIN.DINGIR-*kán*,[44] NIN.DINGIR-*pa*,[45] and NIN.DINGIR-*ša-an*.[46] Also, the noun has only one rare indication of a determinative to specify that it is a female as is common in other cases of cultic functionaries (the use of LÚ and MUNUS).[47] It seems to me that it is quite clear that the scribes related to the functionary bearing this title as a special and separate known persona.

At this stage I would say that there is no need to read NIN.DINGIR.DINGIR and we can easily maintain the accusative case form NIN.DINGIR-*an*. In the specific version of the Old Hittite text of the KI.LAM festival under discussion, the NIN.DINGIR is mentioned together with the king and queen sitting down for the ritual and drinking to the gods, while the cult personnel serve the king, queen and the NIN.DINGIR, and the musicians play music and the singers sing. The main singers in this text are the LÚ^{MEŠ} *ḫali(ya)ri-* "cantors."[48] The verb indicating their singing is a Sumerogram with an Akkadian complement SÌR-*RU* (*RU* stands for the ending of the Akkadian verb *ZAMARU*). There are three other groups of singers mentioned. One of the other groups of singers in the text is the well-attested group of women cultic singers, the MUNUS^{MEŠ} *zintuḫi-*. Their name is spelled MUNUS^{MEŠ} *zi-in-tu-ḫi-eš*.[49] They appear in this OH text three times (iii 20′, 38′, iv 5′), and also in the KI.LAM festival texts published by Singer, five or six times.

Returning to line KBo 38.12 iv 12′–14′ describing the ending of a cultic ritual; the NIN.DINGIR takes or places some bread from/on the table. "They (the

42 NIN.DINGIR-*an* DUMU^{MES} É.GAL *ḫar-kán-zi*.
43 It is possible to read NIN.DINGIR-*RI* a form of the Akkado-Sumerian.
44 NIN.DINGIR-aš-ma-kán KUB 58.61 rev. iv 19.
45 KBo 21.90 obv. i 7′: NIN.DINGIR-pa a-ra-a-i.
46 KBo 21.97; KBo 30.153 obv. ii 10: NIN.DINGIR-ša-an *QA-TAM* zi-ik-k[i-iz-zi] "The NIN.DINGIR places her hand forth."
47 We have once only – ^{d}NIN.DINGIR in KBo 45.76 6′, and once ^{MUNUS}NIN.DINGIR-*aš* in KBo 22.175 iii 9′ (NS), (with dupl. KUB 58.54 iii 10′).
48 See Puhvel, *HED* 3 (1991): 30–31. In this text (KBo 38.12+) they appear at least four times.
49 See Kloeckhorst 2008: 1038 for the meaning of the word *zintuḫi-* "girl" (maybe of Ḫattic origin) since it is correlating with the Sumerogram ^{MUNUS}KI.SIKIL.

table men) take it away, and they go". The group of cultic functionaries LÚ^{MEŠ} *ḫapieš*, who are mainly dancing, also leave. A break follows, ending with what Groddek reads ^{M}]^{EŠ}, and Weeden reads $^{\text{MUNUS.}}$]^{MEŠ} preceding the NIN.DINGIR-*an*.

Firstly I would agree with Groddek for the ending of the broken place preceding the NIN.DINGIR. It must be]*eš*. I insist that it is –]*eš* sign and not ^{M}]^{EŠ}, since there is a space between the sign and the NIN.DINGIR. In this text when the sign MEŠ precedes a noun the sign MEŠ is attached to the next noun, see for example the line above, LÚ^{MEŠ} *ḫapieš*.[50] It is easy to see that the words as follows, fit in the broken space:

[MUNUS^{MEŠ} *zi-in-tu-ḫi-*]*eš* NIN.DINGIR-*an* EGIR-*ŠU* SÌR-*RU*
"and the *zintuḫi*-wom]en sing of/towards the NIN.DINGIR behind her"

The *zintuḫi*-women are mentioned in the ritual several times and are also known to appear with the NIN.DINGIR in other rituals.[51] This group of cult personnel is always described as singing when they accompany the NIN.DINGIR. They are mentioned in the ritual on this fragment on lines 5′–6′ singing in Ḫattian as on the previous column iii 20′. A similar scene appears at the end of a ritual in KBo 10.27 v 27′–33′ (CTH 649)[52]:

27' [ma-a]-an-ma-kán pa-ra-a ú-iz-zi
28' [ḫ]u-u-lu-ga-an-ni-ya e-ša ta *I-NA* É ^{KUŠ} kur-ša-aš
29' [-]zi LÚ.MEŠ ḫa-pí-[e-eš] ú-nu-wa-an-te-eš
30' [pé-r]a-an-še-et i-ya-an-ta LÚ.MEŠ ^{URU} A-nu-nu-wa
31' [SÌR-*RU*] MUNUS.MEŠ zi-[in]-tu-ḫi-ia-aš EGIR-*ŠU* SÌR-*RU*
32' [LÚ.MEŠ a]r-kam-mi-ya-li-e-eš ^{GIŠ} ar-kam-mi
33' [gal-gal-tu]-u-ri GUL-aḫ-ḫa-an-ni-an-zi
[Whe]n she comes forth, [. . .] and she sits down in the carriage, and into the temple of the *kurša*-bag[she go]es. The adorned *ḫapiya*-men [in f]ront of her proceed. The men of the city of Anunuwa [sing]. The *zintuḫi*-women sing behind her, [and the a]*rkami*-men beat the *arkami*-instrument.

There is still a grammatical difference between KBo 38.12 iv 12′–14′:

[MUNUS.MEŠ *zi-in-tu-ḫi-*]*eš* NIN.DINGIR-*an* EGIR-*ŠU* SÌR-*RU*

---

50 As for the sign –]*eš* read by Weeden as MEŠ, if it were a plural determinative, in comparison with the other attestation in that specific OH text there should have been no space between the MEŠ sign and the noun it precedes. In the case of the NIN.DINGIR there is clear space between the –eš and the NIN, and the vertical for MEŠ cannot be seen in the photo (contra Weeden).
51 KBo 10.27 v 27′–33′; KBo 17.101 iii, iv; KBo 19.163 iv; 19.161 iv; KBo 21.90 obv. 13′–21′; KBo 21.91, 7′; KUB 11.32 + 20.17 iv 9′–14′ / 25.51 iv 8′ / 48.17; KUB 56.46.
52 On these rituals of the NIN.DINGIR in relation to the Sun-goddess see Steitler 2017: 90–91.

and KBo 10.27 v 31′:

[ ] MUNUS.MEŠ *zi-in-tu-ḫi-ia-aš* EGIR-*ŠU* SÌR-*RU*

The appearance of the "NIN.DINGIR-an" in the Old Hittite text can be taken as an accusative case. Another example with the verb SÌR-*RU* is found with the meaning of singing of/about at the beginning of the myth of Ullikumi, where the name of ^{d}Kumarbi appears in the accusative form (^{d}*Kum[arb]in išḫamiḫḫi* in KUB 33.96 i 4) "I shall sing of the god Kumarbi." The line for the NIN.DINGIR would then mean: "They will sing of the NIN.DINGIR behind her." It is however more plausible to see it as a rare case of Old Hittite "accusative of direction."[53] The meaning then would be "They sing to/towards the NIN.DINGIR behind her."

I therefore maintain my conclusion that the NIN.DINGIR was the title for only one priestess at a time in the Hittite royal house. It can be compared with the title *Tawananna* that was only given to the acting queen for her lifetime.[54]

4 Conclusion

The NIN.DINGIR was a daughter of the Hittite king and the sister (NIN) of the crown-prince (DUMU.LUGAL) or the daughter of the previous king and the sister of the ruling king. She was a priestess in an equal way to the MUNUS.LUGAL "queen," who was titled in the cult either *Tawananna-* or AMA.DINGIR-*LIM*. Both of them, mother and daughter/sister, were priestesses to all the gods of the kingdom, and worshiped them at state festivals in different locations especially during the New Kingdom. While the queen ruled over all royal activity including being involved in political issues, the NIN.DINGIR according to text evidence appears only in cultic activities. As the queen through her position as a ruler had control of possessions such as houses and revenue from transactions and especially wealth used for cultic activity as described by Siegelová (2015), thus the NIN.DINGIR had resources for cultic activity. The Old Hittite documents prescribing the cultic performance of the NIN.DINGIR point to the origin of her role being in the ancient myth of the *purulli-* festival, which explained that the universe was

53 For this form, see Hoffner and Melchert 2008: 248–49.

54 For the Hittite title Tawananna, see Collins 2007: 98–101. Regarding the debate on the original language of the female title Tawananna in correlation with the title for the male ruler T/Labarna as being Ḫattian language or Luwian language, see Soysal (2005) for supporting Ḫattian language; but for supporting Luwian origin for *tabarna* "(the) powerful (one)" and *tawananna* "(the) righteous (one)," see Melchert above footnote 16.

controlled by the Storm-god, the very same god who entrusted the kingdom into the hands of the Hittite king. Her title suggests understanding the Hittite royal family as a replica of the family of the gods on earth. Through the family worship of all the divine families of the gods, they received the support of the divine world for their rule.

The fact that the sister of a ruling king was involved in royal turmoil might suggest that a sister's son had a right to become an heir to the throne. The evidence for a family supports the reading of the relevant Sumerograms in Hittite as NIN.DINGIR rather than EREŠ.DINGIR.

Bibliography

Archi, Alfonso. 1998. The High Priestess, dam-dingir, at Ebla. Pp. 43–53 in *'Und Mose schrieb dieses Lied auf': Studien zum Alten Testament und zum alten Orient: Festschrift für Oswald Loretz zur Vollendung seines 70. Lebensjahres mit Beiträgen von Freunden, Schülern und Kollegen / unter Mitwirkung von Hanspeter Schaudig*, ed. Manfried Dietrich and Ingo Kottsieper. AOAT 250. Münster: Ugarit Verlag.

Beckman, Gary. 1995. Royal Ideology and State Administration in Hittite Anatolia. Pp. 529–43 in *Civilizations of Ancient Near East*, Vol. 1, ed. Jack M. Sasson. New York: Scribner.

Beckman, Gary. 1997. Bilingual Edict of Ḫattušili I. Pp. 79–82 in *Context of Scripture*, Volume 2: Monumental Inscriptions from the Biblical World, ed. William W. Hallo and K. Lawson Younger. Leiden: Brill.

Beckman, Gary. 2002. 'My Sun-God': Reflections of Mesopotamian Conceptions of Kingship among the Hittites. Pp. 15–21 in *Ideologies as Intercultural Phenomena: Proceedings of the Third Symposium of the Melammu Project Held in Chicago*, USA, *October 27–31, 2000*, ed. Antonio Panaino and Giovanni Pettinato. Milan: Università di Bologna & Islao.

Beckman, Gary. 2010. Temple building among the Hittites. Pp. 71–89, 451–55 in *From the Foundations to the Crenellations: Essays on Temple Building in the Ancient Near* East *and Hebrew Bible*, ed. Mark J. Boda and Jamie Novotny. Münster: Ugarit Verlag.

Bilgin, Tayfun. 2018. *Officials and Administration in the Hittite World*. Berlin and Boston: De Gruyter.

Collins, Billie Jean. 2007. *The Hittites and Their World*. Atlanta, GA: SBL Press.

de Roos, Johan. 2007. *Hittite Votive Texts*. Leiden: NINO.

Galmarini, Niccolò. 2014. The Festivals for Mount Puškurunuwa. Pp. 277–95 in *Proceedings of the 8th International Congress of Hittitology, Warsaw, 5–9 September 2011*, ed. Pioter Taracha and Magdalena Kapeluś. Warsaw: Agade.

Gilan, Amir and Alice Mouton. 2014. The Enthronement of the Hittite King as a Royal Rite of Passage. Pp. 99–117 in *Life, Death, and Coming of Age in Antiquity: Individual Rites of Passage in the Ancient Near East and its Surroundings*, ed. Alice Mouton and Julie Patrier. PIHANS 124. Leiden: NINO.

Goedegebuure, Petra. 2006. The Bilingual Testament of Hattusili I. Pp. 222–28 in *The Ancient Near East: Historical Sources in Translation*, ed. Mark W. Chavalas. Malden, MA and Oxford: Blackwell Publishing.

Groddek, Detlev. 2004. *Eine althethitische Tafel des KI.LAM-Festes. International Journal of Diachronic Linguistics and Linguistic Reconstruction*. Supplements, volume 1. München: Peniope.
Hoffner, Harry A. 2009. *Letters from the Hittite Kingdom*. Atlanta, GA: SBL Press.
Hoffner, Harry A. 2013. 'The King's Speech': Royal Rhetorical Language. Pp. 137–53 in *Beyond Hatti: A Tribute to Gary Beckman*, ed. Billie Jean Collins and Piotr Michalowski. Atlanta, GA: Lockwood Press.
Hoffner, Harry A. and Craig Melchert. 2008. *A Grammar of the Hittite Language (part 1: reference grammar)*. Winona Lake, IN: Eisenbrauns.
Hutter, Manfred. 2003. Aspects of Luwian Religion. Pp. 216–19 in *The Luwians*, ed. Craig, H. Melchert. Leiden and Boston: Brill.
Klinger, Jürg. 2009. The Cult of Nerik: Revisited. Pp. 97–107 in *Central-North Anatolia in the Hittite Period: New Perspectives in Light of Recent* Research. *Acts of the International Conference Held at the University of Florence (7–9 February 2007)*, ed. Franca Pecchioli Daddi, Giulia Torri, Carlo Corti. Studia Asiania 5: Roma.
Kloekhorst, Alwin. 2008. *Etymological Dictionary of the Hittite Inherited Lexicon*. Leiden and Boston: Brill.
McMahon, Gregory. 1991. *The Hittite State Cult of the Tutelary Deities*. AS 25. The Oriental Institute of the University of Chicago.
Melchert, Craig. 2003. *The Luwians*. Leiden and Boston: Brill.
Nakamura, Mitsuo. 2002. *Das hethitische nuntarriyašḫa-Fest*, PIHANS 94. Leiden: NINO.
Pecchioli Daddi, Franca. 2014. Messengers of the Gods: NIN.DINGIR and Tetešhapi. *Die Welt des Orients* 44: 289–300.
Schwemer, Daniel. 2016. Quality Assurance Managers at Work: The Hittite Festival Tradition. Pp. 1–30, in *Liturgie oder Literatur? Die Kultrituale der Hethiter im transkulturellen Vergleich. Akten eines Werkstattgesprächs an der Akademie der Wissenschaften und der Literatur Mainz, 2.–3. Dezember* 2010, ed. Gerfrid G. W. Müller. Wiesbaden: Harrassowitz.
Siegelová, Jana. 2015 Die hethitische Königin und die Wirtschaft der Krone. Pp. 239–50 in *Saeculum: Gedenkschrift für Heinrich Otten anlässlich seines 100. Geburtstags*, ed. Andreas Müller-Karpe, Elisabeth Rieken, Walter Sommerfeld. StBoT 58. Wiesbaden: Harrassowitz.
Singer, Itamar. 1983–4. *The Hittite KI.LAM Festival*. StBoT 27–28. Wiesbaden: Harrassowitz.
Singer, Itamar. 2002. *Hittite Prayers*. Atlanta, GA: SBL Press.
Soysal, Oğuz. 2005. On the Origin of the Royal Title *Tabarna/Labarna*. *Anatolica* 31: 189–209.
Steinkeller, Piotr. 1999. On Rulers, Priests, and Sacred Marriage: Tracking the Evolution of Early Sumerian Kingship. Pp. 103–37 in *Priests and Officials in the Ancient Near East: Papers of the Second Colloquium on the Ancient Near East: The City and its Life held at the Middle Eastern Culture Center in Japan (Mitaka, Tokyo)*, ed. Kazuko Watanabe. Heidelberg: C. Winter.
Steitler, Charles W. 2017. *The Solar Deities of Bronze Age Anatolia: Studies in Texts of the Early Hittite Kingdom*, StBoT 62: Wiesbaden: Harrassowitz.
Stol, Marten. 2016. *Women in the Ancient Near East*. Translated by Helen and Mervy Richardson. Boston and Berlin: De Gruyter.
Süel, Aygül and Mark Weeden. 2019. MRS Woman(?): A Busy Hittite Lady from Ortaköy: Possible Evidence for the Hittite word for 'Woman.' Pp. 984–1004 in *Acts of the IXth International Congress of Hittitology, Çorum, 08–14 September 2014* (vol. 2), ed. Agül Süel. Çorum Governorate: Provincial Directorate of Culture and Tourism Publications.
Taggar-Cohen, Ada. 2006a. *Hittite Priesthood*. Theth 26. Heidelberg: Winter Verlag.

Taggar-Cohen, Ada. 2006b. The NIN.DINGIR in the Hittite Kingdom: A Mesopotamian Priestly Office in Hatti? *AoF* 33/2: 313–27.

Taggar-Cohen, Ada. Forthcoming. Hittite Royal Administrative Concept and its Representation in Cultic Texts: The Implementing of Cosmic Order, in *It All Began with Stratigraphy and Chronology: Archaeology in Central Anatolia: Festschrift Dedicated to Sachihiro Omura on his 75th Birthday*, ed. Çiğdem Maner, Mark Weeden, Masako Omura, Kimiyoshi Matsumura; Wiesbaden: Harrassowitz.

Taracha, Piotr. 2017. *Two Festivals Celebrated by a Hittite Prince (CTH 647.I and II-III): New Light on Local Cults in North-Central Anatolia in the Second Millennium BC*. StBoT 61. Wiesbaden: Harrassowitz.

Tischler, Johann. 2016. *Hethitische Texte in Transkription* KUB *56 und KUB* 57. DBH 49. Wiesbaden: Harrassowitz.

Torri, Giulia. 2010. The *Scribal School* of the Lower City of Ḫattuša and the Beginning of the Career of Anuwanza, Court Dignitary and Lord of Nerik. *Quaderni di Vicino Oriente* 5: 383–96.

Torri, Giulia. 2015. Remarks about the Transmission of Festival Texts Concerning the Cult of Lelwani (based on the Fragment KBo 13.216 + KBo 56.89 (+) KBo 56.90). Pp. 289–300 in *Saeculum: Gedenkschrift für Heinrich Otten anlässlich seines 100. Geburtstags*, ed. Andreas Müller-Karpe, Elisabeth Rieken, Walter Sommerfeld. StBoT 58; Wiesbaden: Harrassowitz.

Torri, Giulia and Susanne Görke. 2014. Hittite Building Rituals Interaction Between Their Ideological Function and Find Spot. Pp. 287–300, in *Life, Death, and Coming of Age in Antiquity: Individual Rites of Passage in the Ancient Near* East *and Adjacent Regions*, ed. Alice Mouton and Julie Patrier. Leiden: NINO.

Van den Hout, Theo P. J. 1995. *Der Ulmitešub Vertrag: Eine prosopographische Untersuchung*. StBoT 38. Wiesbaden: Harrassowitz.

Van den Hout, Theo P. J. 1997. The Telipinu Proclamation. Pp. 194–98 in *Context of Scriptures* 1. Leiden: Brill.

Van den Hout, Theo P. J. 2009. Reflections on the Origins and Development of the Hittite Tablet Collections in Ḫattuša and their Consequences for the Rise of Hittite Literacy. Pp 71–96 in *Central-North Anatolia in the Hittite Period: New Perspectives in Light of Recent Research*, ed. Franca Pecchioli Daddi, Giulia Torri, and Carlo Corti. Studia Asiana 5. Rome: Herder.

Van den Hout, Theo P. J. 2012. Administration and Writing in Hittite Society. Pp. 41–58 in *Archives, Deposits and Storehouses in the Hittite World: New* Evidence *and New Research*, ed. Maria Elena Balza, Mauro Giorgieri, and Clelia Mora. Studia Meditterranea 23. Genova: Italian University Press.

Van den Hout, Theo P. J. 2015. In Royal Circles: The Nature of Hittite Scholarship. *Journal of Ancient Near Eastern History* 2: 203–27.

Van den Hout, Theo P. J. 2020. *A History of Hittite Literacy: Writing* and Read*ing in Late Bronze-Age* Anatolia *(1650–1200 BC)*. Cambridge University Press.

Vigo, Matteo. 2016. Sources for the Study of the Role of Women in the Hittite Administration. Pp. 328–53 in *The Role of Women in Work and Society in the Ancient Near East*, ed. Brigitte Lion and Cécile Michel. Boston and Berlin: De Gruyter.

Weeden, Mark. 2011a. *Hittite Logograms and Hittite Scholarship*. StBoT 54. Wiesbaden: Harrassowitz.

Weeden, Mark. 2011b. Adapting to New Contexts: Cuneiform in Anatolia. Pp. 597–617 in *The Oxford Handbook of Cuneiform Culture*, ed. Karen Radner and Eleanor Robson. Oxford: Oxford University Press.

Ulla Koch

The Roles of Women in the Practice of Ancient Mesopotamian Divination

Simply put, divination is a way to communicate with the supernatural. The dialogue can either be initiated by humans or by the gods themselves. A person in doubt may ask the divine realm for assurance, confirmation, or answers, or the gods may wish to warn, instruct, or reassure their subjects. Divination may take a multitude of forms from prophecy uttered by an initiated specialist under the influence of psychedelic drugs to an emperor soberly throwing dice to help him make up his mind. For practical reasons, here I apply the distinction by Plato and Cicero between artificial and natural divination – leaving all other classifications aside. In Cicero's definition, artificial divination relies on amassed special knowledge about how to read signs, because the gods do not speak in the vernacular but rely on ants or stars to indicate their decisions by means of a complicated code. Natural divination on the other hand is often direct speech, a mostly un-coded communication with the divine (Cicero, *Cicero on Divination De Divinatione*, Book 1. 56). Here the human mind is the medium selected to transmit the divine messages. By artificial divination in Mesopotamia, I understand the forms of divination which were underpinned by the omen compendia, scholia, and other forms of learned cuneiform literature. The main genres were, of course, extispicy, astrology, and the various forms of omens derived from everyday events, births, human appearance, and other haphazard phenomena. Certainly, artificial divination need not be written down and it exists in oral form in the anthropological present. I am convinced that forms of artificial divination existed outside of the scholarly world, also in ancient Mesopotamia – perhaps practiced by women. Still, we can but speculate about them.

Mesopotamian artificial divination belonged to the domain of higher scholarly education, which was a man's world. As attested to in the Old Babylonian and Neo-Assyrian periods, when the sources for divination are most plentiful, diviners trained as scholars were invariably men (Cryer 1994: 138, 209, 213). There is simply no exception. The divination texts from the first millennium BCE are highly specialized and would have taken many years of study to master – thus practically excluding women from access for this reason alone, since literacy among women at this period was not high and basic reading and writing skills would not have helped them deciphering the texts. (It certainly took some effort for this woman to master them.) Women may have served as scribes and healers for other women for reasons of decorum; but they never served the

https://doi.org/10.1515/9781501514821-010

court as scholars or were educated along with their brothers in the expertise of their father. Even in the Old Babylonian period, where at least some women would learn to read and write and the divination texts themselves were still written in simple Akkadian syllabics, women appear not to have practiced or studied these forms of divination (Halton and Svärd, 2017) Evidently, it was more than literacy that prevented women from practicing the art of divination such as culturally specific gender roles and religious beliefs about cultic purity and taboo. The "Qualifications of the Babylonian Diviner" is specifically directed at men, the possibility of a woman performing extispicy is not envisaged (Lambert 1998). A formula, attested only twice, safeguarding an extispicy was "disregard that a woman has written it and placed it before you" (SAA 4: 321 rev. 4–5; 322 rev. 6–7). The *ezib*-formulae include all kinds of taboos that the diviner may have broken unwittingly as well as faulty performance of the ritual. He may have stepped on something unclean, an unclean person may have stepped on the site of divination or touched the sheep, the diviner might have had nightmares, or jumbled the prayers – the gods are asked not to let all this influence their judgment. A woman writing a question ranked along with these potential sources of disfavor. What role did this woman play? Was she the client or a scribe? Does the formulation mean she wrote the query, or did she dictate it?

The barriers to women becoming diviners may, of course, also have been due to the constraints to women in a patriarchal society.

What culturally specific values were in play probably varied over the centuries, certainly, it is not a given that a patriarchal society *per se* deprives women of the role of diviner. Just as in the anthropological present, women can function as the primary diviners of a traditional society, so they did in antiquity. In Hittite society, for instance, female diviners were involved in state matters and were consulted by high and low. The ^{MUNUS}ŠU.GI – literally "old one" or "old woman," appears to be used as a title for women practicing oracular divination and performing purification and apotropaic rituals. The term is often translated as "wise woman" and one can argue that wisdom and age are often perceived to be correlated. The term bears no relation to the epithets of the Sumerian goddesses with divination abilities, for instance the epithet "wise woman," and probably did not invoke associations of Geštinanna, Gula, or Nanše ((Hamori, 2015) The cultural and temporal distance was, in my opinion, too great. The "Old Ones" served at court and counseled the king and queen as well as private citizens. Their divination expertise was simply called "task" or "product," written with the Sumerogram KIN, representing the Hittite aniyatt-. KIN can equal Akkadian *šipru* ("message, task, product," etc.) or *têrtu*, which is the most frequently used Akkadian term for the answer to a divination inquiry, (most often) by extispicy. The performance of the oracle was recorded in terse accounts, almost like extispicy reports, which simply state the significant signs and the diviner's conclusions. The oldest known report on a KIN-oracle stems from the 16th century BCE, the Old Hittite period. It was performed using a set of symbolical objects which were manipulated in some way to form different arrangements. The objects had names that indicated their significance. The technique used by the "Old Ones" is reminiscent of the technique used by the modern-day basket diviners, but we do not know very much about how it worked or what the conceptual framework was.[1]

However, in Mesopotamia women made an appearance as clients throughout the periods in which artificial divination is attested. Mesopotamian queens and the wives of Old Assyrian merchants consulted the diviners on behalf of their family, but they do not demonstrate knowledge of the particulars. Obviously, when their position made it possible, women took an interest in this powerful access to knowledge and security which so permeated every aspect of their culture. Both queens and wives of well-to-do citizens certainly did.[2]

Divine Female Specialists in Divination

The divine realm reflects the human world, but it often does so exactly by breaking the boundaries which constrain human intercourse. While the supreme god may have murdered his granny and the most revered goddess behave a vile-tempered and headstrong teenager, who kills her suitors, this is seldom acceptable behavior for an earthly *pater familias* and his off-spring. Thus, the role goddesses played as diviners, which they did especially in Sumerian mythology, may not reflect directly on everyday human practice. Still, that goddesses could play an active role in the domain of divination is evidence of a cultural link between the female gender and communication with the divine.[3]

---

1 For the KIN oracle, see Beal (2002) and especially Warbinek (2019).

2 SAA 9: 5 contains an oracle to the queen mother. See e.g., Nissinen (2013: 40) and Halton and Svärd (2017: 188–197) for a collection of women reporting and querying oracles. SAA 4: 321 and 322, two copies of a query made by an unnamed woman to the god Manlaharbanni. Frahm (2004: 45) suggests she is the wife of Ashurbanipal, Libbāli-šarrat.

3 I will not venture into the discussion of Sumerian versus Semitic gender roles, but restrict myself to noting that contrary to Akkadian, Sumerian does not distinguish between gods and goddess in writing nor in language. Asher-Greve and Westenholz (2013: 19) note that the Sumerians feminized cultural institutions such as writing.

While female diviners and exorcists are difficult to find, divination and exorcism were among the domains which goddesses shared with gods from the very earliest periods, and the practice of dream interpretation was dominated throughout the millennia by goddesses. The Sumerian pantheon included a potent and varied wealth of goddesses, who ruled over all aspects of life, culture, and nature. As described by Asher-Greve and Westenholz (2013: 294), this profusion of goddesses was reduced as their cities vanished or lost importance in the second millennium BCE. Perhaps their demise was not alone due to the decline of their shrines and cult centers. As the population shifted to the north and the influx of new peoples in the second millennium BCE brought new ideas to the area, ideas about gender and religion are also likely to have altered.

Even though the names of all these goddesses were not necessarily forgotten, their individual characters paled, a development which is reflected in the syncretism and fusion that began in the Old Babylonian period (Asher-Greve and Westenholz 2013: 288). The Babylonian deities associated with cultural knowledge including artificial divination were male. Šamaš and Adad were of course the gods involved in extispicy *par excellence*, and according to one tradition, they were the gods who revealed the secrets of all kinds of divination to mankind, according to another it was Ea.[4]

The gentle goddess Nanše was protector of the weak, patron of fish and waterfowl, dwelling in the open sea, responsible for weights and measures, and then she was the dream interpreter of the gods.[5] She had her own female dream interpreter with the title **ensi** (Huber Vulliet 2019: 384). In Cylinder A, Gudea describes how he sees Ningirsu in a dream which he did not quite understand, and he decided to ask Ningirsu's sister, the goddess Nanše, to interpret his bewildering nocturnal vision (Zgoll 2002). But first he goes to ask Ningirsu and then Gatumdug, whether they approve of his plan to consult Nanše. Getting their assent involved rituals stretching over two days and a night. When he comes before Nanše:

> The ruler raised his head high in the courtyard of the goddess from Sirara. He offered bread, poured cold water and went to Nanše to pray to her: "Nanše, mighty lady, lady of most precious (?) powers, lady who like Enlil determine fates, my Nanše, what you say is trustworthy and takes precedence. You are the interpreter of dreams among the gods, you are the lady of all the lands. Mother, my matter today is a dream."[6]

4 See (with references to previous literature) Koch-Westenholz (1995: 74).
5 Heimpel (1998–2001) with references to the literature cited here.
6 Translation ETCSL, https://etcsl.orinst.ox.ac.uk/cgi-bin/etcsl.cgi?text=t.2.1.7#.

Gudea refers to Nanše as a "wise dream-interpreter in her own right" (Cylinder A ii 1), but apparently, she was not to be approached directly. The second dream, which Gudea incubates during his construction work, he does not take to Nanše, but instead he performs extispicy on a white kid, presumably to validate that his dream indeed was a communication from Ningirsu. This time he understands the dream without the help of a dream-interpreter.

Presumably, it was a human **ensi**, who spoke the words of Nanše when she explained Gudea's first dream to him. In the Hymn to Nanše A, a human dream-interpreter takes part in the New Year's celebrations preparing silver cups for Nanše. It is unfortunately not certain, whether this person was male or female, it could well be a woman, but it might just as well be a man (Heimpel 1998–2001: 154). After the Ur III period Nanše all but vanishes. She makes rare appearances in learned texts, lexical lists, and rituals.

Ningirsu had promised Gudea both a sign and a pure star to indicate his wishes. Indeed, the first dream includes a vision of a young woman: "who held a stylus of refined silver in her hand, who had placed it on a tablet with propitious stars and was consulting it, was in fact my sister Nisaba. She announced to you the holy star auguring the building of the house" (Cylinder A v 22-vi 2). This must be a reference to a form of astrology even if it probably reflects the selection of a propitious time according to the celestial clock, a *mazel tov*, rather than omen astrology in the form known from *Enūma Anu Enlil* and reports the Neo-Assyrian court astrologers. It could also simply be a reference to time keeping and the use of the fixed stars to realign the lunar calendar with the seasons. Nisaba's relation to time keeping is evident from her epithet as the one who together with Suen counts the days.[7] Keeping track of the calendar – and perhaps even of favorable times for beginning an undertaking – would be a natural skill for the "unsurpassed overseer" (**ugula nu-diri**) directing the activities of the agricultural annual cycle.

Nisaba was the goddess of grain and the scribal arts, including knowledge of "heavenly stars" (**mul an**). Despite her affinity with the configurations of the stars of the sky, she was not associated with divination of any sort. Somehow, one gets the impression of Nisaba as a strangely ethereal goddess – more of a concept than a goddess in the flesh (or whatever gods are made of). She does not seem to have had a regular public cult apart, presumably, from her temple **E$_2$-mul-mul** ("House of the stars") in the city of Ereš. Unfortunately, Ereš disappears almost complete from the record after the Early Dynastic period and is has

7 *Lugal-e* 721. See also the discussion of third millennium astrology in Koch-Westenholz (1995).

not yet been identified. Its cults were transferred to Nippur. So far, offerings and a cella devoted to her appear only to be found in Nippur and references to her cult only occur up until the end of the Old Babylonian period. An institution called **E_2-geštug$_2$-^{d}nisaba** was probably not her temple but rather, "House-of-Wisdom-of-Nisaba" was a poetic generic name for scribal institutions (Michalowski 1998–2001: 577–78). Nisaba was never completely forgotten as the patroness of the scribal arts, even when it was not her primary role anymore (Asher-Greve and Westenholz 2013: 19, 272). Together with Kusu and Ningirima she formed a triad of goddesses, mistresses of ritual purification, who continued to be invoked cultic ceremonies throughout the centuries (Asher-Greve and Westenholz 2013: 118–21).

The mother-goddess Nintur was a specifically a goddess of birthing, like Ninḫursag, with whom she fused (Asher-Greve and Westenholz 2013: 241–42), and, like Nanše, she was a perhaps a patroness of divination. However, there are no pre-Sargonic mentions of her association with divination. The famous passages from a Šulgi hymn quoted by Michalowski seem to me to be the only attestations of Nintur as a goddess of divination, in this case extispicy:

> I am a ritually pure diviner, I am Nintu(r) of the written lists of omens! For the proper performance of the lustrations of the office of high priest, For singing the praises of the high priestess and (their) selection for (residence in) the gipar, For the choosing of the Lumaḫ and Nindingir priests by holy extispicy, For (decision to) attack the south or strike the north, For opening the storage of (battle) standards, For the washing of lances in the "water of battle," And for making wise decisions about rebel lands, The (ominous) words of the gods are most precious, indeed! After taking a propitious omen from a white lamb – an ominous animal – At the place of questioning water and flour are libated; I make ready the sheep with ritual words. And my diviner watches in amazement like a barbarian. The ready sheep is placed in my hand, and I never confuse a favorable sign with an unfavorable one.[8]

Nintur is not described as associated with divination in the entry on the goddess in the *Reallexikon der Assyriologie*. Additionally, it is unclear to me why the author of the hymn chose to associate Šulgi with Nintur when he described the king's abilities as a diviner (Michalowski 2006). That Nintur should have played a role as a goddess of extispicy is not attested anywhere else.

The description of the kind of extispicy that Šulgi performed is quite in accordance with the practice as it is attested in the Old Babylonian and later

8 Translation by Michalowski (2006: 247–249) concerning the translation of **giri$_3$-gen-na inim uzu-ga-ka** as "written lists of omens."

material, but it is different from earlier Sumerian references to extispicy.[9] The sacrificial animal is a white sheep, not a goat as in Sumerian extispicy practice, however, the purposes for divination are common to Sumerian and Akkadian forms of extispicy, namely religion and war. The "written list of omens" that is mentioned in the Šulgi hymn is a neologism and no omen compendia in Sumerian have ever been found. A stronger argument against Sumerian extispicy being like the Akkadian "omenology" is that the technical terminology of extispicy is Akkadian rather than Sumerian, whereas disciplines borrowed from Sumerian are heavily if not entirely written in Sumerograms. The Sumerians practiced extispicy, but in a different way. That this should be so is hardly surprising considering that extispicy is one of the most popular forms of divination and has been invented independently all over the world.

In literary texts goddesses played a role as dream interpreters as well. Famously, in the *Gilgamesh Epic* the hero's divine mother, Ninsun, interprets her son's dreams. In *Dumuzi's Dream*, Dumuzi awakens terrified and calls for his sister, Geštinana:

> Bring, bring, bring my sister! Bring my Geštinana, bring my sister! Bring my tablet-knowing scribe, bring my sister! Bring my song knowing singer, bring my sister! Bring my skillful girl, who knows the meaning of words, bring my sister! Bring my wise woman, who knows the portent of dreams, bring my sister! Let me relate my dream to her! (Alster 1978: 55).

Geštinana was also known in Sumerian as Ama-geštinana and Nin-geštinana ("Mistress of the vine") (Asher-Greve and Westenholz 2013: 95). Under the Kassite dynasty she was invoked as Nin-geštinana and kept her title as the surveyor scribe of heaven and earth.

Along with other goddesses, Geštinana was associated with extispicy in the Old Babylonian period:

> Enter, O Šamaš, lord of judgment; enter, O Adad, lord of extispicy prayer and divination (*bērum*); enter, O Sîn, lord of the crown, and Išhara, lady of divination, who dwells in the holy chamber, Geštinana, registrar of the gods, herald of Anu; Nergal, lord of the weapon. (YOS 11: 13–15)[10]

Nisaba and Geštinana still played the role of divine scribe and surveyor, and the goddess Išḫara was described as lady of divination (*bīru*). However, she is never invoked as the main addressee, Šamaš and Adad take center stage. After the Old Babylonian period, Nabû assumed preeminence as the god of wisdom

9 I will not venture into a discussion of the time of composition of the Šulgi hymns or whether the author of the hymns was a native Sumerian speaker. I merely observe that the description of extispicy reflects Babylonian practices.

10 Starr (1983: 30), collated by Lambert (1998: 154).

and writing, but these goddesses continued to play minor parts in the extispicy rituals into the first millennium. Geštinana's Akkadian counterpart was Bēlet-ṣēri. In the first millennium description of the qualifications of Babylonian diviners, the place of divination is described as "the place of Ea, Šamaš, Asalluḫi, and Bēlet-ṣēri, the surveyor of heaven and earth, the beloved of her brothers."[11] During the extispicy ritual she was represented by a small leather bag (*tukannu šeḫru*) that was placed on the ground. She is also mentioned in the rituals of the diviner known from Ashurbanipal's libraries.[12] Išḫara has the epithets "lady of judgement and divination" (*be-let di-nim u b*[*i-ri*]) in one of the prayers of the diviner where she is exhorted to enter after Šamaš, Adad, Nergal, and Ištar, and then she herself is followed by Bēlet-ṣēri.[13]

In a way she is reminiscent of the Muses, the personified arts, and sciences, which remained popular in European art up until a couple of centuries ago. Just like we know that no Mesopotamian women practiced studying favorable constellations on tablets, whether they were fashioned from clay or lapis-lazuli,[14] women did also not perform any of the classical arts personified by the Muses, at least not originally, but the culture of male practitioners perceived the art that they were devoted to as feminine in gender.

Earthly Women as Practitioners of Divination

Generally, more examples of male than female diviners of any kind are attested. The evidence pertaining to female involvement with divination is sparse compared to that of men, but it is not non-existent. Even though the picture we can draw is very fragmentary, we do see women engaged in various forms of natural divination alongside men. Indeed, the only kinds of divination where women make an appearance as performers are prophecy, oneiromancy (dream-interpretation), and necromancy – all forms of natural divination.

It is not uncommon; indeed, it is found across cultures modern and ancient, that women in possession of special knowledge or special access to the supernatural were required not to bear children – officially at least. Women who are

11 Lambert (1998: 149 ll. 35–36).

12 Zimmern (1901: 98), where she is mentioned with a leather bag but in broken context, collated by Lambert (1998: 154).

13 Zimmern (1901: 202 no.87). The passage can be reconstructed from the parallel Sm. 802.

14 As does Nisaba – very suitable material for a star map, see the Hymn to Nisaba A 1–2, ETCSL 4.16.1

dedicated as cultic functionaries or oblates often are. The *nadītus* are a curious case in point. Their title which is derived from *nadû* the primary meaning of which is "abandoned", or "fallow", suggests that a *nadītu* was considered set apart and not expected to reproduce. Indeed, most of the *nadītus* of Šamaš stayed cloistered in the *gagû* at Sippar and, even though they were allowed to marry, were supposed to only adopt, and not bear their own children. The *nadītus* of Marduk, on the other hand, were allowed natural children and could move around (Barberon 2014). In the Hebrew Bible women who act as diviners and prophets are always described as childless (Hamori 2015: 119–220). This does not seem to have been the case in Mesopotamia. Neither were the women ever described as living outside of other social norms, with the possible exception of a certain Yadida, a crazy woman, *lillatum*, who receives an ordinary garment in a distribution list from Mari (Nissinen et al. 2003: no. 55 l. 42′). Otherwise, they were either cult functionaries who received stipends or ordinary women leading ordinary lives.

Ominous dreams and prophetic ecstasy could be experienced by anybody, not just by male and female professional prophets. A valid prophecy may just as well be a vision that occurred in the night to a person without any specific qualifications or some other form of inspired divine revelation. Professional dreamers and lay persons may have rituals performed to induce dreams; but rituals to induce an exaltation, an altered state of mind in which a prophet speaks for a divinity, appear only to have been practiced by people with a cultic function. This did not exclude ordinary people to fall into trance and prophesy as we shall see. When it came to natural divination there were no boundaries between status and sexes, slave and free, men, women, and the possible cross-gender *asinnu* all could experience and report utterings of the divine. According to Nissinen's survey of gender distribution of prophets in the texts in his collection of citations (Nissinen et al. 2003) there is a tendency towards female prophets becoming more common in the first millennium, as well as a tendency towards gods and prophets being of the same sex. In Mari about two-thirds of prophets are male, whereas in the Neo-Assyrian sources two thirds are female (Lion 2012). There is a similar difference between male and female gods whose utterances are cited: In Mari, male deities prevail: a total of 34 prophecies stem from gods, whereas goddesses only speak 18 times. In the Neo-Assyrian sources, Ištar appears 30 times in her various incarnations, and just 8 male deities are cited. The combination of a male prophet with a male deity is found 26 times, against a male prophet speaking for a female deity, which is attested just 14 times. Female prophets speak for a female deity 15 times, whereas a female prophet only speaks for male deities 7 times. So, both sexes could speak for a god of either sex, with a tendency towards a match in sex. Ištar in her many incarnations gathers ground over the male deities in the Neo-Assyrian sources at the same time as female prophets become more frequent than male. However, it must be kept in mind that the sample is very small.

The titles of persons practicing natural divination changed, and presumably so did the methods they used, their status, and how and by whom they were consulted. Only the seer, the *bārû,* who was the specialist of impetrated oracle (i.e. questions put to the gods in ritual settings), retained his title for two millennia, even though his art of extispicy underwent a similar development as that of other practitioners of divination. It is tempting to ascribe the changes in titulary and practice found in natural divination to its detachment from the conservative written traditions. The titles of female diviners were invariably the same as that of their male counterparts.

Contrary to those titles affiliated with natural divination, the titles of the male professionals consistently performing scholarly divination did not change. These experts held titles of *bārû,* "seer" specialist in forms of provoked divination like extispicy, *ṭupšarru*, "scribe," *āšipu* "exorcist" or *gallû* "cantor;" they were all experts in forms of unprovoked divination, i.e. sign reading, like astrology, and the associated apotropaic rituals. The title *ṭupšār Enūma Anu Enlil* came into use in the first millennium for scholars primarily practicing forms of observational divination such as astrology as well as astronomy, but the older titles remained in use. The female versions of the two professions, exorcist (*āšiptu*) and seer (*bārītu*), are attested but very rarely. In the Old Assyrian material, a female diviner by the title *bārītu* appears but she does not seem to practice the art of extispicy, *bārûtu.* Apart from that, the titles are only known from the anti-witchcraft ceremony *Maqlû* III 39–46:

> Incantation. Witch, murderess, denouncer, sorceress, exorcist (*ašiptu*), ecstatic (*eššebûtu*), snake charmer, bewitcher, the *qadištu*-votary, the nun, the Ištar-votary, the *kulmašītu*-votary. Huntress of the night, espier of the daytime (Abusch 2016: 305).

A single manuscript from Uruk has *ba-ri-tu*$_4$ instead of *ba-a-a-ar-tu*$_4$, "diviner of the night" instead of the "huntress of the night" which is attested in four others (Abusch 2016: 86), an understandable mistake given that the previous guises of the witch all are titles of women with religious roles. Like the *āšiptu*, the female ecstatic, *eššebûtu,*[15] and her male counterpart also only make their appearance in rituals and lexical lists. It is characteristic for the anti-witch rituals to present the witch as someone with the special powers of a person serving the gods, and outdated titles did not lose their potency. Mesopotamian society believed in the existence of witches, but nobody claimed to be one.

15 Also in *Maqlû* IV: 90, 132, VI: 18, VII: 99", see Abusch (2016: 322, 324, 337, 362).

Whereas an *eššebûtu* ecstatic undoubtedly practiced and walked the streets at some point in history (KAR 26 25), the title of *āšiptu* is not yet attested for a mortal woman. The goddess Gula refers to herself as a healer, diviner, and exorcist. She proudly states that "no one has made my cuneiform signs simple, but I . . . [every] one of them," evidently an uncommon feat for a female being.[16] Women might be able to write and sometimes act as healers, *asûtum*, for the ladies at court,[17] but their mastery of the art of writing was limited.

Prophecies could be validated by divination, where the prophet was represented by his/her hem and hair. The statistical material from the Mari letters is of course quite limited, but women (ordinary women and prophets) are with certainty put to the test eight times out of 18 instances, whereas men (ordinary men and prophets) are tested four times out of 30. Once a man is declared to be reliable, *taklu*, so no check was deemed necessary.[18] Prophecies by *asinnus* are just reported three times, all validated in some way. These numbers indicate that women and the possibly cross-gender *asinnus* were considered less reliable as mouthpieces for the gods.

The Old Assyrian Seer and Questioner

Bārītum and the *šā'iltum*, the female "seer" and the female "questioner" are the only type of diviners attested to in the Old Assyrian correspondence of any sex. They were certainly consulted by women but probably also by men even though this is never explicitly stated. Neither is exactly what kind of divination they practiced ever mentioned explicitly.[19] The male counterpart of the *šā'iltum*, the *šā'ilum*, practiced necromancy and oneiromancy, whereas the male counterpart of the *bārītum*, the *bārûm*, practiced extispicy, lecanomancy, and other kinds of artificial divination. The *bārītum*[20] is so far only known form Old Assyrian sources, and there are scattered references to the *šā'iltum* also in Old Babylonian texts and in a couple of literary texts in Standard Babylonian. Elsewhere, the *šā'ilu* is often mentioned together with *bārû*, which makes sense since the two

16 A hymn to Gula quoting her praising herself and her spouse Ninurta, Lambert (1967: 128:183).

17 Female healers at the court of Mari, see Ziegler (1999: 29).

18 Nissinen et al. (2003: no. 38) An ordinary man reporting his own dream.

19 References to diviners and divination in the Old Assyrian correspondence is limited. Apart from TC 1: 5 (Michel (2001) no. 348, BIN 6: 93 (Michel (2001) no. 333, and KTS 1: 25a (Michel (2001: no 325), I know only of kt 94/k 1759, which is unpublished but should appear in Larsen (2010-) volume d.

20 To the references in CAD add kt 94/k 1759. Larsen personal communication.

kinds of divination would supplement each other. It is quite likely that the *bārītum* performed an impetrated oracle, it could be lecanomancy or another form of low-cost ritual, and that the *šā'iltum* was a necromancer and probably also a dream-interpreter. The letter cited below clearly suggests that at least one, and perhaps both, of the diviners consulted the spirits of the dead.

In an oft-quoted letter to Imdīlum from his sister Tarām-Kūbi and his wife Šīmat-Aššur, he is exhorted to return home to Assur:

> Here (in Assur) we have consulted female questioners, female seers, and the spirits; the god Aššur keeps telling you: "you love money and hate your life!" Couldn't you please the god Aššur in the city (Assur)? If you please as soon as you have read this letter, visit Aššur and save your life! Why don't you send me the price of my fabrics?[21]

This early evidence for the importance of work-life balance speaks to us across the millennia, the women's concern is immediately intelligible. They do not ask him for his decision, nor suggest he check the validity of the divination they have resorted to, evidently, they assumed it would carry weight. Without further ado, they, as good businesswomen themselves, end the letter on a business-like note. Michel suggests that the reason why we only have a few letters from Imdīlum's wife is that he in fact returned home. It is rather appealing to think that he listened to the voice of Aššur and his concerned relative.

Two of the famous tradesman Pušu-kēn's kinswomen, his sister and niece(?), wrote to him concerning the health of the wives of two of Pušu-kēn's associates:

> The young women of Puzur-Ištar and Uṣur-ša-Aššur became ill and nearly died. We went to the female questioners and the god said this: "Immediately remove the votive offerings." We would like them to be ready by summer. Please ask your servants (i.e., associates) whether to remove them or not. We await your instructions before removing them.[22]

Here, the god's instruction was not to be followed unless the menfolk agreed (Michel 2009: 147–48). There could be several explanations for this, for instance that the women in question were the responsibility of their husbands, there is no reason to suspect that it reflected the status or the method of divination.

There is one more direct reference to the *šā'iltu* in a letter from an economically troubled woman, Zikri-elka, to Ḫattītum:

> Ever since I went to Waḫšušana, I have gotten angry five times! Please consult the female questioner down there (in Assur) and send me instructions.[23]

21 TC 1 5. Michel (2001: no 348) .
22 KTS 1 25a. Michel (2001: no. 325).
23 BIN 6 93. Michel (2001: no. 333).

As has been pointed out often, only women refer to these diviners in their letters, but since no other practitioners of divination are mentioned in the correspondence, I believe men also benefitted from their services. For instance, the merchant Aššur-idī often quotes the words of the gods, Aššur and Aššurītum, admonishing his son:

> Please, please heed the words of the gods! Do not renounce the decision that the gods have drawn up for you, if you renounce it, you will perish! (Larsen 2002: no. 14).[24]

Exactly how he came to know what the gods thought about the matter is never stated, but I see no reason why he should not have consulted the female diviners. His tone of voice, concern, and references to the will of the gods are, for all intents and purposes, the same as the ones that are found in the letters from women with reference to divination.

There is no evidence that either of the two kinds of female diviners were consulted in practice after the Old Babylonian period.

Ur III and Old Babylonian Ecstatics and Respondents

Maḫḫūtum/maḫḫûm, the female and male "ecstatic," is a title that is also commonly translated as "prophet." Apart from the female dream interpreter, the **ensi** that was mentioned above, the earliest certain evidence for mortal women acting as diviners stems from the early second millennium. Sumerian titles for female diviners are preserved in lexical lists and may reflect earlier practice, but there is still no direct evidence for how and when prophecy was used. Male and female prophets are mentioned in texts from Larsa, where they are referred to by their Sumerian titles (MUNUS) LÚ GUB.BA, *maḫḫûm/maḫḫūtum* in Akkadian. Two distribution lists from Larsa mention a MUNUS LÚ GUB.BA. One is prophetess of Inana of Zabalam who receives 1/72 (TCL 10: 39 11), and the other is prophetess of Ningišzida (TCL10: 69). However, most attestations come from the royal archives at Mari where the *maḫḫû* and *maḫḫūtu*. In other sources from the Old Babylonian down to the Neo-Babylonian period, the title *maḫḫūtu/maḫḫû* still appears with reference to a cult functionary and prophet, often associated with incarnations of Ištar, especially Ištar of Arbela, but also with other deities.

---

24 In nos. 15–16 Aššur-idī also cites the gods.

From the letters and other documents from Mari many aspects of the function, status, and prophecies of the ecstatics can be gleaned. The ecstatics rarely themselves reported directly to the court, rather their oracular speech was reported by officials, temple personnel, or the royal family, whom they might approach themselves with news or demands from their god (e.g., Nissinen et al. 2003: no. 31).

The ecstatics belonged to the staff of the temples of various deities in different cities and would enter ecstasy mainly in their temple (van der Toorn 2000: 80). Presumably there was some kind of ritual associated with attaining the altered state of mind and an ecstatic could fail to reach ecstasy, at least according to a fragmentary ritual of Ištar (Nissinen et al. 2003: nos. 51 and 52). They would rise and stand when making their pronouncements which were classified as *têrtum* or *ṭēmum*, "oracles" or "messages," as were answers obtained through impetrated divination like extispicy. This makes sense, since extispicy and prophecy both required the god to be present, and just as the speech of the prophet was considered direct communication, so the signs on the entrails were the verdict written there by the gods. It appears that they could also pronounce prophecies outside the temple as described in the rather dramatic description of an ecstatic of Dagan, who is said to have asked for a lamb belonging to the king. He devours this lamb raw before pronouncing an oracle (*ṭêrtum*) in the assembly of the elders at the city gate (Nissinen et al. 2003: no. 16).

Another kind of prophet, who are primarily attested in the Mari letters but who were also present in the neighboring kingdom of Aleppo and Babylon, are the *apiltum/āpilum*, the male and female "respondents" (Lion 2012: 153). The *āpilu* is mentioned in texts from Nuzi,[25] and perhaps also in a Middle Babylonian omen text from Assur, by which time it is doubtful that they still practiced.[26] The respondents were linked to various gods and were presumably also cultic functionaries. Their title suggests that they were part of a ritual performed to obtain a divine response, an oracle answer, to a given situation. A prophecy from Adad for Zimri-Lim clearly points in this direction. Adad declares that:

> If you go to war, do not go without an oracle (*ṭêrtum*), when I am present in my oracle you can go. If it is not this way, do not go out the gate! (Nissinen et al. 2003: no. 2 ll. 12′-17′).

25 Unless the *apīlu* mentioned in Nuzi is something entirely different, cf. CAD s.v. B.

26 Heeßel (2012: 109–111) no. 22 l. 16′. Heessel translates "prophet" rather than "nay-sayer" (with CAD s.v.) folllowing Lion (2000).

The respondent of Dagan, Lupaḫḫum, reports the answer to the question "what if the king enters a treaty with the man of Ešnunna without asking the god?" Dagan took a dim view of this (Nissinen et al. 2003: no. 17 ll. 29–40). Exactly what kind of ritual was performed is unfortunately unknown, but it took place in the temple. Like the ecstatics the respondents would "rise" or "stand" when they were ready to speak for the god. They recited the speech of the deity, sometimes in first person, often in quite elaborate detail. Presumably they stood directly by the cult image and the words were perceived as coming directly from the divinity's own mouth (van der Toorn 2000: 80–82). Perhaps the ritual could be a procedure mentioned in two letters where one or more male and female prophets are "given signs to drink" to answer questions concerning going on a campaign and worries about the intentions of king Hammurabi of Babylon (Nissinen et al. 2003: nos. 17 and 23). The prophets were able to answer a series of questions lucidly, so they were presumably not too drunk. These answers could be referred to as an *igerrûm* which is the term for ominous speech (Nissinen et al. 2003: no. 17 l. 6). The respondent of Adad, Lupaḫḫum, was sent to Tuttul to ask Dagan for his support. He gives Dagan the message "to Dagan of Terqa entrust me" and "they answered" with a favorable message (*ṭēmum*) (Nissinen et al. 2003: no. 9). The king had a servant stationed at the temple in Terqa to make sure he received all prophecies, *igerrûm*, made there (ARM 26: 196 ll. 8–10). Nur-Sîn assures Zimri-lim that he reported all "words spoken by a male and female respondent" (Nissinen et al. 2003: no. 1 ll. 34–37).

While the *āpilu*, male respondents, are mentioned more frequently than the ecstatics, the *āpiltum* is referred to just twice, far less than her male counterpart, and she also less frequently than the ecstatic (*muḫḫûtum*) in the Mari correspondence (Lion 2012: 151–52; see Table 1). This indicates that female ecstatics were more common than female respondents, whereas the reverse was true of her male counterpart.

Table 1: Male and female respondents and ecstatics attested at Mari.

āpiltum	āpilum	muḫḫûtum	muḫḫûm
2	15	4	9

Three times oracles are reported by an *asinnu*. Two named *asinnū* occur in the Mari letters, Šēlebum and Ili-ḫaznaya, both prophesize for Annītum, Ištar's most warlike incarnation (ARM 26 197, 198, 212 and 213. Their prophecies concern cultic matters: Annītum was not pleased with the state of her provisions, and warfare and the taking of enemy prisoners. Their messages, *ṭēmum*, were obtained by entering a state of ecstasy (*mâḫu*) (Nissinen et al. 2003: no. 23). Twice their message is to be validated by making an inquiry (extispicy) by their hem and hair, once the letter writer explains that the oracles that he himself had obtained were similar. The *asinnu* is often mentioned alongside the *kurgarrû*, these two cultic functionaries are notoriously difficult to really get a grip of and have spawned much discussion. They both lived as devotees of the goddess Ištar. Their functions changed and fused over the centuries, and they are also associated with the *kalû*, who is perceived as cross-gendered. Similarly, both the *asinnu* and the *kurgarrû* are commonly interpreted as trans-sexual in some way (Becking 2007: 56). The evidence for castration or self-mutilation is very circumstantial and there is no real evidence that they were homosexual or transvestite. The *asinnu* and *kurgarrû* took part in various temple rituals in the Ištar cult. They played a role as jesters at the Hellenistic *Akītu* festival in Babylon.[27] Jesters commonly are perceived as being outside the normal bounds of society and are thus in the unique position of being able and expected to question its norms – whether this reflects on their appearance of bisexual beings must remain speculation. It is beyond doubt that the goddess Ištar/Inana was at the same time the incarnation of female alluring sexuality and male aggression and protective powers. She transcended, or rather united, two complementary sides of human nature as expressed by gender ideals. It was in her power to change right to left, left to right, man to woman and woman to man. For instance, as Venus she changed her sex according to her position in relation to the sun. Still, it is invariably expressed with the feminine form of the adjective: "she is male." However, the *asinnu* as gender-bender has recently been rejected by Zsolnay (2013), as an example of the overemphasis on the role of transgender in Mesopotamian prophecy in modern research (Stökl 2013).

As far as I can tell, there is no difference between the kind of messages male and female prophets may relay. The topics of the prophecies are war, cultic matters, and rarely more personal concerns of the king or the letter writer. The gods pronounce reassurance, warnings, demands, and instructions independent of the gender of their medium.

---

27 Pongratz-Leisten (1994: 230–231). For a discussion of the *asinnu* as prophet and his appearance in other rituals, see e.g., Zsolnay (2013).

Neo-Assyrian Proclaimers

By the Neo-Assyrian period, the titles *muḫḫû/muḫḫūtu* (the equivalent to Old Babylonian *maḫḫû/maḫḫūtu*) were outdated and largely replaced by *raggintu/raggimu*, the male and female "proclaimer." The older title is rarely attested, but there is no reason to assume that the *raggintu* and the *maḫḫūtu* were two different functionaries (Nissinen 1989: 9; Huffmon 2000: 57). There is only a single certain reference to female ecstatics, which is in a decree of expenditures for various ceremonies at the Aššur temple. Here the brewers are allotted barley to produce beer for the presence of the prophetesses at a ceremony called the divine council (SAA 12: 69 obv. 27–31). What they did at the ceremony besides drinking beer is not mentioned anywhere. Esarhaddon referred to all the favorable signs that inaugurated his accession, including messages from prophets, *šipir maḫḫê*. Ashurbanipal cited favorable prophecies along with other kinds of divination when he undertook building activities, and when he was faced with the attacks of Manneans and Elamites. Undoubtedly, all these prophecies reflect the oracle of Ištar of Arbela, as suggested by Nissinen (1998: 9–10). It is only in this phrase that the activities of ecstatics are ever mentioned in the Neo-Assyrian period.

Raggintu/raggimu, the "proclaimer," was the Neo-Assyrian colloquial term for prophet. Unlike the sources from Mari, the Neo-Assyrian prophecies are mostly known from compilations (published in SAA 9), not from letters or reports. This means that we know even less about the cultic setting or possible accompanying rituals. A *raggintu* in Babylon prophesized in "the assembly of the country," presumably in public, to the advantage of the substitute king (SAA 10: 353), whom she had also addressed directly previously. Another letter (SAA 13: 37) mentions a female proclaimer making her pronouncement in the temple, again in Babylonia. An astrologer complains that Esarhaddon summoned male and female proclaimers to the court when he himself is so much more deserving (SAA 10: 109). Van der Toorn argues that the proclaimers generally did not make their prophecies inside the temple and that the ubiquitous self-introduction of the god speaking, e.g., "I am Ištar of Arbela," was therefore necessary. Outside the temple away from the cult statues there would be no other way for the audience to know which god was addressing them (van der Toorn (2000: 82–84). The forlorn scholar, Urad-Gula, describes asking a *raggimu* for council in vain (SAA 10: 294), indicating that the proclaimers had private clients and could be consulted on matters on a smaller scale than politics.

Two women appear in the Neo-Assyrian corpus as prophets but with the title *šēlūtu* "votaress." One is a votaress of the king (SAA 16: 1 v 10), another of Ištar of Arbela (SAA 13: 148).

The compilations are written in Neo-Assyrian dialect and have literary qualities. The collection SAA 9: 1 and perhaps SAA 9: 3 were used as source material for the writers of Esarhaddon's inscription (Nin. A) (Nissinen 1998: 31). Parpola assumes that they were not subject to much editing but rendered as spoken, and the compilations were all written by the same scribe (Parpola (1997: LV and LXVII). The very few reports of prophecies quoted in letters are brief and often use metaphorical language.[28] They are also generally concerned with specific problems rather than the more overarching reassurances of the prophecies in the collection. In SAA 13: 37 a female proclaimer is reported to have made a prophecy about a throne from a temple: "Let the throne go! I will catch the enemies of my king with it!" The throne was needed for the substitute king ritual and evidently there were some problems procuring it for the ceremony. In SAA 13: 144 a female proclaimer prophesized on behalf of a deity: "Why have you given the [. . .] grove to the Egyptians? Say to the king that they be returned to me, and I will give total abundance [to] his [. . .]."

Other Ecstatics and Dream Interpreters

The *zabbu* and *zabbatu* were a kind of ecstatic who prophesized while in a frenzy, perhaps falling to the ground and rolling in the dust (CAD s.v.). *Zabbu* could be used to refer to a crazy person as in the curse formula of a *kudurru*, where the "ecstatic" is mentioned as one of the persons you are not supposed to hand the document over to (Reschid and Wilcke 1975: 56). The title is otherwise only known from rituals, the omen series *Šumma ālu*, and lexical lists. In the lexical lists they are typically equated with the *maḫḫû*.

We do not know much about them, and I will not venture a guess as to when they practiced. They could be consulted by private persons, as a paragraph in the quite beautiful prayer to Ištar of Uruk shows:

> May the ecstatic tell you, may the dream-interpreter recount to you, may the night-watches relate, that I did not weep, that I did not lie down, did not groan, did not arise, that my tears fell into my food.[29]

28 SAA 9: 8 is a brief report on a single prophecy, no name/sex of the prophet, the god proclaims: "I have come from the mace. The snake in it I have hauled out and cut in pieces," referring to the Elamites. In SAA 10: 353, the god says: "I have revealed the polecat . . . ."

29 Ebeling (1953) 29d-e. See Lambert (1959: 126–128). LKA 29d ii 2–5: *zab-bu liq-ba-kim-ma šab-ru-u li-šá-na-ki* en.nun.meš *ša* ge$_6$ *lid-bu-ba-nik-ki ki-i la ab-ku-ú la at-ti-lu la uš-ta-ni-ḫu la at-ba-ma*.

The sufferer calls the two types of diviners and the night itself as witnesses before Ištar of his restless sorrowful nights. Just like Šubši-mešrê-Šakkan, he has in vain sought divinatory answers to why he is struck down.[30]

In a prolonged ritual to cure a private person who has been struck by a demon or another kind of evil, both the male and female ecstatic are mentioned. The ritual is to be performed in the month of Dumuzi when Ištar makes the people mourn for Dumuzi. When the family is gathered, Ištar is to be summoned and offered sumptuous gifts, including a star of gold. The male and female ecstatics (*zabbu*) and the male and female prophets (*maḫḫû*) are given food as part of the offerings to Ištar and Dumuzi, but they do not play any active part in the ritual.[31] Neither is there any evidence that ecstatics were associated with the cult of deities.[32]

The male ecstatic is mentioned among other types of priests, prophets, diviners, and women with special functions (midwife, harlot) in *Šumma ālu*[33] and in lexical lists. One omen reads: "If there is a lot of ecstatic activity in a land: that land will collapse into ruins."[34]

Šabrâtu and *šabrû*, female and male dream interpreter, are only very rarely attested. The words could be derived from *barû*, but that is not certain (see CAD s.v.). From the one instance where it is used within a longer context, it seems that it was the *šabrû* themselves who dream, rather than interpret the dreams of others. Ashurbanipal reports that a *šabrû* lay down and had a dream or vision in the night after the king had entreated Ištar of Arbela to stand by him. He reported the words of Ištar, which are supportive and encouraging. Presumably, Ashurbanipal's worries about the Elamite king Teumman were formulated as part of a ritual to induce the vision – at least, the two events must have been connected, even if it is not stated explicitly. Similarly, a *šabrû* has a dream which confirms Sin's support in the fight against the faithless brother Šamaš-šumu-ukin.[35]

---

30 The righteous sufferer in *Ludlul bēl nēmeqi*. Lambert (1960: 44–45).

31 LKA 69; 70; TuL no. 11. The manuscript from Ashurbanipal's libraries K 02001+ contains a duplicate. The ms. has not been published after K 02001 has been joined and unfortunately no photos are available.

32 The title read as *za-a[b]-bu ša* ^{d}*Aš-šur* on a *pazūzu* head is rather to be read *ṣa-ra*$^{!}$*-pu*, cf. Klengel-Brandt (1968).

33 Sm 322:5′, 23′, (obv.!) published in Köcher and Oppenheim (1957–58: 71).

34 K 3969+ (CT 40 45-46 l. 19). An excerpt from *Šumma ālu*.

35 Prism inscriptions, RINAP 5, Ashurbanipal 3 v 49, 4 v 1′, 6 vi 31′, 7 v 127. See rinap/rinap5 (upenn.edu) and Nissinen (1998: 55–58).

Ordinary Women

Women without any specific religious role or title could also serve as mouthpieces for the divine. In ARM 26: 210, a woman, wife of a (free) man, asks Kibri-Dagan to convey a message from Dagan to Zimrilim. A servant girl is reported to have fallen into a trance in the temple of Annunītum and spoken words of reassurance to the king (ARM 26 214). Zimri-Lim received admonishments from his close female relatives based on their own dreams. Queen Addu-duri, Zimri-lim's mother, reports a dream she had, in which Belet-ekallim has left her temple and Dagan has also gone away. There are no prophetic contents as such and the gods are absent, but the theme is clearly a sort of warning. She goes on to quote a prophetess of Annunītum, who warns the king to be careful (ARM 26: 237).[36] Zimri-lim's daughter reports a dream concerning the naming of a baby girl (ARM 26: 239). In the Mari letters, dreams and visions by named and unnamed private individuals are quoted most often to exhort the receiver of the lẹtter to act in a certain way. A woman named Zunana writes to king Zimrilim about how Dagan spoke to her. In accordance with Dagan's commands, the king should help her getting her maid back, who had been abducted by one of his men. From the context, it is impossible to tell what form the communication with Dagan took, it might have been a dream as suggested by Durand (ARM 26: 232), direct inspiration, or a form of artificial divination. Under any circumstances, Zunana is confident enough to transmit the words of Dagan directly, and she does not appeal to the king to have their validity tested by extispicy.

Women who were affiliated with a temple, but were not prophets *per se*, could also report oracles, *ṭertum*, they had experienced (Nissinen 2013: 41). For instance, a *qammatum* of Dagan of Terqa reports that:

> The peacemaking of the man of Ešnunna is false: beneath straw water runs! I will gather him into the net that I knot. I will destroy his city and I will ruin his wealth which come from time immemorial (Nissinen et al. 2003: no. 7 ll. 11–19).[37]

The title *qammatu* is only known from Mari from three letters, which probably refer to the same incident. One letter specifically concerns the hem and hair of the *qammatum*, which the king had apparently requested to verify the oracle.

Women who did not bear the title *raggintu* could speak on behalf of Ištar of Arbela. The prophecy in SAA 16: 1 iii 1′-5′ is spoken by Ilussa-amur, a woman from the inner city (Assur). Another famous example is the prophecy "by the

36 See Nissinen (2013: 41). Nissinen understands it as an example of a palace woman acting as a prophetess.

37 The same event is mentioned in nos. 9 and 13.

mouth of the woman Bayâ, 'son'(!) of Arbela" (SAA 16: 1 ii 40), the discrepancy has been seen as an indication of the transgender nature of some prophets.

While anybody could report a portentous omen, reports of prophecy by non-professionals are uncommon in the Neo-Assyrian corpus. One Neo-Assyrian letter (SAA 16: 59) mentions a slave girl who has been in a trance for some time and has uttered favorable prophecies for Nusku of Harran in favor of the conspirator Sasî. These were to be tested by extispicy and were evidently very unreliable.[38] So, if not common, it was possible for quite ordinary women to be taken seriously as ecstatic prophets. It is well known that failing to report divine messages in whatever form was considered treason. The succession treaty of Esarhaddon includes a duty to report any unfavorable words, whether uttered by friend or foe, or by the mouth of prophet, of a questioner of the divine word, or any human being at all. It is tempting to understand the last three as uttering adverse prophecies rather than plots of rebellion (SAA 2 6 ll. 108–122).

Conclusion

Female diviners are attested throughout the ancient world, sometimes playing a very prominent role performing artificial divination like the Hittite "Old Ones," or as human mouthpieces for God, like the Hebrew prophetesses. In ancient Mesopotamia, women are only attested as active diviners within prophecy and oneiromancy. There is little indication that visions seen by women were in any way less valuable than those seen by men, even though it has been noted that verification by the prophet's hem and hair are twice as common for women and *asinnus* as for men (Hamori 2012). However, throughout the millennia they were media for divine communication via dreams or visions on a par with men. If they practiced other forms of divination this is virtually unattested with the single mention of female seers in an Old Assyrian source as a possible exception. Natural divination is a form of communication with the divine which utilizes the human mind itself as its medium. It can appear without warning – as a spontaneous message from gods, or it can be the result of a ritual intended to render the human consciousness prepared to receive the divine messages – or conjure a vision, a dream, or a ghost. The prophecies could be answers to specific concerns (primarily by the answerers) or spontaneous warnings or requests from the gods.

38 See the discussion by Nissinen (1998: 159–53).

Apparently, contact with the divine was not dependent on a person's gender, rank, economical, or social position. Whereas the examples from the Hebrew Bible may point to a discomfort with women crossing the boundaries of the social and religious accepted female roles and the authority lent by acting as a conduit for the divine, there is no evidence for this being the case in Mesopotamia, even as society and religious norms changed. There does not seem to be any difference between the kind of dreams or oracles men, or women might convey, neither is there any real evidence that female and male practitioners of natural divination were treated or perceived differently. Throughout the millennia, the sex of the human receptacle was of no importance when it came to communication with the divine.

Bibliography

Abusch, I. Tzvi. 2016. *The magical ceremony Maqlû: A critical edition.* Leiden: Brill.

Alster, Bendt. 1978. *Dumuzi's Dream.* København: Akademisk Forlag.

Asher-Greve, Julia M. and Joan G. Westenholz. 2013. *Goddesses in Context: On Divine Power, Roles, Relationships and Gender in Mesopotamian Textual and Visual Sources.* Fribourg / Göttingen: Academic Press / Vandenhoeck & Ruprecht.

Beal, Richard H. 2002. Hittite Oracles. Pp. 57–81 in *Magic and Divination in the Ancient World,* ed. L. Ciraolo and J. Seidel. Leiden: Brill / Styx.

Barberon, Lucile. 2014. To Dedicate or Marry a Nadîtu-Woman of Marduk in Old Babylonian Society. Pp. 267–74 in *La famille dans le Proche-Orient ancien: réalités, symbolismes et images. Proceedings of the 55e Rencontre Assyriologique Internationale,* L. Marti and J. Llop. Pennsylvania: Penn State University Press.

Becking, Bob. 2007. The Prophets as Persons. Pp. 53–63 in *Hearing Visions and Seeing Voices Psychological Aspects of Biblical Concepts and Personalities,* ed. G. Glas, M.H. Spero, P.J. Verhagen, and H.M. van Praag. Dordrecht: Springer Netherlands.

Cryer, Frederick H. 1994. *Divination in Ancient Israel and its Near Eastern Environment: A Socio-Historical Investigation.* Sheffield: JSOT Press.

Ebeling, Erich. 1953. *Literarische Keilschrifttexte aus Assur.* Berlin: Akademie-Verlag.

Frahm, Eckart. 2004. Royal Hermeneutics: Observations on the Commentaries from Ashurbanipal's Libraries at Nineveh. *Iraq* 66: 45–50.

Halton, Charles and Saana Svärd. 2017. *Women's Writing of Ancient Mesopotamia: An Anthology of the Earliest Female Authors.* New York: Cambridge University Press.

Hamori, Ester J. 2012. Gender and the Verification of Prophecy at Mari. *Die Welt des Orients* 42: 1–22.

Hamori, Ester J. 2015. *Women's Divination in Biblical Literature: Prophecy, Necromancy, and other Arts of Knowledge.* New Haven: Yale University Press.

Heeßel, Nils P. 2012. *Divinatorische Texte II: Opferschau-Omina.* Wiesbaden: Harassowitz.

Heimpel, Wolfgang. 1998–2001. Nanše. A. *RlA* 9: 152–60.

Huber Vulliet, Fabienne. 2019. *Le personnel cultuel à l'époque néo-sumérienne (ca. 2160-2003 av. J.-C.)*. BPOA, 14. Madrid: Consejo Superior de Investigaciones Científicas.

Huffmon, Herbert B. 2000. A Company of Prophets: Mari, Assyria, Israel. Pp. 47–70 in *Prophecy in its ancient Near Eastern context: Mesopotamian, biblical, and Arabian perspectives*, ed. M. Nissinen. Atlanta, GA: Society of Biblical Literature.

Klengel-Brandt, Evelyn. 1968. Ein Pazuzu-Kopf mit Inschrift. *OrNS* 37: 81–84.

Koch-Westenholz, Ulla. 1995. *Mesopotamian Astrology. An Introduction to Babylonian and Assyrian Celestial Divination*. Copenhagen: Museum Tusculanum Press.

Köcher, Franz and A. Leo Oppenheim. 1957–58. The Old-Babylonian Omen Text VAT 7525. *AfO* 18: 62–77.

Lambert, Wilfred G. 1959. The Sultantepe Tablets. A Review Article, review of *The Sultantepe Tablets*, I, by O.R. Gurney and J.J. Finkelstein. *RA* 53: 119–38.

Lambert, Wilfred G. 1960. *Babylonian Wisdom Literature*. Oxford: Clarendon.

Lambert, Wilfred G. 1967. The Gula hymn of Bullutsa-rabi. *OrNS* 36: 105–32.

Lambert, Wilfred G. 1998. The Qualifications of Babylonian Diviners. Pp. 141–58 in *Festschrift für Rykle Borger zu seinem 65. Geburtstag am 24. Mai 1994: Tikip santakki mala bašmu*, ed. S.M. Maul. CM, 10. Groningen: Styx.

Larsen, Mogens T. 2002. *The Aššur-nāda Archive*. Leiden: NINO.

Larsen, Mogens T. 2010. *Kültepe Tabletleri VI-a The Archive of the Salim-Assur Family* Volume I: *The First Two Generations*. Ankara: Türk Tarih Kurumu.

Lion, Brigitte. 2000. Les mentions de "prophètes" dans la seconde moitié du IIe millénaire av J.-C. *RA* 94: 21–32.

Lion, Brigitte. 2012. Prophète et prophétesses en Mesopotamie. Pp. 147–67 in *Femmes médiatrices et ambivalentes: Mythes et imaginaires*, ed. A. Caiozzo and N. Ernoult. Paris: Colin.

Michalowski, Piotr. 1998–2001. Nisaba. A. *RlA* 9: 575–79.

Michalowski, Piotr. 2006. How to read the liver – in Sumerian. Pp. 247–58 in *If a Man Builds a Joyful House: Assyriological Studies in Honor of Erle Verdun Leichty*, ed. E. Leichty and A.K. Guinan. CM, 31. Leiden: Brill.

Michalowski, Piotr and Erica Reiner. 1993. *Letters from early Mesopotamia*. WAW, 3. Atlanta, GA: Scholars Press.

Michel, Cécile. 2001. *Correspondance des marchands de Kanis au début du IIe millňaire avant J.-C.* Paris: Éditions du Cerf.

Michel, Cécile. 2009. Les filles consacrées des marchands assyriens. *Topoi Suppléments* 10: 145–63.

Nissinen, Martti. 1998. *References to Prophecy in Neo-Assyrian Sources*. SAAS, 7. Helsinki: Neo-Assyrian Text Corpus Project.

Nissinen, Martti. 2013. Gender and Prophetic Agency. Pp. 23–58 in *Prophets male and female gender and prophecy in the Hebrew* Bible, *the Eastern* Mediterranean, *and* the *ancient Near East*, ed. J. Stökl and C.L. Carvalho. Atlanta, GA: Society of Biblical Literature.

Nissinen, Martti, Robert K. Ritner, C.L. Seow, and Peter Machinist. 2003. *Prophets and prophecy in the ancient Near East*. Atlanta, GA: Society of Biblical Literature.

Lambert, Wilfred G. 1998. The Qualifications of Babylonian Diviners. Pp. 141–158 in *Tikip santakki mala bašmu. Festschrift to Rykle Borger zu seinem 65. Geburtstag am 24. Mai 1994*, ed S. M. Maul. Groningen: Styx.

Parpola, Simo. 1997. *Assyrian prophecies*. SAA, 9. Helsinki: Helsinki University Press.

Pongratz-Leisten, Beate. 1994. *Ina Šulmi Īrub: Die Kulttopographische und ideologische Programmatik der akītu-Prozession in Babylonien und Assyrien im 1. Jahrtausend v. Chr.* BaF, 16. Mainz: Philipp von Zabern.

Reschid, Fawzi and Claus Wilcke. 1975. Ein 'Grenzstein' aus dem ersten (?) Regierungsjahr des Königs Marduk-šāpik-zēri. *ZA* 65: 34–62.

Starr, Ivan. 1983. *The Rituals of the Diviner.* Malibu: Undena Publications.

Stökl, Jonathan. 2013. Gender "Ambiguity" in Ancient Near Eastern Prophecy? A Reassesment of the Data Behind a Popular Theory. Pp. 59–80 in *Prophets male and female gender and prophecy in the Hebrew* Bible, *the Eastern* Mediterranean, *and* the *ancient Near East*, ed. J. Stökl and C.L. Carvalho. Atlanta, GA: Society of Biblical Literature.

van der Toorn, Karel. 2000. Mesopotamian Prophecy between immanence and transcendence: A Comparison of Old Babylonian and Neo-Assyrian Prophecy. Pp. 71–88 in *Prophecy in its ancient Near Eastern context: Mesopotamian, biblical, and Arabian perspectives*, ed. M. Nissinen. Atlanta, GA: Society of Biblical Literature.

Warbinek, Livio. 2019. Was the Hittite MUNUS.ENSI a Dream Interpretress? *KASKAL* 16: 53–74.

Zgoll, Annette. 2002. Die Welt im Schlaf sehen – Inkubation von Träumen im antiken Mesopotamien. *Die Welt des Orients* 32: 74–101.

Ziegler, Nele. 1999. *Le Harem de Zimri-lim.* FM, 4. Paris: SEPOA.

Zimmern, Heinrich. 1901. *Beiträge zur Kenntnis der babylonischen Religion: Die Beschwörungstafeln Surpu. Ritualtafeln für den Wahrsager, Beschwörer und Sänger.* Leipzig: J.C. Hinrichs'sche Buchhandlung.

Zsolnay, Ilona. 2013. The Misconstrued Role of the *Asinnu* in Ancient Near Eastern Prophecy. Pp. 81–100 in *Prophets male and female gender and prophecy in the Hebrew* Bible, *the Eastern* Mediterranean, *and the ancient Near East*, ed. J. Stökl and C.L. Carvalho. Atlanta, GA: Society of Biblical Literature.

Part III: **Goddesses**

Sophus Helle

Enheduana's Invocations: Form and Force

A fundamental element of ancient poetry – be it hymns, prayers, or myths – is the use of invocations.[1] In poetry about or addressed to a divine figure, invocations serve to summon the deity into the text, centering them as the subject or recipient of the poem. At the same time, invocations mark a distance between the speakers and the gods, who are addressed not as nearby interlocutors but as far-away, all-mighty figures to be apostrophized and praised. The invocation is thus a moment of exceptional poetic force, reaching out to a distant deity and inviting them into the text.

The importance of invocations for ancient poetry too often goes unnoticed. While there is some scholarship on the religious significance of invocations in cuneiform poetry (for example, what their format can tell us about ancient conceptions of the divine), their literary role has not received the same attention.[2] This may be because modern eyes too easily skip past an address to a deity ("Oh Inana!") to reach what seems at first to be the core of the poem: its storyline, images, allusions, tropes, and so on. For many modern readers, there is something *empty* about invocations (Culler 1977: 59–60). They bear no meaning in themselves, they do not advance the plot, often they do not even describe the deity but merely repeat their name or titles. Invocations seem trimmable. When studying ancient poems, they are the parts that one is most tempted to overlook – but, as I argue in this essay, scholars ignore invocations at their own peril.

In the following, I analyze the use of invocations in the Sumerian poem **nin me šar$_2$-ra**, known in English as *The Exaltation of Inana*. The poem is commonly attributed to the Old Akkadian high priestess Enheduana – an attribution that would make her the first named author in the history of world literature. The *Exaltation* is a fascinating poem, full of stunning images and meta-poetic reflections. With more than eighty preserved manuscripts, it is also among the best-attested Sumerian poems, and it is practically unique in cuneiform literature for being preserved in its entirety – it has no gaps or lacunae – though it still offers

---

1 I would like to thank Nicole Brisch for her kind and constructive feedback on an earlier draft of this paper. All shortcomings remain my own.

2 On approaches to invocations in cuneiform hymns and prayers from a religious (rather than a literary) perspective, see e.g., Mayer 1976: 39–45, Zgoll 2003: 195, and Lenzi 2010. On the poetics of prayer and religious rituals in the cuneiform world, see e.g., Abusch 1983, Lenzi 2011, Zgoll 2004, Schwemer 2014, and Veldhuis 1999.

https://doi.org/10.1515/9781501514821-011

many other philological challenges, from obscure phrases to hapax legomena.[3] Crucially, the invocations of the goddess Inana that appear in the *Exaltation* are no empty shout-outs: they serve to structure and organize the poem, and lend it a particular poetic force.

My argument falls in two parts, one focused on the poem's structure and one on its literary effects. The first part argues that the *Exaltation* can be divided into six sections based on the form of the narrator's address to Inana: the invocations thus give the poem a previously unnoticed clarity of composition. The second part turns to what role invocations play in the poetics of the text, that is, what literary effects they are used to achieve. I examine four such effects – action, presence, withheld names, and triangulated address – to argue that invocations imbue the *Exaltation* with a singular literary power. The invocations do not merely describe the goddess, as any epithet might – they *move* the audience in their relation to Inana, while also structuring the poem and highlighting its key transitions.

1 The Exaltation of Inana

The *Exaltation* is a hymn to Inana – the Sumerian goddess of war, love, and transformation – that includes an account of how Enheduana was thrown into exile by a usurper named Lugal-Ane. The historical Enheduana was the daughter of the Old Akkadian king Sargon and served as the high priestess of the moon god Nanna in the city of Ur. The *Exaltation* is one of several poems attributed to her by the Old Babylonian scribes, but the earliest preserved manuscripts of those poems date to centuries after her death, meaning that they may have been composed later in her name (see e.g., Civil 1980: 229; Michalowski 1996: 183–85; Glassner 2009; but cf. Foster 2016: 207; Lion 2011: 97; Helle forthcoming). During the Old Babylonian period (19th–17th century BCE), the *Exaltation* became a mainstay of the ancient school curriculum. Students copied out the poem to familiarize themselves with the complexities of literary Sumerian, which is why the poem has survived in so many manuscripts, leading its editor Annette Zgoll

3 The text was first edited by Hallo and van Dijk (1968), an updated edition was published by Zgoll (1997) and a further updated score transliteration can be found in Delnero (2006: 2021–18). All quotations from the text follow Zgoll's edition; the English translations are my own, though they are highly indebted to the French translation by Attinger (2019). I am preparing a book-length study of Enheduana and the poems attributed to her (Helle forthcoming); it will be accompanied by a website that will include a line-by-line translation and exegesis of the *Exaltation*, at enheduana.org/exaltation/.

(1997: 40) to dub it "der erste Bestseller der Weltliteratur." Though it is unclear whether Enheduana composed the *Exaltation* herself, the poem is still a remarkable literary achievement. It yokes together strings of striking metaphors, creating images that are both vivid and obscure. Its word choice is often unusual or archaic, and there are lines that can be read in several contradictory ways at once (Helle 2020: 61). None of these features are unique to the *Exaltation*, but their combination makes it a work of stunning complexity.

The *Exaltation* begins with a hymnic section that extols the might of Inana, describing the fury with which the goddess destroys all who rebel against her. The narrator Enheduana then introduces herself and explains her plight. She has served faithfully as the high priestess of Nanna, but now Lugal-Ane has seized power in Ur, expelled Enheduana from the temple, and driven her into exile. She wanders through the land praying desperately to Nanna, but he does not answer. The situation is described as an open court case that leaves Enheduana suspended in uncertainty, awaiting her judgment (Zgoll 1997). Since Nanna refuses to step in, Enheduana turns to his daughter Inana instead, asking her to intervene and in so doing succeed Nanna as divine arbiter. Enheduana interprets her own ambiguous predicament as Nanna's de facto abdication; meaning that if he will not decide the matter one way or another, he has effectively left the case to Inana: **^{d}nanna li-bi$_2$-in-du$_{11}$-ga za-a-kam bi$_2$-in-du$_{11}$-ga / nin-ĝu$_{10}$ ib$_2$-gu-ul-en i$_3$-mah-en**, "Nanna has said nothing, so he has said: 'It is up to you!' / This has made you greater, my lady, this has made you the greatest" (ll. 133–134). In other words, since Nanna has issued no verdict in Enheduana's case, he has deliberately left the matter to Inana, paving the way for the goddess's rise to power, if only she is willing to seize her chance.

In other words, Enheduana must convince Inana to rule in her favor, but also to rule in the first place, and so replace her father as a ruler among gods. But Enheduana faces one more challenge, and a particularly daunting one at that: she has lost her eloquence. Her power of speech, with which she used to soothe the angry gods, has disappeared. This is the real crisis of the narrative. Without her eloquence, Enheduana will remain unable to persuade Inana and so save herself. The problem is finally remedied by the composition of the poem itself, as the climax of the story describes how Enheduana created the text we have been reading so far and thus regained her poetic powers. The text effectively ends by describing how it came into being, in the narrative equivalent of a snake biting its own tail. In the last eleven lines (ll. 143–53), an epilogue informs us that the hymn was successful, that Inana accepted Enheduana's prayer and intervened on her behalf, and that Nanna approved his daughter's rise to power. Despite its brevity – it is a mere 153 lines – the *Exaltation* is a complex and multilayered text, which reflects on its own composition and the voice of its narrator.

The story is essentially about itself, and about how the characters who are described in the poem are transformed by that poem. All this is narrated in an often unusual and tightly packed poetic language, replete with elliptical references to other myths about Inana.

The first step in any interpretation must be to establish some structure in the poem, but every translation has done so differently. The first editors, William Hallo and J.J.A. van Dijk (1968: 14–35), divided it into eighteen stanzas that are grouped into three main sections, "Exordium," "Argument," and "Peroration" (ll. 1–65, 66–135, and 136–153). In a later edition, Zgoll opted for four main sections (ll. 1–59, 66–73, 74–96, and 100–108), linked by transitional passages, and further divided into fourteen subsections (see the tables in Zgoll 1997: 37–38 and 55). The translation by Benjamin Foster (2016: 331–36) has twelve sections, that by Jeremy Black et al. (2004: 315–20) has fourteen, while that by Pascal Attinger (2019) does not subdivide the text at all. In short, there seems to be no consensus among scholars about how the text is structured. Of course, this need not be a problem: it is often the case for poetic texts that their transitions are so gradual and their structure so complicated that readers will reach different conclusions about how the text is to be subdivided, and Assyriologists will often offer outlines of the literary texts they study.

However, I will argue that the *Exaltation* does in fact mark its internal transitions quite clearly, carefully guiding the audience through the poem and highlighting its every shift in focus. Instead of imposing onto the text such terms as "peroration," taken from the much later tradition of Classical rhetorics, I think it best to follow the poem's own way of treating textual boundaries. Intriguingly, the *Exaltation* marks its subdivisions through invocations. When Enheduana repeatedly addresses Inana with the same phrase, this signals to the audience that a shift is taking place. When we hear a formula that we have come across before, we are to take note: the invocations are the internal thresholds of the poem, the boundary markers that make its structure apparent.

2 Invocations and Structure

The *Exaltation*'s use of repeated invocations first comes into view in l. 6, which begins with the phrase **nin-ĝu$_{10}$**, "My lady!" Fourteen lines later, one finds another line that begins with the same phrase. It is then found again in ll. 27 and 34. The distribution is no coincidence: with the exception of l. 13, every seventh line of the poem's introductory hymn to Inana begins with the phrase **nin-ĝu$_{10}$**. The apparent exception, l. 13, is remarkable for another reason. In place of the expected **nin-ĝu** one finds the phrase **izi bar$_7$-bar$_7$**, "flaming fire," which in cuneiform is written with the sign NE repeated thrice. The beginning of the poem thus consists of five seven-line stanzas, four of which are introduced by the invocation "My lady!" and the last of which begins with the threefold repetition of the same sign. In fact, the audience is warned in advance that the text will be divided into groups of seven lines. The line just before the first occurrence of the phrase **nin-ĝu$_{10}$**, l. 5, reads: **me imin-be$_2$ šu sa$_2$ du$_{11}$-ga**, "You who took hold of the seven cosmic powers!" The number seven can signify totality, implying that Inana has seized *all* cosmic powers (Sumerian **me**), but in this context, it also serves to announce the structure of the immediately following text.

Just after the last of the five stanzas, one finds the following couplet: **ib$_2$-ba nu-te-en-te-en dumu gal ^{d}suen-na / nin kur-ra diri-ga a-ba ki-za ba-an-tum$_3$**, "Your rage cannot be cooled, great daughter of Suen! / Lady, outstanding in the land, who can take anything from your domain (lit.: place)?" (ll. 41–42). This couplet is repeated almost verbatim in ll. 58–59: **u$_3$-sumun$_2$ zi-zi dumu gal ^{d}suen-na / nin an-ra diri-ga a-ba ki-za ba-an-tum$_3$**, "Charging aurochs, great daughter of Suen! / Lady, outstanding in the heavens, who can take anything from your domain (lit.: place)?" The parallel is a satisfying mix of repetition and variation. The first half of the first line is different, and in the second line, the word "heaven" replaces "earth," but otherwise the couplets are identical. In between the couplets, the poem tells of how Inana destroyed two enemies: a mountain she invaded – an external enemy – and a city that rebelled against her – an internal enemy (ll. 42–50 and 51–57, respectively).[4] The two passages begin by invoking the place that is about to be destroyed: **hur-saĝ**, "mountain," is the first word of l. 42; **iri**, "city," is the first word of l. 51. Whereas the previous section was structured by a linear sequence of seven-line blocks, here we find a chiastic structure: a couplet invoking Inana, the destruction of an invaded mountain, the destruction of a rebellious city, and a second, highly similar couplet invoking Inana.

---

4 It is not clear whether Inana invades the mountain, or whether she retaliates against the mountain's invasion of her territory (**ki**): the phrase **hur-saĝ ki-za ba-e-de$_3$-gid$_2$-de$_3$**, l. 43, can mean either "you extended your dominion over the mountain," as Zgoll (1997: 7) reads it, or "the mountain, which (sought to) extend into your dominion," as read by Attinger (2011: 55 n. 33) reads it. Either way, the contrast between the mountain and the city as external v. internal enemies still applies. I read the stanza as an allusion to the myth of *Inana and Ebih*, in which Inana invades and destroys the mountain of Ebih, which is why I prefer Zgoll's interpretation (note that Inana's destruction of the city is motivated by its failure to honor her, just as in *Inana and Ebih*). The grounds for attributing *Inana and Ebih* to Enheduana seem to me extremely slim, but her poems do repeatedly refer to this myth, especially in ll. 110–112 of the *Hymn to Inana*.

The following section is less clear to me. After the second of the repeated couplets, the poem moves into a narrative mode, introducing its narrator Enheduana and describing her reason for beseeching Inana (ll. 60–108). Invocations continue to play a key role, but their repetition is less exact; instead, the narrator seems to switch back and forth between various addressees. Some lines are addressed to Inana, some to Nanna, and some are Enheduana's description of herself. But if one follows these shifts, a subtle pattern emerges. In ll. 60–66, the as yet unnamed narrator invokes Inana, declaring that she will recite a song for her. In l. 67, the narrator introduces herself: **en-me-en en-he$_2$-du$_7$-a-na-me-en**, "I am the high priestess, I am Enheduana." In l. 74, she turns to Nanna, invoking him by name: **^{d}suen.**[5] In l. 81, Enheduana returns to herself: **en-he$_2$-du$_7$-a-na-me-en**, "I am Enheduana." After describing her plight, she invokes Inana once more in l. 91: **^{d}sumun$_2$ zi-ĝu$_{10}$**, "My righteous aurochs!" Finally, she turns back to herself one last time in l. 100, which begins with the word **ĝa$_2$-e**, "I." Briefly put, the fourth, narration section of the *Exaltation* zigzags between self-description and divine invocation. Enheduana addresses Inana, names herself, turns to Nanna, names herself, addresses Inana, and returns to herself once more. Though this structure is perhaps more muddled than the other sections, it does powerfully capture the narrator's sense of anguish as she turns from one god to the other, desperate for either to reply.

The next passage is again clearer, as it is structured by the threefold repetition of the phrase **nin ki-aĝ$_2$ an-na-ĝu$_{10}$**, "My lady, beloved of An!" (ll. 109, 121, and 135; note that in l. 109, it appears as **nin kal-kal-la an-ne$_2$ aĝ$_2$**, "Precious lady, whom An loves!"). This yields three distinct sections that bring the poem to a climactic resolution. In the first, Enheduana describes why her appeal to Inana remains necessary: **di ni$_2$-ĝa$_2$ nu-mu-un-til di kur$_2$ di-ĝu$_{10}$-gin$_7$ igi-ĝa$_2$ mu-un-ni$_{10}$-ni$_{10}$**, "The trial against me is still open! An adverse verdict coils around me, as if it were mine" (l. 117). In the second, the hymn breaks down into a list of epithets that glorify Inana, marked by the epiphoric repetition

5 Not all translators agree that Enheduana turns from Inana to Nanna in these lines. I follow the interpretation by Foster (2016: 333–34) and Black et al. (2004: 318): since Inana is referred to in the third person in ll. 77–80, they parse ll. 74–75 as Enheduana saying to Nanna that he should tell An about her problems with Lugal-Ane. One can then translate **nam-ĝu$_{10}$ ^{d}suen lugal-an-ne$_2$ / an-ra du$_{11}$-mu-na-ab**, as, "My fate, Suen, (namely this) Lugal-Ane—tell it to An." Zgoll (1997: 11) and Attinger (2019: 7) take a different view, seeing these words as still addressed to Inana, leading to a translation such as: "My fate (which concerns) Suen (and) Lugal-Ane—tell it to An." They see ll. 77–80 as An's instruction to Inana, explaining why she is referred to in third person. But regardless of whether the stanza is addressed to Inana or Nanna, my larger point still stands, as the section zigzags between Enheduana invoking the gods (though possibly just Inana) and returning to her own situation.

of the phrase **he$_2$-zu-am$_3$**, "Let it be known!" (ll. 122–132). In the third section, Enheduana describes how she composed the *Exaltation*, which, as noted above, effectively resolves the tension of the narrative. Once again, the crescendo that unfolds in this section is structured by a repeated invocation, as the phrase **nin ki-aĝ$_2$ an-na-ĝu$_{10}$**, "My lady, beloved of An," marks the transition from appeal through climax to resolution.

The final section, ll. 143–153, is clearly set off from the rest of the poem by a grammatical shift, as Enheduana is transformed from a first-person narrator into a third-person character. It seems that by composing the poem and relegating it to the **gala** singer who performs it in l. 140, the author has disappeared from her own text (Helle 2020). The epilogue states that the hymn was successful: Inana accepted Enheduana's prayer (ll. 144–145) and Nanna approved Inana's exaltation (l. 148). The poem has reached a conclusion, as emphasized by the repetition of phrases first found in the prologue. The first couplet of the poem is **nin me šar$_2$-ra u$_4$ dalla e$_3$-a / munus zi me-li$_9$ gur$_3$-ru**, "Lady of all cosmic powers, bright daylight streaming down, / righteous woman dressed in splendor;" which is echoed in the epilogue: **iti$_5$ e$_3$-a-gin$_7$ la-la ba-an-gur$_3$**, "Like a moonbeam streaming down, she was dressed in delight" (l. 147). The text uses the repetition of key phrases (**e$_3$-a** and **gur$_3$**) to mark its circular closure, and the shift from sunlight to moonlight (**u$_4$** to **iti$_5$**) to show that a transformation has taken place. Finally, the epilogue is once more delimited by a repeated invocation of Inana, as its first and last lines both begin with the word **nin**, "lady" (ll. 143 and 153). This is also the very first word in the text, and the word that is repeated every seventh line in the introductory hymn (its repeated appearance in the *Exaltation* is noted by Zgoll 1997: 18–27). In short, this is the defining word of the poem, echoing through the text like a *Leitmotif* and bringing us back each time to the might of Inana.

To sum up, while the *Exaltation* is a challenging text in any number of ways, it can be shown to follow a relatively clear narrative structure, as it marks the shift from one section to the next through repeated invocations of its main characters, especially Inana. By tracking these invocations, six distinct sections emerge, as shown in Table 1. The first is a prologue, which sets the tone for the rest of the poem by describing Inana's cosmic power. The second is a hymn to Inana, emphasizing her role as the goddess of war. The third section is a warning not to disrespect Inana, telling of how she destroyed an enemy mountain and a rebellious city. The fourth section is the main narrative section of the poem, introducing the narrator and explaining her predicament. The fifth section is the climax of the poem, culminating in the composition of the text itself. The sixth section is an epilogue that describes the outcome of the hymn and returns to its opening lines.

Table 1: Overview of the Structure of the *Exaltation*.

Lines	Section	Structure and repeated invocations
1–5	The prologue sets out the overall theme of the poem: Inana's cosmic power.	The text begins with an invocation of Inana: **nin me šar$_2$-ra**, "Lady of all cosmic powers" (l. 1).
6–40	The introductory hymn describes Inana in her role as goddess of war.	A sequential section consisting of five stanzas of seven lines each, four of which begin with the word **nin-ĝu$_{10}$**, "My lady" (ll. 6, 20, 27, and 34).
41–59	The warning to rebels describes Inana's punishment of a mountain and a city that defied her rule.	A chiastic section framed by two matching couplets invoking Inana (ll. 41–42 and 58–59), divided into a section addressed to the mountain (ll. 43–50) and to the city (ll. 51–57).
60–108	The main narrative introduces Enheduana and her reasons for appealing to Inana.	An alternating section, where the narrator turns back and forth between Inana (ll. 60–66), herself (ll. 67–73), Nanna (ll. 74–80), herself (ll. 81–90), Inana (ll. 91–98), and herself (ll. 99–109).
109–42	The climax glorifies Inana through a list of attributes, then describes the poem's composition.	A sequential section, consisting of three subsections introduced by the phrase **nin ki-aĝ$_2$ an-na-ĝu$_{10}$**, "My lady, beloved of heaven!" (ll. 109, 121, and 135).
143–53	The epilogue presents the resolution of the story.	The section refers to the narrator in the third person and repeats key phrases from the prologue. It is framed by the invocation of Inana as **nin**, "lady" (ll. 143 and 153).

The use of repeated invocations to organize the hymn has many parallels in other Sumerian poems. As noted by Jeremy Black (1992), repetitions are often used in oral poetry to structure the text for the benefit of the listening audience, who, unlike a reading audience, cannot turn to a previous page and review information they might have missed. Listeners are locked into a linear mode of reception; they can neither speed up, skip ahead, or go back. The difficulty involved in this mode of reception can be alleviated by "the use of (i) markers that are regularly associated with particular points of a composition (beginning, section boundary, end) and which thereby serve to 'flag' structural features for the listener; and (ii) by the use of repetition as a means of demarcating sections of the narrative structure" (Black 1992: 72) – a description that applies perfectly to the *Exaltation* as well. Black goes on to illustrate his point through a reading of the Sumerian narrative poem *Lugal-e*, which evidences many of the same features, though there, it is not only invocations that are repeated, but all sorts of phrases. An even more exact parallel was pointed out to me by Gina Konstantopoulos (personal communication), namely the Sumerian royal hymn *Iddin-Dagan D*, which after an initial praise of the goddess Nininsina turns to a selection of other deities, including An, Enlil, Ninlil, and Aruru: each god receives eight lines of hymnic praise, all beginning with an invocation of the deity in question. This structure is very similar to the second section of the *Exaltation*, where a repeated invocation is also followed by a fixed number of lines. However, the *Exaltation*'s choice of seven lines may be unusual. In his discussion of verse structure in Sumerian poetry, Herman Vanstiphout (1993) gives examples of distichs, tercets, quatrains, and sextets, but I know of no other Sumerian poems that demonstrably arranges its verses into septets. But there is still much research to be done on the formal structures of Sumerian poetry, so groups of seven lines may yet turn out to be a more common feature than they seem at present.

3 Invocation and Poetics

In what remains of the essay, I will argue that the invocations of the *Exaltation* are used not only to divide the text into sections, but also to lend it a particular poetic force. In this analysis, I am guided by Jonathan Culler's thought-provoking study *Theory of the Lyric* (2015), in which he argues that the traditional focus in literary studies on *hermeneutics* (which asks what the poem means) should be complemented by the older, but as of late neglected focus on *poetics* (which asks what the poem does or seeks to do). In the following, I identify four interlinked aspects of the literary role of invocations as they appear in the *Exaltation*: action, presence, withheld names, and triangulated address.

3.1 Apostrophe as Action

A seminal moment in Culler's study of the lyric tradition and its poetics was an article from 1977 on the apostrophe, a rhetorical device that has much in common with invocations: the apostrophe is an exclamatory address to an absent person or inanimate object. As Culler remarks, apostrophes are an embarrassment to modern poetry. Phrases like "O stars!" have the ring of the ridiculous.

Contemporary poets tend to employ apostrophes only with a touch of irony, and literary critics tend to ignore them altogether. Culler persuasively argues that this sense of suspicion stems from the apostrophe's attempt not just to describe the world but to change it. The apostrophe *does* something: it summons, scolds, or exalts its subject. Since modern poets have grown disenchanted with the idea that poetry can have real-life effects (as Auden famously wrote: "poetry makes nothing happen"[6]), the apostrophe's blatant assertion of poetic efficacy has come to sound like posturing pretense. When we turn to premodern texts, we risk carrying that bias with us, disregarding invocations in ancient literature as nothing more than grandiloquent embellishments.

There can be no question that the *Exaltation* tries to do something, at least according to its internal narrative logic. As described above, the *Exaltation* depicts a situation in which Enheduana has been cast into exile by a revolt and attempts to regain her position in Ur by appealing to Inana. Enheduana's plea to Inana must overcome a series of hurdles to be successful: Inana must take over Nanna's position as arbiter among gods, and Enheduana must reclaim her lost eloquence. These hurdles are finally cleared in the poem's climactic resolution, where Enheduana composes the text we have been reading. In short, the poem is about its own lyrical efficacy. The resolution of the narrative tension – the question of whether Enheduana will be saved and reinstated as high priestess of Ur – depends entirely on whether the plea to Inana is successful, and the plea is nothing other than the text itself (except the last eleven lines of the text, which state that the prayer has achieved its intended effects). The account of Lugal-Ane's insurrection and Enheduana's exile is merely given as background information, a flashback that explains the main action of the text, which is Enheduana's prayer to Inana. In other words, what happens in the poem is the poem itself. The *Exaltation* is not an account of dramatic events – as an epic would be – but an event in its own right.

As Culler observes, the use of the apostrophe in lyric poetry highlights the voicing of the poem as a self-standing action. That is, an address to a person or thing, irrespective of whether that person or thing will ever hear said address, lends the poem the force of an action, which would be lacking from a more static formulation of the same sentiment. In Culler's words, the apostrophe carries "the incalculable force of an event" (Culler 1977: 68). Compare the sentence "Inana is great" with "Oh great Inana!" The former is a descriptive statement that could be spoken by anyone or by no one; it implies no particular speaker

6 This oft-quoted line is from the second section of W.H. Auden's "In Memory of W. B. Yeats."

or recipient and could just as easily be spoken or written. The latter, by contrast, is clearly addressed to Inana and is just as clearly spoken by a personified narrator, whether or not the identity of that narrator is made explicit. Even if the latter sentence appears exclusively in writing, it summons the *idea* of a voice calling out to the goddess. Finally, whereas the former sentence only describes the world, the latter seeks actively to change it, if only the fictional world of the text: it seeks to attract the goddess's attention and enlist her help. In short, the action of the text is its own voicing.

Before moving on, I would like to briefly note that this discussion of "voicing" does not necessarily mean that the *Exaltation* was orally performed.[7] As noted above, the use of repetition as a structural marker to flag transitions is a common feature of oral poetry; furthermore, the *Exaltation* refers to itself as being orally performed by a **gala** priest on the day after its composition (l. 140). However, other aspects of the text indicate a predominantly written circulation. Remember that in l. 13, the invocation **nin-ĝu$_{10}$**, "My lady!" is replaced with the phrase **izi bar$_7$-bar$_7$**, "flaming fire," written NE NE NE. The pun transposes the force of repeated invocations into the medium of writing, by having the copyist write the same sign again and again. But this is an exclusively graphic pun: it does not work if the text is read out, because a recitation must collapse the polysemy of the cuneiform sign into a single pronunciation. At present, the question of whether – or rather, to what extent – the *Exaltation* was orally performed remains difficult to answer. The notion of voicing discussed above thus refers more generally to how the text became voice in the mind of the audience, regardless of whether that happened through performative recitation or internal dictation.

3.2 Creating Presence

In the preceding section, I treated invocations and apostrophes as if they were functionally equivalent, and to an extent, they are. However, a poetic apostrophe to the stars, the winds, or the seasons is not quite the same as a pious invocation of a deity: in the latter case, the speaker assumes that it is at least possible for the deity to hear the prayer and respond, by altering fate in their favor. Alan Lenzi (2011: 12) offers a brief summary of what invocations can be seen as doing in a religious setting: "Just as one might speak one's friend's name aloud in a group to gain their attention before conversing with them, the

7 On the oral performance of Sumerian poetry, see the essays collected in Vogelzang and Vanstiphout 1992, Alster 1992, Delnero 2015, and Wasserman 2021.

invocation is intended to get the supra-human being's attention before the prayer continues." That may be so, but there is also a crucial difference between the two situations: the friend, hearing their name spoken, would turn around and acknowledge one's presence; the deity offers no such immediately visible response. In short, the invocation of a deity is unlike the apostrophizing of an inanimate object in that one can *hope* for the deity's attention; and unlike an address to a friend in that one cannot be *certain* of it.

As a result, the invocation establishes both the presence and the absence of the deity in the text. The absence is the more obvious of the two. The invocation of a divine figure calls attention to the fact that the gods are not here, or at least not certainly here: otherwise, there would be no need to invoke them. An address implies distance – whether it is the short distance to a friend who is talking to someone else, the vast gulf between the poet and the stars, or the ontological distance that separates the supplicant from an omnipresent deity, who may be physically close but is also a radically different kind of being.[8] The Sumerian gods, however, seem not to be omnipresent, and there is a frequent fear in ancient prayers that one's petition may go unheard. Indeed, that is the central drama of the *Exaltation*. Enheduana appeals to Nanna, the god whom she served as high priestess, but Nanna does not answer: **^{d}nanna-ĝu$_{10}$ en$_{3}$-ĝu$_{10}$ ba-ra-an-tar**, "My Nanna does not care for me (lit.: does not ask about me)" (l. 100). In turning to Inana, Enheduana naturally fears that the failure of her plea will repeat itself, asking Inana with obvious anxiety: **ša$_{3}$-zu na-ma-še$_{17}$-de$_{3}$**, "Will your heart not be appeased (lit.: cool down) towards me?" (l. 137). The fact that the gods may or may not be listening gives the invocation an open-ended character, which, in the *Exaltation*, carries a clear element of despair. This angst is especially apparent in the fourth section of the poem, the narrative section, where Enheduana turns back and forth between Inana, Nanna, and herself. That is also the section where Enheduana states that she has lost her eloquence, linking her current lack of rhetorical prowess to the gods' inattention to her words. It is only at the end of the poem, after Enheduana has regained her poetic skills, that Inana is said to have heard her prayer (ll. 143–144).

The invocation thus seeks to overcome the deity's absence (or at least the uncertainty about their attention) by bringing them into the text. It is an attempt

---

8 Another example of such an ontological distance are the statues of gods, which may have been thought to be one of the gods' physical manifestations; see Walter and Dick 2001: 6–8 and Jacobsen 1987 for an opposing perspective. If hymns were ritually performed in the proximity of those statues, their invocations would not need to overcome a physical distance (since the god was close by), but rather the distance in being that separates the human supplicant from the deified statue.

to establish their presence by and through words. The invocation reaches out to a distant figure and cajoles them into closeness, whether physically or metaphorically: some invocations ask the god or goddess to literally approach the supplicant (Sappho's *Ode to Aphrodite* is a memorable example),[9] while others are satisfied with a more figurative kind of presence. The *Exaltation* culminates in an invitation to Inana to join Enheduana in a night-time ritual in the shrine of the Holy Inn, where Enheduana composes the poem (ll. 135–142). We are told that Inana accepted Enheduana's prayer, but it is unclear whether she literally appeared in the Holy Inn. However, the nature of her appearance may not be all that important. In a sense, the invocation creates its own mode of presence – a strictly poetic presence, in which the deity is made manifest through their names, titles, and deeds as they are listed by the speaker. The invocation thus becomes a solution to its own problem, as it gives the deity a textual presence if nothing else.

In short, invocations function as a rhetorical recompense for the physical distance of the deity (whatever the nature of that distance), inviting the god or goddess to appear before the speaker, either physically in a temple or figuratively in the text. Intriguingly, this aspect of invocations is also emphasized in another text that the Old Babylonian scribes attributed to Enheduana: *The Temple Hymns*, an anthology of forty-two hymns addressed to various Sumerian temples. Each hymn glorifies the temple and so, by extension, the deity who lived there and the city in which it stood. Monica Phillips, who is currently preparing a new edition of *The Temple Hymns*, argues that the entire anthology consists of a series of invocations (Phillips 2018; Phillips forthcoming). According to Phillips, each hymn can be thought of as an "extended naming" of the temple in question. The hymns first give the actual names of the temple and then unpacks, interprets, and expands those names to yield a hymnic description of the building as a whole. Phillips argues that this form of invocation was particularly effective in the cuneiform world because names were thought to be a manifestation of the object they referred to. All persons and objects were thought to be present in the world in several ways at once, including their physical body and the writing of their names (Radner 2005; Bahrani 2003, chaps. 4–5). When Enheduana names the temples, she not only describes their glory but also grants them a new channel of existence. In the cuneiform world, naming was therefore an especially effective way for invocations to achieve the textual presence that is their goal. To invoke a deity or a temple by name blurs

9 For a comparison of the *Exaltation* and Sappho's *Ode to Aphrodite*, see Helle 2020: 62.

the distinction between physical and figurative presence I set up above, since the name was seen as a very real, concrete mode of being.

3.3 Withholding Names

The power of names in cuneiform cultures and their fundamental role in another text attributed to Enheduana makes it all the more striking that the *Exaltation* so consistently avoids naming Inana (Zgoll 1997: 156). The goddess is invoked in a myriad of ways, but her name is given only three times in the poem, in ll. 12, 83, and 153. As noted above, Enheduana's authorship is a contested issue: since the earliest manuscripts of her poems date to centuries after the Old Akkadian period, we may be dealing with pseudepigraphic attributions; it is also possible that the historical Enheduana composed either the *Exaltation* or *The Temple Hymns*, but not both. However, regardless of the veracity of these attributions, it is striking that two of the poems that the Old Babylonian scribes attributed to the same author take so different approaches to the poetry of names. Both texts are structured around a series of invocations, but one fashions those invocations around the name of the temple being addressed, while the other withholds the name of its addressee altogether.

No such reticence applies to other gods in the *Exaltation*: the moon god is named as Nanna in ll. 93, 100, 120, 122, 148, as Suen in ll. 41, 48, and 74, and as Dilimbabbar in l. 84; An is named in ll. 14, 15, 19, 59, 75, 76, 85, 86, 94, 109, 121, 135, and 152; the Anuna are named in ll. 34, 113, and 115; Enlil is named in ll. 18 and 95; Ningal in ll. 119 and 149; Ishkur in ll. 10 and 30; and Dumuzi, as Ushumgalana, in l. 111 (see Zgoll 1997: 86 and 156). The absence of Inana's name is all the more striking in contrast to these other deities. Of the three times her name is used, two come with a caveat. In l. 153, she is named as part of the traditional **za$_3$-mi$_2$** formula, which concludes many Sumerian hymns, giving the name of the deity to whom the text is addressed: "[Name of the deity] be praised!" The appearance of Inana's name in this line – while remarkable in contrast to its preceding absence – thus carries the weight of convention. The first time her name is mentioned is more unusual. In l. 12, the narrator says: **^{d}inana-bi me-en**, "You are their Inana!" This strange sentence can be interpreted in several ways. Foster (2016: 331) translates it as "you are their warrior goddess," implying that the word "Inana" is here being used as a title; while Attinger (2019: 3) suggests that it may be a reference to the folk etymology of Inana's name as "mistress of heaven."

One effect of the conspicuous absence of Inana's name is that the poem instead invokes her through a wealth of circumlocutions, of which some were cited in the previous section: "my lady," "great daughter of Suen," "my righteous aurochs," "my lady, beloved of An," and so on. The poem is replete with such indirect forms of address, which, instead of stating Inana's name, summon a particular facet of the goddess. In that sense, absences can be productive, as the withholding of Inana's name allows for a proliferation of titles and epithets that magnify her might. One might also consider what the absence of names tells us about the relation between Enheduana and Inana. The absence of names finds a striking parallel in the Standard Babylonian *Epic of Gilgamesh*, where, as noted by Martin Worthington (2011), the main characters Gilgamesh and Enkidu consistently avoid speaking each other's names, referring to one another instead as *ibrī*, "My friend." Other characters use their names, and they use the names of other characters – just as Enheduana is willing to use the names of any god except Inana. I have suggested elsewhere that the avoidance of names in *Gilgamesh* is used to create an intimate sphere of affection, where the difference between the two friends is gradually blurred (Helle 2021: 171–78). A similar argument can be made for the *Exaltation*, in which we also find a certain intimacy between Inana and Enheduana, culminating in the night-time ritual in the Holy Inn, where Enheduana composes the text to her goddess.[10]

It is possible that there was in cuneiform literature a convention by which the avoidance of names indicates intimacy, but the argument is uncertain even in *Gilgamesh*, and the parallel to the *Exaltation* is shakier still. Indeed, the avoidance of names could just as easily indicate the opposite: Enheduana's humble unwillingness to use Inana's name out of reverence and respect for the goddess. At present, the avoidance of names is hard to pin down. While it is a central aspect of how invocations are used in the *Exaltation*, more study is needed to understand its role. It is also possible that the omission would have been ambiguous already in antiquity, leaving the audience to surmise its meaning in individual ways. That ambiguity would in itself have given the invocations a particular force, the force of intrigue.

10 William Hallo observes that when Enheduana is referred to with the third-person pronoun in the epilogue, it creates an even closer link between the priestess and the as yet unnamed goddess: "the exaltation of Inanna implies at the same time the restoration of Enheduanna, their two fates being so closely linked that in lines 146 f. it is hard to decide whether the narrator [. . .] is speaking of the one or the other" (Hallo and van Dijk 1968: 62).

3.4 Triangulated Address

A feature of invocations that is so obvious as to easily escape analysis is that they focus the attention of the audience on the deity being invoked: in this case, Inana. Accordingly, the previous three sections have paid special heed to the relation between Enheduana and Inana. However, this aspect of invocations is obvious only on the surface; diving deeper into their structure, one finds a more complicated relationship between speaker and addressee. In a poem such as the *Exaltation*, the invocation will always have a double direction: towards the deity being invoked, and towards the audience reading the poem or listening to its performance.

According to Culler (2015: 16), lyric poetry is characterized by a "complexity of the enunciative apparatus," that is, a relation between the voices contained in the text that is anything but straightforward. In lyric poetry, it is often difficult to determine who is speaking to whom, and apostrophes brings these questions to a head. For example, when we come across Shelley's apostrophe "O wild West Wind!", whose voice are we hearing?[11] That of Shelley, his poetic persona, "the speaker," or our own? And to whom are the words directed? The actual wind, the coming revolution for which the wind is a metaphor, or the reader?

Culler (2015: 186–88) notes that apostrophes in particular and lyric poetry in general often operate through what he calls a "triangulated address," meaning that they invoke one addressee in order to be heard by another. Poets may speak to the stars, but they expect their words to reach their readers. In a fortuitous phrase coined by John Stuart Mill (1860: 95), poetry is not heard but *overheard*: in lyric poems, we come across a situation to which we are made obliquely privy, as the poets seem not to address their readers directly but speak to themselves or some other apostrophized entity (Culler 1977: 60). There is a striking example of triangulated address in the climactic section of the *Exaltation*, where Enheduana invokes Inana with a litany of invocations:

an-gin$_7$ mah-a-za he$_2$-zu-am$_3$
ki-gin$_7$ dağal-la-za he$_2$-zu-am$_3$
ki-bal gul-gul-lu-za he$_2$-zu-am$_3$
kur-ra gu$_3$ de$_2$-za he$_2$-zu-am$_3$
sağ ĝiš ra-ra-za he$_2$-zu-am$_3$
ur-gin$_7$ ad$_6$ gu$_7$-za he$_2$-zu-am$_3$
igi huš-a-za he$_2$-zu-am$_3$

11 These are the opening words of Percy Bysshe Shelley's "Ode to the West Wind."

igi huš-bi IL_2-IL_2-i-za he_2-zu-am_3
igi gun_3-gun_3-na-za he_2-zu-am_3
uru_{16}-na nu-še-ga-za he_2-zu-am_3
u_3-ma gub-gub-bu-za he_2-zu-am_3

Let it be known that you are tall as the skies,
let it be known that you are huge as the earth,
let it be known that you destroy the rebel lands,
let it be known that you roar at the enemy,
let it be known that you crush skulls,
let it be known that you eat corpses like a lion,
let it be known that your eyes are terrifying,
let it be known that you glance is terrifying,
let it be known that your eyes flash and flicker,
let it be known that you are stubborn and unruly,
let it be known that you always stand triumphant! (ll. 123–132)

The passage lists Inana's glorious traits and asks that the goddess should "let them be known" (**he_2-zu-am_3**). This passage purports to address Inana, not the audience, but if that is so, the demand seems to be directed at the wrong recipient, since it asks of Inana that people who are not Inana, including the audience, should recognize her might. Culler shows that this kind of misdirection is typical of lyric poetry. Enheduana puts the triangulated address to great effect: the listener who hears the invocation and so comes to know that Inana crushes skulls is effectively recruited into the fulfillment of the narrator's demand. The repetitious, charm-like nature of the passage works to bring the message home, inculcating the might of Inana into the mind of the audience. When Enheduana asks Inana to let her power be known, the unwitting listener is simultaneously fulfilling that request for her: now we know.

Part of the force of invocations thus comes from the split structure they impart to the poem: their simultaneous address to a deity and – if they appear in a literary text that will be heard or read by others – to a larger audience as well. Just as invocations carry a tension between the absence and presence of the deity being invoked, they also carry a tension between the two audiences they hope to reach. Indeed, the double nature of invocations is the premise that underlies my previous analysis of the *Exaltation*'s division into sections. When Enheduana invokes Inana, she is also relaying crucial information to the audience about the shifts and flows of the text: the narrator addresses the goddess with one eye turned to the audience, guiding them through the poem.

4 Conclusion

As I hope to have shown, invocations can play a crucial role in ancient literature. While they may seem at first to be the most marginal elements of the text – brief exclamations that introduce the main characters before the poem moves on to meatier matters – they can change the entire thrust and structure of a composition. They can mark key shifts in the narrative and imbue the poem with dynamism and entrancing tensions; they can capture and redirect the attention of the audience; they can intrigue and compel. Invocations may not advance the plot or give us new information about the subject matter, but that is simply because they are not a description of an event: they are themselves a poetic event, reaching out from the world of the text to summon a divine presence, while also lighting up a path through the poem.

Bibliography

Abusch, Tzvi. The Form and Meaning of a Babylonian Prayer to Marduk. *JAOS* 103: 3–15.

Alster, Bendt. 1972. *Dumuzi's Dream: Aspects of Oral Poetry in a Sumerian Myth.* Mesopotamia 1. Copenhagen: Akademisk forlag.

Attinger, Pascal. 2019. Innana B (Ninmešara) (4.7.2). Available online at: https://zenodo.org/record/2667768#.XhScnRdKgWo

Bahrani, Zainab. 2003. *The Graven Image: Representation in Babylonia and Assyria.* Philadelphia, PA: University of Pennsylvania Press.

Black, Jeremy. 1992. Some Structural Features of Sumerian Narrative Poetry. Pp. 71–101 in *Mesopotamian Epic Literature: Oral or Aural?*, ed. Marianna E. Vogelzang and Herman L.J. Vanstiphout. Lewiston, NY: The Edwin Mellen Press.

Black, Jeremy, Graham Cunningham, Eleanor Robson, and Gábor Zólyomi. 2004. *The Literature of Ancient Sumer.* Oxford: Oxford University Press.

Civil, Miguel. 1980. Les limites de l'information textuelle. Pp. 225–32 in *L'archéologie de l'Iraq: Du début de l'époque néolithique à 333 avant notre ère*, ed. Marie-Thérèse Barrelet. Colloques internationaux du CNRS 580. Paris: Editions du CNRS.

Culler, Jonathan. 1997. Apostrophe. *Diacritics* 7: 59–69.

Culler, Jonathan. 2015. *Theory of the Lyric.* Cambridge, MA: Harvard University Press.

Delnero, Paul. 2006. Variation in Sumerian Literary Compositions: A Case Study Based on the Decad. Unpublished dissertation. Philadelphia: University of Pennsylvania.

Delnero, Paul. 2015. Texts and Performance: The Materiality and Function of the Sumerian Liturgical Corpus. Pp. 87–118 in *Texts and Contexts: The Circulation and Transmission of Cuneiform Texts in Social Space*, ed. Paul Delnero and Jacob Lauinger. Studies in Ancient Near Eastern Records 9. Berlin: De Gruyter.

Foster, Benjamin R. 2016. *The Age of Agade: Inventing Empire in Ancient Mesopotamia.* London: Routledge.

Glassner, Jean-Jacques. 2009. En-hedu-ana, une femme auteure en pays de Sumer, au IIIe millenaire? *Topoi Suppléments* 10: 219–31.

Hallo, William W. and J.J.A van Dijk. 1968. *The Exaltation of Inanna*. YNER 3. New Haven, CT: Yale University Press.

Helle, Sophus. 2020. The Birth of the Author: Co-Creating Authorship in Enheduana's *Exaltation*. *Orbis Litterarum* 75: 55–72.

Helle, Sophus. 2021. *Gilgamesh: A New Translation of the Ancient Epic*. New Haven, CT: Yale University Press.

Helle, Sophus. Forthcoming. *Enheduana: The Complete Poems of the World's First Author*. New Haven, CT: Yale University Press.

Jacobsen, Thorkild. 1987. The Graven Image. Pp. 15–32 in *Ancient Israelite Religion: Essays in Honor of Frank Moore Cross*, ed. Patrick Miller, Paul D. Hanson, and S. Dean McBride. Philadelphia, PA: Fortress Press.

Lenzi, Alan. 2010. Invoking the God: Interpreting Invocations in Mesopotamian Prayers and Biblical Laments of the Individual. *JBL* 129: 303–15.

Lenzi, Alan (ed.). 2011. *Reading Akkadian Prayers & Hymns: An Introduction*. Ancient Near East Monograph 3. Atlanta, GA: Society of Biblical Literature.

Lion, Brigitte. 2011. Literacy and Gender. Pp. 90–112 in *The Oxford Handbook of Cuneiform Culture*, ed. Karen Radner and Eleanor Robson. Oxford: Oxford University Press.

Mayer, Werner. 1976. *Untersuchungen zur Formensprache der babylonischen "Gebetsbeschwörungen."* StPohl SM 5. Rome: Biblical Institute Press.

Michalowski, Piotr. 1996. Sailing to Babylon, Reading the Dark Side of the Moon. Pp. 177–93 in *The Study of the Ancient Near East in the Twenty-First Century: The William Foxwell Albright Centennial Conference*, ed. Jerrold S. Cooper and Glenn M. Schwartz. Winona Lake, IN: Eisenbrauns.

Mill, John Stuart. 1860. Thoughts on Poetry and Its Varieties. *The Crayon* 7: 93–97.

Phillips, Monica L. 2018. "O House!" The Invocation of Temple Names in the Collection of Sumerian Temple Hymns. Paper read at the 64th RAI, Innsbruck.

Phillips, Monica. Forthcoming. *Uniting Heaven and Earth: The Collection of Sumerian Temple Hymns*. Unpublished dissertation. Chicago: University of Chicago.

Radner, Karen. 2005. *Die Macht des Namens: Altorientalische Strategien zur Selbsterhaltung*. Santag 8. Wiesbaden: Harrassowitz Verlag.

Schwemer, Daniel. 2014. "Form Follows Function"? Rhetoric and Poetic Language in First Millennium Akkadian Incantations. *WO* 44: 263–88.

Vanstiphout, Herman L.J. 1993. "Verse Language" in Standard Sumerian Literature. Pp. 305–29 in *Verse in Ancient Near Eastern Prose*, ed. Johannes C. de Moor and Wilfred G.E. Watson. AOAT 42. Neukirchen: Butzon & Bercker.

Veldhuis, Niek. 1999. The Poetry of Magic. Pp. 35–48 in *Mesopotamian Magic: Textual, Historical, and Interpretative Perspectives*, ed. Tzvi Abusch and Karel van der Toorn. AMD 1. Groningen: Styx.

Vogelzang, Marianna E., and Herman L.J. Vanstiphout (eds.). 1992. *Mesopotamian Epic Literature: Oral or Aural?* Lewiston, NY: The Edwin Mellen Press.

Walker, Christopher, and Dick Michael. *The Induction of the Cult Image in Ancient Mesopotamia: The Mesopotamian Mīs Pî Ritual*. State Archives of Assyria Literary Texts 1. Helsinki: Neo-Assyrian Text Corpus Project.

Wasserman, Nathan. 2021. Lists and Chains: Enumeration in Akkadian Literary Texts. Pp. 57–80 in *Lists and Catalogues in Ancient Literature and Beyond: Towards a Poetics of*

Enumeration, ed. Rebecca Lämmle, Cédric Scheidegger Lämmle, and Katharina Wesselmann. Trends in Classics Supplementary Volumes 107. Berlin: De Gruyter.
Worthington, Martin. On Names and Artistic Unity in the Standard Version of the Babylonian Gilgamesh Epic. *Journal of the Royal Asiatic Society* 21: 403–20.
Zgoll, Annette. 1997. *Der Rechtsfall der En-ḫedu-Ana im Lied nin-me-šara*. AOAT 246. Münster: Ugarit-Verlag.
Zgoll, Annette. 2003. Audienz: Ein Modell zum Verständnis mesopotamischer Handerhebungsrituale. Mit einer Deutung der Novelle vom *Armen Mann von Nippur*. *BagM* 34: 181–203.
Zgoll, Annette. 2004. *Die Kunst des Betens: Form und Funktion, Theologie und Psychagogik in babylonisch-assyrischen Handerhebungsgebeten zu Ishtar*. AOAT 308. Münster: Ugarit-Verlag.

Piotr Michalowski

On Language, Gender, Sex, and Style in the Sumerian Language

1 Introduction

Recent years have witnessed a rapid increase in Assyriological research on matters of sex and gender in ancient societies, with a welcome focus on contemporary theoretical perspectives, providing links to other disciplines in the humanities and social sciences.[1] The study of the social, political, legal, economic, and emotive roles of women, or of their images and participation in the literary and educational spheres has gained new prominence,[2] but until now the linguistic expression or indexing of gender in Mesopotamian societies has not attracted the same levels of scrutiny.

In concert with these debates, I here attempt to survey some of the basic information on how gender differentiation was encoded in the Sumerian language, with the expectation that I will be able to explore much of this in more detail elsewhere. Gender, after all, is a classificatory concept laced with emotional, practical, as well as social signification and such categories permeate linguistic expression: as Michael Halliday (1976: 572) expressed it, "in all languages, words, sounds, and structures tend to become charged with social value," and furthermore (p. 580), "social dialects are not necessarily associated with caste or class; they may be religious, generational, sexual, economic (urban/rural), and perhaps other things too. What distinguishes them is their hierarchical character. The social function of dialect variation is to express, symbolize, and maintain the social order; and the social order is an essentially hierarchic one." Ancient Mesopotamian societies were

1 I am grateful to Nicole Brisch and Fumi Karahashi for inviting me to contribute to this volume. Preliminary versions of this essay were presented November 13, 2017, at the celebrations of the 85 Years of Oriental Studies at the University of Warsaw, at Chuo University on February 8, 2018, and at the 232nd annual meeting of the American Oriental Society in Boston, on March 19, 2022; I am grateful to profs. Agata Bareja-Starzyńska and Fumi Karahashi for their kind invitations. A shorter early and very different version was published in Japanese as Michalowski 2019. I am indebted to Pascal Attinger, Jerry Cooper, Jay Crisostomo, and Cécile Michel for generous comments on a draft version, to Simone Willemoes Skjold Sørensen for careful reference checking and to Gonzalo Rubio for kindly standardizing the transliterations of Russian titles. All translations are by the author, unless otherwise indicated.

2 For overviews, see Garcia-Ventura and Svärd 2018; Michel, in press. For a bibliography of works 2002–2016, see Garcia-Ventura and Zisa 2017.

https://doi.org/10.1515/9781501514821-012

saturated with hierarchical distinctions including status and gender and there can be no doubt that this was reflected in language use, be it in Sumerian, Akkadian, Amorite, Aramaic, or whatever tongue or tongues were in use in each place and time. The socio-linguistic embedding of the information described below will require further elaboration; here I do not propose any definitive solutions, only suggestions for further avenues of investigation.

2 Lexical and Morpho-Syntactic Means of Expressing Gender in Sumerian

Although elementary facts about the marking of gender in Sumerian can be found in various modern grammars of the language, no comprehensive study of the matter is available. What follows is a succinct description of the issues involved with some typological perspectives in mind.

The Sumerian language had two distinct canonical noun classes (genders) differentiated by "animacy" but not by sexual gender. This was a covert morphosyntactic feature that was unmarked on noun phrases but recognizable only in case assignment, pronominal and deictic reference, as well as in argument indexing on verbs. Pronouns, of course, provide the fundamental locus of sex/gender distinction (Rose 2013, 2018).

Most languages utilize some form of nominal classification, either by morphological (noun classes) or lexico-syntactic means (Dixon 1968): some have complex systems while others have simple ones, sometimes limited only to two classes and Sumerian belongs to the latter group, what Corbett (2014: 111) categorized as a semantic assignment system. He also observed (p. 124) that in a sample of 256 languages, just over a half have no gender system at all, but among those that do, most are based on sex (84), and only 28 exhibit animacy-based systems. More precisely, as noted by Aikhenvald (2008: 1031) "since gender systems show some correlation with sex, many non-linguists (and a few linguists) erroneously confuse gender and sex. However, sex represents biological categorization, and gender represents grammatical categorization."

In terms of number, two-gender systems were the most common in Corbett's survey (50). Of course, surveys of this kind never consider ancient Near Eastern languages: most of these, as far as they are known, are of this two-gender type and, aside from Afro-Asiatic languages, had gender systems that were not sex based. Barring Indo-European Hittite and Hurrian/Urartaean, these languages without sex-based gender distinctions were isolates (Michalowski 2017), and it is possible that this was an areal feature, although insufficient knowledge and questioning of the very concept of a linguistic area should be kept in mind (e.g., Campbell 2006, 2017, and in general the articles in Hickey 2017).

In modern grammars of Sumerian the two basic noun classes of the language have been variously categorized as *Personenklasse* and *Sachklasse* (Falkenstein 1959: 36 and many after him), personal and non-personal (Jacobsen 1988a: 128; 1988b: 211–12 n. 55; Attinger 1993: 150 [personnel, non-personnel]; Edzard 2003: 29 [person, non-person]; Foxvog 2014: 23), commonly as animate vs. inanimate (e.g., Thomsen 1984: 49; Yoshikawa 1988: 501–502; Diakonoff 1997: 58; Rubio 2007: 1329; Michalowski 2008: 22, Civil 2020: 119 ["in reality the two classes are agents and non-agent entities"], etc.), and most recently as human and non-human (Jagersma 2010: 102). None of these labels are fully appropriate, as the latter well noted. Diakonoff (1967: 54, translation mine) perceptively observed that "the Sumerian language has no genders, but has classes: a class of animate nouns, or, more accurately, of socially-active ones (free people, gods, slaves as individuals, anthropomorphized animals, objects, and concepts), and a class of inanimate nouns, or, more precisely, of socially passive ones (animals, objects, concepts). This socially-passive class includes nouns that denote people and gods, if they express a unified group (collective plural)." Note, however, that proper nouns denoting professions and political rank could be treated as animate or inanimate (collective) depending on time and place.

The animate and inanimate distinction, in linguistic rather than biological formulation, might conveniently be defined invoking Kittilä, Västi, and Ylikoski (2011: 5) who put it thus: "linguistic animacy is typically defined based on an entity's ability to act or instigate events volitionally and on how this is manifested formally in languages," which may be too broad to provide an adequate fit for Sumerian.

Diakonoff's description well illustrates that while semantic concepts such as animacy, personhood, humaneness, and agency were mapped into a simple system of classes, providing some insight into early Mesopotamian worldview, none of these are fully definitional. From a comparative typological perspective, the Sumerian nominal gender assignment system classes might best be labeled as rational and irrational, that is humans, divinities, "demons," etc. as opposed to animals, objects, concepts, and the like. This terminology derives from the Tamil grammatical tradition and is used in the description of Dravidian and other languages (Dixon 1968: 113; Aikhenvald 2000: 276). To be sure, Tamil has a different, much more complex system of noun classification than did Sumerian, but the general distinction holds. As described by Steever (2018: 662), in Tamil "there are two basic genders: 'rational' (*uyartiṇai*) and 'irrational' (*ahRiṇai*) corresponding roughly to human and non-human. Rational nouns are further classified as honorific, masculine and feminine. Nouns referring to deities and men are classified as rational; in some dialects women are classified as rational, in others as irrational. (Children and animals are normally classified as irrational.)" In the future, one might perhaps apply this to Sumerian but to avoid drastically changing a terminology already in use in the discipline and to conform to established linguistic usage, I will retain the animate/inanimate labels here.

2.1 Linguistic Means of Expressing Sexual Gender in Standard Sumerian

In a comprehensive study of noun categorization, Aikhenvald (2000: 19–20), distinguished between noun class and grammatical gender systems of the kind documented in Indo-European or Afro-asiatic. In Sumerian, *nominal sexual gender* was not grammatically marked; when required, it could be expressed by two means: (a) by adding a gender word and (b) by suppletion in a closed small class of nouns, suppletion being understood as the use of two or more phonologically distinct words within the same paradigm. In practical documentary Sumerian writing, sex gender could be recognized by use of masculine or feminine personal names, or by application of kinship terms. A written convention utilizing separate unpronounced classifiers for females and males – a single vertical wedge before masculine and the sign for "woman" preceding feminine personal names – first became current in some parts of Babylonia during the early second millennium for Akkadian writings but this was rarely extended to texts written in Sumerian.

(a) Words such as **dumu**, "son, child (irrespective of gender)," could be defined as feminine by adding the noun **munus**, "woman," as in **dumu munus**, "daughter," in an appositional, non-possessive manner, although in documents the gender word was not always used, either because it was not obligatory and/or because of abbreviation.[3] The unmarked form functioned as the masculine and generic term. In certain contexts, when the distinction needed semantic nuance, highlighting, emphasis, or generically in documents, an equivalent masculine word, **nita/nita$_2$**, "male," could be added, e.g., **dumu nita$_2$**, "male child, heir," **maš$_2$ nita$_2$**, "male goat," or **udu nita$_2$**, "male sheep." With some words both gender words could qualify animate as well as inanimate nouns, as in **dumu munus/nita$_2$**, "female/male child," or $^{\hat{g}e\check{s}}$**gu-za munus/nita$_2$**, "chair for women/men."

3 There are also temporal and geographical differences in usage of such designations, e.g., **dumu munus** first appears in ED IIIa times, when it is extremely rare, but was generally in use in ED IIIb, in Girsu at least. In royal inscriptions, it is very infrequent before the Old Akkadian period (Lion 2009a: 170–71).

Not all nouns could be specified in this manner, however. For example, there is only **diĝir**, "god, goddess, divinity," but ***diĝir munus**, "goddess," was not in general use.[4] For a rare example of the use of the words **munus** and **$nita_2$** to express gender differentiation with words such as **diĝir**, see *Hendursanga Hymn* 85 (Attinger and Krebernik 2005: 42; Konstantopolous 2020: 366):

> imin-be_2-ne diĝir munus nu-me-eš u_3 $nita_2$ nu-me-eš
> "These seven are neither female nor male divine creatures,"

(b) Gender was distinguished in a small, closed group of nouns by means of distinct suppletive feminine and masculine forms. Nominal lexical suppletion was uncommon in Sumerian and was predictively limited to small groups of economically important and most frequently referenced animals and humans. Writing about a similar phenomenon in Italian, Maiden (1992: 306 n. 23) observed: "the suppletive masculine and feminine forms of the names of many higher mammals (for instance toro "bull" vs. mucca "cow") is motivated by the salience of the sex differences."

In Sumerian, the most salient difference of this kind was **lu_2**, "man, human," or **$nita_2$/ninta**, "male," vs. **munus**, "woman," but **lu_2**, "person" (also used like English "one," as in "no one," with a negated verb or in **lu_2 tur**, "person+small" = "little one (as a form of address)." Notable are basic kinship distinctions such as **ama**, "mother," **ad-da**, "father," but **dumu**, "child, son," vs. **dumu munus**, "daughter," without suppletion, as noted above. The various Sumerian local words for "king, lord" such as **lugal**, **$ensi_2$**, or **en**, had a single feminine equivalent **ereš/nin**. In the labeling of the animal kingdom, we find **ab_2**, "cow," vs. **gud**, "bull," **$maš_2$**, "ram," vs. **uz_3/uzud**, "nanny goat," **udu**, "ram," vs. **u_8**, "ewe;"[5] **ur-$ĝir_{15}$**, "dog," vs. **nig**, "bitch;" **anše**, "donkey," vs. **eme_3**, "jenny," etc. In all instances, the male term functioned as the generic label. It needs to be stressed once again that both (a) and (b) were restricted to a small culturally salient group of lexical labels.

(c) At least since the beginning of the second millennium, if not earlier in some areas, most people writing Sumerian were native speakers of Semitic languages, primarily Akkadian. The linguistic expression of gender in these languages was appreciably different than in Sumerian. Most significantly, they

4 A rare poetic word **amalu**, which originally designated a type of cultic practitioner, was occasionally used with the meaning "goddess."
5 For more information on such designations of goat and sheep, see Steinkeller 1995.

distinguished between masculine and feminine genders: in general, the unmarked form of the noun was masculine, while the feminine was marked with the suffix *–(a)t*; gender was also marked in agreement and in personal pronouns. As in other languages, including Sumerian, Akkadian had a limited class of culturally salient suppletive forms, including animal labels, but also differentiating between terms such as *aššatu*, "wife," and *mutu*, "husband," whereas Sumerian has only one generic term, **dam**, "wife, husband, spouse," so that the semantics of such words was somewhat different in the two languages. Most important, unlike in Sumerian, Akkadian verbal affixes identified the sexual gender of the speaker but also of who was spoken to and was spoken about (for a survey of gender in Semitic, including Akkadian, see Hasselbach 2014a, 2014b). This would not have much effect on the pragmatics of face-to-face communication but could create some ambiguity of reference in written forms of expression, sometimes requiring different strategies. This limited formal binary gender oppositions in the lexicon (and morphology in the case of Akkadian) should not be categorically viewed as reflecting all levels of psycho-social perspectives in Mesopotamian societies where sexual gender was not strictly categorized as binary, although such conceptualizations were fluid and often contested, subject to situational and local tribulations, as noted most recently by Konstantopolous (2020).

3 Gender in Written Sumerian Discourse

Another mechanism for marking gender or gender identity in Sumerian written literary discourse was the occasional use of a distinct version of the language by female deities and humans, a variety that has sometimes in the past been described as a women's language, *Frauensprache*, or female genderlect, although such definitions have been questioned of late. In native terminology, this style of Sumerian was designated as **eme sal** (ES).

More precisely, Mesopotamian texts utilized two native socio-linguistic terms varying by adjective to describe varieties of Sumerian discourse: **eme gir$_{15}$** (EG) and **eme sal** (ES).[6] The former, which could perhaps be etymologized as "native language' (Steinkeller 1993: 112–13 n. 9; 2005: 309) or "noble tongue"

6 Much of the evidence points to the reading **šal** rather than **sal**, but for clarity I retain the traditional reading here.

(Cooper 2012: 294), was used from Old Akkadian times on; by the 18th century, if not earlier, it was apparently a designation for what we could label as Standard Literary Sumerian (SLS), most likely for all versions of the language, as expressed in the often-cited *Proverb Collection 2*: 47:

> dub-sar eme gir_{15} nu-mu-un-zu-a a-na-am_3 nam(-)dub-sar-ra-ni
> "A scribe who does not know the Sumerian language – what kind of scribe is he?"

I would stress that there is no reason to posit an opposition between ES and EG as is done in most discussions of the Sumerian language; the former was taxonomically subordinate to the latter.

3.1 Emesal: General Characteristics

The best description of ES to date with a listing of the known ES words is to be found in Schretter (1990); the publication of many new texts and progress in the understanding of the Sumerian language suggests that it may be time for a full update. For a critical evaluation of work since then, see the overview of Garcia-Ventura (2017); among the important recent contributions to the debates about ES (which the present essay builds on), see e.g., Rubio (2001: 269–71; 2009: 31–32), Löhnert (2014), Matini (2021), and now, most notably, Schretter (2018) and Matuszak (2021: 195–217). It is important to note that texts designated as Emesal have various mixtures of ES and SLS forms; indeed, sometimes a line or passage contains only one word of explicitly written ES, and, of course, we cannot always know how logographically written words may have been read. One of the few non-liturgical literary texts written largely in ES is the 18th c. *Dialog Between Two Women B* (Rubio 2009: 31, now edited with detailed commentary in Matuszak 2021).

The main distinctions between these two styles of Sumerian were based on phonological substitutions (Schretter 2018: 172), but these were not always regular, and the same SLS "phoneme" could match more than one Emesal equivalent. Thus, for example, SLS /ĝ/ was substituted by ES /m/ (SLS **ĝar** ~ ES **mar**; "to place"), SLS /d/ = ES /z/ (SLS **udu** ~ ES **eze**, "sheep," SLS /z/ = ES /š/ (SLS **zi** ~ ES **ši**,"breath, life"), or SLS /š/ = ES /n/ (SLS **a-nir** = ES **a-še-er**, "lament"). I reluctantly use the word "phoneme" here and stick to conventional representations of the words of the language in recognition our inadequate understanding of Sumerian phonology and phonetics.

Some Emesal words were either reduced or expanded versions of standard Sumerian counterparts, e.g., ES **ze_2** ~ SLS **dun**, "to warp wool." **umun** ~ **en**, "lord, king," may perhaps be explained as resulting from a form of reduplication

(> ***en.en**), or prefixing (>***mu.en**). A small number of basic terms are inexplicable, e.g., SLS **nin/ereš** ~ ES **gašan**, "queen, mistress," **gu-za** ~ **aš-te**, "chair, **a-na** ~ **ta**, "what?," or $\mathbf{e_2}$ ~ **ma**, "house, temple." The origins of such lexical distinctions cannot be traced at present. Moreover, Emesal was characterized by specific characteristic usages of cuneiform script such as the extensive use of syllabic writings, some of which seem specific to Emesal, or the utilization of visually similar signs such as $\mathbf{uru_2}$ (URU×U_4), "city," where standard Sumerian usually has **e/iri** (URU), presumably representing two different words, although, to complicate matters, $\mathbf{uru_2}$ could also occur in Standard Sumerian texts, sometimes alternating with the latter in different manuscripts of the same composition.[7]

Certain limited semantic sets may have been driven by word building patterns but tinged with game playing. Consider the use of a prefix **mu**- to make male designations such as ES **mu-lu** ~ SLS $\mathbf{lu_2}$, "man, person," **mu-tin** ~ **nita/ninta**, "young man," or **mudna** ~ **ĝešdana**, "betrothed man," where **mu**- may have been a classifier, equivalent to SLS $\mathbf{lu_2}$, as in $\mathbf{mu\text{-}zuh_2}$, "thief," which was equivalent to SLS $\mathbf{lu_2\text{-}zuh}$. The word $\mathbf{lu_2}$ by itself could carry this prefix (ES **mu-lu**), bringing to mind an early Sumerian derivational morpheme **nu**- used to create professional names such as $\mathbf{nu\text{-}kiri_6}$, "gardner" ($\mathbf{kiri_6}$ = "orchard"), presumably related to $\mathbf{lu_2}$ (Edzard 1962). If this were not enough, there was also the ES **mu-(i/uš)**, "penis," and synecdochally "male," that replaced SLS **ĝiš**$_3$ as well as the homonym **ĝeš**, "wood, tree." The ludic aspect of such language games is significant.

3.2 Origins of Emesal

It is difficult to trace the use of Emesal back in time. Strictly speaking, this style is not attested before the Old Babylonian period (ca. 17th-18th c. BCE), although its usage in cult can be inferred for earlier times. There have been attempts to trace it at least as far back as the Early Dynastic IIIa of the third millennium, but Matuszak (2021: 216–17) has convincingly shown that the available data do not support this. Cooper (2006) and Gabbay (2011b) have gathered evidence of **gala** practitioners chanting to the accompaniment of the **balaĝ** drum in Ur III times, but it is only a supposition that they already did so in ES. The earliest securely dated examples of ES are embedded in 18th c. copies of poems ascribed to the reigns of the early second millennium Ur III rulers Ur-Namma,

---

7 For a syllabic rendition of ES $\mathbf{uru_2}$, perhaps /**uri**/ or /**ura**/, see e.g., VS 10: 179 rev. 2 ($\mathbf{u_4\text{-}ra}$ = Akk. *a-lu*).

Šulgi, and Šu-Sin.[8] In one of these the goddess Inana sings a love song to Šulgi in ES (*Šulgi Hymn X*, ll. 14–41; Klein 1981: 136–39; Attinger 2022), but later in the same poem (ll. 49–72) she speaks a blessing in standard Sumerian; we shall return to this example below. It is important to recall that this poem, even in its Old Babylonian guise, preserves traits that suggest it was composed in Ur III times, as noted by Sallaberger (1993: 150 n. 708) who collected information on ES usage in that period. It is therefore of particular interest here.

A female, perhaps Inana, sings of love to the king in ES (*Šulgi Hymn Z*) but also to his son and successor (*Šu-Sin Hymn B*) as well as in lullaby for one of Šulgi's son's (*Šulgi N*). The earliest known such Ur III example is inserted in a single line in the poem or song *Ur-Namma F* (l. 3) that concerns Šulgi's father. One must keep in mind, however, that all these works of literature associated with Ur III kings are preserved exclusively 18th c. BCE Old Babylonian tablets: the precise dates of origin and levels of later alteration and redaction are unknown. Instructive, however, are the allusions in the poem *Death of Ur-Namma* to the ES cultic **balaĝ** prayer Edinausaga, well known from later times (Wilcke 1988: 248; Cooper 2006: 42).

Wilcke (1976a: 208) has noted that two poems concerning the god Ninurta have short ES passages: a lament sung by the mother goddess in *Lugale* (see below) and in a two-line quote from the goddess Ninlil in *Angim* (ll. 110–112). The latter is first documented in Old Babylonian and much later versions, but one witness of the former is probably Ur III in date.[9] If, as Hallo (1976: 184–85), Wilcke (1976a: 208) and many others have hypothesized, the roots of these poems lay in late third millennium Girsu, perhaps in the time of King Gudea who reigned closely before Ur-Namma, this might provide some indication of prior literary use of ES.

Other early evidence is ambiguous, at best. In the poem *The Curse of Agade* (l. 202), composed in Ur III times, if not slightly earlier, one reads that the old women who survived the catastrophe that afflicted the city and its polity cried out "Woe, my city" (**a uru$_2$-ĝu$_{10}$** [or -**ma$_3$**]), which may be a signal that they were exclaiming in ES or even chanting an ES style lament prayer (Cooper 2006: 41). This expression was commonly used by goddesses in the city laments, in the *Lament over Ur* (LUr), the *Lamentation over the Destruction of Sumer and Akkad* (LSUr), and the *Nippur Lament* (NL), usually as **a uru$_2$-ĝu$_{10}$**,

---

8 Wilcke 2010: 10–11 cautiously proposes that the writing **im-ma-al**, "wild cow," the 21st c. poem *Gudea Cyl. B* iv 8: may be the earliest attestation of an ES word, but the term was not limited to ES; see Veldhuis 2002: 72 (and now Schretter 2018: 180).

9 Ni 4138 (ISET 2, p. 23); see Rubio 2000: 212 w. n. 39. There is a possibility that this was an archaizing later copy of an Ur III version, but that is of no importance to us here.

"Woe, my city," or as **a uru$_2$ gul/hul-la/a**, "Woe, the destroyed city," but also in the ES cultic prayers sung by **gala** chanters. As noted above, however, the **uru$_2$** sign is not necessarily diagnostic. The same equivocality tempers the interpretation of an entry in an Ur III (or very early Old Babylonian) literary catalog providing the opening line of an otherwise unattested poem (Hallo 1963: 170, l. 39): **ur-saĝ piriĝ huš uru$_2$ me gal-gal**, "O warrior, ferocious lion (of$^?$) the city of great divine rites," which may or may not have been written in ES. Finally, there is the case of an Ur III or early OB cylinder with a hymn to Inana (Sjöberg 1988). Geller (2002: 89, 95) tentatively read **ga-ša-an**, the ES word for "lady/queen," in the poorly preserved l. i 17, but this reading is unlikely, judging from subsequently published detailed photographs (CDLI P345955).

The earliest actual ES texts discovered up to now were found in the city of Girsu and can only be dated on the basis of paleography and that is hardly a precise science as far as cuneiform is concerned. Krecher (1967a: 19–20; 1967b: 88) believed they could not be later than the time of King Lipit-Ištar of Isin (1936–1926 BCE), probably somewhat older, but this is just conjecture. I would only say, based on an examination of some of the original tablets, that they are post-Ur III (2000–2100), but must be earlier than the oldest currently known dated Old Babylonian literary tablet (CT 58: 27; Michalowski 1995: 50) from around 1890 BCE.

3.3 Later History of ES

Old Babylonian 18th and 19th c. BCE elite urban schooling, in southern and central Babylonia at least, was primarily focused on SLS, with limited exposure to ES compositions, but those who were destined to become **gala** chanters apparently concentrated on ES as part of their additional studies or during their apprenticeships, although it is difficult to ascertain how many of these chanters were fully literate; most of them likely learned the prayers from their fathers as they prepared to inherit the role. There is more evidence of Old Babylonian ES writing training farther north, in cities such as Sippar, Kish, and Babylon, as opposed to the more limited use of this form of Sumerian in educational practices of Nippur and of southern cities, although this impression may be at least in part due to the way in which these places were excavated or plundered by robbers.

The later history of ES remains to be chartered in detail and there is no comprehensive glossary of the style that would consider the varieties of practice over the millennia. A lexicon of the Seleucid sources of bilingual ES prayers discovered at Uruk was compiled by Oberhuber (1990) but is now very much out of date (see the reviews by Borger 1989/90 and Edzard 1993). An important source of information about one native perspective on ES is a glossary that provided side by side listings of words in both forms of Sumerian as well as their Akkadian equivalents (Veldhuis 2014: 318–20). The earliest known manuscripts of the *Emesal Vocabulary* date from 12th c. Assyria, but it was undoubtedly composed some time earlier (Veldhuis 1996).

Emesal was absent from the Western second millennium Syrian and Anatolian cuneiform traditions based on Mesopotamian models. Its scant traces are accidental at best. To my knowledge, ES may perhaps be attested in only three compositions from the West. The first is a fragmentary tablet from the Hittite capital of Hattuša (KUB 37, 41), possibly a piece of a Dumuzi-Inana composition (Viano 2016: 283). The second is the bilingual *Hymn to Marduk for a King* documented at Ugarit and Emar (Dietrich 1998). Viano (2016: 297) draws attention to three ES forms in this poem: **mu-li-li** for Ninlil (l. 4), **e-re-eš** / **ereš** (l. 6) as the word for "mistress," and **umun** (l. 7, Emar only) for "lord." The first two may not be ES at all, as there is evidence for both the readings **ereš** and **nin** of the NIN sign is SLS (Marchesi 2004: 186–89), and the syllabic rendering of the name of the goddess rendered a reading that was not limited to ES.[10] The third is a unique fragmentary Sumerian text from Emar concerning Inana that includes the ES form **mu-gib** (for **nu-gig**, one of her major epithets).[11] Arnaud (1987: 341), considered it to be part of a mythological text concerning Inana incorporated within an incantation, without any supporting explanation (see also Viano 2016: 321; Zomer 2018: 357 [no. 88]). This may very well be the case, but the generic attribution should perhaps be suspended pending further investigation.[12]

While ES continued to be used in liturgical prayers down to the very end of cuneiform writing, its use in other contexts underwent changes that have yet to be traced in detail. During the second half of the second millennium, lamentation prayers continued to be written in ES, but its incorporation in other types of texts underwent some changes, as described many years ago by Falkenstein (1953), who drew attention to its "promiscuous" (p. 4) usage in bilingual prayers of the

10 Arnaud 1982: 214 was of the opinion that this was the ES name of Enlil, but it was probably just a local syllabic rendering of Mullisu, etc., the readings of **^{d}nin.lil$_2$**, for which see, most recently, Brisch 2016. There are other forms in the Emar version that do not conform to standard SLS, such as **še-er-ga-an-zu** (l. 6), which may have to be explained as an attempt at rendering ES **še-er-ga-al**, or **ši-meš nam-ti-la** (l. 8), equivalent to syllabic **la-le-e nam-ti-la** in Ugarit and Akkadian *la-li ba-la-ṭi*, where ši is an error, perhaps the scribe was thinking of the ES form of **zi**, "life."

11 It is time to retire the ridiculous English translation "hierodule."

12 For a hand copy, see Arnaud 1985: 526. If one can read **naĝa si-a ĝeš-š[inig**$^{??}$ . . ..] in l. 3′, such *materia magica* might bolster the notion that this was an incantation.

Babylonian ruler Kurigalzu I (ca. 1400-1375 BCE) and the Assyrian king Tukulti-Ninurta I (1243-1207 BCE) as well as to the inclusion of ES elements in later royal inscriptions. Veldhuis (2018a: 188–91) in his study of translation in the first millennium bilingual poem *The Elevation of Ištar*, concluded (p. 191) "apart from the royal inscriptions (where Emesal forms are rare), the use of Emesal in bilingual-born texts is mostly Assyrian. One may recall that the Emesal Vocabulary is primarily an Assyrian compilation with only two exemplars from Babylonia. The Emesal inventory of words becomes one more resource to draw on when attempting to write Emegir . . . this happens less in Babylonia and more in Assyria." He also brought attention to the fact that in the *Elevation*, ES forms were used in speeches of male deities, a practice that was exceptional in early second millennium usage. The complexities of later Emesal practice remain to be fully charted.

3.4 Social and Discourse Functions of ES

Attempts have been made to explain the social and discourse function of Emesal by linking it to hypothetical origins. As noted above, in earlier scholarly literature it was usually described as a women's language or sociolect, although both definitions were already critiqued by Schretter (1990: 121–23). Alster (1982) thought that it might be related to the UD.GAL.NUN texts of the Early Dynastic period. Others have sought its origins in regional dialects. Bobrova (in Bobrova and Militariev 1989: 98) suggested that it was originally the dialect of a cultic center of the goddess Inana that spread out in tandem with her cult, but, as noted by Rubio (2001: 271), without sufficient supporting evidence. Bachvarova (2008: 20, see also 1997: 19) hypothesized that it was originally a regional dialect used by women, living in an area where men and women spoke differently, who "developed a supraregional reputation for their lament performances." Bauer (1998: 436) observed that some of the sound changes characteristic of ES appear to have been present in third millennium texts from the Lagash area. This led him to propose that this form of Sumerian was related to, if not based on, the local version of Sumerian, which was hidden from our view by the scribes who wrote in the standard version of the language (see also Krispijn 2000). But, as argued by Wilcke (2010: 9), these features "are neither restricted to the province of Lagaš nor to southern Babylonia."

None of these proposals are convincing. More compelling is Cooper's (2006) argument linking women to funeral songs that were eventually shared with and then appropriated by the mostly male **gala**, suggesting that, etymology aside, perhaps long before the written documentation of ES, there may have been a

Sumerian women's sociolect or, much more likely, a chanting convention that became obsolete, but was preserved in the lamentation prayers of the chanters.

3.5 Emesal as a Genderlect

The one common element in a preponderance of modern views on ES, going back to the very beginnings of the modern study of Sumerian in the nineteenth century, is the hypothesis that it can be ultimately traced back to a form of the language spoken exclusively by women, often designated as a women's language or genderlect (Schretter 1990: 107–15). For example, the great Russian scholar Igor Diakonoff (1997) defended this point of view, comparing the Sumerian situation with the north-eastern Siberian Chukchee language, in which men and women spoke in different forms of the language, an ethnographic analogy that has been questioned by the linguist Gordon Whittaker (2002). More recently, there has been a decided movement away from such conjecture; for example, Gonzalo Rubio (2007: 1370) wrote that "the occurrence of *eme-sal* forms may be determined mostly by the genre of the text, rather than by the gender of the fictional speaker or even the performer," an opinion now shared, to a degree, by Matuszak (2021: 215), although she also speculated that it might have originated in a female genderlect. Veldhuis (2018b: 450–51) was even more forceful, insisting that the currently available documentation in no way supports the notion that those who sang in ES may have been characterized by any "nonnormative sexual identification or activity," describing this as an idea that has been "very slow to die," even though it is not supported by any specific evidence, but relies only on inference.[13] There can be no doubt that that current debates on the matter remain inconclusive but even if it could be demonstrated that at some time **gala** were men who exhibited culturally perceived non-normative sexual behavior, this would not necessarily explain the use of ES in temple ritual practice.

3.5.1 Genderlect

On the face of it, the notion that Emesal was at some time in the history of Sumerian "woman's language," or gender dialect seems hardly farfetched. Linguistic and sociolinguistic perspectives on the concept of genderlect have undergone

13 See also Attinger 2018.

substantial revisions since the term was introduced half a century ago and in recent years has been the subject of much criticism from feminist sociolinguists. This is a vast area of debate, and I can only mention certain basic positions here. One linguist recently defined it in the following manner (Bakker 2019: 136)

> A genderlect constitutes a way of speaking that is limited to one of the sexes. In other words, it refers to a situation in which societies have men and women speak different languages, or, more often, different varieties of the same language. A genderlect refers to systematic and categorical differences between speech BY men and women, or TO men or women. It was for a long time assumed to be extremely rare, limited to a dozen or so cases worldwide, but our database . . . now contains around a hundred cases."

He further (pp. 137–38) explains

> The differences in the speech between men and women may be limited to a handful of conspicuous lexical items, to just a few phonemes, or to some grammatical elements or particles . . . The gender-distinct elements may be few, but they are almost always items of high frequency and salience.

Idiosyncratic gendered language use can take many forms, ranging the full spectrum from subtle intonational elements and word choice to completely different dialect usage, as was already recognized in seventeenth century,[14] and some of this was brought to general attention by Sir James George Frazer (1900, 1901), who sought the origins of gender distinctions in language in such variation, attributing it to exogamy, arguing that in some tribes men married women who spoke different languages, although this was soon disputed by none other than Émile Durkheim (1901); much of this involved reports of what Trechter (1999: 104) has aptly labeled as linguistic exoticism. Since then, many have analyzed the subtle differences between men and women's speech; some have reported more extreme polarities that characterize different dialect usage by men and women as documented in certain North and South American or Australian languages. One such tongue is the now largely extinct Australian Yanyuwa, in which completely different dialects were used by male and female speakers, a phenomenon not shared by any of the surrounding languages (Bradley 1988). Another linguist, Michael Dunn (2000: 305), writing about the very same Chukchi women's language that was so important for Diakonoff's position, expressed it in the following terms: "Most, probably all, languages mark some kinds of social categories with linguistic differences. A common social category to be so marked is gender in the anthropological sense related to sex, rather

14 For an early critical analysis of early Western explorations of "Fraunschprachen" and "Frauendialekten" see Lasch (1907: 95–101).

than in the linguistic sense related to noun class. Gender differences in speech often involve prosodic differences (such as intonation or pitch), the phonetic realization of certain phonemes, or differences in lexical choice."

Linguists influenced by more recent feminist theories have strongly challenged such positions, arguing that gender is not simply binary and is never the sole defining factor in alterations of language styles, but takes its place alongside other social factors such as hierarchies of power, ethnicity, discourse situation, and that "men and women do not form homogeneous groups; therefore, there cannot be one male genderlect and one female genderlect which all men and all women share" (Tenorio 2016: 1194). Noting that most early Western reports about societies in which men and women spoke different languages were focused on the Americas, Trechter (1999: 104) observed, in a review of the data within a broader sociolinguistic perspective informed by gender studies, "although a few Native American languages are reported over and over as possessing gender-exclusive systems, there is considerable doubt that this has ever been the case, and it is more than likely that gender-exclusive systems do not exist in these languages." Dunn (2014: 47), in a recent survey of what he termed gender determined dialect variation in languages, stressed that while such phenomena may be driven by sexual gender to some degree, it is not always the dominating factor and that other social issues such as social rank often outweigh gender in the use of these language forms. But already almost half a century ago, in a classic essay on sex differentiation in language, collecting and classifying what was then described as "women's language or speech," Ann Bodine (1975: 149) exhibited sensitivity to the linguistic ideologies of the people providing information and of those who were gathering it, but also expressed a concern that the social meaning of the reported language differences had not been adequately explored. But perhaps the most vigorous critique of the concept of a separate, strictly applied female genderlect was presented by Motschenbacher (2010) in an essay that was a revised version of one published under the telling title "Can the Term 'Genderlect' be Saved? A Postmodernist Re-definition" (2007). His answer was that it was indeed no longer adequate for sociolinguistic work, but (2010: 58) "it does seem possible to redefine it in postmodern ways, if one understands genderlect as standing for a linguistic style that performatively stages gendered language stereotypes. It is not to be equated with the actual speech behaviour of women and men in the sense of a stable, context-independent gendered variety. Yet, genderlectal features can be part of linguistic behaviour in contexts where speakers have corresponding constructive intentions or where these construction practices belong to the ritualised practice of a community."

In light of Motschenbacher's take on the genderlect issue, one might speculate that there may have been ritualized gendered speech differences that operated within various Mesopotamian languages, including Sumerian at the time when it was still spoken. Moreover, such putative forms of female expression would, in turn, be subject to social differentiation. Elite and perhaps even other types of private houses in early Mesopotamia included a separate set of rooms that were labeled in Old Babylonian literary Sumerian as **ama$_5$** that constituted the domain of women, including the wife of the owner, but also her servants, wet-nurses, nannies, and children: these may have been the places in which women's discourse was prevalent and, if comparative information is relevant here, were probably the loci of language innovation and change. None of this, however, made it into the written record in cuneiform. In this context, it may be useful to cite a highly stylized passage from a royal poem in praise of the goddess Inana, wherein it is said that the divine pair of Enlil and Ninlil entrusted her with the ability to change men into women, women into men, and to exchange gendered symbolism upside down, and with the power to ensure (*Išme-Dagan K*, ll. 25–26)[15]

> eme bunga munus-e e-ne di
> eme munus-e bunga e-ne [di]
>
> Women playing around with baby boy talk,
> Baby boys playing around with women's talk

Here, the rare word **bunga**, "baby," which Bartash (2018: 11) submits might have been a colloquialism, was used playfully to highlight the domestic context, but significantly a woman's way of speaking is not referred to as ES, although it is also obvious that this would make the parallelism impossible. Poetics aside, it is obvious from such citations that ES was not part of everyday women's discourse in the early Mesopotamian literary imagination, even if by the time this poem was composed no mothers or children spoke any kind of Sumerian.

The forms of Sumerian and Akkadian that we encounter were, as already noted, highly formalized means of expression undoubtedly quite different from the ever-shifting local and socially variated and stratified vernaculars of yesteryear. Indeed, one could argue that Motschenbacher's revised definition of "genderlect" could encompass such disparate usages of Emesal as the stereotyped dialog *Two Women B* as well as the emotionally salient ES prayers of the **gala**, but this will require a more complex and nuanced analysis that must be left to another day.

---

15 Römer 1988: 32; Volk 2004: 89 n. 115; Schretter 2018: 175. For **bunga**, see the references in Attinger 2021: 215; also, Volk 2004: 89; Bartash 2018: 11. Since **bunga** was written with the signs NITA.GA, it is possible that it referred more precisely to male babies, which would strengthen the contrast, hence the translation.

4 The Pragmatics of Emesal Usage

The way gender was marked grammatically in Sumerian, as depicted in (2) above, does not overtly identify the sex of interlocutors or of persons being spoken about, and therefore one would expect that the signaling indexing role of ES would play a major role in written texts, identifying speech participants in lieu of sexually distinctive deictic pronominal or morphological elements. This is put in strong relief in the *Dialog Between Two Women B*, the longest non-cultic composition written in ES, where the female identity of the participants is signaled using this style, as analyzed by Matuszak (2021: 212–13). Indeed, as she stresses, the name of one of the interlocutors, which could identify her gender, is never even mentioned and the name of the second one does not even make an appearance until l. 173, and so ES fulfills the signaling function. One area in which the alteration of styles serves to identify speakers are erotic dialogs between the goddess Inana and her lover Dumuzi, where the poetry would be rendered heavy if they were identified again and again, but the identity of each interlocutor is often reinforced by forms of address such as "my sister," or "my brother," which is how lovers called each other in Sumerian (for more detail, see 4.4 below). But this kind of usage is not, in fact, obligatory in Sumerian literature, where goddesses who speak or sing in ES are usually introduced in some manner. Most commonly, the use of ES in direct speech of goddesses was associated with Inana, but it also occurs in addresses by other goddesses such as Nisaba, Nininsina, or Ninšubur. There is little consistency, however, and it is often difficult to ascertain the motivations for putting some of their speeches in ES while at other times they speak SLS. A fascinating example of the sex identity signaling function of ES is an Old Babylonian tablet with a rough scenario for a vocal performance in which a male singer, a male chorus, and a female soloist were involved and the text assigned to the latter was in ES (Mirelman and Sallaberger 2010).

4.1 The gala/*kalû* and ES

Reservations concerning the existence of "women's languages" or feminine "genderlects," and the lack of any traces of ES in non-literary texts cast doubts on existing definitions and characterizations of this form of Sumerian and require a fresh look into just how it was used in Mesopotamian literary texts and cultic performance.

The main source of our knowledge of Emesal is a voluminous set of ritual prayers, often referred to as laments, that were sung or chanted by cultic practitioners designated as **gala**, Akkadian *kalû* (Gabbay 2014a, 2014b: 63–79; Peled 2016a: 92–153; 2016b; Huber Vulliet 2019: 24 et passim [see p. 504]; Keetman 2021: 461–62). The principal function of these prayers was the appeasement of divine anger in the regular temple cult and at critical social liminal moments, sung in daily, periodic, and episodic ceremonies. Such performances are documented as late as the first century BCE, and it is possible that Emesal may have been used in temples and during public rites for centuries more since we know that Mesopotamian religious practices continued in the heartland and in places such as Palmyra, Edessa, and Harran well into first centuries of the Common Era.[16]

As early as the beginnings of the third millennium, if not before, the major cult centers in both the northern and southern parts of Mesopotamia had head ES chanters, called **gala mah**/*galamaḫḫu*, "supreme lamenter," who were clearly of high status (Shehata 2009: 59; Delnero 2015: 99). These elite chanters and ritual and festival organizers as well as the lower **gala**s sung their prayers from memory, but sometimes wrote texts out to prepare for specific ceremonies, which accounts for the fact that unlike standard school texts, the Old Babylonian ES prayers are rarely attested in more than one exemplar and in cases where duplicates are available, it is obvious that the textual contents were quite unstable (Delnero 2015: 88).[17] It is likely that this reflects the ever changing structuring of various types of many early Mesopotamian rituals, including healing and other cultic practices, so that prayers and incantations were arranged in various ways for each performance. Hence many such texts that have survived are but remnants of preparations for specific occasions; early ritual textual remains were as heterogenous as was the use of Emesal.[18]

Although this cannot in any way be proven, it is likely that Emesal was used in everyday and festive temple rituals for hundreds if not thousands of years before they began to be written down in the eighteenth century BCE; indeed, it is more than probable that there was a taboo on setting these texts into clay before that time. It is important to emphasize that outside of the cultic prayers, that is texts that were labeled as Balaĝ, Eršema, and Šuila in native

16 On such survival of Mesopotamian and Mesopotamian-like cults, see e.g., Dalley 1995; Arbel 1999–2005; Dirven 2014.

17 On the upper rank **gala**s and the **gala mah**s as organizers of rites and festivities, including musical matters, in early Mesopotamia, see Michalowski 2006b for Ur III (a wealth of information on this can now be found on various pages of Huber Vulliet 2019 [index p. 504]) and the description of the activities of the *galamaḫḫu* Ur-Utu in Late Old Babylonian Sippar by Tanret and Van Lerberghe 1993 and Tanret 2011.

18 I am preparing a fuller exploration of such matters, with special attention to incantations.

traditions, no other Mesopotamian performative texts such as incantations ever utilized ES.[19]

Judging by personal names, the **gala** chanters were, as a rule, marked as male. There are very rare instances of women fulfilling this role in third millennium documents, or at least people who carried feminine names.[20] The only example from Babylonia proper studied to date is the case of **nin-tigi$_x$(E$_2$.BALAĜ)-i$_3$-du$_{10}$**, who is mentioned several times in Pre-Sargonic texts from Girsu, as part of a group of women engaged in feeding pigs.[21] As noted by Gelb (1975: 72), the writing of the numbers associated with these women differs from those for men, but the one **gala** in the group is associated with the "masculine" numerals. Nevertheless, he observed that this may very well be a feminine name. Gelb's (1975: 64–74) study of the third millennium **gala**s (which he rendered as "cantor") indicates that their social roles were very different than in later times: many were low status, others had higher rank, some young ones could be purchased, they had wives and children, but although he thought that the term referred to an unspecified physical characteristic, he excluded the possibility that they were eunuchs, concluding (p. 73) "the multiple roles of the gala are those of singers, musicians, and cantors, wailers, liturgists or the like. It also seems quite clear that the gala, while men, had certain feminine characteristics which connect them with women."

Much has been written about these chanters since then, and many have speculated about their sexual identities, invoking terms such as third gender, hermaphrodite, or eunuchs who sang it a high-pitched voice (most recently discussed critically by Peled [2016a: 126–29] with earlier literature). All in all, there is little direct evidence to bolster such interpretations; indeed, as well put by Rubio (2001: 270) "that there were eunuchs in ancient Mesopotamia is quite possible, but that the gala-priests were eunuchs may be a modern, naive, and

---

19 On this matter Veldhuis (2018a: 186 n. 7) recently stated "Falkenstein 1953: 10 nt. 58 came up with one single example. More than 60 years later there may well be more, but the occurrence remains very exceptional." For another dubious example, see p. 219 above.

20 Fara: **munus-lu$_2$-nu-še$_3$**, WF 75 rev. ii 8–9, **nin-gu$_2$-gal**, WF 5 rev. ii 8–9; 9 obv. iii 1–2; 13 obv. ii 5–6; 18 obv. vii 12–13; 26 obv. v 2–3; TSŠ 115 obv. i 8–9; Steible and Yıldız 2015: 15 rev. i 8–9. Presargonic: **munus-tur**, BIN 8: 114 obv. i 4 (Zabala?), possibly **nin-ig-gal**, CUSAS 35: 2 obv. ii 2–3 (Adab), possibly **^{d}inin-ur-saĝ**, OSP 1: 63 obv. ii 2–3. For an Old Akkadian or perhaps slightly later example from Tell Suleima, ancient Awal, in the Hamrin region, see al-Rawi 1992. Both al-Rawi (1992: 182) and Peled (2016a: 108) have suggested that the woman may not have functioned as a *kalû*, but only held the office in the form of a prebend. For Lagaš II, see perhaps **munus-uri$_5$^{ki}**, RTC 248 rev. 4–5.

21 Gelb 1975: 71, see, e.g., BIN 8: 345; CT 50: 34; CTNMC 4: 210; 224; DP 112; 237; 22, etc. (for references, see Balke 2017: 351).

unwarranted assumption based on an old case of character assassination." I would add that there are twenty instances in Ur III documents of adult men, more than half of them associated with the military, who acted in some fashion as **gala**s. This has been interpreted in variety of ways: as induction into the office of **gala**, permanent or temporary, as taking part in musical performances, perhaps in the context of marriage ceremonies, etc. (Michalowski 2006b: 51–57). But no matter which view one accepts, it would be pointless to castrate adult men if the goal was to turn them into chanters who sang with high pitched voices, since it would obviously be much too late in their lives for this to have any such effect. But then this also rests on the dubious notion that Emesal singing was characterized by high pitch, based on doubtful etymology (see Appendix).

4.2 Women's Writing

The complexities of an assumed Sumerian gendered language are striking when one considers the fact that there are hardly any traces of Emesal in Mesopotamian women's writing. While almost all cuneiform literature was presumably composed and copied by males – most Mesopotamian texts have no named authors – there are a handful of Sumerian compositions ascribed by tradition to elite female writers, almost exclusively royal daughters, or copied by the few female students who studied writing.[22] The earliest named human "author" was named Enheduana (e.g., Westenholz 1989; Zgoll 1997; Wagensonner 2020; Konstantopoulos 2021). She was the daughter of King Sargon of Agade around 2400 BCE, the first ruler to unify the independent city states of southern Mesopotamia into a large and powerful territorial polity. As part of his strategy to instill cohesion in a political organization made up of formerly independent entities, he appointed his children to head various major temples, including his daughter as the head priestess of the Moon God in the city of Ur, one of the most prestigious centers of Sumer. Later tradition attributed three or more Sumerian poems to her hand, making her not just the earliest woman writer in recorded history, but the

22 In Old Babylonian times, most scribes and students of writing were male, although there were women writing in Sippar (Lion 2008, 2009b). The situation seems to have been quite different up north in Assur and in the Assur diaspora, where female literacy was much more widespread (Michel 2009). Földi (2019) has raised the distinct possibility that Bulllussa-rabi, the author of the great Akkadian language hymn to Gula, known from later copies but likely composed ca. 13th c. BCE, was a woman.

oldest named author of either gender.[23] Indeed, the satirical *Tumal Chronicle* aside (Michalowski 2006a), there were no named male authors in early Mesopotamia outside of literary epistolography.

Three of these poems concern Inana, goddess of carnal love, violence, and war; paradoxically, she was the goddess that most often expressed herself in ES in other literary contexts. One can debate if Enheduana composed all these compositions, an issue that will never be fully resolved, but the matter is less important than the fact that later tradition insisted that she composed them and that poetic creativity in early Mesopotamia was associated with females, be they human or divine (Brisch 2021: 586). Other women authors of Sumerian works included Ninšatapada, another royal daughter and author of a Sumerian poetic literary letter some centuries later (Brisch 2007: 246–53; Peterson 2016: 68–73), as well as Inanaka, member of one of the most prominent families of the city of Nippur, who wrote a poetic letter of petition to the healing goddess Nintinuga that was studied by Old Babylonian pupils (SEpM 19, Kleinerman 2011: 171–73). In all these poems there is only one solitary trace of Emesal: the mythical poem *Inana and Ebih*, one of the works ascribed by some moderns to Enheduana, Inana mentions Mullil, the ES equivalent of the divine name Enlil (l. 167). It is difficult to know what to make of texts such as this, or for example the hymn *Ninisina E*, that have but one ES word.[24] The avoidance of ES by elite women writers may very well be a function of their high status. The style was associated with powerful goddesses, but in the mundane world it appears to have had lower prestige than the standard literary version of Sumerian, in non-ceremonial contexts at least.

Emesal is also absent from the few surviving cases of female written discourse from Ur III times: stylized testimony by women in records of dispute resolutions or in the lone Sumerian everyday letter from the times sent by a woman currently known (Michalowski 2011: 15–17). Of course, one could argue that these Ur III examples were likely written by male scribes, but the fact is that however we may choose to define Emesal, it was a literary language and was never used in administrative or private economic writing.

It is therefore hardly surprising that according to Jana Matuszak (2018: 269), who knows this material better than anyone and has written insightfully on gender and bias in Sumerian literature, the two extant Old Babylonian women's dialogs, although mostly couched in Emesal, were undoubtedly written by men.

---

23 Wilcke (1976b: 12–13) suggests that a love dialog between the moon god Nanna and his wife (TMH NF 4: 7 ii 7 – iii 6) might be ascribed to Enheduana, but in concert with Westenholz (1989: 550 n. 52), I see no reason for this attribution (nor for her authorship of *Inana and Ebih*).

24 **mar-za**, the ES equivalent of SLS **ĝarza**, "rite," in ll. 20, 28?. Note that Rubio (2001: 270) already drew attention to the lack of ES in the works attributed to Enheduana.

4.3 The Users of ES

Cultic practitioners aside, according to standard opinion ES was used in literature in the speech or song of goddesses and, rarely, by mortal women, almost exclusively by ones of low social status. But as already noted, these same female characters are also often cited enunciating in standard Sumerian and it is not immediately obvious if there were any objective reasons for choice of the form of language or if this was driven by the aesthetic, prosodic, or aleatoric motivations of individual authors. There are examples of others seemingly using this variety of Sumerian, such as a fly, a demon and even a male divinity and a cow (Whittaker 2002: 637–38), but these humorous moments mostly consist of citations from cultic texts that were written in Emesal and thus the speakers were not specifically marked in any separate manner by language register. There are also a handful of Emesal "proverbs." These were school exercises used at an early stage of instruction; some resemble what we call proverbs, but others are just short sayings that were used to learn Sumerian. Most of these were written in the standard form of the language and the few Emesal examples are apparently fragments of cultic laments (Gabbay 2011a).

4.4 Alternation Between ES and SLS

The contrast between ES and the standard Sumerian poetic language is best exemplified in the royal hymn known *Šulgi X*, already mentioned above (Klein 1981: 124–66; Attinger 2022). In this poem, as the king entered the temple of Inana, the goddess performed an Emesal song describing her preparations for a sexual union with the royal. Soon after that she decreed his political, cultic, and martial future but this time her speech was in standard Sumerian. Here one must ask: was the use of different language forms dictated here by ideological motivations or was something else at play? Let us look more closely at this poem, which concerns Šulgi, one of the most powerful rulers of ancient Mesopotamia, who was celebrated for centuries after his death in poetry handed down through the generations. In this composition he journeyed from his home in the city of Ur to Uruk, the metropolis sacred to the Inana. Upon his arrival, the king dressed up in finery, full of love (ll. 9–13):

The faithful shepherd Šulgi, heart in love, dressed himself in a ritual garment
And donned a sensuous wig,[25] *as if it were a crown.*
Filled with admiration
Inana looked at him,
Struck a tune of her own accord,
Voicing songwise:
(followed by a long passage [ll. 14–41] in Emesal)

We then read that (ll. 46–48)

Inana, Su'en's daughter
Decreed the future
Of Šulgi, divine Ninsumuna's son:
(followed by an oration in standard Sumerian [ll. 49–72])

There is, to be sure, a difference in tone between the two Inana soliloquies. The first is full of tenderness and bold sexual imagery, while in the second one the goddess offers the royal the prospect of political and military success. Following this, several other deities, including another goddess, address the king in standard Sumerian, but the only Emesal passage is Inana's first discourse. Most important, as already observed by Löhnert (2009: 11–12),[26] she *sang* to him in Emesal, but *spoke* in standard Sumerian – thus the switch of language seems to be motivated here both by content and by mode of elocution: Emesal is associated here with femininity, expressiveness, sensuality, and sexuality but also, significantly, with song as opposed to spoken poetry or prose. This is not, therefore, simply "a woman's speech." Similarly, in *Lugale* (van Dijk 1983), a long heroic poem concerning the exploits of the god Ninurta, the only passages in ES are a lament of the mother goddess Ninmah (ll. 372–379, 383–385), where all of this, or perhaps only the last section, is summarized as a "sacred song" (**šir$_3$ ku$_3$**, l. 387).[27]

Other Inana poems provide some further insight into the matter. The rather unsettling poem that we entitle as *Inana and Šukaletuda* (Volk 1995) describes how the goddess, traveling in the mountains far away from her home in Uruk, was raped while sleeping in the shade of a large poplar tree by a character named Šukaletuda. After various episodes (Volk 1995: 122, 130–32, ll. 239–249),

25 The word is **hi-li**, which has strong sexual connotations, and may refer to a wig or even a form of hairstyle, both symbolic of sensuality; see Galter 2021: 38–45. Attinger 2022: 215 translates the line as "En guise de couronne, il avait placé *un bandeau autour de* (sa) tête," which is also quite possible (I am grateful to the author for providing me with an early version of the article).

26 Also Schretter 2018: 187; see also the observations of Shehata 2009: 251 on Emesal prayers being sung or chanted.

27 This passage was last treated by Worthington 2019: 295–96.

Once day had broken and the Sun God had risen,
The woman examined herself,
Sacred Inana examined herself:
"Ah, who will recompense me?
"Ah, who will pay (?) for what happened to me?
"Should it not be the concern of my own father, divine Enki?" (she exclaimed).
Sacred Inana directed her steps to the Deep in Eridu town
And, because of all this, prostrated herself before him and stretched out her hands to him
(saying): *"Oh Father Enki, I should be recompensed! What's more, someone must pay!*
"Only once you, acting from the Deep, have handed over that man to me
"Will I go back satisfied to my shrine Eana (in Uruk)!"

The passages in italics are in Emesal, the rest is in standard Sumerian. There is no mistaking the deep hurt and anguish expressed here by Inana, as she seeks retribution for the horrendous deed perpetrated by Šukelatuda, and this distress was expressed in Emesal. Eventually, the perpetrator was handed over to the goddess who took her vengeance, sentencing him to death. In a remarkable follow-up to the end of the story, we read, this time exclusively in standard Sumerian, as Inana explains to Šukaltuda:[28]

"Come now, you shall die, but because of me your name will never be forgotten.
"Because your name shall live on in song, the songs will be sweet,
"Because young singers shall perform them enjoyably in the king's palace,
"Because shepherds shall sing them sweetly turning their butter churn,
"Because young shepherd shall carry your name to where they graze their sheep,
"And so a desert dwelling shall be your home."

Inana attained retribution but promised her tormentor eternal renown – the kind of memory reserved for great kings and mythic heroes – but one that would always be associated with her. Šukaletuda was to be remembered, ironically, in song, but her promise, vengeance taken cold, was not expressed in Emesal.

There are two other fragmentary myths concerning Inana, but none of the passages in which she speaks in them are in Emesal. But there is still another poem in which our goddess is a protagonist, this one labeled as *Inana and Bilulu*.[29] This unusual composition, known only from a single manuscript, belongs to a cycle of texts that dealt with the complex relationship between Inana

28 Ll. 296–301. Inana's speech encompassed at least 5 or 6 more lines, but these are too fragmentary for translation.

29 The original edition is by Jacobsen and Kramer 1953. For a more modern transliteration and translation, see the internet edition by the Electronic Text Corpus of Sumerian Literature (http://etcsl.orinst.ox.ac.uk/cgi-bin/etcsl.cgi?text=c.1.4.4&display=Crit&charenc=gcirc#). The line numbering follows the newer rendition. The text has also been recently translated in Gadotti 2014a: 47–51; see also Ceccarelli 2019: 117–18.

and her lover and sometime paramour Dumuzi, who was doomed to the netherworld, in some texts for only half the year. At one point in the story Dumuzi escaped the netherworld demons sent to capture him and hid in the house of an old woman named Bilulu, who betrayed him to his pursuers, and so the goddess retaliated against the old woman who had deceived her beloved. The beginning of the story the text is poorly preserved: it appears that Inana cried bitterly over her mate, apparently already aware of what has already transpired, or overtaken by bad premonitions. She then asks her mother for permission to go out looking for the shepherd. Her lament as well as her request have only scattered words in Emesal. Once she had found out what had happened (ll. 75–80),

> The Queen composed a song for her husband, fashioned for him a song,
> Sacred Inana composed a song for Dumuzi, fashioned for him a song (in Emesal):
> *"O you, now laid low, shepherd, laid low, you stood guard over them,*
> *"Dumuzi, now laid low, you stood guard over them,*
> *"Lord-Lion-of-the-Sky-(God), now laid low, you stood guard over them,*
> *"Working from sunup you stood guard over my sheep,*
> *"Lying down only by night, you stood guard over my sheep!"*

At the very end she twice sings another lament in Emesal (ll. 155–161, 166–173), which begins with the words,

> *A lament over you, a lament over you, a lament I want to declare,*
> *A lament for you, a lament over you a lament I want to declare,*

but there is a narrative in between the two that is quite revealing. These four ES lines contain the voice of the author/reciter of the tale:

> *Thus, the warrior goddess proved worthy of her betrothed,*
> *Thus, sacred Inana proved worthy of shepherd Dumuzi!*
> *It was granted to Inana to make good his resting place,*
> *It was granted to Inana to avenge him!"*

This interlude, inserted between the two ES Inana laments, could be taken as an indication that the poem may have been intended to be recited or performed by a woman, but unless this is a hypercorrection, it is more likely that the conclusion was to be sung rather than recited so that the author's (male$^{?}$) voice blended in with the laments.

Here once again Emesal is associated with highly emotional moments, but also with song, although it is difficult to know if the differences in the level of ES usage between the various quotations are indicative of emotive differences or are simply graphic. The situation is somewhat different in a set of short love poems concerning Inana and Dumuzi that include highly erotic episodes (Sefati 1998; Rubio 2001). Some were expressed in first person by Inana in standard Sumerian, while in others used Emesal, among those that are couched in the form of a dialog some of them distinguished between the identities of the two lovers by using different linguistic forms, but others do not. Therefore, while the use of ES was linked to eroticism and gender in such poems, this does not seem to have been obligatory and the disparities may be indicative of different origins of individual compositions or may signal pragmatic issues that elude us. A few examples will suffice. In *Inana-Dumuzi A* the protagonists are identified and then in his first address, the sun god Utu acknowledges his sister Inana directly, but in the ensuing dialog the two are recognizable only by the content of the speeches and the use of ES by the goddess. In other dialogs such as *Inana Dumuzi B and C*, the lovers are not overtly specified: the one who speaks is marked only by use of ES for the young woman and by such expressions as "my sister," "my brother." The cleverest and most telling exploitation of language difference is embedded in *Dumuzi-Inana H*. The young woman speaks first, in ES, identifying herself as Inana, describing her wonderful day singing and dancing in the streets and her assignation with Dumuzi, but worries about what to tell her mother when she gets home. Her lover provides her with an excuse; here is a translation of ll. 13–20, with the ES passages once again marked in italics (Sefati 1998: 186–87, ll. obv. 13–20)

> Let me teach you, o let me teach you!
> O Inana, it is I who will teach you women's lies (you will tell her):
> *"My girlfriend was dancing with me in the square.*
> *"She ran around playfully with me, banging on a drum,*
> *"Her songs that were so delightful she sang,*
> *"I spent the day there with her in pleasure and delight."*
> Once you lie so to your mother,
> Then as for us – I can make love with you by moonlight!

Here, in a delightful linguistic role reversal, Dumuzi tells Inana the exact formulation of the lies she is to offer her mother so that they can spend the time making love, embedding the words she is to speak in his own direct speech, instructing her what to say in Emesal![30]

Quite different in tone are several poems or songs associated with Ur III royals that include ES that are known only in later versions. One of these is reminiscent of lullabies, addressed to a "son of Šulgi," albeit it is difficult to

30 For an example of a male repeating a woman's ES speech verbatim, see now *The Old Man and the Young Girl*, ll. 22–23 (Matuszak 2022: 22).

identify the singer, who may have been a mother, wetnurse, or nanny (*Šulgi N*, Kramer 1971; Alster 1971).

Inana was intimately linked with ES in the complex narrative of the *Descent of Inana to the Netherworld* (Attinger 2019b). Here, the goddess always proclaims in ES, but when her sister Ereškigal, the queen of the underworld speaks, with two one-line exceptions, it is always in SLS.[31] This difference is not accidental. Inana, before entering the netherworld, is decked out in all her finery, symbols of her sensuous overt sexuality. Once she enters the great below, she is stripped naked and transformed into a haggard corpse-like creature, but this is only a temporary state, and the ensuing narrative is dedicated to the restoration of her original primal essence. By contrast, her sister Ereškigal, queen of the afterlife domain, is permanently repellant and unattractive described so (ll. 258–262 [Attinger 2019b: 49–50, with a similar depiction in *Gilgamesh, Enkidu, and the Netherworld*, ll. 200–205]; Gadotti 2014b: 158, 166):

> Ereškigal lay there, so (deathly) ill she was,
> She did not unfold a linen cloth over her formidable lap,
> Did not push out her bosom like a flask,
> Her fingers [are] like copper axes,
> [She pulls] the hair from her head like leeks.

The purported reason given by Inana for her visit was the death of her sister's husband Gugalana. There is an obvious contrastive symmetry between the two: Inana is the voluptuous queen of the heavens who engages in sexual activities, whose lover will spend half the year with her, half in the hellish domain of her sister, whose own husband is now dead. Both are, paradoxically, maidens and mothers. But Ereškigal, having been deposed from her throne by her more glamorous sister, is not only a sexless widow in mourning, but an unattractive, deathly ill apparition, devoid of any female charms. It is possible that these conflicting images were reinforced using different language styles: ES used by a supremely female goddess and SLS by a neuter, unattractive person lingering in sickness. Even if Inana was reduced to a similar state in the poem, she retained, deep down, the excessive sensuality that was her quintessence. These tropes are elements in the fuller semantic structure of a poem built around fundamental binary oppositions of cosmic above and below, light and darkness, life and death, and their transgressions. But there is also focus, in the figure of Inana, on sexuality and sensualness and it is here that Ereškigal figures as her mirror image so much so that the queen of the upper regions comes to resemble

31 Ll. 249 and 283, but these lines are only present in source S (= UET 6/1: 10+ 6/3: 433), not in other witnesses; see Attinger 2019b: 92 n. 399, 93 n. 415.

her sororal monstrous double as the narrative unfolds. The use of ES here is not simply a signaling device marking female speech but is hitched to the structural plays of similarity and difference between the two sisters, with SLS symbolizing the relatively unsexed character of the queen of the netherworld.

Sumerian erotic poetic imagery was closely associated with ES, but it was not applied consistently, as can be gleaned from any quick survey of the texts published and discussed by Alster (1993) and Sefati (1998), where Inana sometimes expresses herself in ES and sometimes does not; rarely, in some compositions, as for example in a more recently published fragment (Peterson 2010), we encounter the poet's voice likewise couched in ES. Such sensual associations of ES would clearly require more analysis than can be attempted here.

Other examples of alterations between ES and standard Sumerian are more difficult to parse. Elsewhere, while ES is decidedly associated with Inana, the significance of the use of this style, aside from its obvious gender signaling function is unclear. In *Inana and Enki* (Farber-Flügge 1973) the goddess first praises her feminine charms and sexual attraction and explains that she intends to go to Enki in Eridu and demand the expansion of her powers and some form of sexual activity, and she does so in ES. Once she has received various powers, she brags in direct speech about them, but this is all is SLS (Farber-Flügge 1973: 58–61). As the narrative moves on, there is a dispute about possession of the powers, and the goddess, now indignant, once again switches to ES in her remaining discourses.

As repeatedly mentioned above, some lines of poetry or prose have only one or two Emesal elements. Was this a cue to read the whole line in Emesal? Black (1991: 24 n. 14) observed that "this very slight mixing of Eme-sal forms raises the possibility that texts virtually or even completely written in Eme-gi might be intended to be performed in Eme-sal." If so, what is one to do with longer passages addressed by female deities that only have one or two Emesal words, most often very common ones such **e-ne-eĝ$_3$** (= standard Sumerian **inim/enim**, "word"), as for example in several passages in the myth *Inana and Enki*. As already observed above, in another mythical poem, *Inana and Ebih*, the goddess speaks several times, always in standard Sumerian with uses only one Emesal word – Mullil – the equivalent of the divine name Enlil (l. 167). Much the same can be said about a more prosaic text, purporting to be a stylized song of women workers in a flour mill that likewise only contains the Mullil as the sole ES word, although this composition is currently known to us in fragmentary form (*Song of the Millstone*, Civil 2006: 124, l. A 2); perhaps this version of Enlil's name was an indexing trigger like **uru$_2$**, pointing to the speaker's gender, in this case a miller girl, but one could also speculate, in line with Jeremy Black and others, that in the case of certain texts, reading traditions may have dictated that some whole passages or texts that were not explicitly written in ES had to be spoken or chanted in that style.

But something else may also be at play here: as observed by Matuszak (2016: 241–42), in *Lugale* ll. 457–462 the god Ninurta decrees the future of the sharpening stone and millstone, beginning with the words "A weak lowly worker will be *assigned to you*," where the predicate is **zi$_2$-ig$_3$**, the ES equivalent of SLS **šum$_2$**, "to give." The use of ES by the supremely masculine god Ninurta must surely be demeaning, pointing to the lowly status of female mill workers, leading Matuszak (2016: 242) to the conclusion that "it is not altogether unlikely – though impossible to prove – that the use of Emesal in Ninurta's speech was a means of mockery in itself." Civil's millstone text may very well have been an academic riff on the grand Ninurta poem, but this might also be part of a broader set of denigrating tropes relating to women mill laborers as exemplified by a passage in which one of them expresses herself in ES (Matuszak 2016: 235–36). Even if the nuances escape us, the intersection of ES, feminine gender, and low social status is markedly evident in these tropes. Having said this, it is equally important to stress that not one available cuneiform tablet with Emesal was written by a person whose mother tongue was Sumerian and this is a matter that must always be kept in mind as we consider socio-psychological aspects of linguistic usage. In such contexts, misunderstandings, learning errors, hypercorrection, local performance and instructional differences, as well as individual creativity and innovation surely had roles to play.

One interesting set of instances of ES usage is to be found in the two very different poems recounting how the daughter of the goddess Nisaba came to marry Enlil, designated by their modern titles *Enlil and Ninlil* (Attinger 2019a) and *Enlil and Sud* (Civil 1983; Cavigneaux 2020: 70–74; Mitto and Peterson 2020). In *Enlil and Ninlil*, two female divinities, Nunbaršegunu (Nisaba) and her young daughter Ninlil both speak in ES, but unexpectedly, the narrator's phrase that introduces the mother's initial address to the girl appears to likewise be in ES, using **ša** for SLS **na** (*Enlil and Ninlil*, ll. 13–14):

> ud-ba ki-sikil ama ugu-na *ša* na-mu-un-de$_5$-de$_5$
> dnin-lil$_2$-le dnun-bar-še-gu-nu *ša* na-mu-un-de$_5$-de$_5$
>
> And so, then her birth mother was instructing the maiden,
> Nunbaršegunu was instructing Ninlil (as follows):

In the former, both mother and daughter are quoted speaking in ES, but the situation is quite different in the latter. At the outset of the narrative, Enlil discovers the maiden Sud, apparently standing in the gate of her house in the street; he is immediately stricken with love and proposes to her, even if he seems to be taking her as someone of questionable repute, perhaps even as a sex worker. Sud repels his advances, appalled at being taken for a woman of ill repute, angrily telling him to get out of her sight, and all of this is in ES (ll. 18–21):

> *me-e* ka_2-me-a *še-er-ma-al-bi da-gub* a-ba šu mu-un-kar_2-kar_2
> za-e *ta-zu* [*i-bi_2*] *mu-ma-al ta-aš* gu_2-uš *im-di-di-in*
> [. . .] bi_2-ib-la_2 *i-bi_2-ma_3-ta*
> [. . . a]-ša-an-gar_3 mu-⌈un⌉-ak-ne $murgu_2$ mu-un-na-ne
>
> (So what) if I want to stand proudly at our gate–who dares to insult me?
> What are your intentions? Why have you come here?
> . . . from my sight!
> Others? had already tried to deceive [my mother?] and made her angry.

In a later episode, however, after Enlil has sent the women a messenger apologizing and offering the proper suitably magnanimous marriage proposal, the mother conveys the messenger the exact wording of her answer that he is to repeat to the grand god (ll. 61–73 = 90–102), but these include only one ES word, the first-person pronoun **me-e** (l. 63 = 92). The markedly different use of ES in these two female speeches, on the graphic level at least, is striking: could it be that the fuller use of the style in the young girl's outburst is meant to signal her agitated emotional state?

Such divergent us of Sumerian speech styles by the same goddess can be found elsewhere. For example, in the fragmentary poem *Sin-iddinam C* (Brisch 2007: 138–39, ll. 3′-23′) the healing goddess Ninisina speaks directly to her son Damu in ES, but in a different poem addresses him twice in SLS (*Ninisina A*, ll. 15–16, 27–29, Römer 1969), while also praising herself extensively, likewise not in ES. These texts may have been written at different times and in different places, but truth be told, it is impossible to provide any probable explanation for these differences unless one posits that the goddess was agitated about the health of the king in the fragmentary poem concerning Sin-idinnam and thus in a very emotional state. Such alterations can even be detected within a single text, as in the poem of *Enki and Ninhursaĝ* (Attinger 1984), where the goddesses Ninsikila and Uttu speak in SLS, but there are two lines in ES: after Enki violently sexually abuses the young Uttu, she cries out in ES (l. 186), and when the mother goddess Ninhursaĝ finally curses the violator, she likewise expresses herself emotionally in ES (l. 219).

These two mythological stories about the transgressive activities of the divine pair of Enlil and Ninlil were partly localized in Mesopotamian cities – Nippur and Ereš – but in the transcendent sphere in a dimension inaccessible to human experience. Quite different in tone and narrative is *The Marriage of Martu* that told how the god Martu had acquired a wife: if it were not for the recognizable divine names and the divine classifiers, this narrative, which takes place in the city of Inab in central Babylonia, would appear to be a story about humans rather than divinities. There are two brief ES passages in this story, first, when Martu's mother addresses her son (l. 49), and then towards the very end of the tale (ll. 127–139), someone warns the young goddess, daughter of Numušda, the divine ruler of Inab, not to marry Martu, describing him and his kind in most unflattering terms, the reader has no idea who the speaker is, until in the very last line:

> ma-la-ĝu$_{10}$ ^{d}mar-tu *ta-am$_3$* an-tuku-tuku-un
> O my girlfriend, why ever would you marry Martu?

There is a certain redundancy here – the SLS word **mala(g)** identifies the speaker as female, as does the only ES word **ta-am$_3$**, "why ever?" in her soliloquy.

Finally, mention should be made of five literary city laments that memorialized the collapse of the Ur III kingdom around 2000 BCE and the recovery from the catastrophe that was finalized during the reign of King Išme-Dagan, the fourth ruler of the Isin dynasty whose kings portrayed themselves as successors state of the rulers of Ur. Two of these, the Eridu and Uruk laments (LE and LUk, Green 1978, 1984), are still fragmentary, while a third focused on the city of Nippur (NL, Tinney 1996). The best known are *The Lamentation over the Destruction of Sumer and Ur* (LSUr, Michalowski 1989) and *The Lamentation over the Destruction of Ur* (LU, Samet 2014). These modern titles are somewhat misleading: the former was focused on the moon god Nanna, the titulary deity of Ur, and the latter on his divine wife Ningal, so that they might perhaps be better described as *Nanna's Lament* and *Ningal's Lament*. The circumstances surrounding the composition of these poems are unknown, although it is often suspected that they might have originated in the context of rebuilding celebrations. Gabbay (2014b: 289, also 13–14) recently suggested that the city laments adapted "Emesal materials for royal use in a specific ceremonial circumstance." This may very well be apposite, but the use of ES in these poems is more complex than is often stated.

The city laments were generally composed in SLS but the Eridu and Ur laments contain passages of direct speech by goddesses in ES, but also by the city (Green 1975: 288–89; Samet 2014: 2), although there is occasional bleeding of ES forms into the narrative or even the speeches of male deities here and there.[32]

32 Note that *ālu*, the Akkadian lexical equivalent for "city" was grammatically feminine.

The poorly preserved *Uruk Lament* has no traces of ES.[33] The case of the *Nippur Lament* is perhaps the most complex of all. Much of the first two-thirds has scattered ES words and phrases, suggesting that all of it may have been meant to be recited in that manner, but once the divine quartet of An, Enlil, Enki, and Ninmah decided that the city should be restored, the final third of the poem (ll. 214–323) that describes Enlil's restoration commands, divine compassion, the prayers of King Išme-Dagan, and their divine acceptance, are all written in SLS, with just a single ES word in the very first line of the eighth section.[34] It is difficult to find a rationale for the change in language style between these parts of the lament, but it is possible that it might have signaled a movement in emotional expressivity from woeful lament to acceptance and resolution.

The LSUr, otherwise in SLS, contains about a dozen occurrences of the ES word **uru$_2$**, mostly in the cries of goddesses, although some manuscripts use the SLS **uru/iri**, but also in two other contexts that may signal connections with the cultic ES prayers. At the very outset, in the fifth line, **uru$_2$** is used in a cliché that is characteristic of such prayers, and perhaps most strikingly, in the direct speech of the god Enlil that is filled with pathos. Answering Nanna's pleas for cessation of the catastrophe, Enlil speaks in terms that once again reference the kind of laments normally reserved for the **gala**: "The haunted city (**uru$_2$**) is filled with lamentation, lament reeds grow there!" Such usage of one ES word, as already noted in the discussion of the *Curse of Agade* above, may be generic, signaling affinity with the cultic prayers rather than sexual gender. Moreover, LSUr ends with a three-line ES exhortation addressed to the goddess Ningal that contrasts with the focus on her spouse Nanna in the poem. Various explanations for this have been offered: that these words may have been uttered by a **gala**, or by Ningal, that they might have been addressed to her in her own style, or that this may have been a signal for an ES cultic prayer that was to follow in performance (Michalowski 1989: 108), even if that last solution has not found much favor (Gabbay 2014b: 13 n. 70).[35] There is no such final stanza in LU and the final parts of the other two city laments are not preserved and it is thus impossible to know if this might have been a generic element or not.

It is instructive, in this context, to bring into the discussion a set of poetic works associated with the family travails of a certain Nippurite by the name of Lu-diĝira, possibly imagined as a traveling merchant, whose wife Nawirtum

33 Green (1984: 267) interpreted **i$_3$-bi$_2$** in 2.12′ as ES for "eye" = "observer" (SLS **igi**), but this is the SLS word for smoke; see Attinger 2021: 267 (ref. courtesy of P. Attinger).

34 L. 214 **me-ri**, ES equivalent of **ĝiri$_3$**, "foot/feet."

35 Attinger (2019c: 26) speculated that this as well as the ES ll. 361–362 and 479–481 might be a refrain uttered by a **gala** or a women's choir.

and father Nannaja died and whose mother Šat/Simat-Ištar lived far from his whereabouts. These laments contain but a single ES word each, one of which is once again **uru$_2$**.[36] The *Message of Lu-diĝira to his Mother*, consisting of poetic instructions by the son to a messenger on how to recognize his mother, much happier in tone, is absent any ES words.[37] Once again, one has the impression that just a smattering of ES may signal emotional stress.

To summarize this rather complex description of the main uses of Emesal outside of cultic contexts, it seems that it was almost exclusively with female gender, albeit most often divine, but also with highly emotional poetic moments, with sex and eroticism, primarily from a woman's perspective, and above all with song. The use of ES by mortals in *Two Women B* stands out as unusual, but this may be due to the satirical nature of the composition. It is difficult to account for such a heterogeneous set of characteristics, but it is obvious, once again, that the definition of Emesal as "woman's speech" or "dialect" is much too restrictive to account for all these features.

4.5 Emotive Language

With these facts in mind, rather than view Emesal as a descendant of a genderlect or even as a "genrelect," I would like to take the discussion in a different direction and explore alternative perspectives. If there is one characteristic that is shared by many of the features enumerated above, it would be the adjective "emotive." There are various ways in which languages encode emotive language, best described in the classic essay on the topic by the distinguished linguist Edward Stankiewicz (1964). For him, building on Prague School ideas as interpreted by his teacher Roman Jakobson, the emotive is but one of several functions of language, often expressed by deviations from the normal cognitive use of grammar, sound, or vocabulary as expressive devices. These can take many forms, from use of metaphorical terms, use of specific kinds of lexical compounds, of verbal categories such as aspects or moods, sound repetition, alliteration, or other means. As explained by Stankiewicz (1964: 250), some languages use phonological means to express emotion; thus, for example,

36 *Nannaja Elegy* l. 3 (Sjöberg 1983: 315; ETCSL c.5.5.2), *Nawirtum Elegy* l. 24, **aĝ$_2$**, ES for **niĝ$_2$**, l. 24 (**aĝ$_2$ x-⌜ga-a-ni-ta$^{?}$⌝** [Kramer 1960: 56 (l. 136); ETCSL c.5.5.3] the x is completely broken but a very short sign; all collated on a photograph). Note that this is in a passage with lines ending in **ri**, characteristic of ES prayers.

37 Çığ and Kramer 1976 (ETCSL c.5.5.1), I am preparing a new edition of all three works.

> Among American Indian languages, expressive palatalization is found in Huichol and Sahaptin. In Huichol it is used in affectionate speech, in address to children, and in child-speech, as well as in songs. Emotion is here rendered not only through the alternation of /t, c, n/ with /*t′*, *c′*, *n′*/, but also through the alternation of the voiced /z/ and /r/ (an alveolar trill) with /*s*/ and /*Ø*/ (or *S*), and of /ṛ/ (a retroflex flap) with /*R*/ (an alveolar flap) or with the lateral /*l*/; e.g. *kiyesi* "little sticks" (vs. *kiyezi* "sticks"), *musule* "red and cute" (vs. *muzure* "red"). In Sahaptin, the emotive function is carried by palatals which replace velars, and by /*š*/ or /*l*/ which replace /s/ or /n/ respectively.

In view of this, it is tempting to look at Emesal, whatever its origins, as a formalized non-obligatory means of expressing the emotive language in Sumerian, albeit one associated with women and often with distress or erotic extasy.[38]

Taking this suggestion further, to harken back to the Šulgi hymn I have referred to more than once above, it will be recalled that the two passages in which Inana addressed the king differ not only in the form of language, but also in the mode of elocution: she *sang* to him in Emesal but *spoke* about him in standard Sumerian. This too can be taken as an expression of emotive language; indeed, one could argue that singing is the ultimate vocal expression of emotions. And song, like emotive language in general, is often expressed by alternative linguistic means.

In many societies singing is limited to specific dialects or modes of expression, often simply for technical reasons. In singing one can only hold a note on a vowel, hence it is common to find vocalists assuming features of socio/dialects that have richly colored vowels. For various reasons, the study of the sounds of ES has been focused on its consonantal repertoire, but there are some indications that vowels and glides were modulated in singing. Best known are vocalic performance indications in Late Babylonian cultic prayers (Mirelman 2010; Gabbay and Mirelman 2011), but phonetic spellings of glides, elongated vowels, as well as vowel sequences are occasionally encountered in Old Babylonian ES passages as well (Mirelman and Sallaberger 2010). There is some question as to whether glides were phonemic in SLS, and perhaps in ES as well, so that their usage in singing would be but one more marked element of emotive language.

There are examples of societies in which speech and song must be expressed in different languages or styles. Most dramatically, this recalls the fascinating singing language called Lirasniara or "song-talk" of the Southwest Maluku region of eastern Indonesia that is used exclusively for singing by

38 Much interesting work has been done on the textual and pictorial representations of emotions in Mesopotamia and the ancient Near East; see, most recently, the essays collected by Hsu and Llop Raduà (2020), but it is important to make distinctions between the representation, description, or emulation of emotion and the semiotics of emotional language.

people speaking various languages and dialects (van Engelenhoven 2010). The area is characterized by a wide range of idiolects, dialects, and even mutually unintelligible languages almost all of which belong to the same Austronesian subfamily, as they are all considered to be descended from the same proto-language. All of them, including at least one unrelated language, utilize Lirasniara in song. It may have been created as a jargon used for inter-language communication, but whatever its origin, it was adopted by all, since it shares many features, even if altered, of each.

A structurally different example of linguistic games marking sung verse is represented by the *raivaru* poetry in the Indo-European Dhivehi language of the Maldives archipelago southwest of Sri Lanka. The characteristic device of *raivaru* was syllable or word scrambling, in which syllables could be moved around to create new words and these had to be unscrambled by listeners.

Emesal certainly shares some characteristics of Lirasniara and *raivaru* albeit it in a very different social and linguistic environment.

5 Conclusions

These observations hardly exhaust the topic, but they do strongly suggest, as others have already suspected, that Emesal, as we know it, cannot be simply defined as a form of Sumerian "women's speech" or genderlect. It may very well be that some early spoken varieties of the language included phonological changes for emotive language and that this was formalized for mourning elegies sung by women that were eventually taken over by the **gala**s, in line with Cooper's (2006) hypothesis, but also secondarily formalized for representing the voices of goddesses, and in the case of Inana, only when she was involved in her feminine emotive role rather than in her masculine-like martial and political incarnation. This kind of code-switching is a well-documented stylistic device for expressive prominence but matters of emotional language in Mesopotamian cultures require much more investigation.[39]

The main cultural domain of Emesal – mostly for sung lament prayers – was practiced in early times by cultic specialists who handed down the poems in oral fashion from father to son for countless generations without recourse to

39 As this essay goes to print, a wonderful handbook dealing with emotions in the ancient Near East has just appeared (Sonik and Steiner 2022), too late to be properly referenced here. My impression is that as far as language is concerned, although there is much insight on emotive lexicons, the matter of emotive language is not explored.

writing; indeed, the inscribing of such texts on tablets may have been taboo before the second millennium, as mentioned above. Thus, there must have developed many local and even family traditions of singing before Emesal materials were subject to written redaction and standardization and this may account, in part, for the variations and inconsistencies encountered in the earliest available Emesal prayers. Indeed, as Delnero (2017: 91) has stated, "the content of individual laments – at least during the Old Babylonian Period – was more open to adaptation and modification for oral performance than it was fixed and standardized in a written tradition." Such pragmatic considerations require further investigation of the actual use of different language styles in written and performative discourse, keeping in mind that a preponderance of documentation is dated to times when Sumerian was no longer spoken in the streets. But the definition of the forms of such usage is not a simple matter.

Throughout this essay I have eschewed the terms "dialect," or "register," to designate ES, preferring neutral "type," or, more specifically, "style." The first two have long histories of usage in linguistics, but are problematic for various reasons, most notably because their definitions are very much dependent on how one views such matters as power, hierarchy, ethnicity, or gender in language use, because of different usage in various scholarly traditions and even native language ideologies.[40] I use the plural because it is important to keep in mind that various such ideologies circulate in society, "not as a homogeneous cultural substratum but as dimensions of practices that are deployed in constructing and naturalizing discursive authority" (Briggs 1998: 312). The latter are difficult to tease out from long-dead written traditions, but in the case of Emesal the one Old Babylonian passage in which the label is mentioned may provide some clues.

The acrographic lexical list known as ***Saĝ***, "Head," from its opening entry, was rarely used in Nippur and the south (Veldhuis 2014: 175) but belonged to the northern Old Babylonian school/scholarly tradition in areas where the writing down of ES prayers was more current. In one recension from Babylon, it includes a section with words that begin with the sign **eme**, "tongue, language," including a series of labels for "languages," beginning with Sumerian and Akkadian, followed by those of Elam, of the "Amorites," and of Subir, the latter most likely a reference to Hurrian (Civil, Gurney, and Kennedy 1986: 12 text D iii' 7′-11′ and parallels). Precisely what these labels denoted is a complex matter

40 For a succinct exploration of "register," see Agha 2004; on the definitional complexities of notions such as "sociolect" and "register," see Lewandowski 2010.

that cannot be discussed here, but it is obvious that in the ideological perspective of the compilers of this list, these "ethnic" language labels belonged together. But then the text moves on, in acrographic fashion, to other matters (ll. 12′-15′):[41]

> eme tuku
> eme nu-tuku
> eme ni_2-tuku
> eme sal
> etc.

The meanings of these expressions are somewhat ambiguous; the first two mean literally "having language/tongue," and "not having language/tongue, but later texts render the first in Akkadian as "slanderer," (*muraššu*) and the second as "powerless, poor" (*lā išānû*), while the third may mean something like "respectful talk," or the like. Here ES was clearly grouped separately from major language labels and was not considered to be on the same taxonomic level as "Sumerian" or "Akkadian." A different recension of the list, however, preserved in bilingual form on an unprovenanced tablet, categorizes ES differently, following right after the language labels, either as a transition to the descriptive terms or as the last of the previous section, following after **eme subir** (Civil, Gurney, and Kennedy 1986: 24 iv 30–35). The Akkadian equivalent provided there, *lurû*, is of little help, as it only otherwise occurs three other times in lexical texts and its meaning is unknown.[42] The English translation "person with a thin(?) voice" offered in CAD L: 256 is simply an unsubstantiated guess based on one interpretation of the meaning of the term **eme sal** (see Appendix below). More than this one cannot say, but it is apparent that at least two different language ideologies may have been at work in two variants of the same composition, one that imagined ES as a style and another that grouped it with major language labels, although the latter interpretation is dubious at best. Notably, it was not listed following the general native term for "Sumerian language," **eme** $\mathbf{gir_{15}}$, Akkadian *šumeru/û*. So much for the presently available information on native heuristic views of the matter.

---

41 On this passage, see also Schretter 2018: 179–80, preceded by a discussion of the Sumerian word for "language."

42 Once in another version of the same composition (Civil, Gurney, and Kennedy 1986: 26), and in two other contexts; see CAD L 256: **[l]**$\mathbf{u_2}$ **eme sal** = *lu-ru-*u_2 (Ura 24 "B" iv 14, MSL 12, p. 229) and OBGT III, 222 (PBS 5: 142 iv 2, where one must apparently now read the Sumerian as **⸢eme⸣ [dar-da]r** (Klaus Wagensonner apud Ludwig 2021: 258 and the CDLI photograph P2280710).

If Emesal was not a dialect, register, or genderlect (descendant), then why have I proposed to designate it as a style?[43] In an important discussion of two speech styles used among the Shokleng of Brazil, labeled as "origin-myth telling" and "ritual wailing," Greg Urban (1985: 312) offered a definition that, while lengthy, deserves to be cited in full:

> A speech style is a complex linguistic sign vehicle composed of numerous types of signals that manifests considerable functional richness. First, as a *code*, it can be used to transmit "semantico-referential" (Silverstein 1976) or propositional meaning. Second, as a *style* opposed to other styles, it can be used to highlight or "index" its referential subject matter or the particular context in which it is used. And third, as a complex *signal* composed of numerous discrete signals, it can also relate the subject matter and context to other subject matters and contexts by virtue of the "iconicity" or formal resemblance between its constituent signals (e.g., pronunciation differences, distinct intonational patterns) and other linguistic and nonlinguistic signals employed in the culture.

Moreover, as Urban further observed, speech styles are multifunctional and must be viewed as "an alternative linguistic norm, rather than an individual's deviation from it." Of course, as with all language variation terminology, there are conceptions of style that do not fit our purpose.[44]

Thus, any further study of Emesal must abandon the simple notion of a women's language, in practice or as a mythical source, as I have repeatedly insisted. Looking at it from today's perspective, I would discard much of what I wrote on ES in a short encyclopedia entry (Michalowski 2012, revised version in preparation), and expand on the idea "that its origins, as well as its continuing function, lie not in a regional dialect or a social register of a living language but in a complex nexus of sociolinguistic facts linked to a constellation of cultic practices that involve basic life-changing events, namely, love and death" (Michalowski 2006b: 49), adding that the literary use of ES was heterogeneous and multifunctional albeit orbiting around female gender. Its multifold literary manifestations were located at the complex nexus of emotive exuberance, erotic exaltation, language ideology, power, social roles, and gender – as filtered through different functions of language, in the classic Prague School mode, but also the influence of music and song that characterized this unique form of expression. The locus of ES was in poetics. Indeed, it was song and

---

43 Thorkild Jacobsen (1988a: 131) already used the same term, if in a somewhat different manner, writing "as for the place of Eme-sal in the life of the Ancients, we would suggest that it is a 'style' of Sumerian rather than an actual dialect, a style meant to be ingratiating and so used for requests. As such it was used in laments, and, since wives were often asked to present requests to their husbands, it was often used by women."

44 On this manner of interpreting style, see also Irvine and Gal 2000; Irvine 2001.

emotive language that bridged the divide between the cultic prayers and much of the use of ES in Sumerian poetry, even if the latter differed by focusing on code-switching related to gender.

Most important, from a historical and socio-linguistic perspective Emesal was unique. Some have invoked parallels such as the use of Prakrits in Indian drama (e.g., Falkenstein and von Soden 1953: 29; Whittaker 2002: 638–39), but once one compares the full extent of the heterogeneous variety of social, poetic, and performative contexts of the actual usage of Prakrits, so well described in Andrew Ollet's (2017) fascinating *Language of the Snakes*, the distinctive qualities of these disparate language orders are brought into full relief.

And finally, because discussions of Emesal often speculate that its origins lay in women's ritual funerary wailing, it may be instructive to invoke certain studies of such wailing in other societies. Greg Urban's (1985) essay on language styles among the Brazilian Shokleng people cited above focused on two such distinct styles, women's "ritual wailing" and men's "origin-myth telling," provided a thought-provoking semiotic approach to the way in (p. 328) "which the world . . . and the culture itself, is brought into intellectual and emotional focus." Briggs (1992, 1993), working in a similar but distinct semiotic tradition, studied how women's wailing appropriated men's discourse, at the same time challenging it, but also explored the language ideologies that were part of this process, that is the kind of metapragmatic information that is impossible to reconstruct in a long dead linguistic embedding. Such investigations, as well as more recent cross-cultural examinations of lament traditions by Wilce (2009) and others provide further conceptual frameworks for discovering new aspects of ancient Mesopotamian language ideology, style, and expressions of hierarchy and power, including the use of Emesal.

Thus, there is much about Emesal that remains contested and requires a much broader analysis than can be offered here, but these debates do require us to step back and look for new ways of viewing its formal and sociolinguistic status. While philologists tend to focus on standardized written or everyday language, there is a rich tradition of investigation that encompasses the full array of language use including "secret languages, jargon, cant, argot, children's languages, slang, play-languages, even 'dialect'" (Laycock 1972: 64), not to mention sacred languages, that have been described as special or play languages, sublanguages, and the like. In an important synthetic essay Lasch (1907, summarized by van Gennep 1908), recognized that such language games shared a common typological scheme, suggesting four general sound mechanisms that operated in such language forms (p. 94): (a) paraphrase, (b) loans from other languages, (c) archaisms, and (d) "alteration of words through rearrangement, insertion and reduplication of sounds and syllables." Sapir (1915) and others also drew attention to such “abnormal” forms of speech used for various communicative purposes. Many decades later, linguists returned to the investigation of such matters with special focus on the last category. To avoid some of the value-laden labeling of such linguistic practices, Laycock (1969: 14) introduced the term ludling, derived from Latin *ludus* and *lingua* but also, in a modern extension of the work of Lasch, recognized that they had specific linguistic features in common, regardless of their often-multifunctional sociolinguistic functions. Focusing on sound manipulation, he defined five principal mechanisms at work: expansion, contraction, substitution, rearrangement, and polysystemic. In subsequent years, there has been much formal focus on the phonetic and phonological aspects of ludlings (e.g., Baghemil 1988, 1995; Voux 2011). Even if mainstream linguists have often neglected such matters, the literature on the subject is substantial, written by specialists in several disciplines (e.g., summary in Sherzer and Webster 2014). Emesal must undoubtedly be considered as a unique substitution (but also polysystemic) ludling, albeit one that has come down to us in a formalized written version. The classification of Emesal as a ludling is not simply a pedantic labeling exercise – that would be uninteresting. Rather, it links it to a whole universe of language practices and provides the only workable typological comparative explanation of the phonological nature and the multifunctional use of the style that I am aware of, providing a framework for understanding the various uses of Emesal, as a poetic nonobligatory signal of sexual identity, as a marker of emotive language, its use in song, as well as its generic cultic practice.

As Aikhenvald and Storch (2019: 4) wrote, introducing a collection of essays of secret languages, “alongside the everyday language style, there can be special speech styles employed in different genres (e.g., in poetry, songs, abusive language, mocking, and so on), special ways of speaking used for ritual communication (e.g., in initiation, mourning, and within important activities such as hunting or fishing), politeness strategies and respectful registers (e.g., indirect communication with elders), as in-group modes of speech (e.g., youth languages), and play languages.” Such linguistic exuberance undoubtedly filled the cities and countryside of Mesopotamia, that were multilingual to various degrees and were in constant contact with surrounding areas. Their inhabitants spoke not only different languages and dialects, but also utilized different styles and registers based on various hierarchies, be they social or gendered, including professional jargons, hypothetical anti-languages such as thieves or prostitute jargons, trade languages to communicate across linguistic barriers, and possibly even creoles and mixed languages, not excluding analogies to the later *lingua franca* used in the pre-modern Mediterranean area by speakers of separate languages, and a variety of ludlings as well.[45] The invention and development of writing created a powerful new communication and control tool and preserved a unique discursive universe for millennia, but the dominance of a standardized written version of the Sumerian also acted in a hegemonic manner to silence much of the rich heteroglossic abundance of the civilization, with the sole exception of Emesal, which, in turn, was undoubtedly standardized as well, so that what we read is bit a fragment of a much richer complex linguistic style that in its heyday lived a vigorous everchanging life. I hope to pursue all this further in a larger study, unconstrainted by the limits of the genre of the book chapter essay.

Appendix: The Label Emesal

The word Emesal occurs rarely in cuneiform sources, mostly as a descriptive term describing Sumerian entries in lexical lists. To my knowledge, it is not attested in a single Old Babylonian narrative context other than in the one mentioned above. It occurs in an incompletely preserved line in the *Examination Text D* that Sjöberg (1972: 126–27, l. 14) translated as "to have superior knowledge in Sumerian, to learn . . . .., [to learn] Emesal" in his edition of the text.[46] Like the other three "examination texts," this composition has come down to us exclusively in the form of first millennium bilingual source; Andrew George (2009: 111) seems to imply that they were originally composed in Old Babylonian times, but for now this can only remain hypothetical.

Early on in the history of Assyriology, **eme sal** was translated literally as "woman's tongue" or "language," but that would have been **eme munusa** (**eme munus.ak**) in Sumerian (for a critique of such characterizations, see Whittaker 2002). The reading of the second sign is assured by writings such as **eme sal-la** in the subscript of the *Emesal Vocabulary*. The word appears for the first time in the Old Babylonian acrographic lexical list Sag cited above. Often

45 Many studies of creoles and creolization focus on much later European-based versions, but there are and have been Arabic-based creoles and mixed languages (e.g., Owens 2001), the earliest of which can be traced back to the 11th c. CE (Thomason and Elgibali 1986, with an interesting discussion of creoles outside of the European trade expansion). On *lingua franca*, see Mallette 2014 and now Nolan 2020. On mixed languages, see conveniently Mazzoli and Sippola 2021. On possible Late Bronze and Early Iron Age creoles and trade languages in the Levant, see, e.g., Davis, Maeir; Hitchcock 2015: 157.

46 **niĝ$_2$-zu diri-ga eme gir$_{15}$ zu-zu-de$_3$ eme-[x] zu eme sal [zu-zu-de$_3$$^?$]** = *iḫ-zu šu-tu-ru šu-me-ru a-ḫa-zu* KAB-*lit la-m*[*a-du* x x x x]. The reconstruction of the line and the translation are somewhat uncertain.

mentioned are two Akkadian words that have been considered as copies from Sumerian referencing Emesal.

The *Chicago Assyrian Dictionary* in its E volume (p. 148) includes the entry *emesallu*, "fine taste(ing)," that is supposedly associated with Emesal (e.g., Edzard 2003: 171 thin = high-pitched, etc.); von Soden (1981: 214) even translated it as "Frauensalz" (Jacobsen 1988a: 131, who considered it to mean "salt narrowing the tongue," reflecting articulatory matters), but properly speaking, there was no such word with these meanings in Akkadian. It is almost exclusively found in magical and medical texts as qualifying salt and was a later version of *mēsallu* (CAD M/2 28), as evidenced by the only known Old Babylonian example written as *me-e-sal-la* in a magical text of unknown provenience cited in the entry and now edited by Wasserman (2020: 449–50, commentary). A medical commentary from fourth century BCE Uruk demonstrates that even quite late in the cuneiform tradition the aquatic connotations of this ingredient were recognized, perhaps as a folk etymology, but did not associate it with any form of linguistic expression: "*emesallu* salt refers to salt from midriver" (**mun** *eme-sal-lim*: **mun** *ša*$_2$ *lib*$_3$*-bi nāri*(id$_2$), BRM 4: 32 l. 13, Geller 2010: 169, 172).

The second such word is the adverb *ummisalla*, which occurs only once in the great 1st millennium *Šamaš Hymn* l. 134 (Lambert 1960: 134; CAD U, 120); and although its exact meaning is unknown, the context guarantees that it had nothing to do with any kind of language phenomenon, including any reference to Emesal, as observed by Lambert (1960: 322).

The adjective **sal(a)**, or more properly **šal(a)**, meant "thin, narrow, sleek, thinly spread out" but the semantics of "fine" in some European languages, has been transferred uncritically to Sumerian. In English, a well-honed thin blade is "fine," and a fine song is a nice one, and a thin voice is a high pitched one, but in Sumerian **sal** only corresponded in meaning to the former two, not the latter. Therefore, one cannot translate **eme sal** as "noble/fine language;" some would translate "thin = high pitched voice," but I am highly skeptical because much of this is transferred from dubious hypotheses about the "nonmasculine" status of ES singers, speculatively attributing to them high pitched singing voices, a matter discussed above. To put it bluntly, there is no documented reason to posit that ES prayers were sung in high pitch.[47]

47 For a very different opinion see now Ludwig (2021), who argues in favor of associations of ES with thin or croaky voice. This came to my attention too late to be given a fair reading in the present discussion.

The only example known to me of the adjective qualifying **eme** is in *Debate between Bird and Fish* 84 (Mittermayer 2019: 72–73), where the context leaves no doubt that physical characteristics, not language characteristics are in play:

> a_2[?]-ur_2 gu_2-$guru_5$ ĝiri_3 su-ul-su-ul ka ha-la eme šal-šal
> "Clipped wings, very crippled feet, split[?] mouth, very thin tongue"

To conclude, as far as I can determine, no secure etymology for the term **eme sal** can be offered at the present time.

Bibliography

Agha, Asif. 2004. Registers of Language. Pp. 23–45 in *A Companion to Linguistic Anthropology*, ed. Alessandro Duranti. Malden: Blackwell Publishing.

Aikhenvald, Alexandra Y. 2000. *Classifiers: A Typology of Noun Categorization Devices*. Oxford: Oxford University Press.

Aikhenvald, Alexandra Y. 2008. Gender and Noun Classes. Pp. 1031–45 in *Morphologie: Ein internationales Handbuch zur Flexion und Wortbildung*, ed. Geert E. Booij, Christian Lehmann, Joachim Mugdan, and Stavros Skopeteas. Berlin/New York: De Gruyter Mouton.

Aikhenvald, Alexandra Y., and Anne Storch. 2019. Creativity in Language: Secret Codes, Special Styles and Linguistic Taboo. *International Journal of Language and Culture* 6: 1–9.

Alster, Bendt. 1971. On the Sumerian Lullaby. *RA* 65: 170–71.

Alster, Bendt. 1982. Emesal in Early Dynastic Sumerian? What is the UD.GAL.NUN-Orthography? *ASJ* 4: 1–6.

Alster, Bendt. 1993. Marriage and Love in the Sumerian Love Songs. Pp. 15–27 in *The Tablet and the Scroll: Near Eastern Studies in Honor of William W. Hallo*, ed. Mark E. Cohen, Daniel C. Snell, and David B. Weisberg. Bethesda, MD: CDL Press.

Arbel, Daphna V. 1999–2005. Junctions of Traditions in Edessa: Possible Interaction between Mesopotamian Mythological and Jewish Mystical Traditions in the First Centuries CE. *ARAM* 12: 335–56.

Arnaud, Daniel. 1982. Les Textes cunéiformes suméro-accadiens des campagnes 1979–1980 à Ras Shamra-Ougarit. *Syria* 59: 199–222.

Arnaud, Daniel. 1985. *Recherches au pays d'Aštata, EMAR VI/2: Textes sumeriens et accadiens. Planches. 2.* Synthèse 18. Paris: Éditions Recherche sur les Civilisations.

Arnaud, Daniel. 1987. *Recherches au pays d'Aštata, EMAR VI/4. Textes de La bibliotheque: transcriptions et traductions*. Synthèse 28. Paris: Éditions Recherche sur les Civilisations.

Attinger, Pascal. 1984. Enki et Ninḫursaĝa. *ZA* 74: 1–52.

Attinger, Pascal. 1993. *Eléments de linguistique sumérienne. La construction de du_{11}/e/di "dire."* OBO, Sonderband. Fribourg/Göttingen: Editions Universitaires/Vandenhoeck & Ruprecht.

Attinger, Pascal. 2018. Un gala coquet. *NABU* 2018: 113–14, no. 68.

Attinger, Pascal. 2019a. Enlil et Ninlil (1.2.1). https://zenodo.org/record/2667749.

Attinger, Pascal. 2019b. La descente d'Innana dans le monde infernal (1.4.1). https://zenodo.org/record/2599619.
Attinger, Pascal. 2019c. La lamentation sur Sumer et Ur (2.2.3). https://zenodo.org/record/2599623.
Attinger, Pascal. 2021. *Glossaire sumérien–français, principalement des textes littéraires paléobabyloniens*. Wiesbaden: Harrassowitz.
Attinger, Pascal. 2022. Sulgi X. *AoF* 49: 197–242.
Attinger, Pascal, and Manfred Krebernik. 2005. L'Hymne à Ḫendursaĝa (Ḫendursaĝa A). Pp. 21–104 in *Von Sumer bis Homer. Festschrift für Manfred Schretter zum 60. Geburtstag am 25. Februar 2004*, ed. Robert Rollinger. AOAT 325. Münster: Ugarit-Verlag.
Bachvarova, Mary R. 1997. The Literary Use of Dialects: Ancient Greek, Indic and Sumerian. Pp. 7–22 in *CLS 33: Papers from The Panels on Linguistic Ideologies in Contact*, Universal Grammar, *Parameters and Typology, the Perception of Speech and other Acoustic* Signals, *April 17–19*, 1997, ed. Kora Singer, Randal Eggert, and Gregory Anderson. Chicago: Chicago Linguistic Society.
Bachvarova, Mary R. 2008. Sumerian *Gala* Priests and Eastern Mediterranean Returning Gods: Tragic Lamentation in Cross-Cultural Perspective. Pp. 18–52 in *Lament: Studies in Ancient* Mediterranean *and* Beyond, ed. Ann Suter. Oxford: Oxford University Press.
Bagemihl, Bruce. 1988. Alternate Phonologies and Morphologies. Ph.D. Dissertation. University of British Columbia.
Bagemihl, Bruce. 1995. Language Games and Related Areas. Pp. 697–712 in *The Handbook of Phonological Theory*, 1st ed., ed. John Goldsmith. Cambridge, MA: Blackwell.
Bakker, Peter. 2019. Intentional Language Change and the Connection between Mixed Languages and Genderlects. *Language Dynamics and Change* 9: 135–61.
Balke, Thomas E. 2017. *Das altsumerische Onomastikon. Namengebung und Prosopographie nach den Quellen aus Lagas*. Dubsar 1. Münster: Zaphon.
Bartash, Vitali. 2018. Sumerian "Child." *JCS* 70: 3–25.
Bauer, Josef. 1998. Der vorsargonische Abschnitt der mesopotamischen Geschichte. Pp. 431–585 in Josef Bauer, Robert K. Englund, and Manfred Krebernik, *Mesopotamien. Späturuk-Zeit und Frühdynastische Zeit*, ed. Pascal Attinger and Markus Wäfler. OBO 160/1. Fribourg/Göttingen: Editions Universitaires/Vandenhoeck & Ruprecht.
Black, Jeremy A. 1991. Eme-sal Cult Songs and Prayers. Pp. 23–36 in *Velles Paraules: Ancient Near Eastern Studies in Honor of Miguel Civil on the Occasion of his Sixty-Fifth Birthday*, ed. Piotr Michalowski, Piotr Steinkeller, Elisabeth C. Stone, and Richard L. Zettler. *AuOr* 9. Sabadell: AUSA.
Bobrova, Larissa V., and Alexander Y. Militariev. 1989. Towards the Reconstruction of Sumerian Phonology. Pp. 96–105 in *Lingvističeskaya rekonstrukciya i drevneĭšaya istoriya Vostoka: Materialy k diskussiyam na Meždunarodnoĭ konferencii (Moskva, 29 maja 2 ijunja 1989 g.), Cast '1.* Moscow: Nauka.
Bodine, Ann. 1975. Sex Differentiation in Language. Pp. 130–51 in *Language and Sex: Difference and Dominance*, ed. Barrie Thorne and Nancy Henley. Rowley, MA: Newbury House Publishers.
Borger, Rykle. 1989/90. Review of Oberhuber 1990. *AfO* 36/37: 126–31.
Bradley, John. 1988. Yanyuwa: 'Men speak one way, women speak another.' *Aboriginal Linguistics* 1: 126–34.

Briggs, Charles L. 1992. 'Since I am a Woman, I will Chastise my Relatives': Gender, Reported Speech, and the (Re)production of Social Relations in Warao Ritual Wailing. *American Ethnologist* 19: 337–61.

Briggs, Charles L. 1993. Personal Sentiments and Polyphonic Voices in Warao Women's Ritual Wailing: Music and Poetics in a Critical and Collective Discourse. *American Anthropologist* 95: 929–57.

Briggs, Charles L. 1998. "You're a Liar – You're Just Like a Woman!" Constructing Dominant Ideologies of Language in Warao Men's Gossip. Pp. 308–44 *in Language Ideologies: Practice and Theory*, ed. Bambi B. Schieffelin, Kathryn A. Woolard, and Paul V. Kroskrity. Oxford: Oxford University Press.

Brisch, Nicole Maria. 2007. *Tradition and the Poetics of Innovation: Sumerian Court Literature of the Larsa Dynasty (c. 2003-1763 BCE)*. AOAT 339. Münster: Ugarit-Verlag.

Brisch, Nicole Maria. 2016. Ninlil (Mulliltu, Mullissu, Mylitta) (goddess). *Ancient Mesopotamian Gods and Goddesses*, Oracc and the UK Higher Education Academy. [http://oracc.museum.upenn.edu/amgg/listofdeities/getinanna/]; accessed Jan. 9, 2022.

Brisch, Nicole Maria. 2021. The Marginalization of Priestesses in Ancient Mesopotamia. Pp. 585–94 in *Pearls, Politics and Pistachios: Essays in Anthropology and Memories on the Occasion of Susan Pollock's 65th Birthday*, ed. Aydin Abar et al. Berlin: ex oriente.

Campbell, Lyle. 2006. Areal Linguistics: A Closer Scrutiny. Pp. 1–31 in *Linguistic Areas: Convergence in Historical and Typological Perspective*, ed. by Yaron Matras, April McMahon, and Nigel Vincent. New York: Palgrave Macmillan.

Campbell, Lyle. 2017. Why is it so Hard to Define a Linguistic Area? Pp. 19–39 in *The Cambridge Handbook of Areal Linguistics*, ed. Raymond Hickey. Cambridge: Cambridge University Press.

Cavigneaux, Antoine. 2020. Les traditions littéraires suméro-akkadiennes à Suse. Fragments littéraires susiens (suite). *RA* 114: 63–102.

Ceccarelli, Manuel. 2019. Die ‚Alte Weise' und die ‚weise Frau' im alten Mesopotamien. *Fabula* 60: 100–31.

Civil, Miguel. 1983. Enlil and Ninlil: The Marriage of Sud. *JAOS* 103: 43–66.

Civil, Miguel. 2006. The Song of the Millstone. Pp. 121–38 in *Šapal tibnim mû illakū: Studies Presented to Joaquín Sanmartín on the Occasion of His 65th Birthday*, ed. Gregorio Del Olmo Lete, Lluís Feliu, and Adelina Millet Albà. AuOr Supplementa 22. Sabadell: AUSA.

Civil, Miguel, edited by Lluís Feliu. 2020. *Esbós de gramàtica sumèria: An Outline of Sumerian Grammar*. Barcino monografia orientalia 14. Barcelona: Edicions de la Universitat de Barcelona.

Civil, Miguel, Oliver R. Gurney, and Douglas Kennedy. 1986. *The Sag Tablet: Lexical Text in the Ashmolean Museum. Middle Babylonian Grammatical Texts. Miscellaneous Texts*. MSL SS 1. Rome: Pontificium Institutum Biblicum.

Cooper, Jerrold S. 2006. Genre, Gender, and the Sumerian Lamentation. *JCS* 58: 39–47.

Cooper, Jerrold S. 2012. Sumer, Sumerisch (Sumer, Sumerian). *RlA* 13: 290–97.

Corbett, Greville G. 2014. Gender Typology. Pp. 87–130 in *The Expression of Gender*, ed. Greville G. Corbett. The Expression of Cognitive Categories 6. De Gruyter Mouton.

Çığ, Muazzez, and Samuel Noah Kramer. 1976. The Ideal Mother: A Sumerian Portrait. *Belleten* 40: 413–21.

Dalley, Stephanie. 1995. Bel at Palmyra and Elsewhere in the Parthian Period. *ARAM* 7: 137–51.

Davis, Brent, Aren M. Maeir, and Louise A. Hitchcock. 2015. Disentangling Entangled Objects: Iron Age Inscriptions from Philistia as a Reflection of Cultural Processes. *IEJ* 65: 140–66.
Delnero, Paul. 2015. Texts and Performance: The Materiality and Function of the Sumerian Liturgical Corpus. Pp. 87–118 in *Texts and Contexts: The Circulation of Cuneiform Texts in Social Space*, ed. Paul Delnero and Jacob Lauinger. SANER 9. Berlin/Boston: de Gruyter.
Delnero, Paul. 2017. The Silences of the Scribes, Pt. II: An Unfinished Enlil Lament from Nippur. Pp. 80–102 in *The First Ninety Years. A Sumerian Celebration of Miguel Civil*, ed. Lluís Feliu, Fumi Karahashi, and Gonzalo Rubio. SANER 12. Boston/Berlin: De Gruyter.
Diakonoff, Igor Mikhailovich. 1967. Shumerskiĭ yazyk [The Sumerian Language]. Pp. 35–84 in I. M. Diakonoff, *Yazyki drevneĭ Peredneĭ Azii* [The Languages of the Ancient Near East]. Moscow: Nauka.
Diakonoff, Igor Mikhailovich. 1997. External Connections of the Sumerian Language. *Mother Tongue* 3: 54–62.
Dietrich, Manfred. 1998. *bulut̩ bēlī* "Lebe, mein Köning!" Ein Krönungshymnus aus Emar und Ugarit und sein Verhältnis zu mesopotamischen und westlichen Inthronisationsliedern. *UF* 30: 155–200.
van Dijk, J. 1983. *LUGAL UD ME-LÁM-bi NIR-ĜÁL. Le récit épique et didactique des Travaux de Ninurta, du Déluge et de la Nouvelle Création. Texte, traduction et introduction*, 2 vols. Leiden: Brill.
Dirven, Lucinda. 2014. Religious Continuity and Change in Parthian Mesopotamia: A Note on the Survival of Babylonian Traditions. *JANEH* 1: 201–29.
Dixon, R. M. W. 1968. Noun Classes. *Lingua* 21: 104–25.
Dunn, Michael. 2000. Chukchi Women's Language: A Historical-Comparative Perspective. *Anthropological Linguistics* 42: 305–28.
Dunn, Michael. 2014. Gender Determined Dialect Variation. Pp. 39–67 in *The Expression of Gender*, ed. Greville G. Corbett. The Expression of Cognitive Categories 6. De Gruyter Mouton.
Durkheim, Émile. 1901. Rejoinder to Frazer 1900. *Année sociologique* 4: 364–65.
Edzard, Dietz Otto. 1962. Sumerische Komposita mit dem 'Nominalpräfix' nu. *ZA* 55: 91–112.
Edzard, Dietz Otto. 1993. Review of Oberhuber 1990. *ZA* 83: 301–302.
Edzard, Dietz Otto. 2003. *Sumerian Grammar*. HbO 1/71. Leiden/Boston: Brill.
van Engelenhoven, Aone. 2010. Lirasniara, the Sung Language of Southwest Maluku (East-Indonesia). *Wacana, Journal of the Humanities of Indonesia* 12: 143–61.
Falkenstein, Adam. 1953. Zur Chronologie der sumerischen Literatur. Die nachaltbabylonische Stufe. *MDOG* 85: 1–13.
Falkenstein, Adam. 1959. *Das Sumerische*. HbO I, 2/1-2, 1. Leiden: Brill.
Falkenstein, Adam, and Wolfram von Soden. 1953. *Sumerische und akkadische Hymnen und Gebete*. Zürich: Artemis-Verlag.
Farber-Flügge, Gertrude. 1973. *Der Mythos "Inanna und Enki" unter besonderer Berücksichtigung der Liste der me*. StPo 10. Rome: Biblical Institute Press.
Fiekl, Garrett. 2019. Scrambling Syllables in Sung Poetry of the Maldives. *Anthropological Linguistics* 61: 364–88.
Foxvog, Daniel A. 2014. *Introduction to Sumerian Grammar*. Self-published; available from Amazon.com.
Földi, Zsombor J. 2019. Bullussa-rabi, Author of the Gula Hymn. *KASKAL* 16: 81–83.
Frazer, James G. 1900. Suggestion as to the Origin of Gender in Language. *Fortnightly Review* 67: 79–90.

Frazer, James G. 1901. Men's Language and Women's Language. *Man* 1: 154–55.
Gabbay, Uri. 2011a. Lamentful Proverbs or Proverbial Laments? Intertextual Connections Between Sumerian Proverbs and Emesal Laments. *JCS* 63: 51–64.
Gabbay, Uri. 2011b. Laments in Garšana. Pp. 67–74 in *Garšana Studies*, ed. David I. Owen. CUSAS 6. Bethesda: CDL Press.
Gabbay, Uri. 2014a. The *kalû* Priest and *kalûtu* Literature in Assyria. *Orient* 49: 115–44.
Gabbay, Uri. 2014b. *Pacifying the Hearts of the Gods: Sumerian Emesal Prayers of the First Millennium BC*. HES 1. Wiesbaden: Harrassowitz.
Gabbay, Uri, and Sam Mirelman. 2011. Two Summary Tablets of Balaĝ Compositions with Performative Indications from Late-Babylonian Ur. *ZA* 101: 274–93.
Gadotti, Alhena. 2014a. The Feminine in Myths and Epics. Pp. 28–58 in *Women in the Ancient Near East: A Sourcebook*, ed. Mark Chavalas. London/New York: Routledge.
Gadotti, Alhena. 2014b. *Gilgamesh, Enkidu, and the Netherworld and the Sumerian Gilgamesh Cycle*. UAVA 10. Boston/Berlin: de Gruyter.
Galter, Hannes D. 2021. Veil and Headscarf: Five Aspects of a Cultural Phenomenon. Pp. 21–72 in *Headscarf and Veiling Glimpses from Sumer to Islam*, ed. Roswitha Del Fabbro, Frederick Mario Fales, and Hannes D. Galter. Antichristica 30. Studi Orientali 12. Venice: Edizioni Ca'Foscari.
Garcia-Ventura, Agnès. 2017. Emesal Studies Today: A Preliminary Assessment. Pp. 145–58 in *The First Ninety Years. A Sumerian Celebration of Miguel Civil*, ed. Luís Feliu, Fumi Karahashi, and Gonzalo Rubio. SANER 12. Boston/Berlin: De Gruyter.
Garcia-Ventura, Agnès, and Saana Svärd. 2018. Theoretical Approaches, Gender, and the Ancient Near East: An Introduction. Pp.1–13 in *Studying Gender in the Ancient Near East*, ed. Saana Svärd and Agnès Garcia-Ventura. University Park: Eisenbrauns.
Garcia-Vantura, Agnès, and Giselle Zisa. 2017. Gender and Women in Ancient Near Eastern Studies: Bibliography 2002–2016. *Akkadica* 138: 37–67.
Gelb, I. J. 1975. Homo Ludens in Early Mesopotamia. *Studia Orientalia* 46: 43–76.
Geller, Markham J. 2002. The Free Library Inanna Prism Reconsidered. Pp. 87–100 in *Riches Hidden in Secret Places: Ancient Near Eastern Studies in Memory of Thorkild Jacobsen*, ed. Tzvi Abusch. Winona Lake: Eisenbrauns.
Geller, Markham J. 2010. *Ancient Babylonian Medicine: Theory and Practice*. Malden: Wiley-Blackwell.
van Gennep, Arnold. 1908. Essai d'une théorie des langues spéciales. *Revue des études ethnographiques et sociologiques* 6/7: 327–37.
George, Andrew R. 2009. *Babylonian Literary Texts in the Schøyen Collection*. CUSAS 10. Bethesda: CDL Press.
Green, Margaret Whitney. 1975. Eridu in Sumerian Literature. Ph.D. Dissertation. University of Chicago.
Green, Margaret Whitney. 1978. The Eridu Lament. *JCS* 30: 127–67.
Green, Margaret Whitney. 1984. The Uruk Lament. *JAOS* 104: 253–79.
Halliday, Michael A. K. 1976. Anti-Languages. *American Anthropologist* 78: 570–84.
Hallo, William W. 1963. On the Antiquity of Sumerian Literature. *JCS* 83: 167–76.
Hallo, William W. 1976. Towards a History of Sumerian Literature. Pp. 181–203 in *Sumerological Studies in Honor of Thorkild Jacobsen on his Seventieth* Birthday, *June 7, 1974*, ed. Stephen J. Lieberman. AS 20. Chicago: The Oriental Institute of the University of Chicago.
Hasselbach, Rebecca. 2014a. Agreement and the Development of Gender in Semitic (Part 1). *ZDMG* 164: 33–64.

Hasselbach, Rebecca. 2014b. Agreement and the Development of Gender in Semitic (Part 2). *ZDMG* 164: 319–44.
Hickey, Raymond (ed.). 2017. *The Cambridge Handbook of Areal Linguistics*. Cambridge: Cambridge University Press.
Hidalgo Tenorio, Encarnación. 2016. Genderlect. Pp. 1193–196 in *The Wiley-Blackwell Encyclopedia of Gender and Sexuality Studies*, ed. Nancy A. Naples. Malden: Wiley-Blackwell.
Hsu, Shih-Wei, and Jaume Llop Raduà (eds.). 2020. *The Expression of Emotions in Ancient Egypt and Mesopotamia*. CHANE 116. Leiden: Brill.
Huber Vulliet, Fabienne. 2019. *Le personnel cultuel à l'époque néo-sumérienne (ca. 2160 – 2003 av. J.-C.)*. BPOA 14. Madrid: Consejo Superior de Investigaciones Científica.
Irvine, Judith. 2001. "Style" as Distinctiveness: The Culture and Ideology of Linguistic Differentiation. Pp. 21–43 *Stylistic Variation in Language*, ed. Penelope Eckert and John R. Rickford. Cambridge: Cambridge University Press.
Irvine, Judith, and Susan Gal. 2000. Language Ideology and Linguistic Differentiation. Pp. 35–84 in *Regimes of Language: Ideologies, Polities, and Identities*, ed. Paul Kroskrity. Santa Fe: School of American Research Press.
Jacobsen, Thorkild. 1988a. Sumerian Grammar Today. *JAOS* 108: 123–33.
Jacobsen, Thorkild. 1988b. The Sumerian Verbal Core. *ZA* 78: 161–220.
Jacobsen, Thorkild, and Samuel N. Kramer. 1953. The Myth of Inanna and Bilulu. *JNES* 12: 160–88.
Jagersma, Bram. 2010. A Descriptive Grammar of Sumerian. Ph.D. Dissertation. Universiteit Leiden.
Keetman, Jan. 2021. Review of Gabbay 2014b. *AfO* 54: 460–62.
Kittilä, Seppo, Katja Västi, and Jussi Ylikoski. 2011. Introduction to Case, Animacy and Semantic Roles. Pp. 1–26 in *Case, Animacy and Semantic Roles*, ed. Seppo Kittilä, Katja Västi, and Jussi Ylikoski. Typological Studies in Language 99. Amsterdam: John Benjamins.
Klein, Jacob. 1981. *Three Šulgi Hymns: Sumerian Royal Hymns Glorifying King Šulgi of Ur*. Ramat-Gan: Bar Ilan University Press.
Kleinerman, Alexandra. 2011. *Education in Early 2nd Millennium BC Babylonia: The Sumerian Epistolary Miscellany*. CM 42. Leiden/Boston: Brill.
Konstantopoulos, Gina. 2020. My Men Have Become Women, and My Women Men: Gender, Identity, and Cursing in Mesopotamia. *WdO* 50: 358–75.
Konstantopoulos, Gina. 2021. The Many Lives of Enheduana: Identity, Authorship, and the "World's First Poet." Pp. 57–76 in *Presentation and Perception of Powerful Women in the Ancient World: Perception and (Self)Presentation. Proceedings of the 8th Melammu Workshop, Kassel, 30 January – 1 February 2019*, ed. Sebastian Fink and Kerstin Droß-Krüpe. Melammu Workshops and Monographs 4. Münster: Zaphon.
Kramer, Samuel Noah. 1960. *Two Elegies on a Pushkin Museum Tablet: A New Sumerian Literary Genre*. Moscow: Oriental Literature Publishing House.
Kramer, Samuel Noah. 1971. u$_5$-a a-u$_5$-a: A Sumerian Lullaby (with Appendix by Thorkild Jacobsen). Pp. 191–205 in *Studi in onore di Edoardo Volterra*, vol 6, ed. Luigi Aru et al. Milan: Casa Editrice Dott. A. Giuffrè.
Kraus, Flora. 1924. Die Frauensprache bei den primitiven Völkern. *Imago* 10: 296–313.
Krecher, Joachim. 1967a. Die sumerischen Texte in "syllabischer" Orthographie. *ZA* 58: 16–65.

Krecher, Joachim. 1967b. Zum Emesal-Dialekt des Sumerischen. Pp. 87–110 in *Heidelberger Studien zum Alten Orient. Adam Falkenstein zum 17. September 1966*, ed. Dietz O. Edzard. Wiesbaden: Otto Harrasowitz.

Krispijn, Theo J. H. 2000. The Change of Official Sumerian in the City State of Lagash. *ASJ* 22: 153–75.

Lambert, Wilfred G. 1960. *Babylonian Wisdom Literature*. Oxford: Oxford University Press.

Lasch, Richard. 1907. Über Sondersprachen und ihre Entstehung. *Mitteilungen der Anthropologischen Gesellschaft in Wien* 37 (3. Folge, 7. Bd.): 89–101, 140–162.

Laycock, Don. 1969. Sublanguages in Buin: Play, Poetry and Preservation. *Pacific Linguistics* 22: 1–23.

Laycock, Don. 1972. Towards a Typology of Ludlings, or Play-Languages. *Linguistic Communications: Working Papers of the Linguistic Society of Australia* 6: 61–113.

Lewandowski, Marcin. 2010. Sociolects and Registers – a Contrastive Analysis of Two Kinds of Linguistic Variation. *Investigationes Linguisticae* 20: 60–79.

Lion, Brigitte. 2008. Les femmes et l'écrit en Mésopotamie: auteurs, commanditaires d'inscriptions et scribes. Pp. 53–68 in *Las culturas del Próximo Oriente Antiguo y su expansión mediterránea: textos de los Cursos de Postgraduados del CSIC en el Instituto de Estudios Islámicos y del Oriente Próximo 2003 – 2006*, ed. Josué Javier Justel Vincente, Juan Pablo Vita, and José Angel Zamora López. Saragossa: Instituto de Estudios Islámicos y del Oriente Próximo.

Lion, Brigitte. 2009a. Sexe et genre (2). Des prêtresses fils de rois. Pp. 165–82 in *Femmes, cultures et sociétés dans les civilisations méditerranéennes et proche-orientales de l'Antiquité*, ed. Françoise Briquel-Chatonnet, et al. Topoi Orient-Occident, Supplément 10. Lyon: Maison de l'Orient méditerranéen / Paris: De Boccard.

Lion, Brigitte. 2009b. Les Femmes scribes de Sippar. Pp. 289–303 in *Femmes, cultures et sociétés dans les civilisations méditerranéennes et proche-orientales de l'Antiquité*, ed. Françoise Briquel-Chatonnet, et al. Topoi Orient-Occident, Supplément 10. Lyon: Maison de l'Orient méditerranéen / Paris: De Boccard.

Löhnert, Anne. 2009. *"Wie die Sonne tritt heraus!": eine Klage zum Auszug Enlils mit einer Untersuchung zu Komposition und Tradition sumerischer Klagelieder in altbabylonischer Zeit*. AOAT 365. Ugarit-Verlag.

Löhnert, Anne. 2011. Manipulating the Gods. Lamenting in Context. Pp. 402–17 in *The Oxford Handbook of Cuneiform Culture*, ed. Karen Radner and Eleanor Robson. Oxford: Oxford University Press.

Löhnert, Anne. 2014. Was reden die da? Sumerisch und Emesal zwischen Alltag und Sakralität. *WdO* 44: 190–212.

Ludwig, Marie-Christine. 2021. Ein neues zweisprachiges altbabylonisches Vokabular aus Ur. *AoF* 48: 250–267.

Maiden, Martin. 1992. Irregularity as a Determinant of Morphological Change. *Journal of Linguistics* 28: 285–312.

Mallette, Karla. 2014. Lingua Franca. Pp. 330–44 in *A Companion to Mediterranean History*, ed. Peregrine Horden and Sharon Kinoshita. Malden/Oxford: Wiley Blackwell.

Marchesi, Gianni. 2004. Who Was Buried in the Royal Tombs of Ur? The Epigraphic and Textual Data. *OrNS* 73: 153–97.

Maslov, Boris. 2013. The Dialect Basis of Choral Lyric and the History of Poetic Languages in Archaic Greece. *Symbolae Osloenses: Norwegian Journal of Greek and Latin Studies* 87: 1–29.

Matini, Giovanna. 2021. Gli inni in Emesal e il loro impiego nel culto della Mesopotamia antica. Pp. 39–59 in *Miti, culti, saperi: Per un'antropologia religiosa della Mesopotamia antica*, ed. Claus Ambos and Gioele Zisa. Nanaya: studi i materiali di antropologia e storia delli religioni 1. Palermo: Museo Pasqualino.

Matuszak, Jana. 2016. "She is not fit for womanhood": The Ideal Housewife According to Sumerian Literary Texts. Pp. 228–54 in *The Role of Women in Work and Society in the Ancient Near East*, ed. Brigitte Lion and Cécile Michel. SANER 13. Berlin: De Gruyter.

Matuszak, Jana. 2018. Assessing Misogyny in Sumerian Disputations and Diatribes. Pp. 259–72 in *Gender and Methodology in the Ancient Near East: Approaches from Assyriology and Beyond*, ed. Stephanie Lynn Budin, Megan Cifarelli, Agnès Garcia-Ventura, and Adelina Millet Albà. Barcino Monographica Orientalia 10. Barcelona: Edicions Universitat de Barcelona.

Matuszak, Jana. 2021. *"Und du, du bist eine Frau?!" Editio princeps und Analyse des sumerischen Streitgesprächs 'Zwei Frauen B.'* UAVA 16. Wiesbaden: Harrassowitz.

Matuszak, Jana. 2022. A Complete Reconstruction, New Edition and Interpretation of the Sumerian Morality Tale 'The Old Man and the Young Girl.' *ZA* 112: 1–35.

Mazzoli, Maria, and Eeva Sippola. 2021. Mixed Languages from Core to Fringe. Pp. 1–26 in *New Perspectives on Mixed Languages: From Core to Fringe*, ed. Maria Mazzoli and Eeva Sippola. Language Contact and Bilingualism 18. Boston/Berlin: De Gruyter Mouton.

Michalowski, Piotr. 1989. *The Lamentation over the Destruction of Sumer and Ur*. MC 1. Winona Lake: Eisenbrauns.

Michalowski, Piotr. 1995. Review of *Sumerian Literary Texts* by B. Alster and M. J. Geller. *JNES* 54: 49–51.

Michalowski, Piotr. 2006a. The Strange History of Tumal. Pp. 145–65 in *Approaches to Sumerian Literature: Studies in Honour of Stip (H.L.J. Vanstiphout)*, ed. Piotr Michalowski and Niek Veldhuis. CM 35. Leiden/Boston: Brill.

Michalowski, Piotr. 2006b. Love or Death? Observations on the Role of the Gala in Ur III Ceremonial Life. *JCS* 58: 49–61.

Michalowski, Piotr. 2008. Sumerian. Pp. 6–46 in *The Ancient Languages of Mesopotamia, Egypt and Aksum*, ed. Roger D. Woodward. Cambridge: Cambridge University Press.

Michalowski, Piotr. 2011. *The Correspondence of the Kings of Ur: An Epistolary History of an Ancient Mesopotamian Kingdom*. MC 15. Winona Lake: Eisenbrauns.

Michalowski, Piotr. 2012. Emesal (Sumerian Dialect). Pp. 2387–2388 in *The Encyclopedia of Ancient History*, 1st ed. Roger S. Bagnall et. al. Malden: Blackwell Publishing Ltd.

Michalowski, Piotr. 2017. Ancient Near Eastern and European Isolates. Pp. 19–58 in *Language Isolates*, ed. Lyle Campbell. London/New York: Routledge.

Michalowski, Piotr. 2019. 時に古の女神, 時に古の男性が用いたシュメール語のエメサル [The Sometime Voice of Goddesses and Men: The Emesal Version of the Ancient Sumerian Language]. *Chuo University Kiyō (History)* 64: 23–47 (in Japanese, translated by Fumi Karahashi).

Michel, Cécile. 2009. Les femmes et l'écrit dans les archives paléo-assyriennes. Pp. 253–72 in *Femmes, cultures et sociétés dans les civilisations méditerranéennes et proche-orientales de l'Antiquité*, ed. Françoise Briquel-Chatonnet, et al. Topoi Orient-Occident, Supplément 10. Lyon: Maison de l'Orient méditerranéen / Paris: De Boccard.

Michel, Cécile. 2009. In press. Gender Identity and the History of Ancient Mesopotamia: The Case of the Old Assyrian Sources. In *Identity in Mesopotamia: Sources and Methodology*, ed. Trudi Tanaka and Louise Quillien. University Park: Eisenbrauns.

Mirelman, Sam. 2010. Performative Indications in Late Babylonian Texts. Pp. 241–64 in *Musiker und Tradierung: Studien zur Rolle von Musikern bei der Verschriftlichung und Tradierung von literarischen Werken*, ed. Regine Pruzsinszky and Dahlia Shehata. Wiener offene Orientalistik 8. Vienna: LIT.
Mirelman, Sam, and Walther Sallaberger. 2010. The Performance of a Sumerian Wedding Song (CT 58, 12). *ZA* 100: 177–96.
Mittermayer, Catherine. 2019. *'Was sprach der eine zum anderen?' Argumentationsformen in den sumerischen Rangstreitgesprächen*. UAVA 15. Berlin/Boston: Walter de Gruyter.
Mitto, Tonio, and Jeremiah Peterson. 2020. A Neo-Babylonian Fragment of a Bilingual Version of Enlil and Sud. *KASKAL* 17: 258–71.
Motschenbacher, Heiko. 2007. Can the Term 'Genderlect' be Saved? A Postmodernist Redefinition. *Gender and Language* 1: 255–78.
Motschenbacher, Heiko. 2010. Redefining Genderlect. Pp. 45–60 in *Language, Gender and Sexual Identity: Poststructuralist Perspectives* by Heiko Motschenbacher. IMPACT: Studies in Language and Society 29. Amsterdam/Philadelphia: John Benjamins.
Nolan, Joanna. 2020. *The Elusive Case of Lingua Franca: Fact and Fiction*. Cham: Palgrave Macmillan.
Oberhuber, Karl. 1990. *Sumerisches Lexikon zu "George Reisner, Sumerisch-babylonische Hymnen nach Thontafeln griechischer Zeit (Berlin 1896)" (SBH) und verwandten Texten*. Innsbrucker Sumerisches Lexikon (ISL) des Instituts für Sprachen und Kulturen des Alten Orients an der Universität Innsbruck Abt.1. Sumerisches Lexikon zu den zweisprachigen literarischen Texten. Innsbruck: Institut für Sprachwissenschaft der Universität.
Ollet, Andrew. 2017. *Language of the Snakes: Prakrit, Sanskrit, and the Language Order of Premodern India*. Los Angeles: University of California Press.
Owens, Jonathan. 2001. Creole Arabic: The Orphan of All Orphans. *Anthropological Linguistics* 43: 348–78.
Peled, Ilan. 2016a. *Masculinities and Third Gender: The Origins and Nature of an Institutionalized Gender Otherness in the Ancient Near East*. AOAT 435. Münster: Ugarit-Verlag.
Peled, Ilan. 2016b. Visualizing Masculinities: The Gala, Hegemony, and Mesopotamian Iconography. *NEA* 79: 158–65.
Peterson, Jeremiah. 2010. A Fragmentary Erotic Sumerian Context Featuring Inana. *AuOr* 28: 253–57.
Peterson, Jeremiah. 2016. The Literary Corpus of the Old Babylonian Larsa Dynasties: New Texts, New Readings, and Commentary. *StMes* 3: 1–89.
al-Rawi, F.N.H. 1992. Two Old-Akkadian Letters Concerning the Offices of *kala'um* and *nārum*. *ZA* 82: 180–85.
Rose, Françoise. 2013. Le genre du locuteur et de l'allocutaire dans les systèmes pronominaux: genre grammatical et indexicalité du genre. *Bulletin de la Société de Linguistique de Paris* 108: 381–417.
Rose, Françoise. 2018. A Typology of Languages with Genderlects and Grammatical Gender. Pp. 211–46 in *Non-Canonical Gender Systems*, ed. Sebastian Fedden, Jenny Audring, and Greville G. Corbett. Oxford: Oxford University Press.
Römer, Willem H. Ph. 1969. Einige Beobachtungen zur Göttin Nini(n)sina auf Grund von Quellen der Ur III-Zeit und der altbabylonischen Periode. Pp. 279–305 in *lišān mitḫurti. Festschrift Wolfram Freiherr von Soden zum 19 VI. 1968 gewidmet von Schülern und*

Mitarbeitern, ed. Wolfgang Röllig and Manfred Dietrich. AOAT 1. Kevelaer: Verlag Butzon & Bercker / Neukirchen-Vluyn: Neukichener Verlag.
Römer, Willem H. Ph. 1988. Sumerische Hymnen, II. *BiOr* 45: 24–60.
Rubio, Gonzalo. 2000. On the Orthography of the Sumerian Literary Texts from the Ur III Period. *ASJ* 22: 203–25.
Rubio, Gonzalo. 2001. Inanna and Dumuzi: A Sumerian Love Story. *JAOS* 121: 268–74.
Rubio, Gonzalo. 2007. Sumerian Morphology. Pp. 1327–79 in *Morphologies of Asia and Africa*, ed. Alan S. Kaye. Winona Lake: Eisenbrauns.
Rubio, Gonzalo. 2009. Sumerian Literature. Pp. 11–75, 446–62 in *From an Antique Land: An Introduction to Ancient Near Eastern Literature*, ed. Carl S. Ehrlich. Lanham: Rowman & Littlefield.
Sallaberger, Walther. 1993. *Der kultische Kalender der Ur III-Zeit*, vol. 1. UAVA 7/1. Berlin: de Gruyter.
Samet, Nili. 2014. *The Lamentation over the Destruction of Ur*. MC 18. Winona Lake: Eisenbrauns.
Sapir, Edward. 1915. *Abnormal Types of Speech in Nootka*. Technical report, Canadian Department of Mines Geological Survey Memoir 62, Anthropological Series 5. Ottawa: Government Printing Bureau.
Schretter, Manfred K. 1990. *Emesal-Studien: sprach- und literaturgeschichtliche Untersuchungen zur sogenannten Frauensprache des Sumerischen*. Innsbrucker Beiträge zur Kulturwissenschaft, Sonderheft 69. Innsbruck: Institut für Sprachwissenschaft der Universität Innsbruck.
Schretter, Manfred. 2018. Zum Umgang babylonischer Gelehrter mit dem Emesal-Dialekt. Pp. 171–93 in *Mehrsprachigkeit. Vom Alten Orient bis zum Esperanto*, ed. Sebastian Fink, Martin Lang, and Manfred Schretter. dubsar 2. Münster: Zaphon.
Sefati, Yitschak. 1998. *Love Songs in Sumerian Literature: Critical Edition of the Dumuzi-Inanna Songs*. Ramat-Gan: Bar-Ilan University Press.
Shehata, Dahlia. 2009. *Musiker und ihr vokales Repertoire. Untersuchungen zu Inhalt und Organisation von Musikerberufen und Liedgattungen in altbabylonischer Zeit*. GBAO 3. Göttingen: Universitätsverlag.
Sherzer, Joel, and Anthony K. Webster. 2014. Speech Play, Verbal Art, and Linguistic Anthropology. *Oxford Handbook Topics in Linguistics* (online edn, Oxford Academic, 5 Dec. 2014), https://doi.org/10.1093/oxfordhb/9780199935345.013.33, accessed 5 Aug. 2022.
Silverstein, Michael. 1976. Shifters, Linguistic Categories, and Cultural Description. Pp. 11–55 in *Meaning in Anthropology*, ed. Keith H. Basso and Henry A. Selby. Albuquerque, NM: University of New Mexico Press.
Sjöberg, Åke W. 1972. In Praise of the Scribal Art. *JCS* 24: 126–31.
Sjöberg, Åke W. 1983. The First Pushkin Museum Elegy and New Texts. *JAOS* 103: 315–20.
Sjöberg, Åke W. 1988. A Hymn to Inanna and her Self-Praise. *JCS* 40: 165–86.
Sonik, Karen, and Ulrike Steiner (eds.). 2022. *The Routledge Handbook of Emotions in the Ancient Near East*. London/New York: Routledge.
von Soden, Wolfram. 1981. *Akkadisches Handwörterbuch*, 3 vols. Wiesbaden: Harrassowitz.
Stankiewicz, Edward. 1964. Problems of Emotive Language. Pp. 239–64 in *Approaches to Semiotics: Cultural Anthropology, Education, Linguistics, Psychiatry, Psychology: Transactions of the Indiana University Conference on Paralinguistics and Kinesics*, ed.

Thomas Sebeok, Alfred S. Hayes, and Mary Catherine Bateson. Janua Linguarum Series Maior 15. The Hague: Mouton.
Steever, Sanford B. 2018. Tamil and the Dravidian Languages. Pp. 653–71 in *The World's Major Languages*, 3rd ed., ed. Bernard Comrie. New York: Routledge.
Steible, Horst, and Fatma Yıldız. 2015. *Wirtschaftstexte aus Fara II. Texte der Viehverwaltung von Šuruppak.* WVDOG 143. Wiesbaden: Harrassowitz.
Steinkeller, Piotr. 1993. Early Political Development in Mesopotamia and the Origins of the Sargonic Empire. Pp. 107–29 in *Akkad: The First World Empire: Structure, Ideology, Traditions*, ed. Mario Liverani. Padua: Sargon.
Steinkeller, Piotr. 1995. Sheep and Goat Terminology in Ur III Sources from Drehem. *BSA* 8: 49–70.
Steinkeller, Piotr. 2005. The Priestess égi-zi and Related Matters. Pp. 301–10 in *"An Experienced Scribe Who Neglects Nothing": Ancient Near Eastern Studies in Honor of Jacob Klein*, ed. Yitschak Sefati et al. Bethesda: CDL Press.
Tanret, Michel. 2011. Learned, Rich, Famous and Unhappy: Ur-Utu of Sippar. Pp. 270–87 in *The Oxford Handbook of Cuneiform Culture*, ed. Karen Radner and Eleanor Robson. Oxford: Oxford University Press.
Tanret, Michel, and Karel Van Lerberghe. 1993. Rituals and Profits in the Ur-Utu Archive. Pp. 435–49 in *Ritual and Sacrifice in the Ancient Near East: Proceedings of the International Conference Organized by the Katholieke Universiteit Leuven from the 17th to the 20th of April 1991*, ed. Jan Quaegebeur. OLA 55. Leuven: Peeters.
Thomason, Sarah G., and Alaa Elgibali. 1986. Before the Lingua Franca: Pidginized Arabic in the Eleventh Century A.D. *Lingua* 68: 317–49.
Thomsen, Marie-Louise. 1984. *The Sumerian Language: An Introduction to its History and Grammatical Structure.* Mesopotamia 10. Copenhagen: Akademisk Forlag.
Tinney, Steve. 1996. *The Nippur Lament: Royal Rhetoric and Divine Legitimation in the Reign of Išme-Dagan of Isin (1953-1935 B.C.).* OPSNKF 16. Philadelphia: Samuel Noah Kramer Fund.
Trechter, Sara. 1999. Contextualizing the Exotic Few: Gender Dichotomies in Lakhota. Pp. 101–19 in *Reinventing Identities: The Gendered Self in Discourse*, ed. Mary Bucholtz, Anita C. Liang, and Laurel Sutton. Oxford: Oxford University Press.
Urban, Greg. 1985. The Semiotics of Two Speech Styles in Shokleng. Pp. 311–29 in *Semiotic Mediation: Sociocultural and Psychological Perspectives*, ed. Elisabeth Mertz and Richard J. Parmentier. Orlando: Academic Press.
Veldhuis, Niek. 1996. A Nippur Emesal Vocabulary. *ASJ* 18: 229–34.
Veldhuis, Niek. 2002. Studies in Sumerian Vocabulary: ^{d}nin-ka$_{6}$; immal/šilam; and še$_{21}$.d. *JCS* 54: 67–77.
Veldhuis, Niek. 2014. *History of the Cuneiform Lexical Tradition.* Münster: GMTR 6. Ugarit-Verlag.
Veldhuis, Niek. 2018a. Translation in The Elevation of Ištar. Pp. 183–206 in "The Scaffolding of Our Thoughts:" *Essays on Assyriology and the History of Science in Honor of Francesca Rochberg*, ed. C. Jay Crisostomo, Eduardo A. Escobar, Terri Tanaka, and Niek Veldhuis. AMD 13. Boston/Leiden: Brill.
Veldhuis, Niek. 2018b. Gender Studies and Assyriology: Expectations of an Outsider. Pp. 447–60 in *Studying Gender in the Ancient Near East*, ed. Saana Svärd and Agnès Garcia-Ventura. University Park: Eisenbrauns.

Viano, Maurizio. 2016. *The Reception of Sumerian Literature in the Western Periphery.* Antichistica. Studi orientali 9/4. Venice: Edizioni Ca'Foscari.

Volk, Konrad. 1995. *Inanna und Šukaletuda. Zur historisch-politischen Deutung eines sumerischen Literaturwerkes.* SANTAG 3. Wiesbaden: Harrassowitz Verlag.

Volk, Konrad. 2004. Vom Dunkel in die Helligkeit: Schwangerschaft, Geburt und frühe Kindheit in Babylonien und Assyrien. Pp. 71–92 in, *Naissance et petite enfance dans l'Antiquité. Actes du colloque de Fribourg, 28 novembre – 1er décembre* 2001, ed. Véronique Dasen. OBO 203. Fribourg: Academic Press / Göttingen: Vandenhoeck & Ruprecht.

Voux, Bert. 2011. Language Games. Pp. 722–50 in *The Handbook of Phonological Theory*, 2nd ed., ed. John Goldsmith, AlanYu, and Jason Riggle. Oxford: Wiley Blackwell.

Wagensonner, Klaus. 2020. Between History and Fiction – Enheduana, The First Poet in World Literature. Pp. 38–45 in *Women at the Dawn of History*, ed. Agnete W. Lassen and Klaus Wagensonner. New Haven: Yale Babylonian Collection.

Wasserman, Nathan. 2020. A Hybrid Magical Text from the Böhl Collection. *BiOr* 77: 446–58.

Westenholz, Joan. 1989. Enheduanna: En-Priestess, Hen of Nanna, Spouse of Nanna. Pp. 539–56 in *DUMU-E$_2$-DUB-BA-A: Studies in Honor of Åke W. Sjöberg*, ed. Herman Behrens, Darlene Loding, and Martha T. Roth. OPFSNKF 11. Philadelphia: The University Museum.

Whittaker, Gordon. 2002. Linguistic Anthropology and the Study of Emesal as (a) Women's Language. Pp. 633–44 in *Sex and Gender in the Ancient Near East: Proceedings of the 45th Rencontre Assyriologique Internationale*, vol. 2, ed. Robert Whiting und Simo Parpola. Helsinki: Neo-Assyrian Text Corpus Project.

Wilce, James M. 2009. *Crying Shame: Metaculture, Modernity, and the Exaggerated Death of Lament.* Malden: Wiley-Blackwell.

Wilcke, Claus. 1976a.Formale Gesichtspunkte in der sumerischen Literatur. Pp. 205–316 in *Sumerological Studies in Honor of Thorkild Jacobsen on his Seventieth* Birthday, *June 7, 1974*, ed. Stephen J. Lieberman. AS 20. Chicago: The Oriental Institute of the University of Chicago.

Wilcke, Claus. 1976b. *Kollationen zu den sumerischen literarischen Texten aus Nippur in der Hilprecht-Sammlung Jena.* Abhandlungen der Sächsischen Akademie der Wissenschaften zu Leipzig, Philologisch-Historische Klasse 65/4. Berlin: Akademie Verlag.

Wilcke, Claus. 1988. König Šulgis Himmelfahrt. Pp. 245–55 in *Festschrift Lászó Vajda*, ed. M Claudius Müller and Hans-Joachim Paproth. Münchner Beiträge zur Völkerkunde 1. Munich: Hirmer.

Wilcke, Claus. 2010. Sumerian: What We Know and What We Want to Know. Pp. 5–76 in *Language in the Ancient Near* East. *Proceedings of the 53e Rencontre Assyriologique Internationale*, ed. Leonid Kogan, Natalia Koslova, Sergey Loesov, and Serguei Tishchenko. BuB 4/1. Winona Lake: Eisenbrauns.

Worthington, Martin. 2019. Of Sumerian Songs and Spells. *AoF* 46: 270–300.

Yoshikawa, Mamoru. 1988. For a Better Understanding of Sumerian Grammar. *BiOr* 45: 499–509.

Zgoll, Annette. 1997. *Der Rechtsfall der En-ḫedu-Ana im Lied nin-me-šara.* AOAT 246. Münster: Ugarit-Verlag.

Zomer, Elyze. 2018. *Corpus of Middle Babylonian and Middle Assyrian Incantations.* LAS 9. Wiesbaden: Harrassowitz.

Troels P. Arbøll

Venomous Scorpions and Venerable Women: The Relationship Between Scorpions, the Goddess Išḫara, and Queens in the Neo-Assyrian Period

Caution is key when encountering scorpions.[1] Yet, the people in ancient Babylonia and Assyria lived closely together with these animals, and scorpions appear to have been a common sight in cities as well as private houses (Pientka-Hinz 2011). Perhaps as a result of observing the animal's nature on a daily basis, the scorpion became synonymous with central aspects of life (Zernecke 2008; Pientka 2004). As will be suggested below, the scorpion was a symbol for fertility and motherhood, but also death and divine power in ancient Mesopotamia. It was linked to the goddess Išḫara, who was known as the married aspect of Ištar, and the scorpion represented Išḫara on earth as well as on the night sky in the guise of the constellation Scorpius (Niederreiter 2008: 59–62; Stol 2000: 118). Furthermore, the creature was used as a symbol by the Neo-Assyrian queens (Svärd 2015: 74–75; Radner 2012). While previous studies have illuminated central aspects of the role scorpions played in Babylonia and Assyria, it is still possible to further nuance our understanding of how these animals were perceived.

This article examines the scorpion in the Neo-Assyrian period. By reviewing its use as an image for the terrestrial and astral aspects of the goddess Išḫara and the Neo-Assyrian queens, as well as its uses in magic and medicine, it is possible to identify cultural metaphors, which illuminate the role it played in Mesopotamian thought in the first millennium BCE. The first section surveys the available evidence for studying scorpions in ancient Mesopotamia. In the second section, the relationship between the scorpion and the goddess Išḫara, and the use of

1 This article was written as part of a postdoctoral fellowship at the University of Copenhagen generously funded by the Edubba Foundation and it was revised during a Junior Research Fellowship at the University of Oxford, Linacre College generously granted by the Carlsberg Foundation. I would like to thank the anonymous reviewer and the editors of the volume for their meticulous and helpful comments, as well as the participants of the "Women and Religion in Ancient Mesopotamia Workshop" in November 2015 and the STAKU seminar in September 2018 at the University of Copenhagen for fruitful discussions in relation to my presentations of the material in this article. Furthermore, I am grateful to wildlife zoologist Sophie Lund Rasmussen for guidance in finding further information on scorpion biology and behavior.

https://doi.org/10.1515/9781501514821-013

scorpions as queens' marks in a Neo-Assyrian context, are discussed. On the basis of medical prescriptions and incantations dealing with scorpions, I will examine the relationship between the animal's venom and physiology in the third section. An excursus in the fourth section investigates the related goddess Ištar of Kidmuru and her relationship to pregnancy. Section five scrutinizes the astral aspect of Išḫara, namely the constellation known as Scorpius, in order to identify the effects it had on society. A conclusion is offered in section six.

1 Scorpions in Ancient Mesopotamia

Scorpions (GÍR.TAB, *zuqaqīpu*) were common in Mesopotamia and they must have been observed regularly in cities and houses. Perhaps reflecting this reality, numerous ominous occurrences involving scorpions are listed in *Šumma ālu* as well as the 1st subchapter of Sa-gig.[2] Many types of scorpions with differing colors were differentiated in ancient Mesopotamia, as exemplified by the lexical list **Ur$_5$-ra** tablet 14.[3] While it is difficult to correlate the historical evidence with modern taxonomy, we know at least two species of venomous scorpions native to Iraq, namely the Deathstalker Scorpion (*Leiurus quinquestriatus*) and the Fattail Scorpion (*Androctonus crassicauda*).[4]

2 Tablets 30–31 in *Šumma ālu* were devoted to occurrences involving scorpions (Freedman 2006; see Pientka-Hinz 2011: 578). *Šumma ālu* concerns everyday phenomena in the immediate environment of a man and his house (Koch 2015: 233–62; see also Guinan 2014: 117–18; Guinan 1996). However, an empirical basis for *Šumma ālu* as such seems unlikely (Rochberg 2011: 623–24). For the first subseries of Sa-gig, see Heeßel 2001–02; Labat 1951: 8–11. As a result of such observations, *namburbi*-rituals to undo negative omens caused by scorpions also existed (e.g., Koch 2015: 261–62; Maul 1994: 344–48; Caplice 1965: 121–23). Scorpions are also mentioned in the physiognomic omen series (Böck 2000: 93, 245, 251, 267, 273). The appearance of the intestines as a scorpion in haruspicy is also attested, e.g., Nougayrol 1972: 143–45; see also Koch-Westenholz 2000: 33. For *šumma tīrānu* in the *bārûtu*-series, see Koch 2015: 95–96, 327; Heeßel 2011.

3 Pientka-Hinz 2011: 577; Pientka 2004: 395; Landsberger 1962: 39–40; Landsberger 1934: 28–29, 136–37. As discussed by George (2016: 113), a flying scorpion is attested, although it cannot have been a "zoological reality." Accordingly, the ancient scholarly taxonomy of scorpions differed from modern science.

4 Chippaux and Goyffon 2008: 72; Shalita and Wells 2007; Fet et al. 2000: 72–73, 155–57; Lucas and Meier 1995: 212–13; see also Gilbert 2002: 41–42. In the Al-Anbar province, various scorpions, including both the Deathstalker and Fattail Scorpion, were observed in 2009 (Fadhil et al. 2009: 38). See also Pientka-Hinz 2011: 576–77. Though they have distinct appearances, they are both venomous.

Scorpions must have been found regularly underneath people's beds.[5] A number of seal impressions from various periods display a scorpion in relation to a fertile woman or underneath the bed, and such depictions probably refer to a couple's married aspect (Stol 2016: 434; Winter 2012: 355–56; Zernecke 2008: 109–112; Stol 2000: 118 and n. 46; see below). A Neo-Assyrian scorpion incantation provides further information as to the creature's common places of residence, and in this recitation the scorpion is called: "the wolf of the storeroom, the lion of the larder." And in an Old Babylonian scorpion incantation, its physical appearance and qualities are described as follows: "It is green in the *thornbush*(?), it is silent in the sand, it is venomous in the brick mold."[6] This image is easily recognized today in the Deathstalker Scorpion depicted in Figure 1.

Figure 1: Deathstalker scorpion *Leiurus quinquestriatus*, Negev desert, Israel (Photo by Ester Inbar, available from https://commons.wikimedia.org/wiki/User:ST).

5 A number of omens in *Šumma ālu* concern a scorpion on a man's bed (Freedman 2006: 136–37 tablet 30 ll. 35′-36′). A line from a Sumerian myth describes a world where scorpions and snakes did not yet exist (Foster 2002: 275–76).

6 For the Neo-Assyrian incantation, see CT 38 pl. 38 (CDLI no.: P424963) obv. 59: ÉN *bar-bar ur-ši ni-ši a-bu-us-*[*si*], Pientka 2004: 394 and n. 41; Foster 2005: 861; see also George 2016: 111–16; Freedman 2006: 158–159; Scurlock 2002: 362; Maul 1994: 344–48; Lambert 1976–80; Caplice 1965: 121–23. For the Old Babylonian incantation, see SEAL no. 7167; Wasserman and Zomer 2022: 254; Pientka 2004: 389 and n. 1; Foster 2005: 861; Nougayrol 1972: 141–42 obv. 7–9, *wa-ru-uq i-na ba-aš-tim* 8 *ša-ḫur i-na ba-ṣí* 9 *im-ta* ⌜*i*⌝*-šu i-na na-al-ba-ni*. Note the following phrase in George 2016: 113 obv. 1–2: "Yellow in the open, black at home," ⌜*wa*⌝*-ru-uq ša ṣe-*⌜*e*⌝*-*[*tim*] 2 *ṣa-li-im ša bi-t*[*im*]. See also the various entries under scorpion incantations in SEAL; Wasserman and Zomer 2022: 229–71; Finkel 1999: 234–41.

2 Scorpions and the Goddess Išḫara

The scorpion was the animal of the goddess Išḫara. The animal can therefore be observed on numerous Middle Babylonian *kudurrus* representing this goddess (Toscanne 1917; Prechel 2009). Additionally, prebendaries in the service of Išḫara incised drawings of scorpions on at least two Late Babylonian loan documents.[7] While Išḫara was originally a north-Syrian goddess (Prechel 1996; Prechel 2009), she was known in central Mesopotamia via the Atra-ḫasīs Myth as the married aspect of Ištar:

> When, to institute marriage, they heed Ištar in the house of [the father-in-law]; let there be rejoicing for nine days, let them call Ištar Išḫara.[8]

Furthermore, her temple was called the "house of the womb" (*bīt šassūri*), clearly alluding to motherhood (Stol 2000: 118 and n. 47; Prechel 1996: 161; see also May 2018a: 266 n. 118). Išḫara was also linked to fertility through her presence in potency incantations (Stol 2000: 118 and n. 45; Biggs 1967: 22–23, 44–45). Scorpions functioned as the symbol of motherhood and they were related to fertility.[9] When the scorpion gives birth, it carries around its young on the back (Warburg 2011; Pientka 2004: 396–97), and the female scorpion was called "She who picks up the scorpion" (*tārīt zuqaqīpi*; Radner 2012: 691; Pientka 2004: 396–97). Underlining this caring aspect, the nominal form of the verbal root *tarû* "to raise, pick up" was also used to denominate a nanny (Radner 2012: 691; see CAD T: 232–33). Consequently, the image of a mother who is potentially dangerous and protecting her offspring with a venomous "weapon"

---

7 Baker 2004: 16 and n. 79 nos. 210 and 240. I would like to thank Heather Baker for drawing my attention to these texts.

8 Translation by Lambert and Millard 1969: 64–65 ll. 301–304: *i-nu-ma*$^{!}$ *<a-na> aš-š[u-ti] ù mu-tu-ti* ^{302} *i-na bi-it [e-mi ra-bé]-⌜e⌝ i-ta-ʾi-du iš-tar* ^{303} 9 *u_4-mi [li-iš-š]a-ki-in ḫi-du-tum* ^{304} *iš-tar [li-it-ta-a]b-bu-ú* ^{d}*iš-ḫa-ra*, see Foster 2005: 238 ll. 300–304 for a slightly different translation. Išḫara is also mentioned in the 2nd tablet of the Epic of Gilgamesh in connection to a marriage (George 2003: 168, 178–79, 190, 562–63). Stol (2016: 532) calls Išḫara "the goddess of marital love", see Zernecke 2008: 113 n. 37 with further references; van Buren 1944: 5–6. She is also mentioned in *Šurpu*, see Reiner 1958: 17. For Išḫara in other periods, see Menzel 1981: 73; Prechel 1996; Prechel 2009; Meinhold 2009: 69–71. In Egypt, the goddess Selqet had a scorpion-like symbol, and she was related to infants and watching over a person's mortal remains (von Känel 1984; Spieser 2001). Furthermore, her name was connected to breathing, likely on account of symptoms connected to envenomation (von Känel 1984: 830–31; Spieser 2001: 251). I would like to thank Thomas Christiansen and Sofie Schiødt for making me aware of this goddess.

9 Zernecke 2008; Stol 2000: 118; Prechel 1996; van der Toorn 1996: 173; van Buren 1937–39; see Koch 2015: 38.

must have provided a powerful motif. Thus, the scorpion and Išḫara both represented fertility, birth and motherhood.[10]

Perhaps as a result of the scorpion's association with motherhood, fertility, and awe-inspiring power, it was also used as a symbol of the Neo-Assyrian queens.[11] Many small objects, some of a personal nature, were excavated in the queens' tombs and the women's quarter in the North-West palace in Nimrud.[12] The objects often contain an engraved scorpion in addition to an inscription (al-Rawi 2008: 129, 137; see Hussein 2016: 22–23 and n. 51). Also, examples of queens' seals feature scorpions (Radner 2012: 687–88, 693). For example, the seal shown in Figure 2 belonged to Hamâ, who was the queen of Shalmaneser IV and buried in Tomb 3. This seal likely displays the queen in front of the goddess Gula or Išḫara with a dog or lion in front of her and a scorpion behind her (Spurrier 2017: 160 n. 45; Hussein 2016: 33 and n. 67, pl. 133a).

The symbol was used to mark objects as belonging to royal women, but also to mark it as part of queens' households (Macgregor 2012: 73). Yet, it remains uncertain what role, if any, the queens served in Išḫara's cult.[13] The scorpion illustrates domestic life and combines the concepts of life (renewal, birth), family (motherhood, womanhood), and death (venom). Scorpions were therefore important for the metaphoric expression of the Mesopotamian understanding of the world. The connection between Išḫara and marriage, expressed in contemporary texts such as a potency incantation, as well as the allusions to fertility and motherhood made the use of the scorpion as a symbol of married women ideal.[14]

10 I have focused on these aspects of Išḫara, though she should not be reduced to a goddess of fertility or motherhood alone.

11 See with further references May 2018a: 266 n. 118; Stol 2016: 531–32 and n. 91; Svärd 2015: 74–75; Macgregor 2012: 73–76; Radner 2012: 690–93; Meinhold 2009: 242–43, 251; Prechel 2009; Niederreiter 2008: 59–62 and n. 24; Melville 2004: 50–51. A liver omen seems to connect a woman's jealousy with a scorpion (Stol 2016: 687 and n. 19; Koch-Westenholz 2000: 143). The women of the Assyrian court have been the subject of a variety of recent studies, e.g., May 2018a; Spurrier 2017; Stol 2016: 514–17, 527–48; Svärd 2015; various papers in Chavalas 2014; Kertai 2013; Macgregor 2012; Radner 2012; Barjamovic 2011: 48–57; Melville 2004; Ornan 2002. Generally, mothers in royal harems must have fiercely advocated their children's interests within these cutthroat environments.

12 Svärd 2015: 74; Macgregor 2012: 73–76; Radner 2012: 690–93; Melville 2004: 50–51; Ornan 2002: 470–71; see the articles in Curtis et al. 2008 concerning the queens' tombs in Nimrud. At the Old Babylonian court at Mari, the harem woman Beltani owned a number of jewels shaped like scorpion tails (Stol 2016: 44 and n. 220).

13 May 2018a: 266 n. 118; Svärd 2015: 74–75.

14 Note that Svärd (2015: 74) questions the identification of the scorpion as a reference to Išḫara on the royal women's items.

Figure 2: Drawing of Queen Hamâ's seal (Spurrier 2017: 158 fig. 8, used with permission).

3 Scorpion Venom and Magico-Medical Treatments

Some species of scorpions can inject venom (Akkadian *imtu*) through their sting, which have a variety of physical effects. From a modern perspective, local symptoms include pains, swelling, redness and burning sensations, and among the systemic symptoms are sluggishness, paralysis, muscle rigidity, nausea, vomiting, renal failure, organ failure, respiratory failure, convulsions, abdominal pain, diarrhea, involuntary eye movement, dilation of pupils, priapism, excessive salivation, hypothermia, as well as heart attack.[15] Due to the effects of venom in general, the concept *imtu* was considered to be awe-inspiring in ancient Mesopotamia, and it was used in incantations as a metaphor to establish the effects of various illnesses or demons.[16] This concept was also connected to the regulation

15 These symptoms primarily describe the possible effects of venomous stings from the Deathstalker and Fattail Scorpion. See Bawaskar and Bawaskar 2012: 48–50; Chippaux and Goyffon 2008: 76; Dehesa-Davila et al. 1995: 228–30; Sofer 1995; Sofer et al. 1994: 973–74.

16 E.g., in relation to the illness *maškadu*: "It took half the venom of the snake (and) it took half the venom of the scorpion," BAM 124 col. iv 14: *mi-šil im-ti šá* MUŠ *il-qé mi-šil im-ti šá* GÍR.

of fluids in the human body via a metaphoric relationship to bile (Akkadian *martu*).[17] Furthermore, some symptoms, such as "paralysis" (*šimmatu*) that were commonly experienced with stings, became classified as illnesses.[18] The scorpion was also related to the child murdering demoness Lamaštu, and it appears on amulets intended to ward her off (Wiggermann 2000: 234, 239, 341). While few species of scorpions have a fatal sting, children are especially susceptible to die from envenomation (Chippaux and Goyffon 2008: 76–77; Sofer et al. 1994: 973). Therefore, the image of a scorpion on some amulets against Lamaštu probably points to the scorpion's motherly aspect as well as its venom. Scorpion incantations seem generally to focus on the scorpion's physical appearance, where it appears, its behavior, or motifs associated with fertility (see George 2016: 111–16). Scorpions were therefore used metaphorically to designate potency in connection to the awe-inspiring qualities of its venom, in order to explain the power and effects of illnesses and demons.[19]

Some of the very visible effects of envenomation may have been used to establish certain scorpion metaphors. The name for the scorpion in Akkadian, *zuqaqīpu*, is derived from the verbal root *zaqāpu* "to erect, to point upward."[20] The *zuqaqīpu* has therefore been translated as the "erector", because its venomous stinger stands erect when confronted with danger (Pientka 2004: 391). This verbal root, however, could on rare occasions be used to describe a penis

TAB *il-qé* (Arbøll 2018: 268–69 and n. 29; see Zomer 2018: 273–74; Collins 1999: 238–49, 253–59). Other examples include Lamaštu's venom, which is occasionally described in a similar manner (Farber 2014: 156–57 l. 127; Pientka 2004: 399). See also Scurlock 2014a: 562–63, 565. Furthermore, scorpions could in some instances sting a deity, see George 2016: 112. This could indicate that their venom was strong enough to affect the gods. For additional scorpion incantations, see SEAL; Wasserman and Zomer 2022: 229–71 Finkel 1999: 234–41. The demon Pazuzu is also depicted with a scorpion stinger (Heeßel 2002: 20).

17 Arbøll 2020: 79–83; 2021: 181. Maybe the excessive salivation, which could be a symptom of scorpion envenomation, contributed to the belief that venom could affect fluids in the body.

18 E.g., Geller 2018: 301 l. 32, 309; Abusch and Schwemer 2011: 57; Böck 2007: 266–67, 299.

19 A number of divine beings with scorpion features are known from ancient Mesopotamia, among these the scorpion men in the Epic of Gilgamesh tablet IX (George 2003: 668–71). For other "scorpion-men", see Scurlock 2002: 363–64; Wiggermann 1992: 144, 147, 149, 179–80. In the humorous *aluzinnu*-text, a jester burns down a house to exorcise it, and he states: "But the haunt of the house, the serpent and the scorpion, are not spared", ms D ii 15: MAŠKIM *šá* É *šá-a-šú* MUŠ *ù* GÍR.TAB-*ma ul in-ne-zib* (Foster 2005: 809; Foster 1974: 77; see Scurlock 2002: 379–80). For rituals involving Scorpius, see Abusch et al. 2016: 304–8; Abusch and Schwemer 2011: 15, 19, 188–89, 197; Farber 1977: 157–58. For apotropaic rituals, see n. 1; Pientka-Hinz 2011: 578.

20 For possible meanings of the Sumerogram GÍR.TAB as, e.g., "burning dagger," see Pientka-Hinz 2011: 577.

(AHw: 1512–13; see Pientka 2004: 393 and n. 38). Although the verbal root is rarely used to describe the male erection, I believe it may represent a literal description. Scorpion venom could cause priapism, an involuntary and painful erection, and this symptom may provide an additional reason for the scorpion's name.[21] Therefore, *zuqaqīpu*, "the erector," could literally refer to the penis, and by extension to fertility.[22] A number of so-called *araḫḫi*-incantations ("I impregnate myself") also incorporate motifs of sexuality, agriculture, and fluidity, and some were likely intended to be cast on oil for anointing someone (Arbøll 2018: 270 with further references). They were used in connection to scorpion stings, love magic, fertility, illnesses of the "strings" (*šerʾānu*), and witchcraft.[23] By combining the *araḫḫi*-incantations' themes with the metaphors related to scorpions, these dualistic animals were also used to designate potency in a healing context.

Medical texts describe a scorpion's sting by use of the verb *zaqātu* "to sting, hurt (said of a stinging pain)." This verb was also used to describe the effects of other afflictions, e.g., various renal and rectal ailments.[24] In general, only a limited number of medical texts against scorpion stings are known from ancient Mesopotamia, and these prescribe the application of various substances directly to the sting or mixtures for drinking.[25] Furthermore, relatively few

21 Although this symptom mainly occurs in "older" children (Sofer et al. 1994: 976), it is also attested in adults in relation to scorpion stings from, e.g., the Fattail Scorpion (Bawaskar and Bawaskar 2012: 49). As I have argued elsewhere (Arbøll 2020: 76–79), the effects of venom on the human body were useful for the conceptualization of how severe medical symptoms manifested themselves.

22 The allusions to sexuality in connection to scorpions seem to have been evident already in the earliest incantations, see Krebernik 1984: 9–12.

23 Arbøll 2018: 269–70; Abusch 2016: 169–70, 263, 350; Cavigneaux 1999: 258–59; Cooper 1996.

24 Geller 2005: 48–49, 54–57, 64–67, 127, 136–37, 168–69, 188–89, 192–95, 208–9, 212–13, 220–21; for other ailments, see Arbøll 2018: 276 and n. 61; Salin 2017: 36–39, 44–45; Scurlock 2014a: 14 and 20 l. 37, 30 and 35 l. 35, 199 and 204 l. 72′, 208 and 210 l. 32, 652 and 659 l. 13; Scurlock and Andersen 2005: 287–88, 365. Whether or not the pains and cramps experienced during childbirth were associated with the pains of a scorpion sting remains uncertain, but such a relationship could further underline a connection to motherhood.

25 E.g., Arbøll 2020: 327–329; George 2016: 164–65; see Pientka-Hinz 2011: 578–79; Scurlock and Andersen 2005: 366; Finkel 1999: 213; Scheil 1918. Treatments for scorpion stings are also mentioned in the "Exorcist's Manual" (Geller 2018: 299 l. 19) and the "Assur Medical Compendium" (Steinert et al. 2018: 215 l. 78).

medical prescriptions make use of ingredients derived from scorpions.[26] However, the relationship between scorpions and potency may have influenced the reasoning behind the following medications for problems in the testicles: "If a man is ill at his testicle(s), you crush a dried scorpion, he drinks it in beer and he will live," and: "If a man <is ill> in one testicle, you soak a living scorpion <in> a hardened vessel with oil . . ."[27] Perhaps attesting to the use of scorpions in rituals, a four-sided Middle Babylonian prism from Ḫattuša (KBo 1 no. 18) contains two incantations (col. iv 14′-20′, 21′-23′) intended "to seize a scorpion" and "to expel a scorpion."[28] However, our primary information on the treatment of scorpion stings originates within or in connection to incantations.[29] A common remedy appears to have been the application of dough to specific places of the body, perhaps to relieve the pain, but also to transfer the evil associated with the sting to the dough so it could be removed (George 2016: 4–6, 48). However, a patient might also be given a potion to drink (George 2016: 115).

The effects of venom resulted in several physical symptoms, which served as a basis for establishing some of the scorpion's metaphoric relationships with various other illnesses and demons; they also underline the scorpion's fertility aspect. Themes encountered in incantations, especially the *araḫḫi*-motifs, alongside the limited use of parts of scorpions in medical prescriptions seem to emphasize its relationship to potency.

26 E.g., BAM 499 col. iii 3′ (= AMT 4,1 col. iii 3′), which prescribes the use of various ingredients including "bile of a scorpion" (ZÉ ⸢GÍR.TAB⸣) for an ointment. However, scorpions do not have gallbladders, and the recipe must refer to a different fluid. See also Chalendar 2016: 101.

27 BAM 396 col. iv 13–14: DIŠ NA ŠIR-*šú* GIG GÍR.TAB ḪÁD.DU *ta-sàk* ^{14} *ina* KAŠ NAG-*ma i-ne-eš*; BAM 396 col. iv 15: DIŠ ⸢NA *ina*$^{?}$ ŠIR DIDLI⸣ <GIG> GÍR.TAB TI.LA <*ina*> DUG.KAL Ì.GIŠ DIR (Scurlock 2014a: 544–46; Geller 2005: 40–41; Pientka 2004: 400 and nn. 85–86). Scurlock (2014: 544) focuses on the idea that scorpion stings can produce numbness, and this quality would be beneficent to transfer to the ill testicles via the application of an actual scorpion. For a related remedy involving a live scorpion, see Geller 2005: 101 col. iv 23′.

28 Col. iv 20′: *ša* GÍR$^{!}$.TAB *ṣa-ba-tim*; col. iv 23′: *an-nu-tu*$_4$ *ša pa-ša-ar* ⸢GÍR$^{!}$⸣.TAB (Zomer 2018: 273–76). Additionally, the text contains an incantation likely against *maškadu*-illness (col. i 1′-10′), two incantations related to a snake (col. 1 19′-21′ and 25′-28′), and spells against insect(s) and flies (col. 1 11′-18′). For this text, see also Arbøll 2018: 269; SEAL nos. 7295 and 7296. See Cunningham 1997: 66 for a text alluding to carrying a scorpion.

29 SEAL no. 7167; George 2016: 98–100, 102–104, 109–16; Finkel 1999: 234–39; see van Dijk and Geller 2003: 14–18; Cavigneaux 1999: 254; Cunningham 1997: 40, 97, 113, 139, 142–43, 152–54, 156–58; Krebernik 1984: 8–12.

4 Excursus: Ištar of Kidmuru and Pregnancy

The deity Ištar also had a poorly recognized aspect linked to fertility. Ištar was known as the goddess of (sexual) love and war (Westenholz 2007), although she occasionally played a role in relation to motherhood.[30] Furthermore, an aspect of her, called Ištar of Kidmuru, may have played a role when attempting to conceive a child. She is mentioned in a Neo-Assyrian letter as the "Queen of Kidmuru" (^{d}*šarrat Kidmuri*). With all probability, this goddess should be identified as Ištar of Kalḫu.[31] Yet, it remains uncertain what the word Kidmuru/Kidmuri actually means (Porter 2004: 43). The Kidmuru temple in Nimrud was located to the east of the North-West Palace.[32] As emphasized by Reade (2002: 145), the temple likely existed before Assurnaṣirpal II's time, and it was presumably regarded as a separate structure. And although divine inhabitants of the temple may have included Enlil, Šamaš, and Aššur, Ištar was the main occupant (Reade 2002: 145). More important for the present discussion is the document SAA 10: 294, which is also known as the letter of the "Forlorn Scholar" (Parpola 1993: 231–34; 1987). Among the topics addressed in this long and scholarly text, the sender Urad-Gula, the son of the king's personal advisor Adad-šumu-uṣur of the influential Nabû-zuqup-kēnu family (May 2018b with references; Radner 2017: 221–23), writes as follows:

---

30 Westenholz 2007: 336, 339–40. The Lady of Nineveh (= Ištar/Mullissu) is "the mother who bore me" in Assurbanipal's hymn to the Ištars of Nineveh and Arbela (SAA 3: 3, esp. ll. 14–16; see also Meinhold 2009: 238–39; Parpola 1997: XXXVI, XL, 18, 40 n. 9). In a prophecy, the Lady of Arbela (= Ištar) is called Assurbanipal's "nurse" (Parpola 1997: 39). For select Assyrian aspects of Ištar, see Maul 2017: 337, 341, 350, 355; Meinhold 2009; Lambert 2004; Porter 2004. Ištar of Assur also had a relationship to fertility and motherhood through some votive objects found there (Stol 2016: 639 and n. 64; Meinhold 2009: 245–62).

31 Parpola 1993: 380; see also SAA 10: 197 obv. 11. For references to objects from the temple with this title, see Reade 2002:154; Albenda 1991: 44, 46, 49, 50, 53. Ištar is described as "the great lady dwelling in the house of the Kidmuri, lady of Kalaḫ," ll. 1–2: *ana* ^{d}MÙŠ NIN GAL-*ti a-šib-at* ^{2} É *kid*$_{9}$*-mu-ri* NIN URU *kal-ḫi* . . ., in an inscription located on an incense-burner$^{?}$ originally placed in the temple gate (Reade 2002: 152). Ištar of Kidmuru is also referenced alongside Ištar of Nineveh and Ištar of Arbela in some royal inscriptions, e.g., an Assurbanipal inscription listing gods who commanded Esarhaddon to name him as successor (Porter 2004: 42–43 and n. 9; Borger 1996: 15 ll. A I 11–21, 208; RIMA 2: 359–360 no. A.0.101.109). For a *šangû*-priest of the Kidmuru temple, see Menzel 1981: 207; van Driel 1969: 178. For further references to Kidmuru, see Cole and Machinist 1998: 126 and n. to no. 154; Westenholz 1970: 27.

32 See Russell 2017: 438 with further references. A reconstructed description of the temple is available in Reade 2002: 154. For other finds in the temple than the ones discussed here, see Reade 2002: 154–156. See Konstantopoulos (2015: 182–83) for a discussion of a temple to the Sebettu possibly located in connection to the Kidmuru temple.

> I have visited the Kidmuru temple and arranged a banquet, (yet) my wife has embarrassed me; for five years (she has been) neither dead nor alive, and I have no son.[33]

The episode recounted in the letter has previously been interpreted as an indication that Urad-Gula's wife was unable to have children (Radner 2017: 223). For unspecified reasons, Urad-Gula chose the Kidmuru temple as the place to remedy this situation via divine intervention.[34] As will be discussed below, this specific temple or goddess seems to have held a role in connection to conceiving a child (Parpola 1987: 277).

One specific find in the temple may support the hypothesis that the temple of Kidmuru had a connection to pregnancy, namely the Middle Assyrian text Rm 376, originally published by Lambert (1965). This text was excavated in the Kidmuru temple in Nimrud (Reade 2002: 155; Reade 1986: 218; see Zomer 2018: 41 and n. 123; cf. Lambert 1965: 283). Although the manuscript is partially broken, it contains incantations against *maškadu*-illness (col. ii 1–11), Lamaštu (col. ii 12–18), a spell concerning the Cow of Sîn (col. ii 19–36), and a female evil possibly related to Lamaštu (col. iv 1–32).[35] I have recently argued that Rm 376 was a compendium intended for use during (troublesome) births (Arbøll 2018: 270–72; see also Zomer 2018: 233–35). As the only text known to have been excavated in the Kidmuru temple, it is therefore noteworthy it was concerned with birth and pregnancy.[36] Considering the presumed Middle Assyrian age of the temple (Reade 2002: 145), it is striking that the text was written in a Middle Assyrian ductus and it was burned in antiquity in a manner typical of Middle Assyrian tablets (Lambert 1965: 283). Thus, the Kidmuru temple may have been connected to pregnancy before the Neo-Assyrian period.

In sum, the sparse evidence tentatively supports the hypothesis that Ištar of Kidmuru's temple was connected to fertility and childbirth, and by association Ištar of Kidmuru may have played a role in such matters. However, further evidence to support this suggestion is currently lacking.

---

33 Translation by Parpola, SAA 10: 294 rev. 23–25: . . . *ina* É *kid-mur-ri e-ta-rab*[!] *qa-re-e-tu e-ta-pa-áš* [24] MÍ *ši-i ta-ad-dal-ḫa-an-ni* 5 MU.AN.NA.MEŠ *la*[!]*-a mu-ʾa-a-tu la ba-la-ṭu* [25] *ù* DUMU[!]*-a-a la-áš-šú* . . .

34 The word used to describe the banquet is *qarētu* (CAD Q: 240–42; AHw: 917–18). Parpola (1987: 277) identifies such banquets as having been offered by private individuals with the aim of increasing progeny.

35 Zomer 2018: 270–72, 326–30; Veldhuis 1991: 4–5, 10–11, 63; Lambert 1965: 284–85. Note that the incantation against *maškadu*-illness in col. ii 10 makes use of a similar phrase as the *araḫḫi*-incantations discussed in Section 3 (Zomer 2018: 270–72).

36 Black (2008: 261) suggested that the Kidmuru temple could have had a library.

5 The Astral Aspect of Išḫara

Returning to Išḫara, she had an astral aspect named “the Scorpion” (^{mul}GÍR.TAB), which I refer to as “Scorpius” in order to differentiate it from other representations of scorpions. The astronomical compendium Mul-apin describes the constellation as follows:

> The Scorpion (i.e., Scorpius), Išḫara, goddess of all inhabited regions. The breast of Scorpius: Lisi, Nabû. The two stars which stand in the sting of Scorpius: Šarur and Šargaz.[37]

The constellation became visible on the morning of the 5th of the month *Araḫsamnu* (October-November), and the breast of Scorpius became visible on the 15th of the same month (Watson and Horowitz 2011: 190; Hunger and Pingree 1999: 65; 1989: 44). Recently, Anna Zernecke (2008: 117–20) has suggested that the autumn rise of Scorpius on the morning horizon signaled the time to begin sowing fields, as the earth was typically cultivated in the fall.[38] As such, the metaphor of fertility expressed through the scorpion combined with Išḫara as the married Ištar, connects well with the idea of ploughing fields and consummating these by providing seed for the coming grain.[39] The relationship between scorpions, fertility, and agriculture is superbly illustrated on an Old Akkadian

---

37 Watson and Horowitz 2011: 189 ll. Iii 29–32; Hunger and Pingree 1989: 38–39 ll. ii 29–32: DIŠ ^{mul}GÍR.TAB ^{d}*iš-ḫa-ra be-let da-ád-me* [30] DIŠ ^{mul}GABA GÍR.TAB ^{d}*li*$_9$-*si*$_4$ ^{d}AG [31] DIŠ 2 MUL.MEŠ *šá ina zi-qit* ^{mul}GÍR.TAB GUB.MEŠ-*zu* [32] ^{d}*šár-ur*$_4$ *u* ^{d}*šár-gaz*. See also Pientka-Hinz 2011: 579–80; Hallo 2008: 238; Scurlock 2002: 368; Hunger and Pingree 1999: 61, 71, 77–78, 93, 98, 108–109, 149, 275. In addition, the horns of Scorpius were known as “the Scales” (*zibānītu*), and Scorpius was part of the 15 stars of Ea (Watson and Horowitz 2011: 65; Hunger and Pingree 1989: 33, 38–39). Mul-apin likely functioned as a reference work, and it contained information on various planets, stars, and constellations in addition to some omens. See also Koch-Westenholz 1995: 131–32, 164; Reiner and Pingree 1981: 8. In the “Great Star List” Išḫara is listed as Ištar, queen of all lands, and Scorpius is listed as Išḫara as well as Išḫara Tiamat (i.e. the divine sea) (Koch-Westenholz 1995: 188–89). In a Late Babylonian astral explanatory text for “Marduk’s Address to the Demons”, Scorpius is called “Išḫara, the sea” (Wee 2016: 162–63). It remains uncertain how to interpret these relationships. A connection between water, venom, and bile is discussed in Arbøll 2020: 79–83; 2021.

38 Other texts, such as the “Farmer’s Instructions,” support the idea of astronomical phenomena signaling the time to sow the fields (Zernecke 2008: 117 and n. 64; Civil 1994: 30–31 ll. 38–39, 79). For sowing fields in the fall and harvesting in the spring, see Postgate 1992: 167–69.

39 It is possible farmers would generally have encountered scorpions when ploughing fields. Motifs of fertility can be found in connection to Ištar in, e.g., Ištar’s Descent (Lapinkivi 2010: 26–27, 31 ll. 77–80 and 87–90), though it is mainly her relationship to Dumuzi that provides a connection to plant fertility (e.g., Jacobsen 1976: 62–63).

cylinder seal (As.31:660) shown in Figure 3. The seal likely depicts two deities ploughing, of which one holds the plough and the other drives the span consisting of a snake-like dragon(?) and a lion (Zernecke 2008: 109–10 Figure 3; von der Osten-Sacken 1999: 268 and n. 23, 273, 278 Figure 10; Frankfort 1955: 49, pl. 62 no. 654). The lion may indicate Ištar was invoked in this scene.[40] The god driving the span has one arm on the plough and one arm extending into a scorpion.

Figure 3: Old Akkadian cylinder seal from Tell Asmar (drawing by the author after Frankfort 1955: pl. 62 no. 654).

This focus on astronomical phenomena coupled with cultivating activities is perhaps reflected in an omen involving wind in Mul-apin: "[If . . .] Scorpius becomes visible and the South wind blows: this year will be good."[41] Consequently, we should expect an emphasis to be placed on Scorpius in other astrological

40 Ištar was described as a lion in the Old Akkadian period with fierce and motherly qualities (see Foster 2016: 138).

41 Watson and Horowitz 2011: 204; Hunger and Pingree 1989: 116 l. iii 52: [DIŠ x] ^{mul}GÍR.TAB IGI IM.U$_{18}$ DU MU BI SIG$_5$. Note also the following related advice in Mul-apin: "On the 5th of *Araḫsamnu* the Scorpion becomes visible, on the 15th the breast of the Scorpion; on the day they become visible [you obser]ve the wind that [blows]," Watson and Horowitz 2011: 94, 195 ll. IIi 68–71; Hunger and Pingree 1989: 79 ll. i 32–33: DIŠ *ina* ^{iti}APIN UD.5.KAM ^{mul}GÍR.TAB UD.15.KAM ^{mul}GABA GÍR.TAB ^{33} IGI.MEŠ *ina u$_4$-me* IGI.MEŠ IM *šá* [DU-*ku* ŠE]Š-*ár*. The compendium also carries specific recommendations to determine which wind blows, see Watson and Horowitz 2011: 102; Hunger and Pingree 1989: 87. For Scorpius in *Enūma Anu Enlil*, see tablets 50 and 51 in Reiner and Pingree 1981: 36–37, 56–57, 60–61; see also Hunger and Pingree 1999: 52. In these instances, the rise of Scorpius appears to be related to economy.

texts. One of the best sources for understanding applied astrology remains the Neo-Assyrian reports written by astrologers to the Neo-Assyrian king published by Hermann Hunger (1992).[42] I have been able to identify at least 24 reports as well as letters to the Assyrian king from his scholars, in which Scorpius is referenced.[43] The manuscripts show that various astral events could affect Scorpius in a positive or negative manner. The texts consist of observations reported to the king as well as citations from astrological texts, such as *Enūma Anu Enlil*.[44]

One aspect that affects Scorpius negatively is the presence of Mars within the constellation.[45] At least seven examples are known of such observations, and the message is clear: "It is a bad sign" (SAA 8: 53 rev. 4) and "let the king guard himself" (SAA 8: 387 rev. 5–6). Two reports cite an evil omen concerning the "Plough star" (^{mul}APIN), though evidently dealing with Mars, and when the planet moves into Scorpius the omen states:

> If the Plough star comes close to Scorpius: the ruler will die from a sting of a scorpion – variant: he will be seized in his palace – after him his son will not take the throne; the mind of the land will change, the land will get another lord, and the dwelling of the land will not become stable; lamentation of the great gods for the land.[46]

---

42 For discussions of the Neo-Assyrian astrologers' methods of working, see Robson 2011; Veldhuis 2010.

43 SAA 8: 53 rev. 2–4; 55 obv. 7-rev.8; 66 rev. 1′-4′; 85 rev. 1–3; 113 obv. 7-rev. 1; 147 obv. 1–2 and rev. 2–4; 185 rev. 3–5; 219 obv. 1–6; 370 rev. 3–7; 371 rev. 2; 386 obv. 1–13; 387 obv. 3-rev. 6; 430 obv. 1–5; 466 obv. 1–4; 480 obv. 7-rev. 1; 502 obv. 7–14 and obv. 17-rev. 3; 504 obv. 3-rev. 5; 545 obv. 1′-4′; 547 obv. 1′-4′; 550 obv. 3–5; SAA 10: 8 obv. 21–27; 12 obv. 6–10; 149 obv. 3′-rev. 6′. In addition, Scorpius is mentioned in a broken context in SAA 8: 559 rev. 2. Mul-apin was in use in this period as well, as evidenced by the copies found in contemporary libraries (e.g., Hobson 2009). See also Brown 2000: 93, 276.

44 An example of this can be found in the two relevant passages concerning Scorpius in SAA 8: 147 obv. 1–2 = observation, and rev. 2–4 = omen "from the series" (*iškāru*). For serialized and extraneous omens, see Rochberg-Halton 1984; see also Koch 2015: 31–32, 53–54, 181; Brown 2000: 158. For the astronomical-astrological series *Enūma Anu Enlil*, see Koch 2015: 163ff; see also Brown 2000: 255–56.

45 SAA 8: 53; 85; 219; 387; 502; SAA 10: 8; 12. See also Hunger and Pingree 1999: 130–32. Brown (2000: 105–106, 145, 156) states that Scorpius was "an ill-boding constellation."

46 Translation by Hunger, SAA 8: 502 rev. 1–3: DIŠ MUL.APIN *ana* ^{mul}GÍR.TAB TE NUN *ina zi-qit* ^{mul}GÍR.TAB ÚŠ KI.MIN *ina* É.GAL-*šú* ^{2} DAB-*bat* [EGIR-*šú* DUMU]-*šú* AŠ.TE NU DAB-*bat* UMUŠ KUR MÌN-*ni* KUR$^{?}$ EN MÌN-*ma* TUK-*ši* KI.TUŠ KUR NU GI.NA ^{3} I.^{d}UTU DINGIR.MEŠ GAL.MEŠ *ana* KUR. Almost the exact same omen can be found in SAA 8: 219 obv. 1–5: DIŠ MUL.APIN *ana* ^{mul}GÍR.[TAB TE] ^{2} NUN *ina zi-qit* GÍR.TAB [BA.ÚŠ] ^{3} EGIR-*šú* DUMU-*šú* AŠ.TE N[U DAB-*bat*] ^{4} UMUŠ KUR MÌN-*ni* KUR EN MÌN-*ma* [TUK-*ši*] ^{5} *ku-dúr* KUR NU GI.NA I.^{d}UTU DIN[GIR.MEŠ GAL.MEŠ *ana* KUR]. See Brown 2000: 70–71, 74; Koch-Westenholz 1995: 142–43.

Mars was generally considered evil and the planet had a sinister character in astrology (Koch-Westenholz 1995: 128–29; see Hunger and Pingree 1999: 130–31; Brown 2000: 70–72). The association between Mars' presence in Scorpius and the ruler dying from a scorpion sting makes logical sense, seeing as the scorpion represented Scorpius (see Brown 2000: 106). However, the presence of Venus (SAA 8: 55), Saturn (SAA 8: 386), or Mercury (SAA 8: 504) in close proximity to Scorpius also seems to have been considered negative (see Brown 2000: 67–70; Hunger and Pingree 1999: 116–38; Koch-Westenholz 1995: 122–27). Other planets in close proximity to Scorpius were therefore considered undesirable, perhaps due to the added radiance (see, e.g., SAA 8: 113). This idea may have constituted a response to the common knowledge that although scorpions lived among people, they should preferably be left in darkness.

Scorpius itself, or parts of the constellation, could also be darkened (GI_6). Such sightings could signal "reconciliation (and peace) in the land" (SAA 8: 113; 371; 504; 545). Yet, if Scorpius was "obscured" this constituted a bad omen (*adir*, SAA 8: 502 obv. 13; see Brown 2000: 153 n. 364). Furthermore, specific darkened regions combined with illuminated parts of Scorpius could indicate that "rain and flood will be early in the land."[47] Overabundant rains and floods could pose a problem to agricultural activities, and, as such, these outcomes related to the dual nature of the scorpion as a bringer of life as well as death. The relationship between scorpion venom and bile (*martu*, see above) as a water regulating fluid may have added further value to the hermeneutical foundation behind the connection between Scorpius and rain.

The "sting" of Scorpius, meaning the metaphoric lower abdomen with a venomous stinger, consisted of the stars Šarur and Šargaz, which were also known as the deified weapons of Ninurta.[48] Two omens relate to these stars

47 SAA 8: 504, the full omen reads obv. 8: A.AN *u* A.KAL *ina* KUR *i-ḫar-ru-pu* . . . For planets in relation to Scorpius and causing floods, see also SAA 8: 55; 113.

48 Cooper 1978: 76–79 and 122 ll. 129–30, "On my right, I bear my Šarur, on my left, I bear my Šargaz." Šarur is the most important of Ninurta's weapons, see Wisnom 2019: 40–42, 133–137, 173–174; Annus 2002: 25, 70, 84, 99 n. 278, 126, 157, 180. In a Late Babylonian astrological commentary to "Marduk's Address to the Demons," Šarur is explained as "rectifier of the wronged" (*muštēšir ḫablim*) and Šargaz as "the weapon of Marduk" (Wee 2016: 162–63; Lambert 2013: 497). The two stars are also mentioned in the "Great Star List" as one of the seven twins (Koch-Westenholz 1995: 198–99). Both weapons are referenced and explained in an explanatory text as Šarur "gatherer of totality" and Šargaz "killer of totality" (Livingstone 1986: 54–55). For Šarur, see also Jacobsen 1987: 237 n. 7; Cooper 1978: 159. Only Šarur is mentioned as Ninurta's weapon in the myths Lugale (Seminara 2001; van Dijk 1983) and the second tablet of the Epic of Anzû (Annus 2001: 24 ll. 70 and 86, 25 ll. 102 and 124; Foster 2005: 474–76). The sting of Scorpius was called Pabilsag in two reports (SAA 8: 502; 550), although Mul-apin writes: "The star which stands

having gained radiance, which results in the following apodosis: "the weapons of Akkad are raised" (SAA 8: 185; 370; see 502). The added radiance to this specific area therefore invoked the aggressive aspect of the scorpion.

If a halo surrounded the moon and Scorpius stood inside it (and gained radiance), the following apodosis is attested: "*entu*-priestesses will be made pregnant; men – variant: lions – will rage and block off the traffic of the land."[49] While the pregnancy of an *entu*-priestesses surely attests to the fertility expressed by the scorpion,[50] the second part of the apodosis seems less fortuitous (see Brown 2000: 77 n. 206). On the other hand, if the sting of Scorpius surrounds the appearing moon, possibly like a halo, then "the flood will [come]" (SAA 8: 66). And finally, if Scorpius comes close to the moon and stands there, then the king's reign will be long (SAA 8: 430; 466). Thus, the relationship between Scorpius and the moon is less clear.

Išḫara's astral aspect, Scorpius, was connected to sowing fields and achieving an abundant harvest. Added radiance to Scorpius invoked one or more negative aspects related to the scorpion's inherent metaphors. In general, ordinary illumination of the constellation or a darkening was regarded as neutral or slightly positive in the ominous occurrences referenced in scholars' reports and letters to the Neo-Assyrian king. The strengthening or obscuring of Scorpius' radiance, however, had a concrete negative effect on fertility, general behavior, and kingship on earth.

6 Conclusion

The scorpion was a dualistic animal in ancient Mesopotamia, and it encompassed aspects of fertility and motherhood, as well as an awe-inspiring power potentially leading to death. As such, it was used as a marker for the ideal

behind them (i.e. Šarur and Šargaz): Pabilsag," Watson and Horowitz 2011: 189; Hunger and Pingree 1989: 39 l. ii33. Furthermore, the Sebettu (Pleiades) were called the "sons of Išḫara" in a late astronomical text, see May 2018a: 266 n. 118; Konstantopoulos 2015: 369.

49 The translation largely follows the one published by Hunger, SAA 8: 147 rev. 2–4: DIŠ 30 TÙR NIGÍN-*ma* ^{mul}GÍR.TAB *ina* ŠÀ-*šú* GUB ^{3} NIN.DINGIR.RA.MEŠ *uš-taḫ-ḫa-a* ^{4} NITA.MEŠ KI.MIN UR.MAḪ.MEŠ IDIM.MEŠ-*ma* A.RÁ KUR KUD.MEŠ; a similar omen is attested in SAA 8: 480.

50 Note that the title *entu*-priestess is problematic in a Neo-Assyrian context, and that such priestesses may (in some periods) have lived in chastity (CAD E: 172–73; see Svärd 2018: 126; Stol 2016: 448, 566–68, 570, 573). Thus, it is possible that the pregnancy of an *entu*-priestess was considered negative. See also Cooper 2016: 211 n. 4; Scurlock 2014b: 106 and n. 23.

mother, carrying and nursing its young, while protecting it with the deadliest of weapons. The scorpion was the animal of the goddess Išḫara, the married aspect of Ištar. Perhaps as a result of the associations between the scorpion's symbolisms and Išḫara, this animal also represented the Neo-Assyrian queens. In medicine, scorpion venom was used as a metaphor for establishing the effects of illnesses and demons due to the fluid's threatening qualities. In addition, the scorpion's name, "the erector" (*zuqaqīpu*), may have originated in the visibility of a possible symptom of scorpion envenomation, namely priapism. A limited number of medical treatments are known against scorpion stings, and the application of ingredients derived from scorpions seems to underline its symbolic qualities. Finally, Išḫara's astral aspect, the constellation Scorpius, was used as a marker for sowing fields in the autumn. The references to this constellation within the Neo-Assyrian astrological reports reflect the dualistic nature of the scorpion. Although the constellation itself does not appear to have been malicious, added radiance to Scorpius was interpreted as evil omens, which resulted in negative associations with the scorpion's relationship to fertility, procreation, and death.

Bibliography

Abbreviations follow the CDLI Abbreviations for Assyriology http://cdli.ox.ac.uk/wiki/abbreviations_for_assyriology (accessed 23/09/2019), with the addition of SEAL for *Sources of Early Akkadian Literature*, ed. M. P. Streck and N. Wasserman <http://www.seal.uni-leipzig.de> (accessed 12/06/2022).

Abusch, Tzvi. 2016. *The Magical Ceremony Maqlû: A Critical Edition*. Ancient Magic and Divination 10. Leiden and Boston: Brill.

Abusch, Tzvi and Daniel Schwemer. 2011. *Corpus of Mesopotamian Anti-Witchcraft Rituals Volume One*. Ancient Magic and Divination 8/1. Leiden and Boston: Brill.

Abusch, Tzvi, Daniel Schwemer, Mikko Luukko, and Greta van Buylaere. 2016. *Corpus of Mesopotamian Anti-Witchcraft Rituals Volume Two*. Ancient Magic and Divination 8/2. Leiden and Boston: Brill.

Albenda, Pauline. 1991. Decorated Assyrian Knob-Plates in the British Museum. *Iraq* 53: 43–53.

Annus, Amar. 2001. *The Standard Babylonian Epic of Anzu*. State Archives of Assyria Cuneiform Texts 3. Helsinki: The Neo-Assyrian Text Corpus Project.

Annus, Amar. 2002. *The God Ninurta in the Mythology and Royal Ideology of Ancient Mesopotamia*. State Archives of Assyria Studies 14. Helsinki: The Neo-Assyrian Text Corpus Project.

Arbøll, Troels P. 2018. Tracing Mesopotamian Medical Knowledge: A Study of *maškadu-* and Related Illnesses. Pp. 261–284 in *Sources of Evil. Studies in Mesopotamian Exorcistic*

Lore, ed. Greta van Buylaere, Mikko Luukko, Daniel Schwemer, and Avigail Mertens-Wagschal. Ancient Magic and Divination 15. Leiden and Boston: Brill.

Arbøll, Troels P. 2020. *Medicine in Ancient Assur: A Microhistorical Study of the Neo-Assyrian Healer Kişir-Aššur*. Ancient Magic and Divination 18. Leiden and Boston: Brill.

Arbøll, Troels P. 2021. A New Look at Eels and their Use in Mesopotamian Medicine. Pp. 179–192 in *Animal Encounters in the Ancient Near East*, ed. Laerke Recht and Christina Tsouparopoulou. McDonald Institute Conversations. Cambridge: McDonald Institute for Archaeological Research.

Baker, Heather D. 2004: *The Archive of the Nappāḫu Family*. Archiv für Orientforschung Beiheft 30. Wien and Horn: Institut für Orientalistik der Universität Wien and F. Berger & Söhne G.m.b.H.

Barjamovic, Gojko. 2011. Pride, Pomp and Circumstance: Palace, Court and Household in Assyria 879–612 BCE. Pp. 27–61 in *Royal Courts in Dynastic* States *and Empires*, eds. Jeroen Duindam, Tülay Artan, and Metin Kunt. Rulers and Elites 1. Leiden and Boston: Brill.

Bawaskar, Himmatrao S., and Pramodini H. Bawaskar. 2012. Scorpion Sting: Update. *Journal of the Association of Physicians of India* 60: 46–55.

Biggs, Robert D. 1967. *ŠÀ.ZI.GA. Ancient Mesopotamian Potency Incantations*. Texts from Cuneiform Sources 2. Locust Valley: J. J. Augustin Publisher.

Black, Jeremy. 2008. The Libraries of Kalhu. Pp. 261–266 in *New Light on Nimrud. Proceedings of the Nimrud Conference 11th–13th March 2002*, ed. John E. Curtis, Henrietta McCall, Dominique Collon, and Lamia al-Gailani Werr. London: British Institute for the Study of Iraq and The British Museum.

Borger, Rykle. 1996. *Beiträge zum Inschriftenwerk Assurbanipals: Die Prismenklassen A, B, C = K, D, E, F, G, H, J und T sowie andere Inschriften*. Wiesbaden: Harrassowitz Verlag.

Böck, Barbara. 2000. *Die Babylonisch-Assyrische Morphoskopie*. Archiv für Orientforschung Beiheft 27. Wien: Selbstverlag des Instituts für Orientalistik der Universität Wien.

Böck, Barbara. 2007. *Das Handbuch Muššuʾu "Einreibung": Eine Serie sumerischer und akkadischer Beschwörungen aus dem 1. Jt. vor Chr.* Biblioteca del Próximo Oriente Antiguo 3. Madrid: Consejo Superior de Investigaciones Científicas.

Brown, David. 2000. *Mesopotamian Planetary Astronomy-Astrology*. Cuneiform Monographs 18. Groningen: STYX Publications.

van Buren, E. Douglas. 1937–39. Scorpions in Mesopotamian Art and Religion. *AfO* 12: 1–28.

van Buren, E. Douglas. 1944. The Sacred Marriage in Early Times in Mesopotamia. *OrNS* 13: 1–72.

Caplice, Richard. 1965. Namburbi Texts in the British Museum. I. *OrNS* 34: 105–31 and pls. 15–18.

Cavigneaux, Antoine. 1999. A Scholar's Library in Meturan?. Pp. 253–76 in *Mesopotamian Magic: Textual, Historical, and Interpretative Perspectives*, ed. Tzvi Abusch and Karel van der Toorn. Ancient Magic and Divination 1. Groningen: STYX Publications.

Chalendar, Vérène. 2016. What Reality for Animals in the Mesopotamian Medical Texts? Plant vs Animal. *Anthropozoologica* 51: 97–103.

Chavalas, Mark W. (ed.) 2014. *Women in the Ancient Near East*. London and New York: Routledge.

Chippaux, Jean-Philippe, and Max Goyffon. 2008. Epidemiology of Scorpionism: A Global Appraisal. *Acta Tropica* 107: 71–79.

Civil, Miguel. 1994. *The Farmer's Instructions. A Sumerian Agricultural Manual.* Aula Orientalis, Supplementa 5. Barcelona: Editorial AUSA.
Cole, Steven W., and Peter Machinist. 1998. *Letters from Priests to the Kings Esarhaddon and Assurbanipal.* State Archives of Assyria 13. Helsinki: Helsinki University Press.
Collins, Timothy J. 1999. Natural Illness in Babylonian Medical Incantations Volume I-II. Ph.D. Dissertation. The University of Chicago.
Cooper, Jerrold S. 1978. *The Return of Ninurta to Nippur.* Analecta Orientalia 52. Rome: Pontificium Institutum Biblicum.
Cooper, Jerrold S. 1996. Magic and M(is)use: Poetic Promiscuity in Mesopotamian Ritual. Pp. 47–57 in *Mesopotamian Poetic Language: Sumerian and Akkadian*, ed. Marianna E. Vogelzang and Herman L. J. Vanstiphout. Cuneiform Monographs 6. Groningen: STYX Publications.
Cooper, Jerrold S. 2016. The Job of Sex: The social and economic role of prostitutes in ancient Mesopotamia. Pp. 209–227 in *The Role of Women in Work and Society in the Ancient Near East*, ed. Brigitte Lion and Cécile Michel. Studies in Ancient Near Eastern Records 13. Boston and Berlin: De Gruyter.
Cunningham, Graham. 1997. *'Deliver me from Evil'. Mesopotamian Incantations 2500–1500 BC.* Studia Pohl 17. Rome: Editrice Pontificio Instituto Biblico.
Curtis, John E., Henrietta McCall, Dominique Collon, and Lamia al-Gailani Werr (eds.) 2008. *New Light on Nimrud. Proceedings of the Nimrud Conference 11th–13th March 2002.* London: British Institute for the Study of Iraq and The British Museum.
Dehesa-Davila, Manuel, Alejandro C. Alagon, and Lourival D. Possani. 1995. Clinical Toxicology of Scorpion Stings. Pp. 221–238 in *Handbook of Clinical Toxicology of Animal Venoms and Poisons*, ed. Jurg Meier and Julian White. Boca Raton, New York, London, and Tokyo: CRC Press.
van Dijk, Jan. 1983. *LUGAL UD ME-LÁM-bi NIR.GÁL: Le récit épique et didactique des Travaux de Ninurta, du Déluge et de la Nouvelle Création. Texte, traduction et introduction. Tome II: Introduction à la reconstruction du texte Inventaire des Textes. Partition, copies des originaux.* Leiden: E. J. Brill.
van Dijk, Johannes J. A., and Markham J. Geller. 2003. *Ur III Incantations from the Frau Professor Hilprecht-Collection, Jena.* Texte und Materialien der Frau Professor Hilprecht Collection 6. Wiesbaden: Harrassowitz Verlag.
van Driel, Govert. 1969. *The Cult of Aššur.* Assen: van Gorcum & Comp. N. V. and Dr. H. J. Prakke & H. M. G. Prakke.
Fadhil, Omar, Mudhafar A. Salim, and Ibrahem M. Abd. 2009. *Key Biodiversity Survey of Central and Western Iraq.* Sulaimani: Nature Iraq.
Farber, Walter. 1977. *Beschwörungsrituale an Ištar und Dumuzi: attī Ištar ša ḫarmaša Dumuzi.* Wiesbaden: Franz Steiner Verlag GMBH.
Farber, Walter. 2014. *Lamaštu: An Edition of the Canonical Series of Lamaštu Incantations and Rituals and Related Texts from the Second and First Millennia B.C.* Mesopotamian Civilizations 17. Winona Lake, Indiana: Eisenbrauns.
Fet, Victor, W. David Sissom, Graeme Lowe, and Matt E. Braunwalder. 2000. *Catalog of the Scorpions of the World (1758–1998).* New York: The New York Entomological Society.
Finkel, Irving L. 1999. On Some Dog, Snake and Scorpion Incantations. Pp. 213–50 in *Mesopotamian Magic: Textual, Historical, and Interpretative Perspectives*, ed. Tzvi Abusch and Karel van der Toorn. Ancient Magic and Divination 1. Groningen: STYX Publications.

Foster, Benjamin R. 1974. Humor and Cuneiform Literature. *JANES* 6: 69–85.

Foster, Benjamin R. 2002. Animals in Mesopotamian Literature. Pp. 271–88 in *A History of the Animal World in the Ancient Near East*, ed. Billie J. Collins. Handbuch der Orientalistik 64. Leiden, Boston, and Köln: Brill.

Foster, Benjamin R. 2005. *Before the Muses: An Anthology of Akkadian Literature. Volume I-II* [Third Edition]. Bethesda, Maryland: CDL Press.

Foster, Benjamin R. 2016. *The Age of Agade. Inventing Empire in Ancient Mesopotamia*. Oxon and New York: Routledge.

Frankfort, Henri. 1955. *Stratified Cylinder Seals from the Diyala Region*. Oriental Institute Publications 72. Chicago: The University of Chicago Press.

Freedman, Sally M. 2006. *If a City is Set on a Height. The Akkadian Omen Series Šumma Alu ina Mēlê Šakin Volume 2: Tablets 22–40*. Occasional Publications of the Samuel Noah Kramer Fund 19. Philadelphia: The University Museum.

Geller, Markham J. 2005. *Renal and Rectal Disease Texts*. Die babylonisch-assyrische Medizin in Texten und Untersuchungen 7. Berlin and New York: De Gruyter.

Geller, Markham J. 2018. The Exorcist's Manual (KAR 44). Pp. 292–312 in *Assyrian and Babylonian Scholarly Text Catalogues*, ed. Ulrike Steinert. Die Babylonisch-assyrische Medizin in Texten und Untersuchungen 9. Boston and Berlin: De Gruyter.

George, Andrew R. 2003. *The Babylonian Gilgamesh Epic: Introduction, Critical Edition and Cuneiform Texts Volume I-II*. Oxford: Oxford University Press.

George, Andrew R. 2016. *Mesopotamian Incantations and Related Texts in the Schøyen Collection*. Cornell University Studies in Assyriology and Sumerology 32. Bethesda, Maryland: CDL Press.

Gilbert, Allan S. 2002. The Native Fauna of the Ancient Near East. Pp. 3–78 in *A History of the Animal World in the Ancient Near East*, ed. Billie J. Collins. Handbuch der Orientalistik 64. Leiden, Boston, and Köln: Brill.

Guinan, Ann K. 1996. Left/Right Symbolism in Mesopotamian Divination. *SAAB* 10/1: 5–10.

Guinan, Ann K. 2014. Laws and Omens: Obverse and Inverse. Pp. 105–122 in *Divination in the Ancient Near* East. *A* Workshop *on Divination Conducted during the 54th Rencontre Assyriologique Internationale, Würzburg, 2008*, ed. Jeanette C. Fincke. Winona Lake, Indiana: Eisenbrauns.

Hallo, William W. 2008. MUL.APIN and the Names of Constellations. Pp. 235–53 in *Studies in Ancient Near Eastern World View and Society Presented to Marten Stol on the Occasion of his 65th Birthday, 10 November 2005, and his Retirement from the Vrije Universiteit Amsterdam*, ed. Robartus J. van der Spek. Bethesda, Maryland: CDL Press.

Heeßel, Nils P. 2001–02. 'Wenn ein Mann zum Haus des Kranken geht . . .': Intertextuelle Bezüge zwischen der Serie *šumma ālu* und der zweiten Tafel der Serie SA.GIG. *AfO* 48–49: 24–49.

Heeßel, Nils P. 2002. *Pazuzu. Archäologische und philologische Studien zu einem altorientalischen Dämon*. Ancient Magic and Divination 4. Leiden, Boston, and Köln: Brill and Styx.

Heeßel, Nils P. 2011. 'Sieben Tafeln aus sieben Städten' – Überlegungen zum Prozess der Serialisierung von Texten in Babylonien in der zweiten Hälfte des zweiten Jahrtausends v. Chr. Pp. 171–96 in *Babylon. Wissenskultur in Orient und Okzident*, eds. Eva Cancik-Kirschbaum, Margarete van Ess, and Joachim Marzahn. Topoi Berlin Studies of the Ancient World 1. Berlin and Boston: De Gruyter.

Hobson, Russell. 2009. A Copy of MUL.APIN from a Private Library at Ashur (VAT 9429). *Journal of Ancient Civilizations* 24: 35–39.

Hunger, Hermann. 1992. *Astrological Reports to Assyrian Kings*. State Archives of Assyria 8. Helsinki: Helsinki University Press.

Hunger, Hermann, and David Pingree. 1989. *MUL.APIN: An Astronomical Compendium in Cuneiform*. Archiv für Orientforschung Beiheft 24. Horn: Verlag Ferdinand Berger & Söhne Gesellschaft M. B. H.

Hunger, Hermann, and David Pingree. 1999. *Astral Sciences in Mesopotamia*. Handbuch der Orientalistik 44. Leiden, Boston, and Köln: Brill.

Hussein, Muzahim M. 2016. *Nimrud: The Queens' Tombs* [Translated by M. Altaweel]. Baghdad and Chicago: Iraqi State Board of Antiquities and Heritage and The Oriental Institute of the University of Chicago.

Jacobsen, Thorkild. 1976. *The Treasures of Darkness. A History of Mesopotamian Religion*. New Haven and London: Yale University Press.

Jacobsen, Thorkild. 1987. *The Harps that Once . . . : Sumerian Poetry in Translation*. New Haven and London: Yale University Press.

von Känel, Frédérique. 1984. Selqet. Pp. 830–834 in *Lexikon der Ägyptologie Band V. Pyramidenbau – Steingefäße*, eds. Wolfgang Helck and Wolfhart Westendorf. Wiesbaden: Otto Harrassowitz.

Kertai, David. 2013. The Queens of the Neo-Assyrian Empire. *Altorientalische Forschungen* 40: 108–24.

Koch, Ulla S. 2015. *Mesopotamian Divination Texts: Conversing with the Gods. Sources from the First Millennium BCE*. Guides to the Mesopotamian Textual Record 7. Münster: Ugarit-Verlag.

Koch-Westenholz, Ulla S. 1995. *Mesopotamian Astrology: An Introduction to Babylonian and Assyrian Celestial Divination*. Carsten Niebuhr Institute Publications 19. Copenhagen: Museum Tusculanum Press.

Koch-Westenholz, Ulla S. 2000. *Babylonian Liver Omens: the Chapters Manzāzu, Padānu and Pān tākalti of the Babylonian Extispicy Series mainly from Aššurbanipal's Library*. Carsten Niebuhr Institute Publications 25. Copenhagen: Museum Tusculanum Press.

Konstantopoulos, Gina V. 2015. They are Seven: Demons and Monsters in the Mesopotamian Textual and Artistic Tradition. Dissertation. Michigan: The University of Michigan.

Krebernik, Manfred. 1984. *Die Beschwörungen aus Fara und Ebla: Untersuchungen zur ältesten keilschriftlichen Beschwörungsliteratur*. Texte und Studien zur Orientalistik 2. Hildesheim, Zürich, and New York: Georg Olms Verlag.

Labat, René. 1951. *Traité dkkadien de diagnostics et prognostics médicaux I-II*. Collection de Travaux de l'Académie Internationale d'Historie des Sciences 7. Paris and Leiden: Academie Internationale d'Historie des Sciences and Brill.

Lambert, Wilfred G. 1965. A Middle Assyrian Tablet of Incantations. Pp. 283–88 in *Studies in Honor of Benno Landsberger on His Seventy-Fifth Birthday April 21, 1965*, ed. Hans G. Güterbock and Thorkild Jacobsen. Assyriological Studies 16. Chicago: The University of Chicago Press.

Lambert, Wilfred G. 1976–80. Išḫara. *RlA* 5: 176–77.

Lambert, Wilfred G. 2004. Ištar of Nineveh. *Iraq* 66: 35–39.

Lambert, Wilfred G.2013. *Babylonian Creation Myths*. Mesopotamian Civilizations 16. Winona Lake, Indiana: Eisenbrauns.

Lambert, Wilfred G., and Alan R. Millard. 1969. *Atra-ḫasīs: The Babylonian Story of the Flood*. Oxford: Oxford University Press.

Landsberger, Benno. 1934. *Die Fauna des Alten Mesopotamien nach der 14. Tafel der Serie ḪAR-RA = ḫubullu*. Abhandlungen der philologisch-historischen Klasse der Sächsischen Akademie der Wissenschaften 6. Leipzig: Verlag von S. Hirzel.

Landsberger, Benno. 1962. *MSL VIII/2. The Fauna of Ancient Mesopotamia. Second Part. ḪAR-ra = ḫubullu Tablets XIV and XVIII*. Materialien zum Sumerischen Lexikon 8/2. Rome: Pontificium Institutum Biblicum.

Lapinkivi, Pirjo. 2010. *The Neo-Assyrian Myth of Ištar's Descent and Resurrection*. State Archives of Assyria Cuneiform Texts 6. Helsinki: The Neo-Assyrian Text Corpus Project.

Livingstone, Alasdair. 1986. *Mystical and Mythological Explanatory Works of Assyrian and Babylonian Scholars*. Oxford: Oxford University Press.

Lucas, Sylvia M., and Jürg Meier. 1995. Biology and Distribution of Scorpions of Medical Importance. Pp. 205–19 in *Handbook of Clinical Toxicology of Animal Venoms and Poisons*, ed. Jurg Meier and Julian White. Boca Raton, New York, London, and Tokyo: CRC Press.

Macgregor, Sherry L. 2012. *Beyond Hearth and Home. Women in the Public Sphere in Neo-Assyrian Society*. States Archives of Assyria Studies 21. Helsinki: Neo-Assyrian Text Corpus Project.

Maul, Stefan M. 1994. *Zukunftsbewältigung: Eine Untersuchung altorientalischen Denkens anhand der babylonisch-assyrischen Löserituale (Namburbi)*. Baghdader Forschungen 18. Mainz: Verlag Philipp von Zabern.

Maul, Stefan M. 2017. Assyrian Religion. Pp. 336–58 in *A Companion to Assyria*, ed. Eckart Frahm. Hoboken and Chichester: Wiley Blackwell.

May, Natalie N. 2018a. Neo-Assyrian Women, Their Visibility, and Their Representation in Written and Pictorial Sources. Pp. 249–88 in *Studying Gender in the Ancient Near East*, eds. Saana Svärd and Agnès Garcia-Ventura. University Park: Eisenbrauns.

May, Natalie N. 2018b. The Scholar and Politics: Nabû-zuqup-kēnu, his Colophons and the Ideology of Sargon II. Pp. 110–64 in *Proceedings of the International Conference Dedicated to the Centenary of Igor Mikhailovich Diakonoff (1915–1999)*, ed. Natalija V. Kozlova. Transactions of the State Hermitage Museum 95. St. Petersburg: The State Hermitage Publishers.

Meinhold, Wiebke. 2009. *Ištar in Aššur. Untersuchung eines Lokalkultes von ca. 2500 bis 614 v. Chr.* Alter Orient und Altes Testament 367. Münster: Ugarit-Verlag.

Melville, Sarah C. 2004. Neo-Assyrian Royal Women and Male Identity: Status as a Social Tool. *JAOS* 124: 37–57.

Menzel, Birgitte. 1981. *Assyrische Tempel. Band I-II*. Studia Pohl 10/I-II. Rome: Biblical Institute Press.

Niederreiter, Zoltán. 2008. Le role des symbols figures attributes aux membres de la Cour de Sargon II: Des emblems créés par les letters du palais au service de l'idéologie royale. *Iraq* 70: 51–86.

Nougayrol, Jean. 1972. Textes Religieux (II). *RA* 66: 141–145.

Ornan, Tallay. 2002. The Queen in Public: Royal Women in Neo-Assyrian Art. Pp. 461–77 in *Sex and Gender in the Ancient Near East: Proceedings of the 47th Rencontre Assyriologique Internationale, Helsinki, July 2–6, 2001*, ed. Simo Parpola and Robert M. Whiting. Helsinki: The Neo-Assyrian Text Corpus Project.

von der Osten-Sacken, Elisabeth. 1999. Vögel beim Pflügen. Pp. 265–78 in *Landwirtschaft im Alten Orient. Ausgewählte Vorträge der XLI. Rencontre Assyriologique Internationale Berlin, 4.-8.7.1994*, ed. Horst Klengel and Johannes Renger. Berliner Beiträge zum Vorderen Orient 18. Berlin: Dietrich Reimer Verlag.

Parpola, Simo. 1987. The Forlorn Scholar. Pp. 257–78 in *Language, Literature, and History: Philological and Historical Studies Presented to Erica Reiner*, ed. Francesca Rochberg-Halton. American Oriental Series 67. New Haven: Amerian Oriental Society.

Parpola, Simo. 1993. *Letters from Assyrian and Babylonian Scholars*. State Archives of Assyria 10. Helsinki: Helsinki University Press.

Parpola, Simo. 1997. *Assyrian Prophecies*. State Archives of Assyria 9. Helsinki: Helsinki University Press.

Pientka, Rosel. 2004. Aus der Wüste ins Schlafzimmer – Der Skorpion. Pp. 389–404 in *Nomades et Sédentaires dans le Proche-Orient Ancien: Compte rendu de la XLVIe Rencontre Assyriologique Internationale (Paris, 10–13 juillet 2000)*, ed. Christophe Nicolle. Amurru 3. Paris: Éditions Recherche sur les Civilisations.

Pientka-Hinz, Rosel. 2011. Skorpion. *RlA* 12: 576–80.

Porter, Barbara N. 2004. Ishtar of Nineveh and Her Collaborator, Ishtar of Arbela, in the Reign of Assurbanipal. *Iraq* 66: 41–44.

Postgate, John N. 1992. *Early Mesopotamia. Society and Economy at the Dawn of History*. London and New York: Routledge.

Prechel, Doris. 1996. *Die Gottin Ishara. Ein Beitrag zur altorientalischen Religionsgeschichte*. Abhandlungen zur Literatur Alt-Syrien-Palästinas und Mesopotamiens 11. Münster: Ugarit-Verlag.

Prechel, Doris. 2009. Ishara. Pp. 1–2 in *Iconography of Deities and Demons in the Ancient Near East: Electronic Pre-Publication*, eds. J. Eggler and C. Uehlinger <http://www.religionswissenschaft.uzh.ch/idd/prepublications/e_idd_ishara.pdf> (accessed 10/ 12/ 2019).

Radner, Karen. 2012. The Seal of Tašmetum-šarrat, Sennacherib's Queen, and Its Impressions. Pp. 687–98 in *Leggo! Studies Presented to Frederick Mario Fales on the Occasion of His 65th Birthday*, ed. Giovanni B. Lanfranchi, Daniele M. Bonacossi, Cinzia Pappi, and Simonetta Ponchia. Wiesbaden: Harrassowitz Verlag.

Radner, Karen. 2017. Economy, Society, and Daily Life in the Neo-Assyrian Period. Pp. 209–28 in *A Companion to Assyria*, ed. Eckart Frahm. Hoboken and Chichester: Wiley Blackwell.

al-Rawi, Farouk N. H. 2008. Inscriptions from the Tombs of the Queens of Assyria. Pp. 119–38 in *New Light on Nimrud. Proceedings of the Nimrud Conference 11th–13th March 2002*, ed. John E. Curtis, Henrietta McCall, Dominique Collon, and Lamia al-Gailani Werr. London: British Institute for the Study of Iraq and The British Museum.

Reade, Julian. 1986. Archaeology and the Kuyunjik Archives. Pp. 213–22 in *Cuneiform Archives and Libraries. Papers read the 30e Rencontre Assyriologique Internationale Leiden, 4–8 July, 1983*, ed. Klaas R. Veenhof. Nederlands Historisch-Archaeologisch Instituut te Istanbul 57. Leiden: Nederlands Historisch-Archaeologisch Instituut te Istanbul.

Reade, Julian. 2002. The Ziggurrat and Temples of Nimrud. *Iraq* 64: 135–216.

Reiner, Erica. 1958. *Šurpu. A Collection of Sumerian and Akkadian Incantations*. Archiv für Orientforschung Beiheft 11. Osnabrück: Biblio Verlag.

Reiner, Erica, and David Pingree. 1981. *Babylonian Planetary Omens: part Two. Enūma Anu Enlil, Tablets 50–51*. Bibliotheca Mesopotamica 2. Malibu: Undena Publications.

Robson, Eleanor. 2011. Empirical Scholarship in the Neo-Assyrian Court. Pp. 603–30 in *The Empirical Dimension of Ancient Near Eastern Studies*, eds. Gebhard J. Selz and Klaus Wagensonner. Wien: LIT Verlag.

Rochberg, Francesca. 2011. Observing and Describing the World Through Divination and Astronomy. Pp. 618–36 in *The Oxford Handbook of Cuneiform Culture*, ed. Karen Radner and Eleanor Robson. Oxford: Oxford University Press.

Rochberg-Halton, Francesca. 1984. Canonicity in Cuneiform Texts. *JCS* 36: 127–44.

Russell, John M. 2017. Assyrian Cities and Architecture. Pp. 423–52 in *A Companion to Assyria*, ed. Eckart Frahm. Hoboken and Chichester: Wiley Blackwell.

Salin, Silvia. 2017. 'Stinging Pain' in Assyro-Babylonian Medical texts: Some Considerations. *JMC* 29: 35–48.

Scheil, Vincent. 1918. Notules. *RA* 15: 75–86.

Scurlock, JoAnn. 2002. Animals in Ancient Mesopotamian Religion. Pp. 361–88 in *A History of the Animal World in the Ancient Near East*, ed. Billie J. Collins. Handbuch der Orientalistik 64. Leiden, Boston, and Köln: Brill.

Scurlock, JoAnn. 2014a. *Sourcebook for Ancient Mesopotamian Medicine*. Writings from the Ancient World 36. Atlanta, Georgia: SBL Press.

Scurlock, JoAnn. 2014b. Medicine and healing magic. Pp. 101–43 in *Women in the Ancient Near East*, ed. M. W. Chavalas. London and New York: Routledge.

Scurlock, JoAnn, and Burton R. Andersen. 2005. *Diagnoses in Assyrian and Babylonian Medicine: Ancient Sources, Translations, and Modern Medical Analyses*. Urbana and Chicago: University of Illinois Press.

Seminara, Stefano. 2001. *La Versione Accadica del Lugal-e*. Materiali per il Vocabolario Sumerico 8. Rome: Università degli Studi di Roma "La Sapienza".

Shalita, Eric A., and Ryan D. Wells. 2007. Treatment of Yellow Scorpion (*Leiurus quinquestriatus*) Sting: A Case Report. *Journal of the American Pharmacists Association* 47/5: 616–19.

Sofer, Shaul. 1995. Scorpion envenomation. *Intensive Care Med* 21: 626–28.

Sofer, Shaul, Eliezer Shahak, and Moshe Gueron. 1994. Scorpion Envenomation and Antivenom Therapy. *The Journal of Pediatrics* 124/6: 973–78.

Spieser, Cathie. 2001: Serket, protectrice des enfants à naître et des défunts à renaître. *RdE* 52: 251–64.

Spurrier, Tracy L. 2017. Finding Hama: On the Identification of a Forgotten Queen Buried in the Nimrud Tombs. *JNES* 76: 149–74.

Steinert, Ulrike, Strahil V. Panayotov, Markham J. Geller, Eric Schmidtchen, and J. Cale Johnson. 2018. AMC Text Edition. Pp. 209–19 in *Assyrian and Babylonian Scholarly Text Catalogues*, ed. Ulrike Steinert. Die babylonisch-assyrische Medizin in Texten und Untersuchungen 9. Boston and Berlin: De Gruyter.

Stol, Marten. 2000. *Birth in Babylonia and the Bible: Its Mediterranean Setting*. Cuneiform Monographs 14. Groningen: STYX Publications.

Stol, Marten. 2016. *Women in the Ancient Near East* [Translated by H. Richardson and M. Richardson]. Boston and Berlin: De Gruyter.

Svärd, Saana. 2015. *Women and Power in Neo-Assyrian palaces*. State Archives of Assyria Studies 23. Helsinki: The Neo-Assyrian Text Corpus Project.

Svärd, Saana. 2018. Women in Neo-Assyrian Temples. Pp. 117–33 in *Neo-Assyrian Sources in Context*, ed. Shigeo Yamada. State Archives of Assyria Studies 28. Helsinki: The Neo-Assyrian Text Corpus Project.

van der Toorn, Karel. 1996. *Family Religion in Babylonia, Syria and Israel: Continuity and Change in the Forms of Religious Life*. Studies in the History and Culture of the Ancient Near East 7. Leiden, New York, and Köln: E. J. Brill.

Toscanne, Paul. 1917. Sur la figuration et le symbole du scorpion. *RA* 14: 187–203.

Veldhuis, Niek. 1991. *A Cow of Sîn*. Library of Oriental Texts 2. Groningen: Styx Publications.

Veldhuis, Niek. 2010. The Theory of Knowledge and the Practice of Celestial Divination. Pp. 77–92 in *Divination and Interpretation of Signs in the Ancient World*, ed. Amar Annus. Oriental Institute Seminars 6. Chicago: The Oriental Institute of the University of Chicago.

Warburg, Michael R. 2011. Pre- and Post-Parturial Aspects of Scorpion Reproduction: A Review. *European Journal of Entomology* 109: 139–146.

Wasserman, Nathan, and Elyze Zomer. 2022. *Akkadian magic Literature. Old Babylonian and Old Assyrian Incantations: Corpus – Context – Praxis*. Leipziger Altorientalistische Studien 12. Wiesbaden: Harrassowitz Verlag.

Watson, Rita, and Wayne Horowitz. 2011. *Writing Science before the Greeks: A Naturalistic Analysis of the Babylonian Astronomical Treatise MUL.APIN*. Culture and History of the Ancient Near East 48. Leiden and Boston: Brill.

Wee, John Z. 2016. A Late Babylonian Astral Commentary on *Marduk's Address to the Demons*. *JNES* 75/1: 127–67.

Westenholz, Aage. 1970. *berūtum, damtum*, and Old Akkadian KI.GAL: Burial of dead enemies in Ancient Mesopotamia. *AfO* 23: 27–31.

Westenholz, Joan G. 2007. Inanna and Ishtar in the Babylonian world. Pp. 332–47 in *The Babylonian World*, ed. Gwendolyn Leick. New York and London: Routledge.

Wiggermann, Frans A. M. 1992. *Mesopotamian protective Spirits. The Ritual Texts*. Cuneiform Monographs 1; Groningen: STYX and PP Publications.

Wiggerman, Frans A. M. 2000. Lamaštu, Daughter of Anu. A Profile. Pp. 217–52 in *Birth in Babylonia and the Bible: Its Mediterranean Setting*, Marten Stol. Cuneiform Monographs 14. Groningen: STYX Publications.

Winter, Urs. 2012 [1983]. *Frau und Göttin. Exegetische und ikonographische Studien zum weiblichen Gottesbild im Alten Israel und in dessen Umwelt*. Jerusalem and Tübingen: SLM Press and Tobiaslib [Orbis Biblicus et Orientalis 53. Fribourg and Göttingen: Academic Press and Vandenhoeck & Ruprecht].

Wisnom, Selena. 2019. *Weapons of Words: Intertextual Competition in Babylonian Poetry*. Culture and History of the Ancient Near East 106. Leiden and Boston: Brill.

Zernecke, Anna E. 2008. Warum sitzt der Skorpion unter dem Bett? Überlegungen zur Deutung eines altorientalischen Fruchtbarkeitssymbols. *Zeitschrift des Deutschen Palästina-Vereins (1953-)* 124/2: 107–27.

Zomer, Elyze. 2018. *Corpus of Middle Babylonian and Middle Assyrian Incantations*. Leipziger Altorientalistische Studien 9. Wiesbaden: Harrassowitz Verlag.

Carolina López-Ruiz

The Networks of Ashtart-Aphrodite and the Archaic Mediterranean *Koiné*

The goddesses Aphrodite and Ashtart and their local equivalents acted as catalysts of cultural and economic exchange in the entire Mediterranean, in a crucial period when Phoenicians, Greeks, and others intensified and expanded their networks from the Levant and Cyprus to the Aegean, Italy, and Iberia. At least in the realm of the divine, stories and cult of female figures attribute them an important role as cultural and even economic mediators and enablers, even if real women are underrepresented in this role in myth and epic. This is due at least in part to authorial-literary constraints and the *mentalité* behind a literary culture that mostly excluded women from heroic action. Goddesses, on the other hand, were not constrained by these social boundaries, or even by gender stereotypes. Although Ashtart and Ishtar were invoked to protect and foster sexuality, fertility, and birth in general, they were also agents of prosperity in the male-dominated realm of trade and navigation. On the mythical plane, we can also think of Artemis and Athena in Greece, and Anat, Ashtart, and Ishtar in the Canaanite and Mesopotamian world, as hunter, soldier, and warrior figures respectively.[1] Thus goddesses, as opposed to female human figures, can more aptly bridge the male and female worlds and oversee aspects of society that integrated female actors in a world dominated by their male counterparts.

Leaving aside gender issues, my goal in this essay is to highlight these goddesses' place in the pan-Mediterranean commercial and colonial networks. Comparative mythology and archaeological data help us follow the trail of a feminine divine figure who had a major role in helping diverse communities structure their human social and economic relations. If we consider the divine realm, stories about Ishtar, Anat, Athena, even Aphrodite and Hera often form

1 Although the "Fertility" goddess label is not without its problems (Hackett 1989) as a blanket term, the connection of goddesses such as Aphrodite, Ashtart, and Ishtar with sexuality, the family realm, and motherhood is well established from cultic and literary sources (see comments below). On the other hand, Baal, Tarhun, Marduk, and other male weather-storm gods are related to the seasons and fertility of the land, and productive rain as opposed to the salty water and destructive force of the sea (e.g., for the theme of the storm god's combat with the sea, Ayali-Darshan 2020).

https://doi.org/10.1515/9781501514821-014

mythological clusters around which Greek and Near Eastern features overlap.[2] The following is a brief *tour de force* (by no means a complete study of this phenomenon), to show that in areas where Phoenicians, Greeks, and others encountered each other, the goddess Ashtart and her incarnations as Aphrodite, Tanit, Venus, and other local goddesses were often at the heart of the hybrid cultures of these communities, whether in cultic nodes or through mythology attached to the different areas.[3] Not surprisingly, the Phoenicians are intimately tied to this phenomenon. The figure of Herakles provides the closest, better-known, model for this sort of pan-Mediterranean network. As Herakles was assimilated to the Tyrian god Melqart (a form of Baal), in his Phoenician or Greek form his cult and his stories marked colonies and trading posts from east to west as a founding figure and divine patron. As the mythological Herakles travelled the Mediterranean he set an example for the explorers and conquerors to follow. But while the "networks of Melqart" have received some attention (Bonnet 1988; Malkin 2011: 119–41; Álvarez 2018) his female counterparts have not.

1 The Levant and Cyprus

Let us begin with the Levant and work our way towards the western Mediterranean. Well known among specialists in the Near East are the roles of Ishtar and Ashtart as patroness of sanctuaries, often linked to industrial areas, for instance harbors and smelting workshops, tied to the function of sanctuaries as nodes of economic exchange (Celestino and López-Ruiz 2016: 147, 212–13; Snell 1997). The Phoenician goddess Ashtart (in Greek "Astarte") was prominent in the main Phoenicians cities where she was revered also under local hypostases, normally as the consort of the principal male god, some form of the storm god Baal (e.g., overview in Xella 2019). Despite the scarce archaeological remains of Iron Age Phoenician temples, we still have ample epigraphical and archaeological testimonies of the goddess. At the sanctuary of Eshmoun outside Sidon (Bustan el-Sheikh), the healing god is paired with Ashtart and the goddess' throne, flanked with sphinxes, presides over the main monumental precinct and its

2 Studies of Aphrodite and her Near Eastern overlaps include Budin 2003; Cyrino 2010; Eisenfeld 2015; Currie 2016: esp. 160–78; López-Ruiz 2015: 378–80 (for Aphrodite's origins), 2016 (for Cyprus), 2022.

3 For the postcolonial concept of "hybridity" and "hybrid practices" applied to areas affected by cultural and economic contact in the ancient Mediterranean, see van Dommelen 2006; Hodos 2006.

healing pools. At Tyre, where the famous temple of Melqart dominated the religious landscape, and securely-identified ritual installations for the goddess are still lacking, the cult of Ashtart must have been strong as well; as a goddess that represents life and regeneration, she complemented the divine quality of Melqart, who underwent a ritual death and rebirth called *egersis* by Greco-Roman sources.[4] At Byblos, the fertility goddess was known as Baalat Gubal, "Lady of Byblos," whether a hypostasis of Ashtart or a goddess with separate origins and identity.[5]

But as it often happens, we have more evidence for Phoenician religion and ritual outside Lebanon, especially on Cyprus. When the Phoenicians settled there in the ninth century BCE or earlier, they encountered a prehistoric (Neolithic) goddess of fertility that dominated the island's cultic landscape. She was easily assimilated to Ashtart and later to Aphrodite (DCPP, s.v. "Astarté"; Young 2005).[6] The aniconic worship of the goddess at Paphos as a betyl also marks the Semitic traits of her cult, given the Phoenician tendency to aniconism (e.g., empty thrones, betyls, cippi, etc.) (Doak 2015). At Kition, Enkomi, and Paphos, major temples dating to the Late Bronze Age were now rebuilt and (re)dedicated to Ashtart as a goddess associated with metal work, a fundamental industry in Cyprus (the "copper island") and with seafaring, fundamental for Phoenician and Greek trade. Kition's sacred complex provides the best example of these aspects of her cult. Besides the typically-Levantine features of open-air altars, sacred pools, and gardens, the goddess is clearly association with harbors (a feature adopted by Aphrodite too; see below). Specifically, at Kition part of the temple complex in the Bamboula area lies next to the harbor ramparts that have been excavated. In turn, already in the Bronze Age building ("Temple 4") anchor stones had been used for the walls' foundations, and in later phases (Temple 1) the walls were engraved with depictions of sailing boats.

---

4 Paus. 10.4.6. According to Josephus the cult was established by Hiram I of Tyre (*AJ* 8.5.3, *Ap*. 1.118–19; cf. possible allusion in 1 Kings 18.27; cf. Eudoxus F284b). Some see this ritual as a harvest or "first fruits" festivals of the type attested more broadly in Syro-Palestine and in the Greek world. See Burkert 1985: 66–68; Stager 2014: 13–14; Lipiński 1995: 226–43.

5 For the "Lady of Byblos" as a proper name, see Zernecke 2013. In Philon of Byblos's cosmogony she is called Baaltis (Euseb. *Praep. evang.* 1.10.35), and appears as a sister of Ashtart and Rhea and identified with Dione, all of them wives of Kronos/El (*Praep. evang.* 1.10.22). See Attridge and Oden 1981: 88 nn. 100–101, pp. 91–92 n. 132. It is unclear whether this Dione is the same as the mother of Aphrodite in the *Iliad* (with Zeus).

6 She appears as "Wanassa" (Mycenaean for "Lady"), "Paphian," "Cypriot" (Kyprian), and Golgia in epigraphical sources, and not as "Aphrodite" until the fourth century (López-Ruiz 2016: 244–45).

Most significantly, the Cypriot goddess was since prehistory in association with a blacksmith god. This detail most evidently bridges the Phoenician and Greek traditions. A series of horned or smiting gods standing on bronze ingots ("ox-hide" shape ingots) have appeared in cult sites also associated with the fertility goddess (e.g., at Enkomi). The horned altars found at some of her cultic places (e.g., Kition) may also be linked with the horned male god, although the goddess' symbolic repertoire included the moon and its crescent "horns" since very early on. This "ingot-god," in any case, reflects a very old partnership between blacksmithing and fertility deities, which may lie behind the odd (but popular) Homeric story where Aphrodite is Hephaistos' wife, only mentioned once in the *Odyssey* (*Od.* 8.266–366).

2 The Aegean

The love/fertility goddess jumped from Cyprus and the Cypro-Phoenician realm to Greece in the Iron Age, a trajectory that was part of the Greeks' own narrative about the goddess' origins. In fact, Aphrodite is probably the divinity most consistently associated with the Near East in antiquity. Her affinity with other love/fertility goddesses, such as Mesopotamian Ishtar, Egyptian Isis, and Phoenician Ashtart is evident in mythology and iconography and is assumed without much problem in scholarship. But more interesting is in fact that from Hesiod to the *Homeric Hymns* and Herodotos, the Greeks themselves associated Aphrodite with Cyprus and the Levant (e.g., *Od.* 8.362–363; *Hom. Hymh Aphr.* 58–67; Hdt. 1.105.3; Diod. Sic. 5.75.5; Paus. 1.14.7). Herodotos, in so many words, states that the goddess was the same as Syro-Phoenician Ashtart and that she was imported by Phoenicians to Greece via Cyprus.[7] Deeply aware of and interested in the overlap between Near Eastern and Greek religions, throughout Book 2 Herodotos draws connections between Greek and Near Eastern gods (Hdt. 2.43–64; cf. López-Ruiz 2015: 371–73); there he traces the goddess to the cult of Aphrodite Ourania ("Heavenly Aphrodite") in Askalon in Syro-Palestine. According to him this was "the oldest of all the temples of the goddess, for even the temple in Cyprus originated from there. As for the one on Kythera, it was Phoenicians

7 For the early history of Aphrodite and her connection with earlier local fertility deities and Cyprus, see Budin 2003: chs. 5–6 for Cyprus; Cassio 2012: 414; Burkert 1985: 153; López-Ruiz 2015: 378–80. Other general studies are Pirenne-Delforge 1994; Cyrino 2010.

who founded it, who came from this same land of Syria" (Hdt. 1.105.3).[8] He also proposes a Phoenician presence at Thebes, Thera, and Thasos, although, unlike for Cyprus, no clear archaeological footprint of a long-term presence of Phoenicians has been detected so far in these sites (cf. Paus. 1.14.7, 3.22.1 on Kythera).

Aphrodite's two most common epithets in Greek epic are "Kypris" ("Cypriot"), "Kyprogeneia" ("Cyprus-born"), and "Kythereia." As we have seen, the Cypriot connection is well established and overlaps with the Cypro-Phoenician realm. The epithet "Kythereia," on the other hand, was since antiquity believed to point to her cultic transfer from Cyprus to the west, linking her to the island of Kythera, south of the Peloponnese. The oldest account of Aphrodite's origins in Hesiod's *Theogony* (*Th.* 185–206) already contains these elements: Aphrodite emerges from the foam produced by Ouranos' genitals, after his son Kronos had thrown them into the sea, and as soon as she appears she goes first to Kythera and then reaches Cyprus (*Th.* 192–193); here Hesiod reverses the east-to-west trajectory, placing the Greek island first on her journey, and also uses the geographical points to explain her epithets "Cypris" and "Kythereia."

The entire birth-of-Aphrodite passage in Hesiod is a bridge between Greek and Near Eastern traditions in more than one way: first, the episode is framed by what is probably the most striking Near Eastern motif in the *Theogony*, the castration of the Sky (attested in Hurro-Hittite mythology), from which Aphrodite is a result; this bloody act separated Heaven and Earth and began the succession of gods (López-Ruiz 2010: 87–94). This specific passage is also a feast of etymologies and puns, including the alleged connection of the name of Aphrodite with *aphros* "foam," most likely a popular etymology.[9] Without a Greek name, and given that she does not appear in Mycenaean texts, scholars agree that Aphrodite may very well be an "imported" goddess from the Levant or Cyprus, as the Greeks themselves thought. A Semitic origin of her Greek name, however, has not been convincingly established.[10] On the other hand, her epithet "Kythereia" might hide a Northwest Semitic etymology. As it has been argued, her title may reflect a pre-Hesiodic tradition from the Late Bronze Age or early Iron Age, in

---

8 Translations are mine unless noted. At 8.5.2 Pausanias follows a different tradition, attributing the sanctuary at Paphos to the Arcadian Agapenor on his return from Troy. In *de Dea Syria* 4–6, Lucian distinguishes between the cult of Astarte/Ashtart in Sidon and that of Aphrodite of Byblos (on the "The Lady of Byblos," see below).

9 The name would be formed from the older Indo-European root for "foam" or "cloud" (cf. Indic **abrha*) and the suffix *dj-* (cf. Greek *dios/dia*), related to both "brightness" and the name of Zeus. Cyrino 2010: 23–26.

10 West postulated the origin of the name "Aphrodite" in a Cypro-Phoenician cult title *prazit* ("or the like"), from a hypothetical Canaanite word, cf. Hebrew *perazah*, "village," so "Lady of the Villages." West 2000: 138. Others propose a connection between the names of Aphrodite and

which she was paired with the Northwest Semitic artisan and blacksmithing god, Kothar (López-Ruiz 2022). The Canaanite *kṯr* is most familiar as the Ugaritic figure Kothar-wa-Hasis (literally "Skilled and Wise"), who appears in the epics fashioning weaponry for heroes as well as a building a palace for Baal and making furniture and bowls for Athirat/Asherah, the mother of the gods and spouse of El/Ilu: "the Skilled one goes up to the bellows, with tongs in the hands of Hasis. He casts silver, he pours gold . . . "[11] Centuries later, this craftsman god was present in the Phoenician world. Although we have very little by way of Phoenician literature preserved, we know he survived as a mythological "culture figure" until Roman times, as attested in fragmentary Phoenician cosmogonies.[12]

Finally, other motifs surrounding Hesiod's Aphrodite reveal Levantine aspects. Her birth from Ouranos, the sky in Hesiod's version, which is absent from the Homeric tradition,[13] seems to be a narrative explanation of the "heavenly" attribute that Ashtart and Aphrodite shared. The Phoenician goddess was invoked as "Queen of Heaven" in the Levant, and Aphrodite, as Herodotos emphasizes, was known as Ourania ("heavenly") in the Greek world, particularly in contexts where she is associated with the Phoenician origins of her cult.[14] Hesiod's verses also play with the goddess' relationship with the sea, reflected in her later epithets "Limenia," "Euploia," "Pontia" ("of the harbor," "of the good navigation," "of the sea"), which is also a prominent feature in Ashtart's Northwest Semitic imagery. In other words, Hesiod may or may not have been aware of the Ashtart-like aspects interwoven into his account, but all the same his myth accounted for the goddess' popular associations with Sky, Cyprus, the sea, and sexuality, all features shared by the Greek and Near Eastern goddesses.

Ashtart, although through unclear linguistic mechanisms (just by general similarity): Dowden 2007: 48; Cyrino 2010: 26. Cf. West's (2000: 135–36) dismissal of the possible equation.

11 *Baal Cycle*. CAT 1.4.1 Translation by Smith and Pitard 2009 (with commentary at 399–426).

12 BNJ 790 F2 (Eusebios *P.E.* 1.10.11–12). Philo's Khousarthis in P.E. 1.10.43 (BNJ 790 F10) is probably another variant of the same. See Attridge and Oden 1981; Kaldellis and López-Ruiz 2009. "Chousor" or "the opener" appears as a cosmic figure in the cosmogony attributed to Mochos: BNJ 784 F4 (Damaskios, *De principiis* 125 c [I p. 323 Ruelle; III 166 Westerink]; Eudemos in Wherly fr. 150). See López-Ruiz 2009.

13 In Homer and the *Homeric Hymn* she is assumed to be the daughter of Zeus, but her mother is Dione in one passage (*Il.* 5.170–171), which has received much attention for its Near Eastern parallels (see footnote 5 above). Cf. also Apollodoros' *Library* 1.3.1.

14 The epithet is attested in epigraphical and literary sources, e.g., Hdt. 1.105.3, Pausanias 1.14.7 on a Ourania in Athens and her cult in Cyprus and the Levant (probably from Herodotos). In Plato's *Symposium* (180d) Phaedrus distinguishes between the elevated and the carnal/popular love, through the figures of Aphrodite "Ourania" and Aphrodite "Pandemos." For the cult of Aphrodite in Athens, see Rosenzweig 2004.

The overlap between cultic and mythological aspects of the Greek and Near Eastern love goddesses are abundantly attested beyond Hesiod. For the sake of space, I will only mention the instances in which Aphrodite is portrayed as a "Mistress of Beasts" (*potnia therôn*), both in iconography and in the *Hymn to Aphrodite* (68–74). This quality, evident in the case of Ashtart and Ishtar, is in the Greek world more frequently attributed to Artemis. The depiction of Aphrodite in the battlefield, emulating Anat or Ishtar, is also awkward.[15] Moreover, besides her tie to the sea (see above), the Greek goddess also shares with Ashtart her association with birds, especially doves and sparrows (West 1997: 56–57; Budin 2003; Currie 2016: 167). Finally, Aphrodite is intimately linked with a "dying and rising" lover, Adonis, who situates her squarely in the Syro-Palestinian realm. Both the figure of Adonis, with his Semitic name, and the story-pattern, mirror the Babylonian traditions regarding Inanna/Ishtar and Dumuzi/Tammuz.[16] In fact, in the very multi-cultural scenario of Cyprus, local stories combined these elements, as we see in a Syriac text where the love/fertility goddess (called Baaltis, i.e., Baalat/Ashtart) is entangled in a tragic love story involving Tamuz and Kothar (Adonis and Hephaistos).[17] In this odd text, the craftsman and metalworking god appears as a partner of the fertility goddess, in an explicitly Cypro-Phoenician context.

As we have seen, the mythology about Aphrodite's birth, the Greek's perception of her origins in the East, and her general qualities, all make her a goddess who represents the Greek and Near Eastern encounter of cultures and religion. On the other hand, her ties with metalwork and Hephaistos (and his Semitic counterpart Kothar) situates her even more at the center of cultural exchange. Crafts, metalwork, and trade gave impetus to the expansion of the

---

15 E.g., *Il.* 5.352–430, a passage filled with Near Eastern overtones, especially compared with the theme of Gilgamesh and Ishtar in Tablet 6 of the epic: West 1997: 361–62; Burkert 1992: 96–99; Cassio 2012: 418–23.

16 Adonis' cult flourished at Byblos and Cyprus and spread to the Greek world, especially Athens and Alexandria: Burkert 1985: 177; Parker 1996: 160; cf. Brown 1995: 245; West 1997: 57. Lucian, *de Dea Syria* 6, links the "Aphrodite of Byblos" with the rites of Adonis. The alleged practice of sacred prostitution, generally associated with Ishtar's and Ashtarte's cult, is still not well understood and much debated, and is, in any case, not so-far attested for the Greek world, excepting in the one allusion in Strabo 8.6.21 to the temple of Aphrodite at Corinth.

17 The Syriac text is preserved in a single manuscript in Hebrew script. It is attributed to the second-century CE bishop and apologist Melito of Sardis, and although some scholars believe the text is based on a Greek source, it ultimately draws on Aramaic tradition. See Van Rompay 2011 for more details; Brown 1995: 245. Cf. Franklin 2015: 468–86 on Cypro-Byblian interfaces especially in relation to Kothar and Kinyras. On Kythereia and Kothar, see López-Ruiz 2022.

Phoenician and Greek networks across the Mediterranean. It is not by coincidence that these goddesses mark many of the nodal points of these networks. The economic importance of sanctuaries as safe havens for commercial agreements and international displays of wealth need little emphasis. And in the Greek world, it is often feminine divine figures who oversee the major international sanctuaries and economic centers: besides Aphrodite, we can highlight the role of Hera as patron of important centers of exchange (another goddess that bears aspects of Hathor and Isis), as best exemplified in the great Heraion of Samos, the Argive Heraion, and the Heraion at Perachora in the Gulf of Corinth. At Corinth, a hub of commerce in the archaic period, the most famous sanctuary was that of Aphrodite on the steep acropolis (Akro-Corinth); and at Sparta the sanctuary of Artemis Ortheia was the recipient of ivories and terracottas that show Levantine influence and suggest the presence of Phoenician workshops in the "*uber*-Greek" polis. These are a few cases in which the Love Goddess encapsulates the intimate contact with the Near East, whether this is reflected in archaeological sites or mythologies and iconography. The mechanism of *interpetatio* or mutual identification of these goddesses (e.g., Ashtart as a Phoenician form of Hera, Aphrodite, or Artemis), helped open up a space for mutual trust among these communities in contact, which allowed commercial interaction and collaboration (Parker 2017). As in the case of the hubs dedicated to Melqart/Baal and the Greek Herakles, the sense of an identifiable and respectable divine supervision facilitated transactions and agreements across cultures and languages.

3 The Central and Western Mediterranean

Moving further west, we find extraordinary testimonies of the assimilations of this goddess precisely at key centers for local-Levantine interactions. A shared feature of sites associated with the cult of Ashtart is their location along the coast often by or overlooking the sea (Bloch-Smith 2014: 167, 191). At Pyrgi in coastal Etruria, a unique inscription in Etruscan and Phoenician languages formalizes a shared dedication, inscribed in gold around 500 BCE, of a sanctuary to both Uni (akin to Roman Juno) and Ashtart. The sanctuary seemingly served as the main sacred space in this harbor-town at the gateways to the Etruscan metal-rich region. In Tas-Silġ, in Malta, layers of cultic installations and votive inscriptions also illustrate how "merchants and travellers celebrated the multifaceted Astarte, the goddess on the move and the goddess of the land, or (. . .) the goddess of the sea and agricultural production all in one" (Vella and

Anastasi 2019: 563; cf. Lipiński 1995: 153–54; Day 2002: 131–32). Something similar may have occurred at the famous Greco-Semitic shrine at Kommos, on the southern shore of Crete, which linked routes from the Levant, Cyprus, Egypt, and Greece (Shaw 1989).

With the foundation of Carthage, Ashtart finds a new home in North Africa, both as the Tyrian Ashtart and under the guise of the goddess Tanit.[18] The foundation of the new metropolis itself is marked by the goddess' supervision: the famous Elissa (Virgil's Dido), one of the single cases of a female city-founder, was wife to the Tyrian Acerbas, a priest of "Hercules" (the Roman rendering of Melqart). After her husband is murdered by her own brother king Pygmalion of Tyre, Elissa and her retinue flees westwards. Tellingly, their first stop is Cyprus, where the Phoenician "expatriates" are joined by the priest of Jupiter/Baal and devotees of Ashtart, who will help them start the new city (Justin, *Epitome of Trogus* 18.5). Even if she is not said to be a priestess of Ashtart, she is a powerful queenly figure and city founder – we can almost see the couple as representatives on earth of the Melqart-Ashtart pair. It is following this tradition that Virgil makes Juno the main goddess in Carthage in his own version of the foundation, written under Augustus: for the Romans Juno (Greek Hera) represented Tanit-Ashtart (we already noted their identification in the Pyrgi inscription). For Virgil she was the archenemy of Aeneas and Rome and the protector of Carthage. Aeneas, in turn, was protected by Venus (the Roman version of Aphrodite), who was his mother according to Greco-Roman myth, initiating a genealogy that branched up to Augustus' own family. The Romans somehow split the qualities of the Love Goddess and the Queen of Heaven into two goddesses, Venus and Juno, but it is clear that both are of paramount importance in the foundation legend of both Carthage and Rome. It is around a colonization and love story that Virgil choses to articulate his epic, capturing in a past affair the future love-hate relationship between Rome and Carthage (*Aeneid* 1.418–457). We can follow the colonial and trading "networks of Ashtart" to Sardinia and Sicily too, where the sacred precincts called "tophets" were dedicated to Baal Hammon and Ashtart or Tanit, and where the temple of Ashtart at Eryx in northwest Sicily became in a highly contested site, caught in between Phoenician, Greek, and Roman cultures; indeed the Romans appropriated it as a temple to Venus and were prompt to build a temple of Venus Ericina in Rome itself during the Second Punic War; the timing makes clear the recognition of the

18 Tanit is attested in the Punic (i.e., western) realm, while in the Phoenician mainland only in Serepta so far. Her name is perhaps related to "lamenting" (*tny*): Lipiński 1995: 199–200; DCCP s.v. "Tanit."

Punic goddess and their anxiety to gain her favor (as Venus) (Lietz 2012; Miles 2010: 403–404 n. 50), a type of contest better attested in regard to the cult and propagandistic use of Herakles as embodying Greek-Roman Herakles/Hercules and Phoenician Melqart (Miles 2010: 99).[19]

Finally, the evidence takes us as far west as Iberia, where we also find the pan-Mediterranean phenomenon of the cult of Ashtart-Aphrodite and her local versions. Again, this extensive overlap with colonial and economic networks is only comparable to that of Melqart. In Iberia, native and Phoenician cultures met since the ninth century BCE and interacted with special intensity during the eighth and seventh centuries. From the island of Ibiza to the Guadalquivir Valley the nodal points of exchange are marked by cults that feature a Melqart-Baal type of god and a fertility goddess generally identified with Ashtart, sometimes explicitly, through inscriptions, and more often just by her iconography: we can single out the votive dedication to Ashtart from El Carambolo near Seville; the graffiti scratched on elephant tusks transported in a ship wrecked in the eastern coast of Spain (Bajo de la Campana); and the ubiquitous iconography of fertility and life-death cycles, such as rosettes and lotus flowers (e.g., Carmona *pithoi*, ivory "palettes") (Navarro Ortega 2021). Also associated with Ashtart and Melqart are the boat models deposited in shrines and the depiction of boats (model from El Carambolo, ivory box from El Turuñuelo), providing a nice parallel with the iconography of boats in the Cypriot temples mentioned at the beginning of this essay. In turn, altars in "ox/bull-hide" shape have appeared in several sacred spaces in areas where Phoenician influence run deep in the archaic period (the area known in antiquity as Tartessos), again pointing to the local assimilations of Baal and Ashtart in areas of colonial and commercial contact, as the gods were in the Levant associated with bulls and the crescent-moon's "horns" as symbols of fertility (Celestino and López-Ruiz 2016: 214–66).

4 Final Remarks

Although it is beyond the scope of this essay (and of my expertise) to hypothesize on the implications of this pattern for our understanding of gender roles in the ancient Mediterranean, I hope to have shown that Ashtart and her iterations became mediating figures for the cultural transactions that transformed the

---

19 Bloch Smith (2014) offers a good overview of the cultic evidence for Ashtart in and outside the Levant, with some discussion of the goddess' overlap with other female divine entities.

Mediterranean in the eighth-seventh centuries BCE, when the first global pan-Mediterranean culture emerged.

To close on a less dry note, however, I offer a final reflection inspired by the representation of Aphrodite in two ancient sources. In Plato we find the idea that there were two kinds of Aphrodites, the "Heavenly" one (Ourania) and the popular one (Pandemos).[20] I want to suggest that, in these networks, such a goddess, often mapped onto local fertility or queenly goddesses, possessed both the authoritative and the mundane, pragmatic qualities that appealed to those involved in economic transactions. She also represented and stimulated the human interactions (including men and women) that allowed for these communities to adjust and grow, economically and culturally, from the mixed, multilingual, multicultural family nucleus to the larger social group, which coalesced around the household, the workshop, the temple, and the harbor. Women were not, moreover, alien to the world of "small commerce," as they constituted essential consumers of jewelry, ivories, perfumes, amulets, cosmetics and oils, pottery for cooking and display, and were instrumental themselves in the production of textiles and possibly other domestic and luxury items that entered the cycle of economic exchange. This goddess and her iterations were, in other words, essential for the wellbeing of the household and its integration in the community. We can imagine that their narratives were at home in the realm of domestic storytelling, as well as of household rituals, from weddings and childbearing to rites of passage and female-led funerary rites. To this "small feminine world" we are transported in a passage from the Homeric *Hymn to Aphrodite*, when Aphrodite herself tells Anchises, Aeneas' father:

> Your language as well as mine I know well; for a Trojan nurse raised me in the palace, who reared me since I was a small child, taking me from my dead mother's arms. So it is that I also know your language well. (*Hymn to Aphrodite* 113–116)

As the "Queen of Heaven" interacted and made love with Anchises, conceiving the founder of the future Roman empire, she blurred the lines between the realms of the divine and the human, the political and the domestic, and indeed the Greek and the foreign.

20 Plato's *Symposium* (180d). See note 14 above. Cupid and Venus also act in both heavenly ways and mundane ways as they manipulate Psyche "the Soul" in Apuleius, *Golden Ass*, books 4–6. For this and other Aphrodite-Venus related stories, see selection of texts in López-Ruiz 2017: 383–467.

Abbreviations

Abbreviations for Greek of Roman authors follow the Oxford Classical Dictionary conventions: Hornblower, Simon, and Antony Spawforth (eds.). 2005. *Oxford Classical Dictionary*, 3rd ed. Oxford). https://oxfordre.com/classics/page/abbreviation-list/

BNJ *Brill's New Jacoby* (*Fragments of Ancient Historians*, editor in chief: Ian Worthington). http://referenceworks.brillonline.com/entries/brill-s-new-jacoby

DCPP Lipiński, E. (ed.) 1992. *Dictionnaire de la Civilisation Phénicienne et Punique*. Paris.

Bibliography

Álvarez Martí-Aguilar, Manuel. 2018. The Network of Melqart: Tyre, Gadir, Carthage, and the Founding God. Pp. 113–50 in *Warlords, War, and Interstate Relations in the Ancient* Mediterranean, *404 BC-AD* 14, ed. Toni Ñaco and Fernando López-Sánchez. Leiden: Brill.

Attridge, Harold W. and Robert A. Oden, Jr. 1981. *Philo of Byblos:* The Phoenician History. *Introduction, Critical Text, Translation, Notes*. Washington, DC: The Catholic Biblical Association of America.

Ayali-Darshan, Noga. 2020. *The Storm-God and the Sea. The Origin, Versions, and Diffusion of a Myth throughout the Ancient Near East.* Tübingen: Mohr Siebeck.

Bloch-Smith, Elizabeth. 2014. Archaeological and Inscriptional Evidence for Phoenician Astarte. Pp. 167–94 in *Transformations of a Goddess: Ishtar-Astarte-Aphrodite*, ed. David T. Sugimoto. Fribourg: Academic Press; Göttingen: Vandenhoeck and Ruprecht.

Bonnet, Corinne. 1988. *Melqart: Cultes et mythes de l'Héraclès tyrien en Méditerranée.* Studia Phoenicia 8. Leuven: Peeters.

Brown, John P. 1995. *Israel and Hellas*. Volume 1. BZAW 231. Berlin and New York: De Gruyter.

Budin, Stephanie. 2003. *The Origin of Aphrodite*. Bethesda, MD: CDL Press.

Burkert, Walter. 1985. *Greek Religion*. Cambridge, MA: Harvard University Press.

Burkert, Walter. 1992. *The Orientalizing Revolution: Near Eastern Influence on Greek Culture in the Early Archaic Age*, translated by Margaret E. Pinder and Walter Burkert. Cambridge, MA: Harvard University Press.

Burkert, Walter. 2004. *Babylon, Memphis, Persepolis: Eastern Contexts of Greek Culture*. Cambridge, MA: Harvard University Press.

Cassio, Albio Caesare. 2012. Kypris, Kythereia and the Fifth Book of the *Iliad*. Pp. 413–26 in *Homeric Contexts: Neoanalysis and the Interpretation of Oral Poetry*, ed. Franco Montanari, Antonios Rengakos, and Christos Tsagalis. Berlin and Boston: De Gruyter.

Celestino Pérez, Sebastián and Carolina López-Ruiz. 2016. *Tartessos and the Phoenicians in Iberia*. Oxford: Oxford University Press.

Currie, Bruno. 2016. *Homer's Allusive Art*. Oxford: Oxford University Press.

Cyrino, Monica S. 2010. *Aphrodite. Gods and Heroes of the Ancient World*. London and New York: Routledge.

Day, John. 2002. *Yahweh and the Gods and Goddesses of Canaan*. Sheffield: Bloomsbury.

Doak, Brian R. 2015. *Phoenician Aniconism in its Mediterranean and Near Eastern Contexts*. Atlanta, GA: SBL Press.

Dowden, Ken. 2007. Olympian Gods, Olympian Pantheon. Pp. 41–55 in *A Companion to Greek Religion*, ed. Daniel Ogden. Malden, MA: Wiley-Blackwell.
Eisenfeld, Hanne. 2015. Ishtar Rejected: Reading a Mesopotamian Goddess in the *Homeric Hymn to Aphrodite*. *Archiv für Religionsgeschichte* 16.1: 133–62.
Franklin, John C. 2015. *Kinyras the Divine Lyre*. Center for Hellenic Studies 70. Cambridge, MA: Harvard University Press.
Hackett, Jo Ann. 1989. Can a Sexist Model Liberate Us? Ancient Near Eastern "Fertility" Goddesses. *Journal of Feminist Studies in Religion* 5.1: 65–76.
Hodos, Tamar. 2006. *Local Responses to Colonization in the Iron Age Mediterranean*. London and New York: Routledge.
Kaldellis, Anthony and Carolina López-Ruiz. 2009. (BNJ 790) Philon of Byblos. In *Brill's New Jacoby* (online edition), ed. Ian Worthington.
Lietz, Beatrice. 2012. *La dea di Erice e la sua diffusione nel Mediterraneo: un culto tra Fenici, Greci e Romani*. Pisa: Edizioni della Normale.
Lipiński, Edward. 1995. *Dieux et déesses de l'univers phénicien et punique*. Leuven: Peeters.
López-Ruiz, Carolina. 2009. (BNJ 784) Laitos (Mochos). In *Brill's New Jacoby* (online edition), ed. Ian Worthington.
López-Ruiz, Carolina. 2010. *When the Gods Were Born: Greek Cosmogonies and the Near East*. Cambridge, MA: Harvard University Press.
López-Ruiz, Carolina. 2015. Gods: Origins. Pp. 369–82 in *The Oxford Handbook of Greek Religion*, ed. Esther Eidinow and Julia Kindt. Oxford-New York: Oxford University Press.
López-Ruiz, Carolina. 2016. "Religión en Chipre/Religion in Cyprus. Pp. 81–90 (English 243–47) in La colección chipriota del Museo de Montserrat, ed. Javier Uriach. Barcelona: Museu de Montserrat.
López-Ruiz, Carolina (ed.). 2017. *Gods, Heroes, and Monsters: A Sourcebook of Greek, Roman, and the Near Eastern Myths in Translation*. 2nd revised edition. Oxford and New York: Oxford University Press.
López-Ruiz, Carolina. 2022. From Kothar to Kythereia: Exploring the Northwest Semitic Past of Aphrodite. Pp. 253–373 in *"Like 'Ilu Are You Wise": Studies in Northwest Semitic Languages and Literatures in Honor of Dennis G. Pardee*, ed. H. H. Hardy II, Joseph Lam, and Eric D. Reymond. Chicago: The Oriental Institute.
Malkin, Irad. 2011. *A Small Greek World: Networks in the Ancient Mediterranean*. Oxford: Oxford University Press.
Miles, Richard. 2010. *Carthage Must Be Destroyed: The Rise and Fall of an Ancient Civilization*. London: Penguin.
Navarro Ortega, Ana D. 2021. *Astarté en el extremo occidente: la diosa de El Carambolo*. Seville: Universidad de Sevilla.
Parker, Robert. 1996. *Athenian Religion: A History*. Oxford: Oxford University Press.
Parker, Robert. 2017. *Greek Gods Abroad: Names, Natures, and Transformations*. Oakland, CA: University of California Press.
Pirenne-Delforge, Vinciane. 1994. *L'Aphrodite grecque*. Kernos suppl. vol. IV. Athens and Liège: Presses universitaires de Liège.
Rosenzweig, Rachel. 2004. *Worshipping Aphrodite: Art and Cult in Classical Athens*. Ann Arbor: The University of Michigan Press.
Shaw, Joseph W. 1989. Phoenicians in Southern Crete. *American Journal of Archaeology* 93: 165–83.

Smith, Mark S. and Wayne Pitard. 2009. *Ugaritic Baal Cycle, Volume 2: Introduction with Text, Translation and Commentary of KTU/CAT 1.3–1.4*. Leiden: Brill.
Snell, Daniel C. 1997. *Life in the Ancient Near East: 3100–332 BCE*. New Haven: Yale University Press.
Stager, Lawrence. 2014. *Rites of Spring in the Carthaginian Tophet*. Eighth BABESH Byvanck Lecture. Leiden: The Babesch Foundation.
van Dommelen, Peter. 2006. The Orientalizing Phenomenon: Hybridity and Material Culture in the Western Mediterranean. Pp. 135–52 in *Debating Orientalization: Multidisciplinary Approaches to Change in the Ancient Mediterranean*. Monographs in Mediterranean Archaeology 10, ed. Corinna Riva and Nicholas Vella. London and Oakville: Equinox.
Van Rompay, Lucas. 2011. Meliton the Philosopher. Pp. 284–85 in *The Gorgias Encyclopedic Dictionary of the Syriac Heritage*, ed. Sebastian P. Brock, Aaron M. Butts, George A. Kiraz, and Lucas van Rompay. Piscataway, NJ: Gorgias Press.
Vella, Nicholas and Maxine Anastasi. 2019. Malta and Gozo. Pp. 553–68 in *The Oxford Handbook of the Phoenician and Punic Mediterranean*, ed. Carolina López-Ruiz and Brian R. Doak. Oxford: Oxford University Press.
West, Martin L. 1997. *The East Face of Helicon: West Asiatic Elements in Greek Poetry and Myth*. Oxford: Oxford University Press.
West, Martin L. 2000. The Name of Aphrodite. *Glotta* 76: 133–38.
Xella, Paolo. 2019. Religion. Pp. 273–92 in *Oxford Handbook of the Phoenician and Punic Mediterranean*, ed. Carolina López-Ruiz and Brian R. Doak. Oxford: Oxford University Pres.
Young, Philip H. 2005. The Cypriot Aphrodite Cult: Paphos, Rantidi, and Saint Barnabas. *Journal of Near Eastern Studies* 64: 23–44.
Zernecke, Anna E. 2013. The Lady of the Titles: The Lady of Byblos and the Search for her 'True Name.' *Die Welt des Orients* 43: 226–42.

Nozomu Kawai

The Lioness Goddess Statuary from the Rock-Cut Chambers at Northwest Saqqara and Their Cult in Middle Kingdom Egypt

1 Introduction

The excavation by the Japanese archaeological mission from Waseda University at a rocky outcrop in Northwest Saqqara yielded a number of terracotta and clay statues in two rock-cut chambers on the southeastern slope of the outcropping.[1] They were found with fragments of wooden statues, a number of Middle Kingdom pottery sherds, and plant micro remains. The most distinguished statuary among them are those representing a lioness goddess, which will be the main topic of this article.

Four terracotta statues and two clay statues depicting either a lioness goddess or lioness were found in a rock-cut chamber, while the remaining clay lioness goddess statues were found in a separate rock-cut chamber. Notably, one of the terracotta statues was inscribed with the Horus name and prenomen of Khufu, along with the prenomen of Pepy I. They were found with Middle Kingdom pottery, but the statues themselves were apparently repaired several times in antiquity.

In this article, I will reconstruct the life history of these lioness goddess statues from the Fourth Dynasty to the end of the Middle Kingdom and relate it

1 This paper is a fully revised version of the papers presented earlier at: the international symposium "Sakhmet Ominipotent" in Luxor, Egypt organized by Hourig Sourouzian and Betsy M. Bryan in March, 2017; the workshop on Women's Religious and Economic Roles in Antiquity at Chuo University in November, 2017; as well as an invited lecture at the symposium "Goden van Sakkara" at the National Museum of Antiquities in Leiden in November, 2018. All of the papers are slightly different, but I have combined and expanded upon them in this single article. I am grateful to Dr. Hourig Sourouzian and Prof. Betsy M. Bryan for inviting me to the symposium and to Prof. Fumi Karahashi for inviting me to the workshop and to contribute the article to this volume. Thanks are due to Dr. Lara Weiss for inviting me to present a lecture for the precious symposium at the National Museum of Antiquities, Leiden.

I would like to thank Prof. Betsy M. Bryan, Dr. Hourig Sourouzian, and Dr. Kazumitsu Takahashi for reading the manuscript and providing invaluable comments. Thanks are due to Mr. Nicholas Brown for improving my English manuscript. Finally, I would like to thank Prof. Sakuji Yoshimura, President at Higashi Nippon International University for giving me the opportunity to study and publish the material from the excavation at Northwest Saqqara.

https://doi.org/10.1515/9781501514821-015

to the cult of the lioness goddess in this part of the Memphite Necropolis. First, I will explain the archaeological context of the lioness goddess statuary with the other associated finds. Second, I will describe their style, date, reuse, collapse or destruction, ancient restorations, rearrangement and ritual burial. Finally, I will propose the nature of the cult of lioness goddess at this remote outcropping at Northwest Saqqara.

2 Excavations at a Rocky Outcropping at Northwest Saqqara

Our excavation site is situated approximately 1.5 kilometers to the northwest of the Serapeum in Saqqara (Figures 1 and 2). The presence of archaeological remains at this remote outcropping was unknown until we were granted permission to work there by the former Supreme Council of Antiquities in 1991. Since then, a Japanese mission from Waseda University has been conducting excavations at this site. Due to the shape of this outcropping, stretching in an east-west direction, colleagues of the Czech Mission called it the "Lion Hill." It would be reasonable to compare the hill to the statue of the recumbent lioness that are discussed later on.

Excavations at the site revealed a number of important archaeological remains and artifacts in this remote outcropping (Figures 2 and 3). This includes a layered stone structure and its substructure dating to around the end of the Early Dynastic Period and the early Third Dynasty in the Old Kingdom (Yoshimura, Kawai, and Kashiwagi 2005; Yoshimura and Kawai 2006; Kawai 2011a), a Middle Kingdom rock-cut chamber (Yoshimura, Kawai, and Kashiwagi 2005), a mud-brick structure constructed by Amenhotep II and subsequently modified by Thutmose IV (Yoshimura and Takamiya 2000; Yoshimura and Saito 2003), the mortuary chapel of Prince Khaemwaset (Yoshimura and Takamiya 2000; Takamiya, Kashiwagi, and Yoshimura 2011), and the tomb chapel of his daughter Isisnofret (Kawai 2011b and 2014). They indicate that this outcropping was a very significant place throughout the Pharaonic period.

Figure 1: Map of Abusir and Saqqara ©Institute of Egyptology, Waseda University/Institute of Egyptian Archaeology, Higashi-Nippon International University.

Figure 2: The rocky outcropping at Northwest Saqqara. Photo by the author. ©Nozomu Kawai.

3 The Archaeological Context of the Statuary of Lioness Goddess

The main focus of this article is the lioness goddess statuary found in two rock-cut chambers designated A and B on the southeastern slope of the outcropping (Figure 3).

Chamber A consists of a forecourt and a subterranean chamber (Figures 3–5) (Yoshimura, Kawai, and Kashiwagi 2005: 388–89). The rectangular forecourt measures about 3 meters wide and 5 meters long. There are four small postholes in the floor, probably made for something like a temporary kiosk. Beside the rear wall of the forecourt, a rectangular shallow pit was cut, leading to the entrance of the subterranean chamber. It is composed of two rooms: a transverse hall and an inner hall, arranged in a T-shaped plan. The chamber is completely undecorated. The entrance passage was sealed by a pile of limestone blocks covered with gypsum plaster from the inside, but the upper left part had already been breached. The clearance inside and the forecourt of the rock cut chamber revealed a number of statue fragments made of clay, terracotta, and wood, as well as Middle Kingdom pottery and botanical remains. No human remains were found in the chamber.

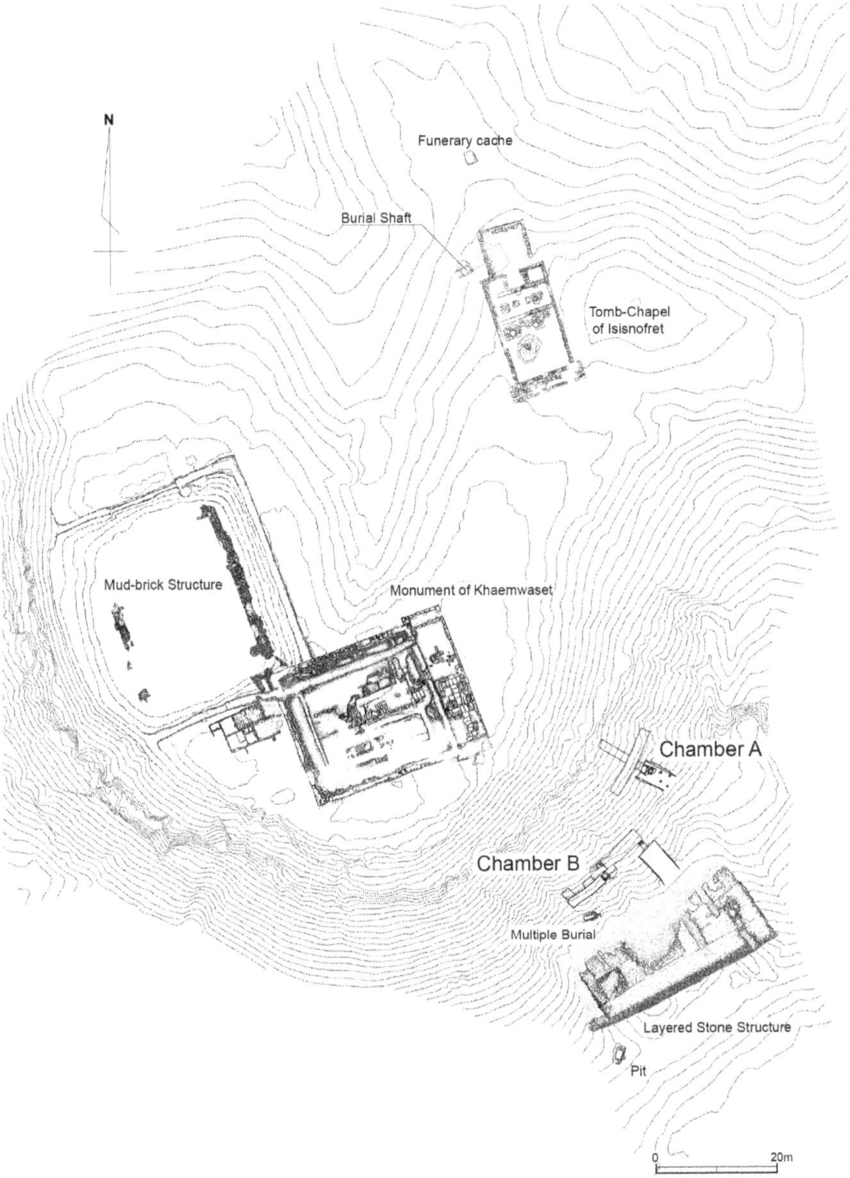

Figure 3: Map of the site ©Institute of Egyptology, Waseda University/Institute of Egyptian Archaeology, Higashi-Nippon International University.

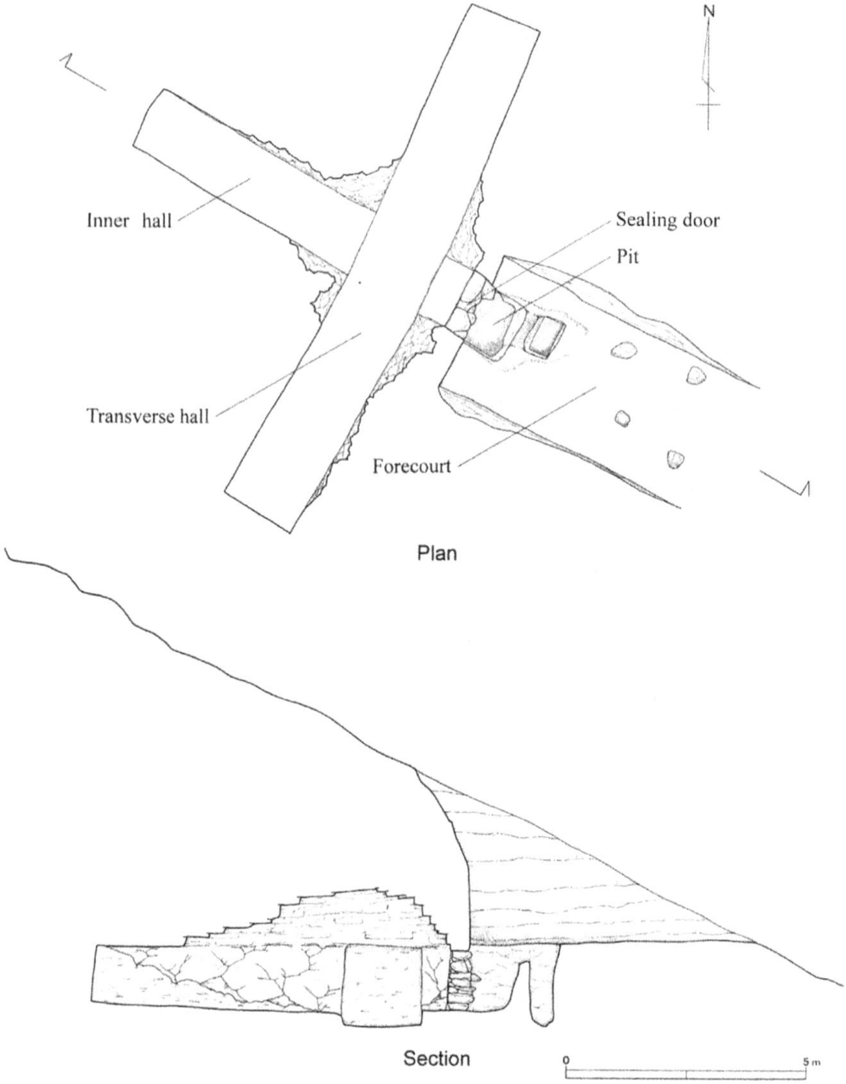

Figure 4: Plan and section of Chamber A ©Institute of Egyptology, Waseda University/Institute of Egyptian Archaeology, Higashi-Nippon International University.

When the terracotta or clay statue fragments were reconstructed, it was found that four of the statues represented a standing lioness goddess, two were recumbent lions, and the remainder were human busts with their hands on their heads. It was not possible to reconstruct a single statue from the fragments of wooden statues recovered from the excavation (Figure 6). Notably, a

Figure 5: The forecourt and entrance of Chamber A ©Institute of Egyptology, Waseda University/Institute of Egyptian Archaeology, Higashi-Nippon International University.

wooden statuette of a naked child-king wearing the *nemes* headdress and putting a finger to his mouth was found; similar to the small figures of child-kings attached to the back slab of a lioness goddess statue.

The pottery assemblage from the Chamber A dates to the Middle Kingdom, from the Twelfth Dynasty to the end of the Thirteenth Dynasty.[2] One especially diagnostic Middle Kingdom pottery type discovered was a small cup known as "Pyramid Ware." It is skillfully thrown and shaped, coated all over with a fine thick red ochre coating, and polished to a weak shine, even under its base. Susan Allen (1998: 47–48) argues that this ware developed from the reign of Senwosret II onward into the Thirteenth Dynasty. It is also notable that most of

2 We dated the pottery sherd found in this chamber from the Twelfth Dynasty to the early Thirteenth Dynasty (Kawai, Takahashi, and Yazawa 2012: 150 Figure 3). David Aston (2020: 3), however, suggested that the pottery sherds found in this chamber could date from the Twelfth Dynasty on the basis of the excavations at Kom Rabi'a in Memphis (Bourriau and Gallorini 2016: 39–206). I would like to thank Dr. David Aston for sending a copy of his article.

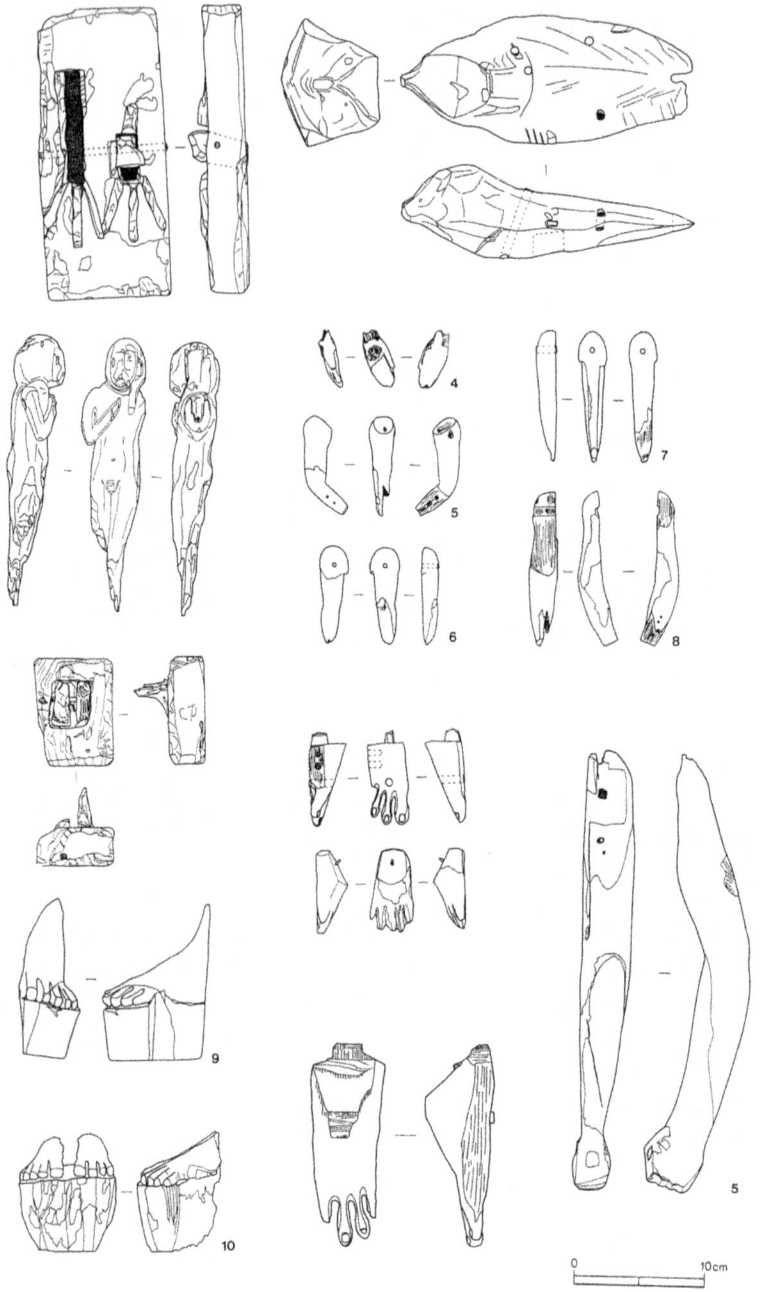

Figure 6: Fragments of wooden statues from Chamber A ©Institute of Egyptology, Waseda University/Institute of Egyptian Archaeology, Higashi-Nippon International University.

the bowls and dishes have a white slip on their rims, probably indicating purification. Ahmed Fahmy suggested that 84% of the plant macro remains from this rock-cut chamber belong to grain, such as wheat and barley, and 11% is Christ's thorn wood; all are known as important funerary offerings (Fahmy, Kawai, and Yoshimura 2014).

The other rock-cut chamber, Chamber B, is located at approximately 10 meters to the south of Chamber A (Figures 3 and 7). This originally was the subterranean chamber belonging to the layered stone structure dating from the end of the Second Dynasty to the beginning the Third Dynasty (Kawai 2011a: 804–22). In the Middle Kingdom, the chamber was probably reused as a cult sanctuary when a new entranceway was opened to the forecourt to the south (Figure 8) and a new chamber seems to have been dug to the west of the original shaft (Yoshimura, Kawai, and Kashiwagi 2005: 376–78, 380–84). In fact, Middle Kingdom pottery and other artifacts were concentrated in these areas. In the forecourt, two pot stands with dishes upon them were found intact and *in situ*, showing that the forecourt was used as an offering ritual place (Yoshimura, Kawai, and Kashiwagi 2005: 377–78).

The Middle Kingdom objects include a number of pottery vessels with organic remains, wooden statue fragments, fragments of a clay statue of a lioness goddess, and fragments of mud sealings, one of which bears the impression of *sḫmty* enclosed within a S-spiral pattern.[3] The pottery assemblage is strikingly similar to that found in the Chamber A, suggesting the same date from the middle of the Twelfth Dynasty to the end of the Thirteenth Dynasty (Yoshimura, Kawai, and Kashiwagi 2005: 380). The pottery assemblages from both Chambers A and B clearly show funerary characteristics, as has been discussed already.[4]

The clay statue of a lioness goddess was reconstructed from numerous fragments found both inside the chamber and in the forecourt to the south of Chamber B. This statue is similar stylistically to the other clay lioness goddess statues deposited in Chamber A. In total, we found in the two rock-cut chambers nine statues consisting of five terracotta statues and four clay statues in total. Seven represent either a lioness goddess or recumbent lioness, while two represent human busts (Figures 9 and 10).

---

3 It is noteworthy that the impression of sxmty can mean not only "double crowns" but also a *nisbe* meaning "associate with power," or it could be dual, meaning "double divine powers," which may be associated with a goddess or goddesses. See Yoshimura, Kawai, and Kashiwagi 2005: 378–80 and Figure 13.

4 For the funerary pottery in the Middle Kingdom, see Allen 2009.

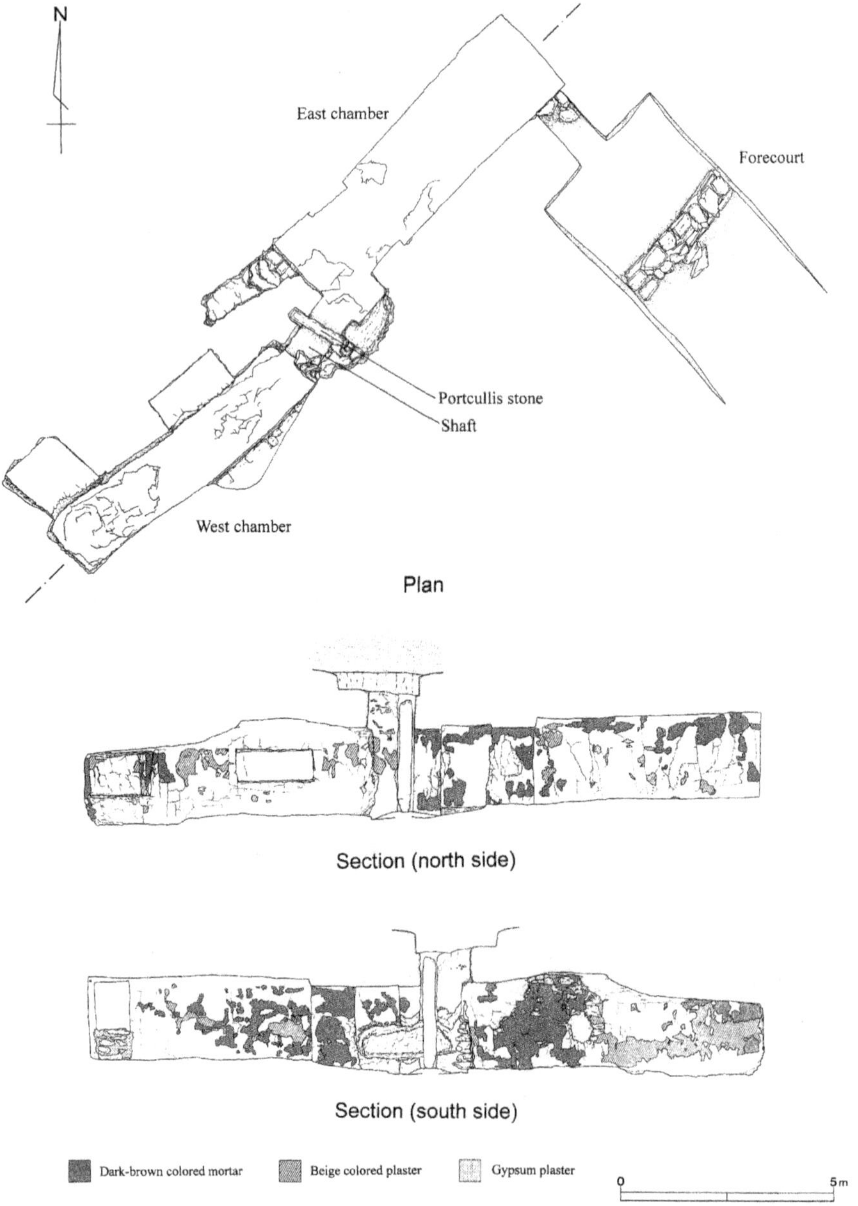

Figure 7: Plan and section of Chamber B ©Institute of Egyptology, Waseda University/Institute of Egyptian Archaeology, Higashi-Nippon International University.

Figure 8: The Middle Kingdom entrance of Chamber B ©Institute of Egyptology, Waseda University/Institute of Egyptian Archaeology, Higashi-Nippon International University.

4 The Terracotta Lioness Goddess and Lioness Statuary

In the following, I would like to discuss the life history of the lioness goddess and lioness statues made of terracotta, which seem to have been produced at the same time due to the same material, style, and manufacture technique.

The lioness goddess designated no. 1 (Figures 9.1 and 10) flanked by two small figures of a child-king.[5] The color of the statue appears to be red-brown, being very finely finished, and completely polished over with red hematite (red ocher).[6] The goddess's statue has a well-modelled head and body, with carefully rendered details such as facial features and wigs, and smoothly finished surfaces. The goddess wears a typical female tripartite wig of the Old Kingdom and a sheath dress, and her arms along her body.

5 Dimensions: H. 99.5 cm, W. 28.5 cm, D. 26.2 cm (as restored). It was restored by Richard Jaeschke and is now registered as JE 99681 at the Egyptian Museum, Cairo.

6 Red color was painted on the Old Kingdom pottery lion from Hierakonpolis, now in Ashmolean Museum, Oxford (E.189).

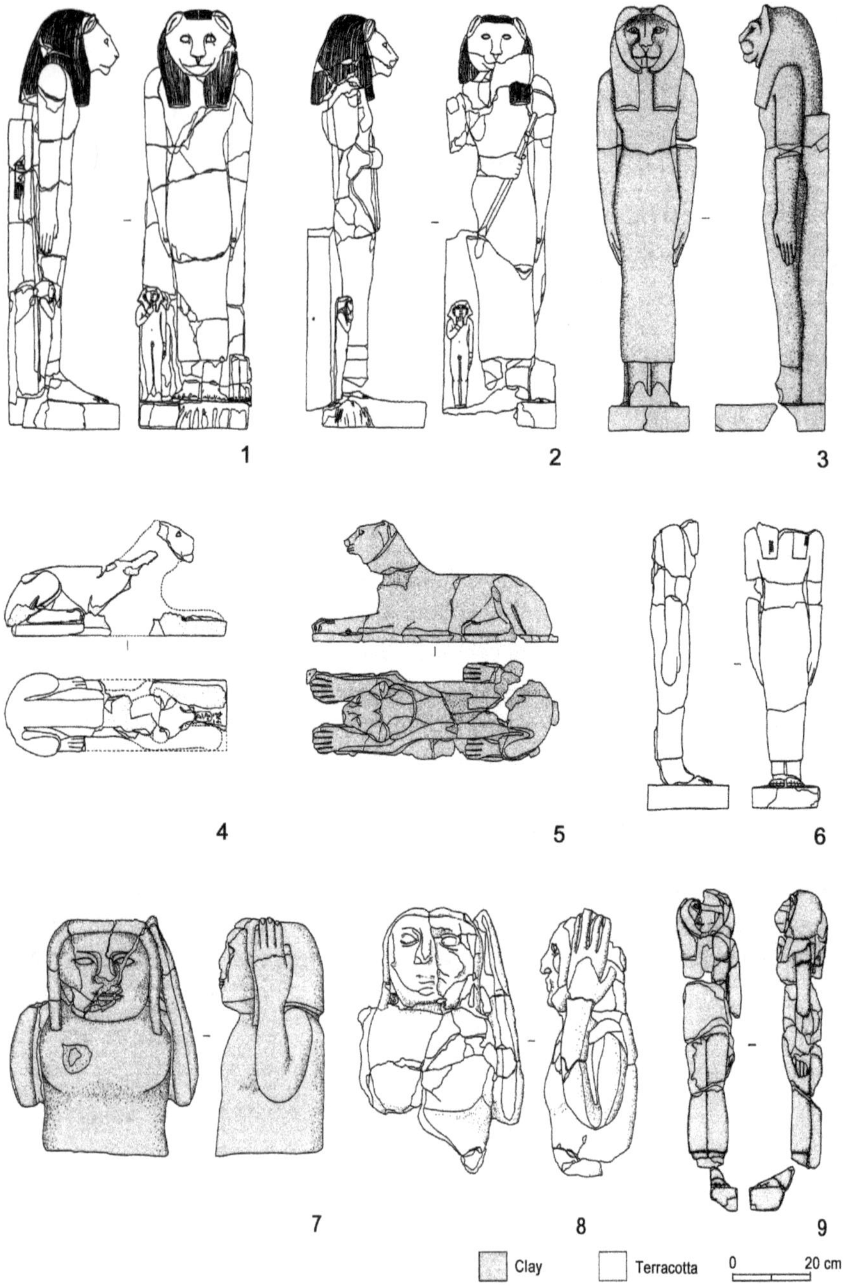

Figure 9: Terracotta and clay statues from Chambers A and B ©Institute of Egyptology, Waseda University/Institute of Egyptian Archaeology, Higashi-Nippon International University.

Figure 10: Terracotta and clay statues from Chambers A and B ©Institute of Egyptology, Waseda University/Institute of Egyptian Archaeology, Higashi-Nippon International University.

Of the two small figures of a child-king only the right figure has most of the body preserved. The figure of the child-king wears the *nemes* headdress and puts a finger up to his mouth, creating a visual allusion to the king in the guise of Horus (Figure 11).[7] On the right side of the back slab, near the right hand of the goddess, the Horus name of Khufu, *Mḏdw*, is inscribed, identifying the child-king represented on the right side as a figure of King Khufu (Figure 12). We also found a cartouche of Khufu on the back surface of the statue's back slab, which was not mentioned in previous reports (Figure 13). Furthermore, the child-king wears a distinctive type of *nemes* headdress dating to the Fourth Dynasty (Stadelmann 1998: 361–63). On the left side of the goddess, both the legs and feet of a small figure of Pepy I remain attached to a socket cut into the base of the statue (Figure 14). Actually, the small figure stands beyond the edge

Figure 11: Figure of King Khufu ©Institute of Egyptology, Waseda University/Institute of Egyptian Archaeology, Higashi-Nippon International University.

7 Spell 378 of the Pyramid Texts mentions " . . . Horus the young boy with his finger in his mouth . . . " See Allen 2005: 88.

Figure 12: Horus name of Khufu ©Institute of Egyptology, Waseda University/Institute of Egyptian Archaeology, Higashi-Nippon International University.

of the base of the statue, which clearly suggests that the figure was not originally intended and was a later addition. On both sides of the feet are the two cartouches containing Pepy I's prenomen, *Mry-Rˁ* (Figure 14). However, they were, in fact, covered over with red-brown plaster when the fragments were uncovered. It should be noted that the red-brown plaster was also observed in different places, such as cracks and hollows, and may have originally been used as a kind of glue for restoration in antiquity. Thus, it would seem that the statue was restored several times after it was completed. On the basis of the scale of the remaining portion of the figure of Pepy I, a similar sized child-king, like Khufu, might have stood to the right.[8] The ancient restoration was also indicated by the traces of pinkish powder-like mortar in several cracks all over the body. Since the fragmented surfaces were not really weathered, it seems that restoration was undertaken shortly after the damage occurred. Several parts of

8 Both king figures could have originally been approximately 27.5 cm in height.

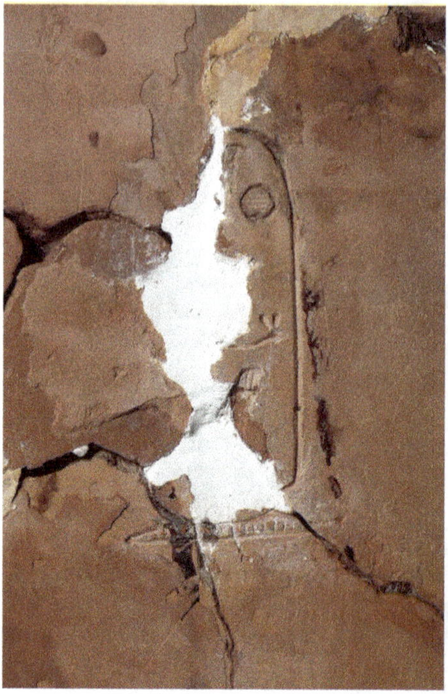

Figure 13: Cartouche of Khufu ©Institute of Egyptology, Waseda University/Institute of Egyptian Archaeology, Higashi-Nippon International University.

the statue show traces that look like the remnants of a liquid dripped on it, probably an oil of some kind. I assume that this is evidence of the anointment of the statue during a ritual. On the backside of the back slab, there are some joined fragments of terracotta where traces of liquid are missing (Figures 15 and 16), suggesting that these portions were added to restore the statue.

Like the cartouches of Pepy I on the pedestal of his figure, the Horus name of King Khufu on the side of the back slab was completely covered with red-brownish mortar when it was found. Protruding remains of the same mortar on the sides of the back slab covering a portion of Khufu's Horus name indicate that the statue was inserted into something like a niche when it was in use at a later phase of its life history. A mortise for a tenon was probably used to join it with a different material at the same time. When this modification of the statue was in effect in the final phase of its usage, the names of both kings Khufu and Pepy I were no longer relevant. This phase was most probably in the Middle Kingdom, before the interment of the statue in the rock-cut chamber. But why

Figure 14: Figure of Pepy I ©Institute of Egyptology, Waseda University/Institute of Egyptian Archaeology, Higashi-Nippon International University.

did the names of the kings become insignificant? I will discuss the answer for this question later.

The next statue is the other terracotta statue of a lioness goddess designated #2 (Figures 9.2 and 10).[9] This statue is almost exactly the same size as statue #1 and represents the same stylistic features, but here the lioness goddess holds a papyrus scepter (wAD). No inscription can be identified on the remaining part of the back slab of this statue. However, the portion where Khufu's Horus name is inscribed on the other statue is not preserved here. Therefore, it is possible that Khufu's name was once inscribed on the now missing portion. The figure of a child-king at the right of the goddess also wears the *nemes* headdress and holds a finger to his mouth (Figure 17). A statue base inscribed with the name of Pepy I at the left of the goddess is attached to the pedestal of the lioness goddess statue (Figure 18). Here, his body is also missing, except for the tips of his feet. Again,

9 Dimensions: H. 100.5 cm, W. 29.4 cm, D. 30.5 cm. It was restored by Richard Jaeschke and is now registered as JE 99682 at the Egyptian Museum, Cairo.

Figure 15: Back of the statue with remnants of liquid or oil ©Institute of Egyptology, Waseda University/Institute of Egyptian Archaeology, Higashi-Nippon International University.

the name of Pepy I, which was obscured with red-brownish mortar, was found only after we cleaned the base of the small figure. It seems that this statue, like the first mentioned above, was once broken and then restored, since red-brown powder-like mortar was observed in the cracks and hollows. This statue also has the same traces of the liquid that was dripped on its surface. Although there is no thick layer of protruding remains of mortar on the sides of the back slab, as on the other statue, a mortise for a tenon is present on one side of the back slab. This also indicates that this statue was also joined to something like a niche, similar to the other statue.

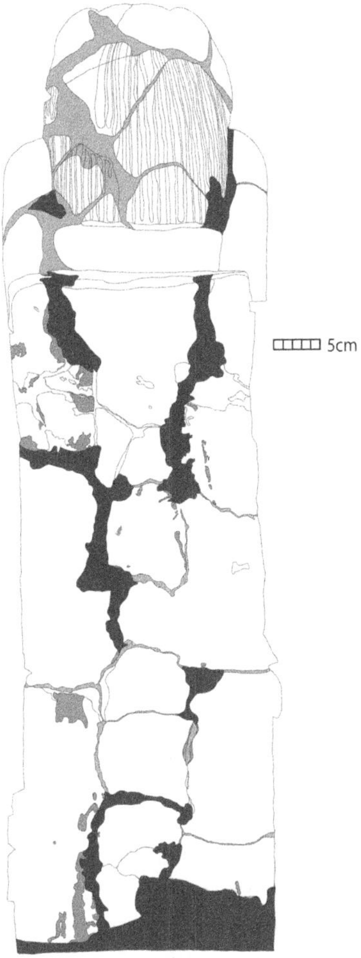

Figure 16: Back of the statue with remnants of liquid or oil ©Institute of Egyptology, Waseda University/Institute of Egyptian Archaeology, Higashi-Nippon International University.

The third statue is also a terracotta statue, but slightly smaller in scale; it most likely represents a lioness goddess standing upon a rectangular base, though its head does not survive (Figures 9.6 and 10).[10] This statue does not have a back slab, which may have resulted in instability. Several cracks on the body of the statue show some evidence of ancient restoration. Like the other terracotta statues of the lioness goddess, red-brownish plaster is observable for ancient restoration, but very thin fine linen was also applied to some cracks (Figure 19). After putting linen in cavities and joining the fragments with

10 Dimensions: H. 64 cm, W. 20.4 cm, D. 20.4 cm.

Figure 17: Figure of probably King Khufu standing to the right of lioness goddess statue #2 ©Institute of Egyptology, Waseda University/Institute of Egyptian Archaeology, Higashi-Nippon International University.

mortar, the broken parts seem to have been covered with gesso. The base was restored by filling the cracks with plaster. Although the statue does not have a back pillar, there is a long rectangular incision at the center of the back of the statue. This incision contains brownish mortar and pieces of wood to join the broken pieces together.

A terracotta statue of a recumbent lioness was identified after joining the broken fragments together and the name of King Khufu appears between the paws of the lioness (Figures 9.4, 10, 20, 21).[11] Khufu's name is inscribed in front

11 Dimensions: L. 61.8 cm, W. 19.1 cm, H. 29 cm (as restored). It was restored by Richard Jaeschke and is now registered as JE 99683 at the Egyptian Museum, Cairo. The author identified some parallels of the terracotta recumbent lion statues from Koptos in the Petrie Museum of Egyptian Archaeology at UCL (UC 34867, see Adams 1986: 38–40, pls. XXV-XXVII) and from Abydos in the Ashmolean Museum of Archaeology at Oxford (E.4499A-J). I am grateful to Prof. Stephen Quirke at UCL and Dr. Liam Macnamara at Oxford for permitting me to examine them.

Figure 18: Figure of Pepy I attached to the base of lioness goddess statue #2 ©Institute of Egyptology, Waseda University/Institute of Egyptian Archaeology, Higashi-Nippon International University.

of a figure under the chin of the lioness. Therefore, the figure may have represented King Khufu himself, though most of his body is now missing. Only a part of his left leg and the phallus remain.[12] This figure seems to represent Khufu nude and in a squatting position, which resembles a calcite statuette of Pepy I in the Egyptian Museum, Cairo (JE 50616).[13] Therefore, this statue shows a child-king protected by his divine mother, the recumbent lioness. The front part of the pedestal appears to show traces of dripped liquid. Perhaps this may

The so-called pottery lion from Hierakonpolis in the Ashmolean (E.189) can be another example of the parallels, although it exhibits a slightly different appearance.

12 In the previous report, we did not mention the presence of part of phallus, which was not recognized. See, Yoshimura, Kawai, and Kashiwagi 2005: 390. Thus, Hourig Sourouzian (2010: 859) mentioned that this small monument gives us the first known example of a statue type, after an exceptional appearance in the Middle Kingdom (Cairo CG 391), will be frequently exemplified in the New Kingdom.

13 Cf. Romano 1997: 252–54, Figures 54–58.

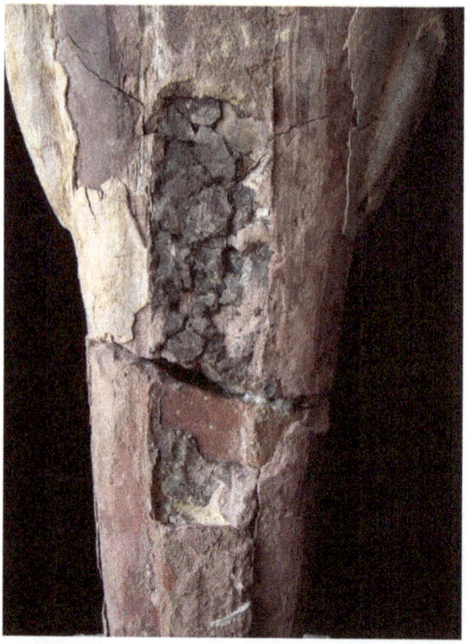

Figure 19: Ancient restoration on the back of the smaller scaled terracotta statue of lioness goddess statue ©Institute of Egyptology, Waseda University/Institute of Egyptian Archaeology, Higashi-Nippon International University.

Figure 20: Terracotta recumbent lioness ©Institute of Egyptology, Waseda University/Institute of Egyptian Archaeology, Higashi-Nippon International University.

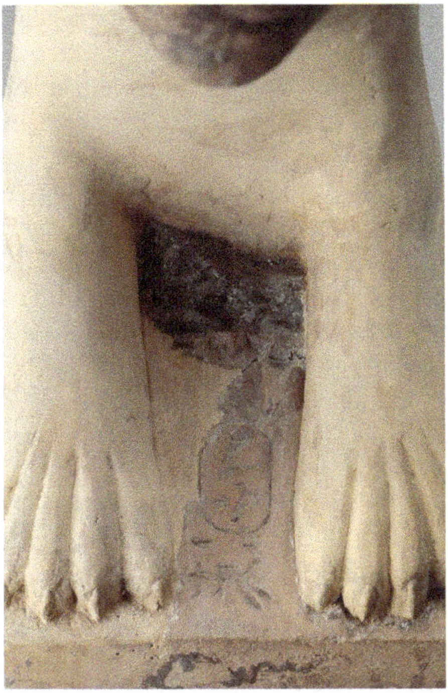

Figure 21: The area between the paws of the recumbent lioness ©Institute of Egyptology, Waseda University/Institute of Egyptian Archaeology, Higashi-Nippon International University.

have been the remnant of a ritual performed on the statue, like the other terracotta statues of the standing lioness goddess mentioned above. Likewise, there is a small hole, which was probably a mortise for a tenon in order to attach it to something like a frame.

5 The Clay Statues of a Lioness Goddess and Lioness

Now I would like to discuss the clay statuary consisting of two standing statues of a lioness goddess and the statue of a recumbent lioness. The larger standing lioness goddess clay statue found in Chamber A measures approximately 1 meter in height (Figures 9.3 and 10), corresponding to the height of the two standing terracotta lioness goddess statues.[14] The second, and smaller standing clay statue was found broken and scattered in Chamber B and its forecourt (Figures 9.9 and 10). Over ten pieces of the fragments could be joined and make up a statue of approximately 85 centimeters in height.[15] They both are made of Nile Silt mixed with chaff. Their arms are stretched downward, and both have a narrow back pillar on the backside. The two statues show different proportions and renderings of the facial features from those statues made of terracotta. The representation of these standing clay statues is simpler than that of the two terracotta statues of lioness goddesses. The eyes and mouth on both statues are painted in black. The similarity of the material, proportion, style, and treatment of both clay statue suggests that they are of contemporary production, most probably dating to the Middle Kingdom.

A statue of a recumbent lioness made of clay measures almost exactly the same size as the other recumbent lioness statue made of terracotta (Figures 9.5 and 10).[16] Stylistically, however, the facial feature of the clay recumbent lioness resembles that of other lioness statues dating to the Middle Kingdom, such as a lion gargoyle from the pyramid complex of Senwosret I and from Coptos.[17]

6 The Identification of the Lioness Goddess Represented in the Statuary and Its Meaning

As for the identification of the lioness goddess represented in the terracotta and clay statuary, there is no clear evidence to identify a particular deity, due to the lack of texts on them. As already mentioned, the terracotta lioness goddess statuary dates to the Old Kingdom due to the presence of the names of Khufu to the original phase of production. The lioness goddess likely represents Bastet, the most ancient and prominent lioness goddess in the Third Millennium BC, who has the epithet "Mistress of Ankhtawy (*nbt-ꜥnḫ-tꜣwy*)"[18] in the Memphite area

14 Dimensions: H. 100 cm, W. 23.5 cm, D. 20 cm.

15 Dimensions: H. 85 cm, W. 18.2cm, D. 18.5 cm.

16 Dimensions: L. 66 cm, W. 22.8 cm, H. 27.5 cm.

17 Arnold 1988: 81, Figure 31; Pls. 57, 101; Lacovara 2005: 160 (UC 14319).

18 The toponym dominates an area at Memphis, but it remains still uncertain whether it is the name of a district of the town itself or of the necropolis of the city, i.e. Saqqara. For a summary of the scholarly discussion about the localization and character of Ankhtawy, see Sandman Holmberg 1946: 214–15. In the Late Period Ankhtawy was used for the necropolis of Memphis: Ray 1976: 146 n. 2.

since the Old Kingdom.[19] In Giza, Bastet was represented with Khufu's son Khafre in a dyad from the northern entrance of his Valley Temple,[20] where Khafre is mentioned "Beloved of Bastet, living forever" (Hölscher 1912: 17 Abb. 7). Additionally, there is an unprovenanced dyad showing a lioness goddess made of limestone now in Hildesheim (Seidel 1996: 10–12 Taf. 2; Friedman 2008: 116 Figure 8, 126). Seidel (1996: 12) assumes it represents Bastet with a king on the basis of the break at her left shoulder suggesting the presence of a second figure of equal size and dates the statue to the reign of Khufu at the earliest. If his assumption is correct, this will be yet another dyad of a lioness goddess and a king from the reign of Khufu, in addition to our two terracotta statues, which were originally the dyads of Bastet and Khufu. It seems that Bastet was a divine protector and mother of the king and a prominent lioness goddess like Hathor in the Fourth Dynasty.

Bastet is often represented as the lioness goddess holding the papyrus scepter, as shown in statue #2 (Figures 9.2 and 10).[21] The papyrus scepter was connected specifically to the violent and Hathoric aspects of the lioness goddesses (Kaplony 1983: 160–64). Bastet is considered a lioness goddess who embodies the Eye of the Sun (Re), with her inherent aggressive and violent nature, as the daughter of Re, as well as peaceful and gentle mother duplicity. She exhibits her aspect of a pacified lioness, of fecundity and prosperity, as an incarnation of the Distant Goddess (or Wandering Goddess),[22] who approaches the alluvial valley from the desert wadis during the inundation season at the beginning of the year, in order to give birth to or feed her offspring. This is represented in the small figures of the child-king Khufu on the terracotta lioness goddess statues and the child-king Khufu between the paws of the terracotta recumbent lioness. In the hands of Bastet, who controls dangers at the time of the renewal of the year, that papyrus scepter is the symbol of her power to grant the re-birth of the king and guarantee his life.

Apparently, the terracotta lioness statues were produced for the same purpose: the representation of the lioness goddess Bastet as the divine mother and

---

19 The connection between the most well-known lioness goddess Sekhmet and Ankhtawy does not seem to antedate the Middle Kingdom. See Lange 2016: 304. The author once assumed the lioness goddess represented in the statuary is Sekhmet. But this assumption was changed to Bastet in the paper presented in the 11[h] International Congress of Egyptologists in Florence in 2015.

20 Seidel 1996: Pl. 3a (Cairo CG11); Hölscher 1912: 16–17. The head of Bastet is missing, but she is identified by the text inscribed on the throne: BAstt, nbt-anxw "Bastet, Lady of Life."

21 Borchardt (1913: pl. 35) in the temple of Sahura; Borchardt (1907: 94 Figure 72) in the temple of Nyuserra.

22 Darnell 1995; Pinch 2002: 71–74, 90–91, 96 n. 23; Richter 2010.

protector of King Khufu, perhaps representing a wish for his divine rebirth alongside the feet or under the chin of this divine mother goddess, and showing an intimate relationship between mother and child. It is well known that the lioness goddess functioned as the divine mother and protector of the king, as shown by other sources, such as the Pyramid Texts[23] and by scenes in the royal mortuary complexes of the Old Kingdom depicting a lioness goddess suckling or embracing the king.[24]

Later, Pepy I added his own figures of the same size as Khufu's to these Fourth Dynasty dyad statues of the lioness goddess with King Khufu. This strikingly reinforces the special relationship between the Fourth and Sixth Dynasties; now a great lioness goddess is shown framed by two kings represented as children – Khufu on one side and Pepy I on the other. The symmetry ensures that Pepy I enjoyed the status of a child-king protected by a divine mother shared with Khufu. This "remodeling" of statues bears witness to works carried out during the Sixth Dynasty. Therefore, it seems that the kings of the Sixth Dynasty, as well as the high elite, already looked back with nostalgia and respect to the past grandeur of the Fourth Dynasty kings. The problem is that we cannot know the original placement and function of these terracotta statues of a lioness goddess, but it is certain that they were placed somewhere in a cultic setting, due to the remnants of anointment preserved on them. It should also be noted that all the standing statues were broken at some moment and carefully restored in antiquity, although we do not know whether they were restored at the time when Pepy I reused the statues, or sometime before.

The names of Khufu and Pepy I on the two standing statues were completely plastered over at a later stage, sometime before they were ritually buried in the rock-cut chambers during the Middle Kingdom. It is assumed that these terracotta statues together with the recumbent lioness statue, in their latter stage of use, stood inserted into a rectangular cavity, such as niche or wooden frame. This is based on the thick layer of protruding mortar on the sides of the back slab of a standing statue and the presence of the mortises for tenons on a side of the back slab of each statue. As for the terracotta statue of the lioness goddess in a slightly smaller scale, it is difficult to know for certain whether it was made at

23 See note 7 above.

24 For example, see a relief showing a lioness goddess suckling the king on the block found in the valley temples of Niuserre (Borchardt 1909: 39–41, Berlin 17911) and a small fragment showing the king posed nose to nose with a lioness goddess in the Valley temple of Snefru at Dahshur (Fakhry 1959–61, I: Figure 141). Ćwiek (2003: 176–87) carried out a comprehensive study on royal reliefs in royal mortuary temples of the Old Kingdom and discusses the scene of suckling and embracing the king.

the same time as the other terracotta statues. Finally, by the time of the final stage when these terracotta statues were buried, similar lioness goddess statues made of clay were produced for the new ritual setting context in the Middle Kingdom, discussed further below.

7 The Human Bust Statues

Two human busts were found together with the other terracotta and clay statues of lioness goddess in Chamber A.[25] Each depicts a man with a full beard and locks of hair, holding his hands over his ears on both sides of the head. Like the lioness goddess statues, they are made of terracotta and clay respectively (Figures 9.7, 9.8, 10). Yet the clay and firing of the terracotta human bust is coarser than that of the terracotta lioness goddess statues, and the quality of the terracotta human bust statue is not as good as that of the lioness goddess statues. The inside of both statues is hollow and there is a circular hole on the top of the head. These human busts themselves do not give us clear evidence for dating. As far as I am aware, there are no parallels of this kind of terracotta or clay bust from the Old Kingdom. There are similar types of terracotta busts from the Middle Kingdom, which depict female mourners.[26] Peter Dorman mentions that certain bag-shaped jars were transformed into human shapes, by the addition of hand-modeled elements to produce 'mourner' jars during the Middle Kingdom (Dorman 2002: 14). Therefore, it is reasonable to assume that the date of the terracotta human bust falls within the Middle Kingdom, although the terracotta lioness goddess statues clearly date to the Old Kingdom. Unlike the terracotta figurines showing female mourners, each of the two human busts from Chamber A depicts a man with a beard and locks of hair, a typical representation of foreigners known from other statues depicting foreign enemies from earlier periods of ancient Egypt.[27] Particularly, the locks of hair are the most distinctive Libyan ethnic icon in Egyptian art, and the hair locks are associated with Libyans at all periods,[28] in addition to Pyramid Text Spell 412 that

---

25 Dimensions for the terracotta human bust statue: H. 66.5 cm, 46.5 cm, D. 24 cm.; Dimensions for the clay human bust statue: H. 59 cm, W. 32 cm, D. 28.5 cm.

26 See, for example, one provenance unknown in Berlin (ÄM 9695) (Oppenheim et al. 2015: 223); one provenance unknown at the Louvre (Andrew et al. 1995).

27 For example, a statue base with enemy heads dating to the Third Dynasty (Staatliche Sammlung Ägyptischer Kunst, München ÄS 6300). See Ziegler 1999.

28 Bates 1914: 134–37. For the Libyan wearing a sidelock in the Niuserre "Libyan Scene," see Borchardt 1907: 49 Figure 31.

mentions "like the lock which is upon the head of *Mnṯiw* (Libyan)."[29] If the human busts represent Libyans, why were they deposited with the lioness goddess statues with the kings in Chamber A? This issue should be left open for discussion in the future.

8 The Dual Symbolism of the Terracotta and Clay Statuary

If we look at all the statues made of terracotta and those made of clay from Chambers A and B together, the same images were depicted in both materials (Figures 9 and 10). I suggest that the clay statues of lioness goddess and recumbent lioness were made as the counterparts of the terracotta statues, in order to create a dual symbolic meaning[30] of *Ḏsr* and *Km*: red and black in ancient Egyptian, considered as the most basic colors that formed the primary palette alongside white.[31]

The terracotta lioness goddess statues were polished over with red hematite (red ocher), indicating they were intentionally colored. The color red was considered the color of the desert, and symbolized destruction or chaos. It was also used to represent the fiery nature of the sun, the Eye of Re, which the goddess Bastet embodied. The red color also strengthens the protective role usually associated with the image of the lion. Red or red-brown was the color of the Nile when the waters of the inundation receded and the underlying ground appears closer, which would have formed a striking visual parallel to the red-ocher blood color of the beer used to pacify the Distant Goddess.[32] The black color of mud was a symbol of fertility and regeneration or resurrection, due to the abundance provided by the dark, black silt of the annual inundation of the Nile.

Therefore, these colors are meaningful for the lioness goddess. It is likely that they were intentionally arranged to create dual symbolism in their Middle

---

29 See, Allen 2005: 87. Allen translated Mntiw as Northern Bedouin. I would rather follow Darnell's interpretation of MnTiw as Libyan. See Darnell 1995: 68–90.

30 For the dual symbolism in ancient Egypt, see for example Servajen 2008.

31 For the colors red and black in ancient Egypt, see Ćwiek 2014: 120, and for the color symbolism in ancient Egypt, see Robins 2001; Sist 2016.

32 A later version of the myth of the Distant Goddesss, "The Destruction of Humankind" in the Book of the Heavenly Cow, mentions that the lioness goddess Sekhmet ("The Powerful One") is tricked into drinking red-colored beer and thus became pacified. See: Richiter 2010: 159; Pinch 2002: 74–75.

Kingdom context. Accordingly, the Old Kingdom terracotta lioness goddess statues were integrated into the new context of the symbolic ritual setting of the Middle Kingdom. Thus, I assume that the names of Khufu and Pepy I of the terracotta statues were no longer relevant and were covered with red-brownish plaster, which was considered appropriate for this new arrangement. Then at the same time, terracotta and clay human busts were produced to make a dual symbolism for this new symbolic ritual setting context.

9 The Cult Ritual for Bastet and Statue Burial in the Rock-Cut Sanctuary at Northwest Saqqara

An extensive cult debris deposit of Middle Kingdom pottery sherds was recovered to the south of the layered stone structure (Figure 22) (Yoshimura, Kawai, and Kashiwagi 2005: 399–400; Kawai, Takahashi, and Yazawa 2012: 156–60).

Figure 22: The Middle Kingdom cult activities in the rock cut sanctuary at Northwest Saqqara ©Institute of Egyptology, Waseda University/Institute of Egyptian Archaeology, Higashi-Nippon International University.

These pottery sherds date from the mid Twelfth Dynasty to the end of the Thirteenth Dynasty. The deposit's ceramic assemblage corresponds to the date of the Middle Kingdom pottery from Chambers A and B. The ceramic assemblage from the debris shows that most of the pottery is miniature. The ceramic repertoire of the cult debris displays distinctive functions. More than 80% of the assemblage consists of small beakers and small dishes. This suggests that the material was related to a very specific and repetitive type of activity. An extremely high volume of this pottery type suggests that the presentation of liquid offerings would have been conducted on a continual basis. Josef Wegner (2000: 112) suggested that the principal function of this type of small beaker may well have been as a beer container. The overall assemblage of pottery vessels from this cult debris deposit is very similar to that from the contemporary funerary temples (Wegner 2000: 111–13). It is assumed that these pottery vessels were the containers for the offering cult ritual to the lioness goddess worshipped in the rock-cut sanctuary on the slope of the outcropping (Kawai, Takahashi, and Yazawa 2012: 160). They might have been discarded from the Middle Kingdom rock-cut sanctuary after the offering activities.

After the cult ritual activities ceased in the rock-cut sanctuary towards the end of the Thirteenth Dynasty, the divine statues of the lioness goddess and human busts were ultimately ritually buried in the rock cut chambers. This is based on the archaeological context with the funerary nature of the pottery vessels, both from the rock-cut chambers and cult debris deposit, and the botanical evidence found in the rock-cut chambers mentioned above. When we found the terracotta and clay lioness statuary in the rock-cut chambers, they were all found scattered as fragments. As I have already discussed, apparently the terracotta statues were already broken into pieces and restored several times in antiquity before their final burial in the rock-cut chambers during the Middle Kingdom. However, if we look at the clay lioness goddess statues and recumbent lion, it seems that they were deliberately broken. For example, the large clay lioness goddess statue that measures 1 meter in height has a horizontal split in the middle of the body (Figure 9.3). This cannot be caused either naturally or accidentally. The shorter clay lioness goddess statue has four almost equally spaced splits on the body (Figure 9.9). The clay recumbent lioness has a slit in the middle of the body and the paws are broken (Figure 9.5). It is possible that they were deliberately broken at the time of burial and the terracotta counterparts must have been broken likewise. If this was the case, the intentional destruction of the divine statuary can be interpreted as dismemberment of the divine body, like that of Osiris, the god of the dead and lord of the hereafter. Literally, the breaking and dismembering of the statuary meant the 'death' of the statue itself. I assume that these statues seem to have been deactivated at their ritual burial at the end of the Thirteenth Dynasty, at the desert sanctuary of Bastet in Northwest Saqqara. There are other parallels that suggest a similar ritual killing of cult statues. In the temple of Ptah at Karnak, the statue of the god Ptah was buried, fragmented and out of use at the bottom of the pit toward the back of the temple (Charloux et al. 2017: 1202). According to the excavators, Ptah was assimilated with Osiris in a regeneration phase and his tomb was the territory forbidden to everyone (Charloux et al. 2017: 1202). Likewise, the terracotta and clay statues of the lioness goddess Bastet were assimilated with Osiris at their ritual burial in the rock-cut chambers, that were deliberately sealed and eventually used as caches for the divine statues.

10 The Sacred Landscape of the Rock-Cut Sanctuary at Northwest Saqqara

The rock-cut sanctuary at Northwest Saqqara is located approximately 1.5 kilometers into the desert, away from the cultivation in the east. This suggests the nature of the cult of the lioness goddess Bastet, who embodies the Eye of the Re and Distant Goddess, since we know that several cult places are located in the desert wadis such as the Speos Artemidos for the goddess Pacht (Takacs 2019), El-Kab (Wadi el-Hallel) for Nekhbet-Hathor (Richter 2010), Hathor in Hierakonpolis (Friedman et al. 1999), Hathor in Dendera (Richter 2010), and so on. The locations of these small rock-cut temples and sanctuaries near the wadis in the desert offer the clearest evidence for their use in the festival celebrating the return of the Eye of Re/Distant Goddess at the beginning of the New Year and the inundation of the Nile. Constant de Wit (1951: 285) noted that lioness deities could be closely connected to desert wadis and their entrances. Furthermore, Derchain (1991: 85 and 87) pointed out the wadis were areas where the presence of lionesses would not be rare at the beginning of the inundation. Takacs (2019: 314) rightly suggested the lioness statues and recumbent lioness figure from Northwest Saqqara might strengthen this connection between lionesses and lioness-form deities and desert cult places.[33] The rocky outcropping at Northwest Saqqara where the rock-cut chambers are hewn is the highest point in the area and dominates the landscape; situated on the western bank of the Wadi Abusir, which was the main access to the Saqqara Necropolis starting in the Early Dynastic

33 This idea was already presented in my paper at the 11th International Congress of Egyptologists in Florence in 2015.

Period (Reader 2017). Notably, the rock-cut chambers entrances face towards the wadi, which is strongly connected with the lioness goddess related to the Eye of Re and Distant Goddess. The outcropping also overlooks the Lake of Abusir[34] in the area of the boundary between the desert and alluvial plain. The inundation would reach this lake at the beginning of the New Year, and this event was considered as the return of the Eye of Re/Distant Goddess. It should be noted that the shape of the outcropping appears like a recumbent lion or lioness stretching an east-west direction (Figure 2). It does not seem coincidental that the ancient Egyptians saw the outcropping as a sacred place for the lioness goddess. Sometimes, temples are found near natural features of the landscape that might inspire associated sacred significance, such as el-Qurn on the West Bank of Thebes, the Hathor shaped rock-cliff of Deir el-Bahri (Donohue 1992), the desert landscapes at Abydos and Amarna (Wegner 2007; Richards 1999), and the uraeus shaped outcropping of Gebel Barkal (Kendall 2004).[35]

The location of the rock-cut sanctuary at Northwest Saqqara that yielded the divine statuary, especially of the lioness goddess Bastet, clearly indicates that it was at one time the sanctuary of Bastet who embodied the Eye of Re and Distant Goddess. The extensive cult debris deposited during the Middle Kingdom in front of the layered stone structure must have been the remnant of offering ritual activities. At the end of the series of ritual activities ranging from the mid Twelfth Dynasty to the end of the Thirteenth Dynasty, the divine statues, including lioness goddesses, recumbent lioness, as well as the human bust statues, were ritually buried and sealed within the rock-cut chambers.

11 Conclusion

To conclude my paper, I would like to present the life history of the lioness goddess statues through the ages, showing the changes in their function in relation to the cult at Northwest Saqqara.

The terracotta lioness goddess statues were originally made to represent the dyad of the goddess Bastet and King Khufu as her divine child during the Fourth Dynasty. In the Sixth Dynasty, Pepy I added his small figures to the two statues of the lioness goddess to reinforce his special relationship with Khufu.

---

34 The Lake of Abusir has been identified with the *pḏw-š* related to the god Sokar that mentioned in the Pyramid Texts. See Gaballa and Kitchen 1969: 5 n. 6.

35 For the most recent discussion on the natural pyramids, including el-Qurn in Thebes, see Ejsmond 2018.

At least in the Fourth and Sixth Dynasties, these statues of Bastet with the kings manifested the goddess's nature as divine mother and protector of the kings. This may also represent a wish for their divine rebirth alongside the feet or under the chin of their mother goddess. Sometime after this triad was created, the two statues of the lioness goddess were both intentionally broken and shortly thereafter carefully restored.

By the end of the Middle Kingdom, the names of Khufu and Pepy I on the terracotta statues of Bastet and recumbent lioness were completely plastered over. These terracotta statues appear to have stood inserted into a rectangular cavity, such as niche or wooden frame, in their final stage of use. This is based on the presence of a thick layer of protruding mortar on the sides of the back slab of a standing statue, and the presence of the mortises for tenons on a side of the back slab of each standing statue of Bastet as well as on the base of the recumbent lioness. I suggest that the clay statues of the lioness goddess and recumbent lioness were made as the counterparts to the terracotta statues. This was done in order to create dual symbolic meaning of dSr and Km, red and black in ancient Egyptian during the Middle Kingdom. Additionally, two human busts made of terracotta and clay, respectively, were made during the Middle Kingdom to enhance the statue group and ritual cult place. From the mid Twelfth Dynasty to the end of the Thirteenth Dynasty, the rock-cut sanctuary at Northwest Saqqara was the focal point of the worship of Bastet as the Eye of Re and Distant Goddess in the Abusir-Saqqara necropolis. The offering rituals were performed in front of the rock-cut sanctuary in this new arrangement during the Middle Kingdom. The pottery assemblage of the midden of the offering activities suggest that they are similar to that of contemporary funerary temples.

Finally, when the rock-cut sanctuary ceased to function as the place of worship, all of the divine statues were ritually destroyed and buried with the funerary pottery vessels and plants within the rock-cut chambers. The statues of Bastet were assimilated with Osiris during their ritual burials. The rock-cut chambers were deliberately sealed and eventually became a cache of the buried divine statues.

Bibliography

Adams, Barbara. 1986. *Sculptured Pottery from Koptos in the Petrie Collection*. Warminster: Aris & Philips.

Allen, James. 2005. *The Ancient Egyptian Pyramid Texts*. Atlanta: Society of Biblical Literature.

Allen, Susan. 1998. Queen's Ware: Royal Funerary Pottery in the Middle Kingdom. Pp. 39–48 in *Proceedings of the 7th International Congress of Egyptologists, Cambridge, England*, ed. Christopher J. Eyre. Orientalia Lovaniensia Analecta 82. Leuven: Peeters.
Allen, Susan. 2009. Funerary Pottery in the Middle Kingdom: Archaism or Revival? Pp. 319–39 in *Archaism and Innovation: Studies in the Culture of Middle Kingdom Egypt*, ed. David P. Silverman, William K. Simpson, Josef Wegner. New Heaven and Philadelphia: Yale University and University of Pennsylvania.
Andrew, Guillemette, Marie-Hélène Rutschowscaya, and Christiane Ziegler (eds.). 1997. *Ancient Egypt at the Louvre*. Paris: Hachette.
Arnold, Dieter. 1988. *The Pyramid of Senwosret I*. New York: Metropolitan Museum of Art.
Aston, David A. 2020. Putting One's Feet up Under The Palm Trees: Some Examples of Ceramic Sculpture from Tell el-Dab'a Locus 81. Pp. 1–15 in *Text-Bild-Objekte im archäologischen Kontext: Festschrift für Susanne Bickel*, ed. Kathrin Gabler, Rita Gautschy, Luka Bohnenkämper, Hanna Jenni, Clémentine Reymond, Ruth Zillhardt, Andrea Loprieno-Gnirs, and Hans-Hubertus Münch. Hamburg: Widmaier Verlag.
Borchardt, Ludwig. 1907. *Das Grabdenkmal des Ne-user-rea*. Leipzig: J.C. Hinrichs.
Borchardt, Ludwig. 1909 *Das Grabdenkmal des Königs* Nefer-i'r-keA-*ra*, Leipzig: J.C. Hinrichs.
Borchardt, Ludwig. 1913 *Das Grabdenkmal des Königs Śa3ḥu-rea*. Band II: Die Wandbilder, 2 vols. Leipzig: J.C. Hinrichs.
Bourriau, Janinue and Carla Gallorini. 2016 *The Survey of Memphis VIII. Kom Rabia. The Middle Kingdom and Second Intermediate Period Pottery*. Excavation Memoir 108, London: Egypt Exploration Society.
Charloux, Guillaume, Christophe Thiers, Mohammad Abd Al-Aziz, and Mona Ali Abady Mahmoud. 2017. The Afterlife of Egyptian Statues: A Cache of Religious Objects in the Temple of Ptah at Karnak. *Antiquity* 91/359: 1189–204.
Ćwiek, Andrzej. 2003. Relief Decoration in the Royal Funerary Complexes of the Old Kingdom: Studies in the Development, Scene Content and Iconography. Ph.D. Dissertation. Warsaw University.
Ćwiek, Andrzej. 2014. Red and Black World. *Studies in Ancient Art and Civilization* 18: 119–33.
Darnell, John. 1995. Hathor Returns to Medamud. *Studien zur Altägyptischen Kultur* 22: 47–94.
Derchain, Phillip. 1991. La lionne ambiguë. Pp. 85–91 in *Les divins chats d'Égypte: un air subtil, un dangereux parfum*, ed. Luc Delvaux and Eugène Warmenbol. Leuven: Peeters.
Donohue, V.A. 1992. The Goddess of the Theban Mountain. *Antiquity* 66/253: 871–85.
Dorman, Peter. F. 2002. *Faces in Clay: Technique, Imagery, and Allusion in a Corpus of Ceramic Sculpture from Ancient Egypt*. Mainz: Verlag Phillip von Zabern.
Ejsmond, Wojciech. 2018. Natual Pyramids of Ancient Egypt. *Ägypten und Levante* 28: 169–80.
Fahmy, Ahmed Gamal-El-Din, Nozomu Kawai, and Sakuji Yoshimura. 2014. Archaeobotany of Two Middle Kingdom Cult Chambers at Northwest Saqqara. Pp. 141–49 in *Archaeology of African Plant Use*, ed. Chris J. Stevens, Sam Nixon, Mary Anne Murray, and Dorian Q. Fuller. London: UCL Institute of Archaeology Press.
Fakhry, Ahmed. 1959–61. *The Monuments of Sneferu at Dahshur*. Vol. I, *The Bent Pyramid*. Vol. II, *The Valley Temple*. Cairo: General Organization for Government Printing Office.
Friedman, Florence, D. 1998. The Menkaure Dyad(s). Pp. 109–44 in *Egypt and Beyond: Essays Presented to Leonard H. Lesko upon his Retirement from the Wilbour Chair of Egyptology at Brown University June 2005* ed. Stephen E. Thompson and Peter Der Manuelian.

Providence (RI): Department of Egyptology and Ancient Western Asian Studies, Brown University.
Gaballa, Gaballa A. and Kenneth A. Kitchen. 1969. *The Festival of Sokar. Orientalia* 38: 1–76.
Hölscher, Uvo. 1912. *Das Grabdenkmal des Königs Chephren*. Leipzig: J. C. Hinrichs.
Kaplony, Peter. 1983. Der Schreiber das Gotteswort und die Papyruspflance. Mit Neuen Untersuchungen zum Unterägyptischen Königtum. *Zeitschrift für Ägyptische Sprache und Altertumskunde* 110: 143–73.
Kawai, Nozomu. 2011a. An Early Cult Centre at Abusir-Saqqara? Recent Discoveries at Rocky Outcrop in North-west Saqqara. Pp. 801–28 in *Egypt at its Origins 3. Proceedings of the Third International Conference "Origin of the State: Predynastic and Early Dynastic Egypt," London, 27th July–1st August 2008*, ed. Renée F. Friedman and Peter N. Fiske. Leuven: Peeters.
Kawai, Nozomu. 2011b. The Tomb of Isisnofret at Northwest Saqqara. Pp. 497–511 in *Abusir and Saqqara in the Year 2010*, ed. Miroslav Bárta, Fillip Coppens, and Jaromir Krejčí. Prague: Czech Institute of Egyptology.
Kawai, Nozomu. 2014. The New Kingdom Tomb Chapel of Isisnofret at Northwest Saqqara. Pp. 69–90 in *Quest for the Dream of the Pharaohs: Studies in Honour of Sakuji Yoshimura*, ed. Jiro Kondo. Supplémenr aux annals du service des antiquités de l'Égypte. Chaier No. 43. Cairo: Ministry of Antiquities.
Kawai, Nozomu, Takahashi Kazumitsu, and Yazawa Ken. 2012. Middle Kingdom pottery from the WasedaUniversity excavations at north-west Saqqara 2001–2003. Pp. 147–60 in *Handbook of pottery of the Egyptian Middle Kingdom II: The Regional Volume*, ed. Robert Schiestl and Anne Seiler. DÖAWW 72. CCEM 31. Vienna: Austrian Academy of Science Press.
Kendall, Timothy. 2004. The Monument of Taharqa on Gebel Barkal. *Meroitica* 21: 1–6.
Lacovara, Peter. 2005. Lion gargoyle. P. 160 in *Excavating Egypt*, ed. Betsy T. Trope, Stephen Quirke, and Peter Lacovara. Atlanta (GA): Michael C. Carlos Museum, Emory University.
Lange, Eva. 2016. The Lioness Goddess in the Old Kingdom Nile Delta: A Study in Local Cult Topography. Pp. 301–24 in *Sapientia Felicitas: Festschrift für Günter Vittmann zum 29. Februar 2016*. ed. Sandra L. Lippert, Maren Schentuleit, and Martin A. Stadler. Montpellier: Universite Paul Valéry.
Oppenheim, Adela, Dorothea Arnold, Dieter Arnold, and Kei Yamamoto. 2015. *Ancient Egypt Transformed The Middle Kingdom*. New Haven (CT) and London: Yale University Press.
Pinch, Geraldine. 2002. *Handbook of Egyptian Mythology*. Santa Barbara (CA): ABC-CLIO.
Ray, John. D. 1976. *The Archive of Ḥor*. Texts from Excavations 2. London: Egypt Exploration Society.
Reader, Colin. 2017. An Early Dynastic Ritual Landscape at North Saqqara: An Inheritance from Abydos?*Journal of Egyptian Archaeology* 103: 71–87.
Romano, James F. 1998. Sixth Dynasty Royal Sculpture Pp. 235–303 in *Les critères de datation stylistiques à l'Ancien Empire*, ed. Nicholas Grimal. Cairo: Institut Français d'Archéologie Orientale.
Richards, Janet. 1999. Conceptual Landscape in the Nile Valley. Pp. 83–100 in *Archaeologies of Landscape: Contemporary Perspectives*, ed. Wendy Ashmore and A. Bernard Knapp. Malden (MA): Blackwell.

Richter, Barbara. A. 2010. On the Heels of the Wandering Goddess: The Myth and the Festival at the Temples of the Wadi el-Hallel and Dendera. Pp. 155–86 in *Ägyptologische Tempeltagung 8: Interconnections Between Temples*, ed. Monika Dolinska and Horst Beinlich. Königtum, Staat und Gesellschaft Früher Hochkulturen 3,3. Wiesbaden: Harrassowitz Verlag.

Sandman Holmberg, Maj. 1946. *The God Ptah*. Lund: C. W. K. Gleerup.

Seidel, Mathias. 1996. *Die Königliche Statuengruppen I. Die Denkmäler vom Alten Reich bis zum Ende der 18. Dynastie*. Hildesheim Ägyptologische Beitrage 42. Hildesheim: Gerstenberg.

Servajean, Frédéric. 2008. Duality in *UCLA Encyclopedia of Egyptology*, ed. Willke Wendrich, Jacco, Dielenman, Elizabeth Frood, and John Bains. Los Angeles (CA): UCLA. http://digital2.library.ucla.edu/viewItem.do?ark=21198/zz0013x9jp.

Sourouzian, Hourig. 2010. Old Kingdom Sculpture. Pp. 853–81 in *A Companion to Ancient Egypt*, vol. II, ed.Alan B. Lloyd. West Sussex: Wiley-Blackwell.

Stadelmann, Rainer. 1998. Formale Kriterien zur Datierung der Königlichen Plastik der 4. Dynastie. Pp. 353–87 in *Les critères de datation stylistiques à l'Ancien Empir*, ed. Nicholas Grimal. Cairo: Institut Français d'Archéologie Orientale.

Takacs, Daniel.V. 2019. The Pakhet of Speos Artemidos and Wadi Batn el-Baqara. *Studien zur Alt Ägyptischen Kultur* 48: 283–315.

Takamiya, Izumi. H., Hiroyuki Kashiwagi, and Sakuji Yoshimura. 2011. Khaemwaset and His Monument at North Saqqara: A Record of Multiple Aspects of "the First Egyptologist" Pp. 401–21 in *Times, Signs, and Pyramids: Studies in Honour of Miroslav Verner on the Occasion of His Seventieth Birthday*, ed. Vivienne G. Callender, Ladislav Bareš, Miroslav Bárta, Jiri Janák, and Jaromir Krejčí. Prague: Czech Institute of Egyptology.

Wegner, Josef. 2000. The Organization of the Temple *Nfr-k3* of Senwosret III at Abydos. *Ägypten und Levante* 10: 85–125.

Wegner, Josef. 2007 From Elephant-Mountain to Anubis-Mountain? A Theory on the Origins and Development of the Name Abdju. Pp. 459–76 in *The Archaeology and Art of Ancient Egypt. Essays in Honor of David B. O'Connor*, vol. II, ed. Zahi Hawass and Janet Richards. Cairo: Ministry of Antiquities, Egypt.

Yoshimura, Sakuji and Nozomu Kawai. 2006. A new early Old Kingdom layered stone structure at Northwest Saqqara. Pp. 363–374 in *The Old Kingdom Art and Archaeology: Proceedings of the Conference held in Prague*, May *31 – June 4, 2004*, ed. Miroslav Bárta. Prague: Czech Institute of Egyptology.

Yoshimura, Sakuji and Masanori Saito. 2003. Waseda University Excavations in Egypt and Recent Works at North Saqqara. Pp. 574–81 in *Egyptology at the Dawn of the Twenty-first Century: Proceedings of the Eighth International Congress of Egyptologists, Cairo, 2000*, ed. Z. Hawass. Cairo: American University in Cairo Press.

Yoshimura, Sakuji, and Izumi H. Takamiya. 2000. Waseda University excavations at North Saqqara from 1991 to 1999. Pp. 161–72 in *Abusir and Saqqara in the Year 2000*, ed. Miroslav Bárta and Jaromir Krejčí. Prague: Czech Institute of Egyptology.

Yoshimura, Sakuji, Nozomu Kawai, and Hiroyuki Kashiwagi. 2005. A Sacred Hillside at Northwest Saqqara: A Preliminary Report on the Excavations 2001–2003. *Mitteilungen des Deutschen Archäologischen Instituts Abteilung Kairo* 61: 361–402.

Ziegler, Christiane. 1999. Statue Base with Enemy Heads. P. 174 in *Egyptian Art in the Age of the Pyramids*. New York: Metropolitan Museum of Art.

Index

Divine Names

Adad 166, 169–170, 176–177, 202
Ama'NIN-Geštinana. *See* Geštinanna
An 169, 194n5, 195, 197, 202–203, 240
Anat 289, 295
Annunītum. *See* Ištar
Anu. *See* An
Anuna 202
Aphrodite 8, 201, 289–296, 298–299
Artemis 289, 295–296
Aruru 197
Asalluḫi 170
Ashtart-Aphrodite 289
Aššur 58–59, 174–175, 179, 272
Aššurītum 175
Aštart. *See* Ištar
Athena 289
Athirat/Asherah 294
Atra-Ḫasīs 266

Baal 9, 289_{1}, 290–291, 294, 296–298
Baalat Gubal 291
Baal Hammon 297
Baba 28, 30, 96
Bastet 9, 326–327, 330, 333–335
Belet-ekallim 182
Bēlet-ṣēri *See* Geštinanna
Bilulu 232–233

Dagan 102, 176–177, 182
Damu 238
Dido 297
Dilimbabbar 202
Dumuzi 169, 181, 202, 219, 225, 233–234, 274_{39}, 295

Ea *See* Enki
El/Ilu 294
Elissa 297
Emar 127
Enki 133, 166, 170, 232, 236, 238, 240, 274_{37}
Enlil 123–124, 128_{24}, 129–130, 132, 134, 166, 197, 202, 219, 224, 229, 236–238, 240, 272, 276
Ereškigal 126, 235
Eshmoun 290
Euploia. *See* Aphrodite

Gatumdug 34_{50}, 166
Geštinana. *See* Geštinanna
Geštinanna 164, 169–170
Gugalana 235
Gula 164, 173, 228_{22}, 267

Hathor 296, 333–334
Hephaistos 292, 295
Hera 289, 296–297
Horus 303, 316, 318–319
Ḫalmaššuitt 142, 149_{30}, 150–152

Illuyanka 150
Inana. *See* Inanna
Inanna 8, 100_{19}, 117_{60}, 127, 132, 149, 175, 178, 189–196, 198, 200–205, 217–220, 224–225, 229–236, 243, 295
Iškur. *See* Adad
Išḫara 169–170, 263–264, 266–267, 274, 278–279
Ištar 2, 8–9, 170–171, 175–182, 220, 263–264, 266, 272–275, 279, 289–292, 294–198
Isis 292, 295
Ištara. *See* Ištar

Kothar 294–295
Kronos 291_{5}, 293
Kusu 168
Kythereia. *See* Aphrodite.

Lamaštu 269, 273
Limenia. *See* Aphrodite
Lugalaba 122
Lugalmudakush 31

https://doi.org/10.1515/9781501514821-016

Maitreya 82
Marduk 72, 122, 171, 219, 274_{37}, 277_{48}, 289_{1}
Martu 239–240
Melqart. *See* Baal
Mezzulla 150
Mullil. *See* Enlil.
Mullissu. *See* Ninlil.

Nabû 169
Nanaya 71–72
Nanna 7, 95–107, 109–117, 133, 167, 169, 181, 190–191, 193–195, 198, 200, 202–203, 229_{23}, 231, 239–240, 273
Nanše 35–36, 164, 166–168
Nergal 126, 169–170
Ningal 99, 101, 116, 202, 239–240
Ningirima 168
Ningirsu 34_{49}, 127, 166–167
Ningišzida 175
Ninḫursag 168, 238
Nininsina 197, 225, 238
Ninlil 56, 197, 217, 219, 224, 237–238
Ninmah 168, 231, 240
Ninsikila 238
Ninsun 169
Ninšubur 225
Nintinuga 229
Nintud/r. *See* Ninmah.
Ninurta 7, 96_{2}, 121–125, 128–129, 131–133, 135, 173_{16}, 217, 231, 237, 277
Nisaba 167–168, 170n14, 225, 237
Numušda 239
Nunbaršegunu. *See* Nisaba
Nuska 123_{5}, 183
Nusku *see* Nuska.

Osiris 332–333, 335

Pazuzu 269_{16}
Pontia. *See* Aphrodite

Re 327, 330, 333–335

Sakhmet 303_{1}, 327_{19}, 330_{32}
Sekhmet. *See* Sakhmet
Selqet 266
Sîn/Suen. *See* Nanna
Sud. *See* Ninlil
Sutīti 71–72
Šamaš 46_{4}, 47, 166, 169–171, 238, 250, 272

Tammuz. *See* Dumuzi
Tanit 8, 190, 297
Tarhun 289_{1}
Tetešḫapi 147, 149–150
Tyrian Ashtar. *See* Ištar

Ushumgalana 202
Uttu 238
Utu 102

Venus 8, 178, 190, 297–298, 299_{20}

Zeus 291_{5}, 293_{9}, 294_{13}

Geographical Names

Agade. *See* Akkade
Akkade 98, 217, 228, 240
Aleppo 176
Arbela 175, 179, 181–183, 272_{30}
Arinna 142, 152
Askalon 292
Assur 6, 56, 174, 176, 182, 228_{22}, 272_{30}

Babylon 63, 64_{3}, 70, 122, 176–179, 218, 244
Borsippa 5, 63–66, 71–74, 77
Byblos 291, 293_{8}, 295_{16}

Calah. *See* Nimrud
Chang'an 81, 86–87

Dawiniya 149
Dongu *see* Luoyang.

Ebla 127, 145_{11}
Edessa 226
Emar 219
Enkomi 291–292
Eridu 108, 113_{48}, 117_{59}, 232, 236, 239
Ereš 167, 238
Ešnunna 177, 182, 275

Gaeš 105, 111, 113
Girsu 25, 96, 107–108, 110, 114–115, 212_{3}, 217–218, 227

Harran 183, 226
Henei 86
Huaizhou 86
Ḫarranašši 148
Ḫattuša 147–148, 153–154, 219, 271
Ḫupišna 152

Irisaĝrig 107–108, 110
Isin 101, 218

Jerusalem 56

Kalḫu. *See* Nimrud
Kanesh 4
Kangju 85
Khotan 84
Kidmuru 264, $272–273_{31}$
Kish 218
Kition 291–292
Kuššar 154_{39}
Kythera 292, 293

Lagash 25, 28–30, 31_{30}, 32, 36–38, 40–41, 98–99, 115_{55}, 220, 227_{20}
Landa 152
Larsa 102, 104, 175
Luoyang 81–82, 84–85, 87–88
Lušna 152
Luxor 303_{1}

Mari 144_{6}, 171, 173, 175–177, 179, 182, 267_{12}
Memphis 309, 326_{18}

Nenašša 152
Nimrud 48, 49_{11}, 56, 267, 272–273
Nina 29_{18}
Nineveh 47, 49, 53, 57–59, 272_{30}
Nippur 7, 96_{2}, 122–126, 128–135, 168, 217–218, 229, 239–240, 244
Nuzi 176

Palmyra 226
Paphos 291
Paršuḫanta 152
Peloponnese 293
Puzriš-Dagan 107–117, 125
Pyrgi 296

Saqqara 303–304, 326_{18}, 331, 333–334
Sidon 290
Sippar 63, 171, 218, 226_{17}, 228_{22}
Sumer 217, 228, 239
Susa 65–66, 71, 73

Tas-Silġ 296
Tell Asmar. *See* Ešnunna
Tell el-Amarna 126
Terqa 177, 182
Thebes 293
Thera 293
Thasos 293
Troy 293_{8}, 299
Tuttul 177
Tuwanuwa 152
Tyre 53, 58, 291, 297

Ugarit 219
Umma 100_{15}, 126
Ur 7, 98–99, 101–107, 109–111, 114–117, 133, 190–191, 198, 217, 228, 230, 239
Uruk 63, 172, 180, 218, 230, 232, 239–240, 250

Xijing 85

Yamatai-koku 16

Zabalam 175
Zallara 152

Personal Names

Alla 33
A-Ab-Ba 102
Agubnidu 34_{50}
Ama-nagar 34_{50}

Ama-numun-zi 31_{29}
Amar-Suenra-kiaganna 110
Amar-šuba 34_{48}
Ana-muḫḫi-Nabû-taklāk 71
Ana-Nabû-taklāk 75
Andiya 5, 63–64, 73, 75–77
Anuwanza 147
Aššur-idī 175
Aššur-nīrka-da"inni 53_{23}
Atete 75

Balāṭu 65
Baraaranu 31–32, 34
Barairnun 33
Bayâ 183
Bazuzu 66, 68
Bēl-aṣûa 68
Bēl-ēṭer 75–76
Bēl-ibni 68–69
Bēl-iddin 68–69, 71–72
Bēl-zēra-iddin 68–69
Bodhiruci 84
Bolun 85–86
Bullussa-rabi 228_{22}

Chuyi 85
Cicero 163

Degan 85–86
Dharmaruci 84
Dudu 29_{19}, 32–33

Enagazianna 105–106, 113
Enanedu 102–105
Enannepada 98
Enannatumma 101–103, 105
Enḫeduana. *See* Enḫeduanna
Enḫeduanna 8, 98, 135, 189–192, 193_{4}, 194–196, 198, 200–205, 228–229
Eniggal 32_{35}, 34, 36
Enkidu 203, 235
Enmahgalanna 100, 109, 115
Enmegalanna 106
Enmenanna 98
En-Nanna-Amar-Suen-kiagra 106
En-Nanna-ra-kal-la 110
Ennirgalanna 99, 104
Ennirzianna 99–100, 101_{20}, 109–110, 115
Enšakiag-Nanna 102–103
Enuburzianna 99–100, 104, 107, 115
Etellum 103

Fabao 85–86
Faming 85
Fazang 85–86, 88
Fuli 85–86

Gan-Baba 31_{29}
Ganshubur 35–36
Geme-Nanše 29_{21}
Geme-ub-ku-ga 31
Gišgal-ir-nun 33_{45}
Gubi 36
Gūzānu 75

Halhal 34, 36
Herakles 9, 290, 296–298
Herodotus 1, 292, 294
Hesiod 292–295
Homer 292, 294, 299
Hongjing 85–96
Huileng 85
Huiyan 85–86
Ḫantili 153
Ḫattītum 174

Iddin-Marduk 72_{32}
Iddin-Nabû 66–67
Iddinaya. *See* Iddin-Nabû
Ili-ḫaznaya 177
Ilussa-amur 182
Imdīlum 174
Inanaka 229
Itti-Marduk-balāṭu 73_{32}

Jia Yingfu 85–86

Kibri-Dagan 182
Kugepa 32–33

Lala 36
Li Zhi 81

Lu-Baba 34_{50}
Lugal-Ane 190–191, 194, 198
Lugalshasu 33
Lupaḫḫu 177
Lu-Utu 126

Marduk-balāssu-iqbi 70
ME-Enlil. *See* Enuburzianna
Munussaga 29_{19}
Muršili 153

Nabû-aḫḫē-iddin 66
Nabû-erība 70–71
Nabû-ēṭir 74–77
Nabû-kuṣuranni 70
Nabû-nādin-šumi 70
Nabû-silim 75
Nabû-tāriṣ 71
Nabû-uṣuršu 75
Nāṣiru 75
Nergal-nāṣir 68
NI-a-a 28
Ninbur 32–33, $34_{46, 50}$
Ninburšuma. *See* Ninbur
Nindar 34_{50}
Ninmezida 29_{19}
Ninšatapada 229
Nin-šu-sikil 31_{29}
Ninuma 36
Nūptaya 73_{32}
Nur-Sîn 177

Papa 36
Pei Xuanzhi 87–88
Plato 163, 299
Pušu-kēn 174
Puzur-Ištar 174

Rē'indu 5, 63–74, 77
Rēmūt-Bēl 65–67, 69–73

Sa_6-sa_6 32
Sag-Ningirsuda 36
Sig_4-ki-be_2-gi_4 35–36
Sig_4-ki *see* Sig_4-ki-be_2-gi_4.
Śikṣānanda 84, 86

Šaddinnu 74
Šīmat-Aššur 174
Šubši-mešrê-Šakkan 181
Šubur-Baba 29_{21}
Šukaletuda 231–232

Tarām-Kūbi 174
Tuṭṭanapšum 132, 134

Urad-Gula 179
Ubār 75
Urbanu 68
Ur-Bilgames 110, 116
Ur-e-muš 32
Ur-Ningublaga 116
Ur-Utu 226_{17}
Uṣur-ša-Aššur 174

Vergil 297

Weishu 86

Xinggan 85
Xinxing 87
Xuangui 85

Yang Gongren 88
Yijing 84, 86

Zhijing 85
Zikri-elka 174
Zunana 182

Professional Titles

Apiltum 176–177
Asinnu 173, 177–178, 183
Ama-Dingir 145–146, 148_{23}, 156
Amalu 213_4
Ašipu 172–173

Bārītum 172–174
Bishou 85

Dingir-Munus 213
Dumu-Lugal. *See* Taḫukanti

Egi-zi(-anna) 96, 101_{21}
En-^{d}Nanna 107
EN-priestess 95–107, 110–118, 123, 133–134
Ensi 20_{14}, 28_{14}, 125, 166–167, 175, 213
Entum 129–130, 132–135, 278
Ereš-Dingir 31, 33, 39, 96, 117, 124_{9}, 126–130, 135, 141_{1}, 143, 156, 160, 213, 216, 219

Gala 195, 199, 216, 218, 220–221, 224–228, 240, 243
Gašan 127, 216

Ḫaliyari-men 150, 157
Ḫapiya-men 150, 158

Igiṣītu 134

Kaiguogong 85
Kalû *See* Gala
Kurgarrû 178

Lugal 127, 144–146, 153, 213
Lukur 31, 33, 39, 96, 122, 125_{17}, 128_{22}, 131, 134–135

Maḫḫūtum 175, 177, 179–181
Maškim 111–112
Menea 150
Munus-Lugal. *See* Tawananna
Munus-ŠU.GI 164

Naditum 26, 122, 128_{22}, 131, 134, 171
NIN. *See* NIN.DINGIR
NIN.DINGIR 7, 121–135, 141, 143–151, $152n_{36}$, 153–160, 195–196, 202, 216, 219
NIN-Dingir ^{d}Nin-urta 124–125, 132
Nin ensi-ka-me (Ruler's Sisters) 31
Nu-gig 128, 134_{32}

Qammatu 182

Raggintu 179, 182

Sa_{12}-du_{5} 32_{37}
Sanga 29, 34–36, 145–147, 149–150
Šā'iltum 173–174
Šabra 110, 116
Šēlūtu 179

Tabarna 146
Taḫukanti 144, 146, 150, 153, 159
Taizi zhongshe 85
Taklu 173
Tawananna 144–146, 153, 159
Tupšarru 172

Ugbabtum 129–130, 133–134
Umun 215, 219
^{d}UTU-ŠI 144

Xianshou 85

Zabbatu 180–181
Zintuḫi-women 149–150, 157–158
Zirru 105, 128_{22}, 130
Zhengyi 85
Zhuiwen 85

Royal Names

Abi-Sare 102
Adad-Nērārī II 46
Addu-duri 182
Amar-Suen 100, 105, 111_{44}, 113
Ambaris 48, $49_{11, 13}$
Amenhotep II 304
Amris *See* Ambaris
Aššurbanipal 45, 50_{17}, 51–55, 57–59, 165_{2}, 170, 179, 181, 272_{30}
Aššurnaṣirpal II 46_{3}, 51, 52n22, 53, 55–56, 272
Ašmunikkal 144_{7}
Augustus 297

Ba'alu 53–54_{25}
Baranamtara 28, 29_{17}
Bartatua 47

Dimtur 28_{14}

Enentarzi 28_{14}, 29_{19}, 31_{29}
Enlilbani 131
Esarhaddon 46–47, 50–51, 53, 57, 179–180, 183, 272_{31}

Gaozong 81
Gilgamesh 169, 203, 235, 266_{8}, 269_{19}, 295_{15}
Gudea 167, 217
Gungunum 102–103

Himiko 16, 19
Hamâ 267–268
Hammurabi 134, 177
Hezekiah 52
Ḫattušili I 148_{23}, 153, 154_{39}
Ḫattušili III 147_{21}
Ḫullī 48

Ibbi-Sîn 101_{20}, 118
Išbi-Erra 101_{21}
Išme-Dagan 101–103, 239–240

Khafre 327
Khufu 303, 316–319, 322–323, 326–328, 331, 334–335
Kudur-Mabuk 102, 104
Kurigalzu 220

Libbāli-Šarrat 54_{28}, 165_{2}
Lipit-Ištar 102, 104, 134_{32}, 218
Lubarna 52_{22}, 53
Lugalanda 28, $29_{20, 21}$, 35

Madyes 47
Marduk-bēl-usāte 46_{3}
Marduk-zākir-šumi 46_{3}
Mullissu-mukannišat-Nīnua 53_{23}
Muršili I 153

Nabonidus 103–104
Nabû-šuma-ukīn I 46
Naram-Sîn 97–98, 132

Pepy I 303, 316–320, 323, 328, 331, 334–335

Rīm-Sîn 102–104, 131

Samsuiluna 131
Sargon 98, 104, 190, 228
Sargon II 46, 48, $49_{11, 13}$
Sasa 28
Sennacherib 46, 49–52, 57
Senwosret I 326
Senwosret II 309
Šalmaneser III 46_{3}, 51, 53, 56
Šalmaneser IV 51, 57, 267
Šalmaneser V 48
Sin-idinnam 238
Sûmû-El 103
Šamaš-šumu-ukin 181
Šamšī-Adad V 46
Šulgi 96, 99–100, 104, 112, 168–169, 217, 230–231, 234–235, 242
Šulmu-bēli-lušme 46_{4}
Šusanqu 49–50
Šu-Sîn 110, 217

Telipinu 152
Teumman 181
Thutmose IV 304
Tiglath-pileser III 48
Tudḫaliya IV 147_{21}
Tukultī-Ninurta I 220
Tukultī-Ninurta II 46_{3}, 51, 55

Uallî 52, 59
Ur-Baba 98, 115_{55}
Ur-Namma 99, 134_{32}, 216–217
Urtaku 46
Urukagina 28, 29_{21}

Warad-Sîn 102–104, 131_{30}
Wu Zetian 6, 81–89

Xerxes 63, 72

Zimrilim 176–177, 182

Temple Names

Bīt šassūri 266

Dabiankong 84–85
Dafuxian 82, 84, 88
Dayun 82, 86
Dongtaiyuan 88
Dublamah 111

Eana 232
E_2-Babbar$_2$ 36
E'igišugalamma 132
E_2-mul-mul 167
Enunmah 99, 102
Ešumeša 132
Ezida 65, 68–69, 72, 74–75

Foshouji 82, 84–85

Huadu 86, 88–89

Karzida 105–106, 108–110, 111_{44}, 112–115

Qingchan 85

Xitaiyuan 85, 88

Printed in the USA
CPSIA information can be obtained
at www.ICGtesting.com
JSHW011314141024
71656JS00020B/144

9 781501 523601